5th Workshop on e-Commerce and NLP (ECNLP 2022)

Dublin, Ireland
26 May 2022

ISBN: 978-1-7138-6736-4

Printed from e-media with permission by:

Curran Associates, Inc.
57 Morehouse Lane
Red Hook, NY 12571

CURRAN ASSOCIATES INC. proceedings.com

Some format issues inherent in the e-media version may also appear in this print version.

Association for Computational Linguistics
209 N. Eighth Street
Stroudsburg, Pennsylvania 18360

Phone: 1-570-476-8006
Fax: 1-570-476-0860

acl@aclweb.org

Additional copies of this publication are available from:

Curran Associates, Inc.
57 Morehouse Lane
Red Hook, NY 12571 USA
Phone: 845-758-0400
Fax: 845-758-2633
Email: curran@proceedings.com
Web: www.proceedings.com

ECNLP 2022

The 5th Workshop on e-Commerce and NLP

Proceedings of the Workshop

May 26, 2022

Introduction

It is our great pleasure to welcome you to the Fifth Workshop on e-Commerce and NLP (ECNLP).

This workshop focuses on intersection of Natural Language Processing (NLP) and e-Commerce. NLP and information retrieval (IR) have been powering e-Commerce applications since the early days of the fields. Today, NLP and IR already play a significant role in e-Commerce tasks, including product search, recommender systems, product question answering, machine translation, sentiment analysis, product description and review summarization, and customer review processing. With the exploding popularity of chatbots and shopping assistants -- both text- and voice-based -- NLP, IR, question answering, and dialogue systems research is poised to transform e-Commerce once again.

The ECNLP workshop series was designed to provide a venue for the dissemination of late-breaking research results and ideas related to e-commerce and online shopping, as well as a forum where new and unfinished ideas could be discussed. After four successful editions since 2019, we are happy to host ECNLP 5 at ACL 2022 and once again bring together researchers from both academia and industry.

We have received a larger number of submissions than we could accept for presentation. ECNLP 5 received 52 submissions of long and short research papers. In total, ECNLP 5 featured 29 accepted papers (56% acceptance rate). The selection process was competitive and we believe it resulted in a balanced and varied program that is appealing to audiences from the various sub-areas of e-Commerce.

We would like to thank everyone who submitted a paper to the workshop. We would also like to express our gratitude to the members of the Program Committee for their timely reviews, and for supporting the tight schedule by providing reviews at short notice.

We hope that you enjoy the workshop!

The ECNLP Organizers May 2022

Organizing Committee

Organizing Committee

Shervin Malmasi, Amazon, USA
Surya Kallumadi, Lowe's Companies, Inc, USA
Nicola Ueffing, eBay, Germany
Eugene Agichtein, Emory University, USA
Oleg Rokhlenko, Amazon, USA
Ido Guy, Meta AI, Israel

Program Committee

Program Committee

Ahsaas Bajaj
Adrian Benton, Google
Giuseppe Castellucci, Amazon
Dumitru Clementin Cercel, University Politehnica of Bucharest
Lei Chen, Rakuten Institute of Technology, The University of Tokyo
Young-joo Chung
Marcus D. Collins, Amazon
Leonard Dahlmann
Li Dong, Amazon
Besnik Fetahu, Amazon
Ciro Greco
Jongseok Han
Ohnmar Htun
Fei Hu, Microsoft
Manoj Balaji J
Ajinkya Kale
Sudipta Kar, Amazon
Shahram Khadivi, eBay Research
Tracy Holloway King, Adobe Systems
Vinayshekhar Bannihatti Kumar, Amazon
Saar Kuzi, Amazon
Gal Lavee
Jeong Min Lee, Facebook AI
Amita Misra, Amazon
Sudipto Mukherjee, Microsoft
Varun Nagaraj Rao, University of Southern California
Indraneil Paul, Amazon
Arushi Prakash
Alexandre Salle, VTEX
Salim Sazzed
Venkat Srinivasan
Daniel Stein
Sandesh Swamy, Amazon
Jacopo Tagliabue, Coveo
Liling Tan, Amazon
Chen Zhang
Jie Zhao

Table of Contents

DEFTri: A Few-Shot Label Fused Contextual Representation Learning For Product Defect Triage in e-Commerce

Ipsita Mohanty
Walmart Global Tech
Sunnyvale, California, USA
ipsita.mohanty@walmart.com

Abstract

Defect Triage is a time-sensitive and critical process in a large-scale agile software development lifecycle for e-commerce. Inefficiencies arising from human and process dependencies in this domain have motivated research in automated approaches using machine learning to accurately assign defects to qualified teams. This work proposes a novel framework for automated defect triage (DEFTri) using fine-tuned state-of-the-art pre-trained BERT on labels fused text embeddings to improve contextual representations from human-generated product defects. For our multi-label text classification defect triage task, we also introduce a Walmart proprietary dataset of product defects using weak supervision and adversarial learning, in a few-shot setting.

1 Introduction

In large e-commerce organizations, there are many defects generated periodically with a massive pool of software teams and developers spread across geographies to pick from, each with unique domain specialization. Most organizations have a large pool of human triaging agents responsible for routing these product defects across various teams within the organization. However, large-scale software releases are time-sensitive, and effective defect assignments are a critical component in the process that is prone to bottlenecks. Determining the most suitable team to own a defect may require several attempts; thus, wasting time to diagnose a defect not in the team's domain of specialty and, overall, negatively impacting the defect resolution throughput.

Prior industry research work on automated defect triage has primarily focused on using the traditional machine learning approaches. However, with the recent surge of state-of-the-art pre-trained language models, one under-explored field of application is operations in agile software development. In the defect triage, handling scenarios require Natural Language Understanding to utilize the context of the defects logged by human testers, to predict all the teams associated with resolution. The current defect triage process is primarily human-agents driven. This work integrates an automated defect triage framework, DEFTri using product defect's contextual features to achieve operational excellence within Walmart's software development lifecycle.

We propose a novel framework, DEFTri to perform an automated defect triage using contextual representations of human-generated defect texts. We use Walmart's proprietary data of product defects curated by product managers, program managers, and beta-testers to train our models. We use domain-specific lexicons to generate labeled training data using weak supervision in a few shot settings. We further use adversarial learning to increase our training sample size while increasing the robustness of our models. We propose our model architecture for fine-tuning pre-trained BERT (Devlin et al., 2018) for our multi-label classification task. Finally, we consolidate our experiments, analyze the results and discuss future research work.

2 Related Work

Prior research work on defect triage (Choquette-Choo et al., 2019; Mani et al., 2018; Soleimani Neysiani et al., 2020) mostly focuses on using traditional machine learning and RNNs on word vector representations of text using BOW, Word2Vec, Tfidf, etc. Another recent research relies on graph representation learning for defect triage (Wu et al., 2021). This paper proposes a graph recurrent convolution network with a joint random walk mechanism-based architecture. Also, several recent research on label embedding (Xiong et al., 2021; Liu et al., 2021; Si et al., 2020) has shown promising results for learning the text and label representation in the same latent

Proceedings of The Fifth Workshop on e-Commerce and NLP (ECNLP 5), pages 1 - 7
May 26, 2022 ©2022 Association for Computational Linguistics

space. We further the research by proposing a novel architecture to derive superior contextual text representations using state-of-the-art language model BERT for multi-label defect triage.

Most of these published research benchmarks are on open-source defect report datasets - Eclipse and Mozilla (Lamkanfi et al., 2013). However, these datasets are focused on technical errors generated during system failures and do not mimic our use case. Our product defects are comprehensive user testing reviews consisting of natural language, technical and domain-specific text. In the real world, gathering labeled data is hard and expensive. Hence, we propose a methodology to generate a robust proprietary multi-label training dataset using weak supervision and adversarial learning.

3 Data

Our primary dataset is a proprietary in-house dataset consisting of actual defect reviews generated by beta testers for one of our major software releases. We rely on defect title and description fields to create the text corpus and text labels to identify the teams uniquely. Each defect could have multiple associated teams and vice versa. For our research, we have 3485 samples as a train set and 85 samples as the test set with 15 unique team labels for our multi-label dataset. Refer Table 1. We have 4-5 human-expert annotated defects corresponding to each team label in our low-resource setting. Our data preparation pipeline follows the below steps,

3.1 Generate Labeled Data Using Weak Supervision

Despite the success of fine-tuning pre-trained language models, one bottleneck is the requirement of labeled data. These labeled training data were expensive and time-consuming to create. It required human annotators with domain expertise to read through each defect review and assign team labels accordingly. Every change in labeling guidelines, team orientation, or use case changes necessitated re-labeling. Hence, we used Snorkel label model (Ratner et al., 2017) to generate weak labels for our training data. We apply 25 labeling functions (LFs) to unlabelled training data using a snorkel pipeline. Refer Table 2.

3.2 Generate Synthetic Data Using Adversarial Learning

Machine learning algorithms are often vulnerable to adversarial examples that have imperceptible alterations from the original counterparts but can fool the state-of-the-art models (Jin et al., 2019; Dong et al., 2021).To increase the robustness, model training can be done using adversarial examples (Goodfellow et al., 2014; Gowal et al., 2021). We use Textattack framework (Morris et al., 2020) on 30% of our data, chosen at random to generate synthetic data for training our models and append these synthetic examples to our train set. We use embedding recipe of the framework that augments text by replacing words with neighbors in the counter-fitted embedding space, with a constraint to ensure their cosine similarity is at least 0.8. For every sampled defect, we produce 2 augmented defect texts by altering 10% of original text words, while preserving the team labels . Refer Table 3

3.3 Fix Data Imbalances

We found that the final training data created using the above techniques were imbalanced. This issue was because the product defects were likely skewed towards a specific defect associated with a more significant and frequently tested domain vs. a rarely occurring one. We also noticed that defect reviews for features related to new team labels are getting introduced into the environment on an ongoing basis. To resolve the skewness, we used Multilabel Synthetic Minority Over-sampling Technique (MLSMOTE) (Charte et al., 2015) w.r.t the team labels with minimal data representation.

4 Model

The multi-team-labels defect classification task in this research can be summarized with S as the tuple set. d_i and t_i represents the ith defect denoted as D and its corresponding team-labels denoted as T. N, n and m are the total number of defects, the length of the ith defect text and the number of teams-labels of the ith document, respectively.

$$S = \{(d_i, t_i)\}_{i=1}^{N}, D = \{d_i | d_i = \{d_1, d_2, , d_n\}\}, T = \{t_i | t_i = \{t_1, t_2, , t_m\}\}$$

Our framework, DEFTri aims at assigning team-labels to its corresponding defects based on the conditional probability P(t_i|d_i).

Defect Text Corpus (Anonymized Excerpts)
...For a store only query like XXX i am seeing available for scheduled pickup as the stack title on FE when i don't have a slot booked.This stack title should just reflect the XXX query like ios and web..Incorrect XXX mapping (number mapped to XXX..
...I cant add XXX to my cart from order details from my previous canceled order. There is no actionable CTA.There is an add to cart CTA for the XXX. See attached video. Using ios XXX...

Table 1: Samples of Defect Text Corpus.

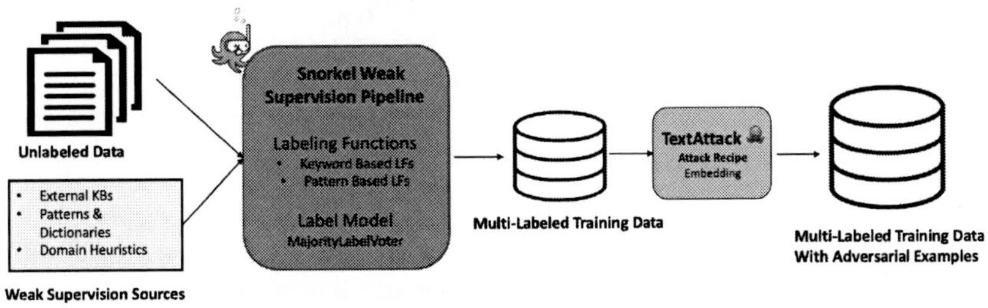

Figure 1: DEFTri Data Generation Methodology

Rule	corpus->labels (Anonymized)
Keyword	'android' or 'ios' -> [Team-LabelA]
Pattern	'*search*' -> [Team-LabelB, Team-LabelC]

Table 2: Example LFs For Snorkel pipeline

4.1 Pre-Trained Model

For our fine-tuning, we use BERT pre-trained transformer embedding from Hugging Face's Transformers library (Wolf et al., 2020).BERT base uncased embeddings are case insensitive and are pre-trained on the English language self-supervised using two objectives - masked language modeling (MLM) and Next Sentence Prediction (NSP). These embeddings were introduced in the original BERT (Devlin et al., 2018) paper and serve as baseline embeddings for our models.

4.2 Approach

For our DEFTri framework, we propose 2 novel implementations to derive superior contextual representations from product defect text, that help in improved multi-label defect classification task. We denote the defect corpus(title and description) tokens as D_i and their corresponding token embeddings as E_{Di}, where K is the total number of words in the input defect and D_K represents the last token. Similarly, let L_j be the team label text of the jth team of the overall 15 teams, corresponding to the defect corpus. Finally, we derive the positional embedding using BERT and apply classification layer with activation to the last layer of the hidden state at the [CLS] token.

4.2.1 Label Fused Model with [SEP]

We utilize the sentence pair configuration of BERT for text input. We concatenate the team labels text as Sentence A and concatenate the Defect title and description text as Sentence B, both separated by a [SEP] token. Refer Figure 2

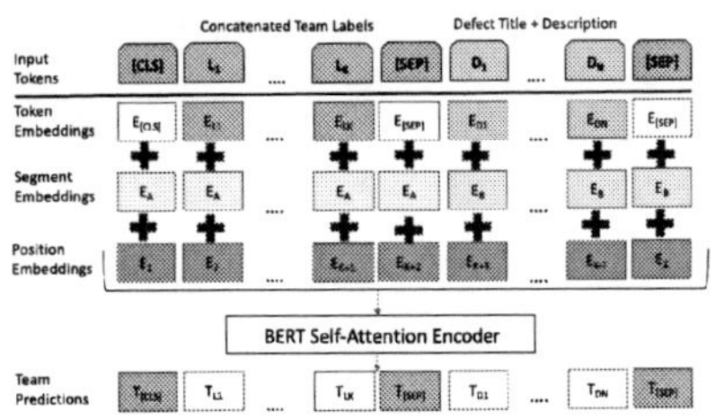

Figure 2: DEFTri LabelFuse Model with [SEP]

4.2.2 Label Fused Model without [SEP]

For our second implementation, we concatenate the team labels text along with Defect title and description text as a single Sentence A, without any [SEP] token as input. Refer Figure 3

Defect Text (Anonymized)	Adversarial Defect Text (Anonymized)
Price showing inconsistently	Price displaying inconsistently
Final cost by weight not showing on search tiles	Final prices by weight not showing on search tiles
Spacing on Nutrition Label is too large	Spacing on Nourishment Label is too large

Table 3: Sample cases of Defect text vs Adversarial Defect Text.

Model	Macro-F1	Accuracy
BERT+Linear	0.8123	0.8134
BERT+BiLSTM	0.8206	0.8216
BERT+LabelFuse w/o [SEP]+Linear	0.8144	0.8153
BERT+LabelFuse w/o [SEP]+BiLSTM	**0.8236**	**0.8245**
BERT+LabelFuse w [SEP]+Linear	0.8137	0.8150
BERT+LabelFuse w [SEP]+BiLSTM	0.8229	0.8241

Table 4: DEFTri Experiments Results For Contextual Multi-TeamLabel Classification on Real Product Defects

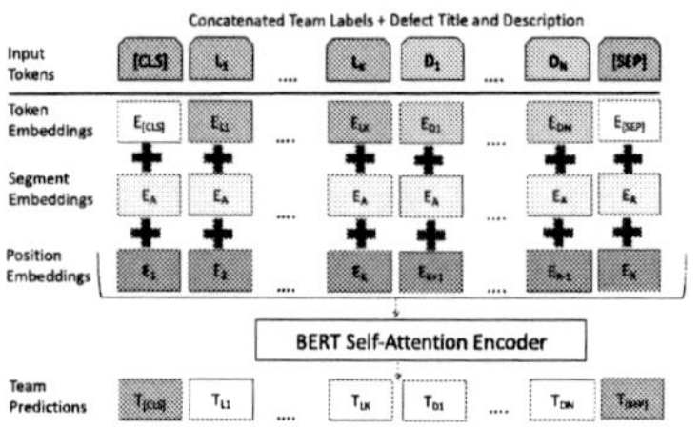

Figure 3: DEFTri LabelFuse Model w/o [SEP]

4.3 Classification Head

We experimented with two different dense layers for the classification head - Linear and BiLSTM. Refer Table 5

Classification Heads		Dense Layer		Linear Layer	
Type	Activation	In	Out	In	Out
Linear	Tanh	768	768	768	15
BiLSTM	ReLU	768	256	512	15

Table 5: DEFTri Classification Head Configurations

4.4 Loss Function and Optimizer

For model training we use PyTorch implementation of BCEWithLogitsLoss as our loss function and AdamOptimizer as our optimizer. BCEWithLogitsLoss combines a Sigmoid layer and the Binary Cross Entropy Loss in one single class. In case of multi-label classification the loss can be described as,

$$l_t(x, y) = L_t = \{l_{1,t}, ..., l_{N,t}\}^T,$$
$$l_{n,t} = -w_{n,t}[p_t y_{n,t} \cdot log\sigma(x_{n,t}) + (1 + y_{n,t}) \cdot log\sigma(x_{n,t})]$$

where t=15 and represents the number of team-labels , n is number of sample in the batch and p_t is the weight of the positive answer for team-label t.

4.5 Hyper-Parameters

We use a set of hyper-parameters for our experiments. We used manual search for hyper-parameter search and the best model was chosen based on the best top-1 accuracy yielded in the validation data. Refer Table 6

HParams	Values
Dropout	0.1
Max Sequence Length	512
Batch-Size	16
Learning Rate	1e-5
Weight Decay	0.01
Adam epsilon	1e-6
Epochs	10

Table 6: DEFTri Hyper-Parameters

5 Experiments

As baseline and our proposed architecture, we use the pre-trained bert-base-uncased model (Wolf et al., 2020; Vaswani et al., 2017). We perform a total of 6 experiments for our models under 3 different settings (1) baseline fine-tuned BERT model with no fused labels (2) fine-tuned BERT with fused labels without [SEP] token and (3) fine-tuned BERT with fused labels with [SEP] token, using 2 classification heads combinations e.g Linear and BiLSTM. Refer Table 4 and Appendix A.1

For data preprocessing step, the corpus is converted to lowercase and tokenzied with one-hot-encoded labels.Our deep learning model is then trained to predict multiple team-labels for each test sample. At inference time, the model takes in an input of text corpus of defect and predicts a vector of probabilities for each of the 15 team-labels. We used a confidence threshold of 0.55 for our probability vector to obtain a binary vector for comparison with ground-truth.

Measuring accuracy on exact binary vector matching for multi-label classification is too penalizing because of the low tolerance for partial errors. Therefore, we divide our predictions by classes. For each of the team-labels in our dataset, we calculate the number of false positives (FP), false negatives (FN), true positives (TP), true negatives (TN). Finally, to obtain our Accuracy, we sum up the values across each team-labels as below,

$$Accuracy = \frac{\sum TP_t + \sum TN_t}{\sum FP_t + \sum FN_t + \sum TP_t + \sum TN_t}$$

where T=15 and represents the number of team-labels in our dataset and TP_t, TN_t, FP_t , FN_t represents values of TP, TN, FP, FN for t^{th} team-label. Similarly, we used macro-F1 (F1) scores based on averaged value of precision and recall calculated over all team-labels as below,

$$Precision_t = \frac{TP_t}{FP_t + TP_t}$$

$$Recall_t = \frac{TP_t}{FN_t + TP_t}$$

$$F1 = 2 \times \frac{\frac{1}{T}\sum Precision_t \times \frac{1}{T}\sum Recall_t}{\frac{1}{T}\sum Precision_t + \frac{1}{T}\sum Recall_t}$$

6 Analysis

Based on our experiments, we observed that label-fused contextual learning-based fine-tuned BERT models significantly outperformed the base model using only the context of the defect text. The performance boost over the base BERT pre-trained fine-tuned model is because of the context in the label embeddings used in addition to the defect text in the label-fused models, which optimizes on the alignment of features, which makes it possible to classify better. Our team labels were short meaningful English words vs abbreviations which made fused embeddings better for classification when paired as a sentence with the defect texts as inputs. We observed that label-fused model without [SEP] token performed better that with [SEP] token which could have been because of the unnatural formation of Sentence A, where a bunch of team labels are concatenated together.

Also, with the addition of synthetically generated data using adversarial examples for model training, we achieved an average accuracy improvement of 2.69% across our models vs. using the original data only. However, during our experiments we observed that the performance was sensitive towards the choice of text corpus sequence length and perturbation percentage for data augmentation made, during model training. A higher percentage of perturbations combined with a lower sequence length of text corpus negatively impacted performance.

7 Future Work

Fine-tuning language models with weak supervision definitely solves the challenge of low labeled data availability. However, the models performance definitely suffers from error-propagation of pseudo-labels generated during the process. Recent research in contrastive self-regularized self-training approach (Yu et al., 2020) and GAN-BERT in adversarial setting (Croce et al., 2020) have shown promising results for fine-tuning BERT-based language models with weak supervision. Also, Contrastive learning and Adversarial Learning approaches applied to various NLP tasks have demonstrated improvement over fine-tuning on BERT-based models (Mohanty et al., 2021; Pan et al., 2021). To further our research, we would improve upon these approaches.

8 Conclusion

In this work, we proposed a novel framework, DEFTri for automated defect triage using contextual representations of human-generated defect reviews at Walmart. We discussed our methodology of generating a new proprietary labeled dataset by using weak supervision and adversarial learning, in a few shot setting. We presented two label-fused model approaches for fine-tuning pre-trained BERT. As hypothesized, the experimental results show that our approach improves the multi-label text classification task for defect triage. We also proposed our future work of implementing contrastive learning for fine-tuning using weak supervision.

Acknowledgments

The author would like to thank colleagues in the Omni Customer Experience org. at Walmart Global

Tech for all their support and encouragement.

References

Francisco Charte, Antonio J. Rivera, María J. del Jesus, and Francisco Herrera. 2015. Mlsmote: Approaching imbalanced multilabel learning through synthetic instance generation. *Knowledge-Based Systems*, 89:385–397.

Christopher A. Choquette-Choo, David Sheldon, Jonny Proppe, John Alphonso-Gibbs, and Harsha Gupta. 2019. A multi-label, dual-output deep neural network for automated bug triaging. *CoRR*, abs/1910.05835.

Danilo Croce, Giuseppe Castellucci, and Roberto Basili. 2020. GAN-BERT: Generative adversarial learning for robust text classification with a bunch of labeled examples. In *Proceedings of the 58th Annual Meeting of the Association for Computational Linguistics*, pages 2114–2119, Online. Association for Computational Linguistics.

Jacob Devlin, Ming-Wei Chang, Kenton Lee, and Kristina Toutanova. 2018. BERT: pre-training of deep bidirectional transformers for language understanding. *CoRR*, abs/1810.04805.

Xinshuai Dong, Luu Anh Tuan, Min Lin, Shuicheng Yan, and Hanwang Zhang. 2021. How should pre-trained language models be fine-tuned towards adversarial robustness? *CoRR*, abs/2112.11668.

Ian J. Goodfellow, Jean Pouget-Abadie, Mehdi Mirza, Bing Xu, David Warde-Farley, Sherjil Ozair, Aaron Courville, and Yoshua Bengio. 2014. Generative adversarial networks.

Sven Gowal, Sylvestre-Alvise Rebuffi, Olivia Wiles, Florian Stimberg, Dan Andrei Calian, and Timothy A. Mann. 2021. Improving robustness using generated data. *CoRR*, abs/2110.09468.

Di Jin, Zhijing Jin, Joey Tianyi Zhou, and Peter Szolovits. 2019. Is BERT really robust? natural language attack on text classification and entailment. *CoRR*, abs/1907.11932.

Ahmed Lamkanfi, Javier Pérez, and Serge Demeyer. 2013. The eclipse and mozilla defect tracking dataset: A genuine dataset for mining bug information. In *2013 10th Working Conference on Mining Software Repositories (MSR)*, pages 203–206.

Huiting Liu, Geng Chen, Peipei Li, Peng Zhao, and Xindong Wu. 2021. Multi-label text classification via joint learning from label embedding and label correlation. *Neurocomputing*, 460:385–398.

Senthil Mani, Anush Sankaran, and Rahul Aralikatte. 2018. Deeptriage: Exploring the effectiveness of deep learning for bug triaging. *CoRR*, abs/1801.01275.

Ipsita Mohanty, Ankit Goyal, and Alex Dotterweich. 2021. Emotions are subtle: Learning sentiment based text representations using contrastive learning. *CoRR*, abs/2112.01054.

John X. Morris, Eli Lifland, Jin Yong Yoo, and Yanjun Qi. 2020. Textattack: A framework for adversarial attacks in natural language processing. *CoRR*, abs/2005.05909.

Lin Pan, Chung-Wei Hang, Avirup Sil, Saloni Potdar, and Mo Yu. 2021. Improved text classification via contrastive adversarial training. *CoRR*, abs/2107.10137.

Alexander Ratner, Stephen H. Bach, Henry R. Ehrenberg, Jason Alan Fries, Sen Wu, and Christopher Ré. 2017. Snorkel: Rapid training data creation with weak supervision. *CoRR*, abs/1711.10160.

Shijing Si, Rui Wang, Jedrek Wosik, Hao Zhang, David Dov, Guoyin Wang, Ricardo Henao, and Lawrence Carin. 2020. Students need more attention: Bert-based attentionmodel for small data with application to automaticpatient message triage. *CoRR*, abs/2006.11991.

Behzad Soleimani Neysiani, Seyed Morteza Babamir, and Masayoshi Aritsugi. 2020. Efficient feature extraction model for validation performance improvement of duplicate bug report detection in software bug triage systems. *Information and Software Technology*, 126:106344–106363.

Ashish Vaswani, Noam Shazeer, Niki Parmar, Jakob Uszkoreit, Llion Jones, Aidan N. Gomez, Lukasz Kaiser, and Illia Polosukhin. 2017. Attention is all you need. *CoRR*, abs/1706.03762.

Thomas Wolf, Lysandre Debut, Victor Sanh, Julien Chaumond, Clement Delangue, Anthony Moi, Pierric Cistac, Tim Rault, Rémi Louf, Morgan Funtowicz, Joe Davison, Sam Shleifer, Patrick von Platen, Clara Ma, Yacine Jernite, Julien Plu, Canwen Xu, Teven Le Scao, Sylvain Gugger, Mariama Drame, Quentin Lhoest, and Alexander M. Rush. 2020. Huggingface's transformers: State-of-the-art natural language processing.

Hongrun Wu, Yutao Ma, Zhenglong Xiang, Chen Yang, and Keqing He. 2021. A spatial-temporal graph neural network framework for automated software bug triaging. *CoRR*, abs/2101.11846.

Yijin Xiong, Yukun Feng, Hao Wu, Hidetaka Kamigaito, and Manabu Okumura. 2021. Fusing label embedding into bert: An efficient improvement for text classification. In *Findings of the Association for Computational Linguistics: ACL/IJCNLP 2021, Online Event, August 1-6, 2021*, pages 1743–1750. Association for Computational Linguistics.

Yue Yu, Simiao Zuo, Haoming Jiang, Wendi Ren, Tuo Zhao, and Chao Zhang. 2020. Fine-tuning pre-trained language model with weak supervision: A contrastive-regularized self-training approach. *CoRR*, abs/2010.07835.

A Appendix

A.1 Experiment Setting

We ran all our experiments on a Google Cloud Platform using a n1-standard-16 machine with NVIDIA Tesla V100 GPUs.

Interactive Latent Knowledge Selection for E-commerce Product Copywriting Generation

Zeming Wang [1]* **Yanyan Zou** [2], **Yuejian Fang** [1], **Hongshen Chen** [2], **Mian Ma**[2], **Zhuoye Ding**[2] and **BO Long** [2]

[1]School of Software and Microelectronics, Peking University, Beijing, China

[2]JD.com, Beijing, China

wzm@stu.pku.edu.cn, fangyj@ss.pku.edu.cn,
{zouyanyan6,chenhongshen,mamian,dingzhuoye,bo.long}@jd.com

Abstract

As the multi-modal e-commerce is thriving, high-quality advertising product copywriting has gain more attentions, which plays a crucial role in the e-commerce recommender, advertising and even search platforms. The advertising product copywriting is able to enhance the user experience by highlighting the product's characteristics with textual descriptions and thus to improve the likelihood of user click and purchase. Automatically generating product copywriting has attracted noticeable interests from both academic and industrial communities, where existing solutions merely make use of a product's title and attribute information to generate its corresponding description. However, in addition to the product title and attributes, we observe that there are various auxiliary descriptions created by the shoppers or marketers in the e-commerce platforms (namely human knowledge), which contains valuable information for product copywriting generation, yet always accompanying lots of noises. In this work, we propose a novel solution to automatically generating product copywriting that involves all the title, attributes and denoised auxiliary knowledge. To be specific, we design an end-to-end generation framework equipped with two variational autoencoders that works interactively to select informative human knowledge and generate diverse copywriting. Experiments on real-world e-commerce product copywriting datasets demonstrate that our proposed method outperforms various baselines with regard to both automatic and human evaluation metrics.

1 Introduction

Traditional e-commerce platforms solely present a list of products to customers. Nowadays, as the multi-modal recommender systems are thriving, the e-commerce platform ecosystem has also been enriched with multi-modal forms, such as product advertising copywriting and product living videos. Especially, the product advertising copywriting plays an important role in the e-commerce recommender, advertising and search platforms, which is able to improve the customers' shopping experience. Instead of only showing the product title, a well-written product description can interest the customer hugely and save their time from clicking every product and reading the long-and-complex product details. Hence, this work focuses on the problem of automatic product copywriting generation, which aims to generate a textual description for a product, highlighting the attractive properties of the product. Such a task is always framed as a sequence-to-sequence problem (Chen et al., 2019).

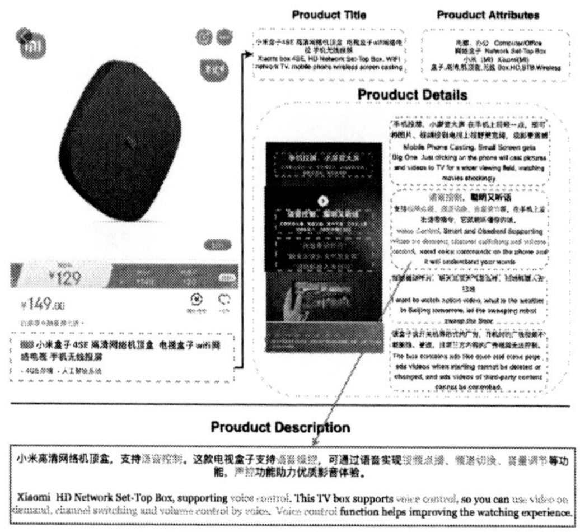

Figure 1: An example of product copywriting generation from our dataset, including product title, attribute, details as well as the product description.

The product title and a list of product attributes are always taken as the main model input to generate the product copywriting, exemplified by Figure 1. Recently, Chen et al. (2019) proposed to involve the external knowledge (i.e., Wikipedia) into the product title and attributes during the generation process of product copywriting. However, the

*Work done during internship at JD.com.

Proceedings of The Fifth Workshop on e-Commerce and NLP (ECNLP 5), pages 8 - 19
May 26, 2022 ©2022 Association for Computational Linguistics

external knowledge and customer reviews are not always available. For example, thousands of newly released products are emerging in the e-commerce platforms, where the external or the customer reviews are not accessible while automatically generating advertising copywriting is critical for such new products to improve the click-through rate and the conversion rate.

In practice, we observe that each product (e.g., the hot and newly released items) is accompanied with various product details in the e-commerce platforms (e.g., Taobao, JD, and Amazon). The product title and associated attributes summarize the main information of a product, while the product details comprise of auxiliary advertising descriptions created by shoppers and marketers which contain salient information that highlight the product properties with advertising phrases (i.e., human knowledge) and thus are beneficial to improving the quality of the generated copywriting. Exemplified by Figure 1, the product title and attributes summarize the main functions of "Xiaomi box SE", while the product details elaborate the product with slogans that are attractive to customers, like "voice control" and "switch channels and adjust the volume by voice". Unfortunately, we also observe that such human knowledge also contains redundant pieces, like "I want to watch action video", which might harm the quality of the generated copywriting. One recent work (Zhang et al., 2021) simply concatenated all the product details with product title and attributes as the model input, without considering the noises contained by the product details. In this work, we propose to select the salient knowledge from the auxiliary product details before we feed such information, associated with product title and attributes, into the model.

To be specific, we propose an **I**nteractive **L**atent **V**ariables model based on **T**ransformer architecture (Vaswani et al., 2017) (i.e., **ILVT**), which is designed to select knowledge from noisy product details and incorporate the selected knowledge into the process of product copywriting generation. To enhance the connection between the process of the knowledge selection and copywriting generation, we sample latent variables from prior description and knowledge latent space separately. During generation phase, ILVT will firstly sample the description latent variable from the description distribution conditioned on the product title and attributes, then sample the knowledge latent variable from knowledge distribution conditioned on product details and the description latent variable. With the interactive latent variables, ILVT can also generate copywritings with strong diversity. Without latent variable modules, ILVT degenerates into transformer with copy mechanism, which is a traditional method for copywriting generation in e-commerce platform (Zhang et al., 2021). To the best of our knowledge, this is the first work that selects knowledge from product details to improve the generation quality and diversity in product copywriting generation task.

Dataset Size	220,000
Average length of product title	44.93
Average length of attribute set	7.75
Average length of product details	838.39
Average length of human knowledge	111.38
Average length of product copywriting	81.16

Table 1: Data statistics for the JDK dataset.

To evaluate our proposed method, we collected a Chinese product copywriting dataset from the JD platform, named **JDK**. The dataset consists of 220,000 instances, each of which comprises of a product's title, attributes, details as well as the corresponding description. Results on such dataset shows that our proposed method obtains the best performance compared to all baselines, in terms of both automatic and human evaluations.

2 Proposed Method

2.1 Dataset Construction

We collected a Chinese product copywriting generation dataset, named JDK, from the e-commerce platform, JD[1], one of the biggest Chinese e-commerce platforms. The dataset consists of 220K products, covering 30 categories, such as digits and clothing. Each product instance is associated with a product title, a set of attributes, product details created by advertising experts, as well as the product copywriting published by professional writers. We randomly split the whole datasets into three parts, 200K for training, 10K each for test and validation. The product title and attributes summarize the main characteristics of the product. On average, the number of Chinese tokens in product title is 44.93, and the size of the attribute set is 7.75. However, the average number of tokens before pre-processing in the product details is 838.39, which is much larger than the average length of the

[1] https://www.jd.com/

copywriting, i.e., 81.16. The average length of the human knowledge now is 111.38 tokens. Table 1 lists the detailed statistics about this dataset.

We observed that the product details, created by advertising experts, contain ample and heterogeneous information, such as the advertising slogans in textual form, the product size in numbers and specification with particular usage examples. Simply feeding all product details might harm the generation performance. Thus, a heuristic method is introduced to filter out the apparently noisy pieces in collected product details. We split the whole detail paragraph K_{total} into fragments KF following the heuristic rule γ (i.e., the stop symbols) and keep the fragments whose length is between 10 and 64 tokens to remove some useless pieces, such as instructions for usage.

$$K_{total} \xrightarrow{\gamma} KF = \{K_{frag_1}, K_{frag_2}, ..., K_{frag_m}\}$$

where m is the number of fragments that varies for different products. We adopted the Sentence-Bert (Reimers and Gurevych, 2019) to obtain the contextual representation for each fragment $K_{frag_i} \in KF$, denoted as E_{frag_i}. We feed the contextual representations of KF into the K-Means clustering algorithm (MacQueen et al., 1967), where fragments with similar semantics are clustered into the same group:

$$\{E_{frag_1}, \cdots, E_{frag_m}\} \xrightarrow{\mathcal{K}} KP = \{K_1, \cdots, K_{|K|}\}$$

where each $K_i \in KP$ is a group of fragments with similar semantics and we concatenated all fragments in the same group in an alphabetical order to obtain a single sequence, i.e. a text containing human knowledge. For simplicity, we manually set $|K| = 6$ for the number of clusters.

Likewise, we applied Sentence-Bert to obtain the contextual representation of each knowledge text $K_i \in KP$ and the corresponding product description D, denoted as R_{K_i} and R_D, respectively. We calculate the cosine similarity between R_{K_i} and R_D. The cluster with the highest similarity score will be considered as a pseudo knowledge K_{pse}.

$$K_{pse} = \max_{K_i \in KP} cos < R_{K_i}, R_D >$$

where $cos < \cdot >$ means the function of cosine similarity. Finally, for each copywriting instance, we have a set of knowledge in the size of 6, one of which is labeled as pseudo knowledge.

2.2 Problem Formulation

With a product title, attribute sets and its corresponding commodity details, the objective of our method is to utilize the intrinsic information firstly, and then select an appropriate knowledge from details. Finally, diverse and accurate product description will be generated. Given a product, the e-commerce platforms often describes such a product from multiple aspects, including the product title T, a set of attributes A, and the product details KP. The product title T describes the product in a short text, represented as a sequence of words $T = \{t_1, t_2, ..., t_{|t|}\}$. The attribute set A consists of $|A|$ attributes $A = \{a_1, a_2..., a_{|A|}\}$ that captures the product properties from different aspects. The product details $KP = \{K_1, K_2, ..., K_{|KP|}\}$ are essentially a human knowledge pool, composed of advertising description created by advertising experts. Each advertising description $K_i \in KP$ is a sequence of words $K_i = \left\{k_i^1, k_i^2, ..., k_i^{|K_i|}\right\}$. Figure 1 demonstrates an example.

In this work, we aim to select the most salient knowledge from the product details KP, and then incorporate such knowledge with product title T and attributes A to generate diverse and high-quality product copywriting.

2.3 Framework

In order to better guide the knowledge selection process and enhance the relationship between the target copywriting and corresponding selected knowledge, we utilize an interactive variational autoencoder framework (Kingma and Welling, 2014) to inject the description latent variable to the knowledge latent distribution, followed by selecting the salient knowledge and generating the description sequentially as follows:

$$\begin{aligned} p_\theta(K, D|A, T) = \int_{z_d} \sum_{z_k} & p_\theta(D|z_d, K, A, T) \\ & \cdot p_\theta(K|z_d, A, T, KP) \\ & \cdot p_\varphi(z_k|z_d, KP) \cdot p_\varphi(z_d|A, T) dz_d \end{aligned}$$

where z_k and z_d are latent variables for knowledge and product copywriting, respectively. $p_\varphi(z_d|A, T)$ and $p_\varphi(z_k|z_d, A, T)$ are their conditional priors. Since the knowledge selection is a discriminative task with limited choices, z_k is suitable for a categorical distribution (Jang et al., 2017), while the z_d follows an isotropic Gaussian distribution (Kingma and Welling, 2014). From the perspective of the

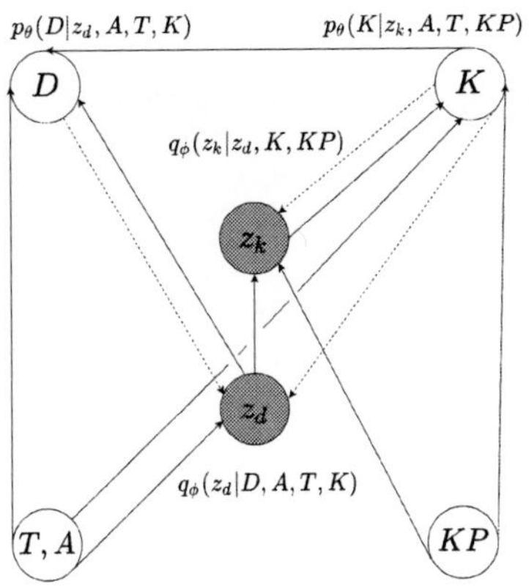

Figure 2: The graphical representation of the propossed ILVT model. Dotted line belongs to posterior distribution solely.

product description writing process, we assume that the product copywriting contains pivot information that points out what kind of information from the product knowledge pool KP (i.e., product details) is useful for copywriting generation. Thus, the latent variable z_d sampled from $p(z_d|A, T)$ is based on the intrinsic product information (i.e., product title and attributes) and $z_k \sim p(z_k|z_d, KP)$ is dependent on z_d. During the training phase, a variational posterior $q_\phi(\cdot)$ is used to maximize the Evidence Lower Bound (ELBO) as follows:

$$\begin{aligned}
&\mathcal{L}_{ILVT} = \\
&- D_{KL}[q_\phi(z_d|D, A, T, K)||p_\varphi(z_d|A, T)] \\
&- D_{KL}[q_\phi(z_k|z_d, K, KP)||p_\varphi(z_k|z_d, KP)] \\
&+ E_{z_k \sim q_\phi(z_k|z_d, K, KP)}[\log p_\theta(K|z_k, A, T, KP)] \\
&+ E_{z_d \sim q_\phi(z_d|D, A, T)}[\log p_\theta(D|z_d, A, T, K)]
\end{aligned}$$

where θ, ϕ and φ are the parameters of the generation, posterior and prior modules. The generative process can be described as:

- Step 1: sample the description latent variable $z_d \sim p_\varphi(z_d|A, T)$.
- Step 2: sample the knowledge latent variable $z_k \sim p_\varphi(z_k|z_d, KP)$.
- Step 3: select the most salient knowledge $K \sim p_\theta(K|z_k, A, T, KP)$.
- Step 4: generate the product copywriting $D \sim p_\theta(D|z_d, A, T, K)$.

The description latent variable z_d contributes to the knowledge latent variable z_k explicitly, and z_k influences z_d via common target knowledge K and back propagation implicitly. We show the graphical model of the single-track interaction in Figure 2.

2.4 Encoding Layer

We adopt the Transformer (Vaswani et al., 2017) encoder as the encoding layer.

Basic Product Representation For simplicity, we concatenate the product title T and its associated attributes $A = \{a_1, a_2, ..., a_{|A|}\}$ (ordered in alphabet) into a single sequence to get basic product information as:

$$P = [T; a_1; a_2; ...; a_{|A|}]$$

where ";" stands for sequence concatenation. The basic product embedding in the first layer $E^{(0)}$ is the sum of the word embeddings $WE(\cdot)$ and the positional encoding $PE(\cdot)$:

$$E_P = WE(P) + PE(P)$$

The initial product embedding will go through multi-layers and the output of i-th layer is:

$$E_P^{(i)} = FFN(MHA(E_P^{(i-1)}, ..., E_P^{(i-1)}))$$

where $MHA(\cdot, \cdot, \cdot)$ means multi-head self-attention function and $FFN(\cdot)$ is the position-wise fully connected feed-forward network. The final representation of product basic information (i.e., product title and attributes) defined as:

$$H_P = avgpool(E_P^{(N)})$$

where $E_P^{(N)}$ is the the final representation from the N-th encoder layer, and $avgpool$ is the average pooling operation (Cer et al., 2018).

Product Description Representation Following the same procedures, we can obtain the initial and final representations of the product description (i.e., copywriting), denoted as E_D and H_D.

Product Knowledge Representation The product knowledge pool (i.e., the product details) is a list of advertising descriptions created by advertising experts, $KP = \{K_1, ..., K_{|KP|}\}$. To obtain the representation of the knowledge pool, for each advertising descriptions $K_j \in KP$, we consider all the word embedding, positional embedding description segment embedding:

$$E_{K_j} = WE(K_j) + PE(K_j) + SE(j)$$

where j stands for the description position in the knowledge pool, and SE is the segment embedding which can be learned during the training phase. The representation of i-th encoder is calculated as:

$$E_{K_j}^{(i)} = FFN(MHA(E_{K_j}^{(i-1)}, \cdots, E_{K_j}^{(i)}))$$

The final representation of the whole knowledge pool is then defined as:

$$H_{KP} = [avgpool(E_{K_0}^{(N)}), \cdots, avgpool(E_{K_{|KP|}}^{(N)})]$$

It is worthy noting that there are no available annotations of the most salient knowledge, however, which is necessary during training phrase. Thus, we designed a simple algorithm to construct the pseudo label for the knowledge selection for each product. According to the pseudo annotations, we denote the selected knowledge as K_{pse}, whose hidden representation is denoted as $H_K = avgpool(E_K^{(N)})$.

2.5 Interactive Latent Variable Layer

To build the relationship between the knowledge selection and copywriting generation, we design a pair of interactive latent variables, i.e., the description latent variable and the knowledge latent variable, to influence each other.

Description Latent Variable To make the generated copywriting more diverse and guide the selection phase, we learn a Gaussian distribution with the intrinsic product information.

For the posterior, inspired by Kim et al. (2018) we calculate hidden representations $H_{D_{atten_K}}$ and $H_{K_{atten_D}}$ for enhancing the relation between description and pseudo knowledge, as

$$H_{D_{atten_K}} = avgpool(Softmax(\mathcal{Q}_D \mathcal{K}_K))$$
$$\mathcal{Q}_D = W_Q E_D$$
$$\mathcal{K}_K = W_K E_K$$

where W_Q, W_K is parameters. $H_{K_{atten_D}}$ is calculated similarly. We concatenate the hidden representations $H_{D_{atten_K}}, H_{K_{atten_D}}$ with H_P, H_D, H_K as H_{des} and feed into a MLP layer to calculate parameters μ and σ of the posterior distribution:

$$\begin{cases} \mu = MLP(H_{des}) \\ \sigma = Softplus(MLP(H_{des})) \end{cases}$$

$$H_{des} = [H_D, H_P, H_K, H_{D_{atten_K}}, H_{K_{atten_D}}]$$

so the posterior Gaussian distribution can be then described as:

$$q_\phi(z_d|D, A, T, K) = N_\phi(z_d|\mu, \sigma I)$$

For the prior distribution, we only utilize the basic product representation H_P and calculate parameters μ' and σ' similar to the posterior processing:

$$p_\varphi(z_d|A, T) = N_\varphi(z_d|\mu', \sigma' I)$$

$$\begin{cases} \mu' = MLP(H_P) \\ \sigma' = Softplus(MLP(H_P)) \end{cases}$$

In the training phase, we use the reparameterization trick(Kingma and Welling, 2014) since the stochastic sampling from the latent distribution is non-differential. In order to approximate the distributions of the posterior and prior representation, we introduce the KL divergence loss (Kullback and Leibler, 1951).

Knowledge Latent Variable In order to strength the relationship between the selected knowledge and corresponding description, we inject the description latent variable z_d to the knowledge latent space and thus get the interactive VAEs model. Since knowledge selection is a discriminate task, we utilize the Categorical distribution (Jang et al., 2017) for knowledge latent space.

We then calculate the hidden representation $H_{KP_{atten_{z_d}}}$ via attention method:

$$H_{KP_{atten_{z_d}}} = Softmax((W_d z_d) H_{KP}^T) H_{KP}$$

In the training phase, we feed $H_{KP_{atten_{z_d}}}$ and z_d with the total and pseudo knowledge representations H_{KP}, H_K together into a MLP layer to compute the parameters π for posterior categorical distribution. By removing the H_K, we obtain the parameters π' for prior distribution.

$$\pi = MLP[z_d, H_K, H_{KP}, H_{KP_{atten_{z_d}}}]$$
$$\pi' = MLP[z_d, H_{KP}, H_{KP_{atten_{z_d}}}]$$

The posterior and prior distributions can be then described as:

$$q_\phi(z_k|z_d, K, KP) = Cat_\phi(\pi)$$
$$p_\varphi(z_k|z_d, KP)) = Cat_\varphi(\pi')$$

We also introduce the KL divergence loss and reparametrization trick. We use gumbel-softmax (Jang et al., 2017; Maddison et al., 2017) as the categorical distribution is discrete.

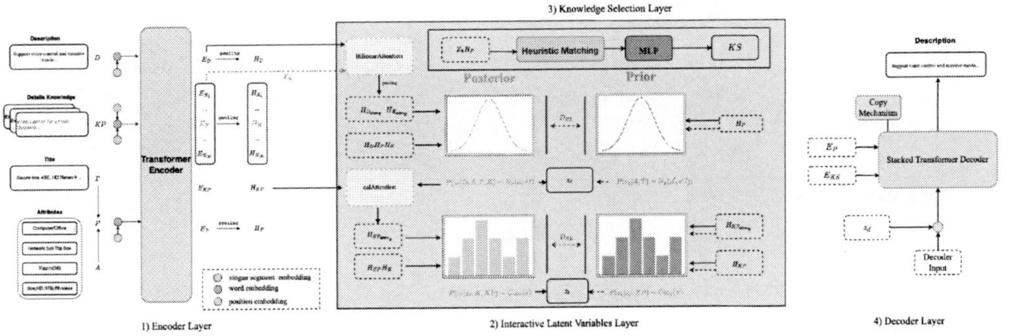

Figure 3: The architecture of the proposed ILVT model.The solid line denotes the training procedure, while the dotted line denotes the inference process.

2.6 Knowledge Selection

Motivated by Mou et al. (2016), we adopt the heuristic matching algorithm to select the target salient knowledge from all the product details. After getting the knowledge latent variable z_k sampling from the posterior distribution and prior distribution in training and generation stage, respectively, we compute the hidden representation for knowledge selection as:

$$H_{sel} = [H_P, z_k, |H_P - z_k|, H_P \odot z_k]$$

where $\odot$ stands for the element-wise multiplication. The selected knowledge is denoted as $KS \in KP$, whose representation H_{KS} can be obtained through the encoder layers where only the word and positional embeddings are taken as input, similar to the product title and attributes.

The selection embedding H_{sel} will be fed into a MLP layer to predict the index ID_{KS} of the corresponding target knowledge KS.

2.7 Decoder Layer

We inject the basic product information (i.e., title and attributes) $E_P^{(N)}$, the generation latent variable z_d, and the selected knowledge $E_{KS}^{(N)}$ into a stacked transformer decoder module with the copy mechanism to generate the product copywriting.

We also try different ways to combining the VAE modules with transformer decoder. Similar to Fang et al. (2021); Li et al. (2020a), we empirically observed that the best choice is to element-wisely add the latent variable z_d with the word and positional embeddings of each word, before fed into the decoder, to generate the copywriting. The copy mechanism is used to copy words in the selected knowledge and the input product information (i.e., title and attributes). The probability of generating token d_t at t-th step is computed as:

$$P(d_t) = \lambda_1 P_{cp}(d_t|KS, P) + \lambda_2 P_{voc}(d_t|z_d, KS, P)$$

where λ_1 and λ_2 are the coordination probability. P_{voc} is the output from the stacked transformer decoder layers and P_{cp} represents the copy logits, defined as:

$$P_{cp}(d_t|*) = \sum_{i:t_i=D_t} \alpha_{t,i}$$

where $*$ stands for either P or KS.

3 Experiments

We conducted experiments on the JDK dataset.

3.1 Baseline Models

We compare our model with several baselines:

- **CONVSEQ2SEQ** (Gehring et al., 2017) is a sequence-to-sequence model with convolutional neural networks for text generation.
- **TRANSFORMER** (Vaswani et al., 2017) is an encoder-decoder architecture relying on self-attention mechanism.
- **KOBE** (Chen et al., 2019) incorporates knowledge extracted from exogenous database into the copywriting generation model.
- **PTRANS** (Vaswani et al., 2017; See et al., 2017) is a transformer-based generation model with copy mechanism, which is the backbone architecture of this ILVT. In other words, ILVT without latent variable modules is degenerated into PTRANS.

For the model CONVSEQ2SEQ, TRANSFORMER and PTRANS, in addition to the baseline version,

Model	BLEU	BLEU-1	BLEU-2	BLEU-3	BLEU-4	DIST-1	DIST-2
ConvSeq2Seq	12.60	**29.57**	12.11	5.91	3.19	39.50	62.27
+ALL	11.16	26.82	10.46	4.86	2.50	40.42	63.24
+RAND	12.41	29.32	11.72	5.62	2.99	39.85	63.36
+PSE	12.67	29.25	12.09	6.03	3.33	40.20	63.48
Transformer	12.09	28.96	11.41	5.31	2.69	37.41	59.22
+ALL	12.24	29.18	11.61	5.42	2.73	35.23	55.59
+RAND	12.14	29.09	11.47	5.32	2.69	35.63	56.31
+PSE	12.35	29.46	11.73	5.47	2.75	36.46	57.59
Kobe*	14.07	27.20	14.82	8.83	5.40	38.12	60.17
PTrans	14.82	29.15	15.84	8.56	5.72	40.76	65.84
+ALL	13.65	28.41	12.13	8.54	5.52	40.50	65.27
+RAND	15.11	29.27	16.03	9.31	5.82	42.59	70.49
+PSE	15.70	30.25	16.47	10.07	6.01	42.66	70.58
ILVT	**15.24**	29.22	**16.14**	**9.66**	**5.93**	**44.57**	**74.80**

Table 2: Automatic evaluation results on the JDK dataset. $*$ represents that the model takes as input the pseudo labelled knowledge due to the system design. The best results, including the one for PTrans+PSE, are highlighted with underline. The highest scores, except the ones for PTrans+PSE, are highlighted in bold.

we also consider the following three variants that treat the product details with different strategies:

+ALL: takes all knowledge KP as input.

+RAND: randomly picks $K_i \in KP$ as input.

+PSE: takes as input the pseudo labelled knowledge K_{pse} as input.

All variants also take as input the product title and attributes. Specifically, in this case, Kobe also considers the pseudo labelled knowledge as the one from the external database.

4 Implementation Details

We implement our models on the Tesla V100 GPUs. For the transformer-based model, the hidden units is 512 and feed-forward hidden size is 2048. Both the encoder and decoder has 6 layers with 12 heads. The beam size is 5. The sentence length of title, attributes, description and knowledge are 128, 64, 128 and 512 tokens, respectively. The dropout rate is 0.1. We choose the Adam optimizer with β_1 = 0.9 and β_2 = 0.998. The warm-up step is set to 4000 and learning rate is 0.0001. The batch size is 32. To avoid the KL-vanishing problem, we choose KL-annealing trick (Bowman et al., 2016) with the α=0.00025 and β = 6.25 for both two VAEs. Hyperparameters are set based on the performance of the validation set.

4.1 Automatic Evaluation

For the automatic evaluations, we consider both the quality and diversity of output text generated by different systems:

BLEU (Papineni et al., 2002): To verify the effectiveness of models in selecting useful knowledge from noisy details and the ability of improving the generation quality, we reported BLEU-1,2,3,4 and the arithmetic mean of above values as BLEU.

Distinct (Li et al., 2016): We calculated the number of distinct n-grams for Distinct-1,2 as Dist-1,2 to measure the diversity of generated copywriting.

The automatic evaluation results on the JDK dataset are listed in Table 2. ILVT beats all baselines in BLEU but PTrans+PSE that can be seen as the model utilizing the ground truth knowledge label. Compared with PTrans+ALL and PTrans+RAND, ILVT improves 1.59 and 0.13 BLEU score individually, illustrating that ILVT is able to extract effective knowledge. In terms of Kobe that uses the pseudo labelled knowledge, ILVT achieves notable improvement in all automatic metrics, which shows that ILVT can take better advantage of the selected knowledge for improving generation quality. Also, ILVT significantly improves the generation diversity, beating all baselines in Distinct-1 and Distinct-2 , demonstrating that the interactive latent variables contribute to the diversity of generated product copywritings.

Model	BLEU	BLEU-1	BLEU-2	BLEU-3	BLEU-4	DIST-1	DIST-2
ILVT	**15.24**	**29.22**	**16.14**	**9.66**	**5.93**	**44.57**	**74.80**
- Copy Mechanism	14.96	29.19	15.98	9.26	5.44	43.22	71.14
- Description Distribution	14.30	29.10	14.73	8.26	5.13	41.93	64.13
- Knowledge Distribution	14.39	29.17	14.93	8.35	5.13	42.65	70.24
- above all	12.23	29.19	11.63	5.40	2.71	35.93	56.71

Table 3: Model ablation study on JDK dataset. -Copy Mechanism: removing copy mechanism. -Description Distribution: removing description latent variable. -Knowledge Distribution: removing knowledge latent variable.

Model	Corr.	Dive.	Cohe.
CONVSEQ2SEQ+PSE	3.52	3.28	3.52
TRANSFORMER+PSE	3.73	3.33	3.29
PTTRANS+PSE	4.21	4.24	4.49
KOBE	4.39	3.85	4.14
ILVT	**4.77**	**4.62**	**4.51**

Table 4: Human evaluation results on the JDK dataset. All baselines input pseduo selected knowledge. Corr.: Correctness, Dive.: Diversity, and Cohe.: Coherence.

4.2 Effect of Pseudo Label

As shown in Table 2, compared the variant without knowledge to the one considering all product details (denoted by +ALL), the BLEU of CONVSEQ2SEQ (+ALL) and PTRANS (+ALL) drop significantly, which demonstrates that the product details contain harmful pieces, i.e., noises. However, simply feeding all product details into TRANSFORMER, the BLEU is improved. The performance drop of PTRANS might be caused by the copy mechanism that copies noisy words from the product details. Reverse scenario happens to TRANSFORMER and PTRANS. We can attribute this to the effect of attention mechanism that can denoise knowledge implicitly, while the copy mechanism may copy noise from input details. Taking all three variants, i.e., +ALL, +RAND and +PSE, we observe that simply picking a random knowledge text from the product details can improve the quality and diversity of the generated text for the most cases. Moreover, adopting the pseudo labelled knowledge results in the best performance. The above observations demonstrate that the product details (i.e., human knowledge) contain salient and informative knowledge but also tremendous noises. Thus, it is necessary to perform knowledge selection.

4.3 Ablation Study

We also conducted the ablation study by removing particular modules, including copy mechanism, description latent variable and knowledge selection module with knowledge latent variable. Results are listed in Table 3. The absence of the copy mechanism hurts both the generation quality(BLEU) and diversity(Distinct). We observe the prominent impact in automatic evaluation metrics without the description distribution, affirming it is helpful to enhance selecting informative knowledge from prior information and generating copywriting with good coherence and diversity. When removing the knowledge latent variable from the framework and selecting knowledge only based on the product representation, both BLEU and Distinct drop significantly. It demonstrates the interactive latent variable contributes to select knowledge and enhance generation quality.

4.4 Human Evaluation

We also consider the model preference in terms of three criteria for human evaluations, as follows:

- **Correctness**: How correct the generated copywriting describes the product information?
- **Diversity**: How diverse the output is?
- **Coherence**: How coherent the copywriting is to the recommended product?

We invited six native Chinese speakers as volunteers to judge the quality of generation results with a score from 1 (worst) to 5 (best). The result of human writings is 5 for reference. We choose the average of all volunteers for each criteria for the same copywriting as human evalution score. We randomly selected 200 instances from test split, each instance contains the product title, attributes, commodity details with labeled pseudo knowledge and the generated result. We only evaluate baselines with pseudo knowledge in order to compare fairly. The average scores of human evaluation are shown in Table 4, from where we can see that ILVT outperforms all baselines. In the correctness criterion, our model get an average score of 4.77, which indicates that ILVT can extract useful information from nosie and generate informative copywritings. In the diversity criterion, the improvement is 0.38, comparing with the best baseline model PTRANS+PSE, which proves that our model is able to generate more diverse results with the interactive knowledge and description latent variables. The Fleiss's kappa scores (Fleiss, 1971) among all volunteers is 0.529.

4.5 Case Study

The case study is performed to investigate how IVLT utilizes the auxiliary product details (i.e., human knowledge) to generate diverse and informative product copywriting. For fair comparisons, we only choose baselines with pseudo knowledge for fair comparison, namely CONVSEQ2SEQ+PSE, TRANSFORMER+PSE, KOBE and PTRANS+PSE. As shown in Table 5 in Appendix, the baselines tend to generate general and vague results mainly from the title and attributes, such as "宽松(loose and comfortable stereotype)" and "圆领(round collar)", while the product details are ignored. Rather, ILVT generates more diverse copywriting guided by the product details, such as "青春的活力气息(the vitality of youth)", "运动风(sport fashion)" and "打破了纯色的单调性(breaks monotony of solid color)", which are attractive to customers. Such a running example demonstrates that the ILVT is able to well utilize the selected knowledge to make the generation more diverse and informative, thanks to the interactive latent variables that enhance the connection between knowledge selection and copywriting generation.

5 Related Work

Product Copywriting Generation. The task of product copywriting generation has gained considerable attentions with various systems proposed to automatically generate product descriptions. Wang et al. (2017) presented a statistical framework and template-based method. Shao et al. (2019) proposed a Planing-based Hierarchical Varitional Model that decomposed the long product copywriting generation into several dependent sentence generation sub-tasks. Chen et al. (2019) proposed a transformer-based generation model which utilized the user categories of items and the knowledge collected from external database. (Li et al., 2020b) construted a list of salient attributes and keywords incorporated with visual information from a product picture to generate the copywriting. Zhang et al. (2021) simply concatenated the short advertising phrases written by experts with the product title and attributes to generate product copywriting. We are different from such work by involving dominant knowledge-selection rather than simply incorporating information from external sources, and we make a selection in an end-to-end fashion.

Variational Autoencoders. Variational Autoencoders (i.e., VAEs) (Kingma and Welling, 2014) have been widely used in a plenty of natural language generation tasks, such as dialogue generation (Zhao et al., 2017), text summarization (Li et al., 2017) and neural machine translation (Zhang et al., 2016). VAEs aims at incorporating posterior information to capture the high variability during training phase and reducing the KL Divergence(Kullback and Leibler, 1951) between the prior and the posterior. Traditional VAE models used RNNs (Zhang et al., 2016; Shao et al., 2019; Lee et al., 2020). Lin et al. (2020); Li et al. (2020a); Fang et al. (2021) incorporated the latent variables from VAEs with transformer. However, both RNNs-based and transformer-based VAEs face the problem of KL-vanishing. Bowman et al. (2016); Fu et al. (2019); Shao et al. (2021) changed the weight of KL-divergence to solve the KL-vanishing problem. Shao et al. (2021) studied the balance between diversity and relevance from the generation results with KL-vanishing in e-commerce situation. This paper adopts the VAEs to dynamically model the input product title, attributes as well as the human-written advertising knowledge to extract the salient parts from the advertising descriptions and also inject the selected knowledge into the generated product copywriting, so that the diversity and the quality can be improved.

6 Conclusion

This work studies a novel problem on how to generate informative and diverse product copywriting with auxiliary human-created product details. We propose an interactive latent variables model based on transformer architecture, ILVT, which allows to select salient knowledge from the noisy product details. To better evaluate ILVT model, we construct a large Chinese product copywriting dataset, JDK. Extensive experiments demonstrate that our proposed model outperforms the baselines with regard to both automatic and human evaluation, illustrating that ILVT can select outstanding knowledge and improve the generation quality and diversity.

Acknowledgements

We would like to thank the anonymous reviewers for their thoughtful and constructive comments. Yanyan Zou is the corresponding author.

References

Samuel R. Bowman, Luke Vilnis, Oriol Vinyals, Andrew M. Dai, Rafal Józefowicz, and Samy Bengio. 2016. Generating sentences from a continuous space. In *Proceedings of The 20th SIGNLL Conference on Computational Natural Language Learning*.

Daniel Cer, Yinfei Yang, Sheng-yi Kong, Nan Hua, Nicole Limtiaco, Rhomni St John, Noah Constant, Mario Guajardo-Céspedes, Steve Yuan, Chris Tar, et al. 2018. Universal sentence encoder for english. In *Proceedings of the 2018 Conference on Empirical Methods in Natural Language Processing*.

Qibin Chen, Junyang Lin, Yichang Zhang, Hongxia Yang, Jingren Zhou, and Jie Tang. 2019. Towards knowledge-based personalized product description generation in e-commerce. In *Proceedings of the 25th ACM SIGKDD International Conference on Knowledge Discovery & Data Mining*.

Le Fang, Tao Zeng, Chao-Chun Liu, Liefeng Bo, Wen Dong, and Changyou Chen. 2021. Transformer-based conditional variational autoencoder for controllable story generation. *arXiv preprint arXiv:2101.00828*.

Joseph L Fleiss. 1971. Measuring nominal scale agreement among many raters. *Psychological bulletin*, 76(5):378.

Hao Fu, Chunyuan Li, Xiaodong Liu, Jianfeng Gao, Asli Celikyilmaz, and Lawrence Carin. 2019. Cyclical annealing schedule: A simple approach to mitigating kl vanishing. In *Proceedings of the 2019 Conference of the North American Chapter of the Association for Computational Linguistics: Human Language Technologies*.

Jonas Gehring, Michael Auli, David Grangier, Denis Yarats, and Yann N Dauphin. 2017. Convolutional sequence to sequence learning. In *International Conference on Machine Learning*. PMLR.

Eric Jang, Shixiang Shane Gu, and Ben Poole. 2017. Categorical reparameterization with gumbel-softmax. In *International Conference on Learning Representations*.

Jin-Hwa Kim, Jaehyun Jun, and Byoung-Tak Zhang. 2018. Bilinear attention networks. In *Advances in Neural Information Processing Systems*.

Diederik P. Kingma and Max Welling. 2014. Auto-encoding variational bayes. In *International Conference on Learning Representations*, volume abs/1312.6114.

Solomon Kullback and Richard A Leibler. 1951. On information and sufficiency. *The annals of mathematical statistics*, 22(1):79–86.

Dong Bok Lee, Seanie Lee, Woo Tae Jeong, Donghwan Kim, and Sung Ju Hwang. 2020. Generating diverse and consistent qa pairs from contexts with information-maximizing hierarchical conditional vaes. In *Proceedings of the 58th Annual Meeting of the Association for Computational Linguistics*.

Chunyuan Li, Xiang Gao, Yuan Li, Xiujun Li, Baolin Peng, Yizhe Zhang, and Jianfeng Gao. 2020a. Optimus: Organizing sentences via pre-trained modeling of a latent space. In *Proceedings of the 2020 Conference on Empirical Methods in Natural Language Processing*.

Haoran Li, Peng Yuan, Song Xu, Youzheng Wu, Xiaodong He, and Bowen Zhou. 2020b. Aspect-aware multimodal summarization for chinese e-commerce products. In *International Conference on Learning Representations*.

Jiwei Li, Michel Galley, Chris Brockett, Jianfeng Gao, and William B. Dolan. 2016. A diversity-promoting objective function for neural conversation models. In *Proceedings of the 2016 Conference of the North American Chapter of the Association for Computational Linguistics: Human Language Technologies*.

Piji Li, Wai Lam, Lidong Bing, and Zihao Wang. 2017. Deep recurrent generative decoder for abstractive text summarization. In *Proceedings of the 2017 Conference on Empirical Methods in Natural Language Processing*.

Zhaojiang Lin, Genta Indra Winata, Peng Xu, Zihan Liu, and Pascale Fung. 2020. Variational transformers for diverse response generation. *arXiv preprint arXiv:2003.12738*.

James MacQueen et al. 1967. Some methods for classification and analysis of multivariate observations. In *Proceedings of the fifth Berkeley symposium on mathematical statistics and probability*, volume 1, pages 281–297.

Chris J. Maddison, Andriy Mnih, and Yee Whye Teh. 2017. The concrete distribution: A continuous relaxation of discrete random variables. In *International Conference on Learning Representations*.

Lili Mou, Rui Men, Ge Li, Yan Xu, Lu Zhang, Rui Yan, and Zhi Jin. 2016. Natural language inference by tree-based convolution and heuristic matching. In *Proceedings of the 54th Annual Meeting of the Association for Computational Linguistics*.

Kishore Papineni, Salim Roukos, Todd Ward, and Wei-Jing Zhu. 2002. Bleu: a method for automatic evaluation of machine translation. In *Proceedings of the 40th Annual Meeting of the Association for Computational Linguistics*.

Nils Reimers and Iryna Gurevych. 2019. Sentence-bert: Sentence embeddings using siamese bert-networks. In *Proceedings of the 2019 Conference on Empirical Methods in Natural Language Processing*.

Abigail See, Peter J Liu, and Christopher D Manning. 2017. Get to the point: Summarization with pointer-generator networks. In *Proceedings of the 55th Annual Meeting of the Association for Computational Linguistics*.

Huajie Shao, Jun Wang, Haohong Lin, Xuezhou Zhang, Aston Zhang, Heng Ji, and Tarek Abdelzaher. 2021. Controllable and diverse text generation in e-commerce. In *Proceedings of the Web Conference 2021*, pages 2392–2401.

Zhihong Shao, Minlie Huang, Jiangtao Wen, Wenfei Xu, and Xiaoyan Zhu. 2019. Long and diverse text generation with planning-based hierarchical variational model. In *Proceedings of the 2019 Conference on Empirical Methods in Natural Language Processing*.

Ashish Vaswani, Noam Shazeer, Niki Parmar, Jakob Uszkoreit, Llion Jones, Aidan N Gomez, Łukasz Kaiser, and Illia Polosukhin. 2017. Attention is all you need. In *Advances in Neural Information Processing Systems*.

Jinpeng Wang, Yutai Hou, Jing Liu, Yunbo Cao, and Chin-Yew Lin. 2017. A statistical framework for product description generation. In *Proceedings of the Eighth International Joint Conference on Natural Language Processing*.

Biao Zhang, Deyi Xiong, Jinsong Su, Hong Duan, and Min Zhang. 2016. Variational neural machine translation. In *Proceedings of the 2016 Conference on Empirical Methods in Natural Language Processing*.

Xueying Zhang, Yanyan Zou, Hainan Zhang, Jing Zhou, Shiliang Diao, Jiajia Chen, Zhuoye Ding, Zhen He, Xueqi He, Yun Xiao, et al. 2021. Automatic product copywriting for e-commerce. *arXiv preprint arXiv:2112.11915*.

Tiancheng Zhao, Ran Zhao, and Maxine Eskénazi. 2017. Learning discourse-level diversity for neural dialog models using conditional variational autoencoders. In *Proceedings of the 55th Annual Meeting of the Association for Computational Linguistics*.

A Case Study

Product Title	中国风圆领印花时尚宽松大码T恤女款夏季新款显瘦短袖黑色印花预售t恤 Chinese style, round neck printing fashion, loose T-shirt, for women in new summer fashions, looking slim with short sleeves and black printing, pre-sale T-shirt
Attribute Set	服饰内衣；T恤；风虎；圆领；印花；时尚；宽松；大码；女；夏季；新款；短袖 Clothing underwear; T-shirt; recluserecluse; Round neck colla; Printing; Fashion; Loose; Large size; Women; Summer; New Fashion; Short sleeves
Product Details	柔软爽滑的面料，妙意由心。轻松穿搭出洒脱情懒的气质 Soft and smooth fabric, wonderful intention. Wear out of a free and lazy temperament easily 大而松的肥袖口与紧致的小圆领，非常宽松的直腰身的线条 Large loose fat cuffs and tight colla, a very loose straight line of the wasit 不限体型,有奇特的减龄效果 No restriction on figures, with a peculiar age-defying effect 本款中国风与运动风结合的时尚宽松大恤将青春潮流注入中国风加人灵动的运动风潮 The Chinese and sporty loose fashion shirt infuses the youth trend into Chinese style, adding spirited sport fashion 搭配棒球帽运动鞋,个性又潮流 Matching with baseball cap and sneakers, cool and fashionable 不对称的斜印花犹如猛虎 Asymmetrical printing looks like an fierce tiger
ConvSeq2Seq+PSE	宽松版型遮肉显瘦，这款T恤采用宽松的版型设计，对身材的包容度很高，微胖身材也能轻松驾驭。经典的圆领设计，贴合颈部线条，穿着舒适自在。 Loose design hiding obesity and showing slim, the T-shirt adopts loose design, unconstrained on figures, slightly chubby body can also handled it easily. The classic round neck design fits the neckline, comfortable for wearing.
Transformer+PSE	圆领印花宽松版型圆领的设计，穿着舒适自在，同时也能修饰颈部线条，凸显修长的脖颈线条。宽松的版型，不挑身材，遮肉显瘦，适合多种身材。 Round neck printing loose design. Round neck design, comfortable for wearing, embellish and highlight the slender neck line. Loose design, unconstrained on figures, hiding obesity and showing slim, suitable for a variety of figures.
KOBE	纯棉面料透气舒适，采用纯棉面料制作而成，触感柔软细腻，具有良好的透气性，穿着舒适不闷热。宽松的版型设计，包容性强，适合多种身材穿着。 Breathable and comfortable cotton fabrics, made of pure cotton fabric, gives a soft and delicate touch. It is comfortable to wear, feeling no hot with good breathability. Loos design, inclusive and suitable for a variety of figures.
PTrans+PSE	中国风印花，这款T恤采用了中国风的印花设计，将中国风的元素融入其中，带来了不一样的视觉美感。宽松的版型设计，遮肉显瘦，轻松打造慵懒随性的时尚风。 Chinese style printing, the T-shirt has a Chinese style printing design, incorporates Chinese elements, providing a different visual aesthetic. Loose design, hiding obesity and showing slim, building a lazy and casual style easily.
ILVT	印花图案更显趣味，衣身点缀大面积的印花图案，打破了纯色的单调性，增添了整体的趣味性，彰显出了青春的活力气息，穿着上身更显运动风。 The printing pattern is more interesting, large area embellished with printing pattern in the clothes breaks monotony of solid color, gives bluethe whole piece a more interesting touch, highlights the vitality of youth, showing greater sport fashion .

Table 5: Case study of ILVT and baselines on JDK dataset. All baselines take as input the product title, attributes and the pseudo labelled knowledge. We highlight the pseudo labelled knowledge in yellow. Words generated from product title and attribute set are highlighted in breaking line and from product details are in double underline. Diverse words generated from selected knowledge in ILVT is highlighted in red color.

Leveraging Seq2seq Language Generation for Multi-level Product Issue Identification

Yang Liu, Varnith Uttam Chordia, Hua Li, Siavash Fazeli,
Yifei Sun, Vincent Gao, Na Zhang
Amazon, Inc.
{yngliun, vchordia, realname, saivash, sunyifei, vincegao, naazhang}@amazon.com

Abstract

In a leading e-commerce business, we receive hundreds of millions of customer feedback from different text communication channels such as product reviews. The feedback can contain rich information regarding customers' dissatisfaction in the quality of goods and services. To harness such information to better serve customers, in this paper, we created a machine learning approach to automatically identify product issues and uncover root causes from the customer feedback text. We identify issues at two levels: coarse grained (L-Coarse) and fine grained (L-Granular). We formulate this multi-level product issue identification problem as a seq2seq language generation problem. Specifically, we utilize transformer-based seq2seq models due to their versatility and strong transfer-learning capability. We demonstrate that our approach is label efficient and outperforms the traditional approach such as multi-class multi-label classification formulation. Based on human evaluation, our fine-tuned model achieves 82.1% and 95.4% human-level performance for L-Coarse and L-Granular issue identification, respectively. Furthermore, our experiments illustrate that the model can generalize to identify unseen L-Granular issues.

1 Introduction

Customer feedback plays a crucial role in continuously improving service quality for e-commerce companies. One important piece of information in customer feedback are the product issues that customers encounter during their order experience, such as product-quality defects and undesired product features. Although negative product experience occurs rarely in mature e-commerce stores, identifying the product issues presented in customer feedback significantly helps sellers understand customers' concerns and facilitates them to further improve customer order experience. As the volume of customer feedback grows rapidly, an automatic and intelligent issue identification system is needed to support the fast-growing e-commerce business. In this paper, we introduce a machine learning solution for multi-level issue discovery by taking advantage of advanced deep language modeling techniques. We show that our approach not only accurately identifies product issues from customer feedback, but also meets the requirements for our use case, which, we believe, is also common to other e-commerce store business.

Identifying product issues from customer feedback has its own unique characteristics as compared to common NLP tasks such as text classification, document summarization, entity extraction, and sentiment analysis. First, we target to extract diverse and dynamic product issues, instead of categorizing them into a fixed set of labels. This is mainly due to three varying factors: the product itself, the customer and the context. Different categories of products naturally have different kinds of issues. Different customers may find different flaws of the same product, depending on their personal taste and preferences; the way they describe issues could vary greatly from one customer to another. In addition, issues are dynamic as different issues emerge and disappear from time to time. For example, a bad local weather can lead to a surge in shipment damage and delivery failure complaints in a short period of time.

Second, to effectively improve customer experience, multi-level issues with different granularity are needed. Higher-level, concise, and consistent issues can be shared with sellers to help them identify trends and hotspots for the flaws in their products; more detailed lower-level issues are needed by business investigators to study root causes of product defects and design treatment accordingly.

The third requirement for product issue identification is about supervised information extraction. Customer feedback often contains contents that are unrelated to product issue. Furthermore, multi-

Proceedings of The Fifth Workshop on e-Commerce and NLP (ECNLP 5), pages 20 - 28
May 26, 2022 ©2022 Association for Computational Linguistics

ple product issues can be tangled or be embedded within one phrase or sentence. Therefore, uncontrolled excerpts from customer feedback can be confusing and overwhelming to downstream users. So our system should focus on product issues and disentangle them to best serve downstream users.

Traditional language processing approaches can not meet all the three requirements discussed above. To start with, traditional classification methods can only produce results from a pre-defined, limited set of labels, and therefore cannot satisfy the first requirement. Unsupervised methods such as topic modeling and clustering, on the other hand, are able to identify diverse patterns varying from a dataset to another and discover new trends. However, it is hard to steer the algorithms to exercise the control over the patterns or type of information they extract from the data. Based on our experience, it is challenging to generate meaningful and highly coherent 'topics' using topic modeling or clustering algorithm based on text embedding techniques. Finally, it is not straightforward to adapt these methods for multi-level issue identification unless we develop multiple models to handle each level individually. For operation efficiency, we prefer to have a single model to complete the whole task so as to minimize model deployment and maintenance cost.

In this paper, we propose an innovative solution by formulating our problem as seq2seq language generation tasks and leveraging deep learning models with multi-task capability to meet all our requirements. In particular, we choose transformer-based seq2seq models as backbone and fine tune them on our data. A single model is trained to generate both the low-level and high-level product issues. Even though the model is trained in a supervised manner with human-annotated data to have better content generation control, as a large-scale language model, the model shows generalization power to discover fine-grained issues from customer feedback that were not seen during training time. To the best of our knowledge, so far it is the most flexible and effective approach for extracting multi-level product issues from e-commerce customer feedback.

2 Related Work

There are various approaches to extract key topics and identify issues from customer feedback. Prior work in this area can be categorized into four major groups: (1) document classification, (2) topic modeling, (3) clustering, and (4) text summarization. Document classification is one of the most well studied NLP tasks, and many deep learning methods (Kim, 2014; Devlin et al., 2018a) have been introduced and excelled at it in recent years. Tong et al. (2018) developed a convolutional neural network to extract reason codes from customer complaints. More recently, Liu et al. (2021a) leveraged BERT-based model to classify different types of fraud elements from Internet fraud complaints. Instead of assigning labels to the entire texts, they map the labels to each paragraph. These methods are not very applicable in the current context since they require a fixed and pre-defined taxonomy.

For topic modeling, latent Dirichlet allocation (LDA) (Blei et al., 2003) is a widely used statistical method for analyzing information in customer reviews and feedback (Mou et al., 2019; Debortoli et al., 2016; Jeong et al., 2019). Zhai et al. (2011) added pre-existing constraints to LDA in order to improve product feature extraction from customer reviews. Bagheri et al. (2014) proposed a Twofold-LDA model to produce topics focused on desired aspects. Srivastava and Sutton (2017) proposed autoencoded variational inference for topic model (AVITM) which yielded much more interpretable topics than LDA. While most traditional topic modeling methods use simple document representations such as the bag-of-words, an alternative approach is to cluster similar documents using document embeddings followed by extracting common topics within each cluster. Du et al. (2016) used GloVe embeddings and K-means clustering for analyzing different aspects in electronics and restaurants reviews. Grootendorst (2020) used BERT embeddings and DBSCAN to create interpretable topics. Although topic modeling and clustering are not constrained to a fixed label set, the results can be inconsistent and incoherent due to unsupervised topic extraction.

One can also pose this problem as a text summarization problem, where a model can generate a summary to present the key information from the input text. Liu et al. (2021b) improved abstractive summarization models for generating summaries about product issues from customer feedback. For our use case, however, it's not clear how to use text summarization to produce multi-level issues and how to disentangle different issues mixed within a summary.

Customer Feedback	L-Granular Issue	L-Coarse Issue
When I received the product, there was no power cable included. The box has been opened previously and the item looks used.	no power cable included, box has been opened, item looks used	missing parts issue, opened box, used condition
Instructions were hard to read, some of it was written in another language. The product also looks different from the picture.	instructions hard to read, written in another language, looks different from picture	instruction issue, not as pictured

Table 1: Example customer feedback texts and L-Coarse & L-Granular issues.

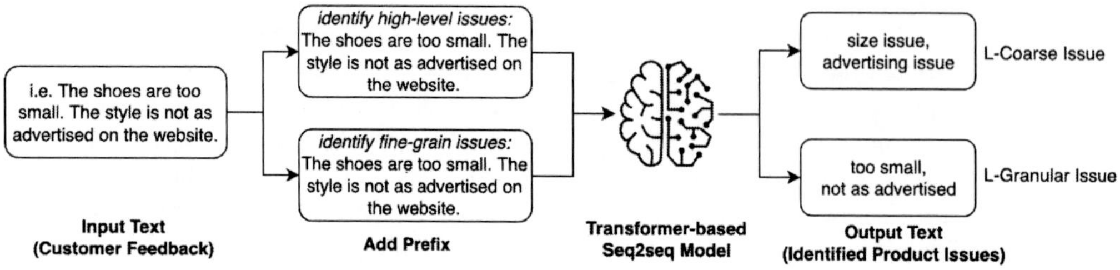

Figure 1: Illustration of multi-level issue generations enabled by multi-tasking models.

3 Proposed Approach

3.1 Multi-level Issue Identification

We aim to have comprehensive issue representations due to the large variety of intents and issues customers can express through customer feedback. One solution is to build a hierarchical architecture. According to the abstraction levels, more detailed and trivial issues will sit on the leaves whereas more general and conclusive issue categories will sit on the branches and major chunks. In this work, we decide to approach the problem starting with a two-level issue representation: L-Coarse and L-Granular.

An L-Granular issue is a faithful representation of the original customer communication and it captures concrete and fine-grain issues in a free form text. We deliberately leave L-Granular issues unaggregated to preserve original customer expression so that they will serve as a solid foundation for subsequent bottom-up aggregation. Each L-Coarse issue is an aggregation of multiple L-Granular issues, which describes an abstract issue shared across multiple customer communications. To fully capture customer concerns and differentiate the nuances among issues, we allow multiple issues, at both L-Coarse and L-Granular levels, for each customer feedback. Table 1 provides three examples of customer feedback together with their corresponding L-Coarse and L-Granular issues[1].

[1]Due to confidentiality, all customer feedback examples in this paper are composed by the authors and are used for demonstration only.

3.2 Seq2seq Learning for Issue Identification

We tackle the issue identification problem using a seq2seq learning approach. In this approach, we format our problem as text-to-text tasks, where the input text is customer feedback and the output text is the literal text representing the identified issues. We fine tune a seq2seq model to capture issues that are relevant to product defects. This approach is illustrated in Figure 1.

Leveraging the versatility of the text-to-text format, Raffel et al. (2019a) and Aribandi et al. (2021) demonstrated the capability and advantage of handling multiple tasks within a single model. They inspired us to take the advantage of these multi-task learning techniques to train a single model to generate both L-Coarse and L-Granular issues simultaneously. As illustrated in Figure 1, we append different customized prefixes to the same input text to distinguish different tasks and pair the prefixed sample with the corresponding target text (L-Coarse or L-Granular issues). The model is trained to produce different levels of issues according to the prefixes in the input. In particular, the prefixes we use are *"identify high-level issues:"* and *"identify fine-grain issues:"* for L-Coarse- and L-Granular-issue generations, respectively. For the target text, we use comma to separate multiple issues for both L-Coarse and L-Granular issues. In our training, we use the natural mix (1:1) of the two task data.

4 Experiments

4.1 Dataset

We collected 9200 samples of negative customer feedback across different post-order communication channels from online e-commerce stores. We asked subject matter experts [2] to identify L-Coarse and L-Granular issues for each customer feedback text with emphasis on extracting the information related to product issues. The annotated dataset contains 70 unique L-Coarse issues and 6906 unique L-Granular issues. The large difference in the numbers of unique issues shows the different characteristics of L-Coarse and L-Granular issues: L-Coarse issues are organized and abstract whereas L-Granular issues are detailed, diverse, and are often in free form. As illustrated in Figure 2, for the distribution of the top 50 L-Coarse issues, it is highly skewed and long tailed. In our experiments, we used human-annotated issues as the target text during model training. The train/test split ratio is 80:20.

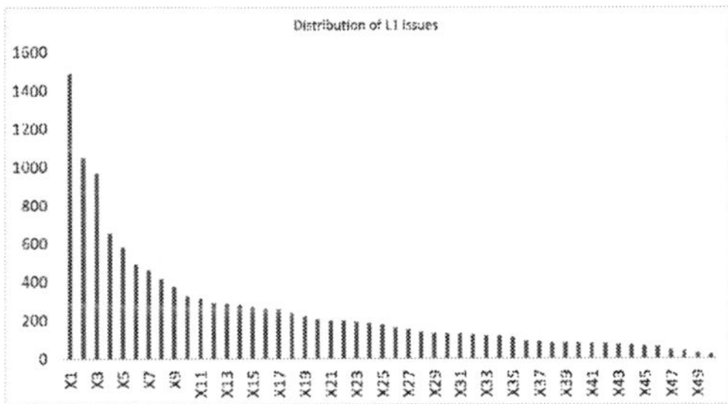

Figure 2: Distribution of anonymized L-Coarse issues.

4.2 Models & Training Settings

We compare three transformer-based seq2seq models: BART (Lewis et al., 2019a), T5 (Raffel et al., 2019a), and Pegasus (Zhang et al., 2020). We adopt the pretrained models from the HuggingFace[3] implementation and fine tune the models on our training dataset.The details regarding the training parameters we used can be found in the appendix C. We implement several training techniques to improve model performance and help the models better adapt to our application:

Auxiliary Tasks Recent studies have shown that multi-tasking helps improve model performance (Raffel et al., 2019a; Aribandi et al., 2021). In our case, in addition to L-Coarse and L-Granular issue generations, we include other NLP tasks into model training. The auxiliary tasks include summarization, token infilling, and classification. Details about the auxiliary tasks can be found in Appendix A.

Sentence & Issue Shuffling A unique characteristic of issue identification is that the order of individual issues does not matter, as long as all relevant issues are correctly identified from customer feedback. This is contrary to conventional language generation tasks, such as summarization and translation, where the order of generated words must follow natural language syntax. Hence, we shuffle both input sentences and target issues during model training to induce the model to learn to ignore the ordering information and achieves better performance.

4.3 Evaluation Metrics

Similarity Measure To evaluate our models' performance, we first measure the similarity between model-generated and human-annotated issues. We employ two sets of metrics to measure both lexical and semantic similarity.

- **Lexical Metrics**: We compute the ROUGE-1 & ROUGE-2 (Lin, 2004) metrics between the model-generated text and human-annotated issues. They measure the overlapping unigrams and bigrams between the texts.
- **Semantic Metrics**: We define two new metrics - **SimCSE Precision & SimCSE Recall** - which evaluate the precision and recall at the customer feedback level, based on the pairwise similarity of the sentence embeddings for model-generated and human-annotated issues. Let the model-generated issues be represented by $X_1, X_2, .., X_I$ and the human-annotated issues by $Y_1, Y_2, .., Y_J$. We measure the pairwise similarity between each issue pair X_i and Y_j ($0 \leq i \leq I$ and $0 \leq j \leq J$) as the cosine similarity of their corresponding SimCSE embeddings (Gao et al., 2021). A similarity higher than a given threshold is considered a match between a pair of issues as seen in equation 1. Based on the number of matches, we are able to compute precision and recall. The threshold (0.7) is chosen based on our

[2] All annotators followed the confidentiality policy when conducting the labeling jobs.

[3] https://huggingface.co/

Model	L-Coarse				L-Granular			
	ROUGE		SimCSE		ROUGE		SimCSE	
	R-1	R-2	P	R	R-1	R-2	P	R
MCML-BERT	-24.1%	-41.8%	-27.5%	-35.7%	-	-	-	-
BART	+1.6%	+0.3%	-3.4%	+4.9%	-2.9%	-4.0%	-7.4%	0.0%
Pegasus	+1.2%	+1.0%	+0.5%	-0.7%	-3.9%	-5.9%	-1.8%	-9.3%

Table 2: Performance comparison. The performance numbers are shown as the difference from the T5 performance. Here R-1 & R-2 refers to ROUGE-1 and ROUGE-2 scores respectively, whereas P refers to precision and R refers to recall.

empirical study on the inter-label similarity distribution.

$$match(X_i, Y_j) = \begin{cases} 1, & \text{if sim}(X_i,Y_j) > 0.7 \\ 0, & \text{otherwise} \end{cases} \quad (1)$$

where sim(X_i,Y_j) is the similarity score between a model generated issue and human-annotated issue. More details with examples on the calculation of this metric can be found in the Appendix B.

Human Evaluation Both ROUGE and SimCSE evaluations have their limitations, i.e. ROUGE score fails to capture semantic similarity while SimCSE evaluation relies on the embedding quality. Both methods are influenced by annotation noise. Thus, we also conduct human evaluation to assess the quality of the model- and human-generated issues. To have an unbiased evaluation, we adopt a double blind approach, where we first shuffle the model outputs and human annotations and then ask human auditors to adjudicate the issues (shuffled) according to the following criteria:

- Rating 1: All the issues are correctly identified.
- Rating 2: At least one issue is missing.
- Rating 3: At least one issue is incorrectly assigned.

5 Results

In this section, we report the results and analysis from our study. To our knowledge there are no publicly-available datasets in e-commerce or performance benchmarks for the problem of multi-level product issue identification. Thus, we conduct the study using our private customer-feedback dataset. Due to confidentiality, we can not report absolute model performance numbers but only relative ones compared to the baseline models.

5.1 Model Performance

First, we compare the performance of different transformer-based seq2seq models, including BART (Lewis et al., 2019b), T5 (Raffel et al., 2019b), and Pegasus (Zhang et al., 2019). We attempted to provide a quantitative comparison between our seq2seq approach and other approaches such as topic modeling and clustering. However, the outputs from these alternative approaches are not directly comparable to ours. Instead, we train a multi-class multi-label classification model for L-Coarse issues using BERT (Devlin et al., 2018b) (MCML-BERT) as a baseline for comparison. We do not apply the classification modeling approach to the L-Granular-issue prediction task due to the large number of L-Granular issues.

Results on the test dataset are provided in Table 2, where we choose T5 as the base model. We observe that for L-Coarse issues, MCML-BERT significantly underperforms in comparison to all the seq2seq models. Among the seq2seq models, for L-Coarse-issue identification, BART and Pegasus perform marginally better than T5. For L-Granular-issue identification, however, T5 shows consistent better performance. Due to the best overall performance of T5, in the following sections, we will focus on the results produced by T5.

5.2 Zero- and Few-shot Learning

As we aim to identify diverse and dynamic issues, it's important for the model to be able to discover novel issues with zero or only few training samples. Here, we examine the zero-shot and few-shot learning capability by varying the amount of samples containing specific issues in the training dataset. Specifically, we select two frequent issues from L-Coarse and L-Granular respectively. We fine-tune T5 using the training dateset containing a fraction of samples with those selected issues, then evaluate the model on the same test dataset.

Table 3 shows the relative model performance (F1-scores) as a function of the fractions of samples

Level - Selected Issue	100% samples	75% samples	50% samples	25% samples	0% samples
L-Coarse - X1	100.0%	98.5%	98.3%	92.2%	0%
L-Coarse - X2	100.0%	77.2%	69.9%	56.1%	0%
L-Granular - X3	100.0%	97.1%	96.0%	90.7%	75.8%
L-Granular - X4	100.0%	95.3%	92.7%	81.5%	68.6%

Table 3: Relative SimCSE F1-score performance with different proportions of training examples containing the selected issues (anonymized).

exposed during model training. In this table, we take the model performance when 100% samples with the selected issues are included in training as baseline. In general, the performance decreases as fewer training samples are included. For L-Granular issues, even when there is no sample of selected issues present during model training, the model is still able to identify the correct issues with a high F1-scores (75.8% and 68.6%). It indicates that the model generalizes well on identifying unseen fine-grained issues from customer feedback. On the other hand, though the model fails to recognize unseen L-Coarse issue (no exposure during training), its detection performance improves quickly: with 25% samples, model's F1-scores rise to 92.2% and 56.1%. This shows that our approach, fine-tuning a pre-trained seq2seq model such as T5, is label efficient.

5.3 Human Evaluation

Human evaluation is performed on 850 records randomly sampled from the test dataset. We ask auditors to evaluate both model-generated and human-annotated issues following double blind auditing procedures (see Section 4.3 for details). We obtain the ratings assigned by auditors for all the samples. We then compute the performance metric that is defined as the (percentage of Rating-1 samples + 0.5 $*$ percentage of Rating-2 samples). Table 4 shows the model performance relative to human annotator. As can be observed from this table, our model achieves 82.1% and 95.4% of human-level performance for L-Coarse and L-Granular issue identification, respectively. Given the complexity and challenges of the tasks, such results indicate the effectiveness of our approach. On the other hand, the better L-Granular performance aligns with our previous observations that model generalizes better on L-Granular issues than L-Coarse issues. We hypothesize that this is due to that fact that L-Granular issues are concrete ones while L-Coarse issues are more abstract, which is more challenging for the model to learn, as also observed in Zeyu Liu (2021).

Issue Level	Relative to Human Performance
L-Coarse	82.1%
L-Granular	95.4%

Table 4: Model performance based on human auditing.

5.4 Ablation Study

We examine the effect of adding auxiliary tasks and sentences & issues shuffling to model training. Here, the baseline model is a T5 model that's fined tuned using only L-Coarse & L-Granular issue identification tasks where the issues are presented in a fixed order.

Additional Training Techniques	L-Coarse	L-Granular
Summarization, Token-infilling, classification	-0.16%	+1.44%
Sentences & issues shuffling	+3.48 %	-0.89%
All tasks above	+4.40 %	+1.33%

Table 5: Effect of auxiliary tasks and sentences & issues shuffling (SimCSE F1-scores).

Table 5 shows the change in SimCSE F1-scores when including the additional training techniques. As can be seen from this table, auxiliary tasks improve L-Granular performance while sentences & issues shuffling gives better performance at the L-Coarse level. We achieve the best overall model performance by combining both set of techniques.

6 Conclusion

In conclusion, we analyzed the challenges in identifying diverse and multi-level product issues from customer feedback. To overcome these challenges, we creatively formulated our problem as a seq2seq modeling problem and leveraged text-to-text transfer learning framework. We utilized multi-tasking to generate product issues at multiple levels using a single model, which minimizes operational cost. Results show that our model performs closely to human on issue identification tasks. We also observed that our approach is label efficient and our model generalizes well to identify unseen L-Granular issues. Our next step is to explore ways to improve our model's performance and generalizability on L-Coarse issue prediction.

References

Vamsi Aribandi, Yi Tay, Tal Schuster, Jinfeng Rao, Huaixiu Steven Zheng, Sanket Vaibhav Mehta, Honglei Zhuang, Vinh Q Tran, Dara Bahri, Jianmo Ni, et al. 2021. Ext5: Towards extreme multi-task scaling for transfer learning. *arXiv preprint arXiv:2111.10952.*

Ayoub Bagheri, Mohamad Saraee, and Franciska De Jong. 2014. Adm-lda: An aspect detection model based on topic modelling using the structure of review sentences. *Journal of Information Science*, 40(5):621–636.

David M Blei, Andrew Y Ng, and Michael I Jordan. 2003. Latent dirichlet allocation. *Journal of machine Learning research*, 3(Jan):993–1022.

Stefan Debortoli, Oliver Müller, Iris Junglas, and Jan Vom Brocke. 2016. Text mining for information systems researchers: An annotated topic modeling tutorial. *Communications of the Association for Information Systems*, 39(1):7.

Jacob Devlin, Ming-Wei Chang, Kenton Lee, and Kristina Toutanova. 2018a. BERT: pre-training of deep bidirectional transformers for language understanding. *CoRR*, abs/1810.04805.

Jacob Devlin, Ming-Wei Chang, Kenton Lee, and Kristina Toutanova. 2018b. Bert: Pre-training of deep bidirectional transformers for language understanding. *arXiv preprint arXiv:1810.04805.*

Hui Du, Xueke Xu, Xueqi Cheng, Dayong Wu, Yue Liu, and Zhihua Yu. 2016. Aspect-specific sentimental word embedding for sentiment analysis of online reviews. In *Proceedings of the 25th International Conference Companion on World Wide Web*, pages 29–30.

Tianyu Gao, Xingcheng Yao, and Danqi Chen. 2021. Simcse: Simple contrastive learning of sentence embeddings. *arXiv preprint arXiv:2104.08821.*

Maarten Grootendorst. 2020. Bertopic: leveraging bert and c-tf-idf to create easily interpretable topics (2020). *URL https://doi. org/10.5281/zenodo*, 4381785.

Byeongki Jeong, Janghyeok Yoon, and Jae-Min Lee. 2019. Social media mining for product planning: A product opportunity mining approach based on topic modeling and sentiment analysis. *International Journal of Information Management*, 48:280–290.

Yoon Kim. 2014. Convolutional neural networks for sentence classification. In *Proceedings of the 2014 Conference on Empirical Methods in Natural Language Processing (EMNLP)*, pages 1746–1751, Doha, Qatar. Association for Computational Linguistics.

Mike Lewis, Yinhan Liu, Naman Goyal, Marjan Ghazvininejad, Abdelrahman Mohamed, Omer Levy, Ves Stoyanov, and Luke Zettlemoyer. 2019a. Bart: Denoising sequence-to-sequence pre-training for natural language generation, translation, and comprehension. *arXiv preprint arXiv:1910.13461.*

Mike Lewis, Yinhan Liu, Naman Goyal, Marjan Ghazvininejad, Abdelrahman Mohamed, Omer Levy, Veselin Stoyanov, and Luke Zettlemoyer. 2019b. BART: denoising sequence-to-sequence pre-training for natural language generation, translation, and comprehension. *CoRR*, abs/1910.13461.

Chin-Yew Lin. 2004. Rouge: A package for automatic evaluation of summaries. In *Text summarization branches out*, pages 74–81.

Tong Liu, Siyuan Wang, Jingchao Fu, Lei Chen, Zhongyu Wei, Yaqi Liu, Heng Ye, Liaosa Xu, Weiqiang Wang, and Xuanjing Huang. 2021a. Fine-grained element identification in complaint text of internet fraud. In *Proceedings of the 30th ACM International Conference on Information & Knowledge Management*, pages 3268–3272.

Yang Liu, Yifei Sun, and Vincent Gao. 2021b. Improving factual consistency of abstractive summarization on customer feedback. In *Proceedings of The 4th Workshop on e-Commerce and NLP*, pages 158–163.

Jian Mou, Gang Ren, Chunxiu Qin, and Kerry Kurcz. 2019. Understanding the topics of export cross-border e-commerce consumers feedback: an lda approach. *Electronic Commerce Research*, 19(4):749–777.

Colin Raffel, Noam Shazeer, Adam Roberts, Katherine Lee, Sharan Narang, Michael Matena, Yanqi Zhou, Wei Li, and Peter J Liu. 2019a. Exploring the limits of transfer learning with a unified text-to-text transformer. *arXiv preprint arXiv:1910.10683.*

Colin Raffel, Noam Shazeer, Adam Roberts, Katherine Lee, Sharan Narang, Michael Matena, Yanqi Zhou, Wei Li, and Peter J. Liu. 2019b. Exploring the limits of transfer learning with a unified text-to-text transformer. *CoRR*, abs/1910.10683.

Akash Srivastava and Charles Sutton. 2017. Autoencoding variational inference for topic models. *arXiv preprint arXiv:1703.01488.*

Ilya Sutskever, Oriol Vinyals, and Quoc V. Le. 2014. Sequence to sequence learning with neural networks. *CoRR*, abs/1409.3215.

Xuesong Tong, Bin Wu, Shuyang Wang, and Jinna Lv. 2018. A complaint text classification model based on character-level convolutional network. In *2018 IEEE 9th International Conference on Software Engineering and Service Science (ICSESS)*, pages 507–511. IEEE.

Yonghui Wu, Mike Schuster, Zhifeng Chen, Quoc V. Le, Mohammad Norouzi, Wolfgang Macherey, Maxim Krikun, Yuan Cao, Qin Gao, Klaus Macherey, Jeff Klingner, Apurva Shah, Melvin Johnson, Xiaobing Liu, Lukasz Kaiser, Stephan Gouws, Yoshikiyo Kato, Taku Kudo, Hideto Kazawa, Keith Stevens, George Kurian, Nishant Patil, Wei Wang, Cliff Young, Jason Smith, Jason Riesa, Alex Rudnick, Oriol Vinyals, Greg Corrado, Macduff Hughes, and Jeffrey Dean. 2016. Google's neural machine translation system: Bridging the gap between human and machine translation. *CoRR*, abs/1609.08144.

Jungo Kasai Hannaneh Hajishirzi Noah A. Smith Zeyu Liu, Yizhong Wang. 2021. Probing across time: What does roberta know and when? In *Findings of the Association for Computational Linguistics: EMNLP 2021*, pages 820—-842.

Zhongwu Zhai, Bing Liu, Hua Xu, and Peifa Jia. 2011. Constrained lda for grouping product features in opinion mining. In *Pacific-Asia Conference on Knowledge Discovery and Data Mining*, pages 448–459. Springer.

Jingqing Zhang, Yao Zhao, Mohammad Saleh, and Peter Liu. 2020. Pegasus: Pre-training with extracted gap-sentences for abstractive summarization. In *International Conference on Machine Learning*, pages 11328–11339. PMLR.

Jingqing Zhang, Yao Zhao, Mohammad Saleh, and Peter J. Liu. 2019. PEGASUS: pre-training with extracted gap-sentences for abstractive summarization. *CoRR*, abs/1912.08777.

A Auxiliary Tasks

- Summarization: We use a customized dataset containing 14k customer-feedback records with human-annotated summaries. For this task, we train the model to mimic human-generated summaries.

- Token Span infilling: It has been recently shown (Devlin et al., 2018a) that a masked language modeling based objective results in superior performance on various downstream tasks. The objective for the model is to predict the missing tokens during model pre-training. We follow a similar approach by randomly replacing spans of token by single sentinel tokens. The target sentence corresponds to all of the dropped-out spans of tokens, delimited by the same sentinel tokens used in the input sequence. The number of samples for this task is 7k.

- Classification: For this auxiliary task, we use a customer-feedback dataset that has been labelled using a fixed set of product-related categories. There are 10k samples in total. We cast this classification problem into a text-to-text format, where the input is the customer feedback text and the output is a text-based label.

B SimCSE Evaluation

For each sample, we compute pairwise cosine similarity base on the SimCSE (Gao et al., 2021) sentence embedding computed for each of the model-generated and human-annotated issues. If the similarity is greater than a threshold for an issue pair, we increment the number of matches by 1, even if there is more than one match for a given issue. The threshold was selected based on L-Coarse and L-Granular intra-issue similarity distributions, i.e., the distribution of all the pairwise cosine similarity between the unique issues from the data. Based on our emperical study, we choose 0.7 as the threshold. Table 6 illustrates the SimCSE precision and recall calculation process. Note that the issues are comma delimited. We can see for the first example in the table although "minor scratches" and "minor cosmetic defects" vary lexically, the two are semantically similar, which is reflected in their greater than 0.7 SimCSE similarity. On the other hand, "minor scratches" has a SimCSE similarity lower than 0.7 with "counterfeit issue" and hence not a match, which is consistent with our intuition. The number of matches includes all the issues with similarity greater than 0.7. Based on the number of matches, we can calculate the instance level precision and recall as usual. Averaging instance level precision and recall, we can obtain precision and recall for aggregated dataset level.

C Training Parameters

For training transfomer-based seq2seq models, we select maximum input text and target text lengths as 512 and 64, respectively. We use a batch size of 40 distributed equally over 8 GPUs, with a learning

Model Output	Human Annotation	# Match
minor scratches	minor cosmetic defects, fitting issue	1
size issue, not as described	size issue, material issue, not as described	2
quality issue	quality issue	1

Table 6: Calculation of the Precision and Recall, with similarity threshold of 0.7 for L-Coarse

rate of 5e-5. We train this setup over 25 epochs on a p3.16xlarge EC2 instance with distributed model and data parallelism to fine-tune the model. During inference we use beam search (Sutskever et al., 2014) to generate the target text sequence with a beam width of 2 and length penalty $\alpha = 2.5$ (Wu et al., 2016).

Data Quality Estimation Framework for Faster Tax Code Classification

Ravi Kondadadi and **Allen Williams** and **Nicolas Nicolov**
Avalara Inc.
255 South King St., Suite 1800
Seattle, WA 98104
{*ravi.kondadadi, allen.williams, nicolas.nicolov*}@*avalara.com*

Abstract

This paper describes a novel framework to estimate the data quality of a collection of product descriptions to identify required relevant information for accurate product listing classification for tax-code assignment. Our Data Quality Estimation (DQE) framework consists of a Question Answering (QA) based attribute-value extraction model to identify missing attributes and a classification model to identify bad quality records. We show that our framework can accurately predict the quality of product descriptions. In addition to identifying low-quality product listings, our framework can also generate a detailed report at a category level showing missing product information resulting in a better customer experience.

1 Introduction

As a global tax compliance company, Avalara enables businesses to use the correct sales tax rate by mapping their product catalogs to a tax code taxonomy built by Avalara. The tax codes, in turn, inform the tax calculation engine how to apply the tax for a transaction. This mapping process is very laborious today due to many reasons. One of the main challenges is the quality of the product catalog data we receive from customers. Many times, this data is quite vague and noisy. This can be caused by many factors.

1. Not enough context about the business: For tax code classification, we only receive a collection of product titles. This product information does not give enough context about the industry in general, causing problems in tax code mapping, especially if the language in the product information is ambiguous. This lack of context results in the mapping team having to talk to the business to get more information about the business and the corresponding industry. This is a very tedious process requiring a lot of manual effort, causing delays in the customer onboarding process.

2. Missing attributes in the product titles and descriptions: Many product descriptions do not have relevant attributes. This makes it hard for the models to map the products in the catalog to applicable tax codes. For example, a clothing product without specific attributes like knitted/crocheted cannot be mapped to the appropriate tax code.

3. Product information contains rare words, and acronyms: If the product information includes words that were not seen before, acronyms or abbreviations, it makes it harder for the model to classify.

4. The industry of the business is unknown or not currently covered by the tax code taxonomy: If the business belongs to a new sector or belongs to an industry with low tax code coverage, the mapping would be more challenging.

A model including these factors to identify the quality of product titles would help the mapping team request additional information for those products from the business and accelerate the onboarding process for that customer.

In this paper, we describe a novel data quality estimation framework which businesses can interact with and provide all relevant information required to map all entries in a product catalog to the corresponding tax codes. Iteratively, the tool can map input product records to tax codes, identify low quality records and present pertinent questions to the user for the bad records. The tool repeats the process until all records are fixed, and the mappings are complete for the entire product catalog.

Next, we discuss our Data Quality Estimation framework. We then describe our methodology and experiments followed by relevant recent work.

Proceedings of The Fifth Workshop on e-Commerce and NLP (ECNLP 5), pages 29 - 34
May 26, 2022 ©2022 Association for Computational Linguistics

2 Data Quality Estimation Framework

In this section, we present details of the Data Quality Estimation framework. The framework includes a tax code classification model, an attribute-value extraction model, and a quality assessment model. Next, we will discuss each of these components in detail.

2.1 Tax Code Classification

The Avalara Tax code system consists of thousands of codes hierarchically organized by categories and the nature of the business. The codes fall into a dozen major categories ranging from products to food and beverages. The automatic tax code classification system is responsible for identifying the appropriate tax code for any given product in a customer's inventory catalog. The tax codes are mapped when the customer is onboarded to the Avalara system. The classification system at Avalara uses a tiered approach where a top-level model predicts the probable category, and then a category-specific model predicts a probable tax code. This approach was chosen predominantly to keep the number of labels for each model down to a manageable number and allow for targeted improvements for each category without interfering with other categories. Each of the models is a BERT (Devlin et al., 2019) model fine-tuned for classification.

2.2 Attribute Value Extraction (AVE)

The most important parts of product information to determine the relevant tax code are the product title and product description. An attribute is a feature that describes a specific property of a product. Some examples of attributes include brand, color, material, etc. An attribute-value is a particular value assumed by the attribute. For example, for the product title *"Apple iPhone 13 Pro, 128GB, Sierra Blue"*, iPhone is the main entity. The corresponding attribute-values are "Apple", "13 pro" and "Sierra Blue". Apple is the brand, "13 pro" is the model and "Sierra Blue" is the color.

The presence of attributes is quite important to classifying a product title to the most relevant tax code. Often, we lack attribute information in the product title data we receive from our customers. This usually results in lot of back and forth with the customer and causes significant delays in the time to fully onboard a customer. A model that can extract attribute-values from product titles and identify missing attributes would be of great help in determining the quality of the customer data.

Input to the attribute-value extraction model would include the product listing and a set of attributes. These attributes come from a tax code ontology developed internally by Avalara that covers a wide range of tax code categories. The tax code classification model is used to identify the relevant category for the product listing. We can then identify the related attributes for that category from the ontology.

For our experiments, we formulated the attribute-value extraction as a Question Answering problem as mentioned in (Wang et al., 2020a). The advantage of a Question Answering (QA) formulation is that it can scale well with more attributes and can work well with unseen attributes in the training data. We can treat the product listing as the document, attribute name as the question and retrieve the value as the answer. We used the MAVE dataset (Yang et al., 2021) for training the QA model. MAVE is a product dataset for Multi-source Attribute-Value Extraction, created by Google. MAVE is the largest product attribute-value extraction dataset by the number of attribute-value examples containing over 3M attribute-value annotations from 2.2M Amazon product descriptions.

2.3 Quality Assessment

The goal of the quality assessment model is to identify the product listings that require more information in order to be correctly mapped to the relevant tax codes. We created a logistic regression (LR) (Cox, 1958) model for this classification task. Our features include prediction probabilities from the tax code classification model, missing attribute information, title length, and category meta data, etc.

Here is an overview of the steps involved in running the framework.

1. First run the current tax code classification model.
2. Remove the records with good predictions based on the prediction probabilities.
3. For the remaining records, run the attribute-value extraction to identify missing attributes.
4. Identify the quality score using the quality assessment model.
5. Generate a detailed report listing relevant questions for each category to cover the ma-

jority of the bad records and share the report with the user for feedback.

6. Repeat steps 1-5 on the updated records set from the user until the number of bad records fall below a predefined threshold.

3 Experimental Results

In this section, we present the evaluation of both the attribute-value extraction and the quality assessment models.

3.1 Attribute-Value Extraction Evaluation

We evaluated various attribute-value extraction methods on two different datasets.

1. MAVE dataset: A random subset of around 10,000 records from MAVE for evaluation.
2. Compliance dataset: A subset of around 1,000 product listings that was manually annotated with attribute-value information.

We compared two different approaches for attribute-value extraction.

1. AVE-FT: This is a hybrid approach of look-up and classification. We created a list of 1,200 most frequent attributes and the possible values they could take. For example, for the attribute "material-type" we included phrases like “plastic”, “pvc”, “synthetic rubber” as possible values. We first check if we can find an attribute-value in the listing using a look-up approach. We used a SpaCy (Honnibal and Montani, 2017) matcher to identify such values. In order to work with attributes that are not in our list, we used a fastText (Bojanowski et al., 2017) model to identify if a product listing contains a specific attribute. The model was trained on our historical data where we know whether a specific attribute is present.
2. AVE-QA: We developed a QA model fine-tuned on a DistilBERT (AVE-QA-DISTILBERT) (Sanh et al., 2019) model on a subset of records from the MAVE dataset as mentioned in (Wang et al., 2020a). We also created a different QA model by fine-tuning on the MiniLM model (AVE-QA-MINILM) (Wang et al., 2020b).

We used the F1-score metric as defined in the SQuAD (Rajpurkar et al., 2016) evaluation dataset for Question Answering.

Attribute-Value Extractor	**MAVE F1-score**	**Compliance set F1-score**
AVE-FT	0.15	0.19
AVE-QA-DISTILBERT	0.95	0.54
AVE-QA-MINILM	0.93	0.63

Table 1: Comparison of various attribute-value extraction methods on the MAVE and Compliance datasets

Table 1 shows the evaluation of various attribute-value extraction methods on the MAVE and the Compliance datasets. We can see that the Question-Answering based models outperformed the FastText baseline on both datasets and MiniLM performs slightly better than Distilbert version. Not surprisingly, both QA models performed well on the MAVE datasets as the QA models were fine-tuned on MAVE. The compliance dataset includes attributes related to domains like Insurance and Medical care whereas the MAVE data was predominantly about e-commerce. Although our performance is currently low on the compliance dataset, we are working on augmenting MAVE with compliance related information and retraining the model with more compliance data.

3.2 Evaluation of Data Quality Estimation

In this section, we compare different configurations of Attribute-value extraction and Data quality assessment for estimating the data quality of a set of product listings. In addition to the Logistic Regression model for quality assessment, we also evaluated two baselines. The first baseline simply predicts the quality based on the prediction probability. The second baseline includes both tax-code level precision (this can be determined from the historical performance of the tax-code) and prediction probabilities. For the evaluation, we used the same sample of 1,000 listings from the attribute-value extraction experiment. The dataset was reviewed by our tax coding experts to classify each listing as good/bad quality. Table 2 shows the evaluation of various data quality estimation methods. For this experiment, we used a threshold of 0.5 for prediction probabilities. It can be seen from the results that our classification model for data quality assessment outperformed the baselines based on prediction probabilities and tax-code level precision. Although adding the missing attribute

Attribute-Value Extractor	Data Quality Estimator	F1-score
None	Pred.Prob. Thresholding	0.755
None	Pred.Prob.+Tax-code precision	0.741
None	Logistic Regression	0.823
AVE-FT	Logistic Regression	0.826
AVE-QA-MINILM	Logistic Regression	0.828

Table 2: Comparison of various data quality estimation models

information to the model did not help, it is useful in explaining why the data is inadequate to our customers.

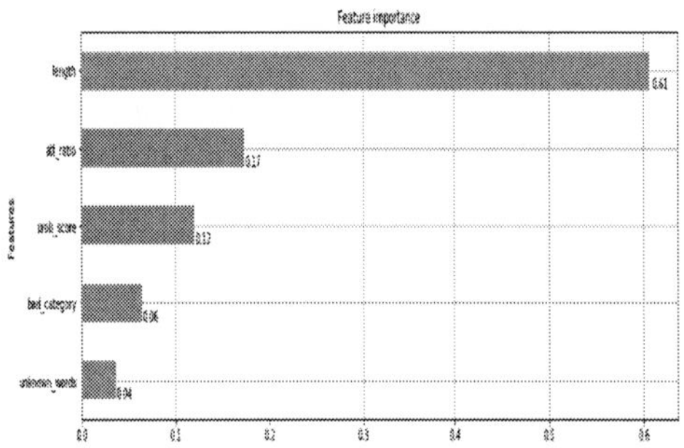

Figure 1: Importance of quality estimation features

Figure 1 shows the importance of various features in the quality estimation model. It can be seen that title length and missing attribute information are the most important features for quality estimation. It also shows that using attribute value extraction model alone is not enough in assessing the data quality of product listings.

We generate a summary report at a category level showing the missing attribute information to help our customers understand how they can enhance their product descriptions. Figure 2 shows a sample screenshot of the detailed report showing missing attribute information at a category level. We are currently working on including this tool in production to estimate the data quality of product catalogs from our customers.

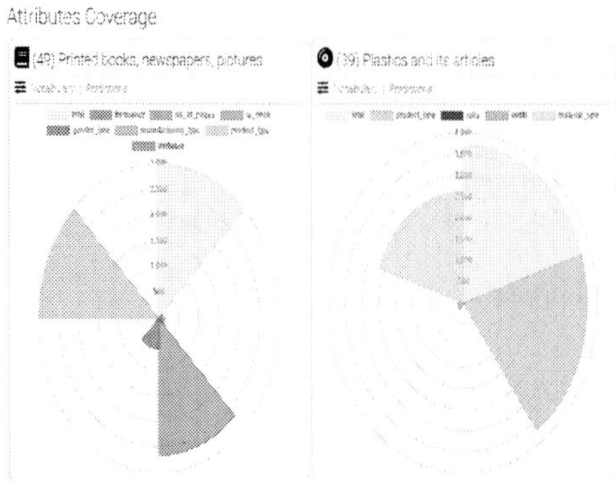

Figure 2: A sample data quality report

4 Related Work

The quality of predictions of a machine learning model is dependent on the quality of the data it is trained on. Poor data results in bad predictions from the model, translating to a poor customer experience. Due to increased usage of data in businesses, researchers have been seeking to define data quality. Batini et al. (2009) compares data quality and assessment methodologies along several dimensions. Pipino et al. (2002), Cai and Zhu (2015) identify various dimensions for defining data quality. ONeill (2020) proposed a decision tree algorithm to predict data quality. Schelter et al. (2018) proposed a declarative API to "unit-test" data. They also discussed methods such as anomaly detection to assess data quality. Active learning (Settles, 2009) has also been used to determine most confusing entries in a dataset. Active learning suggests labeling samples that are most uncertain based on prediction probabilities. But the prediction probabilities are not always good enough to identify data quality and to understand what information is missing from the product listings.

Attribute-value extraction was predominantly solved using rule-based approaches (Nadeau and Sekine 2007; Vandic et al. 2012) in the past. The disadvantage with these methods is that they are domain-specific and require extensive feature engineering. More recently, with the advances in Neural Networks-based methods, approaches like BiLSTM-CRF (Kozareva et al. 2016; Zheng et al. 2018) have been proposed. Wang et al. (2020a) formulated attribute extraction as a Question Answering problem. They proposed a multi-task framework to address generalizability. Yang et al. (2021)

extended this work by adopting an ETC encoder (Ainslie et al., 2020) to generate the contextual embeddings for title and description of the product listing to handle longer descriptions.

5 Conclusion

We presented a novel data quality estimation framework for the e-commerce domain that can identify product listings with incomplete information. The framework includes a Question Answering based attribute-value extraction model trained on the MAVE dataset. We prove that our framework can reliably identify inadequate product listings resulting in faster tax code classification.

Beyond mapping products to tax codes, our framework is applicable to services (in fact, our top-level categories already include a Services group), as well as, utilities/energy, or in general any domain where items can be described in terms of attributes and values. We are applying this framework to other tax code ontologies like the Harmonized Commodity Description and Coding System (HS) which provides codes for traded products as part of international transactions.

6 Acknowledgements

We would like to thank our coworkers Mike Lash and Brandon Van Volkenburgh for helping us with the data annotation. We also would like to thank Vsu Subramanian, and Rajesh Muppalla for their support and valuable feedback.

References

Joshua Ainslie, Santiago Ontañón, Chris Alberti, Vaclav Cvicek, Zachary Kenneth Fisher, Philip Pham, Anirudh Ravula, Sumit K. Sanghai, Qifan Wang, and Li Yang. 2020. Etc: Encoding long and structured inputs in transformers. In *EMNLP*.

Carlo Batini, Cinzia Cappiello, Chiara Francalanci, and Andrea Maurino. 2009. Methodologies for data quality assessment and improvement. *ACM computing surveys (CSUR)*, 41(3):1–52.

Piotr Bojanowski, Edouard Grave, Armand Joulin, and Tomas Mikolov. 2017. Enriching word vectors with subword information. *Transactions of the association for computational linguistics*, 5:135–146.

Li Cai and Yangyong Zhu. 2015. The challenges of data quality and data quality assessment in the big data era. *Data science journal*, 14.

David R Cox. 1958. The regression analysis of binary sequences. *Journal of the Royal Statistical Society: Series B (Methodological)*, 20(2):215–232.

Jacob Devlin, Ming-Wei Chang, Kenton Lee, and Kristina Toutanova. 2019. BERT: pre-training of deep bidirectional transformers for language understanding. In *Proceedings of the 2019 Conference of the North American Chapter of the Association for Computational Linguistics: Human Language Technologies, NAACL-HLT 2019, Minneapolis, MN, USA, June 2-7, 2019, Volume 1 (Long and Short Papers)*, pages 4171–4186. Association for Computational Linguistics.

Matthew Honnibal and Ines Montani. 2017. spaCy 2: Natural language understanding with Bloom embeddings, convolutional neural networks and incremental parsing.

Zornitsa Kozareva, Qi Li, Ke Zhai, and Weiwei Guo. 2016. Recognizing salient entities in shopping queries. In *Proceedings of the 54th Annual Meeting of the Association for Computational Linguistics (Volume 2: Short Papers)*, pages 107–111.

David Nadeau and Satoshi Sekine. 2007. A survey of named entity recognition and classification. *Lingvisticae Investigationes*, 30(1):3–26.

Allen ONeill. 2020. Data quality evaluation using probability models. *arXiv preprint arXiv:2009.06672*.

Leo L Pipino, Yang W Lee, and Richard Y Wang. 2002. Data quality assessment. *Communications of the ACM*, 45(4):211–218.

Pranav Rajpurkar, Jian Zhang, Konstantin Lopyrev, and Percy Liang. 2016. Squad: 100,000+ questions for machine comprehension of text. In *EMNLP*.

Victor Sanh, L Debut, J Chaumond, and T Wolf. 2019. Distilbert, a distilled version of bert: Smaller, faster, cheaper and lighter. arxiv 2019. *arXiv preprint arXiv:1910.01108*.

Sebastian Schelter, Dustin Lange, Philipp Schmidt, Meltem Celikel, Felix Biessmann, and Andreas Grafberger. 2018. Automating large-scale data quality verification. *Proceedings of the VLDB Endowment*, 11(12):1781–1794.

Burr Settles. 2009. Active learning literature survey.

Damir Vandic, Jan-Willem Van Dam, and Flavius Frasincar. 2012. Faceted product search powered by the semantic web. *Decision Support Systems*, 53(3):425–437.

Qifan Wang, Li Yang, Bhargav Kanagal, Sumit Sanghai, D Sivakumar, Bin Shu, Zac Yu, and Jon Elsas. 2020a. Learning to extract attribute value from product via question answering: A multi-task approach. In *Proceedings of the 26th ACM SIGKDD International Conference on Knowledge Discovery & Data Mining*, pages 47–55.

Wenhui Wang, Furu Wei, Li Dong, Hangbo Bao, Nan Yang, and Ming Zhou. 2020b. Minilm: Deep self-attention distillation for task-agnostic compression of pre-trained transformers. *Advances in Neural Information Processing Systems*, 33:5776–5788.

Li Yang, Qifan Wang, Zac Yu, Anand Kulkarni, Sumit Sanghai, Bin Shu, Jon Elsas, and Bhargav Kanagal. 2021. Mave: A product dataset for multi-source attribute value extraction.

Guineng Zheng, Subhabrata Mukherjee, Xin Luna Dong, and Feifei Li. 2018. Opentag: Open attribute value extraction from product profiles. In *Proceedings of the 24th ACM SIGKDD International Conference on Knowledge Discovery & Data Mining*, pages 1049–1058.

CML: A Contrastive Meta Learning Method to Estimate Human Label Confidence Scores and Reduce Data Collection Cost

Bo Dong, Yiyi Wang, Hanbo Sun, Yunji Wang, Alireza Hashemi, Zheng Du
Amazon Alexa AI
{dongbd,yiyiwang,sunhanbo,yunjiwan,arhash,zhengdu}@amazon.com

Abstract

Deep neural network models are especially susceptible to noise in annotated labels. In the real world, annotated data typically contains noise caused by a variety of factors such as task difficulty, annotator experience, and annotator bias. Label quality is critical for label validation tasks; however, correcting for noise by collecting more data is often costly. In this paper, we propose a contrastive meta-learning framework (CML) to address the challenges introduced by noisy annotated data, specifically in the context of natural language processing. CML combines contrastive and meta learning to improve the quality of text feature representations. Meta-learning is also used to generate confidence scores to assess label quality. We demonstrate that a model built on CML-filtered data outperforms a model built on clean data. Furthermore, we perform experiments on de-identified commercial voice assistant datasets and demonstrate that our model outperforms several SOTA approaches.

1 Introduction

Deep neural networks' remarkable capacity for representation learning has resulted in performance gains across a wide range of applications. The majority of these gains are dependent on having high-fidelity data; however, in practice, large-scale datasets are frequently corrupted by noise caused by a variety of factors such as task difficulty, annotator experience, and annotator bias. This is a concern because training data with corrupted labels can adversely affect the performance of deep learning models. Collecting ground truth data to alleviate this problem, on the other hand, has proven both time consuming and costly.

We can broadly enhance model performance on corrupted labels by applying two approaches: improving model robustness and improving quality of feature representation. A number of existing methods such as robust loss function based methods (Wang et al., 2019a; Zhang and Sabuncu, 2018; Ghosh et al., 2017), loss adjustment based methods (Ren et al., 2018; Zheng et al., 2021; Shu et al., 2019), and sample selection based methods (Jiang et al., 2018; Malach and Shalev-Shwartz, 2018; Han et al., 2018), have been proposed to enhance model robustness. In spite of these advances, these methods are primarily concerned with computer vision and lack quality assessment for feature representation.

There are also several approaches to improving the quality of existing feature representations. They do not, however, specifically address the adverse effects of noisy (corrupted) labels in the context of natural language processing (NLP). (Chen et al., 2020; Ghosh and Lan, 2021) proposed a contrastive learning-based approach for improving feature representation quality for computer vision (not NLP) applications through augmentation steps in the feature learning process. (Gao et al., 2021) proposed a contrastive learning-based approach to improving the quality of sentence embedding. However, this approach does not address the problems caused by noise-corrupted labels.

In this paper, we propose a contrastive meta-learning (CML) framework for simultaneously addressing the challenges introduced by corrupted labels, in the context of NLP. Importantly, our framework learns a confidence score for evaluating the quality of annotations. In the real world, the work of data annotators is typically evaluated against ground truth data. The term "ground truth data" refers to validated data labels that have been subjected to multiple passes by data annotators and labelled using majority vote. (Namazifar et al., 2021). We will hereafter refer to a dataset consisting of ground truth labels as a "gold" dataset, contrasting it with a "standard" dataset annotated by a single data associate.

Collecting ground truth data ("gold" datasets) is time consuming and expensive, and sometimes in-

Proceedings of The Fifth Workshop on e-Commerce and NLP (ECNLP 5), pages 35 - 43
May 26, 2022 ©2022 Association for Computational Linguistics

volves heavy engineering efforts (Sun et al., 2020). The confidence score generated by our model offers the potential to perform large-scale evaluations of annotation tasks. Another application of the confidence score generated by our model is to select high-quality data from a noisy dataset.

To address the issue of corrupted labels, we employ meta learning, which combines meta data and training data. Our meta data is comprised of a relatively small number of ground truth labels. The training data consists of unverified annotations (i.e. corrupted labels). Our model also learns an explicit loss-weight function while performing classification, which predicts label confidence scores.

We utilized a meta learning approach (Shu et al., 2019) as our meta module. The meta module is concatenated with the classifier. The meta module learns an explicit loss-weight function in a meta-learning manner. We use the output loss of the classifier as the input to the meta module. The meta module learns confidence scores using a multilayer perceptron on the output loss of the classifier, which reflects the quality of labels and can also improve classifier performance. Each of our training processes contains two steps. The first step consists of using our training data to update the parameters of the classifier, and the second step consists of using our meta data to update the parameters of the meta weight net. To improve the quality of feature representations, we apply contrastive learning to a pretrained BERT model (Gao et al., 2021). Contrastive learning aims to learn effective representations by pulling semantically close neighbors together and pushing apart non-neighbors. In order to have semantically close neighbors, the same sentence pass the pretrained encoder twice to predict the sentence itself with noise introduced by standard dropout layer. In such way, we have two embeddings generated from the same sentence but with slight difference. These two embeddings are "positive pair".

As we mentioned above, current methods (Zheng et al., 2021; Shu et al., 2019) designed to address corrupted labels are mainly geared towards computer vision applications. In addition, their motivation is largely centered around label correction or improving the performance of a classifier. In contrast, in the NLP domain, researchers mainly focus on improving the quality of embeddings or learning representations of text data. Our proposed framework unifies the advantages of current methods and is suitable for NLP. We demonstrate that CML not only addresses concerns stemming from having corrupted labels, but also learns feature representations from raw text data effectively.

Additionally, in real-world applications, we are concerned with the quality of annotations. As such, evaluating the work of annotators presents an important challenge. During the training process, CML learns a confidence score for labels, which can be used to evaluate annotators' work online. In other words, CML offers the potential for scaling the work of data annotators. Furthermore, because CML predicts a confidence score for labels, it can be applied to a wide range of use cases. In many instances only incorrectly labelled data is available and collecting ground truth data is time-consuming and costly. We can therefore use CML to filter high-quality data for such problems, saving both time and money.

To summarize, the main contributions of our work are listed as follows:

- CML combines meta learning and contrastive learning to address the corrupted label issue and feature representation quality issue in tandem.
- CML predicts confidence score for annotated labels which solves the problem of evaluating annotators' work at scale.
- CML can be applied to filter high quality data from raw annotations, which proves to be of the same level of quality as the ground truth data. It reduces costs associated with collecting massive amounts of ground truth data for downstream model development.

The remainder of this paper is organized as follows: We introduce related work in section 2. We then formalize the problem and present our proposed approach in section 3. Next, we present applications and corresponding results of our experiments in section 4 and 5. Finally, we present our conclusion and propose future research directions.

2 Related Work

In this section, we discuss some of the related work in contrastive learning and learning from corrupted labels.

2.1 Learning from Corrupted Labels

Machine learning techniques (Liu et al., 2021, 2019; Dong et al., 2017, 2018; Wang et al., 2020,

2019b; Li et al., 2021; Dong et al., 2019) have been widely applied on labeling tasks. With respect to learning from corrupted labels, a variety of methods have been proposed. Namely, (Zheng et al., 2021) proposes a meta-learning framework for re-weighting and correcting corrupted labels. This method requires a clean dataset (without corrupted labels) alongside a dataset with corrupted labels. The focus of above paper is label correction. It provides an approach to predict a set of weights in label space for each instance. We cannot get a single weight score for each instance directly by using this method. (Li et al., 2017) proposes a distillation framework which uses metadata, including a small clean dataset and label relations in a knowledge graph to learn from corrupted labels. However, in the real world setting, it is difficult to collect sufficient and useful metadata. (Dong et al., 2020) proposes a new loss function which includes an importance weight for training instance. This importance embedding serves the function of finding important training instances. The importance embedding is trained during model training. However, this method is not originally designed for corrupted labels and can not make use of ground truth data and corrupted labels in tandem, in the training process. (Shu et al., 2019) proposes a meta learning method to learn weight score to evaluate label quality. Their approach focuses on corrupted labels and addresses class imbalance issues. It also learns an explicit loss-weight function, parameterized through a multi-layer perceptron during meta-learning.

2.2 Learning Feature Representation

Feature representation quality is a critical factor affecting deep neural network performance. One research direction is contrastive learning. (Chen et al., 2020) proposes a contrastive learning framework which can improve feature representation via contrastive loss with augmented data for computer vision applications. (Ghosh and Lan, 2021) demonstrates that initializing supervised robust methods using representations learned through a contrastive learning framework leads to significantly improved performance with noisy labels. (Kim et al., 2021) proposes a contrastive learning method that uses self-guidance to fine tune BERT, which does not rely on sentence augmentation. (Fang et al., 2020) also fine tune a pretrained language encoder like BERT. This approach uses back-translation as augmentation of input sentence. (van den Oord et al., 2019) designs a contrastive predictive coding method to extract representations from high-dimensional data in a universal unsupervised manner.

3 Approach

3.1 Problem Setting

In this paper, we propose a contrastive meta learning framework(CML). Basically, in learning with corrupted labels, we assume that a small set of data with clean labels and a large set of data with noisy (corrupted) labels are needed (Zheng et al., 2021). Usually due to scarcity and high cost of generating ground truth labels, the relative size of the clean dataset is much smaller than the noisy one. Since a small training set tends to cause overfitting, utilizing a clean dataset alone may lead to creating a model that does not generalize well. On the other hand, training with noisy data is also not a very desirable option since large high-capacity models will fit and memorize the noise (Zhang et al., 2017). Therefore, an effective way to overcome the aforementioned challenges is to build a framework which utilizes both noisy/corrupted data and clean data. Our framework consists of two modules: the main module and meta module. The main module learns feature representations in a contrastive manner and builds a predictive model. At the same time, we also learn a meta module which is a loss weight function. The meta module tries to learn confidence scores for corresponding labels. Our framework allows the main module and meta module to learn from each other.

3.2 Framework

The CML framework (Figure 1) consists of two modules: the main module and the meta module. The main module adopts pre-trained BERT-base in a contrastive manner followed by a dropout layer, a hidden layer, and several fully connected layers to map the input data into a semantic representation. The last layer in the main module is a linear output layer. The meta module is an MLP(multilayer perceptron) network with only one hidden layer. The activation function for all hidden layers is ReLU. The meta module utilizes a small set of clean data to guide the training of all of its parameters.

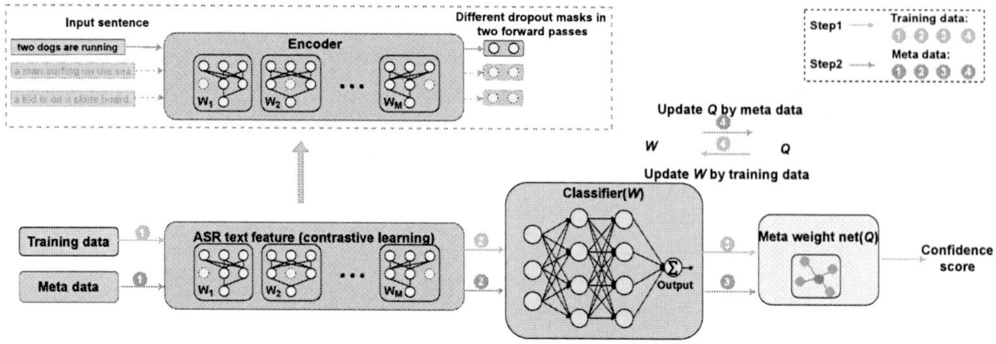

Figure 1: CML framework: one iteration consists of two steps. Both start with contrastive learning that is a pretrained dropout masked BERT, followed by fully connected layers and meta weight net. In the first step, we keep the meta weight net unchanged and only update weight of fine tuned layers. The second step is to feed meta data (ground truth) to update meta weight net with main model's predicted probability as input to meta weight net. In addition, meta weight net learns an explicit loss-weight function to predict label confidence. We demonstrate an example in the figure where contrastive learning takes automatic speech recognition(ASR text) to predict if the recognition is capable to represent the speaker's goal.

3.2.1 Main Module

We fine-tune simCSE framework (Gao et al., 2021) for learning the text feature representation in a contrastive manner. A commonly used contrastive learning setting is as follows, assume we have a collection of paired sentences $S = (\mathbf{x}_i, \mathbf{x}_i^+)$, where $\mathbf{x}_i$ and $\mathbf{x}_i^+$ are semantically related. Then we can use a base encoder $\mathcal{F}(\cdot)$(pre-trained BERT-base) to encode each sentence $\mathbf{x}_i$ as follows

$$\mathbf{e}_i = \mathcal{F}(\mathbf{x}_i) \tag{1}$$

Let $\mathbf{e}_i$ and $\mathbf{e}_i^+$ represent the feature representation of $\mathbf{x}_i$ and $\mathbf{x}_i^+$. The contrastive learning loss function is designed as:

$$l = \sum_{i=1}^{N} log \frac{exp(sim(\mathbf{e}_i, \mathbf{e}_i^+)/\tau)}{\sum_{j=1}^{N} exp(sim(\mathbf{e}_i, \mathbf{e}_j^+)/\tau)} \tag{2}$$

where τ is the temperature parameter and sim is the cosine similarity $\frac{\mathbf{e}_i^\top \mathbf{e}_i^+}{\|\mathbf{e}_i\| \cdot \|\mathbf{e}_i^+\|}$.

In above setting, simCSE let $\mathbf{x}_i^+ = \mathbf{x}_i$. Then use $\mathbf{e}_i^m = \mathcal{F}(\mathbf{x}_i^m)$ to represent the feature representation of $\mathbf{x_i}$ with random mask m for dropout. The same sentence pass to the encoder twice with different dropout masks m, n. The loss function is defined as follows:

$$l = \sum_{i=1}^{N} log \frac{exp(sim(\mathbf{e}_i^{m_i}, \mathbf{e}_i^{n_i})/\tau)}{\sum_{j=1}^{N} exp(sim(\mathbf{e}_i^{m_i}, \mathbf{e}_j^{n_j})/\tau)} \tag{3}$$

We utilize pre-trained simCSE to learn representations of the input sentence in our main module for predicting labels.

3.2.2 Meta Module

Inspired by (Shu et al., 2019), we incorporate a loss-weight function(a multilayer perceptron) into our meta module. This module learns confidence scores which can be used to evaluate the quality of labels. When an input sentence passes the main module, we have a loss computed using the predicted label and the original label. In the meta module, we utilize a small set of clean data to learn a confidence score from the output of the main module. We initialize the parameters $\mathbf{w}$ of the main module and parameters θ of the meta module. In general, our framework is an iterative procedure. For each iteration, it mainly contains two steps. The first step is to update the parameters $\mathbf{w}$ of the main module as equation 4 indicated by feeding biased training data.

$$\hat{\mathbf{w}}^{t+1}(\theta) = \mathbf{w}^t - \alpha \frac{1}{n} \times \sum_{i=1}^{n} G(L_i^{train}(\mathbf{w}^t), \theta^{t+1}) \nabla_{\mathbf{w}} \tag{4}$$

where $\nabla_{\mathbf{w}}$ is computed as follows

$$\nabla_{\mathbf{w}} = \frac{\partial L_i^{train}(\mathbf{w})}{\partial \mathbf{w}} |_{\mathbf{w}=\mathbf{w}^t} \tag{5}$$

The second step is to pass the clean data to update the parameters θ of meta module as equation 6 indicated.

$$\theta^{t+1} = \theta^t - \beta \frac{1}{m} \sum_{i=1}^{m} \frac{\partial L_i^{meta}(\hat{\mathbf{w}^t}(\theta))}{\partial \theta} |_{\theta=\theta^t} \tag{6}$$

After the learning process, we can predict confidence scores for annotated labels by inference from our trained model.

Algorithm 1 CML Learning Algorithm

Input: Biased training data S with batch size m, Unbiased meta data $\hat{S}$ with batch size n, max iterations I

Parameter: Main module parameters $\mathbf{w}$ and meta module parameters θ

Output: Main module parameters $\mathbf{w}$ and meta module parameters θ

Let $t = 0$.
while t in range $[0, I)$ **do**
  $(x, y) \leftarrow$ Sample Mini Batch (S,m)
  $(x^{meta}, y^{meta}) \leftarrow$ Sample Mini Batch ($\hat{S}$,n)
  if Data comes from S **then**
    Fine-tune main module
    update main module parameters $\mathbf{w}$ with equation 4
  else
    update meta module parameters θ with equation 6
  end if
  $t = t + 1$
end while
return $\mathbf{w}$, θ

4 Application

The confidence score obtained from CML's output has an important application for data labeling services: measuring label quality at scale. In the industrial setting, the quality of each annotator's work is measured by ground truth reference, which is usually of limited quantity. Small volumes of gold reference data could cause high variance in assessing annotator's performance. As such, it often requires complex procedures to find root cause of quality issue. Error detection model is broadly used in industry but remains a challenge due to limited ground truth labels.

The confidence score from CML is a promising attempt to solve the aforementioned challenges. In particular we implement the following two applications:

4.1 Application 1

Use confidence scores to generate a quality metric for each label, and shows that these scores manage to distinguish the labels in different levels of quality.

4.2 Application 2

Use the data filtered by the confidence score to build an error detection model and demonstrate that it will produce better results.

Figure	Statistics	P value
Figure 2 (a)	0.834	0.000
Figure 2 (b)	0.752	0.000

Table 1: Kolmogorov–Smirnov test results

5 Evaluation

This section shows the experiment results. We also compare our method to state-of-the-art methods.

5.1 Dataset

In our experiment, we process and de-identify commercial voice assistant dataset that assess goal success rate(GSR). We evaluate the goal category task, i.e. labeling a given utterance to a fixed taxonomy of categories. Text ASR (automatic speech recognition) is used as the input feature. Data is collected from both the standard and gold data. Because the standard data only performs one pass on each task, it contains some corrupted labels. Data collected from the gold data can be conceived as "ground truth" data. It will be the data source from which we will generate synthetic data.

5.2 Application 1

In this experiment, we use synthetic data to show that the confidence score produced by CML is capable to separate the incorrect label from correct label at various noise level.

5.2.1 Synthetic data generation process

We generate synthetic data by flipping labels of gold data with different noise ratios for the training set with corrupted labels. Ambiguous labels are generated by flipping label based on assuming that the gold dataset is "correct". The level of noise is also varied between 0% and 20%. We generate synthetic training data by flipping X% labels to incorrect labels. When the flipping rate is 0, the training data are all ground truth. For the test set, we synthetically flip 50% data to incorrect labels.

5.2.2 Metrics and graph explanations

Figure 2 illustrates the confidence scores for the test dataset. The left figure represents the confidence score learned by CML model with training data containing 0% corrupted labels. The right figure represents the confidence score result learned by CML with training data containing 20% corrupted labels. In Table 1, a Kolmogorov–Smirnov test (Massey, 1951) shows the confidence scores from

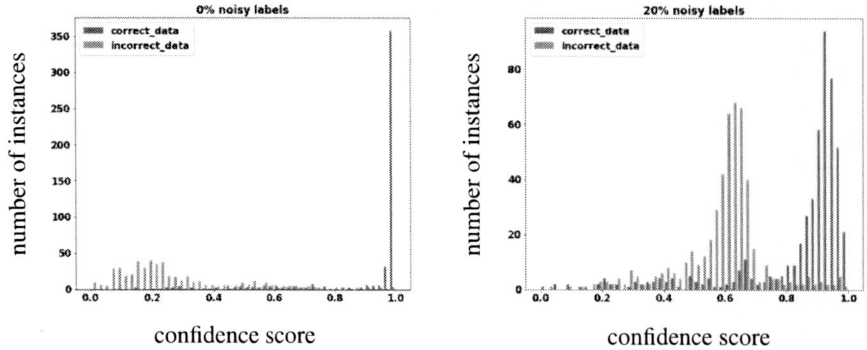

(a) (b)

Figure 2: Confidence score distribution on test set learned from training set with 0%, 20% corrupted labels experiments

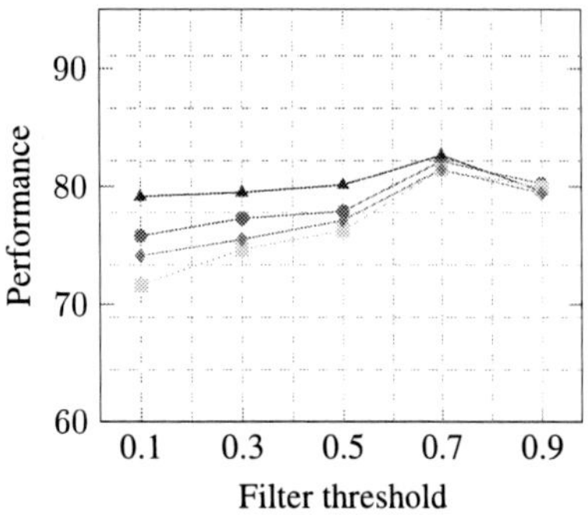

Figure 3: Parameter sensitivity on training data set contains 30% noise (Accuracy, Precision, Recall, F1 score)

the correct labels and the incorrect labels are from different distributions in both scenarios, with the test statistic showing a more extreme value in the 0% noisy label case. From Figure 2 we can see, our learned confidence scores can differentiate correct labels and incorrect labels clearly. In addition, the noise ratio of training set negatively correlate with the level of difference of the confidence scores.

5.3 Application 2

In this experiment, we use both synthetic data and commercial voice assistant data to show that the data filtered by the confidence score works better in error prediction than the same model trained with either the raw training data or the clean data alone.

5.3.1 Synthetic data generation

For the training set, we generate synthetic data similarly as in application 1 by flipping labels of gold data with different noise ratios. We generate training data with 10%, 20%, 30%, 40% and 50% noisy labels. For test set, we synthetically flip 50% labels to incorrect labels.

5.3.2 Experiment setup

The experiment is conducted with the following steps: 1) In a classification task, we train CML to learn the confidence score from the training set, i.e. to predict the correct goal category. 2) We set a threshold to filter good quality data based on the learned confidence score (the threshold is treated as a hyperparameter). 3) Using the filtered training data set, we train a separate BERT-based error detection model. 4) We train the same error detection model using only biased training data. 5) We run the above two models on the same test set and compare their performance. For model evaluation, commonly used metrics such as accuracy, precision, recall, and F1 score are used.

5.3.3 Explain results

Table 2 shows the model performance. The result obtained after CML filtered data outperforms the result obtained using biased training data for all metrics. In addition, based on the last two columns, with the data filtering setup, we select most correct labeled instances and very few incorrect instances. Figure 3 indicates the sensitivity experiment result of threshold for filtering. Figure 3 illustrates that threshold is sensitive for all evaluation metrics.

5.3.4 Real data

We utilize data collected from standard dataset and gold dataset for evaluation. Data collected from standard dataset contains corrupted labels. We design two sets of experiments.

Training set	Accuracy	Precision	Recall	F1 score	#Correct	#Incorrect
Biased training data with 50% noise	40.04	57.54	40.51	43.53	5000	5000
CML Filtered data	**77.38**	**79.57**	**74.81**	**76.33**	4664	902
Biased training data with 40% noise	68.60	73.27	65.01	67.13	6000	4000
CML Filtered data	**79.76**	**81.13**	**77.50**	**77.98**	5590	714
Biased training data with 30% noise	77.36	78.33	72.09	74.51	7000	3000
CML Filtered data	**82.18**	**82.67**	**81.43**	**81.45**	6509	537
Biased training data with 20% noise	80.64	82.61	78.68	80.01	8000	2000
CML Filtered data	**82.98**	**83.30**	**82.26**	**82.17**	7432	350
Biased training data with 10% noise	83.70	**83.55**	82.82	**83.10**	9000	1000
CML Filtered data	**83.72**	83.14	**83.32**	82.77	8353	162

Table 2: Experiment result for synthetic data: compare model built on full data with model built on selected data that are filtered by CML. The number of correct and incorrect in the table stand for the volume of examples with correct and incorrect labels respectively. For instance, 50% noise data contain 5000 correct labeled examples and 5000 incorrect labeled examples. Filtered by CML, we obtain 4664 correct labeled and 902 incorrect labeled examples respectively.

5.3.5 Experiment setup

1) We sample data from the gold dataset (gold-1 of size 3k, and gold-2 of size 6k) to be the unbiased meta data, and sample data from standard dataset (of size 100k) to be the noisy training data. We utilize both of these datasets to train the CML model. We filter the noisy training data by the confidence score learned from CML model, and then build two error detection models with gold-1 data and the filtered data separately. At last we compare the performance on a hold-out gold data set of size 5k. This hold-out data set is used for all the evaluation cases. In a variant of this experiment, we replicate the same process for gold-2. 2) This set of experiment is designed to verify that CML achieves better performance by ingesting small proportion of gold data, compared to model trained on noisy data alone. We sample data from gold dataset of size 3k and sample standard(noisy) data of size 20k.

5.3.6 Experiment results

Comparing row 1 and 3 of Table 3, we demonstrate that the model trained with filtered standard data outperforms the model trained with gold data. This is achieved when the size of noisy training data is 30 folds larger than that of gold data. Comparing rowd 2 and 3, even though the size of the gold data is doubled, the model's performance is still worse than the model trained with filtered standard data. Comparing rowd 4 and 5, we demonstrate that using CML with a noisy training set and small meta data outperforms using noisy training set alone.

In the commercial setting, we hold a large amount of data with corrupted labels. Collecting ground truth data is time consuming and expensive. Based on the above experiment results, CML and its applications provide a economic way to building label error detection model.

Training set	Accuracy	Precision	Recall	F1 score
gold1(3k)	79.42	78.78	78.64	78.70
gold2(6k)	80.72	80.02	**79.93**	79.97
Filtered data	**81.28**	**81.66**	79.44	**80.53**
Biased data	80.20	80.71	77.67	78.02
Biased+meta data	**81.82**	**81.16**	**81.82**	**81.25**

Table 3: Experiment result for real data.
Filtered data: filter from the biased training data(100k).

5.4 Model Evaluation

5.4.1 Data set

For this set of experiment we want to verify the performance of CML. We sample 3k examples from gold dataset as meta data. We also sample 20k examples from standard dataset as noisy training data.

5.4.2 Experiment setting

We evaluate our proposed approach CML against state-of-the-art methods(Shu et al., 2019; Han et al., 2018) for learning with noisy labels. As we mentioned in Section 1, current state-of-the-art methods mainly focus on computer vision domain. We revise the architecture of these two baselines by using pre-trained BERT-base as their main classifiers. We also compare our approach with contrastive learning benchmarks (Gao et al., 2021).

Method	Accuracy	Precision	Recall	F1 score
MetaNet	82.54	82.25	80.79	81.51
simCSE	79.66	80.31	79.65	77.34
Co-teaching	77.00	69.78	76.74	72.73
CML(ours)	**82.82**	**82.86**	**82.58**	**82.71**

Table 4: Experiment result for CML and baselines.

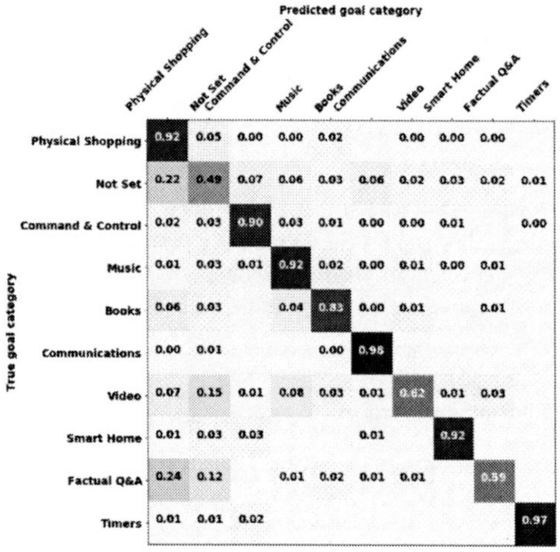

Figure 4: Confusion matrix(goal category prediction with CML)

5.4.3 Experiment results

From Table 4 we can see that our approach outperforms the other three baselines. We not only improve the quality of feature representation, but also improve model performance under noisy label scenario. We also render a confusion matrix for our method as illustrated in Figure 4. As we can see, the "Not Set" category does not perform good since annotators would choose "Not set" category when the category is ambiguous and they are not sure the correct answer. For another example, for "Timers" category, both recall and precision are very high as a result of less ambiguity compared to other categories.

6 Conclusion

In this paper, we propose a contrastive meta learning framework (CML) for estimating human label confidence scores and lowering data collection costs. We use contrastive learning and meta learning to jointly address the main challenges of label scarcity and poor feature representation. We design three sets of experiments with two application settings and three state-of-the-art baseline models to test the effectiveness of our proposed method. Our experiments on a commercial voice assistant GSR dataset show that our method can predict a reliable confidence score for annotations while also effectively lowering the cost of ground truth data collection. Moreover, our proposed method outperforms several SOTA approaches.

References

Ting Chen, Simon Kornblith, Mohammad Norouzi, and Geoffrey Hinton. 2020. A simple framework for contrastive learning of visual representations. In *Proceedings of the 37th International Conference on Machine Learning*, volume 119 of *Proceedings of Machine Learning Research*, pages 1597–1607. PMLR.

Bo Dong, Jinghui Guo, Zhuoyi Wang, Rong Wu, Yang Gao, and Latifur Khan. 2019. Regression prediction for geolocation aware through relative density ratio estimation. In *2019 IEEE International Conference on Big Data (Big Data)*, pages 1644–1649.

Bo Dong, Md Shihabul Islam, Swarup Chandra, Latifur Khan, and Bhavani M. Thuraisingham. 2018. GCI: A transfer learning approach for detecting cheats of computer game. In *IEEE International Conference on Big Data, Big Data 2018, Seattle, WA, USA, December 10-13, 2018*, pages 1188–1197.

Bo Dong, Yifan Li, Yang Gao, Ahsanul Haque, Latifur Khan, and Mohammad M. Masud. 2017. Multistream regression with asynchronous concept drift detection. In *2017 IEEE International Conference on Big Data, BigData 2017, Boston, MA, USA, December 11-14, 2017*, pages 596–605.

Bo Dong, Cristian Lumezanu, Yuncong Chen, Dongjin Song, Takehiko Mizoguchi, Haifeng Chen, and Latifur Khan. 2020. At the speed of sound: Efficient audio scene classification. In *Proceedings of the 2020 International Conference on Multimedia Retrieval*, ICMR '20, page 301–305, New York, NY, USA. Association for Computing Machinery.

Hongchao Fang, Sicheng Wang, Meng Zhou, Jiayuan Ding, and Pengtao Xie. 2020. Cert: Contrastive self-supervised learning for language understanding.

Tianyu Gao, Xingcheng Yao, and Danqi Chen. 2021. Simcse: Simple contrastive learning of sentence embeddings.

Aritra Ghosh, Himanshu Kumar, and P. S. Sastry. 2017. Robust loss functions under label noise for deep neural networks. In *Proceedings of the Thirty-First AAAI Conference on Artificial Intelligence*, AAAI'17, page 1919–1925. AAAI Press.

Aritra Ghosh and Andrew Lan. 2021. Contrastive learning improves model robustness under label noise.

Bo Han, Quanming Yao, Xingrui Yu, Gang Niu, Miao Xu, Weihua Hu, Ivor Tsang, and Masashi Sugiyama. 2018. Co-teaching: Robust training of deep neural networks with extremely noisy labels.

Lu Jiang, Zhengyuan Zhou, Thomas Leung, Li-Jia Li, and Li Fei-Fei. 2018. MentorNet: Learning data-driven curriculum for very deep neural networks on corrupted labels. In *Proceedings of the 35th International Conference on Machine Learning*, volume 80 of *Proceedings of Machine Learning Research*, pages 2304–2313. PMLR.

Taeuk Kim, Kang Min Yoo, and Sang goo Lee. 2021. Self-guided contrastive learning for bert sentence representations.

Yi-Fan Li, Bo Dong, Latifur Khan, Bhavani Thuraisingham, Patrick T. Brandt, and Vito J. D'Orazio. 2021. Data-driven time series forecasting for social studies using spatio-temporal graph neural networks. In *Proceedings of the Conference on Information Technology for Social Good*, GoodIT '21, page 61–66, New York, NY, USA. Association for Computing Machinery.

Yuncheng Li, Jianchao Yang, Yale Song, Liangliang Cao, Jiebo Luo, and Li-Jia Li. 2017. Learning from noisy labels with distillation.

Jie Liu, Wenqian Dong, Qingqing Zhou, and Dong Li. 2021. Fauce: fast and accurate deep ensembles with uncertainty for cardinality estimation. *Proceedings of the VLDB Endowment*, 14(11):1950–1963.

Jie Liu, Jiawen Liu, Wan Du, and Dong Li. 2019. Performance analysis and characterization of training deep learning models on mobile device. In *2019 IEEE 25th International Conference on Parallel and Distributed Systems (ICPADS)*, pages 506–515. IEEE.

Jie Liu, Jiawen Liu, Zhen Xie, and Dong Li. Flame: Aself-adaptive auto-labeling system for heterogeneous mobile processors.

Eran Malach and Shai Shalev-Shwartz. 2018. Decoupling "when to update" from "how to update".

F. J. Massey. 1951. The Kolmogorov-Smirnov test for goodness of fit. *Journal of the American Statistical Association*, 46(253):68–78.

Mahdi Namazifar, John Malik, Li Erran Li, Gokhan Tur, and Dilek Hakkani Tür. 2021. Correcting automated and manual speech transcription errors using warped language models.

Mengye Ren, Wenyuan Zeng, Bin Yang, and Raquel Urtasun. 2018. Learning to reweight examples for robust deep learning. In *Proceedings of the 35th International Conference on Machine Learning*, volume 80 of *Proceedings of Machine Learning Research*, pages 4334–4343. PMLR.

Jun Shu, Qi Xie, Lixuan Yi, Qian Zhao, Sanping Zhou, Zongben Xu, and Deyu Meng. 2019. Meta-weight-net: Learning an explicit mapping for sample weighting.

David Q. Sun, Hadas Kotek, Christopher Klein, Mayank Gupta, William Li, and Jason D. Williams. 2020. Improving human-labeled data through dynamic automatic conflict resolution.

Aaron van den Oord, Yazhe Li, and Oriol Vinyals. 2019. Representation learning with contrastive predictive coding.

Yisen Wang, Xingjun Ma, Zaiyi Chen, Yuan Luo, Jinfeng Yi, and James Bailey. 2019a. Symmetric cross entropy for robust learning with noisy labels.

Zhuoyi Wang, Bo Dong, Yu Lin, Yigong Wang, Md Shihabul Islam, and Latifur Khan. 2019b. Co-representation learning framework for the open-set data classification. In *2019 IEEE International Conference on Big Data (Big Data)*, pages 239–244.

Zhuoyi Wang, Yigong Wang, Bo Dong, Sahoo Pracheta, Kevin Hamlen, and Latifur Khan. 2020. Adaptive margin based deep adversarial metric learning. In *2020 IEEE 6th Intl Conference on Big Data Security on Cloud (BigDataSecurity), IEEE Intl Conference on High Performance and Smart Computing, (HPSC) and IEEE Intl Conference on Intelligent Data and Security (IDS)*, pages 100–108.

Chiyuan Zhang, Samy Bengio, Moritz Hardt, Benjamin Recht, and Oriol Vinyals. 2017. Understanding deep learning requires rethinking generalization.

Zhilu Zhang and Mert R. Sabuncu. 2018. Generalized cross entropy loss for training deep neural networks with noisy labels.

Guoqing Zheng, Ahmed H. Awadallah, and Susan Dumais. 2021. Meta label correction for noisy label learning. In *AAAI 2021*.

Improving Relevance Quality in Product Search using High-Precision Query-Product Semantic Similarity

Alireza Bagheri Garakani, Fan Yang, Wen-Yu Hua, Yetian Chen,
Michinari Momma, Jingyuan Deng, Yan Gao, Yi Sun
Amazon
Seattle, WA, USA
{alirezg,fnam,wenyuhua,yetichen,
michi,jingyua,yanngao,yisun}@amazon.com

Abstract

Ensuring relevance quality in product search is a critical task as it impacts the customer's ability to find intended products in the short-term as well as the general perception and trust of the e-commerce system in the long term. In this work we leverage a high-precision cross-encoder BERT model for semantic similarity between customer query and products and survey its effectiveness for three ranking applications where offline-generated scores could be used: (1) as an offline metric for estimating relevance quality impact, (2) as a re-ranking feature covering head/torso queries, and (3) as a training objective for optimization. We present results on effectiveness of this strategy for the large e-commerce setting, which has general applicability for choice of other high-precision models and tasks in ranking.

1 Introduction

Search is one of the primary means used by customers to find products in e-commerce and therefore it is critical to ensure the relevance quality of search results. A search result may be considered to have low relevance quality (search defect) if it mismatches the customer's query intent. Such defects may range from the mild case of mismatch in brand or color (i.e., substitutes) to the more egregious case of a completely irrelevant result of a different product type. Addressing search defects is a critical task as it can damage customer trust and perception of the e-commerce system, and in general hinder the ability to sell products.

As a simplified view, product search may consist of two distinct phases. First, given a search query, a set of candidate products are determined based on various matchset generation techniques (e.g. lexical/semantic matching, historical associations from past query reformulations, and others). Next, a ranking model is used to generate a score for each (query,product) pair upon which a descending sort determines a ranked list. In the ideal case, the construction of the matchset would be strictly restricted to products that are only relevant to the customer's query, however, this can be challenging to enforce without potentially limiting recall, which itself presents issues that negatively impact search experience. In practice, products in the matchset may still contain complementary or related items to the customer-intended one due to partial matches or from noisy historical associations.

The ranking phase can be used to mitigate the impact of search defects that may exist in the matchset by demoting such results out of the first several pages. In contrast to matchset restrictions, demotion in ranking can be seen as a softer approach since a product will not be entirely eliminated from search results but simply moved beyond the top-results. Given a dataset with relevance labels for query-product pairs, relevance quality can be optimized within ranking to demote products estimated to be less relevant to the customer's query. However, this strategy will have a dependence on similarity measures that often need to favor online efficiency over a higher-precision computationally-expensive counterpart. For example, common ranking features may include query-product lexical/semantic match features and behavioral features that incorporate historical customer interactions; for all these cases, efficient computation over the entire matchset will be required, whether by simple online computations (e.g. TF-IDF, cosine similarity) or by retrieving pre-computed offline (intermediate) results or a combination of both.

In this work we leverage a high-precision model bounded by offline computational resources for addressing our ranking-based task. Specifically, we develop a high-precision cross-encoder BERT model for semantic similarity between customer query and products that is optimized for predicting relevance quality and we survey its effectiveness for three applications where offline-generated scores could be used: (1) as an offline metric for estimat-

Proceedings of The Fifth Workshop on e-Commerce and NLP (ECNLP 5), pages 44 - 48
May 26, 2022

ing relevance quality impact, (2) as a re-ranking feature covering head/torso queries, and (3) as a training objective for optimization. We present results on effectiveness of this strategy for the large e-commerce setting, which has general applicability for choice of other high-precision models (i.e. other than BERT) and tasks in ranking (other than relevance quality).

2 Related Work

Generating textual representations that are effective for downstream tasks is an active area of research that has seen significant improvement in the last several years (Peters et al., 2018; Cer et al., 2018; Devlin et al., 2019). BERT (Devlin et al., 2019) is one such model based on a multi-layer bidirectional Transformer encoder (Vaswani et al., 2017) that has shown state-of-the-art performance on various NLP tasks. In this work, we leverage BERT for two-sentence classification with cross-encoders that is known to have strong predictive performance while at the same time presenting computational challenges for large-scale product search (Humeau et al., 2020; Reimers and Gurevych, 2019). Various strategies can be used towards improving scalability of model inference such as model distillation/compression (Hinton et al., 2015; Sanh et al., 2019; Bucila et al., 2006; Liu et al., 2021; Gordon et al., 2020) and factorizing inputs into separate model paths (i.e. two-tower or bi-encoder models) (Huang et al., 2013; Reimers and Gurevych, 2019; Humeau et al., 2020), but these optimizations typically come at the expense of model performance. For example, using a factorized model enables opportunities to cache pre-computed embeddings and use efficient distance functions on embeddings vectors (e.g. cosine similarity), but this architecture will sacrifice interactions between inputs within early model layers that tend to be helpful. Indeed, the trade-off between precision and inference speed is not limited to BERT nor transformer-based models; in general, higher precision for a given task may be achievable when there is flexibility to use more complex models (e.g. more parameters, ensemble methods), and consume more costly features (e.g. embeddings generated from a secondary model and fed as input). Given its applicability and known computational challenges for our task, in this work we use BERT directly as our high-precision model (i.e. without any computational efficiency optimizations) and apply it for several applications where offline-computed scores are permitted.

3 Query-Product Semantic Similarity

For our task we would like to develop a measure of semantic similarity $g : (Q, A) \to \mathbb{R}$, given an arbitrary query $q \in Q$ and product $a \in A$, where we assume the cardinality of Q and A may be infinite. We select g by favoring a model that maximizes predictive performance bounded by offline resources as opposed to meeting stricter online inference requirements. As mentioned in the previous section, we adopt BERT and frame our problem as two-sentence classification (Devlin et al., 2019) to incorporate textual inputs for the query and product.

For two-sentence classification using BERT as a cross-encoder the input sequence is prepared by prefixing a 'CLS' token followed by the query textual representation, a special separator token ('SEP'), and finally the product textual representation via product title. This input sequence is segmented into sub-words using WordPiece algorithm (Wu et al., 2016) and fed through BERT-base pre-trained model (12 transformer blocks, 768 hidden units, and 12 self-attention heads). We further pre-train the BERT-base model using both Masked LM and Next Sentence Prediction tasks as described in (Devlin et al., 2019) on product metadata such as title and description. For building a classification model, the output embedding for 'CLS' token is passed to a final linear classification layer. All model weights, including transformer block layers, are trained jointly using binary cross-entropy loss. The labeled dataset consisting of judgments tuples (query,product,label) is based on historical query-product samples with relevance judgments (relevant vs irrelevant), which is split into train/validation/test datasets. Table 1 shows a few examples of query-product pairs with their respective model score. Further model improvements (e.g. use of pairwise loss for finetuning, extension beyond BERT to include product images) are applicable for our problem setting but left as future work.

For evaluating relevance quality, we use NDCG metric (Normalized Discount Cumulative Gain) that achieves the highest value of 1 when the rank order respects the ideal relevance label ordering, which is then averaged over all queries. Table 2 shows the performance of our BERT-based classification model benchmarked against a competitive

Table 1: Example query and product inputs with respective BERT-based predictions with higher scores indicating stronger relevance.

Search Query	Product Title (truncated)	Label	Score
blankets for winter double bed soft	... Microfiber Single Comforter ...	exact	0.911
kitchen small storage boxes	... Plastics Polka Container Set ...	exact	0.967
girl jacket for winter	... Women's Slim Fit Joggers ...	irrelevant	0.011

Table 2: Relevance quality (NDCG@16) over competitive GBDT baseline model, including evaluation over query-frequency segments. Table includes BERT model without additional pre-training (sem-noPT), after pre-training (sem), and added as additional feature on top of GBDT baseline.

	Relevance Quality		
Model	Overall	Head+Torso	Tail
sem-noPT	-0.25%	-0.60%	0.18%
sem	-0.13%	-0.59%	0.44%
sem+GBDT	**0.75%**	**0.64%**	**0.89%**

model based on Gradient Boosted Decision Tree (GBDT) (Friedman, 2000) using existing search ranking features (lexical, semantic, and behavioral based) that are either computed in real-time or as part of an offline build. We observe that the BERT-based predictor after pre-training (sem) has significant improvement in the tail-query segment (+0.44%) but sub-par for head+torso queries (−0.59%); this is expected as behavioral features as part of the GBDT baseline model tend to perform well for frequent traffic segments where historical customer behavior signals are available but will be sparse or noisy otherwise. Finally, we build a GBDT-based predictor in a similar manner as the baseline except including our BERT model score as an additional input feature used for feature selection. This final model demonstrates the value brought over the existing set of online-efficient features (+0.75% overall improvement), where gains are seen even for the head-torso query segment suggesting the new feature works in a complimentary way with existing features.

Using this high-precision predictor, we explore several applications in search ranking where we can leverage this model using offline-generated scores for our end task. These are discussed in the next section.

Table 3: Measure of correlation metrics between offline and online measurements for relevance improvement, where offline estimator is baseline or our high-precision predictor.

estimator	Pearson	Kendall
baseline	0.58029	0.20589
sem+GBDT	0.83764	0.59298

4 Applications within Ranking

4.1 Offline Estimation of Relevance Quality

Given that relevance quality is an important metric across search, it is useful to monitor it alongside other important metrics (e.g. revenue, latency) for each experiment that impacts ranking of products and search experience. Here we propose using our semantic predictor for estimating online relevance impact and seek to measure which offline estimator (our high-precision predictor or baseline) better reflects the changes observed for the online metric. We represent our observations as pairs (x_i, y_i) where, for of a given model (treatment) over production (control), x_i is the estimated improvement given an estimator and offline dataset, and y_i is the actual observed improvement as measured by human-judged labels. For our study, our dataset consists of 19 pairs collected from 5 experiments within a 6-month span impacting ranking for a particular marketplace. Our offline estimate is measured on a ranking evaluation dataset of query-product pairs by measuring the improvement in exact probability (output of our semantic predictor) among top results based on the treatment's rank over the control's rank, averaged over all queries. Similar estimation is done for our baseline model, which is a GBDT model trained similar to baseline in section 3. Using this dataset of offline-online impact pairs, we measure Pearson and Kendall correlation coefficients. Table 3 indicates that while neither estimator perfectly reflects online observed values, our high-precision semantic predictor shows significantly improvement over our baseline and, hence, can be used for more effective model selec-

Table 4: Online relevance quality (NDCG@16) of re-ranking models using high-precision semantic model (sem+GBDT) and refreshed baseline over production model.

Model	Relevance Quality
baseline	-0.15% (p=0.39)
sem+GBDT	0.46% (p=0.017)

tion and metric monitoring.

4.2 Feature for Search Re-ranking

We explore using our high-precision model as an input feature for search re-ranking. Re-ranking is a second ranking phase on the top-K results from the preceding (main) ranking phase. Given that our semantic predictor cannot be trivially applied online for the entire matchset due to computational and latency costs, we instead pre-computed semantic scores for more frequent queries and their respective top results and index these scores for fast online retrieval. Specifically, coverage is limited to queries having a predefined number of searches S within the last D days and for their top-P ranked results. For our experiment we re-rank top-16 results where feature coverage exists for head/torso queries (influenced by S and D parameters) and their respective products (by selecting $P >= 16$), however, feature will lack coverage for infrequent queries.

We prepare GBDT predictor models similar to section 3, except the semantic feature used within 'sem-GBDT' is modified to reflect the expected feature coverage online. Results are shown in Table 4, where we observe from online results that we are able to significantly improve NDCG by 0.46% while avoiding regression to revenue, latency, or other guardrails (not shown).

4.3 Objective for Optimization

In this section we prepare primary-phase ranking models and introduce an objective for optimization of search quality. We take the optimization-based approach in ranking, as opposed to feature-based as used for re-ranking usecase, given that offline score pre-computation is no longer practical as it would need to cover the entire matchset (or at least a sizable portion) to be useful. Instead, by using an optimization-based approach we can use full-coverage estimates using our high-precision predictor at training time. Tail queries (e.g. a query never seen before) were strictly not covered in the feature-based re-ranking usecase, but the optimization route can be useful even for this segment by allowing the model to learn associations between other existing ranking features and the task-specific labels generated via our high-precision predictor.

Table 5: Online relevance quality (NDCG@16) of multi-objective ranking model using high-precision semantic predictor as an objective over comparable baseline. Results include query frequency segments. All measurements are statistically significant ($p < 0.05$).

	Relevance Quality		
Exp.	Overall	Head+Torso	Tail
1	0.29%	0.19%	0.44%
2	0.49%	0.52%	0.42%

We use the constraint-based optimization algorithm, AL-LambdaMART (Momma et al., 2020), for the multi-objective formulation:

$$\min_s C^p(s) \;\; s.t. \;\; C^s(s) \leq b \qquad (1)$$

where the cost terms are NDCG-weighted pairwise loss as similarly defined in LambdaMART (Burges, 2010)). In our problem we assume two objectives – relevance quality and revenue – and our modeling goal is to maximize relevance quality $[\min_s C^p(s)]$ while remaining at least flat on revenue relative to the existing production model $[C^s(s) \leq b]$. For the latter, the upperbound value b is set accordingly to achieve this goal using the approach outlined in (Momma et al., 2020). The motivation for having both objectives, despite being generally aligned, is that relevance quality may be one of several factors important for a customer's shopping mission.

We ran 2 online experiments for a particular marketplace against the existing production model. To isolate impact, each experiment included a comparable treatment optimized similarly but without the high-precision semantic score. Results in Table 5 show that in each experiment our semantic treatment is able to achieve higher online relevance impact over the baseline ranking model, while keeping flat on revenue (not shown). Each experiment also showed improvements across all query segments, including tail queries.

5 Conclusion and Future Work

To improve relevance quality in search ranking we applied a high-precision BERT cross-encoder model for semantic similarity in search. We demonstrated three applications where offline-generated scores can be leveraged to improve the end task. This can be viewed as a complementary approach alongside efforts for developing online-efficient models, where the advantages include leveraging higher-precision models and with potentially less development overhead. A follow-up study including benchmarking on public datasets is left as future work.

References

Cristian Bucila, R. Caruana, and Alexandru Niculescu-Mizil. 2006. Model compression. In *KDD '06*.

Chris J.C. Burges. 2010. From ranknet to lambdarank to lambdamart: An overview. Technical Report MSR-TR-2010-82.

Daniel Cer, Yinfei Yang, Sheng-yi Kong, Nan Hua, Nicole Limtiaco, Rhomni St. John, Noah Constant, Mario Guajardo-Cespedes, Steve Yuan, Chris Tar, Brian Strope, and Ray Kurzweil. 2018. Universal sentence encoder for English. In *Proceedings of the 2018 Conference on Empirical Methods in Natural Language Processing: System Demonstrations*, pages 169–174, Brussels, Belgium. Association for Computational Linguistics.

J. Devlin, Ming-Wei Chang, Kenton Lee, and Kristina Toutanova. 2019. Bert: Pre-training of deep bidirectional transformers for language understanding. In *NAACL-HLT*.

Jerome H. Friedman. 2000. Greedy function approximation: A gradient boosting machine. *Annals of Statistics*, 29:1189–1232.

Mitchell Gordon, Kevin Duh, and Nicholas Andrews. 2020. Compressing bert: Studying the effects of weight pruning on transfer learning. In *Proceedings of the 5th Workshop on Representation Learning for NLP*, pages 143–155, Online. Association for Computational Linguistics.

Geoffrey Hinton, Oriol Vinyals, and Jeff Dean. 2015. Distilling the knowledge in a neural network.

Po-Sen Huang, Xiaodong He, Jianfeng Gao, Li Deng, Alex Acero, and Larry Heck. 2013. Learning deep structured semantic models for web search using clickthrough data. ACM International Conference on Information and Knowledge Management (CIKM).

Samuel Humeau, Kurt Shuster, Marie-Anne Lachaux, and Jason Weston. 2020. Poly-encoders: Architectures and pre-training strategies for fast and accurate multi-sentence scoring. In *International Conference on Learning Representations*.

Peiyang Liu, Xi Wang, Lin Wang, Wei Ye, Xiangyu Xi, and Shikun Zhang. 2021. *Distilling Knowledge from BERT into Simple Fully Connected Neural Networks for Efficient Vertical Retrieval*, page 3965–3975. Association for Computing Machinery, New York, NY, USA.

Michinari Momma, Alireza Bagheri Garakani, Nanxun Ma, and Yi Sun. 2020. *Multi-Objective Ranking via Constrained Optimization*, page 111–112. Association for Computing Machinery, New York, NY, USA.

Matthew E. Peters, Mark Neumann, Mohit Iyyer, Matt Gardner, Christopher Clark, Kenton Lee, and Luke Zettlemoyer. 2018. Deep contextualized word representations. In *Proceedings of the 2018 Conference of the North American Chapter of the Association for Computational Linguistics: Human Language Technologies, Volume 1 (Long Papers)*, pages 2227–2237, New Orleans, Louisiana. Association for Computational Linguistics.

Nils Reimers and Iryna Gurevych. 2019. Sentence-BERT: Sentence embeddings using Siamese BERT-networks. In *Proceedings of the 2019 Conference on Empirical Methods in Natural Language Processing and the 9th International Joint Conference on Natural Language Processing (EMNLP-IJCNLP)*, pages 3982–3992, Hong Kong, China. Association for Computational Linguistics.

Victor Sanh, Lysandre Debut, Julien Chaumond, and Thomas Wolf. 2019. Distilbert, a distilled version of bert: smaller, faster, cheaper and lighter. *arXiv preprint arXiv:1910.01108*.

Ashish Vaswani, Noam Shazeer, Niki Parmar, Jakob Uszkoreit, Llion Jones, Aidan N Gomez, Lukasz Kaiser, and Illia Polosukhin. 2017. Attention is all you need. Neural Information Processing Systems.

Yonghui Wu, Mike Schuster, Zhifeng Chen, Quoc V. Le, Mohammad Norouzi, Wolfgang Macherey, Maxim Krikun, Yuan Cao, Qin Gao, Klaus Macherey, Jeff Klingner, Apurva Shah, Melvin Johnson, Xiaobing Liu, Lukasz Kaiser, Stephan Gouws, Yoshikiyo Kato, Taku Kudo, Hideto Kazawa, Keith Stevens, George Kurian, Nishant Patil, Wei Wang, Cliff Young, Jason Smith, Jason Riesa, Alex Rudnick, Oriol Vinyals, Greg Corrado, Macduff Hughes, and Jeffrey Dean. 2016. Google's neural machine translation system: Bridging the gap between human and machine translation. *CoRR*, abs/1609.08144.

Comparative Snippet Generation

Saurabh Jain, Yisong Miao, Min-Yen Kan
National University of Singapore

saurabhjain@u.nus.edu, miaoyisong@gmail.com,
kanmy@comp.nus.edu.sg

Abstract

We model product reviews to generate comparative responses consisting of positive and negative experiences regarding the product. Specifically, we generate a single-sentence, comparative response from a given positive and a negative opinion. We contribute the first dataset for this task of Comparative Snippet Generation from contrasting opinions regarding a product, and a performance analysis of a pre-trained BERT model to generate such snippets.

1 Introduction

The proliferation of opinions on the Web has transformed the way users express their opinions and experiences about aspects of products and services. *Online user reviews* contribute personal opinions, and when aggregated together, these reviews play a crucial role in purchasing decisions. However, due to the large volume of reviews, it can be infeasible for customers to skim all such sources. As users have to navigate through a large pool of opinions to make decisions, *opinion mining and summarization* grows in importance. As such, this area of work has received significant attention.

Many e-commerce platforms provide functionalities to compare products. These functionalities may be template-based and compare products on the basis of information provided by sellers. Comparative opinions from customers, who are experienced users of the product or service, are largely missing from such template-based comparison. On the other hand, question answering systems based on reviews, such as AmazonQA (Gupta et al., 2019), often only tell one side of the story in the response: either positive or negative. In our opinion, there is a demand for compact representations of both positive and negative opinions of products. Such compact textual representation could be enunciated by dialogue agents or shown as a succinct summary to drill-down on in a mobile interface. To the best of our knowledge, no such work has been done yet to provide *comparative responses* regarding a product to a user. We attempt this novel task. We take as input a positive and a negative opinion regarding a product and generate a comparative, single-sentenced fused response, which we call a comparative snippet (Fig. 1).

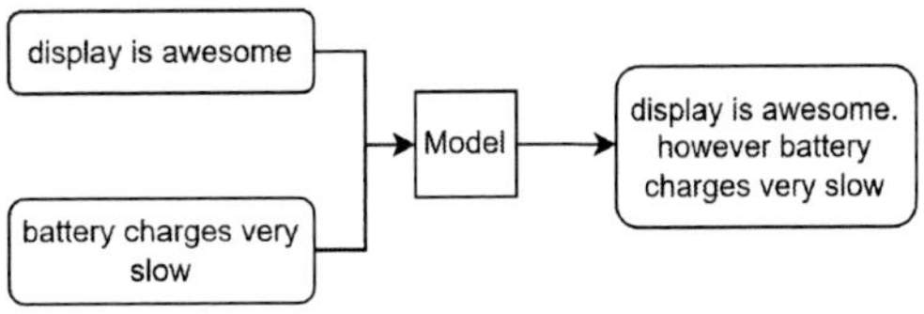

Figure 1: Comparative Snippet Generation: taking a positive and a negative opinion and generating a comparative response.

We extract single-sentence summaries of positive and negative opinions, separately, from reviews of 3,269 products mentioned by the Amazon Reviews Dataset (2018). We chose to base our corpus on this existing dataset to help spur future research on our task that can leverage existing work on the parent dataset. We then combine these positive and negative opinions to generate comparative responses. Our final dataset contains $174,394$ training instances, $19,725$ validation instances, and $21,397$ test instances[1]. We also successfully model positive and negative opinions to generate a comparative response expressing both positive and negative opinions about a target product.

2 Related Work

Sentence Sentiment Detection. Sentiment detection classifies the opinion of a sentence into two classes, *Positive* and *Negative*. Sometimes a third class, *Neutral*, is also included. Early works focus on unsupervised approaches and the use of sentiment lexicons to compute the overall sentiment of a text; e.g., (Turney, 2002). Subsequently, the convo-

[1] https://github.com/WING-NUS/comparative-snippet-generation-dataset

Proceedings of The Fifth Workshop on e-Commerce and NLP (ECNLP 5), pages 49 - 57

lutional neural network (CNN) architecture was introduced to classify the sentiment of sentences Kim (2014). Socher et al. (2011) use recursive neural networks to learn sentiment at varying granularities (i.e., words, phrases, and sentences). Many current well-performing neural models use the attention mechanism (Vaswani et al., 2017; Devlin et al., 2019) to encode a text into a vector representation.

Opinion Summarization. Opinion summarization differs from other summarization tasks in two aspects. First, it cannot rely on reference summaries for training, as it is infeasible to get such meta-reviews. To produce a reference summary for a single product, a reviewer may have to go through hundreds of reviews. Second, due to the subjectivity and conflicting nature of reviews, the notion of information importance applies differently. In this task, output summaries are based on the popularity of opinions. Moreover to be viable, approaches must be flexible with respect to input size as products can be reviewed frequently, resulting in increasing amounts of review content.

Opinion summarization can be either *abstractive* or *extractive*. In abstractive summarization, summaries are generated token-by-token to generate new sentences that articulate prevalent opinions from the inputs. These generated summaries offer a solution to the lack of reference summaries, and can be written in the style of the input reviews. However, prior work have used unrealistically small number of input reviews — 10 or fewer — to generate output summaries Suhara et al. (2020); Amplayo and Lapata (2021). Due to these shortcomings, we chose the alternative style of extractive summarization, which generates summaries by selecting phrases from the inputs. As a foundation, we base our method on Angelidis et al. (2021), who used the Vector-Quantized Variational Autoencoder (VQ–VAE) in their extractive opinion summarization. First introduced by van den Oord et al. (2017), VQ–VAE is used to learn discrete latent variables. It passes encoder output through a discretization bottleneck by lookup in the space of latent code embeddings. Specifically, we use the Quantized Transformer (*cf.* § 3.1), an unsupervised neural model inspired by VQ–VAE, to generate popularity-driven opinions. This method does not depend on vector averaging, nor does it suffer from information loss, which motivates us to use it as it easily accommodates large numbers of reviews.

Sentence Fusion. Sentence fusion combines multiple sentences, which may contain redundancies, into one coherent sentence. The output sentence not only should preserve input information but also any semantic relationships among sentences. Sentence fusion requires understanding the discourse semantics between the input sentences. Previously, feature-based approaches were used to combine sentences due to the lack of annotated data. Recently, a large-scale sentence fusion dataset, DiscoFuse Geva et al. (2019), was introduced, which has enabled the training of neural network-based models for the fusion task. The authors also train the sequence-to-sequence model to fuse the input sentences and find that the trained model succeeds in combining the sentences through structural constructions, but performs badly when fusion involves inserting discourse connectives. Recently, Rothe et al. (2020) uses a BERT-based encoder–decoder model. Although this work improves the accuracy, it struggles in detecting the semantic relationships correctly between the input sentences.

Predicting discourse markers or connecting strings is a sister task of sentence fusion. It is typically utilized as an intermediate step to improve downstream tasks. Ben-David et al. (2020) train a model to learn both the discourse relation and discourse connective together in a multi-task framework. In our work, similar to Rothe et al. (2020), we fuse two sentences together by training a model to learn the appropriate insertion of a discourse connective.

3 Dataset Generation

An instance of our dataset contains positive and negative opinions as an input and a comparative response as an output as shown in Table 2. Since no such dataset is available for reviews, we generate it from scratch. Here, dataset generation includes the tasks of opinion extraction and rule-based response generation sub-tasks. The task of opinion extraction itself includes subtasks of extraction, polarity classification, and summarization of segments.

3.1 Opinion Extraction

Segment Extraction. A sentence of a review may contain more than one opinion. For e.g., *"display was quite bland, didn't enjoy much, but speed was brilliant."* This sentence contains a positive opinion, *"but speed was brilliant"*, and a negative opinion, *"display was quite bland"*. Therefore, as suggested by Angelidis and Lapata (2018), it is

Review	In the end, take this tablet for what it is, a low end budget tablet that runs Lollipop smoothly but has a less than desirable screen resolution.
EDUs	In the end, take this tablet
	for what it is, a low end budget table
	that runs Lollipop smoothly
	but has a less than desirable screen resolution.

Table 1: A review and its extracted segments.

Input	the display is awesome. camera is not good.
Output	the display is awesome. however, camera is not good.

Table 2: An instance of our dataset.

beneficial to process phrases and discourse units extracted from review sentences compared to processing these sentences directly. Hereafter, we refer to these phrases and units as *segments*. We use work done by Feng and Hirst (2014) to extract segments from reviews (as shown in Table 1's example). After extracting segments, we perform the following five post-processing steps to improve overall quality:

1. We remove segments having less than three words, e.g. *"good product"*, *"best product"*, *"very sad"*, etc. Such short segments are not relevant to our work.

2. We remove leading and trailing punctuations; e.g., ".", "!". "," and "-".

3. We remove segments that do not contain at least one noun or pronoun and one main or auxiliary verb; e.g., *"the only problem"*, *"and was destroyed"* and *"which is annoying"*. We use Spacy[2] to extract a noun and a verb from a segment.

4. Since we focus on working with segments with third-person narrative, we discard segments containing first-person words: "i", "me", "my", "myself", "mine", "we", "us", "our", "ourselves". While our *extractive summarization* approach (§3.1) will eventually rank such segments low, we prefer to drop these here for efficiency.

5. If a segment starts with We delete any leading occurrences of "because", "and", "before", "but", "however", "now", "of", "then", "&", "or" from the segment. As an example, we edit *"but it is not that great"* into *"it is not that great"*, by omitting the leading *"but"*.

Segment Sentiment Classification. We next classify each segment into one of two categories, positive or negative. Reviews from different domains may differ in syntactic properties — e.g., length and vocabulary — however, the underlying semantics and discourse properties remain the same. To the best of our knowledge, there are no segment-level polarity-annotated datasets that build from the Amazon Reviews. As such, we use SPOT: Sentiment Polarity Annotation Dataset[3], which contains 197 reviews taken from the Yelp Tang et al. (2015) and IMDB Diao et al. (2014) datasets, annotated with segment-level polarities for positive, neutral, or negative sentiments. AS our work only utilizes positive and negative opinions to generate a comparative response, we discard the neutral segments. We fine-tune BERT Devlin et al. (2019) for polarity classification using the SPOT dataset. Then we classify extracted segments into positive or negative class using the fine-tuned model.

Segment Summarization. Products may have a large number of reviews. In our dataset, the single most-reviewed product has a massive $10,222$ reviews, generating $90,314$ segments – completely infeasible to manually process. Also, many reviews may express the same meaning. These two characteristics strongly motivate the need for a summarization algorithm to extract popular segments. Our summarization algorithm should satisfy the following requirements: 1) it must be unsupervised, since we do not have reference summaries; 2) it must be highly scalable since reviews per product regularly exceed $1,000$ inputs; and 3) it should extract frequently-occurring segments. In the case of reviews, we observe that the popularity of a segment is generally associated with their frequency of repetition. If several reviewers talk about a specific segment, e.g., *"display is very good"*, in their reviews for a product, it becomes a popular segment.

To satisfy these requirements, we employ the

[2] https://spacy.io/

[3] https://github.com/EdinburghNLP/spot-data

Positive	Negative
it is great the display is awesome screen is great meets all expectations this tablet is fantastic	battery life is lackluster camera is not good does have some issues with clearing memory it 's just annoying eventually it refuses to turn on at all

Table 3: Extracted Summaries. This table depicts five segments each of positive and negative opinions from a extracted summary of a product.

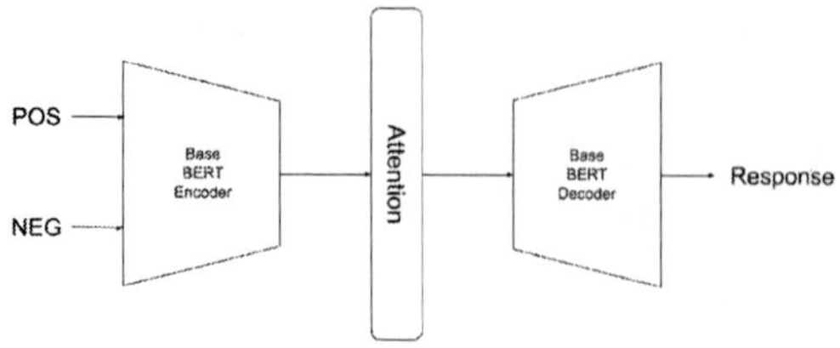

Figure 2: Model Architecture from Rothe et al. (2020).

technique of Angelidis et al. (2021). They train an embedding space consisting of latent codes. Each latent code is a randomly-initialized vector that groups semantically similar segments. Then, a later part of the algorithm extracts top segments from each code which are considered popular segments.

Our work uses a slightly different approach to determine segments to extract. While Angelidis et al. (2021) use a threshold for the total number of words in the desired output summary, our method emphasizes popularity: we select segments for the output summary which are sampled greater than a tunable threshold t times. With an overly high t (e.g., $t = 50$), too few segments are selected; but if set too low (e.g., $t = 5$), the resultant segment quality is often poor and also often syntactically invalid, semantically incomplete or repetitive. We set the threshold to $t = 18$, based on appropriate empirical tuning on our validation set. For each product, we perform summarization on positive and negative opinions separately. Table 3 illustrates a few examples of extracted summaries.

3.2 Rule-based Response Generation

After extracting popular positive and negative segments separately, our final step is to generate the contrastive snippets, conforming to the format exemplified by Table 4.

We first analyzed sampled extracted reviews to understand how users actually combine two contrasting opinions when writing their own reviews. As a result, we inventoried seven common templates that users employ to combine both positive (POS) and negative (NEG) opinions:

1. {POS} . but , {NEG} .
2. {POS} . however {NEG} .
3. {POS} . on the other hand , {NEG} .
4. although {POS} , according to a few users {NEG} .
5. {POS} . yet , some users have also mentioned that {NEG} .
6. {POS} . however , there are people who have complained that {NEG} .
7. {POS} . on the other hand , a few users have complained that {NEG} .

For a given product e, let O_p and O_n represent a set of positive and negative opinions, respectively, extracted by our opinion extraction method. We combine $o_p \in O_p$, and $o_n \in O_n$ using the templates, as illustrated in Table 4, to generate an output response. Then, for each product, we combine each positive segment, o_p, with each negative segment, o_n, present in the respective extracted summaries.

4 Model Architecture

Given a positive opinion $o_p \in O_p$, and a negative opinion $o_n \in O_n$, our task is to generate a response R as shown in Table 4. We use an Encoder–Decoder based architecture similar to Rothe et al. (2020), as depicted in Fig. 2. For the encoder, we inherit BERT Transformer layer implementations which differs slightly than the canonical Transformer layer implementation Vaswani et al. (2017); as BERT replaces the standard RELU with GELU activation (Hendrycks and Gimpel, 2016). The implementation of our decoder is also similar to BERT with two modifications: First, the self-attention mechanism is modified to look only at the left context. Second, an encoder–decoder attention mechanism is added. We initialize both the encoder and decoder with publicly available pre-trained checkpoints from the uncased base model of BERT to learn and decode hidden representations. We join o_p and o_n, respectively, with a *full stop (.)* to make an input sequence. We use *mean cross entropy (MCE)* to compute loss. We fine-tune our model to generate a response fusing a positive and a negative opinion. In the next section, we describe our experimental settings and analyze results in detail.

Input	**Positive Opinion**: it works great. **Negative Opinion**: camera is not good.
Response Format	{POS} . However , some users have also mentioned that {NEG} .
Generated Response	it works great . However , some users have also mentioned that camera is not good .

Table 4: Response generation example: a tuple of consisting of a template-based response, generated from an extracted positive and a negative opinion of a product.

5 Evaluation and Results

Dataset. We use reviews of products from the "Electronics" category of Amazon Reviews Dataset (2018) Ni et al. (2019). We generate our dataset in two phases, following the steps in § 3. In the first phase, we consider reviews of 74 products only and hand-curate segments in the generated summaries. We consider syntactically and semantically valid segments only. In the second phase, we scale the number of products and consider reviews of $3,269$ products. After extracting segments from these reviews, we consider only those segments for the summary generation which have part-of-speech patterns similar to hand-curated segments extracted in the first phase. Thus, we can ensure syntactic validity of the segments. Our final dataset contains $174,394$ training instances generated from reviews of $2,569$ products, $19,725$ validation instances generated from reviews of 321 products, and $21,397$ test instances generated from reviews of 379 products.

5.1 Implementation Details

We use the Transformer architecture in segment summarization model and uncased base BERT architecture for our response generation model.

Segment Summarization. As our summarization model is similar to Angelidis et al. (2021), we retain their settings in our experiments. We use a unigram LM SentencePiece vocabulary of size $32K$[4] to encode opinion segments. Our Transformer has a dimension size of 312, while its feed-forward layers are of size 512. It uses 3 layers and 4 internal heads. The input embedding layer is shared between the encoder and decoder, and $H = 8$ sentence heads are used to represent every sentence. For the quantizer, we set number of latent codes $k = 1024$ and sample $m = 30$ codes for each segment. We use the Adam optimizer (Kingma and Ba, 2015) with an initial learning rate of 10^{-3} and a learning rate decay of 0.9. We disable segments assignments to latent codes for the first 4 epochs as warm–up steps for the Transformer. We train the model for a total of 20 epochs. At prediction time, in two-step sampling, we sample 300 latent codes, and for each code, we sample $n = 30$ segments.

Response Generation. Due to the effectiveness of BERT over Transformers in text generation tasks (Devlin et al., 2019), we use the base BERT model for our encoder and decoder. Since we initialize both the encoder and decoder with uncased base BERT pre-trained checkpoints, our experimental settings are similar to what were used while training the base BERT model. It has 12 layers, hidden size of 768, 12 attention heads, and vocabulary of $\sim 30K$ word pieces. We fine-tune this model for 5 epochs with a batch size of 32. Inputs and outputs are padded to a length of the largest available instance present in training, validation, and test sets.

5.2 Metrics

An output response should be evaluated on the basis of three aspects:

1. Preservation of input information. There should not be any change in positive and negative opinions. The semantic meaning and the syntactic structure of these opinions should be preserved. We use ROUGE-L to evaluate this aspect. It measures the longest common subsequence between an output sentence and a reference sentence. Since we do not modify the positive and negative opinions, the longest common subsequence is identical to one of the input opinions. For example, for an input sentence *"display is awesome. battery takes long time to charge."* and the corresponding output sentence *"display is awesome. however, battery takes long time to charge."*, the longest common sub-sequence is *"display is awesome. battery takes long time to charge."*

2. Quality of output. In this aspect, we

[4] `https://github.com/google/sentencepiece`

Recall	Model Based	Rule Based	Comparison Source
ROUGE-L	0.9876	1.0	Input and predicted output
ROUGE-3	0.8563	1.0	Prediction output and the most similar reference
ROUGE-4	0.7885	1.0	Prediction output and the most similar reference
ROUGE-2	0.8376	1.0	Connecting strings from the prediction output and the most similar reference
ROUGE-3	0.7884	1.0	Connecting strings from the prediction output and the most similar reference

Table 5: Comparative Snippet Generation Model Evaluation (Column 2; "Model Based"). The first row (ROUGE-L) measures input information preservation. The next two rows (ROUGE-3 and -4) measure the quality of predicted outputs, and the last two rows' entries measure the quality of the model-proposed connecting strings.

measure whether the order of words is correct, and connecting string is inserted at the right place. We use ROUGE-3 and ROUGE-4 to measure this aspect. These metrics measure the number of common trigrams and quadgrams between a generated output and a reference. We compare a generated output with each reference separately, and consider the score corresponding to the closest matching reference.

3. Quality of connecting string. This aspect measures whether words in connecting string are in the correct order and represent a valid sentence connector. For example, the connecting string *"on the other hand, some users have also mentioned that"* is of higher quality than the string *"on, some users have also mentioned that"*. We use ROUGE-2 to measure this aspect. Since a valid connecting string may comprise of part of two or more connecting strings, we do not use ROUGE-3 and ROUGE-4 to avoid heavy penalties. We remove those tokens from an output that are also present in the input sentence. We assume that thus remaining sub-string comprises tokens only from connecting strings. We repeat the same for all the references. Then we compute the ROUGE-2 metric between the processed output and references.

5.3 Results and Analysis

Overall Performance. We compute ROUGE-L-recall between input and a generated output to evaluate the model's performance in preserving input information. As shown in Table 5, recall of model-based generations is high: 0.9876; yet less than the perfect rule-based generation method that created the dataset. We consider recall values of ROUGE-3 and ROUGE-4 metrics to measure the quality of generated outputs with respect to the reference outputs. As shown in Table 5, recall values of ROUGE-3, and ROUGE-4 metrics for model-based

Connecting String	%age
but,	0.64%
however	44.68%
on the other hand,	33.65%
yet, some users have also mentioned that	0.86%
although [positive opinion], according to a few users	0.57%
on the other hand, a few users have complained that	10.79%
however, there are people who have complained that	8.82%

Table 6: Distribution of connecting strings for which a prediction output matches with one of the references. This distribution is with respect to the total number of exact matches.

generations are 0.8563, and 0.7885, respectively, which we believe is adequate. Finally, we compute the ROUGE-2 metric specifically confined specifically to the connecting string, in the manner described in (*cf.* § 5.2). As shown in Table 5, the recall of ROUGE-2 for our model-based generation is 0.8376. We believe that the connecting string quality is adequate but can definitely be improved with more careful modelling, and that the connecting string realization is a key component also contributing to overall quality in our second, overall output quality evaluation.

Study on Connective Prediction. We examine the connective prediction in more detail as this is the key aspect that is variable in the generation task. The model's prediction outputs exactly match with one of the references in 13.09% test cases. Table 6 shows distribution of connecting strings corresponding to these exact matches. Our model not only learns to generate comparative responses by fusing positive and negative opinions but also learns to generate new connecting strings by fusing words of two separate connecting strings or by appending a punctuation symbol with a connecting string. Our model fuses an additional 13.94% test cases with newly-generated connecting strings. Table 7 shows the distributional analysis of such

New Connecting String	Percent.
yet, there are people who have complained that	0.07%
but, there are people who have complained that	0.07%
however, some users have also mentioned that	48.74%
but, some users have also mentioned that	0.23%
however,	48.34%
yet,	1.51%
but	0.10%
yet	0.94%

Table 7: Distribution of new connecting strings. This distribution is with respect to the total number of newly-generated connecting strings.

Error Type	Percent.
Incorrect mixing	48.22%
Missing although word	17.82%
Single word "on" insertion	14.65%
Input information modification	19.26%

Table 8: Common generation errors from our pre-trained BERT model's output.

newly-generated connecting strings. We can see that *"however, some users have also mentioned that"* occurs the maximum number of times in such test cases and has been generated by fusing *"however"*, and *"some users have also mentioned that"*. The second most-frequent generated string is *"however,"* in which a comma (",") has been appended to a connecting string.

Our model also generates incorrectly fused sentences. Table 8 shows main types of error. The maximum number of failure cases occur due to incorrect mixing of parts of different connecting strings. In such cases, either an extra word is inserted, or more words are missing from the connecting string. Table 9 depicts top incorrect mixing patterns. In the four patterns, we can see that the first word of negative opinion is inserted in between the connecting string. Our analysis shows that it happens due to the ambiguity present in our training dataset. For example, our training dataset contains connecting strings *"however"*, and *"however, there are people who have complained that"*. In the case of the former, just after the connecting string *"however"*, the model inserts words from the negative opinion. While in the latter case, words from a connecting string are inserted after "however". Therefore, we assume that at prediction time probability of inserting the first word of the negative opinion after *"however"* becomes highest, thus resulting in an incorrect mixing of connecting strings. A similar argument exists for the incorrect cases containing string *"on the other hand"*. Table 10 shows an example of incorrectly mixed connecting string.

The second most common failure case is associated with input information modification. Ideally, a comparative output sentence must contain positive and negative opinions without modification. But our model, sometimes, generates an output sentence that either deletes or repeats one or more words from the input or replaces a word with its synonym or base form (Table 10). As mentioned in the section (*cf.* § 3.2), except one, in all other templates connecting string is inserted between the positive and negative opinions. In case of *although POS, according to a few users NEG*, we also prepend a word *"although"* in the output sentence. Since most of the training instances insert a connecting string only in between, our model does not learn properly to prepend a word *"although"* and thus gives rise to the third most occurring failure cases in which the first word of the positive opinion is repeated instead of prepending a word *"although"*. An example of such a case has been shown in Table 10. The last most occurring errors are associated with single word insertion *"on"* between the positive and negative opinions, as shown in Table 10.

Why not use rules to generate responses if these give better performance? As shown in our results, rule-based generations outperform model-based generations. Therefore, an obvious question arises on the use of model-based generations. Templates used for generating rule-based generations have been manually selected from a random analysis of reviews. But, in the future, we want our model to automatically learn styles of comparative response generations from the given dataset and use these styles to fuse positive and negative opinions. Therefore, we prefer to use model-based generations and improve their accuracy.

6 Conclusion and Future Work

We introduced a novel task of generating a comparative response (or "snippet") regarding a product that combines positive and negative opinions together in a single sentence. As such comparative responses are not easily found in natural review environments, we generate such comparative responses through extractive summaries of product reviews using an unsupervised approach. To spur future research in this area, we have also made our

Incorrect Mixing Pattern	Distribution
however the other hand, [first word from the negative opinion] few users have complained that	9.85%
however [first word from the negative opinion] there are people who have complained that	7.83%
on the other hand, [first word from the negative opinion] few users have complained that	5.83%
on [first word from the negative opinion] there are people who have complained that	7.38%
on, some users have also mentioned that	8.15%
however the other hand,	6.40%

Table 9: Top incorrect mixing patterns. Here percentage is w.r.t. all the failure cases.

Incorrect mixing	Expected	the entire set is comfortable. on the other hand, a few users have complained that right side slides down.
	Predicted	the entire set is comfortable. on the other hand, right few users have complained that right side slides down.
Missing "although"	Expected	although the retractil system works fine, according to a few users the pads are sort of squarish.
	Predicted	the the retractil system works fine, according to a few users the pads are sort of squarish.
Insertion of "on"	Expected	the 415's are a great upgrade from the oem earbuds. but, it is super uncomfortable.
	Predicted	the 415's are a great upgrade from the oem earbuds. on, it is super uncomfortable.
Information modification	Expected	sound is pretty good. but, the movement is actually more like a saw.
	Predicted	sound is pretty good. however, the movement is actually more like a see.

Table 10: Examples of top errors.

dataset public and leveraged the prior Amazon reviews corpus, popular with the research community. Throughout our work we assume that all reviews are genuine and have been written by buyers who have used the product. We investigate and benchmark a baseline model for this task that combines state-of-the-art text representation (BERT) in an encoder–decoder architecture to generate a comparative response. Our analysis of the output results shows that even such a state-of-the-art pre-trained model does not generate perfect responses.

There are limitations of our work that we hope to address in the future. Currently, positive and negative opinions in a generated response may or may not be related to the same aspect. As such, improvements to better generate more naturalistic responses may restrict generation to opinions where both the positive and negative discuss the same product aspect. In future we would also like to quantify the veracity of the opinions and weight them accordingly.

Acknowledgements

We acknowledge the support of NVIDIA Corporation for their donation of the Titan X GPU that facilitated this research.

References

Reinald Kim Amplayo and Mirella Lapata. 2021. Informative and controllable opinion summarization. In *EACL*.

Stefanos Angelidis, Reinald Kim Amplayo, Yoshihiko Suhara, Xiaolan Wang, and Mirella Lapata. 2021. Extractive opinion summarization in quantized transformer spaces. *Transactions of the Association for Computational Linguistics*, 9:277–293.

Stefanos Angelidis and Mirella Lapata. 2018. Multiple instance learning networks for fine-grained sentiment analysis. *Transactions of the Association for Computational Linguistics*, 6:17–31.

Eyal Ben-David, Orgad Keller, Eric Malmi, Idan Szpektor, and Roi Reichart. 2020. Semantically driven sentence fusion: Modeling and evaluation. In *Findings of the Association for Computational Linguistics: EMNLP 2020*, pages 1491–1505, Online. Association for Computational Linguistics.

Jacob Devlin, Ming-Wei Chang, Kenton Lee, and Kristina Toutanova. 2019. BERT: Pre-training of deep bidirectional transformers for language understanding. In *Proceedings of the 2019 Conference of the North American Chapter of the Association for Computational Linguistics: Human Language Technologies, Volume 1 (Long and Short Papers)*, pages 4171–4186, Minneapolis, Minnesota. Association for Computational Linguistics.

Qiming Diao, Minghui Qiu, Chao-Yuan Wu, Alex Smola, Jing Jiang, and Chong Wang. 2014. Jointly modeling aspects, ratings and sentiments for movie recommendation (jmars). *Proceedings of the 20th ACM SIGKDD international conference on Knowledge discovery and data mining*.

Vanessa Wei Feng and Graeme Hirst. 2014. A linear-time bottom-up discourse parser with constraints and post-editing. In *Proceedings of the 52nd Annual Meeting of the Association for Computational Linguistics (Volume 1: Long Papers)*, pages 511–521, Baltimore, Maryland. Association for Computational Linguistics.

Mor Geva, Eric Malmi, Idan Szpektor, and Jonathan Berant. 2019. DiscoFuse: A large-scale dataset for discourse-based sentence fusion. In *Proceedings of the 2019 Conference of the North American Chapter of the Association for Computational Linguistics: Human Language Technologies, Volume 1 (Long and Short Papers)*, pages 3443–3455, Minneapolis, Minnesota. Association for Computational Linguistics.

Mansi Gupta, Nitish Kulkarni, Raghuveer Chanda, Anirudha Rayasam, and Zachary Chase Lipton. 2019. Amazonqa: A review-based question answering task. In *IJCAI*.

Dan Hendrycks and Kevin Gimpel. 2016. Bridging nonlinearities and stochastic regularizers with gaussian error linear units. *ArXiv*, abs/1606.08415.

Yoon Kim. 2014. Convolutional neural networks for sentence classification. In *EMNLP*.

Diederik P. Kingma and Jimmy Ba. 2015. Adam: A method for stochastic optimization. *CoRR*, abs/1412.6980.

Jianmo Ni, Jiacheng Li, and Julian McAuley. 2019. Justifying recommendations using distantly-labeled reviews and fine-grained aspects. In *Proceedings of the 2019 Conference on Empirical Methods in Natural Language Processing and the 9th International Joint Conference on Natural Language Processing (EMNLP-IJCNLP)*, pages 188–197, Hong Kong, China. Association for Computational Linguistics.

Sascha Rothe, Shashi Narayan, and Aliaksei Severyn. 2020. Leveraging pre-trained checkpoints for sequence generation tasks. *Transactions of the Association for Computational Linguistics*, 8:264–280.

Richard Socher, Jeffrey Pennington, Eric H. Huang, Andrew Y. Ng, and Christopher D. Manning. 2011. Semi-supervised recursive autoencoders for predicting sentiment distributions. In *Proceedings of the 2011 Conference on Empirical Methods in Natural Language Processing*, pages 151–161, Edinburgh, Scotland, UK. Association for Computational Linguistics.

Yoshihiko Suhara, Xiaolan Wang, Stefanos Angelidis, and Wang-Chiew Tan. 2020. OpinionDigest: A simple framework for opinion summarization. In *Proceedings of the 58th Annual Meeting of the Association for Computational Linguistics*, pages 5789–5798, Online. Association for Computational Linguistics.

Duyu Tang, Bing Qin, and Ting Liu. 2015. Document modeling with gated recurrent neural network for sentiment classification. In *Proceedings of the 2015 Conference on Empirical Methods in Natural Language Processing*, pages 1422–1432, Lisbon, Portugal. Association for Computational Linguistics.

Peter Turney. 2002. Thumbs up or thumbs down? semantic orientation applied to unsupervised classification of reviews. In *Proceedings of the 40th Annual Meeting of the Association for Computational Linguistics*, pages 417–424, Philadelphia, Pennsylvania, USA. Association for Computational Linguistics.

Aäron van den Oord, Oriol Vinyals, and Koray Kavukcuoglu. 2017. Neural discrete representation learning. In *NIPS*.

Ashish Vaswani, Noam M. Shazeer, Niki Parmar, Jakob Uszkoreit, Llion Jones, Aidan N. Gomez, Lukasz Kaiser, and Illia Polosukhin. 2017. Attention is all you need. *ArXiv*, abs/1706.03762.

Textual Content Moderation in C2C Marketplace

Yusuke Shido
Mercari, inc.
shidoy@mercari.com

Hsien-Chi Toby Liu *
tobbymailbox@gmail.com

Keisuke Umezawa
Mercari, inc.
k-umezawa@mercari.com

Abstract

Automatic monitoring systems for inappropriate user-generated messages have been found to be effective in reducing human operation costs in Consumer to Consumer (C2C) marketplace services, in which customers send messages directly to other customers. We propose a lightweight neural network that takes a conversation as input, which we deployed to a production service. Our results show that the system reduced the human operation costs to less than one-sixth compared to the conventional rule-based monitoring at Mercari.

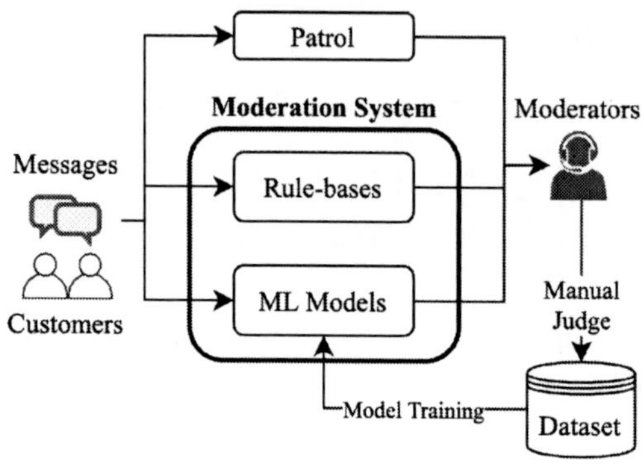

Figure 1: The overview of the moderation system for messages under transaction.

1 Introduction

Mercari is a C2C marketplace app available in Japan and the United States. The application operates along the lines of an online flea market in which any customer can list items for sale and purchase others' listings. To prevent unpleasant customer experiences and unnecessary difficulties, Mercari defines some guidelines for using the platform. If a customer violates the guidelines, moderators from the customer support of Mercari may give them a warning to protect the safety and trustworthiness of the market.

To prevent abuse, platforms try to screen and monitor user-generated content. This is a human-intense task known as content moderation, and some companies like Appen, Facebook, and Pinterest introduced content-based deep learning approaches (Pavlopoulos et al., 2017a; Risch and Krestel, 2020a) to content platforms in recent years. Likewise, Mercari operates such moderation systems for several domains to maintain a safe and enjoyable marketplace.

We observed that most difficulties are encountered while sellers and buyers process with their transactions. In contrast to a normal B2C e-commerce pattern, sellers and buyers need to send messages to complete transactions, even though they are often both inexperienced customers. For example, customers might send messages to each other to provide specialized delivery information. Moderation of user messages is thus a crucial measure to prevent any forms of abuses, e.g. the transmission of offensive messages to others, inducing others to conduct an offline transaction, or even urging buyers to pay upfront via external services. These abuses are commonly detected by keyword-based monitoring or patrol (random inspections made by moderators of the customer support), which has been noted as being extremely limited in terms of scale and efficiency.

In this work, we introduce a scalable textual content moderation system based on machine learning models to perform the message moderation task. [1] Figure 1 shows an overview of our moderation system. In the proposed moderation system, messages with abusive intent or content that violate the terms and conditions could be reported from these three channels: patrol (random inspec-

*Work performed while at Mercari, inc.

[1] We analyzed messages between customers and introduced the machine learning-based system as fraud countermeasures in a legally permissible manner, with the consent and awareness of customers.

Proceedings of The Fifth Workshop on e-Commerce and NLP (ECNLP 5), pages 58 - 62
May 26, 2022

tions), keyword/rule-based monitoring, and predictions made by machine learning (ML) models. In this work, we found that ML models successfully detected potentially-violated messages with a much higher precision compared to the conventional keyword/rule-based monitoring. However, because the type of violations may evolve over time, (e.g., a local government prohibiting the reselling of medical masks during COVID-19) updating ML-based methods in a timely manner following the fluctuations of the marketplace is notably difficult. We preserve the rule-based approach to accommodate the latest types of violations, so that moderators can still quickly revise the monitoring set of keywords and rules, which helps the system detect new domains of violations. In addition, a moderation system cannot tolerate false positives of any misjudged violation which might negatively effect the customer experience. All of the messages considered as potential violations by our moderation system are thus checked manually by moderators. This ensures that the customer experience on the marketplace is not compromised, and also creates a perfect human-in-the-loop cycle. To better detect offending messages and improve on the accuracy of existing ML models, we used these human-checked messages as an accurately-labelled dataset for model re-training.

The contributions of the present work are summarized as follows.

- A scalable machine learning-based violation detection system for content moderation of user-generated conversation is proposed.
- A resilient microservice architecture with high availability to serve violation domain models in an one-vs-rest manner was implemented.
- A human-in-the-loop framework was used successfully to reduce the workloads of moderators in customer support with ML-driven approaches.

2 Related Work

In contrast to typical B2C or B2B2C platforms, in which every item for sale can often be accessed with a single click, communication is inevitable on a C2C platform. Therefore, commercial content moderation plays a vital role in the process of communication to complete transactions successfully (Roberts, 2016).

Because manual content moderation does not scale to large platforms, it is natural to introduce automated content moderation systems. Pavlopoulos et al. (2017b); Risch and Krestel (2020b) investigated the applicability of machine learning-based approaches to the facilitation of content moderation by detecting textual violations using language models.

In the same context, to relieve human resources in the task at Mercari, Ueta et al. (2020) introduced a machine learning-driven item screening system that detects banned listings such as weapons, money, and medicine.

3 Method

3.1 Dataset

Some intents and behaviors, usually stated explicitly by service providers in terms and conditions, are prohibited in our marketplace to prevent unexpected difficulty between sellers and buyers. In this work, we focus on the messages freely exchanged between sellers and buyers until a transaction is completed.[2] The in-house dataset used in this work included the following three features. A **Message**, a text body sent by either the buyer or seller to the other. A positive example of a message that violates the terms and conditions is "Can we continue trading on this site to avoid fees?" This message is prohibited because the writer is trying to induce another customer to conduct the transaction with an external service, which is a violation of the terms of service. To comprehend the context of a conversation, we monitor the most recent five messages. The **Writer** is a label of either the seller or buyer, which indicates who wrote the message. Every message has one writer attribute. **Status** indicates the status of the transaction, e.g. "waiting for payment" or "waiting for shipping". This is an useful feature because exchanging contacts (e.g. SNS accounts) during the transaction have a higher chance to be made with abusive intentions, whereas it is usually normal to do so after the transaction has been completed.

During the creation of the dataset, we deliberately sampled positive and negative data with different sampling ratios, because the majority of messages exchanged on the platform do not vio-

[2] We use data from Japanese version of the Mercari app. We mask user's personal identifiable information, e.g. full names and addresses in the messages, at the pre-processing phase to use for analysis and the machine learning system.

late policy. We acquired raw data of one-year in-transaction conversations and divided them into the first 10 months, as the training set; the following month as the validation set; and the final month for the testing set so that the training results would be robust over time.

For a C2C marketplace like Mercari, we argue that a uniform language model for toxic speech may not fulfill our scenario in which violations may appear in a variety of forms. Violations also occur when users try to make deals offline by sending messages or by threatening other users to make payments upfront, in addition to hate speech. These intents and behaviors are considered as among the targets to be moderated. Considering the variety of violations as our targeted labels, we take the advantage of one-vs-rest classifiers to leverage this multi-label issue (Gunasekara and Nejadgholi, 2018). Thus, the proposed system comprises an assemblage cluster of sub-language models, and is designed to perform inference against a range of specific violation domains in a one-vs-rest fashion.

3.2 Metrics

As noted above, we had a quote for the number of alerts in actual use case. Therefore, we aimed to maximize the precision @K of the model, where K is the capable number of alert for moderators. We monitor the precision @K of running models to detect deterioration of model performance and concept drift (Zliobaite et al., 2016) in actual operation. However, K may vary due to various factors and the policy itself may change depending on the social situation, which causes concept drift. To simplify the experiment, we use the area under the receiver operating characteristic curve (AUROC) and average precision (a.k.a. AUPRC) to compare the models in this work. Also, the extent to which the ML model obviates the need for human labor is the important metric in our scenario. To monitor this, we measured the number of alerts from the ML model required to detect the same number of positives as the rule-base.

3.3 Model Architecture

Our neural network model shown in figure 2 receives three features described in 3.1 and outputs the probability of a violated message. The model extracts textual features using a convolutional neural network (CNN) and flattens the grasped sentence-level features into a 1D feature representation as an input to the subsequent re-

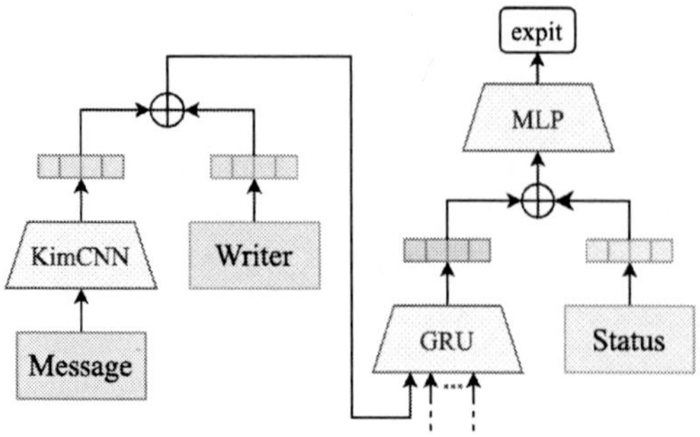

Figure 2: Neural network model architecture.

current neural network (RNN). First, we parse the "Message" input using the fast Japanese morphological analyzer MeCab (Kudo, 2005) with the large dictionary (Toshinori, 2015). We transform the messages to sequences of numeric tokens, and embed them to matrices $\boldsymbol{x}^{(M)} = \left(x_1^{(M)}, \ldots, x_{N_d}^{(M)}\right)$, where $x_i^{(M)} \in \mathbb{R}^{N_s \times d_e^{(M)}}$ is a sequence of word vectors of i-th sentence, N_d, N_s, and d_e are the number of sentences, the length of sentences, and the dimension of embedding space, respectively. We use the word vectors pretrained with word2vec (Mikolov et al., 2013) to perform embedding and optimize the word vectors in the same manner as other model parameters during training. We adopt the convolutional neural network proposed in Kim (2014) (a.k.a. KimCNN) for textual feature extraction because it is lightweight and can reach relatively good accuracy even with a small number of parameters. The d-dimensional textual feature vectors $f_i^{(M)} \in \mathbb{R}^d$ is computed from each $x_i^{(M)}$ using a single KimCNN. The "Writer" feature of i-th sentence and the single "Status" feature are also embedded as d-dimensional vectors $f_i^{(W)}$ and $f^{(S)}$, respectively. The feature of i-th sentence is computed as the sum of the "Message" feature and "Writer" features as $f_i^{(M+W)} = f_i^{(M)} + f_i^{(W)}$. The gated recurrent units (GRUs) (Ballakur and Arya, 2020) compute the feature vector representing the entire conversation $g^{(M+W)} \in \mathbb{R}^d$ from sentence features $\boldsymbol{f}^{(M+W)} = \left(f_1^{(M+W)}, \ldots, f_{N_d}^{(M+W)}\right)$. The GRU is expected to understand the conversation as a sequence of sentences. We use two GRUs, one to enter in forward order and another to enter in reverse order. Finally, the model output $p \in [0, 1]$ is computed from combined feature vector $f^{(M+W+S)} = g^{(M+W)} + f^{(S)}$ using a multi-layer perceptron (MLP). The model parameters

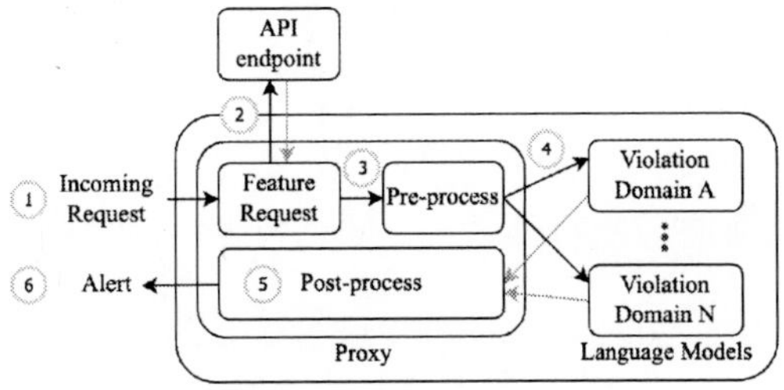

Figure 3: Core components of our ML moderation system.

including embedding vectors are trained by minimizing entropy as $-y \log p - (1-y) \log(1-p)$, where $y \in (0, 1)$ is the true label for the prediction p.

3.4 System Deployment

As one of the largest online marketplace in Japan, Mercari deals with thousands of transaction messages every minute. The system must be robust with high short term capacity to accommodate a variety of language models for each violation domain. Also, it must be easy to add new models and update existing models to keep up with the market situation. Hence, we trained machine learning models in one-vs-rest manner for easy model addition and update, and designed the whole system to serve the models in a horizontal asynchronized pattern (Yusuke, 2020) as shown in Figure 3 to overcome peak traffic. The proxy and each language model components are able to be scaled separately.

Starting from an incoming request sent to the proxy component with a specific message id, the system sends a feature request to the internal API endpoint to fetch the dialogue content as a second step. The proxy component generates feature representations by doing preprocessing over sentences in a given dialogue and sends them to each language model as Steps three and four. Predictions against each violation domain are inferred and returned by the components serving language models as a proxy component again to perform post-processing in Step five. In that step, we send alerts to moderators if the inferred probability surpasses thresholds pre-defined to control the amount of alerts for each violation domain. We also record prediction results for the later human-in-the-loop evaluation.

3.5 Experiments

We conducted experiments to examine whether the data enrichment described in 3.1 improved the performance of the proposed model. Table 1 shows the result of our experiments. We can confirm that using multi-round messages and their additional metadata was effective for the detection of violating messages. In the experiments, we adopted the AdaBound optimizer with a learning rate of 0.001 and decaying learning rate according to the cosine curve. We trained the model for 10 epochs and adopted the weights at epoch, which yielded the best performance on the validation loss. The final performance was evaluated with the testing set.

#M	W	S	AUROC	AUPRC
1			99.4068	97.1052
5			99.6919	98.3702
5		✓	99.6996	98.3793
5	✓		99.6947	98.3733
5	✓	✓	**99.7274**	**98.4194**

Table 1: AUROC and AUPRC score with various features. Here, #M represents the number of message to input to the model and the check mark in column W or S indicates that Writer or Status feature was used. We trained the model three times with different initial weights for each, and adopted average value for the model performance.

In online evaluation, we observe that our model was able to find the same number of positive messages as existing rule-base search methods with $\mathbf{16.05\%}$ of the number of alerts from the rule-base in this violation domain. This means that by replacing the rule-based method with the ML model, the human resources requirements of the system can theoretically be reduced by more than half. However, we preserved rule-bases for the reasons mentioned in Section 1.

4 Conclusion

In this work, we have proposed a scalable ML-based violation detection system designed to accept multi-round user conversations and some categorical features. A variety of violation domains are served as individual components in an one-vs-rest fashion to retain scalability to high volumes of requests and flexibility on targeting domains. In comparison with conventional rule-based monitoring, we have demonstrated that the proposed ML-driven approach successfully reduced the workloads of moderators in customer support to less than one-sixth of their previous levels by automatically detecting abusive messages.

References

Appen. Leveraging ai and machine learning for content moderation [online].

Amulya Arun Ballakur and Arti Arya. 2020. Empirical evaluation of gated recurrent neural network architectures in aviation delay prediction. In *2020 5th International Conference on Computing, Communication and Security (ICCCS)*, pages 1–7. IEEE.

Facebook. How we review content [online].

Isuru Gunasekara and Isar Nejadgholi. 2018. A review of standard text classification practices for multi-label toxicity identification of online content. In *Proceedings of the 2nd workshop on abusive language online (ALW2)*, pages 21–25.

Yoon Kim. 2014. Convolutional neural networks for sentence classification. In *Proceedings of the 2014 Conference on Empirical Methods in Natural Language Processing (EMNLP)*, pages 1746–1751, Doha, Qatar. Association for Computational Linguistics.

T. Kudo. 2005. Mecab : Yet another part-of-speech and morphological analyzer. *http://mecab.sourceforge.net/*.

Tomas Mikolov, Ilya Sutskever, Kai Chen, Greg S Corrado, and Jeff Dean. 2013. Distributed representations of words and phrases and their compositionality. In *Advances in Neural Information Processing Systems*, volume 26. Curran Associates, Inc.

John Pavlopoulos, Prodromos Malakasiotis, and Ion Androutsopoulos. 2017a. Deeper attention to abusive user content moderation. In *Proceedings of the 2017 conference on empirical methods in natural language processing*, pages 1125–1135.

John Pavlopoulos, Prodromos Malakasiotis, and Ion Androutsopoulos. 2017b. Deeper attention to abusive user content moderation. In *Proceedings of the 2017 conference on empirical methods in natural language processing*, pages 1125–1135.

Pinterest. Getting better at helping people feel better [online].

Julian Risch and Ralf Krestel. 2020a. Toxic comment detection in online discussions. In *Deep Learning-Based Approaches for Sentiment Analysis*, pages 85–109. Springer.

Julian Risch and Ralf Krestel. 2020b. Toxic comment detection in online discussions. In *Deep Learning-Based Approaches for Sentiment Analysis*, pages 85–109. Springer.

Sarah T Roberts. 2016. Commercial content moderation: Digital laborers' dirty work.

Sato Toshinori. 2015. Neologism dictionary based on the language resources on the web for mecab.

Shunya Ueta, Suganprabu Nagaraja, and Mizuki Sango. 2020. Auto content moderation in c2c e-commerce. In *2020 USENIX Conference on Operational Machine Learning (OpML 20)*. USENIX Association.

Shibui Yusuke. 2020. Machine learning system design pattern.

Indre Zliobaite, Mykola Pechenizkiy, and Joao Gama. 2016. *An Overview of Concept Drift Applications*, Studies in Big Data, pages 91–114. Springer International Publishing AG, Switzerland.

Spelling Correction using Phonetics in E-commerce Search

Fan Yang, Alireza Bagheri Garakani, Yifei Teng
Yan Gao, Jia Liu, Jingyuan Deng, Yi Sun
Amazon
Seattle, Washington, USA
{fnam,alirezg,yifeit,yanngao,hliujia,jingyua,yisun}@amazon.com

Abstract

In E-commerce search, spelling correction plays an important role to find desired products for customers in processing user-typed search queries. However, resolving phonetic errors is a critical but overlooked area. The query with phonetic spelling errors tends to appear correct based on pronunciation but is nonetheless inaccurate in spelling (e.g., "bluetooth sound system" vs. "blutut sant sistam") with numerous noisy forms and sparse occurrences. In this work, we propose a generalized spelling correction system integrating phonetics to address phonetic errors in E-commerce search without additional latency cost. Using India (IN) E-commerce market for illustration, the experiment shows that our proposed phonetic solution significantly improves the F1 score by 9%+ and recall of phonetic errors by 8%+. This phonetic spelling correction system has been deployed to production, currently serving hundreds of millions of customers.

1 Introduction

Search is critical to provide a great customer shopping experience in E-commerce. Usually, as the first step of the search workflow, spelling correction is responsible to reduce the irrelevant and sparse search results caused by spelling errors in search keywords. In addition, low latency is required considering spelling correction is only part of many modules in the search workflow. Despite the large amount of research on correcting spelling errors (Hládek et al., 2020), addressing phonetic errors is an important, but overlooked area. Phonetic spelling error typically happens when the query has similar pronunciation but is nonetheless inaccurate in spelling (e.g., "bluetooth sound system" vs. "blutut sant sistam" in English). Figure 1 describes the phonetic error percentage of misspelled queries based on a human annotated spelling correction dataset sampled from the Amazon search query log. We find that this type of spelling error dominates in multiple E-commerce markets with various languages, existing mostly on generic item terms (e.g., "nacklesh" vs. "necklace") and brand terms (e.g., "scalkendy" vs. "skullcandy"). This issue might damage customer trust and present greater challenges when E-commerce offers more products (i.e., brand names) with sensational spelling (e.g., Hasbro's Playskool [school]) and attracts customers with low written proficiency.

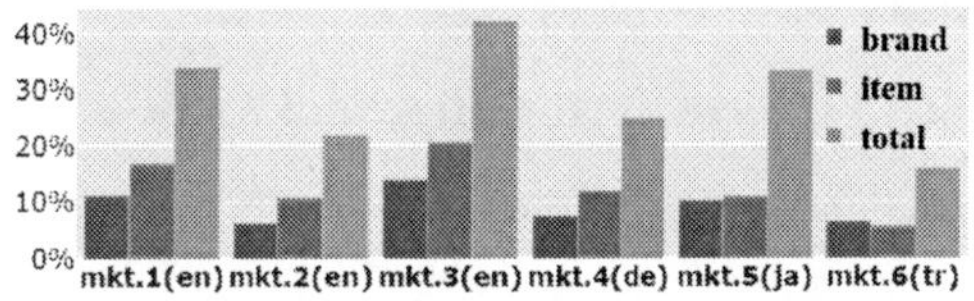

Figure 1: Phonetic error ratio on brand terms (blue), generic item terms (red) or any terms (green) out of all spelling errors in multiple markets (languages).

However, the traditional spelling correction system is not able to address phonetic spelling errors well because it usually searches the correction of given spelling errors up to a certain edit distance (Damerau, 1964) apart (Gorin et al., 1971; Whitelaw et al., 2009), while phonetic spelling errors could lead to large edit distance with variously noisy forms (e.g., EditDist("blutut" vs. "bluetooth")=4).

There exists multiple attempts to address phonetic errors by generating soundslike equivalent candidates based on phonetic algorithms (Atkinson, 2006). Although soundslike equivalent candidates may handle phonetic errors better, they tend to be too noisy to cover the correct spelling of non-phonetic errors in a limited size satisfying low latency requirements (shown in Section 3).

To address these limitations, we propose a generalized spelling correction system that enables us to integrate phonetics into E-commerce search without additional latency cost. It includes a new

Proceedings of The Fifth Workshop on e-Commerce and NLP (ECNLP 5), pages 63 - 67
May 26, 2022 ©2022 Association for Computational Linguistics

hybrid candidate generation method with phonetic mapping as well as an effective candidate ranking method leveraging phonetic signals. In particular, our major contributions include: (1) we propose an effective hybrid candidate generation method, which aims to capture the complementary candidates across edit distance and soundslike based methods to address both phonetic and non-phonetic spelling errors; (2) we propose a flexible candidate ranking stage by leveraging phonetic signals, which tends to rank the correct spelling of phonetic errors to the top; (3) our offline study shows a 9%+ speller overall improvement with an 8% improvement on phonetic errors without additional latency cost by incorporating phonetics into our generalized spelling correction system. To the best of our knowledge, this work is the first to propose an efficient and effective phonetic solution with ablation study in E-commerce search, and this phonetic solution can be easily applied to any automatic spelling correction system with candidate generation or ranking stage.

2 Problem Formulation and Modeling

In this section, we formally define our generalized spelling correction structure using phonetics. Most current search engines detect and correct spelling errors automatically. One of the most popular structures defined by (Kukich, 1992) includes candidate generation and candidate ranking steps based on the noisy channel model (NCM) (Jurafsky and Martin, 2008). The basic idea of NCM is to find the spelling correction C^* given the input query Q and its spelling correction candidates $C = c_1 \ldots c_n$ via the Bayes' Rule:

$$C^* = \arg\max_{c} P(Q|C)P(C), \quad (1)$$

where the language model $P(C)$ represents the probability of the C to be correct, and the error model $P(Q|C)$ represents the chance of the transformation from C to Q. We define NCM score as the logarithm summation of the language and error model score. On top of this popular noisy channel structure, we introduce our generalized spelling correction system using phonetics below.

Hybrid candidate generation: The candidate generation step is to generate the correction candidates given an input query. In our proposed hybrid candidate generation stage, the first step is to leverage an auto-split-combine module tokenizing an input query into tokens and split (combine) tokens when the resulting bigram has a higher probability in the search query log. Second, each token's candidates are generated from the vocabulary dictionary (built from the search query log) up to a certain edit distance. Similar to (Sun et al., 2010; Whitelaw et al., 2009), a trie-based data structure is leveraged that allows to efficiently search within a maximum edit distance (e.g., a common setting is 2 to avoid high latency). Token candidates are sorted based on NCM score built on the search query log limited by a certain size. Caching is applied to avoid duplicated efforts. Considering the potentially large distance introduced by phonetic spelling errors (e.g., EditDist["blutut", "bluetooth"]=4), we design the hybrid candidate generation stage. It additionally includes a phonetic mapping with the key representing the pronunciation and its value being a list of token soundslike candidates, complementing edit-distance based token candidates. Specifically, we leverage phonetic algorithms' encoding (Vykhovanets et al., 2020) to convert the token to the key of the phonetic mapping. The token candidates in the phonetic mapping are extracted from tokenized Amazon product titles sorted by its frequency because Amazon product titles contain rich product information (brands, generic items, etc.), which commonly suffers from phonetic errors. In addition, the top candidates are required to have the same phonetic key, while the remaining candidates can allow a small edit distance of the phonetic key, which introduces noise, but with higher coverage.

Table 1 shows an example of the phonetic mapping in English leveraging Double Metaphone (DM) (Philips, 2000) phonetic algorithm with the phonetic encoding key: "PLTR". Top 10 candidates have the same DM phonetic key "PLTR" and the remaining 30 candidates allow one edit distance. For the given token "blutur" with DM key "PLTR", the correct candidate "bluetooth" is the $13th$ candidate with phonetic key "PLTT".

Top-K	Token Candidates
1-10	"platter","builder","boulder",...
11-40	"leather","holder","bluetooth",...

Table 1: The phonetic mapping of DM phonetic key: "PLTR"

Token candidates compose both edit-distance and phonetic mapping based candidates. Following Eq. (1) to approximately find the top-K query-level

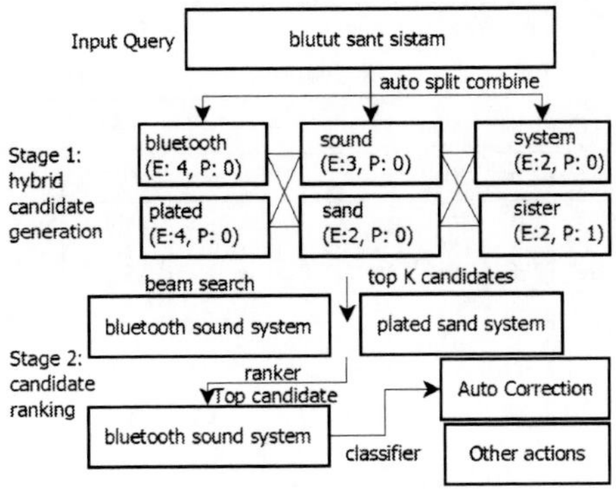

Figure 2: General workflow of spelling correction system. "E": edit distance of the token candidates. "P": edit distance based on phonetic encoding key.

candidates, we leverage the beam search algorithm with the beam search size K, tunable to balance the system latency and its performance. Figure 2 shows the general workflow of the spelling correction system including the hybrid candidate generation stage based on the input query "blutut sant sistam". Take the input token "sant" as an example, "sound" is generated from phonetic mapping, while "sand" is from both edit-distance and phonetic mapping based candidates with maximum edit-distance setting being 2.

Candidate ranking: Although the hybrid candidate generation stage can return candidates with sorted NCM score, we add this candidate ranking stage to flexibly leverage phonetic features and powerful ranking algorithms. Typical ranking features could be candidates' language scores from different sources (e.g., search query log, product titles, etc.) and different types of error scores characterized by the probability of each edit in different edit levels (e.g.,character-level (Mays et al., 1991; Church and Gale, 1991), subword-level (Brill and Moore, 2000) ,phrase-level (Sun et al., 2010)). We specifically add the phonetic distance feature: the edit distance of the phonetic encoding key between the input query and its candidate. The goal of adding this feature is to allow the model to rank the correct candidate of a phonetically misspelled query higher. For the ranking algorithm, the system is flexible to support linear models (e.g., logistic regression (Cox, 1958)), tree based model (e.g., XGBoost (Chen and Guestrin, 2016)) and deep learning models in point-wise and pairwise level. In addition, a classification module can be optionally added after the ranking stage (e.g., (Whitelaw et al., 2009)) to balance between auto-correction and no-correction speller actions. Figure 2 includes the workflow of the candidate ranking stage.

3 Experiments

In this section, we formally evaluate our proposed spelling correction system integrating phonetics. We use IN E-commerce market for illustration. We train and evaluate the candidate ranker based on the human annotated dataset with 30000 query-correction pairs from the search query log. We split 33.33% for training, validating, and testing. The evaluation metric is the F1 score, which is a harmonic mean of the precision and recall. Precision represents the speller's accuracy rate when its action is auto-correction, while recall is defined as the speller's accuracy rate for misspelled queries. We also report the recall of queries with phonetic errors and top percentile (TP) 99 latency of the spelling correction system in milliseconds. We treat the top 1 candidate as the correction of a given input query with auto-correction action when the top 1 candidate is different from the input query, although the system supports more complicated classifiers after the ranking stage. Relative impacts (instead of absolute values) are reported for legal requirements.

We first conduct an ablation study for the candidate ranking module. We apply a standard setting in the candidate generation step that allows 20 edit distance based token candidates with allowed maximum edit distance 2 and beam search size 12. Typical ranking features based on different types of language and error models are included, and we focus on the impact of the phonetic distance feature. Table 2 shows F1 score, recall of phonetic errors (column name: "ph-recall"), and TP99 latency evaluated in the test dataset. Column name "ph-dist" indicates if the phonetic distance feature is added in the ranking model. Row [i] leverages pair-wised logistic regression algorithm, while row [ii, iii] leverage XGBoost LambdaMART algorithm to rank candidates. We have the following observations. First, switching from logistic regression to XGBoost ranking algorithm (comparing row [ii] to row [i]), we find 7%+ improvement on F1 score and 6%+ on recall of phonetic errors with minor latency increase (i.e., 1.5%). The nonlinear structure and the nature of handling feature interaction effects in tree-based models (i.e., XGBoost) might be the reason that our method outperforms linear ranking models (e.g., logistic regression). Second, adding

row	hyperparameter		performance		
	algorithm	ph-dist	F1	ph-recall	TP99
[i]	logistic regression	no	-	-	13
[ii]	XGBoost	no	+7.2%	+6.3%	+1.5%
[iii]	XGBoost	yes	+10.6%	+8.9%	+3.8%

Table 2: Candidate ranking ablation study (c. row[i])

the phonetic distance feature contributes to 3%+ F1 and 2%+ phonetic error recall improvement (comparing row [iii] to row [ii]). This supports our motivation that the phonetic distance feature tends to rank the correct candidate of a phonetically misspelled query higher, improving both the overall F1 score and recall of phonetic errors.

Adopting XGBoost LambdaMART algorithm with phonetic distance feature in the candidate ranking stage, we evaluate the hybrid candidate generation performance in Table 3 (row [i] in Table 3 is row [iii] in Table 2). Columns "ph-s" and "ed-s" represent the size of phonetic mapping and edit-distance based token candidates. Column "beam-s" is the beam search size and "ed-th" is the maximum edit distance allowed for edit-distance based token candidates. Phonetic mapping is created based on DM phonetic algorithm, limiting the top 10 candidates to have same DM phonetic key and allowing maximum 1 edit distance of the phonetic encoding key for the remaining candidates. Row [i] serves as a baseline model without phonetic mapping based token candidates. Row [ii] shows the impact of maximum edit distance setting on edit-distance based token candidates. We find that enlarging the maximum edit distance leads to high latency (371%+ increase) by comparing row [ii] with row [i], but with minor improvement on F1 and phonetic error recall. This indicates resolving phonetic errors (with distant edit distance to the correction) by directly searching the correct spelling within the edit distance threshold is not feasible. Row [iii-vi] shows the impact of adjusting different sizes of phonetic mapping and edit-distance based token candidates. We find that increasing edit-distance based token candidate size (comparing row [iii] to row [i]) leads to minor improvement (F1 + 0.6%, ph-recall +1.9%), but complementing token candidates by adding phonetic-mapping based candidates outperforms baseline by 6%+ on F1 and 5%+ on phonetic error recall (comparing row [iv] to row [i]). If phonetic mapping is the only source of token candidates (comparing row [v] to row [i]), there exists

row	hyperparameter				performance		
	ph-s	ed-s	beam-s	ed-th	F1	ph-recall	TP99
[i]	0	20	12	2	-	-	13.5
[ii]	0	20	12	3	+0.4%	+0.2%	+371%
[iii]	0	40	12	2	+0.6%	+1.9%	+16.3%
[iv]	20	20	12	2	+6.2%	+5.1%	+22.2%
[v]	20	0	12	2	-11.2%	-16.8%	-1.5%
[vi]	40	0	12	2	-6.6%	-8.8%	+23.7%
[vii]	20	20	8	2	**+6.2%**	**+5.4%**	**-3%**
[viii]	20	20	1	2	-5.9%	-8.8%	-20.7%

Table 3: Candidate generation ablation study (c. row[i])

a performance regression on both F1 and phonetic error recall. Furthermore, enlarging the phonetic mapping (row [vi]) is not an optimal solution considering its worse performance than hybrid sources (row [iv]). Then, we select the beam search size (row [vii,viii]) to control the similar TP99 for best F1 and phonetic error recall, compared with baseline (row [i]). The setting in row [vii] achieves 6%+ F1 score and 5%+ phonetic error recall improvement with flat latency. Aggregating the phonetic feature's impact (compare row [vii] in Table 3 to row [ii] in Table 2), the spelling correction system improves the F1 score by 9%+ and phonetic error recall by 8%+ by integrating phonetics into hybrid candidate generation and candidate ranking steps.

We adopt row [i] in Table 2 and row [vii] in Table 3 as baseline speller and phonetic speller for online A/B testing. We find significant business metrics gain without additional latency cost. Moreover, Figure 3 shows an example that the phonetic speller is able to resolve the irrelevant and/or sparse results based on the search query: "blutut sant systam". That is, there are only 82 search results returned by the baseline speller, while more than 9000 results are shown after applying the phonetic speller.

4 Conclusions and Future Work

In this work, we developed a generalized spelling correction system integrating phonetics into both hybrid candidate generation and candidate ranking stages on E-commerce domain. We demonstrated that our proposed phonetic solution improves more than 9% on F1 score and 8% on recall of phonetic errors without additional latency cost. This solution can be applied to any automatic spelling correction system with candidate generation or ranking stage. Online A/B testing showed positive business

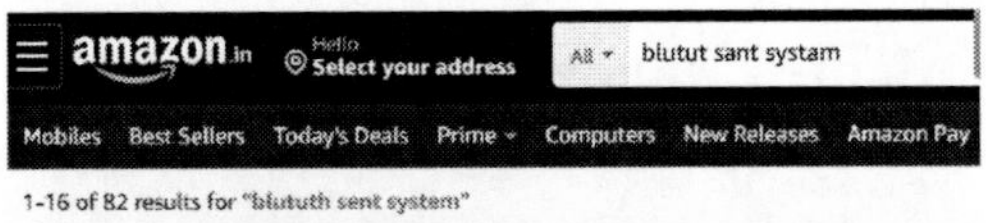

(a) Search results based on baseline speller

(b) Search results based on phonetic speller

Figure 3: Baseline speller vs. phonetic speller for search query: "blutut sant systam"

metrics while reducing sparse/irrelevant search results. Future directions include applying similar phonetic integrating ideas to other spelling correction frameworks (Jayanthi et al., 2020; Park et al., 2021) considering the growing popularity of the use of encoder-decoder deep learning architectures.

References

Kevin Atkinson. 2006. Gnu aspell 0.60. 4.

Eric Brill and Robert C Moore. 2000. An improved error model for noisy channel spelling correction. In *Proceedings of the 38th annual meeting of the association for computational linguistics*, pages 286–293.

Tianqi Chen and Carlos Guestrin. 2016. XGBoost: A scalable tree boosting system. In *Proceedings of the 22nd ACM SIGKDD International Conference on Knowledge Discovery and Data Mining*, KDD '16, pages 785–794, New York, NY, USA. ACM.

Kenneth W Church and William A Gale. 1991. Probability scoring for spelling correction. *Statistics and Computing*, 1(2):93–103.

David R Cox. 1958. The regression analysis of binary sequences. *Journal of the Royal Statistical Society: Series B (Methodological)*, 20(2):215–232.

Fred J Damerau. 1964. A technique for computer detection and correction of spelling errors. *Communications of the ACM*, 7(3):171–176.

RE Gorin, Pace Willisson, Walt Buehring, Geoff Kuenning, et al. 1971. Ispell, a free software package for spell checking files. *The UNIX community*.

Daniel Hládek, Ján Staš, and Matúš Pleva. 2020. Survey of automatic spelling correction. *Electronics*, 9(10):1670.

Sai Muralidhar Jayanthi, Danish Pruthi, and Graham Neubig. 2020. Neuspell: A neural spelling correction toolkit. *arXiv preprint arXiv:2010.11085*.

Daniel Jurafsky and James H Martin. 2008. *Speech & language processing (2nd ed.)*. Prentice Hall.

Karen Kukich. 1992. Techniques for automatically correcting words in text. *Acm Computing Surveys (CSUR)*, 24(4):377–439.

Eric Mays, Fred J Damerau, and Robert L Mercer. 1991. Context based spelling correction. *Information Processing & Management*, 27(5):517–522.

Chanjun Park, Kuekyeng Kim, YeongWook Yang, Minho Kang, and Heuiseok Lim. 2021. Neural spelling correction: translating incorrect sentences to correct sentences for multimedia. *Multimedia Tools and Applications*, 80(26):34591–34608.

Lawrence Philips. 2000. The double metaphone search algorithm. *C/C++ users journal*, 18(6):38–43.

Xu Sun, Jianfeng Gao, Daniel Micol, and Chris Quirk. 2010. Learning phrase-based spelling error models from clickthrough data. In *Proceedings of the 48th Annual Meeting of the Association for Computational Linguistics*, pages 266–274.

Valeriy S Vykhovanets, J Du, and SA Sakulin. 2020. An overview of phonetic encoding algorithms. *Automation and Remote Control*, 81(10):1896–1910.

Casey Whitelaw, Ben Hutchinson, Grace Chung, and Ged Ellis. 2009. Using the web for language independent spellchecking and autocorrection. In *Proceedings of the 2009 Conference on Empirical Methods in Natural Language Processing*, pages 890–899.

Logical Reasoning for Task Oriented Dialogue Systems

Sajjad Beygi, Maryam Fazel-Zarandi[*], Alessandra Cervone, Prakash Krishnan, Siddhartha Reddy Jonnalagadda
Amazon Alexa AI
{beygi, fazelzar, cervon, prakaskr, sjjonnal}@amazon.com

Abstract

In recent years, large pretrained models have been used in dialogue systems to improve successful task completion rates. However, lack of reasoning capabilities of dialogue platforms make it difficult to provide relevant and fluent responses, unless the designers of a conversational experience spend a considerable amount of time implementing these capabilities in external rule based modules. In this work, we propose a novel method to fine-tune pretrained transformer models such as Roberta and T5, to reason over a set of facts in a given dialogue context. Our method includes a synthetic data generation mechanism which helps the model learn logical relations, such as comparison between list of numerical values, inverse relations (and negation), inclusion and exclusion for categorical attributes, and application of a combination of attributes over both numerical and categorical values, and spoken form for numerical values, without need for additional training data. We show that the transformer based model can perform logical reasoning to answer questions when the dialogue context contains all the required information, otherwise it is able to extract appropriate constraints to pass to downstream components (e.g. a knowledge base) when partial information is available. We observe that transformer based models such as UnifiedQA-T5 can be fine-tuned to perform logical reasoning (such as numerical and categorical attributes' comparison) over attributes seen at training time (e.g., accuracy of 90%+ for comparison of smaller than $k_{\max}$=5 values over heldout test dataset).

1 Introduction

Logical reasoning is an important aspect of human thinking and communication. Humans reason over beliefs, preferences, time, facts, and other contextual information to achieve complex tasks, derive meaning, and analyze emotions. Current

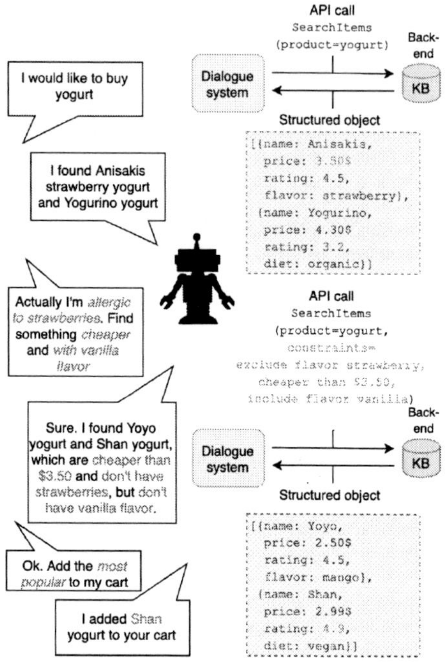

Figure 1: The dialogue system with reasoning ability.

task-oriented dialogue systems, however, only support very limited forms of logical reasoning. More specifically, although reasoning ability has been investigated as part of chatbots (Cui et al., 2020) and question-answering systems (Huang et al., 2019; Chen et al., 2020), in many task-oriented dialogue systems today, the reasoning is mainly focused on determining which slot values are still unknown to the system but are required and elicit them (Guo et al., 2017). However, in realistic task-oriented dialogues, logical reasoning is required to understand the user's request, ask questions that help address the user's task successfully and minimize asking irrelevant questions. The lack of robust, generalizable reasoning capabilities for dialogue systems, requires developers of the system to spend a considerable amount of time implementing these capabilities in external, rule-based and domain spe-

[*] Work done while at Amazon Alexa AI.

Proceedings of The Fifth Workshop on e-Commerce and NLP (ECNLP 5), pages 68 - 79
May 26, 2022 ©2022 Association for Computational Linguistics

cific components. This leads to a poor user experience requiring users to often correct the system's understanding, repeat themselves to ask the same question in different ways, restart the conversation when the system fails to recover from a 'dead-end', or even change their goal.

In this work, we propose to build on recent advances in research on logical reasoning and deep networks (e.g., Dong et al. 2019; Wang et al. 2019; Xie et al. 2019; Clark et al. 2020; Arabshahi et al. 2020) to bring reasoning capabilities to task-oriented dialogue systems. Our primary focus in this work is on mechanisms by which logical reasoning can be learned and used in conversational systems. In this direction, we propose a novel deep learning method to fine-tune pretrained models to reason over numerical and categorical attributes in the dialogue context and present an architecture for the integration of this model in task-oriented dialogue systems. Our objective is for the model to do logical reasoning to respond to queries from the dialogue context when it has all the required information available in the dialogue context without additional external logic (e.g., "Add the most popular to my cart" in Figure 1), extract constraints and inform downstream components when it only has partial context (e.g., "Actually I'm allergic to berries. Find something cheaper and with vanilla flavor" in Figure 1, where cheaper means cheaper than what was shown so far), and not provide an answer when it does not have any relevant information and delegate to the dialogue policy to determine the next action.

We specifically choose to fine-tune transformers since these models operate on language directly, do not impose any structure on the reasoning process (Clark et al., 2020), and we can leverage the knowledge and diversity of language that the pretrained models have already learned. Furthermore, Ding et al. (2020) recently showed that these approaches can outperform neuro-symbolic methods. Our approach is similar to recent works on using transformers as soft reasoners (Clark et al., 2020; Talmor et al., 2020). However, compared to these methods, we focus on use cases relevant to conversational systems and our model goes beyond predicting a true/false response to directly predicting the answer when the model has the information or extract constraints when it has partial information. In this direction, we report experimental results that show using our training method transformers can learn to reason over numerical and categorical attributes in the dialogue context.

Note that although we use transformers for our experiments, our proposed method can be used to generate data and train any other seq2seq model for the same task and be integrated with any dialogue system in a similar manner. Furthermore, our proposed method is different from question-answering or machine reading comprehension in that we are not looking for an answer in a specific passage; rather, we want the model to reason over facts in the dialogue context to draw parallels and conclusions to inform decision making, similar to how humans reason over a multi-turn conversation.

2 Related Work

The approaches for integrating reasoning with deep networks can be categorized into the following.

Reasoning after Semantic Parsing These approaches convert utterances to a semantic representation and feed it to a set of rules or a formal reasoner for reasoning. For example, Kamath and Das (2018) provide examples where given a natural language utterance and context in the form of a relational database, the system first converts the natural language utterance to a SQL query that is then executed using standard SQL grammar to retrieve the answer. This is also similar in approach to how some teams that participated in the WikiSQL task (Victor et al., 2017) developed natural language interfaces for relational databases. However, writing and maintaining rules is not scalable especially as more complex types of reasoning become needed. The data annotation itself becomes hard to manage efficiently as more functionalities need to be supported. Furthermore, deep semantic parsing and reliably extracting attributes and relations and operating on multi-sentence input remains a challenge.

Satisfiability-based Approaches Wang et al. (2019) propose to integrate a differentiable maximum satisfiability solver into the loop of larger deep learning systems, and use this approach to successfully learn logical structures such as the rules of Sudoku. Previous works have shown that temporal reasoning can be modeled as a propositional satisfiability problem (Pham et al., 2008); however, generalizability to other types of reasoning needs further investigation. Although covering a rich class of problems, these approaches impose a structure on the reasoning problem (Clark et al.,

2020), i.e., learning of logical structure specifically as expressed by satisfiability problems.

Neuro-symbolic Approaches Neuro-symbolic systems are hybrid models that leverage neural networks and symbolic reasoning to integrate learning and reasoning. Besold et al. (2017) provide a survey of how symbolic approaches for reasoning are integrated with the machine learning approaches that bring in reasoning. More recently, Dong et al. (2019) propose Neural Logic Machines and apply them to different tasks such as relational reasoning and sorting. Arabshahi et al. (2020) propose an end-to-end differentiable solution that uses a Prolog proof trace to learn rule embeddings from data, and apply their approach to the task of uncovering commonsense presumptions. Similarly, Xie et al. (2019) generate a graph model to embed logic rules into the prediction. However, Ding et al. (2020) show that a fully-learned neural network with the right inductive biases can outperform neuro-symbolic approaches in the context of spatio-temporal interactions between objects.

Transformer Approaches Clark et al. (2020) and Talmor et al. (2020) propose to train transformers to reason over natural language sentences, bypassing a formal representation and show such reasoning over language is learnable. Ding et al. (2020) apply a similar technique to visual question answering and show that their approach outperforms neuro-symbolic approaches. Han et al. (2020) use a similar approach to fine-tune a language model for event temporal reasoning. Our approach builds on top of these works in that we integrate reasoning into task-oriented dialogues and go beyond predicting a true/false response for an input and instead directly predict the answer when the model has the information or extract constraints when it has partial information.

Knowledge Grounding in Dialogue Similar to how Victor et al. (2017) retrieve knowledge from Wikipedia, approaches such as (Ghazvininejad et al., 2018; Neelakantan et al., 2019; Gopalakrishnan et al., 2019) retrieve knowledge from a database to be incorporated into dialogue. These approaches extend the seq2seq approach to condition on the facts present in the knowledge bases. While this is a promising architecture, such approaches are good for applications such as knowledge-grounded open domain chat but not for supporting reasoning in task-oriented dialogues.

Other Approaches There are also other techniques in the literature such as integrating rules defined in first-order logic with knowledge distillation (Hu et al., 2016) that are outside the above categories. There have also been efforts such as CLUTRR (Sinha et al., 2019), bAbI dataset (Weston et al., 2015), Single Rule Test (Richardson et al., 2020), QuaRTz dataset (Tafjord et al., 2019), HotpotQA (Yang et al., 2018), and ROPES (Reasoning over Paragraph Effects in Situations) (Lin et al., 2019), that focus on creating benchmarks for reasoning that measure how well existing systems perform on generalized reasoning.

3 Problem Statement

Task-oriented dialogue systems use a natural language understanding component to extract semantic meaning from the user utterance, and elicit constraints from users to understand their goals in order to provide information, perform a task or provide options and alternatives for users to choose from, retrieved from external knowledge sources (e.g, through API calls). As such, we focus on reasoning over tasks and recommended items in the dialogue which are typically characterized by different attributes, for example, movie names and show-times for a ticket booking scenario. These systems rely on such representations to answer user queries such as *"At what time is Vertigo playing?"* by performing API calls (e.g. *searchTime(movie=Vertigo)*) which return the required information in a structured form (Movie=Vertigo, Times=[12:30-2:30 PM, 3-5 PM], Theater=Cineplex). The required information is then returned to the user in natural language (e.g. *Vertigo is playing today from 12.30 to 2.30 PM and from 3 to 5 PM.*). However, in most currently available task-oriented dialogue systems if the user said next "Book me the earliest one," although this information is already available to the system from the previous API call, given the lack of reasoning abilities the system would either not support such queries, or it would have to make an additional independent API call (e.g., *searchEarliestTime(movie=Vertigo)* or *searchTime(movie=Vertigo, modifier=earliest)*), creating redundant latency in the response and requiring the developer of the system to add APIs/rules to handle these use cases.

Given the above description, our objective is to train a model to learn how to reason over the

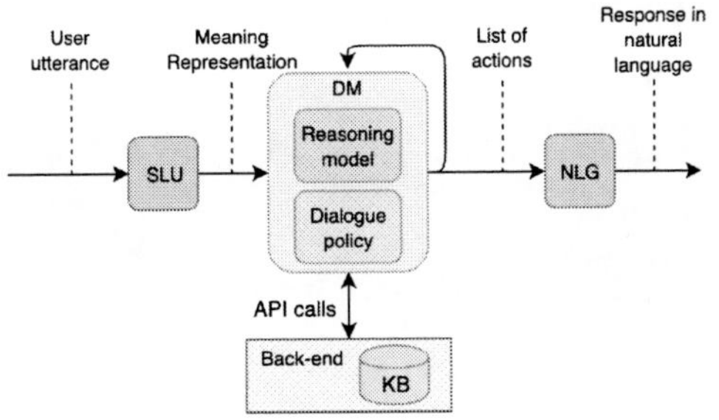

Figure 2: The reasoning model can be easily integrated in task-oriented dialogue architecture, as a component of the Dialogue Manager, i.e., the module in charge of predicting the next system action.

information provided in the context. We assume the following scenarios for each user utterance:

1. Reasoning-required, answer available in the context: The case where the user utterance requires reasoning and it is possible to infer the answer to the user query from the information returned by the previous API calls (e.g., "Give me the earliest one"). Rather than extracting mentions and querying the knowledge base again, in this case the model directly outputs the predicted next system action along with its arguments.

2. Reasoning-required, answer not available in the context: The case where the user utterance requires reasoning, but it is not possible to infer the answer to the user query from the information returned by the previous API calls (e.g., "Show me cheaper options"). In this case the model extracts constraints from the user utterance to be passed to the back-end API.

3. Reasoning-not-required: The case where the user utterance does not require reasoning (e.g., "Please repeat").

In order to support these scenarios, the model needs to learn to 1) compare between different items based on numerical and categorical attributes, 2) compare across a list of numerical values to identify the minimum/maximum value among alternatives, 3) be able to formulate constraints when it is not possible to infer the answer to the user query given the dialogue context but partial inference can be made, and 4) respond no answer when no reasoning is required for answering the user's request.

Figure 2 shows the overall architecture of a dialogue system with the reasoning model. The new model is part of the dialogue manager which predicts the next system action, along side a domain specific dialogue policy. The dialogue policy can predict API calls for retrieving information from a back-end Knowledge Base (KB) or can predict a list of natural language generation (NLG) actions for communicating information to the user (requesting constraints, informing available options, etc.). The reasoning model is added as a modular component that runs along-side the dialogue policy model. Although it would be possible to combine the two models, e.g, by extending the reasoning model to also predict domain specific APIs and actions, we believe that this modular architecture allows the reuse of a trained reasoning model across different domains and tasks.

4 Method

In this work we propose to fine-tune transformers to learn logical reasoning over dialogue context in the form of natural language sentences, bypassing a formal representation and showing such reasoning over language is learnable.

4.1 Data Generation

We describe a general methodology for automatically creating a dataset for logical reasoning in task-oriented dialogue systems. Each example in the dataset is a triple (user-query, context, answer), where the user-query refers to the last user utterance, the context refers to the dialogue context and information returned by API calls to the back-end system (see an example in Figure 1), and the answer refers to the next action to be taken by the dialogue system. The user-query and the context constitute the information given as input to the model, while the answer represents the output.

In order to simulate the context, the objects returned by API calls to the back-end system, we assume an available knowledge base (KB). We further assume that the KB will have different items, identified by an item-name (e.g., *Yogurt Anisakis*), an item-type (e.g., *yogurt*), and a series of attributes, each with an attribute key and value (e.g., *price:* $\$3.40$). For generalizability, we do not assume that all item types have the same attributes, nor that all items of the same type have the same attributes.

The data generation procedure consists of four main steps:

1. Items sampling: In order to construct input-output pairs for training, we first randomly select k items, where $0 \leq k \leq k_{max}$, with the same item-type to create the input context c. While in this work we compare items of the same item-type, this is not a strict requirement of data generation.

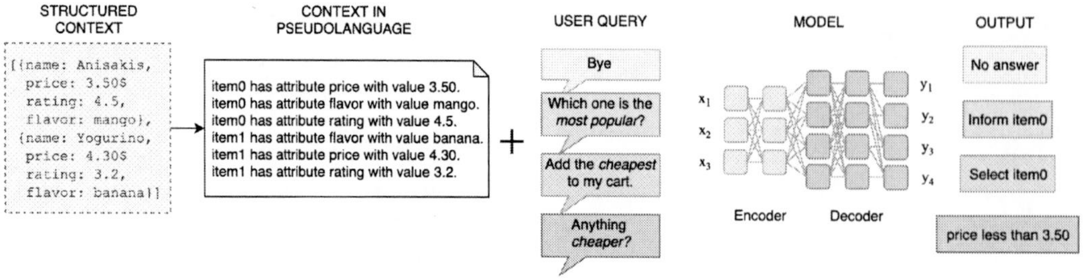

Figure 3: Task structure for the generative model.

The motivation behind this choice is given by a typical scenario of a task-oriented dialogue system where a user might search for a specific object (movie times of Vertigo) and the system would subsequently present different options for that object ("Vertigo is playing today from 12:30 to 2:30 PM and from 3 to 5 PM.").

2. Context conversion to pseudo-language: Once a set of items has been sampled, we transform the structured information (list of triplets) associated to each item into pseudo-language by using a template-based approach, as in Figure 3. Our templates are constructed in a domain-agnostic way, so that they would be directly applicable to other scenarios. We define two main types of statements in pseudo-language, each one associated to a specific template (see first two rows in Table 1). The `IsA` template is used to define the type of an item, while the `HasAttribute` relation is used for triplets expressing the value of a given attribute for the specified item. We note that other templates for the context statements could easily be created to accommodate different scenarios. Finally, we concatenate all the generated statements, after randomizing their order for improving robustness, to form the final input context.

3. Query generation: In this step we generate a set of user queries q suitable for the given context using templates, thus generating several number of different input pairs (c, q_i) where i is an index over possible queries related to the context c. Note that templates for the queries are manually created for each attribute, but they are all agnostic from the domain of the task-oriented dialogue system. Examples of user queries are shown in Table 1. As it can be seen, each template for the user query was associated to the expected output action predicted by the system and the particular reasoning ability involved (e.g., `Inform`). We also consider more complex cases such as *negation*, e.g., "I don't want anything vegan," and *conjunction*, e.g., "Which is the cheapest one and doesn't have strawberry?". Additionally, each template is associated with several different surface form variations to add robustness to the model. Each generated user query is then prepended to the context c. An additional optional post-processing step consists of converting all the numerical values in the user queries from written to spoken format (e.g. *"$3.50"* is converted to *"three dollars fifty"*). This step might be required in the context of a spoken dialogue system scenario, which takes directly as input the output of the Automatic Speech Recognition model.

4. Output creation: In the final step, for each generated input, we automatically create the output by combining the information from each template in regards to the action type to take and calculating the correct answer from the context, e.g., *Yogurt Anisakis is the cheapest.* The output space consists of four main outcomes, as shown in Table 2, depending on whether reasoning is required to respond to the user utterance, and whether the answer is retrievable from the available context. We use the special token `NoAnswer` for user queries that do not require reasoning. When the answer is retrievable from the context and reasoning is re-

Type	Name	Template	Example
Context Statement	IsA	[subject] is [object].	Yogurt Anisakis is a yogurt.
Context Statement	HasAttribute	[subject] has attribute [attribute] with value [value].	Yogurt Anisakis has attribute price with value 3.55.
User Query	Inform	I want something [predicate] [value]. Which one is [predicate]?	I want something cheaper than $5. Which one is the cheapest?
User Query	Inform_TrueFalse	Is [subject] [predicate]?	Is Yogurt Anisakis the cheapest?
User Query	Select	Select [predicate].	Select the cheapest.

Table 1: Examples of templates for context statements (in pseudo-language) and user queries (in natural language)

Reasoning Required	Answer in Context	Action Type	Example	Output
Yes	Yes	Inform	Is the first one cheaper than the second one?	inform <true/false>
Yes	Yes	Inform	Which one is the cheapest?	inform <item_name>
Yes	Yes	Select	Add the cheapest to my cart.	select <item_name>
Yes	No	Constraint	Give me something cheaper	<relation> <attribute> <value>
No	–	No Answer	Find yogurt.	NoAnswer

Table 2: Output space. In cases where there are multiple answers/constraints, they are concatenated with `and`.

User Utterance	Constraint
Give me something vegan.	include diet vegan
I don't want mango.	exclude flavor mango
It should cost $1.50.	equal price 1.50
I want it cheaper than $2	less-than price 2
Anything more popular?	more-than rating 4.5

Table 3: Examples of constraints representation, given as context the one in Figure 2.

quired, we further distinguish between two main cases: `inform`, when the user is simply seeking information (e.g., *"Which one is the cheapest?"*), thus performing an Information-Transfer type of Dialogue Act (see Bunt et al. (2010)), and `select`, when the user is requesting the system to perform a specific action (e.g., *"Add the cheapest to my cart."*), an Action-Discussion Dialogue Act. For the inform action, we also distinguish in the output space between True/False questions and open-answer questions.

In the case of constraint extraction answers, i.e., when the user utterance requires reasoning but the context has partial information, the output consists of the list of constraints extracted from the user query and concatenated with `and`, as shown in Table 3. The constraints extracted from the user query depend on the context, not only in terms of action to take (whether to provide an answer directly or to extract constraints), but also in terms of constraints generation. In the last row of Table 3, for user query ("..more popular?") the reasoning model relies on the context by looking at the ratings of the available products to extract the appropriate rating constraint (e.g, more-than rating 4.5).

4.2 Training Procedure

In order to teach the model rules such as inverse relations and transitivity by example, we investigate the use of appending to the context clues that describe the relations of one or more items. These clues are appended to the final input context during training, but not at inference time. We consider two types of clues: 1) *Comparative clue* describes a comparison of two items in the context along a specific attribute. The template for this clue is: `[subject]` is `[predicate]` `[object]`, where `predicate` refers to the quality regarding which the items are being judged (e.g., "cheaper than", "pricier than", "less than", "equal to"). 2) *Superlative clue* describes an object at the upper/lowest range of a specific attribute. The template for this clue is: `[subject]` is `[predicate]` with value `[value]`. Using the base data generation and clue generation, we are able to construct three types of training scenarios, as follows:

Case I - Clueless context: This scenario uses the base context encompassing the information about the items' different attributes. This is also the scenario we expect at inference time.

Case II - Comparative clues: In this scenario, we sort the items in the base context according to the values of their attributes and append to the base context the comparative relation between pairs of items that are neighbors. The direction of comparison selected is random (e.g. "A is larger than B" or "B is smaller than A") and independent from the user query. This scenario is designed to assess the ability of the model to learn *inverse* relations, since in some queries users will ask for a relation in the opposite direction in regards to the comparative clue in the context (e.g., user asks "Is the second one cheaper than the first one?" while in the context we have "A is pricier than B"), so that the model could learn that these two statements are equivalent. When we have more than two items in context, we can also assess the ability of the model to learn *transitivity*, as we might have cases where the user asks "Is the first one pricier than the third one?" and in the context we have "A is pricier than B" and "B is pricier than C".

Case III - Superlative clues: In this scenario, besides comparative clues, we also add superlative clues to the context to give hints to the model about which item in the context has the extreme value of the attributes (e.g. "A is the cheapest").

We pick the number of items in each context randomly from 0 to k_{max}, so that the model can be robust in its prediction for different number of

Rating	Price	Diet	Flavor
Bounded Numeric	Unbounded Numeric	10	10K

Table 4: Attributes and their catalogs size.

items in the context. We also consider an additional training procedure, which we refer to as Case IV, where we randomly select one of Case I, Case II, or Case III as our context. The random selection of context helps the model to experience all three different cases and by cross learning between different cases, it learns to apply the inverse and transitivity rules for examples with Case I context to draw the right conclusion.

5 Experiments

We showcase our proposed methodology in the context of a dialogue system for a shopping assistant (see Appendix A for an example interaction). We use an ontology for data generation which consists of `item-type` (e.g. yogurt) and `item-name` ("Greek yogurt Anisakis") and each item is characterized by two numerical attributes `price` and `rating`, and two categorical attributes `diet` and `flavor`. This choice of attributes can help us explore and assess the model's performance based on attribute's characteristics. Table 4 summarizes the size of the catalog or range of values for each attribute.

We consider two settings for assessing the logical reasoning capability of transformer models. In the first setting, we fine-tune RoBERTa-base (Liu et al., 2019) with a training dataset generated for reasoning using only numerical attributes. In this setting, we only focus on True/False prediction for each query q given the facts provided in the context c. The objective of this experiment is to understand whether transformer models can learn to reason over numerical attributes. In the second setting, we use a T5 model (Raffel et al., 2019) fine-tuned for the UnifiedQA data (Khashabi et al., 2020), to predict a sequence similar to one given in Table 2. In both cases, we use disjoint catalogs to generate examples for train/dev/test datasets to avoid over-fitting to attribute values.

5.1 True/False Queries

We consider True/False reasoning over attributes such as assessing a conclusion about the comparison of two values of an attribute, or finding minimum or maximum value among list of values of an attribute for several items. Example queries include "is the second item the cheapest one" and "is the first one cheaper than the fourth one". We fine-tune RoBERTa to predict True/False for each (q, c) by adding a classification layer on top of the RoBERTa encoder model to perform binary classification. The training hyper-parameters for fine-tuning this model are provided in Appendix B. For these experiments, we generate 120K samples for train, 5K for dev, and 25K for test set.

Train/Test	I/I	II/II	III/III
2 items	90%	97%	97%
3 items	88%	95%	95%
5 items	77%	91%	93%

Table 5: Roberta-Base model performance for T/F Reasoning over Price and Rating.

Train $\rightarrow$ Test $\downarrow$	Case II (5 items)	Case III (5 items)
Case I, (2 items)	75%	76%
Case I, (3 items)	70%	71%
Case I, (5 items)	67%	69%

Table 6: Train on Case II or Case III with 5 items in all the contexts and test on Case I with 2, 3, or 5 items.

Clueless Training: In this case, we only add `IsA` and `HasAttribute` relations and don't include any clue in the context c in the training data (i.e., Case I). For each generated context, the data generation process attaches all possible forms of queries and the potential true/false label and adds them to training samples. For evaluation, we generate the test samples in a similar fashion. Table 5 summarizes the model performance for predicting the right label for each query given the context with $k \in 2, 3, 5$ number of items in the context. We can see that by increasing the context size (or number of returning items from back-end) the model performance decreases. To understand how well a model with larger k with comparative or superlative clues can generalize to fewer number of items in context, Table 6 shows the performance of a model trained with context size of 5 items using Case II or Case III samples and tested on samples generated by Case I and with $k \in 2, 3, 5$ items. We observe that the model does not generalize to different context sizes if we fix the number of items in the context during model training.

Clue-Aware Training: To resolve the issues in clueless training, we add comparative and superlative clues randomly to each context during the

Train/Test	IV/I	IV/II	IV/III
up-to 5 items	98.70%	99.70%	99.70%

Table 7: Training with CaseIV: Roberta model performance for T/F reasoning over numerical attributes.

training such that the model can learn the inverse and transitivity rules; and also we add random number of items to each individual context (up to k_{max}). Note that we do not add clues to the context during evaluation/inference. Results in Table 7 show the accuracy performance of models trained using samples generated by Case IV and tested on Case I (clue-less), Case II (only comparative clues), and Case III (both comparative and superlative clues) samples. From the results, we observed that adding clues during model training helps the model to achieve better performance.

5.2 Beyond True/False Queries

For this set of experiments, we pick the T5 transformer model which can enable us to perform text-to-text prediction. Similar to (Khashabi et al., 2020), we remove the task prefix that has been used in the original T5 models, since we will use this model only for a single reasoning task within our defined framework. To take advantage of transfer learning from other publicly available question-answering datasets, we start our fine-tuning from the pretrained Unified-QA-T5 small model. We generate 100K samples for training dataset, 5K for dev, and 20K examples for each test set. In our test set we make sure that for each element in Table 8, we have at least 5K examples. Samples are generated as described in Section 4.1. The training hyper-parameters for fine-tuning this model are provided in Appendix B.

In Table 8, we summarize the performance of the fined-tuned model for different scenarios, reporting the results separately for pair of (q, c) such that q can have one (e.g., "Give me something organic') or two attributes (e.g., 'Something cheaper than \$100 but not vegan") about user-preferences. We use the exact-match (EM) accuracy metric to evaluate model performance. We can observe that the model can achieve an EM accuracy of over 90% across all the scenarios. Furthermore, we see that when increasing the number of items in the reasoning context, predicting the correct Inform/Select or Extract output form becomes harder with more attributes in the user query. Evaluating the model performance on all examples (about 8K samples)

# of Attr.s	k_m	Inform/Select	Extract
1	0	–	99.5±0.02%
	1	98.6±0.05%	99.2±0.03%
	2	97.3±0.05%	98.5±0.05%
	3	97.0±0.05%	98.0±0.03%
	4	96.0±0.10%	98.0±0.05%
	5	95.5±0.09%	96.0±0.06%
2	0	–	98.6±0.03%
	1	98.5±0.05%	97.8±0.02%
	2	95.0±0.08%	96.7±0.01%
	3	94.5±0.05%	96.3±0.03%
	4	91.5±0.09%	95.0±0.03%
	5	90.0±0.11%	93.5±0.06%

Table 8: EM accuracy for test sets with different number of attributes, context size, and reasoning task.

from our test set that include spoken form of numerical values in q (e.g., "Give me something cheaper than five dollars"), we observe 95% EM accuracy, showing the ability of the model to compare written form and spoken form versions of numbers. We should note that the accuracy of the model for predicting the cases with no reasoning (e.g., "Checkout please") is important because it makes the integration with the overall dialogue system simpler where the model can delegate to the domain specific dialogue policy. In our experiments, we observe an accuracy of 100% on these cases; however, this value can vary by increasing the size of out-of-domain space/vocabulary.

6 Conclusions

In this paper, we proposed an architecture for the integration of a reasoning model in task-oriented dialogue systems. We formulated the problem as a sequence prediction problem given a user query and context, and presented an approach for generating data and fine-tuning generative models to reason over a set of facts in the dialogue context. We demonstrated our approach for a shopping assistant and reported experimental results for different formulations of the problem. We showed that these models can learn to do logical reasoning to 1) answer questions from the dialogue context when all the information is available, 2) extract constraints when partial information is available, and 3) delegate to the dialogue policy when no reasoning is required.

For future work, we plan to investigate the application of our method to other reasoning tasks (e.g., temporal and spatial reasoning). We also plan to experiment with additional models to compare performances with the ones presented in this work, to further investigate the complexity of the task at hand. Moreover. we would like to test our models on more challenging and realistic testsets, for example by adding noise in the current synthetic data or by performing a data collection with human annotators. Furthermore, we plan to explore how logical reasoning can be used to disambiguate with the user when multiple conclusions can be made.

References

Forough Arabshahi, Jennifer Lee, Mikayla Gawarecki, Kathryn Mazaitis, Amos Azaria, and Tom Mitchell. 2020. Conversational neuro-symbolic commonsense reasoning. *arXiv preprint arXiv:2006.10022*.

Tarek R Besold, Artur d'Avila Garcez, Sebastian Bader, Howard Bowman, Pedro Domingos, Pascal Hitzler, Kai-Uwe Kühnberger, Luis C Lamb, Daniel Lowd, Priscila Machado Vieira Lima, et al. 2017. Neural-symbolic learning and reasoning: A survey and interpretation. *arXiv preprint arXiv:1711.03902*.

Harry Bunt, Jan Alexandersson, Jean Carletta, Jae-Woong Choe, Alex Chengyu Fang, Koiti Hasida, Kiyong Lee, Volha Petukhova, Andrei Popescu-Belis, Laurent Romary, Claudia Soria, and David Traum. 2010. Towards an ISO standard for dialogue act annotation. In *Proceedings of the Seventh International Conference on Language Resources and Evaluation (LREC'10)*, Valletta, Malta. European Language Resources Association (ELRA).

Xiuying Chen, Zhi Cui, Jiayi Zhang, Chen Wei, Jianwei Cui, Bin Wang, Dongyan Zhao, and Rui Yan. 2020. Reasoning in dialog: Improving response generation by context reading comprehension. *CoRR*, abs/2012.07410.

Peter Clark, Oyvind Tafjord, and Kyle Richardson. 2020. Transformers as soft reasoners over language. *arXiv preprint arXiv:2002.05867*.

Leyang Cui, Yu Wu, Shujie Liu, Yue Zhang, and Ming Zhou. 2020. Mutual: A dataset for multi-turn dialogue reasoning. *CoRR*, abs/2004.04494.

David Ding, Felix Hill, Adam Santoro, and Matt Botvinick. 2020. Object-based attention for spatio-temporal reasoning: Outperforming neuro-symbolic models with flexible distributed architectures. *arXiv preprint arXiv:2012.08508*.

Honghua Dong, Jiayuan Mao, Tian Lin, Chong Wang, Lihong Li, and Denny Zhou. 2019. Neural logic machines. *arXiv preprint arXiv:1904.11694*.

Marjan Ghazvininejad, Chris Brockett, Ming-Wei Chang, Bill Dolan, Jianfeng Gao, Wen-tau Yih, and Michel Galley. 2018. A knowledge-grounded neural conversation model. *Proceedings of the AAAI Conference on Artificial Intelligence*, 32(1).

Karthik Gopalakrishnan, Behnam Hedayatnia, Qinlang Chen, Anna Gottardi, Sanjeev Kwatra, Anu Venkatesh, Raefer Gabriel, and Dilek Hakkani-Tür. 2019. Topical-Chat: Towards Knowledge-Grounded Open-Domain Conversations. In *Proc. Interspeech 2019*, pages 1891–1895.

Xiaoxiao Guo, Tim Klinger, Clemens Rosenbaum, Joseph P Bigus, Murray Campbell, Ban Kawas, Kartik Talamadupula, Gerry Tesauro, and Satinder Singh. 2017. Learning to query, reason, and answer questions on ambiguous texts.

Rujun Han, Xiang Ren, and Nanyun Peng. 2020. Deer: A data efficient language model for event temporal reasoning. *arXiv preprint arXiv:2012.15283*.

Zhiting Hu, Xuezhe Ma, Zhengzhong Liu, Eduard Hovy, and Eric Xing. 2016. Harnessing deep neural networks with logic rules. *arXiv preprint arXiv:1603.06318*.

Lifu Huang, Ronan Le Bras, Chandra Bhagavatula, and Yejin Choi. 2019. Cosmos QA: Machine reading comprehension with contextual commonsense reasoning. In *Proceedings of the 2019 Conference on Empirical Methods in Natural Language Processing and the 9th International Joint Conference on Natural Language Processing (EMNLP-IJCNLP)*, pages 2391–2401, Hong Kong, China. Association for Computational Linguistics.

Aishwarya Kamath and Rajarshi Das. 2018. A survey on semantic parsing. *arXiv preprint arXiv:1812.00978*.

Daniel Khashabi, Tushar Khot, Ashish Sabharwal, Oyvind Tafjord, Peter Clark, and Hannaneh Hajishirzi. 2020. Unifiedqa: Crossing format boundaries with a single QA system. *CoRR*, abs/2005.00700.

Kevin Lin, Oyvind Tafjord, Peter Clark, and Matt Gardner. 2019. Reasoning over paragraph effects in situations. *arXiv preprint arXiv:1908.05852*.

Yinhan Liu, Myle Ott, Naman Goyal, Jingfei Du, Mandar Joshi, Danqi Chen, Omer Levy, Mike Lewis, Luke Zettlemoyer, and Veselin Stoyanov. 2019. Roberta: A robustly optimized BERT pretraining approach. *CoRR*, abs/1907.11692.

Ilya Loshchilov and Frank Hutter. 2017. Decoupled weight decay regularization. *arXiv preprint arXiv:1711.05101*.

Arvind Neelakantan, Semih Yavuz, Sharan Narang, Vishaal Prasad, Ben Goodrich, Daniel Duckworth, Chinnadhurai Sankar, and Xifeng Yan. 2019. Neural assistant: Joint action prediction, response generation, and latent knowledge reasoning. *CoRR*, abs/1910.14613.

Duc Nghia Pham, John Thornton, and Abdul Sattar. 2008. Modelling and solving temporal reasoning as propositional satisfiability. *Artificial Intelligence*, 172(15):1752–1782.

Colin Raffel, Noam Shazeer, Adam Roberts, Katherine Lee, Sharan Narang, Michael Matena, Yanqi Zhou, Wei Li, and Peter J. Liu. 2019. Exploring the limits of transfer learning with a unified text-to-text transformer. *CoRR*, abs/1910.10683.

Kyle Richardson, Hai Hu, Lawrence Moss, and Ashish Sabharwal. 2020. Probing natural language inference models through semantic fragments. In *Proceedings of the AAAI Conference on Artificial Intelligence*, volume 34, pages 8713–8721.

Koustuv Sinha, Shagun Sodhani, Jin Dong, Joelle Pineau, and William L Hamilton. 2019. Clutrr: A diagnostic benchmark for inductive reasoning from text. *arXiv preprint arXiv:1908.06177*.

Oyvind Tafjord, Matt Gardner, Kevin Lin, and Peter Clark. 2019. Quartz: An open-domain dataset of qualitative relationship questions. *arXiv preprint arXiv:1909.03553*.

Alon Talmor, Oyvind Tafjord, Peter Clark, Yoav Goldberg, and Jonathan Berant. 2020. Leap-of-thought: Teaching pre-trained models to systematically reason over implicit knowledge. *arXiv preprint arXiv:2006.06609*.

Zhong Victor, Xiong Caiming, and Socher Richard. 2017. Seq2sql: Generating structured queries from natural language using reinforcement learning. *CoRR*, abs/1709.00103.

Po-Wei Wang, Priya Donti, Bryan Wilder, and Zico Kolter. 2019. Satnet: Bridging deep learning and logical reasoning using a differentiable satisfiability solver. In *International Conference on Machine Learning*, pages 6545–6554. PMLR.

Jason Weston, Antoine Bordes, Sumit Chopra, Alexander M Rush, Bart van Merriënboer, Armand Joulin, and Tomas Mikolov. 2015. Towards ai-complete question answering: A set of prerequisite toy tasks. *arXiv preprint arXiv:1502.05698*.

Yaqi Xie, Ziwei Xu, Mohan S Kankanhalli, Kuldeep S Meel, and Harold Soh. 2019. Embedding symbolic knowledge into deep networks. *arXiv preprint arXiv:1909.01161*.

Zhilin Yang, Peng Qi, Saizheng Zhang, Yoshua Bengio, William W Cohen, Ruslan Salakhutdinov, and Christopher D Manning. 2018. Hotpotqa: A dataset for diverse, explainable multi-hop question answering. *arXiv preprint arXiv:1809.09600*.

A Example Interaction with the Shopping Assistant

The following is an example interaction with the shopping assistant with our reasoning model integrated with the dialogue policy.

Speaker	Utterance
User	I want to buy apples
Agent	The top 3 relevant products are: Organic Honycrisp Apple, Organic Gala Apple, and Organic Pink Lady Apple. Which one would you like to add to the cart?
User	Which one is the cheapest?
Agent	The second one, Organic Gala Apple with a price of $2.49.
User	Which one is the most expensive?
Agent	The first one, Organic Honeycripst Apple with a price of $3.99
User	Is the first one cheaper than the second one?
Agent	No. The first one, Organic Honeycripst Apple, costs $3.99 but the second one, Organic Gala Apple, costs $2.49.
User	Is the second one cheaper?
Agent	Yes, that is correct. The second one, Organic Gala Apple, costs $2.49.
User	Give me something cheaper
Agent	Top relevant product is Fuji Apple. Would you like to add it to the cart?
User	Does it cost less than two dollars?
Agent	Yes, that is correct. Fuji Apple costs $1.89.
User	Add it to my cart
Agent	I have added Fuji Apple to your cart. What else would you like to buy?
User	Buy grapes
Agent	The top 2 relevant products are: Red Seedless Grapes and Conventional Cut Grapes. Which one would you like to add to the cart?
User	Is the second one more popular?
Agent	No. The second one, Conventional Cut Grapes has a rating of 4.3 but the first one, Red Seedless Grapes has a rating of 4.5.
User	Add the highest rated one to my cart
Agent	I have added Red Seedless Grapes to your cart. What else would you like to buy?
User	Find cheese
Agent	The top 2 relevant products are: Zola and Muller. Which one would you like to add to the cart?
User	Anything vegan and cheaper than five dollars?
Agent	I couldn't find anything vegan with price less than five dollars. But I found Vegan Artisan cheese with price of $7.99. Would you like to add it to the cart?
User	Sure
Agent	I have added Vegan Artisan cheese to your cart. What else would you like to buy?
User	What's in my cart?
Agent	You have 3 items in the cart with total amount of $12.87. Do you want to hear detailed description?
User	Checkout
Agent	I have placed your order.

B Training Hyper-parameters

In this section, we provide the parameters that are used to fine-tune the transformer models in this work. The following table summarizes the key parameters that are used during the fine-tuning of Roberta-base and UnifiedQA-T5-small pretrained models. For the optimizer, we use AdamW (Loshchilov and Hutter, 2017).

Model	Batch Size	Epoch	Optimizer	Learning Rate	Weight Decay
Roberta-Base	192	15	AdamW	10^{-5}	0.1
UnifiedQA-T5-small	1024	20	AdamW	10^{-5}	0.0

C Discussion

C.1 Generalization to non-synthesis datasets

One of the directions that currently we are working on is to create realistic (human based) conversations with logical reasoning use cases during the interactions with the dialog systems. This type of dataset can help us to evaluate the proposed idea with higher degree of confidence. Since no matter how much one spends time on generating synthetic datasets, there will always be some uncontrolled structures introduced by design of data simulation mechanisms that can corrupt the fair evaluation of deep neural network models and their learning process. However, we believe the True/False scenarios in our current study are less prone to this type of issues and are quite helpful in understating of reasoning capabilities such as negation, numerical comparison, or inclusion/exclusion of categorical values of our proposed algorithm, since model needs to learn the reasoning procedure. In other words, the only way to come up with the right prediction by model is to apply the underlying reasoning procedure to formulate the output True/False results. We will consider: a) better algorithms for generating training data, and b) more realistic general purpose possibly human in the loop training data to make the data generation more general and less domain specific, for future exploration.

C.2 Error Analysis

During our evaluation, we observed that the Transformer models (such as Roberta and T5) performance degrades when the length of the reasoning context increases, i.e., the number of items in the context for reasoning are longer. Also based on the results on Table 8, we see that increasing the number of items in reasoning context leads to performance degradation. Another issue with Transformer models or in general LM models is during the output generation process beyond the

True/False scenario. When the size of the output sequence length increases, e.g., there are several items that all satisfy the user-query. The prediction misses some of the items in the response after the length of the output sequence (number of predicted tokens/words) meets some threshold. This issue is related to both long sequence generation of LM models and also reasoning ability when the multiple items match the user-query's criteria which mostly occurs when the number of items in context are larger.

C.3 Generalization to unseen attribute with common values

One of the aspect that we like to understand is the scalability/generalization of the proposed trained reasoning model to unseen attributes during the test time. There are two possibility for a new attribute: (1) doesn't shares values and keywords that user may use to describe the attribute compared to the attributes that are used during the training process e.g., `color` attribute for experiment in Section 5 [1]. (2) shares same values but keywords that user may use to describe the attribute doesn't overlap with any of the ones used during the training process, e.g., `calorie` [2]. It would be very challenging to teach model in a few-shot manner to learn about attributes from bucket (1). However, based on our initial experiments we have seen that model can easily generalize to the attributes from bucket (2), by fine-tuning to small number of examples in a few-shot manner. For example, we fine-tuned the model which only trained for `diet, flavor, price, and rating` attributes and fine-tuned using only 100 new reasoning context examples which had *calorie* attribute as well. Table 9 summarize the model performance before and after fine-tuning. The test set used for this analysis only has user-query about calories and includes $3K$ examples about Calorie attribute.

Model	EM accuracy
Before fine-tuning	33%
After fine-tuning	80%

Table 9: Model EM accuracy performance before/after fine-tuning to new attribute `calorie`.

[1]For query about the `color` user may use keywords such as: [darker, lighter, warmer, red, blue, ..., etc.] one, and attribute values are red, blue, dark blue, ... etc. which doesn't overlap with none of the attributes that we have already in our training dataset, i.e., `diet, flavor, price, and rating`

[2]For query about the `calories` user may use keywords such as: [healthier, higher calories, more energetic..., etc.] one, and attribute values are numeric value that are shared possibly with `price` and `rating` [considering we have done unit normalization for attributes]

CoVA: Context-aware Visual Attention for Webpage Information Extraction

Anurendra Kumar* **Keval Morabia*** **Jingjin Wang**
Kevin Chen-Chuan Chang **Alexander Schwing**

University of Illinois at Urbana-Champaign
{ak32,morabia2,jingjin9,kcchang,aschwing}@illinois.edu

Abstract

Webpage information extraction (WIE) is an important step to create knowledge bases. For this, classical WIE methods leverage the Document Object Model (DOM) tree of a website. However, use of the DOM tree poses significant challenges as context and appearance are encoded in an abstract manner. To address this challenge we propose to reformulate WIE as a context-aware Webpage Object Detection task. Specifically, we develop a Context-aware Visual Attention-based (CoVA) detection pipeline which combines appearance features with syntactical structure from the DOM tree. To study the approach we collect a new large-scale dataset[1] of e-commerce websites for which we manually annotate every web element with four labels: product price, product title, product image and others. On this dataset we show that the proposed CoVA approach is a new challenging baseline which improves upon prior state-of-the-art methods.

1 Introduction

Webpage information extraction (WIE) is an important step when creating a large-scale knowledge base (Chang et al., 2006; Azir and Ahmad, 2017) which has many downstream applications such as knowledge-aware question answering (Lin et al., 2019) and recommendation systems (Ma et al., 2019; Lin et al., 2020).

Classical methods for WIE, like Wrapper Induction (Soderland, 1999; Muslea et al., 1998; Chang and Lui, 2001), rely on the publicly available source code of websites. The code is commonly parsed into a document object model (DOM) tree. The DOM tree is a programming language independent tree representation of any website, which contains all its elements. It can be obtained using various libraries like Puppeteer. These elements contain information about their location in the rendered webpage, styling like font size, etc., and text if it is a leaf node. State of the art method in WIE (Lin et al., 2020) uses text and markup information and employ CNN-BiLSTM encoder (Rhanoui et al., 2019) on the sequence of HTML nodes obtained from DOM to learn the embedding of each node.

However, using only the DOM tree for WIE is increasingly challenging for a variety of reasons: 1) Webpages are programmed to be aesthetically pleasing; 2) Oftentimes content and style is separated in website code and hence the DOM tree; 3) The same visual result can be obtained in a plethora of ways; 4) Branding banners and advertisements are interspersed with information of interest.

For this reason, recently, WIE applied optical character recognition (OCR) on rendered websites followed by word embedding-based natural language extraction (Staar et al., 2018). However, as mentioned before, recent webpages are highly enriched with visual content, and classical word embeddings don't capture this contextual information. For instance, text in advertising banners may be interpreted as valuable information. For this reason, a simple OCR detection followed by natural language processing techniques is a suboptimal for WIE (Vishwanath et al., 2018).

In response to these challenges we develop WIE based on a visual representation of a web element and its context. This permits to address the aforementioned four challenges. Moreover, visual features are independent of the programming language (*e.g.*, HTML for webpages, Dart for Android or iOS apps) and partially also the website language (*e.g.*, Arabic, Chinese, English). Intuitively, we aim to mimic the ability of humans to detect the location of target elements like product price, product title and product image on a webpage in a foreign language like the one shown in Fig. 1.

For this, we develop a context-aware Webpage

[1] CoVA dataset and code are available at github.com/kevalmorabia97/CoVA-Web-Object-Detection

*These authors contributed equally to this work

Proceedings of The Fifth Workshop on e-Commerce and NLP (ECNLP 5), pages 80 - 90

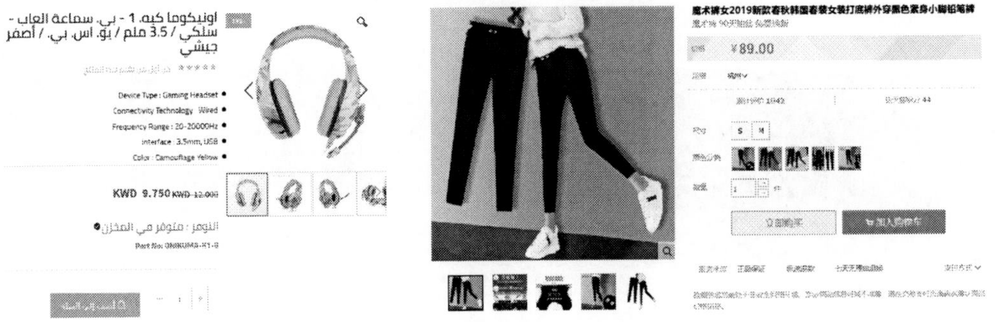

(a) (b)

Figure 1: A person can detect the element for product price, title, and image, w/o knowing (a) Arabic or (b) Chinese

Object Detection (WOD), which we refer to as Context-aware Visual Attention-based detection (CoVA), where entities like prices are objects. Somewhat differently from an object in natural images which can be detected largely based on its appearance, objects on a webpage are strongly defined by contextual information. *e.g.*, a cat's appearance is largely independent of its nearby objects, whereas a product price is a highly ambiguous object (Fig. 2). It refers to the price of a product only when it is contextually related to a product title and a product image. The developed WOD uses a graph attention based architecture, which leverages the underlying syntactic DOM tree (Zhou et al., 2021) to focus on important context (Zhu et al., 2005) while classifying an element on a webpage. Once these web elements are identified, the relevant information *e.g.* price and title can be obtained from the corresponding DOM nodes. These information can then be indexed and used for applications like product search and price comparison across online retailers.

To facilitate this task we create a dataset of 7.7k English product webpage screenshots along with DOM information spanning 408 different websites (domains). We compare the results of CoVA with existing and newly created baselines that take visual features into account. We show that CoVA leads to substantial improvements while yielding interpretable contextual representations.

In summary, we make the following contributions:

1. We formulate WIE as a context-aware WOD problem.
2. We develop a Context-aware Visual Attention-based (CoVA) detection pipeline, which is end-to-end trainable and exploits syntactic structure from the DOM tree along with screenshots. CoVA improves recent state-of-the-art baselines by a significant margin.
3. We create the largest public dataset of 7.7k English product webpage screenshots from 408 online retailers for Object Detection from product webpages. Our dataset is $\sim 10\times$ larger than existing datasets.
4. We show the interpretability of CoVA using attention visualizations (Sec. 6.5)
5. We claim and validate that visual features (without textual content) along with DOM information are sufficient for many tasks while allowing cross-domain and cross-language generalizability. CoVA trained on English webpages perform well on Chinese Webpages (Sec. 6.4).

2 Related Work

Webpage information extraction (WIE) has been mainly addressed with Wrapper Induction (WI). WI aims to learn a set of extraction rules from HTML code or text, using manually labeled examples and counter-examples (Soderland, 1999; Muslea et al., 1998; Chang and Lui, 2001). These often require human intervention which is time-consuming, error-prone (Vadrevu et al., 2005), and does not generalize to new templates.

Supervised learning, which treats WIE as a classification task has also garnered significant attention. Traditionally, natural language processing techniques are employed over HTML or DOM information. Structural and semantic features (Ibrahim et al., 2008; Gibson et al., 2007) are obtained for each part of a webpage to predict categories like title, author, etc. Wu et al. (2015)

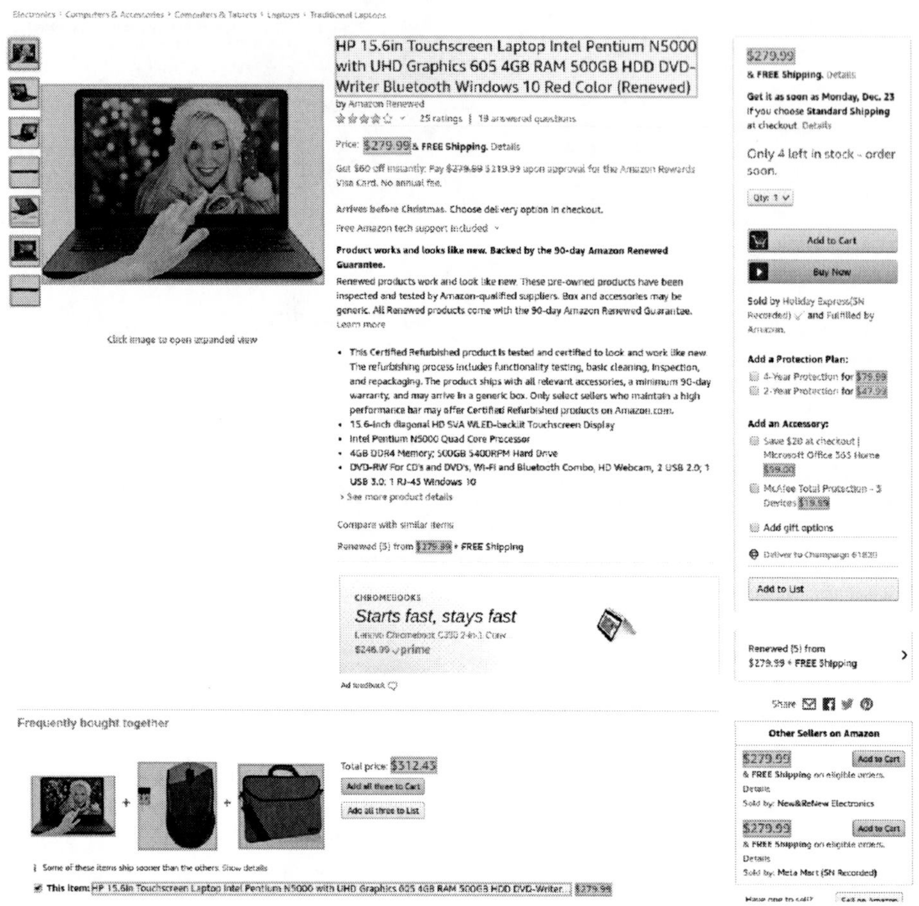

Figure 2: Example webpage showing multiple possible prices (red), but relatively fewer possible title (green) or image (purple)

casts WIE as a HTML node selection problem using features such as positions, areas, fonts, text, tags, and links. Lin et al. (2020) proposes a neural network to learn representation of a DOM node by combining text and markup information. A CNN-BiLSTM encoder is employed to learn the embeddings for HTML node. Hwang et al. (2020) develops a transformer architecture to learn spatial dependency between DOM nodes. Unlike these work which depends on text information, we aim to learn representation of a DOM node using only visual cues. Joshi and Liu (2009) develop a semantic similarity between blocks of webpages using textual and DOM features to extract the key article on a webpage.

Visual features have been extensively employed to generate visual wrappers for pattern extraction. Mostly, these utilize hand-crafted visual features from a webpage, *e.g.*, area size, font size, and type. Cai et al. (2003) develop a visual block tree of a webpage using visual and layout features along with the DOM tree information. Subsequent works use this tree for tasks like webpage segmentation, visual wrapper generation, and web record extraction (Cai et al., 2004; Liu et al., 2003; Simon and Lausen, 2005; Burget and Rudolfova, 2009). Gogar et al. (2016) aims to develop domain-specific wrappers which generalize across unseen templates and don't need manual intervention. They develop a unified model that encodes visual, textual, and positional features using a single CNN.

Object detection (OD) techniques in Computer Vision, which aims to detect and classify all objects, has been extensively studied for natural images. Deep learning methods such as YOLO (Redmon and Farhadi, 2018), R-CNN variants (Girshick et al., 2014; Girshick, 2015; He et al., 2017), etc. yielded state-of-the-art results in OD.

OD methods that can capture contextual information are of particular interest here. Murphy et al. (2006) learn local and global context by object presence and localization and use a product of experts model (Hinton, 2002) to combine them. Kong et al. (2021) proposes a short path context module which transforms the integrated feature maps by considering local feature affinities.

Graph Convolutional Networks (GCN) (Kipf and Welling, 2016) was proposed to learn a node representation while taking neighbors of a node into account. Using it, Liu et al. (2019) represent a visually rich document as a complete graph of text content obtained by passing OCR (Mithe et al., 2013). They employ GCN to learn node representations for each web element.

Recently, **Attention mechanisms** have also shown remarkable ability in capturing contextual information (Bahdanau et al., 2014). Vaswani et al. (2017) propose a transformer architecture for language modeling. Luo et al. (2018) use attention over a BiLSTM-CRF layer for Named Entity Recognition (NER) on biomedical data. Word vectors learned on BERT (Devlin et al., 2018), which use self-attention, have yielded state-of-the-art results on 11 NLP tasks.

Separately, attention has been used for contextual learning in OD (Li et al., 2013; Hsieh et al., 2019; Morabia et al., 2020) and image captioning (You et al., 2016). Attention mechanisms have also been employed over graphs to learn an optimal representation of nodes while taking graph structure into account (Veličković et al., 2017). Moreover, attention permits to interpret result, which is often desired in many applications. We show our visualizations depicting this advantage below (Sec. 6.5).

3 Problem formulation

The DOM tree captures the syntactical structure of a webpage similar to a parse tree of a natural language. Our goal is to extract semantic information exploiting this syntactic structure. We view a leaf web element as a *word* and the webpage as a document with the DOM tree as its underlying parse tree. Formally, we represent a webpage W as the set $W = \{v_1, v_2, \dots, v_i, \dots, v_N, D\}$ where v_i denotes the visual representation of the i-th web element, N denotes number of web elements, and D refers to the DOM tree which contains the relations between the web elements. Our goal is to learn a parametric function $f_\theta(y_i|W, i)$ which extracts a visual representation v_i of the i-th web element from website W so as to accurately predict label y_i of the web element. In the following we consider four labels for a product, *i.e.*, $y_i \in \{\text{product price}, \text{title}, \text{image}, \text{others}\}$. The parameters θ are obtained by minimizing the following supervised classification loss

$$\theta^* = \underset{\theta}{\operatorname{argmin}} \underset{i,W\sim P_W}{\mathbb{E}} \left[\mathcal{L}(f_\theta(y_i|W, i), y_i^*)\right],$$

where $\mathbb{E}$ denotes an expectation, y_i and y_i^* denote the predicted and ground truth labels and P_W denotes a probability distribution over webpages.

Information of a webpage is present in the leaves of the DOM tree, *i.e.*, the web elements i. Web elements are an atomic entity which is characterized by a rectangular bounding box. We can extract the target information y_i from the DOM tree if we know the exact leaf bounding boxes of the desired element. Therefore, we can view WIE as an object detection (OD) task where objects are leaf elements and might contain the desired entity (target). However, identity y_i of a web element is heavily dependent on its context, *e.g.*, price, title, and image of a product are most likely to be in same or nearby sub-tree in comparison to unrelated web elements such as advertisements. Similarly, there can be multiple instances of price-like elements. However, the correct price would be contextually positioned with product title and image (Fig. 2). Therefore, we formulate WIE as a context-aware OD.

We use the DOM tree to identify context for a web element. We represent the syntactic closeness between web elements through edges in the graph (discussed in next section). We then employ a graph attention mechanism (Veličković et al., 2017) to attend to the most important contexts.

4 Proposed End-to-End Pipeline – CoVA

In this section, we present our Context-Aware Visual Attention-based end-to-end pipeline for Webpage Object Detection (CoVA) which aims to learn function f to predict labels $y = [y_1, y_2, \dots, y_N]$ for a webpage. The input to CoVA consists of 1. a screenshot of a webpage, 2. list of bounding boxes $[x, y, w, h]$ of the web elements, and 3. neighborhood information for each element obtained from DOM. It should be noted that bounding boxes of the web elements are relatively accurate and doesn't pose challenges similar to OD for natural images.

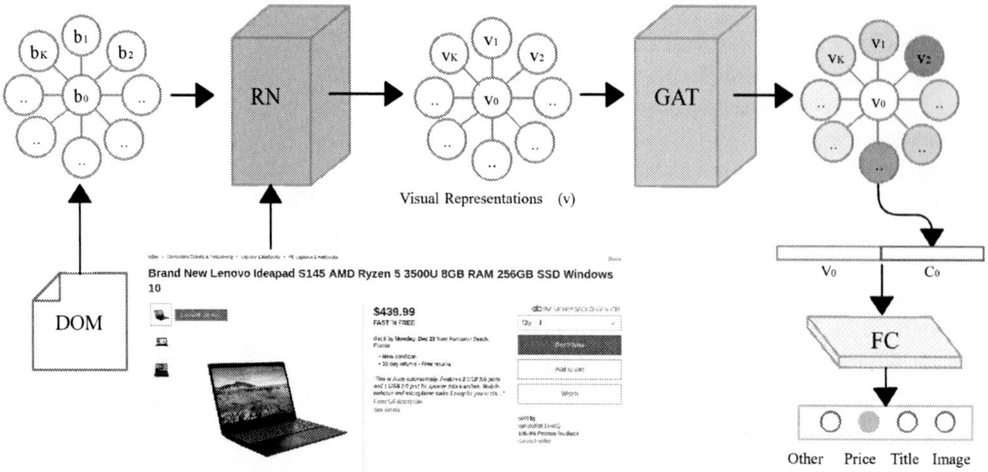

Figure 3: CoVA end-to-end training pipeline (for a single web element). CoVA takes a webpage screenshot and list of bounding boxes along with K neighbors for each web element (obtained from DOM). RN learns visual representation (v_0) while GAT learns contextual representation (c_0) from its neighbor's visual representations.

As illustrated in Fig. 3, this information is processed by CoVA in four stages: 1. the graph representation extraction for the webpage, 2. the Representation Network (RN), 3. the Graph Attention Network (GAT), and 4. a fully connected (FC) layer. The graph representation extraction computes for every web element i its set of neighboring web elements $\mathcal{N}_i$. The RN consists of a Convolutional Neural Net (CNN) and a positional encoder aimed to learn a visual representation v_i for each web element $i \in \{1, \ldots, N\}$. The GAT combines the visual representation v_i of the web element i to be classified and those of its neighbors, *i.e.*, v_k $\forall k \in \mathcal{N}_i$ to compute the contextual representation c_i for web element i. Finally, the visual and contextual representations of the web element are concatenated and passed through the FC layer to obtain the classification output. We describe each of the components next.

4.1 Webpage as a Graph

We represent a webpage as a graph where nodes are leaf web elements and an edge indicates that the corresponding web elements are contextually relevant to each other. A naive way to create graph is by putting edge between every pair of nodes (Liu et al., 2019). An alternative way of creating a graph is to add edges to nearby nodes based on spatial distance. However, web elements vary greatly in shapes & sizes, and two web elements might have small distance but they're contextually irrelevant since they lie in different DOM subtrees. For this, we use the K nearest leaf elements in the DOM tree as the neighbors $\mathcal{N}_i$ a web element i. An edge within the graph denotes the syntactic closeness in the DOM tree.

4.2 Representation Network (RN)

The goal of the Representation Network (RN) is to learn a fixed size visual representation v_i of any web element $i \in \{1, \ldots, N\}$. This is important since web elements have different sizes, aspect ratios, and content type (image or text). To achieve this the RN consists of a CNN operating on the screenshot of a webpage, followed by a Region of Interest (RoI) pooling layer (Girshick, 2015) and a positional encoder. Specifically, RoI pooling is performed to obtain a fixed size representation for all web elements. To capture the spatial layout, we learn a P dimensional positional feature which is obtained by passing the bounding box features $[x, y, w, h, \frac{w}{h}]$ through a positional encoder implemented by a single layer neural net. Finally, we concatenate the flattened output of the RoI pooling with positional features to obtain the visual representation v_i.

4.3 Graph Attention Network (GAT)

The goal of the graph attention network is to compute a contextual representation c_i for each web element i which takes visual information v_i from neighboring web elements into account. However, out of multiple neighbors for a web element, only a few are informative, *e.g.*, a web element having a currency symbol near a set of digits seems relevant. To identify the relational importance we use a Graph Attention Network (GAT) (Veličković et al., 2017). We transform each of the input features by learning projection matrices W_1 and W_2 applied at every node and its neighbors. We then employ self-attention (Lin et al., 2017) to compute the importance score,

$$\alpha_{ij} = \frac{\exp(\text{LeakyReLU}(a^T[W_1v_i||W_2v_j]))}{\sum_{k\in\mathcal{N}_i}\exp(\text{LeakyReLU}(a^T[W_1v_i||W_2v_k]))},$$

where $\cdot^T$ represents transposition, $||$ is the concatenation operation, $\mathcal{N}_i$ denotes the neighbors of web element i. The weights α_{ij} are non-negative attention scores for neighboring web elements of web element i. Finally, we obtain the contextual representation c_i for a web element i as a weighted combination of projected visual representations of its neighbors, *i.e.*, via

$$c_i = \sum_{j\in\mathcal{N}_i} \alpha_{ij}W_2v_j. \quad (1)$$

4.4 Augmenting CoVA with extra features

In scenarios where additional features (*e.g.*, text content, HTML tag information, etc.) are available, CoVA can be easily extended to incorporate those. These features can be concatenated with visual representations obtained from the RN without modifying the pipeline in any other way. We refer to this extended pipeline as **CoVA++**. However, making the model dependent on these features might lead to constraints regarding the programming language (HTML tags) or text language. In Sec. 6.4, we show that CoVA trained on English webpages (without additional features) generalizes well to Chinese webpages.

5 Dataset Generation

To the best of our knowledge there is no large-scale dataset for WIE with visual annotations for object detection. So far, the Structured Web Data Extraction (SWDE) dataset (Hao et al., 2011) is the only known large dataset that can be used for training deep neural networks for WIE (Lin et al., 2020; Lockard et al., 2019). SWDE dataset contains webpage HTML codes which is not sufficient to render it into a screenshot (since it contains links to old and non-existent URLs). Because of this we create a new large-scale labeled dataset for object detection on English product webpage screenshots along with DOM information. We chose e-commerce websites since those have been a de-facto standard for WIE (Gogar et al., 2016; Zhu et al., 2005). Our dataset generation consists of two steps: 1. search the web with 'shopping' keywords to aggregate diverse webpages and employ heuristics to automate labeling of product price, title, and image, 2. manual correction of incorrect labels. We discuss both steps next.

Web scraping and coarse labeling. To scrape websites, we use Google shopping[2] which aggregates links to multiple online retailers (domains) for the same product. These links are uploaded by the merchants of the respective domains. We do a keyword search for various categories, like electronics, food, cosmetics. For each search result, we record the price and title from Google shopping. Then, we navigate through the links to specific product websites and save a 1280×1280 screenshot. To extract a bounding box for each web element, we store a pruned DOM tree. Price and title candidates are labeled by comparing with the recorded values using heuristics. For product images, we always choose the DOM element having the largest bounding box area among all the elements with an <img> HTML tag, although this might not be true for many websites. We correct this issue in the next step.

Label correction. The coarse labeling is only $\sim$60% accurate because 1. price on webpages keeps changing and might differ from the Google shopping price, and 2. many bounding boxes have the same content. To correct for these mistakes, we manually inspected and correct labeling errors. We obtained **7,740 webpages** spanning **408 domains**. Each of these webpages contains exactly one labeled price, title, and image. All other web elements are labeled as 'others'. On average, there are $\sim$90 leaf web elements on a webpage.

Train-Val-Test split. We create a cross-domain split which ensures that each of the train, val and test sets contains webpages from different domains. We observed that the top-5 frequent domains were Amazon, EBay, Walmart, Etsy, and Target. So, we created 5 different splits for 5-Fold Cross Validation such that each of the major domains is present in one of the test splits.

6 Experimental Setup & Results

6.1 Baseline Methods

We compare the results of our end-to-end pipeline CoVA with other existing and newly created base-

[2]shopping.google.com

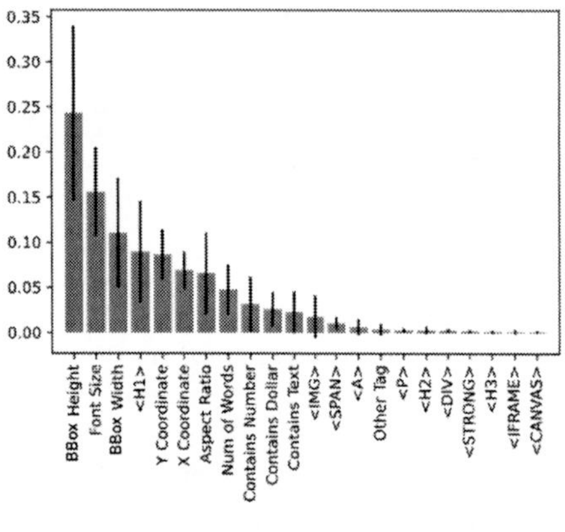

Figure 4: Gini impurity-based importance of features in RF

lines summarized below. Our newly created baselines combine existing object detection and graph based models to identify the importance of visual features and contextual representations.

(Gogar et al., 2016): This method identifies product price, title, and image from the visual and textual representation of the web elements.

Random Forest on Heuristic features: We train a Random Forest classifier with 100 trees using various HTML tags, text, and bounding box features as shown in Fig. 4.

Fast R-CNN*: We compare with Fast R-CNN (Girshick, 2015) to quantify the importance of contextual representations in CoVA. We use the DOM tree instead of selective search (Uijlings et al., 2013) for bounding box proposals. We also use positional features as described when discussing the representation network (Sec. 4.2) for a fair comparison with CoVA. We will refer to this baseline as 'Fast R-CNN*.'

Fast R-CNN* + GCN (Kipf and Welling, 2016): We use GCN on our graph formulation where node features are the visual representations obtained from Fast R-CNN*.

Fast R-CNN* + Bi-LSTM (Schuster and Paliwal, 1997): We train a bidirectional LSTM on visual representations of web elements in preorder traversal of the DOM tree. We use its output as the contextual representation and concatenate it with the visual representation of the web element obtained from Fast R-CNN*.

6.2 Model Training, Inference and Evaluation

In each training epoch, we randomly sample 90% from others. This increases the diversity in training data by providing different contexts for webpages with exactly the same template. We use batch normalization (Ioffe and Szegedy, 2015) between consecutive layers, Adam optimizer for updating model parameters and minimize cross-entropy loss. During inference, the model detects one web element with highest probability for each class. Once the web element is identified, the corresponding text content can be extracted from the DOM tree or by using OCR for downstream tasks.

For CoVA++ we use as additional information the same heuristic features used to train the Random Forest classifier baseline. Unless specified otherwise, all results of CoVA and baselines use the following hyperparameters where applicable: learning rate = 5e-4, batch size = 5 screenshot images, $K = 24$ neighbor elements in the graph, RoI pool output size $(H \times W) = (3 \times 3)$, dropout = 0.2, $P = 32$ dimensional positional features, output dimension for projection matrix W_1, W_2 is 384, weight decay = 1e-3. We use the first 5 layers of a pre-trained ResNet18 (He et al., 2016) in the representation network (RN), which yields a 64 channel feature map. This significantly reduces the parameters in the RN from $12m$ to $0.2m$ and speeds up training at the same time. The evaluation is performed using Cross-domain Accuracy for each class, *i.e.*, the fraction of webpages of new domains with correct class. All the experiments are performed on Tesla V100-SXM2-16GB GPUs.

6.3 Results

As shown in Table 1, our method outperforms all baselines by a considerable margin especially for price prediction. CoVA learns visual features which are significantly better than the heuristic feature baseline that uses predefined tag, textual and visual features. Fig. 4 shows the importance of different heuristic based features in a webpage. We observe that a heuristic feature based method has similar performance to methods which don't use contextual features. Moreover, CoVA++ which also uses heuristic features, doesn't lead to statistically significant improvements. This shows that visual features learnt by CoVA are more general for tasks like price & title detection. Context information is particularly important for price (in comparison to title and image) since it's highly ambiguous and occurs in different locations with varying contexts (Fig. 2). This is evident from the $\sim$8.9% improvement in price accuracy compared to the Fast R-CNN*. Unless stated other-

Method	Params	Price Acc	Title Acc	Image Acc
Gogar et al. (2016)	1.8m	78.1 ± 17.2	91.5 ± 1.3	93.2 ± 1.9
Random Forest using Heuristic features	-	87.4 ± 10.4	93.5 ± 5.3	97.2 ± 3.8
Fast R-CNN* (Girshick, 2015)	0.5m	86.6 ± 7.3	93.7 ± 2.2	97.0 ± 3.6
Fast R-CNN* + GCN	1.4m	90.0 ± 11.0	95.4 ± 1.5	98.2 ± 2.8
Fast R-CNN* + Bi-LSTM	5.1m	92.9 ± 4.6	94.0 ± 2.1	97.6 ± 3.6
CoVA	1.6m	$\mathbf{95.5 \pm 3.8}$	$\mathbf{95.7 \pm 1.2}$	$\mathbf{98.8 \pm 1.5}$
CoVA++	1.7m	$\mathbf{96.1 \pm 3.0}$	$\mathbf{96.7 \pm 2.2}$	$\mathbf{99.6 \pm 0.3}$

Table 1: Cross Domain Accuracy (mean $\pm$ standard deviation) for 5-fold cross validation.

wise, we will discuss results with respect to price accuracy. We observe that CoVA yields stable results across folds ($\sim$3.5% reduction in standard deviation). This shows that CoVA learns features which are generalizable and which have less dependence on the training data. Using GCN with Fast R-CNN* leads to unstable results with 11% standard deviation while yielding a 3.4% improvement over Fast R-CNN*. Fast R-CNN* with Bi-LSTM is able to summarize the contextual features by yielding a $\sim$6.3% improvement in comparison to Fast RCNN*. CoVA outperforms Fast RCNN* with Bi-LSTM by $\sim$2.6% with much fewer number of parameters while also yielding interpretable results. We also obtained top-3 accuracy for CoVA, which are 98.6%, 99.4%, and 99.9% for price, title and image respectively.

6.4 Cross-lingual Evaluation of CoVA

To validate our claim that visual features (without textual or HTML tag information) can capture cross-lingual information, we test our model on webpages in a foreign language. In particular, we evaluated CoVA (trained on English product webpages) using 100 Chinese product webpages spanning across 25 unique domains. CoVA achieves 92%, 90%, and 99% accuracy for product price, title, and image. It should be noted that image has the same accuracy as for English pages. This is expected since images have no language components that the model can attend to.

6.5 Attention Visualizations

Table 1 shows that attention significantly improves performance for all the three targets. As discussed earlier, only few of the contexts are important which are effectively learnt by Graph Attention Network (GAT). We observed that on average, $\sim$20% of context elements were activated (score above 0.05 threshold) by GAT. We also study a multihead attention instead of single head following (Vaswani et al., 2017), which didn't yield significant improvements in our case.

Fig. 5 shows visualizations of attention scores learnt by GAT. Fig. 5(a) shows an example where title and image have more weight than other contexts when learning a context representation for price. This shows that attention is able to focus on important web elements and discards others. Similarly, Fig. 5(b) shows that price has a much higher score than other contexts for learning contextual representation for title.

7 Ablation Studies

Importance of Positional features: Table 2 shows that positional features can significantly improve accuracy for price, title, and image prediction. This also validates that for webpage OD, location and size of a bounding box carries significant information, making it different from classical OD.

Dependence on number of neighbors in graph: Fig. 6 shows the variation in cross domain accuracy of CoVA with respect to the number of neighboring elements K. Note that having 0 context elements is equivalent to our baseline Fast R-CNN*. We observe that, unlike title and image, price accuracy can significantly be improved by considering larger contexts. This is due to the fact that price is highly ambiguous (Fig. 2). We also study the graph construction described by (Liu et al., 2019) where all nodes are considered in the neighborhood of a particular node. This significantly reduced the performance for price (90.7%) and title (92.7%).

8 Conclusion & Future Work

In this paper, we reformulated the problem of webpage IE (WIE) as a context-aware webpage object detection. We created a large-scale dataset for this task and is available publicly. We proposed CoVA

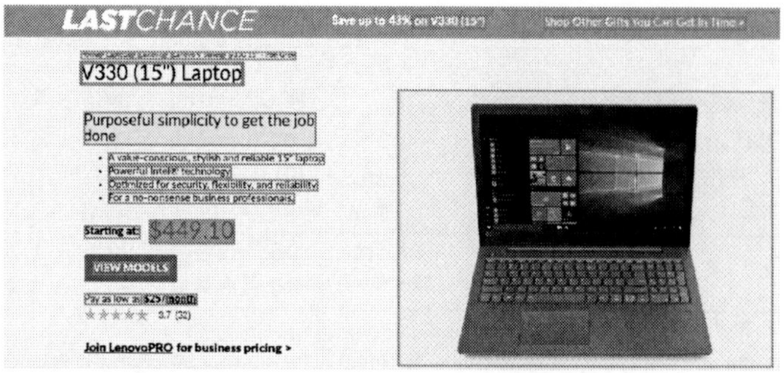

(a)

(b)

Figure 5: Attention Visualizations where red border denotes web element to be classified, and its contexts have green shade whose intensity denotes score. Price in (a) get much more score than other contexts. Title and image in (b) are scored higher than other contexts for price.

Method	Price Accuracy	Title Accuracy	Image Accuracy
CoVA without positional features	89.2 ± 10.3	91.9 ± 1.4	95.9 ± 1.8
CoVA	$\mathbf{95.5 \pm 3.8}$	$\mathbf{95.7 \pm 1.2}$	$\mathbf{98.8 \pm 1.5}$

Table 2: Importance of positional features in RN

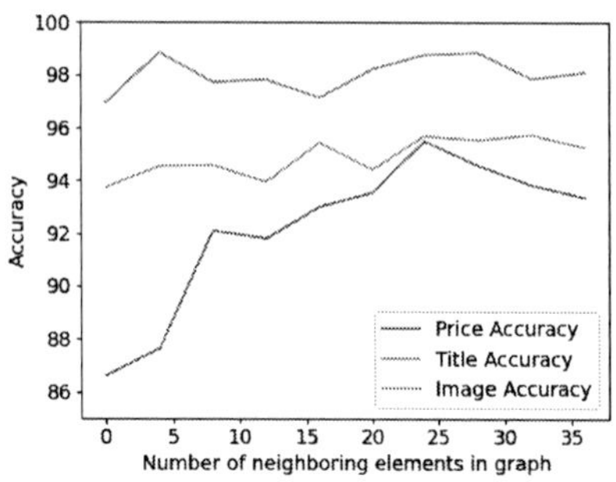

Figure 6: Comparison of context size with accuracy

which uses i) a graph representation of a webpage, ii) a Representation Network (RN) to learn visual representation for a web element, and iii) a Graph Attention Network (GAT) for contextual learning. CoVA improves upon state-of-the-art results and newly created baselines by considerable margins. Our visualizations show that CoVA is able to attend to the most important contexts. In the future, we plan to adapt this method to other tasks such as identifying malicious web elements. Our works shows the importance of visual features of WIE which is traditionally overlooked. We hope that our work will motivate researchers in WIE to employ CV alongwith NLP techniques to solve this important problem.

References

Mohd Amir Bin Mohd Azir and Kamsuriah Binti Ahmad. 2017. Wrapper approaches for web data extraction: A review. In *2017 6th International Conference on Electrical Engineering and Informatics (ICEEI)*, pages 1–6. IEEE.

Dzmitry Bahdanau, Kyunghyun Cho, and Yoshua Bengio. 2014. Neural machine translation by jointly learning to align and translate. *arXiv preprint arXiv:1409.0473*.

Radek Burget and Ivana Rudolfova. 2009. Web page element classification based on visual features. In

2009 First Asian Conference on Intelligent Information and Database Systems, pages 67–72. IEEE.

Deng Cai, Xiaofei He, Ji-Rong Wen, and Wei-Ying Ma. 2004. Block-level link analysis. In *Proceedings of the 27th annual international ACM SIGIR conference on Research and development in information retrieval*, pages 440–447.

Deng Cai, Shipeng Yu, Ji-Rong Wen, and Wei-Ying Ma. 2003. Vips: a vision-based page segmentation algorithm.

Chia-Hui Chang, Mohammed Kayed, Moheb R Girgis, and Khaled F Shaalan. 2006. A survey of web information extraction systems. *IEEE transactions on knowledge and data engineering*, 18(10):1411–1428.

Chia-Hui Chang and Shao-Chen Lui. 2001. Iepad: information extraction based on pattern discovery. In *Proceedings of the 10th international conference on World Wide Web*, pages 681–688.

Jacob Devlin, Ming-Wei Chang, Kenton Lee, and Kristina Toutanova. 2018. Bert: Pre-training of deep bidirectional transformers for language understanding. *arXiv preprint arXiv:1810.04805*.

John Gibson, Ben Wellner, and Susan Lubar. 2007. Adaptive web-page content identification. In *Proceedings of the 9th annual ACM international workshop on Web information and data management*, pages 105–112.

Ross Girshick. 2015. Fast r-cnn. In *Proceedings of the IEEE international conference on computer vision*, pages 1440–1448.

Ross Girshick, Jeff Donahue, Trevor Darrell, and Jitendra Malik. 2014. Rich feature hierarchies for accurate object detection and semantic segmentation. In *Proceedings of the IEEE conference on computer vision and pattern recognition*, pages 580–587.

Tomas Gogar, Ondrej Hubacek, and Jan Sedivy. 2016. Deep neural networks for web page information extraction. In *IFIP International Conference on Artificial Intelligence Applications and Innovations*, pages 154–163. Springer.

Qiang Hao, Rui Cai, Yanwei Pang, and Lei Zhang. 2011. From one tree to a forest: a unified solution for structured web data extraction. In *Proceedings of the 34th international ACM SIGIR conference on Research and development in Information Retrieval*, pages 775–784.

Kaiming He, Georgia Gkioxari, Piotr Dollár, and Ross Girshick. 2017. Mask r-cnn. In *Proceedings of the IEEE international conference on computer vision*, pages 2961–2969.

Kaiming He, Xiangyu Zhang, Shaoqing Ren, and Jian Sun. 2016. Deep residual learning for image recognition. In *Proceedings of the IEEE conference on computer vision and pattern recognition*, pages 770–778.

Geoffrey E Hinton. 2002. Training products of experts by minimizing contrastive divergence. *Neural computation*, 14(8):1771–1800.

Ting-I Hsieh, Yi-Chen Lo, Hwann-Tzong Chen, and Tyng-Luh Liu. 2019. One-shot object detection with co-attention and co-excitation. In *Advances in Neural Information Processing Systems*, pages 2725–2734.

Wonseok Hwang, Jinyeong Yim, Seunghyun Park, Sohee Yang, and Minjoon Seo. 2020. Spatial dependency parsing for semi-structured document information extraction. *arXiv preprint arXiv:2005.00642*.

Hossam Ibrahim, Kareem Darwish, and Abdel-Rahim Madany. 2008. Automatic extraction of textual elements from news web pages. In *LREC*.

Sergey Ioffe and Christian Szegedy. 2015. Batch normalization: Accelerating deep network training by reducing internal covariate shift. *arXiv preprint arXiv:1502.03167*.

Parag Mulendra Joshi and Sam Liu. 2009. Web document text and images extraction using dom analysis and natural language processing. In *Proceedings of the 9th ACM symposium on Document engineering*, pages 218–221.

Thomas N Kipf and Max Welling. 2016. Semi-supervised classification with graph convolutional networks. *arXiv preprint arXiv:1609.02907*.

Yuqiu Kong, Mengyang Feng, Xin Li, Huchuan Lu, Xiuping Liu, and Baocai Yin. 2021. Spatial context-aware network for salient object detection. *Pattern Recognition*, 114:107867.

Gui Li, Cheng Chen, Zheng Yu Li, Zi Yang Han, and Ping Sun. 2013. Web data extraction based on tag path clustering. In *Advanced Materials Research*, volume 756, pages 1590–1594. Trans Tech Publ.

Bill Yuchen Lin, Xinyue Chen, Jamin Chen, and Xiang Ren. 2019. Kagnet: Knowledge-aware graph networks for commonsense reasoning. *arXiv preprint arXiv:1909.02151*.

Bill Yuchen Lin, Ying Sheng, Nguyen Vo, and Sandeep Tata. 2020. Freedom: A transferable neural architecture for structured information extraction on web documents. In *Proceedings of the 26th ACM SIGKDD International Conference on Knowledge Discovery & Data Mining*, pages 1092–1102.

Zhouhan Lin, Minwei Feng, Cicero Nogueira dos Santos, Mo Yu, Bing Xiang, Bowen Zhou, and Yoshua Bengio. 2017. A structured self-attentive sentence embedding. *arXiv preprint arXiv:1703.03130*.

Bing Liu, Robert Grossman, and Yanhong Zhai. 2003. Mining data records in web pages. In *Proceedings of the ninth ACM SIGKDD international conference on Knowledge discovery and data mining*, pages 601–606.

Xiaojing Liu, Feiyu Gao, Qiong Zhang, and Huasha Zhao. 2019. Graph convolution for multimodal information extraction from visually rich documents. *arXiv preprint arXiv:1903.11279*.

Colin Lockard, Prashant Shiralkar, and Xin Luna Dong. 2019. OpenCeres: When open information extraction meets the semi-structured web. In *Proceedings of the 2019 Conference of the North American Chapter of the Association for Computational Linguistics: Human Language Technologies, Volume 1 (Long and Short Papers)*, pages 3047–3056, Minneapolis, Minnesota. Association for Computational Linguistics.

Ling Luo, Zhihao Yang, Pei Yang, Yin Zhang, Lei Wang, Hongfei Lin, and Jian Wang. 2018. An attention-based bilstm-crf approach to document-level chemical named entity recognition. *Bioinformatics*, 34(8):1381–1388.

Weizhi Ma, Min Zhang, Yue Cao, Woojeong Jin, Chenyang Wang, Yiqun Liu, Shaoping Ma, and Xiang Ren. 2019. Jointly learning explainable rules for recommendation with knowledge graph. In *The World Wide Web Conference*, pages 1210–1221.

Ravina Mithe, Supriya Indalkar, and Nilam Divekar. 2013. Optical character recognition. *International journal of recent technology and engineering (IJRTE)*, 2(1):72–75.

Keval Morabia, Jatin Arora, and Tara Vijaykumar. 2020. Attention-based joint detection of object and semantic part. *arXiv preprint arXiv:2007.02419*.

Kevin Murphy, Antonio Torralba, Daniel Eaton, and William Freeman. 2006. Object detection and localization using local and global features. In *Toward Category-Level Object Recognition*, pages 382–400. Springer.

Ion Muslea, Steve Minton, and Craig Knoblock. 1998. Stalker: Learning extraction rules for semistructured, web-based information sources. In *Proceedings of AAAI-98 Workshop on AI and Information Integration*, pages 74–81. AAAI Press.

Joseph Redmon and Ali Farhadi. 2018. Yolov3: An incremental improvement. *arXiv preprint arXiv:1804.02767*.

Maryem Rhanoui, Mounia Mikram, Siham Yousfi, and Soukaina Barzali. 2019. A cnn-bilstm model for document-level sentiment analysis. *Machine Learning and Knowledge Extraction*, 1(3):832–847.

Mike Schuster and Kuldip K Paliwal. 1997. Bidirectional recurrent neural networks. *IEEE transactions on Signal Processing*, 45(11):2673–2681.

Kai Simon and Georg Lausen. 2005. Viper: augmenting automatic information extraction with visual perceptions. In *Proceedings of the 14th ACM international conference on Information and knowledge management*, pages 381–388.

Stephen Soderland. 1999. Learning information extraction rules for semi-structured and free text. *Machine learning*, 34(1-3):233–272.

Peter WJ Staar, Michele Dolfi, Christoph Auer, and Costas Bekas. 2018. Corpus conversion service: A machine learning platform to ingest documents at scale. In *Proceedings of the 24th ACM SIGKDD International Conference on Knowledge Discovery & Data Mining*, pages 774–782.

Jasper RR Uijlings, Koen EA Van De Sande, Theo Gevers, and Arnold WM Smeulders. 2013. Selective search for object recognition. *International journal of computer vision*, 104(2):154–171.

Srinivas Vadrevu, Saravanakumar Nagarajan, Fatih Gelgi, and Hasan Davulcu. 2005. Automated metadata and instance extraction from news web sites. In *The 2005 IEEE/WIC/ACM International Conference on Web Intelligence (WI'05)*, pages 38–41. IEEE.

Ashish Vaswani, Noam Shazeer, Niki Parmar, Jakob Uszkoreit, Llion Jones, Aidan N Gomez, Łukasz Kaiser, and Illia Polosukhin. 2017. Attention is all you need. In *Advances in neural information processing systems*, pages 5998–6008.

Petar Veličković, Guillem Cucurull, Arantxa Casanova, Adriana Romero, Pietro Lio, and Yoshua Bengio. 2017. Graph attention networks. *arXiv preprint arXiv:1710.10903*.

D Vishwanath, Rohit Rahul, Gunjan Sehgal, Arindam Chowdhury, Monika Sharma, Lovekesh Vig, Gautam Shroff, Ashwin Srinivasan, et al. 2018. Deep reader: Information extraction from document images via relation extraction and natural language. In *Asian Conference on Computer Vision*, pages 186–201. Springer.

Shanchan Wu, Jerry Liu, and Jian Fan. 2015. Automatic web content extraction by combination of learning and grouping. In *Proceedings of the 24th international conference on World Wide Web*, pages 1264–1274.

Quanzeng You, Hailin Jin, Zhaowen Wang, Chen Fang, and Jiebo Luo. 2016. Image captioning with semantic attention. In *Proceedings of the IEEE conference on computer vision and pattern recognition*, pages 4651–4659.

Yichao Zhou, Ying Sheng, Nguyen Vo, Nick Edmonds, and Sandeep Tata. 2021. Simplified dom trees for transferable attribute extraction from the web. *arXiv preprint arXiv:2101.02415*.

Jun Zhu, Zaiqing Nie, Ji-Rong Wen, Bo Zhang, and Wei-Ying Ma. 2005. 2d conditional random fields for web information extraction. In *Proceedings of the 22nd international conference on Machine learning*, pages 1044–1051.

Product Titles-to-Attributes As a Text-to-Text Task

Gilad Fuchs
eBay Research, Israel
gfuchs@ebay.com

Yoni Acriche
Bravado, USA
yoni@bravado.co

Abstract

Online marketplaces use attribute-value pairs, such as brand, size, size type, color, etc. to help define important and relevant facts about a listing. These help buyers to curate their search results using attribute filtering and overall create a richer experience. Although their critical importance for listings' discoverability, getting sellers to input tens of different attribute-value pairs per listing is costly and often results in missing information. This can later translate to the unnecessary removal of relevant listings from the search results when buyers are filtering by attribute values. In this paper we demonstrate using a Text-to-Text hierarchical multi-label ranking model framework to predict the most relevant attributes per listing, along with their expected values, using historic user behavioral data. This solution helps sellers by allowing them to focus on verifying information on attributes that are likely to be used by buyers, and thus, increase the expected recall for their listings. Specifically for eBay's case we show that using this model can improve the relevancy of the attribute extraction process by 33.2% compared to the current highly-optimized production system. Apart from the empirical contribution, the highly generalized nature of the framework presented in this paper makes it relevant for many high-volume search-driven websites.

1 Introduction

Many online marketplaces have new-listing forms that include both structured and unstructured input types to help sellers describe their listing[1]. While the unstructured part often includes free-text input boxes for title and description, a pictures upload option, etc., the structured part can include the selection of the listing category from a predefined list, or selecting specific attribute-value pairs (e.g. {"Brand":"Apple", "Color":"Black"}). Of the two, structured input often enables marketplaces a more streamline use of the data, since it requires less preprocessing and allows for more direct usage (via search results filters, etc.). On the flip-side, entering such data is more labor intensive for the sellers, and therefore, more expensive to get. This can also be intricate work for sellers since in most cases there are tens of different possible attribute names for every listing, with some attributes having more than one possible value.

To reduce the seller-inflicted cost of entering listing attribute values we set two solution guidelines: (a) sellers should focus on the top attributes that are expected to impact their listing discoverability. This aims to reduce the number of attributes for which seller attention is required and only focus on those which are likely to be used in the buyer-journey of their target audience. And (b), in an effort to further reduce friction, the marketplace should pre-populate a suggested value for each of these top attributes.

To identify the top attributes in a scalable manner we leveraged the rich historical data of buyer behavior on the eBay website. Like many other search-driven websites, eBay allows buyers to curate search results by applying filters on top of the initial results from the free-text-based query. Logging the filtering selections of buyers, alongside with their post-search actions, allows for an opportunity to learn what are the key attributes that buyers value when searching for the right result. For example, a common buyer behavior is to type a general description in the search box, like "handbag", and then to filter the results using more granular attributes, like "Material", etc. (Figure 1). Following this filtering step, the buyer might click on, and potentially purchase, a specific listing that was a part of the filtered results set. Mapping this buyer journey, from search to filtering and listing-click, allows to learn which attributes are most important for the discovery of every listing.

[1] or service; for simplicity we'll continue with the listing notation.

Proceedings of The Fifth Workshop on e-Commerce and NLP (ECNLP 5), pages 91 - 98
May 26, 2022 ©2022 Association for Computational Linguistics

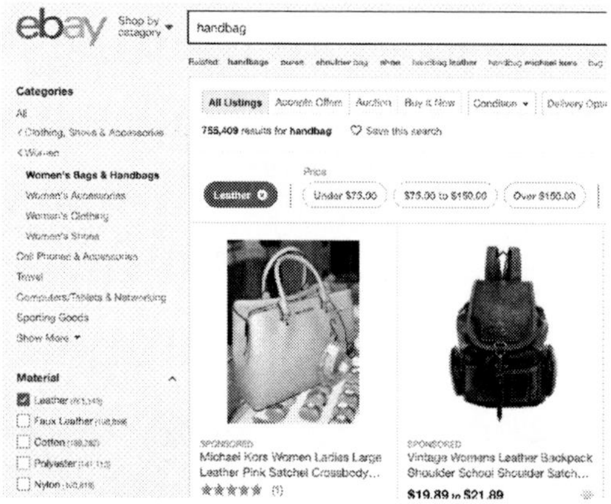

Figure 1: An example of a typical buyer search session. A buyer is searching for "handbag" in the search box (top) and further filters the results by selecting the attribute value "Leather" under "Material" (left).

From a modeling standpoint, to accommodate both of the solution guidelines above, the output set of the model should include the importance ranking of the top attributes and their expected value. As to the model input, in order for the solution to generalize across different downstream tasks, we need to pick a minimal viable data point that all listings have, but yet, that is highly informative. In our case that would be the listing title. Model design can be examined using different lenses; A supervised model based on the historical mapping between listing titles and multiple attribute-value pairs can be modeled as a multi-label text classification (MLTC) task. However, since there is a hierarchical relationship between the attributes and values (since each attribute has a finite list of possible values), the task can also be viewed as a hierarchical multi-label text classification (HMLTC) task. Last, since we care about the importance ranking of the attribute-value pairs, this can also be viewed as a ranking task. Recent Text-to-Text-driven approaches have shown to be highly valuable for various Natural Language Processing (NLP) tasks including MLTC and HMLTC (Nam et al., 2017; Yang et al., 2018; Chang et al., 2018; Li et al., 2018; Lin et al., 2018; Raffel et al., 2019). Inspired by these approaches, we demonstrate using a Text-to-Text framework in a HMLTC ranking task and compare it to other classification models.

Specifically in our case, the use of a Text-to-Text model approach is useful since it allows to produce multiple ranked hierarchical predictions, while separating between the probability score for the attributes and values. This introduces further flexibility to the solution (beyond the scope of the above guidelines) by allowing to report high impacting attributes even if we are uncertain about their expected attribute values. Furthermore, in comparison to approaches such as Named Entity Recognition (NER), a Text-to-Text model does not require the reported top attribute values to exist in the input title. This is useful since sellers are not always mentioning the most valuable attribute values in the listing title. Last, from an empirical standpoint, the Text-to-Text models we trained almost always outperformed models from other approaches (see section 4.2).

To conclude, in this work we suggest a scalable and automatic method for using listing titles to identify the most valuable set of attribute-value pairs by learning from the buyers' filtering behavior. In the next section we describe related work in the field of attribute-value extraction and hierarchical classification tasks. In the following section we describe our data collection methodology and the training procedures used for the four models that we trained. This is followed by a quantitative comparison of the results of the models, and a qualitative evaluation of the results of our best performing one. We conclude by discussing the tradeoffs of our current approach, and describe our plans for future work.

2 Related Work

Various methods are used to automatically extract attribute-value pairs from product-related text. This ranges from manual rules and regular expressions (Petrovski et al., 2014) to more advanced modern learning algorithms (Ghani et al., 2006; Kannan et al., 2011; de Bakker et al., 2013; Melli, 2014; Joshi et al., 2015; Ristoski and Mika, 2016; More, 2016; Petrovski and Bizer, 2017; Majumder et al., 2018; Charron et al., 2016). In contrast to our work, these methods are focusing on extracting the most complete set of attribute-value pairs, or limited to only attribute values which appear explicitly in the product-related text. Apart from (Charron et al., 2016), non of these works have leveraged data from historical user interaction with the attribute-value pairs.

Hierarchical classification has been of wide interest both in computer vision applications and text related tasks. Early work has been focusing on flattening the labels (Cai and Hofmann, 2004; Hayete and Bienkowska, 2005) or on training multiple local classifiers, where the number of classifiers is dependent on the depth of the label hierarchy (Koller and Sahami, 1997; Sun and Lim, 2001; Cesa-Bianchi et al., 2006). More recent studies aimed to train a single neural network which can learn the label hierarchy complexity (Johnson and Zhang, 2015; Peng et al., 2018; Mao et al., 2019), while others combined both a single global network and multiple local classifiers (Wehrmann et al., 2018). Most recently, several works demonstrated that sequence-to-sequence (Seq2Seq) networks are a promising representation for hierarchical text classification tasks (Nam et al., 2017; Lin et al., 2018). However, less focus was given to using Seq2Seq for the ranking of multiple hierarchical label data structures, which are commonly being used, especially in online marketplaces.

3 Methodology

3.1 Datasets

Our training dataset includes information from two major eBay verticals - "Electronics" and "Fashion", where search-filtering activity is most frequent. The data includes roughly 10M and 3M random entities from Fashion and Electronics (respectively), all from the eBay US website. Each training entity includes a listing title and one matching attribute-value pair which was previously used in a single search filtering session to discover that listing. Since the distribution of attribute-value pairs has a long-tail, we reduced the complexity of the task by truncating the data to include only the top 800 most frequent combinations. Doing so, we kept 90% of all of the filtering activity done by buyers (which is considered sufficient coverage for our use case). We used 5% of the data for validation and and model selection, and an additional 5% for test. For non-hierarchical classification experiments we have concatenated attribute-value pairs to a single token (e.g. {"Color":"Black"} was transformed to "Color:Black"). For Seq2Seq hierarchical classification, we kept the pairs as two separated tokens (e.g. "Color Black"). Separating the tokens allows the Seq2Seq model to natively perform hierarchical classification, as the Seq2Seq decoder's predictions are dependent on the previous predicted tokens (e.g. in case the attribute prediction token is "Color" the next token prediction is likely to be a color name, such as "Black"). All tokens in multi-token attribute names or values were concatenated with an underscore as a delimiter. As duplications in the training set represent a frequent, and therefore more important, listing discovery pattern, the data was not deduplicated in any way. For example, the title "Color Clash 100% Genuine Leather Snake Ladies Handbag Tote Shoulder Bag" might appear 20 times in the training data, out of which 12 times it will be coupled with the attribute-value pair {"Material":"Leather"}, 6 times with {"Style":"Tote"} and only 2 times with {"Size":"Large"}. The listing titles dataset was pre-processed by transforming the tokens to lowercase and removing known stopwords and non-alphanumeric characters.

3.2 Model Training

For the Text-to-Text approach we trained a Convolution Neural Network (CNN) Seq2Seq model (Gehring et al., 2017) via the Fairseq framework (Ott et al., 2019). For this we used a CNN architecture, following (Gehring et al., 2017), which consists an embedding layer, positional embedding layer, an encoder with 4 convolutional layers, a decoder with 3 convolutional layers and a kernel width of 3. The output of the each encoder convolutional layer is transformed by a non-linear gated linear units (GLU) (Dauphin et al., 2016) with the residual connections linking between the GLU blocks and the convolutional blocks. Each decoder GLU output undergoes a dot-product based attention with the last encoder GLU block output (see also (Gehring et al., 2017) for more details). Training was done with learning rate of 0.25, gradient clipping (clip-norm) of 0.1, dropout of 0.2, maximum number of tokens in a batch (max-tokens) of 4000 and max number of epochs of 15, with a Nesterov Accelerated Gradient (NAG) optimizer (NESTEROV, 1983) on a single GPU. Prior to training, pre-processing was done with "fairseq-preprocess" to build a vocabulary and binarize the data. For predictions, beam search size was set to 5. We trained two versions of the Seq2Seq models - one with attribute-value labels flattened to a single token (Seq2Seq-single), and the other where we kept their hierarchical structure (Seq2Seq-hierarchical), as described in section 3.1 above. Both versions were trained with the same hyper-parameters.

We tested our Text-to-Text modeling approach for attributes prediction against BERT and ULMFiT models, which have both been shown to be highly beneficial for multiple text classification tasks (Howard and Ruder, 2018; Devlin et al.,

2018). Apart from their past success, we also selected BERT and ULMFiT because they allowed us to test two different types of pre-training and fine-tuning approaches, as described below. For the multi-classification BERT model (Devlin et al., 2018), we used the FastBert library[2] which is based on HuggingFace (Wolf et al., 2019). The model that we fine-tuned was bert-base-uncased which includes 110 million parameters, 12 encoder layers consisting of 12 attention heads per layer and 768 hidden units. Fine-tuning was done for a maximum of 3 epochs with a batch size of 16, learning rate of 5e-5, a maximum sequence length of 128, a LAMB optimizer (You et al., 2019; Lan et al., 2019) and using 4 GPUs.

Next, for the multi-classification ULMFiT (Howard and Ruder, 2018) we used eBay's title corpus to fine-tune an English language model (LM) with an AWD-LSTM architecture (Merity et al., 2017a), which is an LSTM model with tuned dropout hyper-parameters that consists of an embedding size of 400, 3 layers and 1150 hidden activations per layer which were pre-trained on the Wikitext-103 dataset (Merity et al., 2017b) and downloaded from fast.ai[3]. The LM fine-tuning was done using the same data that is described in section 3.1, with a batch size of 64, a dropout set to 0.5, for 2 epochs using one cycle policy (Smith and Topin, 2019) and with a maximum learning rate of 1e-2 and 1e-3 for each on a single GPU. Next, a classifier model was trained while using the fine-tuned LM as an encoder, with a batch size of 64, for 3 epochs on 4 GPUs, using one cycle policy, with a discriminative layer training and gradual unfreezing (Howard and Ruder, 2018). During the first epoch only the last layer was fine-tuned, with a maximum learning rate of 1e-2. For the second epoch we fine-tuned the last two layer groups, with a maximum learning rate ranging between 2.5e-3 and 5e-3, and for the last epoch we fine-tuned all of the layers with a maximum learning rate ranging between 2e-5 and 2e-3. The labels for both BERT and ULMFiT were represented as a single token (see section 3.1 above). We also trained a multi-classification model for both, instead of a multi-label one, since we saw that the latter performed significantly worse.

All models were trained on data from eBay's Electronics and Fashion verticals as described at Section 3.1.

[2]https://github.com/kaushaltrivedi/fast-bert

[3]https://docs.fast.ai/index.html

4 Results

4.1 Evaluation Metrics

As commonly used in similar ranking tasks, we computed Precision at k (Prec@k) and normalized Discounted Cumulative Gain at k (nDCG@k or N@k) for model evaluation. Prec@k is defined as follows:

$$Prec@k = \frac{1}{k}\sum_{l=1}^{k} y_{\mathrm{rank(l)}}$$

Where rank(l) is the index of the l-th highest predicted label and $y \in \{0, 1\}^L$ is the true binary vector. nDCG@k is defined as follows:

$$DCG@k = \sum_{i=1}^{k} \frac{rel_{\mathrm{i}}}{log(i+1)}$$

$$iDCG@k = \sum_{i=1}^{|REL_{\mathrm{k}}|} \frac{rel_{\mathrm{i}}}{log(i+1)}$$

$$nDCG@k = \frac{DCG@k}{iDCG@k}$$

Where $\mathrm{rel_i}$ is the relevance of the result at position i and $\mathrm{REL_k}$ represents the list of relevant documents (ordered by their relevance) in the corpus up to position k. The relevance score of each attribute-value pair per listing title is defined as the number of times it was used by buyers to filter the results, prior of clicking that specific listing.

4.2 Quantitative Evaluation

To compare the performance of the different models we computed the ranking accuracy of each using historic attribute-value pairs that were used by buyers to filter their results, prior of clicking a specific listing. As seen in Table 1, the Seq2Seq-hierarchical model outperformed the other models in most of the test criteria. Interestingly, both of the Seq2Seq models (single and hierarchical) outperformed BERT and ULMFiT in almost all of the metrics, which demonstrates the advantage of using a Text-to-Text frameworks in both hierarchical and non-hierarchical learning tasks.

In theory, the results from Table 1 could be purely due to better attribute value prediction by the Seq2Seq-hierarchical model, and not necessarily because of better attribute ranking. Therefore, to further examine the robustness of these results, we

Table 1: Model performance measured by Precision@k (P@k) and nDCG@k (N@k) comparison of the four models - ULMFiT (ULM), BERT, Seq2Seq-single (S2S) and Seq2Seq-hierarchical (S2S-hier) for the Electronics (Elec) and Fashion (Fash) verticals. Best results are marked in bold.

Data	Metric	BERT	ULM	S2S	S2S -hier
Elec	P@1	54	59.4	61.6	**62.7**
	P@3	33.3	37.2	39.4	**40.1**
	P@5	24.4	26.9	28.7	**29.2**
	N@1	50.6	56.2	58.1	**59.5**
	N@3	56.7	63.4	67.2	**68.3**
	N@5	60.5	66.7	71.1	**72.1**
Fash	P@1	61	62.8	62.8	**63.1**
	P@3	33.8	35.4	36.2	**36.3**
	P@5	23	24.1	**25.2**	**25.2**
	N@1	59.4	61.2	61.2	**61.5**
	N@3	64.7	67.7	68.8	**69**
	N@5	67.7	70.9	**72.6**	**72.6**

disconnected the ranking evaluation from the value prediction one, and tested the above models just on attribute ranking. To conduct this comparison we split the models' concatenated attribute-value predictions to attribute and attribute value predictions (i.e. {"Color:Black"} was split to "color" and "black") and re-computed the evaluation metrics only on the former. As seen in Table 2, the models' performance-ranking is overall consistent with previous experiments, with the Seq2Seq-hierarchical model also outperforming for the attribute ranking task.

In addition, from a pure technical perspective, Seq2Seq was the fastest model to train (x15 faster than BERT and x5 faster than ULMFiT), did not require any pre-trained models, and consisted of

Table 2: Model performance comparison solely for the attributes ranking task. Best results are marked in bold.

Dataset	Metric	BERT Attr	ULM Attr	S2S Attr	S2S -hier Attr
Elec	P@1	92.4	94	93	**94.6**
	P@3	74	76	76.2	**78**
	P@5	51.8	53.8	56	**57.8**
	N@1	78.9	81.9	79.4	**82.1**
	N@3	82.8	85.2	84.3	**86.6**
	N@5	83.1	85.6	85.7	**87.8**
Fash	P@1	95.7	95.5	95.5	**96**
	P@3	61.9	61.2	63.2	**63.6**
	P@5	40.1	40.2	43.2	**43.5**
	N@1	86.2	85.9	87.2	**88**
	N@3	88.3	88.5	89.5	**90.3**
	N@5	87.7	88.4	90.2	**90.7**

only a single training step (unlike ULMFiT, which also required an LM fine-tune step).

To get a sense of the magnitude of impact that the Seq2Seq-hierarchical model could have on eBay's on-site experience, we compared our results to those from eBay's Attribute Extraction Service (AES). AES is a production system that has been highly optimized over the years, and is in charge of automatically extracting attribute-value pairs from titles that sellers provide. Currently it is mostly reliant on extensively curated rules that got added and optimized over the years. To compare the performance of the two methods we used around 15K attribute-value pairs that were used by buyers to filter search results and to discover a specific listing from the Electronics and Fashion verticals. For each we computed whether the attribute extraction method could automatically provide the relevant attribute-value given only the listing's title. This count was later divided by the number of attribute-value pairs to compute a percentage. As seen in Table 3, Seq2Seq-hierarchical led to an overall 33.2% improvement in relevant attribute-value extraction compared to AES.

Table 3: A comparison between eBay's current production system (AES) and the Seq2Seq-hierarchical (S2S-hier) model for the task of relevant attribute-value extraction. The number of attribute-value pairs which were used for the evaluation is denoted as N. For each method we show the percentage of cases that the relevant attribute-value pairs were extracted correctly (as defined by buyer behaviour).

Dataset	N	AES	S2S-hier
Electronics	10,289	58.8%	**71.9%**
Fashion	4,752	40.2%	**67.4%**
Total	15,041	52.9%	**70.5%**

4.3 Qualitative Evaluation

Since Seq2Seq-hierarchical outperformed the other models (Table 1), we focused our qualitative evaluation only on its predictions. Table 4 shows examples of the top predictions of five different listings, ordered by the model likelihood score (descending order).

As seen in Table 4, {"Brand":"Ray-Ban"} was only the 3rd most important attribute-value pair picked by the model for the title "Ray-Ban G-15 Aviator Black Frame Black Classic 58mm". This can be counterintuitive from a domain expertise standpoint, since the latter is clearly a

Table 4: Example of Seq2Seq-hierarchical prediction, including values which are not explicitly mentioned in the title and multi-values attributes. Values are ordered by their importance rank.

Title	Predictions
Ray-Ban G-15 Aviator Black Frame Black Classic	{"Frame Color":"Black", "Lens Color": "Black", "Brand": "Ray-Ban"}
Asus Strix Gaming LGA1151 DDR4 Motherboard	{"Form Factor": "microATX", "Compatible CPU Brand": "Intel"}
DJI Phantom 4 Aerial UAV Drone Quadcopter	{"Camera": "Included", "Features": "4K HD Video Recording"}
Nike Air Max Shoes Men's Size 7-9	{"US Shoe Size (men's)": [8, 8.5, 9, 7.5, 7]}
Men's Slim Fit Coat Jean Denim Jacket Size S-XL	{"Size (men's)": ["M", "L", "XL", "S"]}

more differential attribute-value pair for the category of sunglasses than, for example, {"Frame Color":"Black"}, which was picked first. However, looking at a sample of the search queries that were prior to the filtering steps (not shown here), we see that 93% of them already contained some variation of the term "Ray-Ban" (e.g. "rayban sunglasses", "ray ban sunglasses aviator", "ray-ban aviator"). Therefore most of the search engine's out-of-the-box results already included "Ray-Ban" branded sunglasses, which mitigated the need to further filter by brand. In contrast, only 2% of the queries mentioned the color "black", which explains the frequent buyer behavior of further filtering the results by color after seeing the search results (which included sunglasses from various colors). Such ranking results are in-line with our solution guideline to identify the top attributes that are expected to be used in the listing's buyer-discovery-journey, and therefore, help maximize the listing's chances to be discovered.

In Table 4 we provide further prediction examples which show that our Text-to-Text model does not require the reported top attribute values to be included in the input title. In addition, we evaluated the model's predictions in cases where attributes can include multiple values, like with 'size', and show that the model successfully extracts all of the relevant values from the ranges that appear in the titles. Note that the different likelihood prediction for each size value can serve as proxy to its popularity among buyers.

5 Conclusion

In this paper we demonstrate using filtering behavior data to predict the most relevant listing attribute-value pairs, and the superiority of using a Text-to-Text approach for modeling a hierarchical multi-label text classification (HMLTC) task that combines ranking. We identify several key advantages of this solution framework: First, acquiring the training data we use is a scalable and inexpensive process which does not require manual labor. Therefore, the volume of data collected in high-volume websites is likely to be sufficient for training deep-learning-based models such as Seq2Seq. Second, unlike methods such as NER, using a Text-to-Text approach enables to identify attribute-value pairs that do not necessarily exist in the title, to extract multiple values per attribute (Table 4) and to separately analyze the importance of every possible attribute-value pair. Third, as to the choice of hierarchical modeling, this allows us to separately analyze the likelihood probabilities of the expected attributes and values, which further generalizes the model for additional downstream tasks.

As for classifiers performance, the Seq2Seq models provided better results for most metrics compared to BERT and ULMFiT. Unlike the latter two, the Seq2Seq models didn't use a Transfer Learning approach that leverages a pre-trained Language Models. We suspect that the relatively short length of listing titles (12 tokens on average), combined with the unique jargon in eBay's data, which is hard to fully capture in the fine-tune process, might have negatively impacted the performance of BERT and ULMFiT.

Regardless to the classifier of choice, we keep in mind that the model's attribute ranking is clearly affected by the set of filtering options that were presented to the buyers on the site, and thus, cannot find attribute pairs that have not been historically used for filtering. Therefore, to avoid a closed feedback loop scenario, we would avoid using the model's attribute ranking results as an input to decide these filtering options. Also, to further increase the quality of the attribute ranking we can use a training data that consists of a sample of buyers that were served with a random (or partly random) list of filtering options. Nonetheless, even without this sample, the model can still provide sellers with meaningful information about their potential buyers' current attribute priority ranking.

References

Lijuan Cai and Thomas Hofmann. 2004. Hierarchical document categorization with support vector machines. In *Proceedings of the Thirteenth ACM International Conference on Information and Knowledge Management*, CIKM '04, page 78–87, New York, NY, USA. Association for Computing Machinery.

Nicolò Cesa-Bianchi, Claudio Gentile, and Luca Zaniboni. 2006. Hierarchical classification: Combining bayes with svm. In *Proceedings of the 23rd International Conference on Machine Learning*, ICML '06, page 177–184, New York, NY, USA. Association for Computing Machinery.

Wei-Cheng Chang, Hsiang-Fu Yu, Inderjit S. Dhillon, and Yiming Yang. 2018. Secseq: Semantic coding for sequence-to-sequence based extreme multi-label classification.

Bruno Charron, Yu Hirate, David Purcell, and Martin Rezk. 2016. Extracting semantic information for e-commerce. pages 273–290.

Yann N. Dauphin, Angela Fan, Michael Auli, and David Grangier. 2016. Language modeling with gated convolutional networks.

Marnix de Bakker, Flavius Frasincar, and Damir Vandic. 2013. A hybrid model words-driven approach for web product duplicate detection. In *CAiSE*.

Jacob Devlin, Ming-Wei Chang, Kenton Lee, and Kristina Toutanova. 2018. Bert: Pre-training of deep bidirectional transformers for language understanding.

Jonas Gehring, Michael Auli, David Grangier, Denis Yarats, and Yann N Dauphin. 2017. Convolutional sequence to sequence learning. In *Proc. of ICML*.

Rayid Ghani, Katharina Probst, Yan Liu, Marko Krema, and Andrew Fano. 2006. Text mining for product attribute extraction. *SIGKDD Explor. Newsl.*, 8(1):41–48.

Boris Hayete and Jadwiga Bienkowska. 2005. Gotrees: Predicting go associations from protein domain composition using decision trees. *Pacific Symposium on Biocomputing. Pacific Symposium on Biocomputing*, 10:127–38.

Jeremy Howard and Sebastian Ruder. 2018. Universal language model fine-tuning for text classification. In *Proceedings of the 56th Annual Meeting of the Association for Computational Linguistics (Volume 1: Long Papers)*, pages 328–339, Melbourne, Australia. Association for Computational Linguistics.

Rie Johnson and Tong Zhang. 2015. Effective use of word order for text categorization with convolutional neural networks. In *Proceedings of the 2015 Conference of the North American Chapter of the Association for Computational Linguistics: Human Language Technologies*, pages 103–112, Denver, Colorado. Association for Computational Linguistics.

Mahesh Joshi, Ethan Hart, Mirko Vogel, and Jean-David Ruvini. 2015. Distributed word representations improve NER for e-commerce. In *Proceedings of the 1st Workshop on Vector Space Modeling for Natural Language Processing*, pages 160–167, Denver, Colorado. Association for Computational Linguistics.

Anitha Kannan, Inmar E. Givoni, Rakesh Agrawal, and Ariel Fuxman. 2011. Matching unstructured product offers to structured product specifications. In *Proceedings of the 17th ACM SIGKDD International Conference on Knowledge Discovery and Data Mining*, KDD '11, page 404–412, New York, NY, USA. Association for Computing Machinery.

Daphne Koller and Mehran Sahami. 1997. Hierarchically classifying documents using very few words. In *Proceedings of the Fourteenth International Conference on Machine Learning*, ICML '97, page 170–178, San Francisco, CA, USA. Morgan Kaufmann Publishers Inc.

Zhenzhong Lan, Mingda Chen, Sebastian Goodman, Kevin Gimpel, Piyush Sharma, and Radu Soricut. 2019. Albert: A lite bert for self-supervised learning of language representations.

Wei Li, Xuancheng Ren, Damai Dai, Yunfang Wu, Houfeng Wang, and Xu Sun. 2018. Sememe prediction: Learning semantic knowledge from unstructured textual wiki descriptions.

Junyang Lin, Qi Su, Pengcheng Yang, Shuming Ma, and Xu Sun. 2018. Semantic-unit-based dilated convolution for multi-label text classification.

Bodhisattwa Prasad Majumder, Aditya Subramanian, Abhinandan Krishnan, Shreyansh Gandhi, and Ajinkya More. 2018. Deep recurrent neural networks for product attribute extraction in ecommerce.

Yuning Mao, Jingjing Tian, Jiawei Han, and Xiang Ren. 2019. Hierarchical text classification with reinforced label assignment. In *Proceedings of the 2019 Conference on Empirical Methods in Natural Language Processing and the 9th International Joint Conference on Natural Language Processing (EMNLP-IJCNLP)*, pages 445–455, Hong Kong, China. Association for Computational Linguistics.

Gabor Melli. 2014. Shallow semantic parsing of product offering titles (for better automatic hyperlink insertion). In *Proceedings of the 20th ACM SIGKDD International Conference on Knowledge Discovery and Data Mining*, KDD '14, page 1670–1678, New York, NY, USA. Association for Computing Machinery.

Stephen Merity, Nitish Shirish Keskar, and Richard Socher. 2017a. Regularizing and optimizing lstm language models.

Stephen Merity, Caiming Xiong, James Bradbury, and Richard Socher. 2017b. Pointer sentinel mixture models.

Ajinkya More. 2016. Attribute extraction from product titles in ecommerce. *CoRR*, abs/1608.04670.

Jinseok Nam, Eneldo Loza Mencía, Hyunwoo J Kim, and Johannes Fürnkranz. 2017. Maximizing subset accuracy with recurrent neural networks in multi-label classification. In I. Guyon, U. V. Luxburg, S. Bengio, H. Wallach, R. Fergus, S. Vishwanathan, and R. Garnett, editors, *Advances in Neural Information Processing Systems 30*, pages 5413–5423. Curran Associates, Inc.

Y. E. NESTEROV. 1983. A method for solving the convex programming problem with convergence rate $o(1/k^2)$. *Dokl. Akad. Nauk SSSR*, 269:543–547.

Myle Ott, Sergey Edunov, Alexei Baevski, Angela Fan, Sam Gross, Nathan Ng, David Grangier, and Michael Auli. 2019. fairseq: A fast, extensible toolkit for sequence modeling. In *Proceedings of the 2019 Conference of the North American Chapter of the Association for Computational Linguistics (Demonstrations)*, pages 48–53, Minneapolis, Minnesota. Association for Computational Linguistics.

Hao Peng, Jianxin Li, Yu He, Yaopeng Liu, Mengjiao Bao, Lihong Wang, Yangqiu Song, and Qiang Yang. 2018. Large-scale hierarchical text classification with recursively regularized deep graph-cnn. In *Proceedings of the 2018 World Wide Web Conference*, WWW '18, page 1063–1072, Republic and Canton of Geneva, CHE. International World Wide Web Conferences Steering Committee.

Petar Petrovski and Christian Bizer. 2017. Extracting attribute-value pairs from product specifications on the web. In *Proceedings of the International Conference on Web Intelligence*, WI '17, page 558–565, New York, NY, USA. Association for Computing Machinery.

Petar Petrovski, Volha Bryl, and Christian Bizer. 2014. Learning regular expressions for the extraction of product attributes from e-commerce microdata. In *Proceedings of the Second International Conference on Linked Data for Information Extraction - Volume 1267*, LD4IE'14, page 45–54, Aachen, DEU. CEUR-WS.org.

Colin Raffel, Noam Shazeer, Adam Roberts, Katherine Lee, Sharan Narang, Michael Matena, Yanqi Zhou, Wei Li, and Peter J. Liu. 2019. Exploring the limits of transfer learning with a unified text-to-text transformer.

Petar Ristoski and Peter Mika. 2016. Enriching product ads with metadata from html annotations. In *Proceedings of the 13th International Conference on The Semantic Web. Latest Advances and New Domains - Volume 9678*, page 151–167, Berlin, Heidelberg. Springer-Verlag.

Leslie N. Smith and Nicholay Topin. 2019. Super-convergence: very fast training of neural networks using large learning rates. In *Artificial Intelligence and Machine Learning for Multi-Domain Operations Applications*, volume 11006, pages 369 – 386. International Society for Optics and Photonics, SPIE.

Aixin Sun and Ee-Peng Lim. 2001. Hierarchical text classification and evaluation. In *Proceedings of the 2001 IEEE International Conference on Data Mining*, ICDM '01, page 521–528, USA. IEEE Computer Society.

Jonatas Wehrmann, Ricardo Cerri, and Rodrigo Barros. 2018. Hierarchical multi-label classification networks. In *Proceedings of the 35th International Conference on Machine Learning*, volume 80 of *Proceedings of Machine Learning Research*, pages 5075–5084, Stockholmsmässan, Stockholm Sweden. PMLR.

Thomas Wolf, Lysandre Debut, Victor Sanh, Julien Chaumond, Clement Delangue, Anthony Moi, Pierric Cistac, Tim Rault, R'emi Louf, Morgan Funtowicz, and Jamie Brew. 2019. Huggingface's transformers: State-of-the-art natural language processing. *ArXiv*, abs/1910.03771.

Pengcheng Yang, Xu Sun, Wei Li, Shuming Ma, Wei Wu, and Houfeng Wang. 2018. Sgm: Sequence generation model for multi-label classification.

Yang You, Jing Li, Sashank Reddi, Jonathan Hseu, Sanjiv Kumar, Srinadh Bhojanapalli, Xiaodan Song, James Demmel, Kurt Keutzer, and Cho-Jui Hsieh. 2019. Large batch optimization for deep learning: Training bert in 76 minutes.

Product Answer Generation from Heterogeneous Sources: A New Benchmark and Best Practices

Xiaoyu Shen[1], **Gianni Barlacchi**[1], **Marco del Tredici**[1], **Weiwei Cheng**[1]
Adria de Gispert[1] **and Bill Birne**[1,2]
[1]Amazon Alexa AI
[2]Univeristy of Cambridge
{gyouu, gbarlac, mttredic, weiweic, agispert, willbyrn}@amazon.com

Abstract

It is of great value to answer product questions based on heterogeneous information sources available on web product pages, e.g., semi-structured attributes, text descriptions, user-provided contents, etc. However, these sources have different structures and writing styles, which poses challenges for (1) evidence ranking, (2) source selection, and (3) answer generation. In this paper, we build *a benchmark with annotations for both evidence selection and answer generation covering 6 information sources*. Based on this benchmark, we conduct a comprehensive study and present a set of best practices. We show that all sources are important and contribute to answering questions. Handling all sources within one single model can produce comparable confidence scores across sources and combining multiple sources for training always helps, even for sources with totally different structures. We further propose a novel data augmentation method to iteratively create training samples for answer generation, which achieves close-to-human performance with only a few thousand annotations. Finally, we perform an in-depth error analysis of model predictions and highlight the challenges for future research.

1 Introduction

Automatic answer generation for product-related questions is a hot topic in e-commerce applications. Previous approaches have leveraged information from sources like product specifications (Lai et al., 2018a, 2020), descriptions (Cui et al., 2017; Gao et al., 2019) or user reviews (McAuley and Yang, 2016; Yu et al., 2018; Zhang et al., 2019) to answer product questions. However, these works produce answers from only a single source. While a few works have utilized information from multiple sources (Cui et al., 2017; Gao et al., 2019; Feng et al., 2021), they lack a reliable benchmark and have to resort to noisy labels or small-scaled human evaluation (Zhang et al., 2020; Gao et al., 2021). Furthermore, almost none of them make use of pretrained Transformer-based models, which are the current state-of-the-art (SOTA) across NLP tasks (Devlin et al., 2019; Clark et al., 2020).

In this work, we present a large-scale benchmark dataset for answering product questions from 6 heterogeneous sources and study best practices to overcome three major challenges: (1) evidence ranking, which finds most relevant information from each of the heterogeneous sources; (2) source selection, which chooses the most appropriate data source to answer each question; and (3) answer generation, which produces a fluent, natural-sounding answer based on the relevant information. It is necessary since the selected relevant information may not be written to naturally answer a question, and therefore not suitable for a conversational setting.

Most published research on product question answering is based on the AmazonQA dataset (McAuley and Yang, 2016), which takes the community question-answers (CQAs) as the ground truth. This leads to several problems. (1) CQAs, even the top-voted ones, are quite noisy. Many are generic answers or irrelevant jokes (Gao et al., 2021). (2) CQAs are based more on the opinion of the individual customer who wrote the answer rather than on accompanying sources such as product reviews and descriptions. As such, CQAs are not reliable references for judging the quality of answers generated from these sources (Gupta et al., 2019). (3) There are no annotations for assessing the relevance of the information across multiple data sources. This makes it difficult to evaluate the evidence ranker and generator separately. Some works collect annotations for evidence relevance, but only for a single source and with questions formulated post-hoc rather than naturally posed (Lai et al., 2018a; Xu et al., 2019). To address these shortcomings, we collect a benchmark dataset with the following features: (1) It provides clear annotations *for both evidence ranking and answer*

Proceedings of The Fifth Workshop on e-Commerce and NLP (ECNLP 5), pages 99 - 110
May 26, 2022 ©2022 Association for Computational Linguistics

generation, enabling us to perform in-depth evaluation of these two components separately. (2) We consider a *mix of 6 heterogeneous sources*, ranging from semi-structured specifications (jsons) to free sentences and (3) It represents *naturally-occurring questions*, unlike previous collections that elicited questions by showing answers explicitly.

As sources differ in their volume and contents, collecting training data covering all sources of natural questions and answers is challenging. To get enough positive training signals for each source, we propose filtering community questions based on the model score of a pretrained QA ranker. Questions are only passed for annotation when the confidence scores of top-1 evidence lie within some certain range. This greatly reduces annotation effort by removing most unanswerable questions.

After collecting the data, we apply SOTA Transformer-based models for evidence ranking and answer generation, and present a set of data augmentation and domain adaptation techniques to improve the performance. We show that pretraining the model on the AmazonQA corpus can provide a better initialization and improve the ranker significantly. For evidence ranking, we apply question generation with consistency filtering (Alberti et al., 2019) to obtain large amounts of synthetic QA pairs from unannotated product sources. For answer generation, we propose a novel data augmentation algorithm that creates training examples iteratively. By first training on this augmented data and then finetuning on the human annotations, the model performance can be further enhanced.

As for the model design, we homogenize all sources by reducing them to the same form of input which is fed into a unified pretrained Transformer model, similarly to many recent works of leveraging a unified system for various input formats (Oguz et al., 2020; Su et al., 2020; Komeili et al., 2021). We show that combining all sources within a single framework outperforms handling individual sources separately and that training signals from different answer sources can benefit each other, even for sources with totally different structures. We also show that the unified approach is able to produce comparable scores across different sources which allows for simply using the model prediction score for data source selection, an approach that outperforms more complex cascade-based selection strategies. The resulting system is able to find the correct evidence for 69% of the questions in our test set. For answer generation, 94.4% of the generated answers are faithful to the extracted evidence and 95.5% of them are natural-sounding.

Question: how much weight will it safely hold?

Source	Supporting Evidence	Relevance
Attribute	item_weight:{unit: pounds,value:2.2}	✖
Bullet Point	supports up to 115 pounds	✔
Description	weight limit: 115 lbs.	✔
OSP	if you're looking for an inexpensive way to change up ...	✖
CQA	we put ours on a swingset.	✖
Review	it is sturdy and well made.	✖

Annotated Answer: it can support up to 115 pounds.

Table 1: Annotation example. **Relevance annotation**: Given one question and evidence from heterogeneous sources, judge if each one is relevant to the question. **Answer elicitation**: annotators produce a natural-sounding answer given the question and the evidence that was marked as relevant.

In summary, our contributions are four-fold: (1) We create a benchmark collections of natural product questions and answers from 6 heterogeneous sources covering 309,347 question-evidence pairs, annotated for both evidence ranking and answer generation. This collection will be released as open source. (2) We show that training signals from different sources can complement each other. Our system can handle diverse sources without source-specific design. (3) We propose a novel data augmentation method to iteratively create training samples for answer generation, which achieves close-to-human performance with only a few thousand annotations and (4) We perform an extensive study of design decisions for input representation, data augmentation, model design and source selection. Error analysis and human evaluation are conducted to suggest directions for future work.

2 Benchmark test set collection

We begin by explaining how we collect a benchmark test set for this problem. The benchmark collection is performed in 4 phases: question sourcing, supporting evidence collection, relevance annotation, and answer elicitation. An annotation example is shown in Table 1.

Question sourcing To create a question set that is diverse and representative of natural user questions, we consider two methods of question sourcing. The first method collects questions through Amazon Mechanical Turk, whereby annotators are shown a product image and title and instructed to ask 3 questions about it to help them make hypothetical purchase decisions. This mimics a scenario in which customers see a product for the first time, and questions collected in this way are often general and exploratory in nature. The second method samples questions from the AmazonQA corpus. These are real customer questions posted in the community forum and tend to be more specific and detailed, since they are usually asked after users have browsed, or even purchased, a product. We then filter duplicated and poorly-formed questions. This yields 914 questions from AmazonQA and 1853 questions from Mturk. These are combined to form the final question set.

Collecting Supporting Evidence We gather "supporting evidence" from 6 heterogeneous sources: (1) Attributes: Product attributes in json format extracted from the Amazon product database [1]. (2) Bullet points: Product summaries from the product page. (3) Descriptions: Product descriptions from the manufacturer and Amazon. (4) On-site-publishing (OSP): Publications about products (for example here). (5) CQA: Top-voted community answers. Answers directly replying to questions in our question set are discarded and (6) Review: User reviews written for the product.

Relevance Annotation Annotators are presented with a question about a product and are instructed to mark all the items of supporting evidence that are relevant to answering the product question. Such evidence is defined as relevant *if it implies an answer, but it does not need to directly address or answer a question*. For evidence items from source 1, we directly present the attribute json to annotators. For sources 2∼6, we split the evidence into sentences and present each sentence as a separate item to be considered. There can be a very large number of CQA and Reviews for each product. As manual annotation of these would be impractical, we annotate only the top 40 and 20 evidence from each collection, respectively, as determined by a deep passage ranker pretrained on general-domain QA. Each item of evidence is inspected by 3 annotators and is marked as relevant if supported by at least two of them. In this way, items of evidence are paired with questions for review by annotators. Overall, annotators have inspected 309,347 question-evidence pairs, of which 20,233 were marked as relevant.

[1]We select 320 unique attributes that have diverse structures and hierarchies without standard schema.

Source	#words	available	answerable	N/P
Attribute	5.84	100%	36.10%	22.88
Bullet	12.55	100%	24.95%	5.59
Desc	12.86	98.37%	38.59%	23.97
OSP	17.75	18.98%	4.54%	11.16
CQA	13.32	99.39%	70.61%	13.85
Review	18.37	95.64%	61.16%	2.28
93.72% questions are answerable from at least 1 source.				

Table 2: Benchmark statistics: average number of words per evidence (**#words**), percentage of questions for which the source is available (**available**), percentage of answerable questions (**answerable**) and the negative-positive ratio (**N/P**).

Answer Elicitation In the answer elicitation stage, annotators are presented with a question and an item of supporting evidence that has been marked as relevant. They are required to produce a *fluent, natural-sounding and well-formed* sentence (not short span) that *directly* answers the question. We sample 500 positive question-evidence pairs from each source for answer elicitation (if that many are available). The annotated answers are evaluated by another round of annotation to filter invalid ones. In the end, we obtain 2,319 question-evidence-answer triples for answer generation.

Table 2 shows the collection statistics. Availability differs across sources. Only 19% of questions have available OSP articles, but all products have corresponding Attributes and Bullet Points. 93.72% of questions are answerable from at least 1 out of the 6 sources, indicating these sources are valuable as a whole to address most user questions.

3 Training data collection

For training data collection, a complete annotation of each set of evidence is not necessary; we need only a rich set of contrastive examples. Therefore, we propose to select questions for annotation based on the confidence score of a pretrained ranker (the same ranker we used to select top evidence for CQA and review). We sample 50k community questions about products in the same domain as the testset. We first select questions whose top-1 item of supporting evidence returned by the pretrained ranker has a prediction score of > 0.8. In this way the selected questions have a good chance of being answerable from the available evidence and the approach should also yield enough positive samples from all sources to train the ranker. This selection step is crucial to ensure coverage of low-resource sources, like OSP, which otherwise might have zero positive samples. To avoid a selection process that is biased towards easy questions we further include questions whose top-1 evidence has a score within the range of 0.4∼0.6. Intuitively these questions will pose more of a challenge in ranking the evidence and their annotation should provide an informative signal.

From each out of the 6 sources, we sample 500 questions with prediction score > 0.8 and another 500 questions with scores in the range of $0.4 \sim 0.6$. For each question, we then annotate the top-5 (if available) evidence items returned by the pretrained ranker. This reduces annotation cost relative to the complete annotation that was done for the test set. The final dataset contains 6000 questions with 27,026 annotated question-evidence pairs being annotated, 6,667 of which were positive. We then submit the positive question-evidence pairs for answer elicitation. After filtering invalid annotations as was done for the benchmark collection, we obtain a set of 4,243 question-evidence-answer triples to train the answer generator. For both evidence ranking and answer generation, we split the collected data by 9:1 for train/validation.

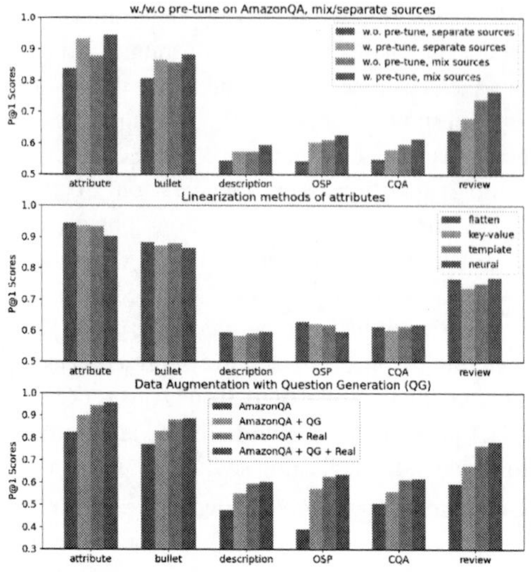

Figure 1: Ablation studies of evidence ranker. From up to down (1) effects of pre-tuning on AmazonQA, mix/separate sources, (2) effects of linearization methods of attributes, and (3) effects of data augmentation by question generation.

4 Model

4.1 Evidence Ranking

Evidence ranking aims to get the best evidence from each of the sources. We build our evidence ranker with the Electra-base model (Clark et al., 2020). The question and evidence are concatenated together and fed into the model. We flatten the json structured from the attribute source into a string before feeding it to the encoder, whereas we split evidence from other sources into natural sentences, so it can be encoded as plain text (training detail in appendix D). We present comparison studies in Figure 1 with the best model configuration. Due to space constraints we report only p@1 scores in Fig 1, with full results in appendix C.

Pre-tuning on AmazonQA Pre-tuning the evidence ranker on similar domains has shown to be important when limited in-domain training data is available (Hui and Berberich, 2017; Hazen et al., 2019; Garg et al., 2020; Hui et al., 2022). For our product-specific questions, the AmazonQA corpus is a natural option to pre-tune the model (Lai et al., 2018b). The corpus contains 1.4M question-answer pairs crawled from the CQA forum. We remove answers containing "I don't know" and "I'm not sure", and filter questions of more than 32 words and answers of more than 64 words. We construct negative evidence with answers to different questions for the same product. The filtered corpus contains 1,065,407 community questions for training. In the training stage, we first finetune the Electra-base model on the filtered AmazonQA corpus and then finetune on our collected training data. As can be seen, *pre-tuning on the AmazonQA corpus improves the p@1 on all sources*. The conclusion holds for both training on mixed sources and individual sources separately.

Mixed sources vs split sources We investigate whether different sources conflict with each other by (1) training a single model on the mixed data from all sources, and (2) training a separate model for each individual source. For the second case, we obtain 6 different models, one from each source. The resulting models are tested on 6 sources individually. We can observe that *mixing all answer sources into a single training set improves the performance on each individual source*. The training signals from heterogeneous sources complement each other, even for sources with totally different structures. p@1 on the semi-structured attribute improves consistently through adding training data of unstructured text. This holds for models with and without pre-tuning on AmazonQA.

Linearization methods In the above experiment, we use a simple linearization method that flattens the json-formatted attributes into a string. We also

selector \ ranker	BM25	AmazonQA	our best
perfect	0.4709	0.7546	0.8338
best-score	**0.2880**	**0.5370**	**0.6986**
highest-score	0.2696	0.5089	0.6888
cascade 1	0.2653	0.5298	0.6791
cascade 2	0.2638	0.5110	0.6715

Table 3: p@1 using different rankers and source selectors.

compare it with 3 other different linearization methods: (1) key-value pairs: Transform the hierarchical json format into a sequence of key-value pairs. For example, the attribute in Table 1 will be transformed into "item_weight unit pounds | item_weight value 2.2". (2) templates: Transform the json by pre-defined templates, e.g. "The [attribute_name] of it is [value] [unit]" and (3) NLG: Transform the json into a sentence by a neural data-to-text model. The results show that *the best performance is achieved by simply linearizing the json into a string*. Although applying the template or neural data-to-text model is closer to a natural sentence, this did not lead to an improvement in p@1. Nonetheless, all these methods have rather similar performance, suggesting *the model can adapt quickly to different representations by finetuning on limited training data and that more complex linearization methods are unnecessary.*

Question Generation Question generation has been a popular data augmentation technique in question-answering. We collect $\sim 50k$ unannotated pieces of evidence from the 6 sources and apply a question generator to generate corresponding questions. The question generator is finetuned first on the AmazonQA corpus and then on our collected training data. We apply nucleus sampling with $p = 0.8$ to balance the diversity and generation quality (Sultan et al., 2020). We further filter the generated questions with our evidence ranker by only keeping those with model prediction scores of > 0.5, which has been shown crucial to get high-quality augmented data (Alberti et al., 2019). We try different finetuning methods and report the results on the bottom of Fig 1, where the "+" means the finetuning order. As can be observed, *finetuning on the augmented data brings further improvement to the model.* A three-step finetuning to gradually bring the model to our interested domain leads to the best performance over all sources.

4.2 Source Selection

Source aims to select the best source to answer after we obtain the top-1 item of evidence from each source. We show results for the following source selectors: (1) **perfect**: oracle selection of the correct item of evidence (if any) in the top-1 pieces of evidence provided from the 6 sources. (2) **best-score**: evidence item with the highest empirical accuracy in its score range which should yield the *upper-bound performance for a selector based on model prediction scores*. (3) **highest-score**: evidence with the highest model prediction score. (4) **cascade 1**: prioritizes evidence from the attribute/bullet sources since they have the highest p@1 scores. If the top-1 evidence item from those two sources has a score of more than ϵ, it is selected. Otherwise, the evidence item with the highest prediction score is selected from the remaining sources and (5) **cascade 2**: prioritizes evidence from attribute, bullet, and descriptions sources since these have better official provenance than user-generated data sources. The selection logic is the same as **cascade 1**. **highest-score** is the most straightforward choice but relies on a comparable score across sources. **cascades 1/2** are also commonly used to merge results from sub-systems. For the **best-score** selector, we split the prediction score range into 100 buckets and estimate the empirical accuracy on the test data. For example the prediction score of 0.924 for the top-1 evidence from an attribute source will fall into the bucket $0.92 \sim 0.93$. In our test set, evidence items from each source will have an empirical accuracy within each score bin [2]. This will lead to an upper-bound approximation of a selector based on prediction scores since we explicitly "sneak a peep" at the test set accuracy. We combine these selectors with 3 evidence rankers: BM25, Electra-based tuned on AmazonQA, and our best ranker (AmazonQA + QG + Real in Figure 1). The results are in Table 3. The thresholds for cascade 1/2 are tuned to maximize the p@1 on the testset.

As our best "fair" ranker, the highest-score selector performs remarkably well, with p@1 only 1% lower than that of the best-score-based selectors. It also outperforms the two cascade-based selectors which prioritize official and high-precision sources. This implies the *the prediction scores across differ-*

[2]By continuing to split the confidence range into more buckets we can make an arbitarily exact approximation to the perfect selector for the test set, but with significant over-fitting.

ent sources are comparable in our model, which might be because our model is trained on a combination of all sources with the same representation. For the model tuned on AmazonQA, where evidence comes solely from the CQA source, the highest-score selector is not as effective as the cascade selectors. For all rankers, even with the best-score-based selector, there is still a large p@1 gap with the perfect selector, suggesting *a further improvement must take into account evidence content*, in addition to the prediction scores.

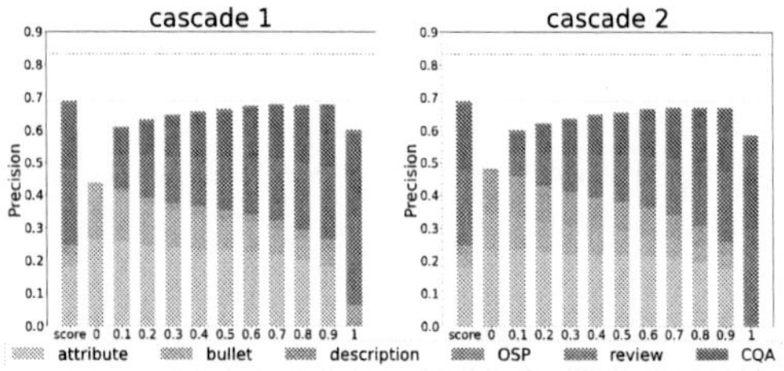

Figure 2: Answer source distribution as the threshold changes when using the cascade selection. Yellow line is with highest-score selector and red line is with a perfect selector.

In Figure 2, we visualize the distribution of selected sources by varying the threshold of two cascade-based selectors. We also show the distribution by using the highest-score selector (score) on the left. As the threshold grows, model precision first grows and then degrades, suggesting *all sources can contribute to answering product questions*. There is no single source that dominates. Although the cascade selection strategy underperforms the highest-confidence selector, it provides us with a flexible way to adjust the source distribution by threshold tuning. In practice, one may want to bias the use of information from official providers, even with a slight reduction in precision.

4.3 Answer Generation

After selecting an evidential item from one source, the role of answer generation is to *generate a natural-sounding answer based on both the question and the evidence*. We build our answer generator with the Bart-large model (Lewis et al., 2020). Similar to the evidence ranker, we take a unified approach for all sources by concatenating both the question and the evidence together (split by the token "|") as the model input. The model is then finetuned on the collected question-evidence-answer (q-e-a) triples. As in training the ranker, we flatten the json structures into strings and process them in the same way as the other sources.

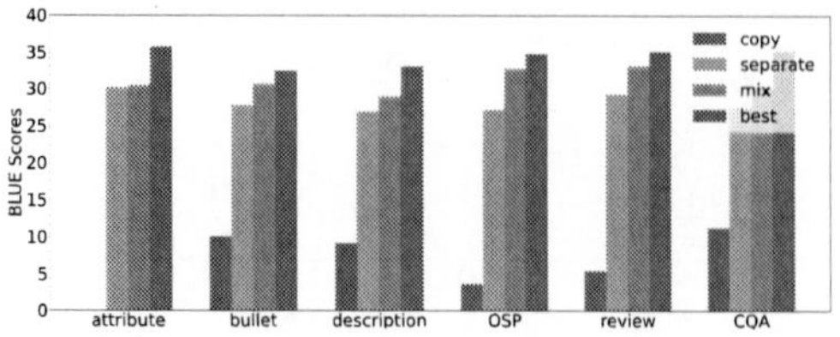

Figure 3: Ablation studies of answer generation. copy evidence vs separate sources/combine sources vs our best model.

Mixed sources vs split sources We experimented with training the generative model on each individual source separately as well as mixing the training data from all sources and training a unified model. We measured the BLEU scores of these systems with results shown in Figure 3, where we also include the results of directly copying the evidence. We can see that *training a unified model to handle all sources improves the performance on all sources*, as is consistent with our findings in evidence ranking. This is not surprising since previous research on data-to-text has also found that text-to-text generative models are quite robust to different variants of input formats (Kale and Rastogi, 2020; Chang et al., 2021). Directly copying the evidence as the answer leads to very low BLEU scores, especially for json-formatted attributes. This indicates *we must significantly rewrite the raw evidence to produce a natural answer*.

Conditional Back-translation (CBT) In our scenario, the AmazonQA contains a large amount of q-a pairs but these do not have corresponding evidence. We can apply a similar idea as back-translation (Sennrich et al., 2016) but further "condition" on the question. Firstly, we train an evidence generator based on our annotated q-e-a triples. The model is trained to generate the evidence by taking the q-a pairs as input. We then apply the model to generate pseudo-evidence e' from the $q-a$ pairs in AmazonQA. The answer generator is then first finetuned on the pseudo $q-e'-a$ triples and then finetuned further on the real $q-e-a$ annotations. It can be considered as a "conditional" version of back-translation where the model is additionally conditioned on the questions. We use nucleus sampling with p=0.8 to generate the evidence e' since the diversity of inputs is important for back-translation (Edunov et al., 2018; Zhao et al., 2019). The results are displayed in Table 4. We can see that *adding the conditional back-translation step improves the BLEU score by nearly 3 points*.

Noisy Self-training (NST) Self-training is an-

Method	BLEU	B-1	B-2	B-3	B-4
Copy	4.0	47.3	22.4	15.9	12.6
Bart-large	30.9	57.6	36.1	24.9	17.6
CBT	33.5	60.3	39.0	27.6	20.5
NST	32.5	59.5	37.3	26.2	19.2
NST + noise	33.2	59.8	38.0	26.9	19.9
Iteration-1	34.3	61.1	39.4	28.0	20.8
Iteration-2	**34.9**	61.1	**39.8**	28.3	21.4
Iteration-3	**34.9**	**61.3**	39.7	**28.6**	**21.6**
Iteration-4	34.7	61.3	**39.8**	28.5	21.3

Table 4: BLEU scores on different methods: copying the input evidence as the answer (**copy**), finetuning Bart-large on training samples (**Bart-large**), Bart-large + conditional back-translation (**CBT**) and Bart-large + noisy self-training (**NST**).

```
(Inilialization) G_e = G_a = Bart-large;
for i=1 to N do
    Finetune G_e on {q − a − e}_real;
    Generate e' with G_e from {q − a}_AmazonQA;
    Finetune G_a on generated
      {q − e' − a}_AmazonQA;
    Finetune G_a on {q − e − a}_real;
    Noisy Self-training (G_a);
    Generate a' with G_a from {q' − e}_QG;
    Finetune G_e on generated {q' − a' − e}_QG;
end
```

Algorithm 1 (Iterative Training Process): G_e is the evidence generator and G_a is the answer generator. $\{q-a-e\}_{real}$,$\{q-a\}_{AmazonQA}$ and $\{q'-e\}_{QG}$ indicate the data from the real annotation, AmazonQA and question generation respectively.

other popular technique in semi-supervised learning (Scudder, 1965). It uses a trained model to generate outputs for unlabeled data, then uses the generated outputs as the training target. In our scenario, however, the unlabeled input data is not readily available since it requires positive question-evidence pairs. We first apply the same question generation model used for evidence ranking to create "noisy" $q' - e$ pairs. The current model then generates an answer a' based on the $q' - e$ pairs. We use beam search with beam size 5 to generate the answers as the generation quality is more important than diversity in self-training (He et al., 2020). A new model is then initialized from Bart-large, first finetuned on the $q' - e - a'$ triples, then finetuned on the real training data. We also experimented with adding noise to the input side when training on the $q' - e - a'$ triples, which has shown to be helpful for the model robustness (He et al., 2020) [3]. As shown in Table 4, NST improves the model performance by over 1 BLEU point. Adding the noise to the input further brings slight improvement.

Iterative Training We further investigated combining the proposed CBT and NST into an iterative training pipeline. The intuition is that CBT can improve the answer generator which then helps NST to generate higher-quality pseudo answers. The higher-quality triples from NST can in turn be used to 'warm up' the evidence generator for CBT. Algorithm 1 details the process. It can be considered a variant of iterative back-translation (Hoang et al., 2018; Chang et al., 2021) with an additional condition on the question and the noisy self-training process inserted in between. It essentially follows a generalized EM algorithm (Shen et al., 2017; Cotterell and Kreutzer, 2018; Graça et al., 2019) where the evidence generator and the answer generator are guaranteed to improve iteratively. We show the results after each iteration in Table 4. As can be seen, the iterative training pipeline further improves generation quality. Most gains are found in the first iteration and the model saturates at iteration 3 with a BLEU score of 34.9.

[3]We apply a similar noise function as in Edunov et al. (2018) that randomly deletes replaces a word by a filler token with probability 0.1, then swaps words up to the range of 3.

Evaluated	Faithfulness (%)	Naturalness (%)
copied evidence	-	15.44
our best	94.39	95.51
human reference	97.00	95.82

Table 5: Human evaluation results.

Human Evaluation We run a human evaluation to assess generation quality of our best generator (iteration-3 from Table 4), human reference and the copied evidence. We evaluate from two perspectives: (1) Faithfulness: A sentence is unfaithful to the evidence if it contains extra or contradictory information, and (2) Naturalness: A sentence is unnatural if it is not fluent; contains additional information that not relevant as an answer; or does not directly reply to the question.

We show the results in Table 5. We can observe that copying the evidence directly leads to a naturalness score of only 0.15, which further confirms that an answer generator is needed for a natural presentation. The generations from our best model improve the naturalness score to 0.9551 and are faithful to the evidence in 94.39% of the cases, only slightly lower than the human references.

4.4 Best Practices

To summarize the best practices, the attribute json strings can be directly flattened and all sources are

Subjectivity of Relevance
Question: what is the snow made of?   **Predicted**: kind of cotton like.
Noise in Attribute Value
Question: is it dark green or brown?   **Predicted**: color: { value:"as shown" }
Overfit to String Match
Q: what is the length of the solder?   **Predicted**: coil of solder is about 1-3/4 long and ...
Uncertain Evidence
Q: can it be machine washed?   **Predicted**: not sure if it is machine washable.

Table 6: Common errors of evidence relevance ranking.

Number accuracy
Q: what's the size of the house?   **E**: item_dimensions: {width:... height:{unit:centimeters, normalized_value:{unit:inches, value:15.35},value:39.}}   **G**: The house is 10.24 × 30.31 × 39 inches
Hallucination when Inference needed
Q: are the dolls with it?   **E**: included_components:{value:"my dreamy doll-house"}   **G**: Yes, it comes with a doll.
Sensitivity to typographical errors
Q: for he many players?   **E**: ages 7 and up, 2-12 players   **G**: this game is for ages 7 and up.

Table 7: Common errors of answer generations.

mixed together and trained with a single unified encoder. The ranker is finetuned on AmazonQA, augmented data obtained by question generation and manually annotated training data in order. Source selection can be performed based solely on the model confidence score and the answer generator can be trained as in Algorithm 1.

5 Error analysis

Based on the human evaluation, we identified the following key problems that exist in the current system. For evidence ranking, the major problems are: (1) **subjectivity of relevance**: It can be subjective to define whether a piece of evidence is enough to answer a given question. The model will sometimes pick a somewhat relevant piece of evidence, even though there could be other, better options that support a more comprehensive answer. (2) **noise in attribute value**: When an attribute value contains uninformative data due to the noise of data sources, the model still may choose it based on its attribute name. (3) **overfitting to string match**: The model tends to select strings similar to the question while ignoring their fine semantics, a common problem from the bias to 'shortcut learning' of neural networks (Geirhos et al., 2020). (4) **uncertain evidence**: The model ranks evidence highly, even if this evidence is an uncertain expression. This can be viewed as a special case of over-fitting to string match. We show examples in Table 6. We can attempt to alleviate errors of type 1 by providing finer-grained labels in the training data instead of only binary signals (Gupta et al., 2019). Error types 2 and 4 could be mitigated by data augmentation, constructing negative samples by corrupting the attribute values or making evidence uncertain. Error type 3 is more challenging. One possible solution is to automatically detect spurious correlations and focus the model on minor examples (Tu et al., 2020). Nevertheless, a fundamental solution to fully avoid Error 3 is still an open question.

For answer generation, we identify the major problems as: (1) **Number accuracy**: The model cannot fully understand the roles of numbers from the limited training examples. (2) **Hallucination if inference is needed**: when it is not possible to generate an answer by simple rephrasing, the model can hallucinate false information. (3) **Sensitivity to typos**: The model is not robust to typos in the question. A tiny typo can easily break the system.

We provide examples of these errors in Table 7. Error types 1 and 3 could be alleviated through data augmentation. We can create new samples to let the model learn to copy numbers properly and learn to be robust to common typos. Another way to reduce number sensitivity could to delexicalize numbers in the inputs, a common strategy in data to text generation (Wen et al., 2015; Gardent et al., 2017). Error type 2 is a challenging open problem in neural text generation. Many techniques have been proposed such as learning latent alignment (Shen et al., 2020), data refinement with NLU (Nie et al., 2019), etc. These could potentially be applied to our task, which we leave for future work.

6 Conclusion

To the best of our knowledge, this work is the first comprehensive study of product answer generation from heterogeneous sources including both semi-structured attributes and unstructured text. We collect a benchmark dataset with annotations for both evidence ranking and answer generation. It will be released to benefit relevant study. We find that the best practice is to leverage a unified approach to handle all sources of evidence together and further experimented with a set of data augmentation techniques to improve the model performance. Error analysis is provided to illustrate common errors, which we hope will lead to inspire future work.

References

Chris Alberti, Daniel Andor, Emily Pitler, Jacob Devlin, and Michael Collins. 2019. Synthetic qa corpora generation with roundtrip consistency. In *Proceedings of the 57th Annual Meeting of the Association for Computational Linguistics*, pages 6168–6173.

Ernie Chang, Xiaoyu Shen, Dawei Zhu, Vera Demberg, and Hui Su. 2021. Neural data-to-text generation with lm-based text augmentation. In *Proceedings of the 16th Conference of the European Chapter of the Association for Computational Linguistics: Main Volume*, pages 758–768.

Kevin Clark, Minh-Thang Luong, Quoc V Le, and Christopher D Manning. 2020. Electra: Pre-training text encoders as discriminators rather than generators. *arXiv preprint arXiv:2003.10555*.

Ryan Cotterell and Julia Kreutzer. 2018. Explaining and generalizing back-translation through wake-sleep. *arXiv preprint arXiv:1806.04402*.

Lei Cui, Shaohan Huang, Furu Wei, Chuanqi Tan, Chaoqun Duan, and Ming Zhou. 2017. Superagent: A customer service chatbot for e-commerce websites. In *Proceedings of ACL 2017, System Demonstrations*, pages 97–102.

Jacob Devlin, Ming-Wei Chang, Kenton Lee, and Kristina Toutanova. 2019. Bert: Pre-training of deep bidirectional transformers for language understanding. In *Proceedings of the 2019 Conference of the North American Chapter of the Association for Computational Linguistics: Human Language Technologies, Volume 1 (Long and Short Papers)*, pages 4171–4186.

Sergey Edunov, Myle Ott, Michael Auli, and David Grangier. 2018. Understanding back-translation at scale. In *Proceedings of the 2018 Conference on Empirical Methods in Natural Language Processing*, pages 489–500.

Yue Feng, Zhaochun Ren, Weijie Zhao, Mingming Sun, and Ping Li. 2021. Multi-type textual reasoning for product-aware answer generation. In *Proceedings of the 44th International ACM SIGIR Conference on Research and Development in Information Retrieval*, pages 1135–1145.

Shen Gao, Xiuying Chen, Zhaochun Ren, Dongyan Zhao, and Rui Yan. 2021. Meaningful answer generation of e-commerce question-answering. *ACM Transactions on Information Systems (TOIS)*, 39(2):1–26.

Shen Gao, Zhaochun Ren, Yihong Zhao, Dongyan Zhao, Dawei Yin, and Rui Yan. 2019. Product-aware answer generation in e-commerce question-answering. In *Proceedings of the Twelfth ACM International Conference on Web Search and Data Mining*, pages 429–437.

Claire Gardent, Anastasia Shimorina, Shashi Narayan, and Laura Perez-Beltrachini. 2017. The webnlg challenge: Generating text from rdf data. In *Proceedings of the 10th International Conference on Natural Language Generation*, pages 124–133.

Siddhant Garg, Thuy Vu, and Alessandro Moschitti. 2020. Tanda: Transfer and adapt pre-trained transformer models for answer sentence selection. In *AAAI*.

Robert Geirhos, Jörn-Henrik Jacobsen, Claudio Michaelis, Richard Zemel, Wieland Brendel, Matthias Bethge, and Felix A Wichmann. 2020. Shortcut learning in deep neural networks. *Nature Machine Intelligence*, 2(11):665–673.

Miguel Graça, Yunsu Kim, Julian Schamper, Shahram Khadivi, and Hermann Ney. 2019. Generalizing back-translation in neural machine translation. In *Proceedings of the Fourth Conference on Machine Translation (Volume 1: Research Papers)*, pages 45–52.

Mansi Gupta, Nitish Kulkarni, Raghuveer Chanda, Anirudha Rayasam, and Zachary C. Lipton. 2019. Amazonqa: A review-based question answering task. In *Proceedings of the Twenty-Eighth International Joint Conference on Artificial Intelligence, IJCAI-19*, pages 4996–5002. International Joint Conferences on Artificial Intelligence Organization.

Timothy J Hazen, Shehzaad Dhuliawala, and Daniel Boies. 2019. Towards domain adaptation from limited data for question answering using deep neural networks. *arXiv preprint arXiv:1911.02655*.

Junxian He, Jiatao Gu, Jiajun Shen, and Marc'Aurelio Ranzato. 2020. Revisiting self-training for neural sequence generation. In *International Conference on Learning Representations*.

Vu Cong Duy Hoang, Philipp Koehn, Gholamreza Haffari, and Trevor Cohn. 2018. Iterative back-translation for neural machine translation. In *Proceedings of the 2nd Workshop on Neural Machine Translation and Generation*, pages 18–24.

Kai Hui and Klaus Berberich. 2017. Transitivity, time consumption, and quality of preference judgments in crowdsourcing. In *European Conference on Information Retrieval*, pages 239–251. Springer.

Kai Hui, Honglei Zhuang, Tao Chen, Zhen Qin, Jing Lu, Dara Bahri, Ji Ma, Jai Prakash Gupta, Cicero Nogueira dos Santos, Yi Tay, et al. 2022. Ed2lm: Encoder-decoder to language model for faster document re-ranking inference.

Mihir Kale and Abhinav Rastogi. 2020. Text-to-text pre-training for data-to-text tasks. In *Proceedings of the 13th International Conference on Natural Language Generation*, pages 97–102.

Mojtaba Komeili, Kurt Shuster, and Jason Weston. 2021. Internet-augmented dialogue generation. *arXiv preprint arXiv:2107.07566*.

Tuan Lai, Trung Bui, Sheng Li, and Nedim Lipka. 2018a. A simple end-to-end question answering model for product information. In *Proceedings of the First Workshop on Economics and Natural Language Processing*, pages 38–43.

Tuan Lai, Trung Bui, and Nedim Lipka. 2020. Isa: An intelligent shopping assistant. In *Proceedings of the 1st Conference of the Asia-Pacific Chapter of the Association for Computational Linguistics and the 10th International Joint Conference on Natural Language Processing: System Demonstrations*, pages 14–19.

Tuan Manh Lai, Trung Bui, Nedim Lipka, and Sheng Li. 2018b. Supervised transfer learning for product information question answering. In *2018 17th IEEE International Conference on Machine Learning and Applications (ICMLA)*, pages 1109–1114. IEEE.

Mike Lewis, Yinhan Liu, Naman Goyal, Marjan Ghazvininejad, Abdelrahman Mohamed, Omer Levy, Veselin Stoyanov, and Luke Zettlemoyer. 2020. Bart: Denoising sequence-to-sequence pre-training for natural language generation, translation, and comprehension. In *Proceedings of the 58th Annual Meeting of the Association for Computational Linguistics*, pages 7871–7880.

Julian McAuley and Alex Yang. 2016. Addressing complex and subjective product-related queries with customer reviews. In *Proceedings of the 25th International Conference on World Wide Web*, pages 625–635.

Feng Nie, Jin-Ge Yao, Jinpeng Wang, Rong Pan, and Chin-Yew Lin. 2019. A simple recipe towards reducing hallucination in neural surface realisation. In *Proceedings of the 57th Annual Meeting of the Association for Computational Linguistics*, pages 2673–2679.

Barlas Oguz, Xilun Chen, Vladimir Karpukhin, Stan Peshterliev, Dmytro Okhonko, Michael Schlichtkrull, Sonal Gupta, Yashar Mehdad, and Scott Yih. 2020. Unified open-domain question answering with structured and unstructured knowledge. *arXiv preprint arXiv:2012.14610*.

Henry Scudder. 1965. Probability of error of some adaptive pattern-recognition machines. *IEEE Transactions on Information Theory*, 11(3):363–371.

Rico Sennrich, Barry Haddow, and Alexandra Birch. 2016. Improving neural machine translation models with monolingual data. In *Proceedings of the 54th Annual Meeting of the Association for Computational Linguistics (Volume 1: Long Papers)*, pages 86–96.

Xiaoyu Shen, Ernie Chang, Hui Su, Cheng Niu, and Dietrich Klakow. 2020. Neural data-to-text generation via jointly learning the segmentation and correspondence. In *Proceedings of the 58th Annual Meeting of the Association for Computational Linguistics*, pages 7155–7165.

Xiaoyu Shen, Youssef Oualil, Clayton Greenberg, Mittul Singh, and Dietrich Klakow. 2017. Estimation of gap between current language models and human performance. *Proc. Interspeech 2017*, pages 553–557.

Hui Su, Xiaoyu Shen, Zhou Xiao, Zheng Zhang, Ernie Chang, Cheng Zhang, Cheng Niu, and Jie Zhou. 2020. Moviechats: Chat like humans in a closed domain. In *Proceedings of the 2020 Conference on Empirical Methods in Natural Language Processing (EMNLP)*, pages 6605–6619.

Md Arafat Sultan, Shubham Chandel, Ramón Fernandez Astudillo, and Vittorio Castelli. 2020. On the importance of diversity in question generation for qa. In *Proceedings of the 58th Annual Meeting of the Association for Computational Linguistics*, pages 5651–5656.

Lifu Tu, Garima Lalwani, Spandana Gella, and He He. 2020. An empirical study on robustness to spurious correlations using pre-trained language models. *Transactions of the Association for Computational Linguistics*, 8:621–633.

Tsung-Hsien Wen, Milica Gasic, Nikola Mrksic, Pei-hao Su, David Vandyke, and Steve J Young. 2015. Semantically conditioned lstm-based natural language generation for spoken dialogue systems. In *EMNLP*.

Hu Xu, Bing Liu, Lei Shu, and Philip S Yu. 2019. Review conversational reading comprehension. *arXiv preprint arXiv:1902.00821*.

Qian Yu, Wai Lam, and Zihao Wang. 2018. Responding e-commerce product questions via exploiting qa collections and reviews. In *Proceedings of the 27th International Conference on Computational Linguistics*, pages 2192–2203.

Shiwei Zhang, Jey Han Lau, Xiuzhen Zhang, Jeffrey Chan, and Cecile Paris. 2019. Discovering relevant reviews for answering product-related queries. In *2019 IEEE International Conference on Data Mining (ICDM)*, pages 1468–1473. IEEE.

Wenxuan Zhang, Qian Yu, and Wai Lam. 2020. Answering product-related questions with heterogeneous information. In *Proceedings of the 1st Conference of the Asia-Pacific Chapter of the Association for Computational Linguistics and the 10th International Joint Conference on Natural Language Processing*, pages 696–705.

Yang Zhao, Xiaoyu Shen, Wei Bi, and Akiko Aizawa. 2019. Unsupervised rewriter for multi-sentence compression. In *Proceedings of the 57th Annual Meeting of the Association for Computational Linguistics*, pages 2235–2240.

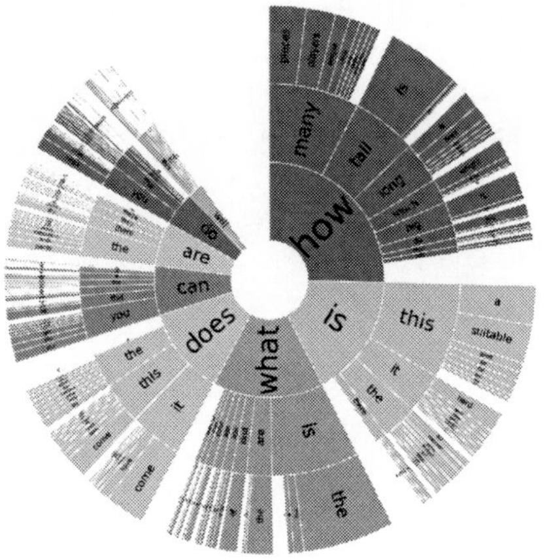

Figure 4: The ngram distribution of prefixes of questions.

A Collected Data

All our collected data have also been manually verified to remove sample with private or offensive information.

In Figure 4, we show the ngram distribution of question prefixes i our collected data. As can be seen, a large proportion of questions are boolean questions starting with "is", "does", "can", "are", "do" and "will". The rest are mostly factual questions like "how many/tall/long ..." and "what ...". Most of them should be able to answer with a short span since there are not many opinion questions like "how is ...", "why ...".

B Instruction for Human Annotation

All annotators are based on the US. We first perform in-house annotation and then estimate the time needed for each annotation. We then set the payment to be roughly 15 USD per hour. The payment is decided based on the average payment level in the US. All annotators are informed that their collection will be made public for scientific research according to the Amazon Mechanical Turk code of rules. The data collection protocol has been approved by an ethics review board.

B.1 Question Collection

Read the given product name and image, imagine you are a customer and are recommended this product. Write one question about it to decide whether or not to purchase this product.

Examples of questions: is it energy efficient? does it require a hub? can I watch sports on this TV? will the plug work with an extension cord?

B.2 Evidence Selection

At the start of each task, the workflow application will present a product, a question about the product and a set of candidates which describe the product. Your annotation task is to mark the proper candidate that contains information to answer the question from the attribute set. If none of the provided candidates contain the information, select "None of the above".

B.3 Answer Generation

Read the raised product question and provided information, write a natural, informative, complete sentence to answer this question. If the provided information cannot address the question, write "none". Make sure the answer is a natural, informative and complete sentence. Do not write short answers like "Yes", "Right", "It is good", etc. Provide enough information to help the asker understand more about the question. If the provided information can only partially answer the question, only reply to the answerable part.

Good Examples:

question: what age range is this product designed for?

Provided information: age_range_description: value:"3 - 8 years

Answer: It is designed for the age range of 3 - 8 years old.

question: how many people can play at one time?

provided information: number_of_players: value:"8

answer: It is designed for 8 players at one time.

Bad Examples:

question: what age range is this product designed for?

Provided information: age_range_description: value:"3 - 8 years

Answer: 3 - 8 years.

question: how many people can play at one time?

provided information: number_of_players: value:"8

answer: 8.

C Full Results of Ranker

We show the full results of our best-performed ranker in Table 8. As can be seen, different sources have different accuracy score. The attribute and bullet point source have the highest accuracy score because the former is more structured, and the latter has a consistent writing style with only a few

Source	MAP	MRR	NDCG	P@1	HIT@5
Attribute	0.965	0.966	0.974	0.943	0.996
Bullet	0.935	0.935	0.952	0.890	0.993
Description	0.648	0.708	0.747	0.611	0.822
OSP	0.667	0.708	0.763	0.579	0.873
Review	0.796	0.860	0.875	0.778	0.966
CQA	0.643	0.750	0.766	0.636	0.897

Table 8: Performance of our best ranker on different sources.

sentences. User reviews also have a high accuracy score. This might be because the candidates of reviews are already the top ones selected by our pretrained ranker. Many of them are already relevant and the negative-positive ratio is low. The model does not have extreme difficulty in handling the user reviews. The model performs worst on the description, OSP and CQA answer source. This might result from the diversity of their writing styles and the high negative-positive ratio, which increase the difficulty. Moreover, these two sources usually depend more on the context to interpret the evidence than other sources. The text description is extracted from the multi-media web page. Simply extracting the text part might lose richer context to interpret the extracted text. Similarly, the CQA usually depends on the community question. If we only extract a sentence from the answer, it might contains references that is not self-contained.

D Training details

For both the generative Bart-large model and the discriminative Electra-base model, we truncate the total input length to 128 subword tokens and select the learing rate from $[5e-6, 1e-5, 3e-5, 5e-5, 1e-4]$. The warm-up step is selected from $[5\%, 10\%, 20\%, 50\%]$ of the whole training steps. For the discriminative model, we choose the best configuration based on the F1 score on the validation set. For the generative model, we choose the best configuration based on the perplexity on the validation set. In the end, we set the learning rate of Electra-base as $3e-5$ and that of Bart-large as $1e-5$. The warm-up step is set as 20% for Electra-base and 10% for Bart-large. The batch size is set as 64 for Electra-base and 16 for Bart-large. For Electra-base, we measure the validation F1 score after finishing every 1% of the whole training steps and stop the model when the valitaion F1 score does not increase for 30% of the whole training steps. For Bart-large, we measure the validation loss every 200 steps and stop the model when the validation loss stops decreasing for 1000 steps. All models are trained once on 8 Nvidia V100 GPUs and the random seed is set as 42.

semiPQA: A Study on Product Question Answering over Semi-structured Data

Xiaoyu Shen, Gianni Barlacchi, Marco del Tredici, Weiwei Cheng and Adria de Gispert
[1]Amazon Alexa AI
{gyouu, gbarlac, mttredic, weiweic, agispert}@amazon.com

Abstract

Product question answering (PQA) aims to automatically address customer questions to improve their online shopping experience. Current research mainly focuses on finding answers from either *unstructured* text, like product descriptions and user reviews, or *structured* knowledge bases with pre-defined schemas. Apart from the above two sources, a lot of product information is represented in a *semi-structured* way, e.g., key-value pairs, lists, tables, json and xml files, etc. These semi-structured data can be a valuable answer source since they are better organized than free text, while being easier to construct than structured knowledge bases. However, little attention has been paid to them. To fill in this blank, here we study *how to effectively incorporate semi-structured answer sources for PQA* and focus on *presenting answers in a natural, fluent sentence*. To this end, we present semiPQA: a dataset to benchmark PQA over semi-structured data. It contains 11,243 written questions about json-formatted data covering 320 unique attribute types. Each data point is paired with manually-annotated text that describes its contents, so that we can train a neural answer presenter to present the data in a natural way. We provide baseline results and a deep analysis on the successes and challenges of leveraging semi-structured data for PQA. In general, state-of-the-art neural models can perform remarkably well when dealing with seen attribute types. For unseen attribute types, however, a noticeable drop is observed for both answer presentation and attribute ranking.

1 Introduction

Product question answering (PQA) is playing an increasingly important role in e-commerce platforms. It is able to greatly improve the online shopping experience since customers do not need to traverse over the detailed web pages to seek information themselves. Traditional approaches built *structured* knowledge bases for product attributes and mapped customer questions into executable queries(Frank et al., 2007; Tapeh and Rahgozar, 2008; Hui et al., 2013; Li et al., 2019). In recent years, with the rapid progress of large-scaled pretrained neural models, many research works have achieved promising results by leveraging only *unstructured* text, like product descriptions, user reviews and community answers (Cui et al., 2017; Gupta et al., 2019; Gao et al., 2019; Zhang et al., 2020). Lying between these two source types, a lot of product information is often organized in a semi-structured form, e.g., key-value pairs, lists and tables from product web pages, json and xml files from internal databases, etc. These semi-structured data can be a valuable answer source since they are better organized and more precise than free text, while being much cheaper to maintain than structured knowledge bases. Nonetheless, few research works have ever considered them and there is no public available dataset for its study. This paper aims to fill in this blank and study *how to effectively incorporate semi-structured answer sources for PQA and present answers in a natural sentence*. To this end, we construct a dataset to benchmark this study. It contains 11,243 product questions about json-formatted semi-structured data [1]. The data contains 320 unique attribute types (size, material, color, etc) spanning a diverse set of semi-structured forms like key-value pairs, lists and hierarchies. Each data is paired with manually annotated text that describes its contents. Table 1 shows some examples from the dataset. Given a question, there are two steps we need to get an answer: (1). **Attribute ranking**: selecting the proper attribute that contains the information to answer the question. Modern pre-trained neural models and QA datasets mainly focus on plain text, so they may not gen-

[1]As json is a standard format for storing data with arbitrary types/schemata, other representations (such as tables or xml files) can be easily mapped to it.

Proceedings of The Fifth Workshop on e-Commerce and NLP (ECNLP 5), pages 111 - 120

eralize well to ranking semi-structured attributes, especially with limited training data. (2). **Answer presentation**: presenting the answer in a fluent sentence. It is not user-friendly to directly present the semi-structured data to customers, especially for applications like voice assistants. We apply data-to-text generation models to convert these data into fluent text.

For attribute ranking, we build our model upon state-of-the-art pre-trained language models. Due to the small size of our training data, we follow the common practice of pre-finetuning the attribute ranker on four large-scale QA datasets: Natural Questions (Kwiatkowski et al., 2019), AmazonQA (McAuley and Yang, 2016), NewsQA (Trischler et al., 2017) and Squad (Rajpurkar et al., 2016). Since these are all based on unstructured text, we also experiment with converting semi-structured attributes into text before being passed to the ranker. Our results show that text-based QA models are quite robust to semi-structured data representations, and can rank attributes correctly with only keyword matching without the extra order information.

For answer presentation, we consider a *question-independent* answer presenter, which is less risky than question-dependent presentation while being more flexible than span extraction or multi-choice selection. We evaluate both a template-based system and a neural sequence-to-sequence generation model. Each template is one or more sentences with gaps that can be filled with pre-defined rules (Deemter et al., 2005). However, semi-structured data does not follow any unified schema, so designing rules to cover all possible data forms or unseen attributes is infeasible. Our neural generation models are initialized with Bart (Lewis et al., 2020) and T5 (Raffel et al., 2020), two representative pretrained models for generative tasks, and fine-tuned on a small set of annotated examples. Compared with the template system, we show the neural approach improves not only the fluency, but also the faithfulness of presented answers.

Finally, we discuss and analyse the challenge of generating factually-correct sentences without hallucinate information, as well as the difficulty of handling unseen attributes in both ranking and answer presentation.

2 Dataset

The data collection contains 3 stages: semi-structured attribute collection, text annotation and question sourcing. This section will explain these three stages in order then present the statistics.

Attribute Collection We obtain the semi-structured attributes of product information from our internal database. These attributes are aggregated from different providers with varied schema. We select 320 unique attribute types from it, filter out information only for internal use and indicator tags containing no actual information like "language_tag", "attribute_id" etc. For each of the 320 attribute types, we randomly sample 20 products containing such attribute from 5M products sold in the US market (The 5M products are randomly sampled from different categories), then extract their attribute instances. After removing duplicate ones, we get 3,316 unique attribute instances in the end. We then preprocess them to lower-case all characters, remove emojis and normalize all floats to contain at most 2 decimals.

Text Annotation After obtaining the semi-structured attributes, we hire annotators from Amazon Mechanical Turk to write a natural sentence for each attribute instance. We restrict to US-based annotators who completed $>$ 500 tasks, out of which more than 97% had been accepted. Before the formal annotation, we did a pilot study with 100 samples. Without extra information, we find 16% of attributes are not understandable to humans, which indicates proper context is necessary to understand the meanings of attributes. Therefore, we also provide the product image and title in the second round of pilot study. By adding the extra information, only 4% of them are not understandable. We then continue with this setting and get all attributes annotated. We also remove all attributes that are not understandable to annotators (usually those that rely on other information to interpret), and end up with 3,191 attribute instances annotated with their description text.

Question Sourcing We collect questions on Mechanical Turk by present annotators with the image, title and rating of the product plus one of its associated attribute instances. Annotators are asked to imagine themselves as potential customers, and their task is to ask four questions about this attribute, which means that the attribute contains the information to answer their question. We explicitly add three criteria that annotators must follow: ques-

Table 1: Examples of question-data-text triples in the dataset. The data features diverse forms of semi-structures like key-value pairs, lists and hierarchies.

Question:	Is the body made out of nylon?
Data (key-value):	fabric_type:{ value:"Body: Nylon/spandex; cup linings:100% polyester;cup pad:100% polyurethane."}
Text:	The body is made of nylon and spandex, the linings in ...
Question:	What kind of devices fit in this?
Data (list):	compatible_devices: {value:"apple ipad mini 4"}; {value:"apple ...
Text:	The product is compatible with apple ipad mini 4, apple ipad air...
Question:	Is this metal?
Data (hierarchy):	blade:{material:[{value:"Plastic"}],length:[{unit:inches,value:3.0}]}
Text:	The blade on this measures 3 inches and is plastic.

tion must be (1) Meaningful, having a reasonable chance of being asked in daily shopping, and not parroted, rigid questions like "what is the [attribute name]"; (2) Diverse, so the three questions must not be paraphrase each other, and (3) Answerable by the attribute, ensuring that the attribute contains the information to answer the questions. After getting these questions, we lower case them and remove duplicate questions about the same products.

Dataset Split and Statistics The dataset will be used to train and evaluate the (1) attribute ranker and (2) answer presenter. For both, we have two test scenarios, one containing only seen attributes with unseen values, and the other containing only unseen attributes to test the model generalization capability. For the unseen scenario, we randomly sample 30 attribute types from all 320 types. We sample 58 instances from them and add into the dev set, while the rest are used as test set. For the seen scenario, we randomly sample 440 instances from the remaining 290 attribute types. 220 of them are added into the dev set and the rest serve as the test set. We use one fixed dev set containing both seen (220) attributes and unseen (58) attributes. All remaining instances serve as training set. Due to the small data size, we perform cross validation to get more reliable results. We repeat the above process ten times with different seeds to get 10 different splits, then train/evaluate on them and average the results. For each question asking about one attribute, we treat all other attribute instances belonging to the same product as negative candidates. The candidate positive-negative ratio is 1:17.89.

3 Attribute Ranking

Attribute ranking aims to select the proper attribute that contains the information to answer the user-posed question.

We start from a tf-idf baseline, which has been shown a strong baseline for sentence matching tasks (Arora et al., 2017). We count the frequency based on the attribute instances on the training set. At test time, we convert question and answer candidate into tf-idf vectors based on the counted frequency, then compute their cosine similarity as the ranking score.

Following the common practice, we also tried concatenating the question and candidate attribute into one sequence then feeding into the Roberta-base encoder (Liu et al., 2019), a Transformer-based neural model pretrained on billions of text. The final classifier is built on top of the representation of the first [CLS] token. The multi self-attention layers of the encoder makes sure each token is able to interact with all other tokens to capture the dependency relations. The model is trained to maximize the likelihood of the positive candidates and minimize that of the negative candidates. As for the input form of the semi-structured attribute, we experimented with 5 forms: (1) **name-only**: only use the attribute name as input. (2) **value-only**: only use the attribute value as input. (3) **linearized**: use the linearized json which concatenates the attribute name and value as input. (4) **template**: use the template system to generate its corresponding text, then use the generated text as input. (5) **neural**: use the neural generator to generate its corresponding text, then use the generated text as input.

Due to the limited size of our training data, we follow a two-step setting (Garg et al., 2020) where the Roberta-base model is first fine-tuned on a large-scale QA dataset, then fine-tuned on our semiPQA training data. This has been shown to improve performance in the low-resource setting (Hazen et al., 2019; Garg et al., 2020). We consider 4 datasets: (1) **NQ**: the Google Natural Questions dataset. We use its sentence selection version (Garg et al., 2020), where its negative samples are categorized into 4 classes to improve the robustness of the model. It contains 61,186 questions from the Google queries for training. (2) **AmazonQA**: QA pairs from the Amazon community QA website (Gupta et al., 2019). We remove answers containing "I don't know", "I'm not sure" etc, and filter questions more than 32 words and answers more than 64 words. Negative candidates are answers about different questions under the same product. It contains 1,065,407 community questions for training. (3) **NewsQA**: QAs about news articles (Trischler et al., 2017). We convert it into sentence selection and drop the span label. For each question, we sample 5 negative sentences not labeled as correct for training. The training dataset contains 75,473 questions. (4) **Squad**: QAs about wikipedia paragraphs (Rajpurkar et al., 2016). We treat sentences containing the ground-truth span as positive and other sentences in the same paragraph as negative. The training dataset contains 87,599 questions. Notably, *all answers in the above 4 datasets are in form of unstructured sentences.*.

We analyzed the performance under three settings: (1) zeroshot where the model is applied directly to the testsets without using our training data, (2) performance on seen attributes after finetuning on the training data and (2) performance on unseen attributes after finetuning on the training data [2]. Precision@1 results are shown in Figure 1. We also computed other metrics like MAP, MRR and HIT@5, but they show a similar trend and are omitted for space limit.

Zeroshot Performance The zeroshot results are visualized in the upper part of Figure 1, where we apply the rankers finetuned on different datasets to directly test on our data. As can be seen, when only the attribute name or value is available, the performance is significantly lower than the others, both for neural models and the tf-idf baseline. This suggests we need information from both the attribute name and value to rank attributes properly. Neither of them are sufficient by its own. *Neural models finetuned on unstructured text can generally adapt well to semi-structured data (linerized form), except for the one finetuned on NQ which performs poorly compared with others.* One reason could be that the negative samples from NQ are finer-grained. It must learn to differentiate between sentences containing correct answer spans

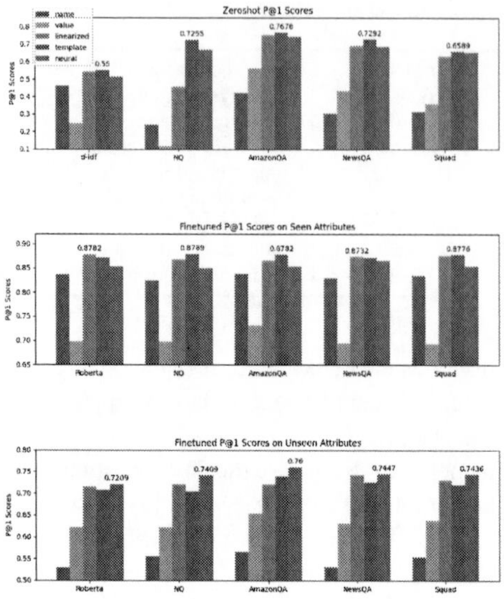

Figure 1: p@1 in zeroshot/finetuned settings.

but talking about irrelevant things, and correct sentences. Therefore, it must rely on the sentence structure to infer the meaning and decide whether it is relevant or not (Garg et al., 2020). When directly tested on semi-structured jsons, it cannot easily interpret non-natural sentences. When finetuned on other datasets like NewsQA, AmazonQA and Squad, negative samples are randomly sampled and hardly contain the correct answer span, so the model might only rely on span detection and do not need well-formed sentences. Using template-generated text leads to the best zeroshot performance for all models, next come the neural-generated text and linearized json which perform slightly worse. Among all datasets used for finetuning, AmazonQA adapts best for all input formats. This is not surprising considering that it is also about product questions and has the largest data size for finetuning.

Finetuned Performance on Seen Attributes The finetuned results on seen attributes is visualized in the middle of Figure 1. "Roberta" indicates the model is initialized with the Roberta-based checkpoint without being finetuned on any other QA datasets in advance. "NQ" indicates that the Roberta-based model is first finetuned on NQ, then finetuned on our training data, same for "AmazonQA", "NewsQA" and "Squad". Similarly to the zeroshot setting, using only the attribute name or

[2]In the zeroshot setting, we only evaluate on the seen attribute split since there is no concept of "seen" or "unseen" for zeroshot evaluation.

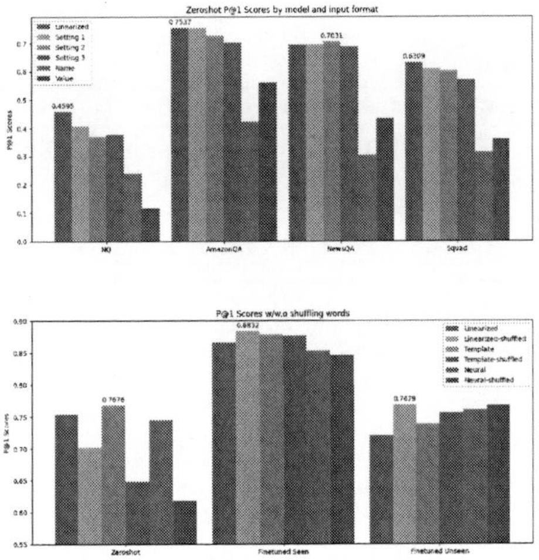

Figure 2: p@1 with varying input formats.

value leads to significantly worse results, although attribute names seem to be more important when finetuning on the training data. *Using the linearized json format and the template-generated text have the best overall performance, achieving a precision score of over 85%. Using more natural and fluent text does not help the ranking performance on seen attributes.* Although neural generated text are of higher-quality according to human evaluations (to be shown in Section 4), this does not make the ranking task easier and leads to performance drop, suggesting that presentation is not a requirement for ranking and can be addressed separately. *Prefinetuning on large-scale text-based QA datasets also does not help the performance on seen attributes*, as the Roberta result already achieves similar performance. The model is able to quickly learn the correspondence between questions and seen attributes even with the limited training data.

Finetuned Performance on Unseen Attributes In the bottom of Figure 1, we show the finetuned performance when testing on unseen attributes. As expected, a significant performance drop is observed for all models, especially when using attribute names only as this is mostly equivalent to classification over unseen labels. *Using neural-generated text as input achieves the best performance in all settings.* We hypothesise that the neural-generated texts are less rigid and more diverse than template-generated or linearised json data, which prevents the model from overfitting. Finetuning from Roberta directly performs the worst on average, and finetuning first on AmazonQA generally leads to a smaller performance drop with respect to seen attributes. The large amount of questions in AmazonQA, though not helpful for seen attributes, do improve the model robustness over unseen attributes.

Analysis As shown above, directly using the linearized json format performs well in the zeroshot setting, which indicates that models finetuned on QA datasets are able to learn to generalize to the json format when finetuning on the sentence format. To investigate this surprising finding, we perform an ablation study in the following settings:

1. Remove all quotation marks plus curly braces from the json.

2. On top of (1), further remove all colons from the json.

3. On top of (2), further shuffle the word order in json.

By gradually removing the structural features of the representation, we aim to evaluate whether the model needs this json structure for attribute ranking. The zeroshot p@1 scores obtained are reported in Figure 2. We also do the same to text generated from the template and neural models.

As can be seen, *removing the json structure does not have a great effect on performance*. Even after shuffling the word orders completely, the performance drop is within 5% for most models. However, removing either the attribute name or value does lead to significant performance drops, which indicates that *the model relies more on semantic matching against both attribute name and value for prediction, rather than on the structure or word order information.*

Finally, the bottom figure shows that in the zeroshot setting, shuffling the word order reduces the performance for both the linearized, template and neural format. The drop is more for template and neural format but less for the linearized json format. This implies the pretrained QA models are more sensitive to word orders in the sentence format than the structured json format. When finetuned on the training data, however, word orders loses importance. Interestingly, when testing on unseen attribute, shuffling the word order even improves model performance. This further confirmed that *for this task, the model does not need to rely on the word order to make predictions, shuffling the word order can even improve the model robustness on generalizing to unseen attributes.*

4 Answer Presentation

The first approach we consider for answer presentation is to use handcrafted templates. However, defining a perfect template for each attribute is challenging due to the lack of a standard schema and templates cannot scale to unseen attributes. With this concern, we also experiment with training a neural data-to-text generator trained with annotated text as the target.

Template System When designing the template system, we aim to capture general rules across different attribute types so that one template can be reusable to other similar attributes. We define each template should contain (1) a precondition specializing when to apply the template, (2) one or several corresponding text with gaps to fill, and (3) a set of rules defining how to fill in the gaps. For example, the following is a template defined from the attribute type *ARE_BATTERIES_REQUIRED*:

```
Precondition: applies if the POS
tag of the attribute
name follows the pattern of
be_NOUN_VERBed.
Rule: (1) If the value is "Y" or
"yes" or "True":
output "It VERBs the NOUN".
(2) Otherwise: output "It does
not VERB the NOUN".
```

where VERBs and VERBed mean the third person singular and past particle form of the verb. For *ARE_BATTERIES_REQUIRED*, VERBs would be "requires" and VERBed is "required". It can also apply to other attribute types following the same pattern like "is_assembly_required" and "is_software_included".

During template construction, we maintain a template bank starting from empty. As we see more attribute types, we check if any template from the bank can be applied, and if so, whether it generates the correct text or whether we need to manually update the template. Otherwise, we create a new template for this attribute type. This process is repeated until we go over all the 320 attribute types three times, to refine, merge and fix the template bank and rules. After these rounds, we end up with a total of 23 distinct templates.

Nevertheless, during the construction process, we realize it is nearly impossible to devise a template system to cover all cases well, even for the limited 320 attribute types that we focus on. The difficulty lies in the following two diversities in the data: (1) linguistic diversity: The attribute values do not follow any strict rule. They can be free text as long as it conveys the meaning, which makes it hard to design general rules even for a single attribute type. (2) structural diversity: The json format is a loose structure. The same semantic meaning can be organized in different ways and hierarchies. Applying one rule for different structures can easily lead to parsing errors. Table 2 shows some examples of different values for the same attribute type. We can see that even for one single attribute, it requires many verbalizing rules to handle different structures and attribute values, let alone extending the template rules to multiple attribute types.

Attribute value	Text
{ value:"gas-powered"}	The product is gas-powered.
{ value:"batteries"}	It runs on batteries.
{ value:"Manual" }	This doesn't have power.
{ value:"NA" }	This doesn't run on any power.

Table 2: Different instances of the attribute type "power_source_type" and human annotated text.

Neural Generator To avoid pre-defined rules and to generalise to unseen attributes, we train a neural generator model initialized either with Bart (Lewis et al., 2020) or T5 (Raffel et al., 2020), two state-of-the-art generative models pretrained on large amount of web text with self-supervised objectives. As input, we feed the linearized json-formatted data [3] and the output is the annotated text.

We further normalize the numbers in both the attribute and text to keep them in a consistent form, to help the model learn their correspondence in the generation task. For example, we turn forms like "1.", "1.0" and "1.00" into 1, and normalize words to numeric values ("one" → "1" etc).

To minimize the changes of hallucination in the generation, we also delexicalize words in the an-

[3] We also tried other input formats like flattening the hierarchical structure, adding instruction prompts (Schick and Schütze, 2020; Liu et al., 2021) etc, but did not find significant improvements.

Model	BLEU	chrF	PARENT-F1	#PARAMs	Faith	Cov	Flu
Performance on Seen Attributes							
Template	-	-	-	-	0.9612	0.9546	3.203
Reference	-	-	-	-	0.9574	0.9728	3.532
Bart-Base	0.3704	0.571	0.36445	139M	-	-	-
Bart-Large	0.3917	0.615	0.38748	406M	-	-	-
T5-Small	0.3267	0.542	0.33128	60M	-	-	-
T5-Base	**0.4061**	0.601	0.38214	220M	-	-	-
T5-Large	0.4060	**0.616**	**0.40806**	770M	**0.9731**	**0.9776**	**3.657**
T5-L (delex)	0.3911	0.604	0.39277	770M	0.9620	0.9640	3.632
Performance on Unseen Attributes							
Reference	-	-	-	-	**0.9401**	**0.8050**	3.520
Bart-Base	0.3386	0.553	0.31463	139M	-	-	-
Bart-Large	0.3541	0.586	0.33292	406M	-	-	-
T5-Small	0.3187	0.512	0.31379	60M	-	-	-
T5-Base	0.3293	0.544	0.33113	220M	-	-	-
T5-Large	**0.3869**	**0.610**	**0.37365**	770M	0.9125	0.9231	**3.610**
T5-L (delex)	0.3696	0.597	0.35275	770M	-	-	-

Table 3: Automatic Metric and human evaluation Results for Answer Presentation

notated text that match with the attribute values, replacing them by a tag in the input attribute, a common technique used in data-to-text generation (Wen et al., 2015; Ferreira et al., 2019; Chang et al., 2020b,a). The tag is the linearized path from the root node (attribute name) to the tag of the value. For example, for the second sentence in Table 1, the text "The product is compatible with ..." will be delexicalized into "The product is compatible for (concatenated) [value]." In the testing phase, after the model decodes the delexicalized text, the tag is then replaced to the corresponding value in the input attribute. While this can provide the model with a clear correspondence between input and output, it also adds the risk of losing the linguistic information like tense, singular/plural after delexicalization.

Automatic Evaluation For the automatic metrics, we report the BLEU (Papineni et al., 2002), chrF (Popović, 2015) and PARENT-F1 (Dhingra et al., 2019) score. The results of automatic metrics are shown in Table 3, where we try different sizes of models and list their number of model parameters (#PARAMs). Generally all the three metrics correlate well with each other. As expected, larger models tend to perform better than smaller models, with a larger difference on unseen versus seen attributes, which suggests that *larger models generalize better than smaller models on unseen attributes*. This could be because larger models are encoded with more language knowledge, which makes them less likely to overfit to the attributes in the training data.

T5-large achieves the best performance across all metrics. Therefore, we train with the delexicalized text as mentioned in Section 4 based on T5-large to see if the delexicalization can improve the performance further (T5-L (delex) in the table). All scores are evaluated on the lexicalized text output, which means that all delexicalized parts have been replaced with the input attribute values so that we can have a fair evaluation.

Delexicalization, unfortunately, does not help with the performance. It lowers down the scores over all metrics compared with directly using the original text as the target. The reason could be that T5 is pretrained with natural text itself. It has no delexicalized slots in its training corpus. Therefore, it fails to adapt well to the format of delexicalized text. Indeed, we find that T-5 sometimes generates text with slot names that do not exist in the input attribute which affects its performance. For future research, it would be interesting to see how to adapt pretrained generative models to delexicalized text, or even directly pretraining large-scaled generative models on delexicalized text.

Human Evaluation We conduct a human evaluation of the generated texts, focusing the following three dimensions: (1) **Faithfulness**, whether the text is faithful to the attribute (binary). (2) **Coverage**, whether the text covers all contents in the attribute (binary). (3) **Naturalness**, whether the text is a natural sentence rather than a machine-generated rigid one. 4-ary score from 1(rigid), 2(slightly rigid), 3(slightly natural) to 4(natural) On seen attributes, we evaluate the T5-large and T5-large with delexicalized text (T5-L (delex)), plus the template system and the annotated reference.

Attribute	From Template	From T5-large
allergen_information: { value:gluten_free }; { value:dairy_free }	allergen warning: the product contains gluten free,dairy free.	this product is gluten free and dairy free.
team_name: { value:"null" }	the team name of the product is null.	this does not have a team name.
speaker_type: {value:"portable bluetooth speakers"}	the product has a portable bluetooth speakers speaker.	this is a portable bluetooth speaker.
installation_type: value:"driver side"	the product is installed using the driver side.	this is installed on the driver side.

Table 4: Example of template-generated texts that are labeled as unfaithful.

Attribute	Reference	From T5-large
size_per_pearl: { value:"iphone" }	it is an iphone.	the product has an iphone size pearl.
switch_type: { value:"rotary switch" }	this has a switch that turns.	the product has a rotary switch.
target_species: { value:"Dog" }	for dogs.	this is for dogs.
installed_size:[{unit: unknown_modifier, value:32.}]	its cache memory installed_size:[{unit: unknown_modifier, value:32.}]	the product has a cache memory of 32 units.

Table 5: Example references which are labeled as unfaithful(first two rows) or unnatural (last two rows).

On unseen attributes, we only evaluate T5-large and the reference since handcrafted templates cannot be applied to unseen attributes at all. From each of 10 data splits, we randomly sample 50 attributes from it such that each model has 500 attribute-text pairs being evaluated. Each pair is evaluated by three annotators. The final scores are averaged over the 500 pairs for each model. We show the results and the agreement score among annotators in Table 3 and Table 6 respectively.

Faithful	**Coverage**	**Natur-4class**	**Natur-2class**
0.97762	0.97402	0.80499	0.92569

Table 6: Agreement Score for Answer Presentation.

Overall, the evaluation has a rather high agreement score. Naturalness has the lowest agreement since it is 4-ary. We also calculate the binary score for naturalness by combining natural and slightly natural into one bucket, and combining rigid and slightly rigid into the other bucket. The agreement score grows to over 0.92 by this means. We then manually checked and corrected all attribute-text pairs that do not have an agreement score of 1 for faithfulness and coverage. For naturalness, as it is a rather subjective metric anyway, we do not correct it. We also manually verified the faithfulness and coverage for the attribute *nutritional_info*, which we find especially hard to be evaluated correctly due to its complexity.

Overall all models have high scores on both faithfulness and coverage, and differences are small. For naturalness, as expected, templates have the lowest score. Using delexicalization underperforms the standard neural model, which is consistent with the findings from the automatic metric scores. We observe two interesting phenomena: (1) Neural models outperform templates even for faithfulness and (2) Neural models outperform human references for faithfulness and naturalness. In Table 4 and 5, we list examples of text generated from templates/references that are labeled as unfaithful/unnatural to the attribute. As can be seen, errors in template-generated texts usually occur because *the templates designed for certain values do not apply to a new value*. Errors in humans references are due to annotation noise, which is usually inevitable. The T5 model outperforms the reference, suggesting that it is able to round up these few annotation errors and learn the general pattern from the most correct references.

5 Conclusion

In this work, we study how to effectively leverage semi-structured data for product question answering. As there is no public datasets for this problem, we collect a dataset containing manually annotated questions together with description text about semi-structured attributes from our internal database. We present empirical results and findings about two key challenges of this problem: attribute ranking and answer presentation . Experiments show that neural models can provide superior text than template systems and perform well for ranking seen attributes, albeit there is still a noticeable drop when it comes to unseen attributes for both ranking and generation.

References

Sanjeev Arora, Yingyu Liang, and Tengyu Ma. 2017. A simple but tough-to-beat baseline for sentence embeddings. In *5th International Conference on Learning Representations, ICLR 2017*.

Ernie Chang, David Ifeoluwa Adelani, Xiaoyu Shen, and Vera Demberg. 2020a. Unsupervised pidgin text generation by pivoting english data and self-training. *arXiv preprint arXiv:2003.08272*.

Ernie Chang, Jeriah Caplinger, Alex Marin, Xiaoyu Shen, and Vera Demberg. 2020b. Dart: A lightweight quality-suggestive data-to-text annotation tool. In *Proceedings of the 28th International Conference on Computational Linguistics: System Demonstrations*, pages 12–17.

Lei Cui, Shaohan Huang, Furu Wei, Chuanqi Tan, Chaoqun Duan, and Ming Zhou. 2017. Superagent: A customer service chatbot for e-commerce websites. In *Proceedings of ACL 2017, System Demonstrations*, pages 97–102.

Kees van Deemter, Mariët Theune, and Emiel Krahmer. 2005. Real versus template-based natural language generation: A false opposition? *Computational linguistics*, 31(1):15–24.

Bhuwan Dhingra, Manaal Faruqui, Ankur Parikh, Ming-Wei Chang, Dipanjan Das, and William Cohen. 2019. Handling divergent reference texts when evaluating table-to-text generation. In *Proceedings of the 57th Annual Meeting of the Association for Computational Linguistics*, pages 4884–4895.

Thiago Castro Ferreira, Chris van der Lee, Emiel van Miltenburg, and Emiel Krahmer. 2019. Neural data-to-text generation: A comparison between pipeline and end-to-end architectures. In *Proceedings of the 2019 Conference on Empirical Methods in Natural Language Processing and the 9th International Joint Conference on Natural Language Processing (EMNLP-IJCNLP)*, pages 552–562.

Anette Frank, Hans-Ulrich Krieger, Feiyu Xu, Hans Uszkoreit, Berthold Crysmann, Brigitte Jörg, and Ulrich Schäfer. 2007. Question answering from structured knowledge sources. *Journal of Applied Logic*, 5(1):20–48.

Shen Gao, Zhaochun Ren, Yihong Zhao, Dongyan Zhao, Dawei Yin, and Rui Yan. 2019. Product-aware answer generation in e-commerce question-answering. In *Proceedings of the Twelfth ACM International Conference on Web Search and Data Mining*, pages 429–437.

Siddhant Garg, Thuy Vu, and Alessandro Moschitti. 2020. Tanda: Transfer and adapt pre-trained transformer models for answer sentence selection. In *Proceedings of the AAAI Conference on Artificial Intelligence*, volume 34, pages 7780–7788.

Mansi Gupta, Nitish Kulkarni, Raghuveer Chanda, Anirudha Rayasam, and Zachary C Lipton. 2019. Amazonqa: A review-based question answering task. *arXiv preprint arXiv:1908.04364*.

Timothy J Hazen, Shehzaad Dhuliawala, and Daniel Boies. 2019. Towards domain adaptation from limited data for question answering using deep neural networks. *arXiv preprint arXiv:1911.02655*.

Kai Hui, Bin Gao, Ben He, and Tie-jian Luo. 2013. Sponsored search ad selection by keyword structure analysis. In *European Conference on Information Retrieval*, pages 230–241. Springer.

Tom Kwiatkowski, Jennimaria Palomaki, Olivia Redfield, Michael Collins, Ankur Parikh, Chris Alberti, Danielle Epstein, Illia Polosukhin, Jacob Devlin, Kenton Lee, et al. 2019. Natural questions: a benchmark for question answering research. *Transactions of the Association for Computational Linguistics*, 7:453–466.

Mike Lewis, Yinhan Liu, Naman Goyal, Marjan Ghazvininejad, Abdelrahman Mohamed, Omer Levy, Veselin Stoyanov, and Luke Zettlemoyer. 2020. Bart: Denoising sequence-to-sequence pre-training for natural language generation, translation, and comprehension. In *Proceedings of the 58th Annual Meeting of the Association for Computational Linguistics*, pages 7871–7880.

Feng-Lin Li, Weijia Chen, Qi Huang, and Yikun Guo. 2019. Alime kbqa: Question answering over structured knowledge for e-commerce customer service. In *China Conference on Knowledge Graph and Semantic Computing*, pages 136–148. Springer.

Xiao Liu, Yanan Zheng, Zhengxiao Du, Ming Ding, Yujie Qian, Zhilin Yang, and Jie Tang. 2021. Gpt understands, too. *arXiv preprint arXiv:2103.10385*.

Yinhan Liu, Myle Ott, Naman Goyal, Jingfei Du, Mandar Joshi, Danqi Chen, Omer Levy, Mike Lewis, Luke Zettlemoyer, and Veselin Stoyanov. 2019. Roberta: A robustly optimized bert pretraining approach. *arXiv preprint arXiv:1907.11692*.

Julian McAuley and Alex Yang. 2016. Addressing complex and subjective product-related queries with customer reviews. In *Proceedings of the 25th International Conference on World Wide Web*, pages 625–635.

Kishore Papineni, Salim Roukos, Todd Ward, and Wei-Jing Zhu. 2002. Bleu: a method for automatic evaluation of machine translation. In *Proceedings of the 40th annual meeting of the Association for Computational Linguistics*, pages 311–318.

Maja Popović. 2015. chrf: character n-gram f-score for automatic mt evaluation. In *Proceedings of the Tenth Workshop on Statistical Machine Translation*, pages 392–395.

Colin Raffel, Noam Shazeer, Adam Roberts, Katherine Lee, Sharan Narang, Michael Matena, Yanqi Zhou, Wei Li, and Peter J Liu. 2020. Exploring the limits of transfer learning with a unified text-to-text transformer. *Journal of Machine Learning Research*, 21:1–67.

Pranav Rajpurkar, Jian Zhang, Konstantin Lopyrev, and Percy Liang. 2016. Squad: 100,000+ questions for machine comprehension of text. In *Proceedings of the 2016 Conference on Empirical Methods in Natural Language Processing*, pages 2383–2392.

Timo Schick and Hinrich Schütze. 2020. Few-shot text generation with pattern-exploiting training. *arXiv preprint arXiv:2012.11926*.

Ali Ghobadi Tapeh and Maseud Rahgozar. 2008. A knowledge-based question answering system for b2c ecommerce. *Knowledge-Based Systems*, 21(8):946–950.

Adam Trischler, Tong Wang, Xingdi Yuan, Justin Harris, Alessandro Sordoni, Philip Bachman, and Kaheer Suleman. 2017. Newsqa: A machine comprehension dataset. In *Proceedings of the 2nd Workshop on Representation Learning for NLP*, pages 191–200.

Tsung-Hsien Wen, Milica Gasic, Nikola Mrkšić, Pei-Hao Su, David Vandyke, and Steve Young. 2015. Semantically conditioned lstm-based natural language generation for spoken dialogue systems. In *Proceedings of the 2015 Conference on Empirical Methods in Natural Language Processing*, pages 1711–1721.

Wenxuan Zhang, Yang Deng, Jing Ma, and Wai Lam. 2020. Answerfact: Fact checking in product question answering. In *Proceedings of the 2020 Conference on Empirical Methods in Natural Language Processing (EMNLP)*, pages 2407–2417.

Improving Specificity in Review Response Generation with Data-Driven Data Filtering

Tannon Kew Martin Volk
Department of Computational Linguistics,
University of Zurich
{kew,volk}@cl.uzh.ch

Abstract

Responding to online customer reviews has become an essential part of successfully managing and growing a business both in e-commerce and the hospitality and tourism sectors. Recently, neural text generation methods intended to assist authors in composing responses have been shown to deliver highly fluent and natural looking texts. However, they also tend to learn a strong, undesirable bias towards generating overly generic, one-size-fits-all outputs to a wide range of inputs. While this often results in 'safe', high-probability responses, there are many practical settings in which greater specificity is preferable. In this work we examine the task of generating more specific responses for online reviews in the hospitality domain by identifying generic responses in the training data, filtering them and fine-tuning the generation model. We experiment with a range of data-driven filtering methods and show through automatic and human evaluation that, despite a 60% reduction in the amount of training data, filtering helps to derive models that are capable of generating more specific, useful responses.

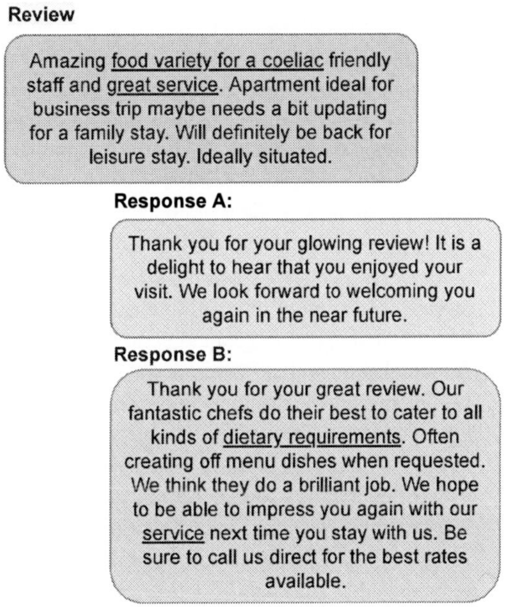

Figure 1: A user-written hotel review with two potentially valid responses. Response A (in blue) is a generic, one-size-fits-all style response, while Response B (in green) addresses and reiterates some, but not all, of the positive points raised in the review.

1 Introduction

Sequence-to-sequence (Seq2Seq) modelling with neural networks has proven to be an extremely popular and effective paradigm for a wide range of conditional text generation tasks (Sutskever et al., 2014; Vinyals and Le, 2015; Nallapati et al., 2016; Lebret et al., 2016, etc.). More recently, the development of large, pre-trained Seq2Seq models (e.g. Lewis et al., 2019) has lowered the bar on the amount of labelled in-domain data required to train models on a particular task and still achieve highly grammatical and fluent text. However, generative models often tend to produce bland and generic text, which significantly inhibits their potential utility (Holtzman et al., 2020). This problem is especially prevalent in tasks with valid many-to-one mappings, where generic outputs occur frequently in the training data; in dialogue modelling it has been referred to as the "I don't know" problem (Khayrallah and Sedoc, 2021).

In this work we consider the task of automatically generating responses to online hospitality reviews. Figure 1 provides an example of the task and presents a user-written hotel review along with two potentially valid responses. While Response B is highly specific, addressing the opening comment of the review and the positive mention of the service, Response A is generic. Such a response would be applicable to a broad range of positive reviews, highlighting the many-to-one problem.

Defining exactly what constitutes a *good* review response is not straightforward. Formal require-

Proceedings of The Fifth Workshop on e-Commerce and NLP (ECNLP 5), pages 121 - 133
May 26, 2022 ©2022 Association for Computational Linguistics

ments such as structure, style, intent and grammaticality are all important to consider, however, in this work we focus on content. Popular web-based review platforms (e.g. Google, Tripadvisor, etc.) recommend that responses should address topics raised in the review specifically. Such an approach is also supported by the Gricean maxims of quantity (be informative) and relation (be relevant) (Grice, 1975). Thus, we aim to avoid generating generic responses such as Response A in Figure 1. Yet, given a lack of constraints in response authorship, a significant portion of data that is available from online platforms consists of generic responses which are potentially of little benefit or even detrimental. In order to derive models that are capable of producing more specific, contentful responses, it is essential to mitigate the negative impact of these generic responses in the training data.

A simple yet effective method for improving a model's performance toward a specific goal is to increase the amount of training examples that exhibit the associated target quality and decrease the amount that do not. However, depending on the objective, this can be difficult. For example, classifying an arbitrary piece of text for specificity is challenging since there is limited consensus on what exactly constitutes specificity (Li et al., 2017b). Nevertheless, we investigate this idea and apply unsupervised scoring techniques to hotel review responses that aim to indicate a text's genericness. Given these scores, we infer suitable thresholds and filter out highly generic training data examples. We find that refining the training data and using just 40% of the original training examples allows us to derive models that are capable of producing fewer generic review responses according to both automatic metrics and human evaluation. Our code to reproduce the data used and relevant experiments is available on GitHub.[1]

2 Background and Related Work

Review Response Generation Thanks to an increasing awareness of the benefits associated with addressing online customer feedback (Proserpio and Zervas, 2018; Li et al., 2017a), there is a growing body of literature on automated review response generation. Previous work in this area has considered various domain applications and extended the basic encoder-decoder architecture to incorporate additional contextual information alongside a review text. Zhao et al. (2019) generate responses for product reviews on an e-commerce platform using tabular product information as additional context, while Gao et al. (2019a) focus on generating responses for smartphone app reviews and incorporate discrete external attribute features, such as the review rating and app category. Kew et al. (2020) later applied the same model to restaurant and hotel reviews in English and German and showed that extensive variability in hospitality responses (compared to app review responses) leads to considerably worse performance according to automatic metrics.

Combating Generic Outputs Considerable work has been dedicated to mitigating generic outputs in dialogue models. One popular approach is to feed the model additional contextual information in order to encourage more 'contentful' responses. Depending on the availability of relevant data, this might include the dialogue history (Sordoni et al., 2015), free text from an external knowledge source (Ghazvininejad et al., 2018; Bruyn et al., 2020), or embedded topic signals derived from the input query (Xing et al., 2017). Meanwhile, a number of works have focused on improving the model architecture (Serban et al., 2016a,b; Zhao et al., 2017; Bao et al., 2019; Gao et al., 2019b) or modifying the decoding strategy (Baheti et al., 2018; Li et al., 2016).

Since generic responses occur with high frequency in the dialogue training data they induce a strong, undesirable bias. Thus, it also makes sense to tackle this problem at its source. Previous work in this direction has aimed to remove uninformative training examples in a *conditional* framework by performing comparisons between source and target pairs (Xu et al., 2018; Csáky et al., 2019). In contrast to dialogue data, review-response pairs typically consist of multiple sentences, resembling paragraphs rather than single sentences. This leads to extensive variance in the surface form on both the source and target side, rendering conditional approaches less suitable. For instance, initial investigations revealed that the best-performing approach presented in Csáky et al. (2019) identifies only 5% of hospitality review-responses as generic. Therefore, in contrast to previous works, we set out to identify generic responses independently of their corresponding source texts to improve our training data.

[1] `https://github.com/ZurichNLP/specific_hospo_respo`

3 Methods

In order to derive models that are capable of producing fewer generic responses, we consider removing them entirely from the training data. Our hypothesis is that generic responses seen often during training encourage the model to learn 'safe' but uninformative responses and are thus detrimental to the model's ability to generate more specific responses. To investigate this, we define three potential methods for scoring a text's genericness within a corpus, operationalising these at the word, sentence and document level. We then derive suitable thresholds for each scoring method and filter training data examples according to their genericness. Formally, given a response text in the training corpus $\mathcal{R} \in \mathcal{T}$, we aim to assign a numerical score $\mathcal{S}$, indicating how unique $\mathcal{R}$ is in relation to all other responses in the corpus.

Lexical Frequency To operationalise our scoring techniques at the word level, we define a response text as a bag of words $\mathcal{R} = \{w_1, w_2, ..., w_m\}$. The frequency distribution of words in natural language corpora tends to follow a long-tailed power law (Zipf, 1935). We exploit this property to easily identify words that occur with such high-frequency that they can be considered to contribute little to no specific information.

Following Wu et al. (2018), a response may then be considered universal if it consists predominantly of words whose rank in the frequency table $\geq n$. Based on this intuition, this scoring method calculates the ratio of high-frequency words to less frequent ones. Specifically for each response text, we compute,

$$\mathcal{S}_{\text{lex\_freq}} = \frac{\sum_{i=1}^{m} \mathcal{I}(w_i)}{m}, \tag{1}$$

where $I(w_i)$ is defined as

$$\mathcal{I}(w_i) = \begin{cases} 1 & \text{if } count(w_i, \mathcal{T}) \geq t \\ 0 & \text{otherwise} \end{cases}. \tag{2}$$

In our experiments, we set a frequency threshold $t = 500$ in order to capture a reasonable amount of generic content words (e.g. 'hotel', 'review', etc.) as well as typical stop words.

Sentence Average Considering only the occurrence of unigrams within a response fails to take into account the effect of larger semantic units that may be considered as generic phrases (e.g. personalised greetings, salutations, expressions of gratitude, etc.). Therefore, we also consider a scoring method aimed at quantifying a response's genericness at the sentence level. To operationalise this method, we define a response text as a bag of sentences, $\mathcal{R} = \{s_1, s_2, ..., s_n\}$. Similar to the lexical frequency-based score described above, given a means of reliably identifying generic sentences, we could simply calculate the ratio of generic to non-generic sentences comprising a response text. However, this is less straightforward since sentences do not share the same distributional property.

Works such as Reimers and Gurevych (2019) and Artetxe and Schwenk (2019) demonstrate that deep contextualised sentence representations work well for a wide range of sentence-level semantic textual similarity (STS) tasks. Inspired by these works, we consider scoring a response sentence for genericness by computing its semantic similarity against a pool of generic example sentences $\mathcal{G} = \{g_1, g_2, ..., g_n\}$.

Initial experiments showed that LSTM baseline models exhibit a strong bias towards generating universal responses with little specificity to the themes raised in reviews. We gathered all response sentences generated more than once by an earlier model, considering them as our pool of generic examples $\mathcal{G}$, and compute the maximum similarity for each $s \in \mathcal{R}$ as follows:

$$\xi(s) = \max_{g \in \mathcal{G}}(\cos(s, g)). \tag{3}$$

Then, we compute average sentence-level genericness as

$$\mathcal{S}_{\text{sent\_avg}} = \frac{1}{n} \sum_{i=1}^{n} \xi(s_i). \tag{4}$$

This method constitutes a two-step approach to improve the training data based on outputs from a less performant model and may be seen as similar to the idea behind the iterative 'data distillation' approach presented by Li et al. (2017b). However, unlike that work, which dealt with sentence-level outputs and compared them directly, we compute the final score for a response text by averaging the genericness scores of its constituent sentences.

LM Perplexity In order to score a response text for genericness at the document level, we rely on a causal language model (LM) and compute the perplexity (PPL) of each response. Intuitively, generic responses that occur frequently and with relatively little variation are less surprising and should thus receive a lower LM PPL in contrast to a highly specific response. Since we do not provide the review text as context, the LM is forced to score the response in isolation, thus maximising surprisal for less generic responses that contain more unexpected events.

To this end, we use a distilled GPT-2 model that is fine-tuned to our domain (Radford et al., 2019; Wolf et al., 2020) and for each training response compute

$$\mathcal{S}_{\text{LM\_PPL}} = \exp(\text{CE}_{\text{LM}}, \mathcal{R}). \quad (5)$$

4 Experiments

4.1 Data Set

Our primary data set comprises a total of 500k unique hotel review-response pairs published on Tripadvisor[2]. We collected data from seven different countries with reviews for more than 7.5k establishments, ranging from luxury hotels to backpacker's hostels and small bed-n-breakfasts. Of the 500k review-response pairs, we take approximately 90% for model training, setting aside 5% for validation purposes and the final 5% for evaluation.

In addition to investigating the proposed techniques on hospitality review responses, we also conduct a small generalisability study on a related data set from a different domain. Specifically, we use the mobile app review responses, originally introduced by (Gao et al., 2019a). These review responses were collected from the Google Play Store and differ considerably in terms of both style and length to those found in the hospitality domain (Kew et al., 2020). Table 1 provides a brief overview of both data sets.

4.2 Training Data Filtration

After having scored each response text in the corpus with the methods described in Section 3, we inspected the distributions of the resulting scores on the training set. Figure 2 shows the distribution of values for each scoring method. As can be seen, the majority of the distributions follow relatively smooth normal distributions, with various degrees of skew, indicating that different scorers appear to detect different qualities. In order to make all experiment runs comparable, we aim to extract the 'best' 40% of training data examples according to each individual scoring method. To derive appropriate thresholds for data filtering, we inspect samples along the range of x-axis values and align these with the following intuitions:

[2]https://www.tripadvisor.com/

Domain	Split	Rev-resp pairs	Sents
Hospitality	Training	450,367	5.4M
	Validation	24,897	299k
	Test	24,736	297k
Mobile Apps	Training	278,374	1.7M
	Validation	14,602	90k
	Test	15,404	95k

Table 1: Overview of the review response data sets used in our experiments. The hospitality domain refers to pairs collected from TripAdvisor, while the mobile app domain refers to the data set introduced by (Gao et al., 2019a). Numbers indicate the size of the training data before performing targeted filtering.

(i) **Lexical frequency** – a higher ratio of high-frequency words indicates more genericness, thus lower is better;

(ii) **Sentence Average** – a higher score indicates a higher degree of generic sentences within a response, thus lower is better;

(iii) **LM PPL** - a lower PPL indicates less surprisal, while a high PPL potentially indicates a large degree of noise and possibly ungrammatical text, thus a mid-range score is better.

Since we filter the training data according to each scoring method independently, it is reasonable to expect that there may be considerable overlap between the resulting training subsets. Figure 3 shows that most overlap occurs between the word and sentence-level scored subsets with 65%, while the LM PPL filtered subset contains only 57% shared examples.

4.3 Model Training and Inference

Our response generation models are built on top of BART (Lewis et al., 2019), a large pre-trained model for Seq2Seq tasks. All models are initialised with the same BART-base model from Hugging Face (Wolf et al., 2020), which comprises six encoder and six decoder layers. We fine-tuned our models with default hyperparameters and an effective batch size of 40 for a maximum of 8 epochs.[3] The best model from each training run was selected according to ROUGE-2 performance on a 25% sample of the validation set.

[3]Depending on the amount of data used, fine-tuning typically runs for two to 5 days on a single 12GB GPU.

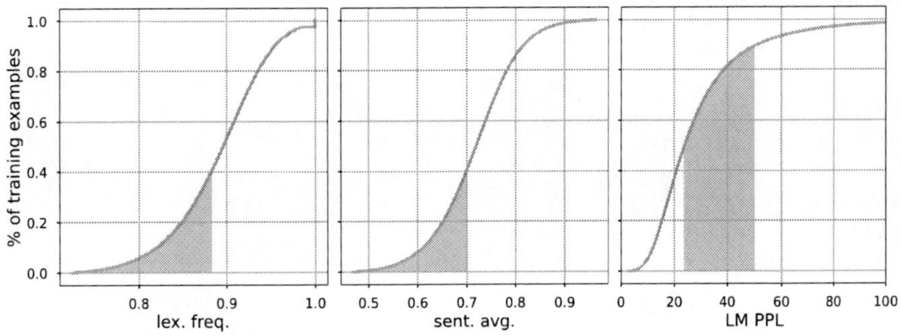

Figure 2: Cumulative distribution plots for each scoring method on the training data. The shaded areas show the 'optimal' 40% of the training data (review-response pairs) identified by the method.

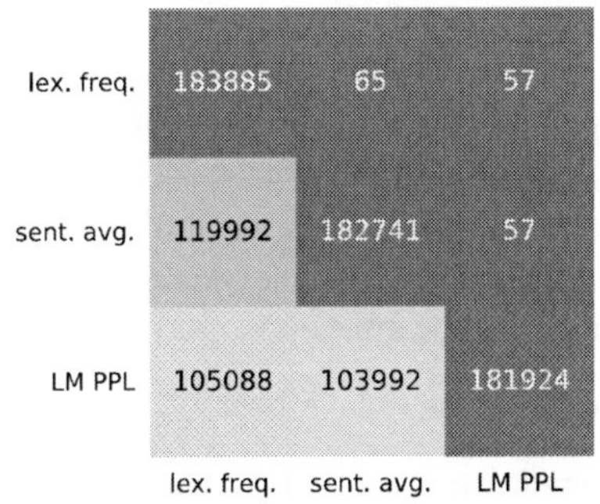

Figure 3: The amount of overlapping examples between each of the three filtered training sets. Numbers in the bottom-left show the raw counts of overlapping target texts, while the numbers in the top-right show the amount of overlap as a rounded percentage.

For all models, inference was performed using standard beam search with k=5 on the full test set, i.e. no filtering is applied to the test set. As a baseline, we use a model fine-tuned on all available training data and compare this to the three experimental systems, each fine-tuned on one of the filtered training sets.

4.4 Evaluation

Evaluating short text-based conversation is inherently difficult since responses are, to a large degree, open-ended. For any given input sequence, the space of potentially valid outputs is extremely large. As a consequence, it is necessary to analyse various characteristics of the generated texts. We employ a selection of automatic metrics that act as approximate but useful indicators of textual quality along multiple axes. In addition, we conduct a human evaluation and compare model outputs in order to measure the effect of different data filtering methods on model performance.

4.4.1 Automatic Metrics

Reference-based Metrics Ground truth responses are unlikely to serve as reliable references for comparison with surface-level or embedding-based automatic metrics due to the open-ended nature of the task. Despite this, and other criticisms (Reiter and Belz, 2009), popular N-gram overlap metrics, such as BLEU have been reported in the relevant literature (Gao et al., 2019a; Zhao et al., 2019). An alternative, easy-to-compute metric is **chrF** (Popović, 2015), which operates on character N-grams rather than full tokens and balances both precision and recall. This makes it considerably more flexible than BLEU, especially for noisy web-based text where spelling errors are common. In addition to reporting chrF against the ground truth responses, we also separately compute chrF using the corresponding input reviews as 'stand-in' references. This provides an approximate measure for specificity in model outputs.

Lexical Diversity and Range Automatically generated review responses should exhibit a decent amount of both inter- and intra-textual diversity. Low inter-textual diversity implies that models repeatedly generate the same or highly similar texts, while low intra-textual diversity indicates that model outputs contain lexical repetitions, possibly as a result of getting stuck in repetitive *de*generate loops (Welleck et al., 2019; Holtzman et al., 2020).

To measure inter-textual diversity, we employ **Self-BLEU** (Zhu et al., 2018). This metric computes for each system-generated output the BLEU score, regarding all other system-generated outputs as makeshift references. Thereby, it effectively measures the amount of textual similarity in terms

	chrF-tgt ↑	chrF-src ↑	DIST-1 ↑	Self-BLEU ↓	Uniq. ↑	Len ↑
Ground truth	-	20.7	75.66	1.18	37649	80.92
Rule-based	19.7	10.1	86.44	55.19	153	35.91
Baseline	30.47	15.87	76.84	24.6	7174	59.39
Lex. freq.	33.6	20.63	74.33	15.37	11859	82.37
Sent. avg.	32.53	20.2	73.46	13.11	11858	75.69
LM PPL	32.63	21.0	74.51	4.24	13366	73.82

Table 2: Model performance under all automatic evaluation metrics considered. Values reported for all BART-based models are averaged over three individual inference runs from models trained with different random seeds to account for potential variation between training runs. Note, metrics reported here are multiplied by 100 where applicable for improved readability.

of N-gram overlap between generated responses. A higher Self-BLEU score indicates less diversity.

For intra-textual diversity, we follow Choi et al. (2020) and use **Distinct-N** (Li et al., 2016). This metric calculates the ratio of unique N-grams to the total number of N-grams generated *within* a text, taking the macro average as the final score. Following Welleck et al. (2019), we also report the total number of **unique** words generated by a model over the entire test set. This provides a simple indicator of a model's lexical range.

Finally, we report the average length of generated texts to provide a rough idea of a model's ability to generate adequate responses under the assumption that shorter responses indicate a greater degree of genericness. Where possible, we also compute these metrics for the human-written ground truth responses in the test set to provide a valuable idea of expected or appropriate values.

4.4.2 Human Evaluation

In order to assess a model's ability to generate fewer generic, one-size-fits-all responses on the basis of training data filtering, we conduct a human evaluation. We sampled 200 reviews from the test set and generated responses with all four models. We then recruited four evaluators, all of whom are familiar with the field of NLP, and asked two evaluators to rate examples 1-100 and the other two evaluators to rate examples 101-200. The evaluation schema was designed to make pairwise comparisons between randomly selected model outputs and asked judges to indicate which response is more specific to the input review. Note that while framing the evaluation question in this way inverts our main aim of reducing generic responses, it simplifies the task for the judges by encouraging them to focus more on the content that *is* generated by the model, rather than what is not. To facilitate decision making and allow for more nuanced judgements, we use a continuous scale that allows evaluators to indicate the degree to which they believe one response is better than the other (Belz and Kow, 2011). Judges were also able to accept or reject both responses if they were equally specific or generic, respectively.

5 Results

Automatic Metrics Table 2 compares model performance under the automatic metrics considered. In addition to the baseline and experimental models discussed above, we also compute automatic metrics for a naïve rule-based baseline, which simply returns a single, hand-crafted response from a small set of candidates based on the rating associated with the input review. These are intended to be highly generic responses that fit the context and thus provide a useful comparison and motivation for more complex approaches.

According to both versions of chrF, all models trained on filtered data sets show considerable gains over the baseline model, trained on the entirety of the data. Specifically, chrF computed against the true target shows smaller improvements over the baseline, while chrF computed against the corresponding source shows a relatively large improvement for all experimental models, bringing the degree of overlap in model outputs much more in line with human-written responses.

DIST-1 shows that intra-textual lexical diversity is consistent against the human-written responses for most models, indicating the lexical repetitions occur within a reasonable range for this relatively restricted domain. Thus, there is no indication that our models are getting stuck in repetitive *de*generate loops (Holtzman et al., 2020).

Self-BLEU reveals considerable variation among all models in terms of the diversity between generated responses. According to this metric, the LM PPL filtering method ensures the most diverse response texts, while both the rule-based and BART baseline generate the least diverse texts by far. Noticeably, the best scoring models are not quite on par with the diversity of human-written responses. However, this is to be expected given that neural models generally stick to generating higher-frequency words (Holtzman et al., 2020). This phenomenon is further indicated by a large discrepancy between the counts of unique lexical items observed.

In terms of average response length, most models under-generate when compared to the human-written ground truth. Here, the baseline models fall the shortest, which may be a useful proxy indicating higher genericness. Meanwhile, the models trained on the lexical frequency-filtered subset show a tendency to generate longer responses. This may be due to the score being directly related to the word count of a text, despite normalisation.

Human Evaluation In analysing the results of the human evaluation, we considered only those examples on which two judges agreed in terms of preference towards a particular response candidate and acceptability. This resulted in 129 valid pairwise comparisons. Following recommendations by Novikova et al. (2018), we derive the overall model rankings using the Bayesian ranking algorithm TrueSkill™ (Herbrich et al., 2007).

According to the results of our human evaluation, all filtering methods help to improve the specificity of model outputs, thereby reducing genericness. Figure 4 depicts the final model rankings derived through applying the TrueSkill™ algorithm to accepted pairwise comparisons from our evaluation. Here, it can clearly be seen that all experimental models outperform the baseline, with a clear tendency towards filtering for genericness based on larger semantic units, i.e. sentence or document-level.

Taken together, the results of our automatic evaluation and the human evaluation strongly suggest that fine-tuning on a filtered subset of data is beneficial, reducing the model's tendency to produce generic responses. In particular, chrF-src and Self-BLEU are useful indicators for gauging relative genericness and diversity of generated texts. Table 5 in Appendix A provides some examples of the

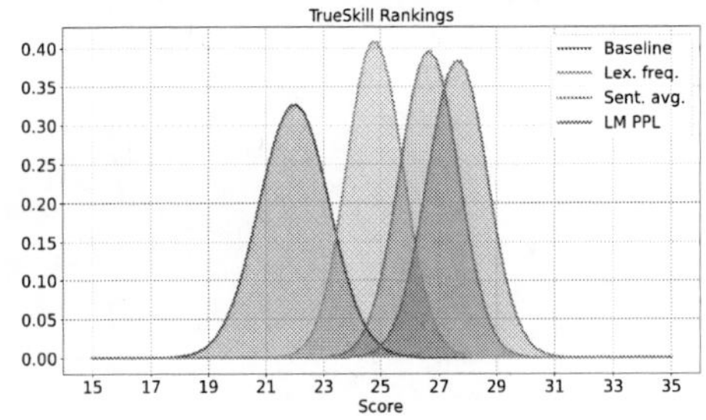

Figure 4: Final model ranking posteriors as computed with TrueSkill™ on 129 human evaluated pairwise comparisons.

responses generated by all models and how they improve in terms of specificity to the input review.

5.1 Ablations

How much filtering is too much filtering? In the above experiments we select thresholds for each filtering method to retain approximately only 40% of the original training data. Results of automatic and human evaluations reveal that the LM PPL method performs best on balance. To investigate the ideal amount of filtering, we train and evaluate additional models by incrementing the lower bound of the target text LM PPL filter to train on different quantities of data. Furthermore, we also consider combining all filtering methods together to train a model on only the least generic responses according to the thresholds set in Section 4.2. The results of these ablations are presented in Table 3.[4]

Comparing the results for the LM PPL filter in isolation, we see that the largest performance gains are achieved when training with between 40 and 80% of the total amount of data. According to metrics used as proxies for specificity, chrF-src, Self-BLEU and Uniq., more aggressive filtering (e.g. 40%) works best with very little cost in terms of chrF-tgt. Meanwhile, extremely aggressive filtering (20%), leads to a large performance drop across the board. Interestingly though, combining all filtering methods to filter aggressively has a more positive impact, suggesting that the overall quality of the training data used can indeed be further improved by considering multiple filtering methods. That said, the relatively high Self-BLEU score indicates that this model tends to generate the same response to different input reviews to a greater extent than those trained on more data.

[4]To reduce the computational cost of ablations, we perform a single training run for these models with a fixed random seed.

	chrF-tgt ↑	chrF-src ↑	DIST-1 ↑	Self-BLEU ↓	Uniq. ↑	Len ↑
20%	27.0	15.3	74.39	31.21	7449	50.46
40%	32.7	21.1	74.54	4.49	13548	73.31
60%	32.8	19.6	74.55	8.08	11405	71.73
80%	32.9	18.9	74.68	12.67	8615	72.96
100%	30.5	15.8	76.95	27.1	7273	59.09
ALL 15%	33.3	22.7	72.29	18.19	14374	83.48

Table 3: Results of ablation runs investigating a) performance as a function of the percentage of data filtered using LM PPL and b) performance as a result of combining *all* filtering methods with the thresholds shown in Figure 2 and training on only the 'best' 15% of the data.

	chrF-tgt ↑	chrF-src ↑	DIST-1 ↑	Self-BLEU ↓	Uniq. ↑	Len ↑
20%	26.0	18.0	83.76	0.31	2362	40.12
40%	29.8	17.5	81.98	1.56	2111	45.04
60%	32.3	16.7	80.91	1.47	1978	49.53
80%	33.5	15.8	80.34	2.72	1545	50.65
100%	35.5	15.5	79.04	2.41	1459	53.67

Table 4: LM PPL filtering at varying thresholds for mobile app review response generation (Gao et al., 2019a).

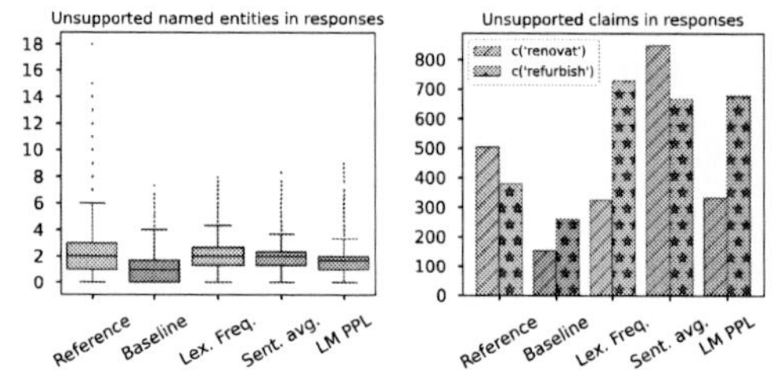

Figure 5: Left: averaged occurrences of named entities in responses that do not appear in the corresponding input review. Right: total occurrences of the stems 'renovat' and 'refurbish' in responses texts.

Generalisability Targeted data filtering is effective for reducing genericness in hospitality review response generation. To investigate whether such an approach generalises to other domains we also consider applying our best performing filtering method to the related task of mobile app review response generation using the data set presented in Gao et al. (2019a). Following the LM PPL approach described in Section 3, we again experiment with a range of thresholds for filtering both low-PPL and overly high-PPL responses from training data. Table 4 shows that targeted filtering in this domain also leads to increased specificity according to automatic metrics used as proxies for measuring genericness.

Are there any side effects? Encouraging a model to consistently produce fewer generic outputs may also have potential side effects. For example, it is possible that this could lead to an increase in hallucinated content that is unsupported by the input and thus may be factually incorrect or misleading. To investigate whether or not the proposed approach compromises the generated outputs in this way, we search for candidate hallucinations in the generated responses and compare their occurrence frequencies to the reference texts and the outputs from the baseline model.

As candidates, we consider named entities, which generally constitute common hallucination errors (Dziri et al., 2021) and mentions of renovations or refurbishments. The latter is observed frequently in hotel review responses as a suitable reply to a criticism about outdated infrastructure or decor. Naturally, the models themselves have no knowledge of whether renovations are planned, so a conservative approach would be to consider all generated responses that mention renovations as hallucinations.

First, we searched review-response pairs for named entities and computed the amount of named entities in the response that do not appear in the corresponding review and are thus 'unsupported'.[5] On the left of Figure 5, we can see that unsupported named entities occur more frequently in the experimental models in contrast to the baseline. Second, we counted occurrences of the stems 'renovat' and 'refurbish' in all response texts. On the right of Figure 5, we can see that all experimental models are guilty of over-producing claims involving renovations or refurbishments and thus could be at risk of generating more factually incorrect claims.

[5]For identifying named entities, we used spaCy (`https://spacy.io/`).

5.2 Discussion and Future Work

Based on the observations from the previous sections, it is clear filtering uninformative instances from the training data is an effective approach to reduce genericness in model outputs for response generation. However, it does not come without risk. Our analysis revealed that generated responses tend to contain more hallucinated content. Thus, further work is required to mitigate this and better ensure the factual accuracy of generated outputs.

While removing generic training examples is effective at reducing unwanted predictive biases, it does not provide any means to steer the amount of genericness. In certain application scenarios, it may be more desirable to be able to control the degree of genericness at inference time in order to handle difficult or ambiguous cases (Li et al., 2017b). To this end, our methods for quantifying textual genericness, might also be used to derive categorical labels for training examples that are provided to the model in order to be able to steer the generation appropriately at inference time (Filippova, 2020; Martin et al., 2020). We leave a detailed investigation in this direction for future work.

We also acknowledge that there is a considerable risk in deploying fully automatic review response generation in online settings. The societal impacts of computer-generated language are still relatively unknown and thus it is unclear what effects such an application may have on customer satisfaction and business-customer relations in e-commerce and online settings. This work is intended to support response authors in improving their efficiency and extending the capabilities.

6 Conclusion

State-of-the-art approaches to conditional text generation involving transfer learning can be adapted to perform a wide range of domain-specific tasks with strong and convincing results. However, the content and quality of a model's outputs largely reflect that of the in-domain data used for fine-tuning. Thus, care should be taken when deciding which data to use for training. In this paper we presented three unconditional scoring techniques for identifying and filtering generic responses in a parallel corpus of review-response pairs. Results of both automatic and human evaluation revealed that this is an effective approach for helping to reduce the production of generic, one-size-fits-all outputs for review response generation in the hospitality domain, as well as for mobile app reviews. We have also shown that such an approach has potential side effects that must be handled appropriately before being utilised in a real-world scenario.

Acknowledgements

This work was partially supported by the Swiss Innovation Agency InnoSuisse as part of the ReAdvisor project (project number 38943.1 IP-ICT) under the direction of Sarah Ebling. We would like to thank Jannis Vamvas, Janis Goldzycher, Nicolas Spring and Noëmi Aepli for their assistance with conducting evaluations and Chantal Amrhein and Rico Sennrich for their valuable feedback. We also thank the anonymous reviewers for their helpful and constructive comments.

References

Mikel Artetxe and Holger Schwenk. 2019. Massively multilingual sentence embeddings for zero-shot cross-lingual transfer and beyond. *Transactions of the Association for Computational Linguistics*, 7:597–610.

Ashutosh Baheti, Alan Ritter, Jiwei Li, and Bill Dolan. 2018. Generating More Interesting Responses in Neural Conversation Models with Distributional Constraints. In *Proceedings of the 2018 Conference on Empirical Methods in Natural Language Processing*, pages 3970–3980, Brussels, Belgium. Association for Computational Linguistics.

Siqi Bao, Huang He, Fan Wang, Hua Wu, and Haifeng Wang. 2019. PLATO: Pre-trained dialogue generation model with discrete latent variable. *arXiv preprint arXiv:1910.07931*.

Anja Belz and Eric Kow. 2011. Discrete vs. Continuous rating scales for language evaluation in NLP. In *Proceedings of the 49th Annual Meeting of the Association for Computational Linguistics: Human Language Technologies*, pages 230–235, Portland, Oregon, USA.

M. D. Bruyn, E. Lotfi, Jeska Buhmann, and W. Daelemans. 2020. BART for knowledge grounded conversations. In *Converse@KDD*.

Byung-Ju Choi, Jimin Hong, David Keetae Park, and Sang Wan Lee. 2020. F$\hat{2}$-Softmax: Diversifying Neural Text Generation via Frequency Factorized Softmax. *arXiv:2009.09417 [cs]*.

Richárd Csáky, Patrik Purgai, and Gábor Recski. 2019. Improving neural conversational models with entropy-based data filtering. In *Proceedings of the 57th Annual Meeting of the Association for Computational Linguistics*, pages 5650–5669, Florence, Italy. Association for Computational Linguistics.

Nouha Dziri, Andrea Madotto, Osmar Zaiane, and Avishek Joey Bose. 2021. Neural Path Hunter: Reducing Hallucination in Dialogue Systems via Path Grounding. *arXiv:2104.08455 [cs]*.

Katja Filippova. 2020. Controlled Hallucinations: Learning to Generate Faithfully from Noisy Data. *arXiv:2010.05873 [cs]*.

Cuiyun Gao, Jichuan Zeng, Xin Xia, David Lo, Michael R. Lyu, and Irwin King. 2019a. Automating App Review Response Generation. In *2019 34th IEEE/ACM International Conference on Automated Software Engineering (ASE)*, pages 163–175, San Diego, USA. IEEE.

Xiang Gao, Sungjin Lee, Yizhe Zhang, Chris Brockett, Michel Galley, Jianfeng Gao, and Bill Dolan. 2019b. Jointly Optimizing Diversity and Relevance in Neural Response Generation. In *Proceedings of the 2019 Conference of the North American Chapter of the Association for Computational Linguistics (NAACL)*, pages 1229–1238, Minneapolis, USA.

Marjan Ghazvininejad, Chris Brockett, Ming-Wei Chang, Bill Dolan, Jianfeng Gao, Wen-tau Yih, and Michel Galley. 2018. A knowledge-grounded neural conversation model. In *Proceedings of the Thirty-Second AAAI Conference on Artificial Intelligence*, pages 5110–5117, New Orleans, USA.

Herbert P Grice. 1975. Logic and conversation. In *Speech Acts*, pages 41–58. Brill.

Ralf Herbrich, Tom Minka, and Thore Graepel. 2007. TrueSkill(TM): A bayesian skill rating system. In *Advances in Neural Information Processing Systems 20*, pages 569–576. MIT Press.

Ari Holtzman, Jan Buys, Li Du, Maxwell Forbes, and Yejin Choi. 2020. The Curious Case of Neural Text Degeneration. *arXiv:1904.09751 [cs]*.

Tannon Kew, Michael Amsler, and Sarah Ebling. 2020. Benchmarking Automated Review Response Generation for the Hospitality Domain. In *Proceedings of Workshop on Natural Language Processing in E-Commerce*, pages 43–52, Barcelona, Spain. Association for Computational Linguistics.

Huda Khayrallah and João Sedoc. 2021. Measuring the 'I don't know' Problem through the Lens of Gricean Quantity. In *Proceedings of the 2021 Conference of the North American Chapter of the Association for Computational Linguistics: Human Language Technologies*, pages 5659–5670, Online.

Rémi Lebret, David Grangier, and Michael Auli. 2016. Neural text generation from structured data with application to the biography domain. In *Proceedings of the 2016 Conference on Empirical Methods in Natural Language Processing*, pages 1203–1213, Austin, Texas. Association for Computational Linguistics.

Mike Lewis, Yinhan Liu, Naman Goyal, Marjan Ghazvininejad, Abdelrahman Mohamed, Omer Levy, Ves Stoyanov, and Luke Zettlemoyer. 2019. BART: Denoising Sequence-to-Sequence Pre-training for Natural Language Generation, Translation, and Comprehension. *arXiv:1910.13461 [cs, stat]*.

Chunyu Li, Geng Cui, and Ling Peng. 2017a. The signaling effect of management response in engaging customers: A study of the hotel industry. *Tourism Management*, 62:42–53.

Jiwei Li, Michel Galley, Chris Brockett, Jianfeng Gao, and Bill Dolan. 2016. A Diversity-Promoting Objective Function for Neural Conversation Models. *arXiv:1510.03055 [cs]*.

Jiwei Li, Will Monroe, and Dan Jurafsky. 2017b. Data Distillation for Controlling Specificity in Dialogue Generation. *arXiv:1702.06703 [cs]*.

Louis Martin, Éric de la Clergerie, Benoît Sagot, and Antoine Bordes. 2020. Controllable sentence simplification. In *Proceedings of the 12th Language Resources and Evaluation Conference*, pages 4689–4698, Marseille, France. European Language Resources Association.

Ramesh Nallapati, Bowen Zhou, Cicero dos Santos, Çağlar Gulçehre, and Bing Xiang. 2016. Abstractive text summarization using sequence-to-sequence RNNs and beyond. In *Proceedings of the 20th SIGNLL Conference on Computational Natural Language Learning*, pages 280–290, Berlin, Germany. Association for Computational Linguistics.

Jekaterina Novikova, Ondřej Dušek, and Verena Rieser. 2018. RankME: Reliable human ratings for natural language generation. In *Proceedings of the 2018 Conference of the North American Chapter of the Association for Computational Linguistics: Human Language Technologies, Volume 2 (Short Papers)*, pages 72–78, New Orleans, Louisiana. Association for Computational Linguistics.

Maja Popović. 2015. chrF: Character n-gram F-score for automatic MT evaluation. In *Proceedings of the Tenth Workshop on Statistical Machine Translation*, pages 392–395, Lisbon, Portugal. Association for Computational Linguistics.

Davide Proserpio and Giorgos Zervas. 2018. Study: Replying to Customer Reviews Results in Better Ratings. *Harvard Business Review*.

Alec Radford, Jeffrey Wu, Rewon Child, David Luan, Dario Amodei, and Ilya Sutskever. 2019. Language Models are Unsupervised Multitask Learners. *OpenAI Blog*, 1(8).

Nils Reimers and Iryna Gurevych. 2019. Sentence-BERT: Sentence embeddings using siamese BERT-Networks. In *Proceedings of the 2019 Conference on Empirical Methods in Natural Language Processing*. Association for Computational Linguistics.

Ehud Reiter and Anja Belz. 2009. An Investigation into the Validity of Some Metrics for Automatically Evaluating Natural Language Generation Systems. *Computational Linguistics*, 35(4):529–558.

Iulian V. Serban, Alessandro Sordoni, Yoshua Bengio, Aaron Courville, and Joelle Pineau. 2016a. Building end-to-end dialogue systems using generative hierarchical neural network models. In *Proceedings of the Thirtieth AAAI Conference on Artificial Intelligence*, AAAI'16, pages 3776–3783, Phoenix, Arizona. AAAI Press.

Iulian Vlad Serban, Alessandro Sordoni, Ryan Lowe, Laurent Charlin, Joelle Pineau, Aaron Courville, and Yoshua Bengio. 2016b. A Hierarchical Latent Variable Encoder-Decoder Model for Generating Dialogues. *arXiv:1605.06069 [cs]*.

Alessandro Sordoni, Michel Galley, Michael Auli, Chris Brockett, Yangfeng Ji, Margaret Mitchell, Jian-Yun Nie, Jianfeng Gao, and Bill Dolan. 2015. A Neural Network Approach to Context-Sensitive Generation of Conversational Responses. *arXiv:1506.06714 [cs]*.

Ilya Sutskever, Oriol Vinyals, and Quoc V. Le. 2014. Sequence to Sequence Learning with Neural Networks. *arXiv:1409.3215 [cs]*.

Oriol Vinyals and Quoc Le. 2015. A Neural Conversational Model. *arXiv:1506.05869 [cs]*.

Sean Welleck, Ilia Kulikov, Stephen Roller, Emily Dinan, Kyunghyun Cho, and Jason Weston. 2019. Neural Text Generation with Unlikelihood Training. *arXiv:1908.04319 [cs, stat]*.

Thomas Wolf, Lysandre Debut, Victor Sanh, Julien Chaumond, Clement Delangue, Anthony Moi, Pierric Cistac, Tim Rault, Rémi Louf, Morgan Funtowicz, Joe Davison, Sam Shleifer, Patrick von Platen, Clara Ma, Yacine Jernite, Julien Plu, Canwen Xu, Teven Le Scao, Sylvain Gugger, Mariama Drame, Quentin Lhoest, and Alexander M. Rush. 2020. HuggingFace's Transformers: State-of-the-art Natural Language Processing. *arXiv:1910.03771 [cs]*.

Bowen Wu, Nan Jiang, Zhifeng Gao, Suke Li, Wenge Rong, and Baoxun Wang. 2018. Why do neural response generation models prefer universal replies? *CoRR*, abs/1808.09187.

Chen Xing, Wei Wu, Yu Wu, Jie Liu, Yalou Huang, Ming Zhou, and Wei-Ying Ma. 2017. Topic Aware Neural Response Generation. In *Proceedings of the Thirty-First AAAI Conference on Artificial Intelligence*, San Francisco, USA.

Xinnuo Xu, Ondřej Dušek, Ioannis Konstas, and Verena Rieser. 2018. Better conversations by modeling, filtering, and optimizing for coherence and diversity. In *Proceedings of the 2018 Conference on Empirical Methods in Natural Language Processing*, pages 3981–3991, Brussels, Belgium. Association for Computational Linguistics.

Lujun Zhao, Kaisong Song, Changlong Sun, Qi Zhang, Xuanjing Huang, and Xiaozhong Liu. 2019. Review Response Generation in E-Commerce Platforms with External Product Information. In *The World Wide Web Conference on - WWW '19*, pages 2425–2435, San Francisco, CA, USA. ACM Press.

Tiancheng Zhao, Ran Zhao, and Maxine Eskenazi. 2017. Learning Discourse-level Diversity for Neural Dialog Models using Conditional Variational Autoencoders. In *Proceedings of the 55th Annual Meeting of the Association for Computational Linguistics (Volume 1: Long Papers)*, pages 654–664, Vancouver, Canada. Association for Computational Linguistics.

Yaoming Zhu, Sidi Lu, Lei Zheng, Jiaxian Guo, Weinan Zhang, Jun Wang, and Yong Yu. 2018. Texygen: A Benchmarking Platform for Text Generation Models. In *The 41st International ACM SIGIR Conference on Research & Development in Information Retrieval*, pages 1097–1100, Ann Arbor MI USA. ACM.

George Kingsley Zipf. 1935. The psycho-biology of language. In *Indogermanische Forschungen*.

A Example Outputs

Review rating: 4 stars	
Review	**Basic clean & lovely** We stayed here whilst doing a road trip between the snowy mountains and Canberra. After doing the caves and coming through Talbingo (beautiful countryside) we were deciding whether to stay in Tumut or Yass or Gundagai. Gundagai had more choices avail. We chose **** due to $ location. There are 3 tiers of accom. Budget $89 basic. Upstairs w a bed shower and a v v tiny tv. Middle +$30 for ground level bigger room and Spa room for $more again. We chose basic as it was 1 night. It was clean. Shower pressure good and comfortable bed. All u need. Wifi didn't happen. Reception was fine. If u don't need large tv and wifi go basic and stay. If u want/need more this wouldn't be the place for you.
Ground truth	Thank you **** for your comments. Our upstairs rooms are small compact rooms and are well priced for the size of room and location (1/2 way between Sydney & Melbourne) downstairs rooms are much more roomy with large flatscreen TV's, parking at the door, spacious bathrooms and of a deluxe standard - worth the extra price for more comfort.
Baseline	Thank you for taking the time to write a review. We are glad you enjoyed your stay with us.
Lex. freq.	Thank you for taking the time to write a review. We are glad that you enjoyed your stay with us. We do offer a range of accommodation options to suit all budgets. Our budget rooms are priced at $89 per night for a standard room and $89 for a superior room. We also offer a variety of room types to suit different needs. We hope to see you again in the future.
Sent. avg.	Thank you for taking the time to write a review of your stay with us at ****. We are sorry to hear that you did not enjoy your stay and that you found the TV to be small. We do have a number of larger TV's in the rooms and we are currently in the process of upgrading them. We hope to see you again in Gundagai.
LM PPL	Thank you for taking the time to write a review. We are glad that you enjoyed your stay with us and found the rooms clean, comfortable and clean. We do offer a range of accommodation at **** and we are sorry that you were not able to experience this during your stay. We hope you enjoyed the rest of your road trip.

Review rating: 3 stars	
Review	**I frequent this hotel for business** Rooms are nice. Great location. Staff should be drug tested. They have some employees that wreak of marijuana... probably will take my business elsewhere. Bye bye. Just say no! This was not an isolated incident.
Ground truth	Thank you for taking the time to comment and I will look into your comments. I am sorry you may take your business elsewhere.
Baseline	Dear Valued Guest, Thank you for taking the time out of your schedule to complete our Guest Survey regarding your recent stay at our hotel. Please know that your feedback is extremely valuable to us and we will utilize your response by continuing to focus on making each and every guest experience the best it can be. We hope to be of service to you in the future. ...
Lex. freq.	Thank you for taking the time to complete our guest survey about your recent experience at ****. Your feedback is critical to our continued improvement and success! We hope you will come back and stay with us again soon. Please contact me personally to arrange your next visit so I can ensure your next stay is nothing less than exceptional. ...
Sent. avg.	Dear Valued Guest, Thank you for taking the time to write a review about your recent stay at ****. I am sorry to hear that your stay was not a pleasant one. We take the cleanliness and safety of our guests very seriously. I have shared your comments with our staff to ensure that this does not happen again in the future. Again, thank you for your review and we hope to see you in the near future. ...
LM PPL	Dear Valued Guest, Thank you for taking the time to provide us with your feedback from your recent stay at ****, a very good place to be. We are happy to hear that you found our rooms to be nice and our location to be great. However, we are very sorry to hear about the incident that occurred during your stay with us. We take the safety and security of all of our guests very seriously and we will be following up with the appropriate departments to ensure this does not happen again. We hope to have the opportunity to welcome you back in the future. ...

Table 5: Example model outputs for reviews of various user ratings (continued on next page). Coloured passages in the responses indicate content that addresses aspects of the input review specifically. We also italicise potentially hallucinated content, which is unsupported by the source text. Note, bold text prefixing a review indicates the review's title. Personalised greetings and salutations are truncated from the response texts, as indicated with ellipsis. Similarly, identifiable information such as personal names and establishment names are anonymised with ****.

Review rating: 2 stars	
Review	**Good for location only. Disappointing overall** Location is great but room faced trash bins and was loud. Also, room was very tiny and looked dated. Windows were tough to close and no air circulation other than the portable fan. Bathroom was hard to even walk in and out of.
Ground truth	We appreciate you taking the time to offer us feedback on your stay. Please allow me to apologise that you did not enjoy your experience on this occasion. ...
Baseline	Thank you for taking the time to write a review. We are sorry to hear that you did not enjoy your stay with us. We hope that you will consider staying with us again in the future.
Lex. freq.	Thank you for taking the time to provide us with a review based on your last experience with us. I would like to apologize if you felt as though we had fallen short of your expectations - please allow me to express my sincerest apologies. We are in the midst of a multi-year renovation project that will touch every corner of our hotel - we hope to warmly welcome you back soon for a stay that is uniquely memorable for all the right reasons.
Sent. avg.	Thank you for taking the time to write a review about your recent stay with us. I am sorry to hear that you did not enjoy your stay. We are in the process of renovating our rooms and hope to have this completed by the end of the year. I hope that you will give us another opportunity to show you that your unsatisfactory stay was an exception. If I can be of any further assistance, please do not hesitate to contact me directly.
LM PPL	Thank you for taking the time to provide a review based on your last experience with us. We would like to apologize for falling short of not only meeting your expectations, but ours as well. It is only through feedback such as yours that we are able to maintain and indeed, where necessary, improve upon the service we provide to our valued guests. We hope to warmly welcome you back soon for a stay that you are most contented with.

Review rating: 1 star	
Review	**False advertising?** Due to the favorable reviews on the Internet we have booked family room (2 rooms with door in between). When we walked in after a full day of driving we were tempted to leave the rooms and continue the trip, as everything but location was disappointing. Rooms were dusty (particularly carpet) and not refurbished for more than 30 years. Beds were short (not king size), uncomfortable and with cheap pillow. Almost every piece of furniture was chipped and broken, bathroom doors couldn't be closed properly, Shower head was falling down. TV reception was terrible. Acoustic insulation was inappropriate. Photo on the Internet is not the proper representation of the motel; I almost took photos to put it on the Internet to show how our rooms looked like. Do not be tempted to come to this nominally 3 star motel. I personally wouldn't give it a single star.
Ground truth	We appreciate all feed back from customers good and bad, and thankyou for taking the time to review. This is the 1st time we have had such a review and feel just a few points should be made. We do not cater for Familys , groups or people under 40 years old, thus the Golden Chain logo, Senior logo and the fact there is nowhere to add children to any internet booking. When presented with a Family as occainionally does happen we open 2 large double rooms with 2 bathrooms 2 lounge rooms and 2 balconies with 100% waterview over ****. and full breakfast for 5 delived to your room for $129 per night. All but these two rooms are Theme rooms completed early 2010 with artworks and decoration valued at $20,000 per room. The risk of damage is too high to have children at the motel. Not all guests like our contingency plan however I beleive it is fair. That said we will look at a standard renovation for these rooms.
Baseline	Thank you for taking the time to write a review. We are sorry to hear that you did not enjoy your stay with us. We have taken all your comments on board and are *currently in the process of refurbishing our rooms*. We hope that you will consider staying with us again in the future.
Lex. freq.	Thank you for taking the time to write a review. We are sorry to hear that you did not enjoy your stay with us. *We do not advertise that we are a 3 star motel*, but we do have a very high standard of cleanliness and customer service. Our rooms are cleaned on a regular basis, and we have never had any issues with any of our carpets. All of our *rooms have been refurbished over the past 3 years*, and our rooms are regularly inspected by our housekeeping team. We have also *recently replaced all of our beds, and are currently in the process of replacing all of the furniture in our rooms...*
Sent. avg.	Thank you for taking the time to write a review. We are sorry to hear that you did not enjoy your stay with us. We do have a wide range of room types to suit all budgets and requirements. We have a variety of different room types available to suit different needs and budgets. *All of our rooms have been refurbished over the last 2 years* and we are sorry that you found the room to be dusty. We would have been more than happy to move you to a different room had we been made aware of your concerns...
LM PPL	Thank you for taking the time to write your review. We are sorry to hear that you did not enjoy your stay with us. Our rooms are cleaned to a very high standard and we are sorry that you found the carpet dusty and uncomfortable. *The carpets in the rooms have been replaced over the last couple of years* and ***we have not received any complaints about the carpet in the room you stayed in.*** We *have not had any complaints regarding the TV reception or the shower head*. We would have been more than happy to move you to another room if you had let us know of your dissatisfaction.

Extreme Multi-Label Classification with Label Masking for Product Attribute Value Extraction

Wei-Te Chen **Yandi Xia** **Keiji Shinzato**
Rakuten Institute of Technology,
Rakuten Group Inc.
{weite.chen, yandi.xia, keiji.shinzato}@rakuten.com

Abstract

Although most studies have treated attribute value extraction (AVE) as named entity recognition, these approaches are not practical in real-world e-commerce platforms because they perform poorly, and require canonicalization of extracted values. Furthermore, since values needed for actual services is static in many attributes, extraction of new values is not always necessary. Given the above, we formalize AVE as extreme multi-label classification (XMC). A major problem in solving AVE as XMC is that the distribution between positive and negative labels for products is heavily imbalanced. To mitigate the negative impact derived from such biased distribution, we propose label masking, a simple and effective method to reduce the number of negative labels in training. We exploit attribute taxonomy designed for e-commerce platforms to determine which labels are negative for products. Experimental results using a dataset collected from a Japanese e-commerce platform demonstrate that the label masking improves micro and macro F_1 scores by 3.38 and 23.20 points, respectively.

1 Introduction

Since organized product data plays a crucial role in serving better product search and recommendation to customers, attribute value extraction (AVE) has become a critical task in the e-commerce industry. Although many studies have treated AVE as named entity recognition (NER) task (§ 2.1), NER-based approaches are not practical in real-world e-commerce platforms. First, NER-based methods perform poorly because the number of attributes (classes) in e-commerce domains is extremely large (Xu et al., 2019). Second, it is necessary to take a further step to normalize extracted values (*e.g., coral to pink*). To reflect extracted values in actual services, e-commerce platform providers need to convert the values into canonical form by referring their own attribute taxonomy that covers attributes and values for the services. Third, extraction of new values is not necessary in many attributes (*e.g., country of origin*). Since it is rare for new values of attributes other than brands to be introduced to the world, it is sufficient to extract the values defined in the attribute taxonomy.

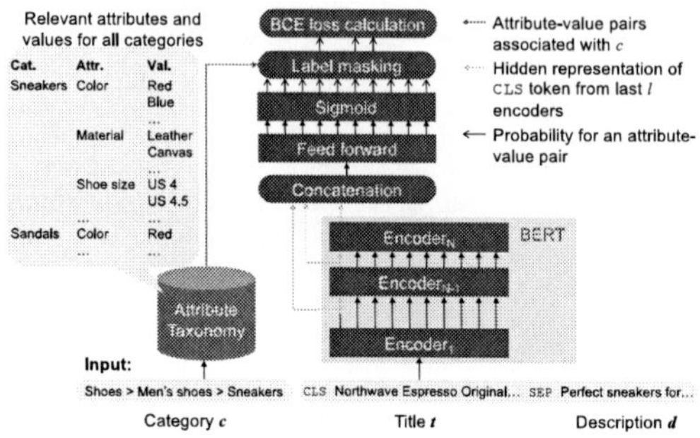

Figure 1: Extreme multi-label classification model with label masking for attribute value extraction.

Given the above reasons, we formalize AVE as extreme multi-label classification (XMC), and design a model that directly predicts possible canonical attribute-value pairs except for brands[1] from given product data. The main problem in solving AVE as XMC is that the number of relevant attribute-value pairs to products is far fewer than that of irrelevant pairs; the majority of attribute-value pairs are regarded as irrelevant (*e.g., ⟨Memory size, 512GB⟩ for sneakers*). To tackle this problem, we propose label masking that mitigates the negative effects of a large amount of irrelevant pairs in training (Figure 1, § 4.2). We detect the irrelevant pairs by referring an attribute taxonomy (§ 3) associated with a real-world dataset we use to train and evaluate models. Through experiments using the dataset, we confirm that our label masking method improves micro and macro F_1 scores by 3.38 and 23.20 points, respectively.

Our contributions can be summarized as follows:

[1]NER-based methods are necessary to extract new values.

Proceedings of The Fifth Workshop on e-Commerce and NLP (ECNLP 5), pages 134 - 140
May 26, 2022

- We formalize AVE as an XMC problem.
- We proposed label masking, a simple and effective method to alleviate the negative impact from irrelevant attribute-value pairs in training (§ 4.2).
- We showed the effectiveness of the label masking using a real-world dataset. It especially performed well on attribute-value pairs at the long tail (§ 5.4).

2 Related Work

2.1 Attribute Value Extraction

There are many attempts based on NER techniques to extract attribute values from product descriptions (Probst et al., 2007; Wong et al., 2008; Putthividhya and Hu, 2011; Bing et al., 2012; Shinzato and Sekine, 2013; More, 2016; Zheng et al., 2018; Rezk et al., 2019; Karamanolakis et al., 2020; Zhang et al., 2020). As Xu et al. (2019) reported, NER-based models perform poorly on a real-world dataset including ten thousand attributes or more.

To deal with a large number of attributes, there is research that introduces question-answering (QA) models for the AVE task (Xu et al., 2019; Wang et al., 2020; Shinzato et al., 2022). These QA-based approaches take an attribute as *query* and a product title as *context*, and extract attribute values from the context as *answer* for the query. Since those models take attributes as input, it is necessary to run the extraction repeatedly on the same product titles with different attributes. Hence, the QA-based approaches are more time-consuming than XMC-based approaches that can predict values for multiple attributes at a time.

2.2 Extreme Multi-Label Classification

To reduce the large output space, previous XMC studies perform label clustering as a separate stage from training classifiers (Wydmuch et al., 2018; You et al., 2019; Chang et al., 2020; Zhang et al., 2021; Jiang et al., 2021; Mittal et al., 2021a,b). For example, XR-Transformer (Zhang et al., 2021) first vectorizes each label with combination of TF-IDF and embeddings of text associated with the label. Then, it applies balanced k-means (Malinen and Fränti, 2014) to these label vectors to generate a hierarchical label cluster tree by recursively partitioning label sets. Instead of k-means, Mittal et al. (2021a) and Mittal et al. (2021b) partition labels into equal sized clusters, and then train a binary classifier per cluster that predicts whether a given text is relevant to labels in the cluster.

Category	Shoes > Men's shoes > Sneakers		
Attributes	Color	Material	Shoe size
Values	• Red • Blue • Green	• Leather • Canvas • Gore-Tex	• US 4 • US 4.5 • US 5

Table 1: Example of attribute taxonomy.

On the other hand, in real-world e-commerce platforms, an attribute taxonomy is available. This can be regarded as label clusters manually tailored by the e-commerce platform providers. Therefore, we simply leverage the existing attribute taxonomy to reduce the size of labels in training through label masking.

3 Attribute Taxonomy

We assume that for each category, attribute taxonomy defines all possible attribute-value pairs that products in the category can take. General attribute-value pairs (*e.g.*, $\langle$*Color, Red*$\rangle$) are defined for multiple categories. Table 1 shows an example of attributes and values defined for the category of sneakers. By referring to the attribute taxonomy, it is possible to determine which attributes and values are relevant or irrelevant to which category of products. For example, from the table, we can see that 512GB of memory size is irrelevant to sneakers.

4 Proposed Method

This section proposes our model based on XMC with label masking for the AVE task. Given a product data $\boldsymbol{x} = \langle c, \boldsymbol{t}, \boldsymbol{d} \rangle$, where c denotes a category, $\boldsymbol{t}$ denotes a title consisting of n tokens ($\{t_1, t_2, \ldots, t_n\}$) and $\boldsymbol{d}$ denotes a description consisting of m tokens ($\{d_1, d_2, \ldots, d_m\}$), respectively, the model returns a set of attribute-value pairs that should be linked with the product data $\boldsymbol{x}$.

Figure 1 depicts the model architecture. As a backbone of the architecture, we employ a pretrained BERT-base model (Devlin et al., 2019), and put a feed forward layer on the top of BERT. As an input to BERT, we construct a string $[\text{CLS}; \boldsymbol{t}; \text{SEP}; \boldsymbol{d}]$ by concatenating $\boldsymbol{t}$, $\boldsymbol{d}$, CLS and SEP; CLS and SEP are special tokens to represent a classifier token and a separator, respectively. Similar with Jiang et al. (2021), we concatenate the last l hidden representations of the CLS token, and then feed the concatenated vector into a feed forward

Category	Title	Description	Attribute-value pairs
靴 > メンズ靴 > スニーカー	ノースウエーブ【northwave】ESPRESSO ORIGINAL RED 男性用 メンズ / 女性用 レディース / スニーカー	製品説明 落ち着いたレッドが象徴的な、足元のアクセントとして最適な1足。軽量ラバーでソールも軽量化された人気カラーのモデル。	⟨ 靴サイズ(cm), 25.0 ⟩, ⟨ 靴サイズ(cm), 26.0 ⟩, ⟨ 靴サイズ(cm), 27.0 ⟩, ⟨ カラー, レッド ⟩
Shoes > Men's shoes > Sneakers	Northwave [northwave] Espresso Original Red Men's / Women's / Sneakers	Product description. These sneakers are the perfect accent for your feet and come in a soft red color. The sole is made of lightweight rubber to reduce weight. It is a popular color.	⟨ Shoe size (cm), 25.0 ⟩, ⟨ Shoe size (cm), 26.0 ⟩, ⟨ Shoe size (cm), 27.0 ⟩, ⟨ Color, Red ⟩

Figure 2: Example of product data. The top shows the original data and the bottom shows its translation.

layer as the representation of the input.

The size of the outputs from the feed forward layer is equal to the total number of labels (attribute-value pairs). The outputs are converted into probability through a sigmoid layer, and then pass to the label masking. To mask labels irrelevant to the given product data x, we refer an attribute taxonomy built for an e-commerce platform. We compute binary cross entropy (BCE) loss over only relevant labels.

In testing, we choose ones whose probability returned from the model exceeds 0.5 among labels relevant to the product data x.

4.1 Preliminary: XMC

XMC is a special case of the multi-label classification problem. What makes XMC unique is its size of a target label set. The label size is 4K to 501K in common XMC datasets (Chang et al., 2020).

Formally, XMC can be defined as follows: Giving a training set $\{(x^{(i)}, y^{(i)})\}_{i=1}^{N}$ where $x^{(i)}$ is the instance, and $y^{(i)} \in \{0,1\}^L$ is the label of $x^{(i)}$ represented by L dimensional multi-hot vectors. L is the size of the label set. $y_j^{(i)} = 1$ indicates that the j-th label is a positive example for x_i. The regular XMC is aimed to learn the function $\sigma_\theta(x) \in \{(0,1) \subset \mathbb{R}\}^L$ which predicts scores in range of [0.0, 1.0] to all labels by giving x. σ tends to be closed to 1.0 to j-th label when $y_j = 1$. The ordinary loss function in XMC is BCE:

$$\mathrm{BCE} = -\sum_{j=1}^{L} (y_j \log \sigma_\theta^j(x) + (1 - y_j) \log (1 - \sigma_\theta^j(x)))$$

BCE loss sums over the log loss among all labels.

4.2 Label Masking

In the AVE task, the number of "hot" labels is extremely small compared to the number of labels defined for the task (L). This means that distribution between positive and negative labels is heavily imbalanced. Such distribution has the negative impact on training classification models because the BCE sums far more loss values from the negative labels.

To alleviate the impact derived from the negative labels, we exploit attribute taxonomy. Since the majority of the negative labels are irrelevant labels to given product data x, we introduce a function $\mathbb{M}$ that returns only relevant labels to x. BCE loss can be rewritten as follows:

$$\mathrm{BCE} = -\sum_{j \in \mathbb{M}(x)} (y_j \log \sigma_\theta^j(x) + (1 - y_j) \log(1 - \sigma_\theta^j(x)))$$

$$\mathbb{M}(x) = \{j : j \in L \wedge l_j \overset{\text{rel}}{\sim} x\}$$

where $l_j \overset{\text{rel}}{\sim} x$ means label l_j is relevant to x. By matching a category of x with categories in the attribute taxonomy, we can obtain all possible attribute-value pairs for x. We regard those pairs as relevant labels to x.

By introducing the function $\mathbb{M}$, BCE loss discards the log loss values from the irrelevant labels. The label masking enables us to train XMC models more properly since (1) it reduces bias in the distribution between positive and negative labels, and (2) the irrelevant labels would not affect the model parameters during back-propagating. This makes the model training more sensitive than normal to misclassification within relevant labels.

5 Experiments

5.1 Dataset

We use product data and attribute taxonomy from Rakuten[2], a large e-commerce platform in Japan. Each product consists of a tuple of category, title, description and a set of attribute-value

[2]https://www.rakuten.co.jp/

	Count
# of product data	1,999,175
# of top categories	38
# of leaf categories	6,796
# of distinct attributes	1,300
# of distinct attribute-value pairs (labels)	7,979
Avg. tokens per title	44.05
Avg. tokens per description	332.04
Avg. # of positive labels	4.42
Avg. # of negative labels	7974.58
Avg. # of relevant labels	489.25
Avg. # of irrelevant labels	7489.75

Table 2: Data statistics. These numbers are calculated from both training and test data.

Hyper parameter	Value
Learning rate	0.0001
Weight decay	0.0
Epoch	5
Batch size	64
Dropout rate	0.1
Max. sequence length	512
Warmup proportion	10%
# of CLS's hidden representations to concat. (l)	5

Table 3: Hyper parameters

pairs. Rakuten manages category and attribute taxonomies, and sellers assign products a category and attribute-value pairs defined in the taxonomies. Figure 2 shows an example of the product data.

For experiments, among product data in Rakuten, we randomly sampled 2,000,446 product data that own one or more attribute-value pairs except brands. We halve this dataset as a 50-50 train/evaluation split. We selected attribute-value pairs appeared in both datasets[3], and removed product data that did not have any selected pairs. Moreover, from the evaluation dataset, we discarded product data whose category did not appear in the training dataset. As a result, the training and evaluation datasets contain 1,000,047 and 999,128 products respectively. Statistics of the dataset are listed in Table 2. We can see that the label masking reduces the size of labels from 7,979 to 489 on average.

5.2 Evaluation Metrics

We use precision (P), recall (R), F_1 score and precision at k (P@k, k = 1,3,5), which is widely used in the XMC tasks.To obtain a top-k list, we regard all prediction results as output regardless of scores.

5.3 Models

We compare the following models:

XR-Transformer XMC model that shows the state-of-the-art performance on datasets commonly used in the XMC field (Zhang et al., 2021). We train the model using the codes released from the authors[4] with default parameters other than max sequence length and batch size. We set 512 for max sequence length and 64 for batch size.

BERT BERT (Devlin et al., 2019) without our label masking. It computes BCE loss from all labels.

BERT with multiple classifiers Model that simply exploits a given category. We design a classifier (feed forward) layer for each category, and put them on the top of a single BERT. Because of this, parameters in BERT are in common with all classifiers. According to the category, we replace a classifier in training and testing. We construct mini-batches to include product data in the same category. As categories, in addition to leaf categories (*e.g., Sneakers*), we also adopt top categories (*Shoes*). This is because the size of training data is not sufficient in some minor leaf categories. By taking top categories, we can expect that the size of training data is enlarged although it increases irrelevant labels to leaf categories assigned in products. The total number of top categories is 38, including shoes, food, furniture and home appliances.

BERT with label masking Our proposed model. It computes BCE loss from only relevant attribute-value pairs to the category of given product data. Unlike BERT with multiple classifiers, this model has a single classifier, and the classifier is trained using product data from all categories.

For fair comparison with our model that assumes a category of the target product to be given, we discard irrelevant labels that the baseline models predict.

We employ a pretrained Japanese BERT-base model and its tokenzier released from Tohoku University[5], and use them in all models. We apply NFKC Unicode normalization[6] to titles and descriptions before the tokenization.

[3]The total number of the un-selected attribute-value pairs is 1,289. These pairs appeared 10 times or less in the sampled product data.

[4]https://github.com/amzn/pecos

[5]https://github.com/cl-tohoku/bert-japanese

[6]https://unicode.org/reports/tr15/

Models	Micro P (%)	Micro R (%)	Micro F_1	Macro P (%)	Macro R (%)	Macro F_1	P@k (%) k = 1	P@k (%) k = 3	P@k (%) k = 5
XR-Transformer	**92.01**	73.80	81.90	45.43	19.93	27.71	90.30	65.68	53.61
BERT	88.77	74.64	81.09	26.57	15.42	19.51	87.59	63.97	52.36
BERT w/ multiple classifiers - leaf	87.79	74.90	80.83	47.24	30.89	37.36	87.79	55.63	44.60
BERT w/ multiple classifiers - top	89.04	79.88	84.21	52.12	34.99	41.87	91.10	65.95	53.75
BERT w/ label masking (ours)	88.90	**80.46**	**84.47**	**52.82**	**35.85**	**42.71**	**91.57**	**66.31**	**54.08**

Table 4: Performance of each model.

Group (# of pairs)	Freq.	Micro F_1		Macro F_1	
High (76)	$[10^4, \infty)$	89.57	(+1.56)	86.15	(+2.31)
Med. (454)	$[10^3, 10^4)$	81.98	(+3.90)	78.58	(+5.24)
Low (1,457)	$[10^2, 10^3)$	70.79	(+10.59)	66.80	(+14.55)
Rare (5,992)	$[1, 10^2)$	53.85	(+33.20)	33.19	(+26.97)

Table 5: Micro and macro F_1 scores of our model for each group of attribute-value pairs. Gains over BERT without label masking are enclosed in parentheses.

For models other than XR-Transformer, we use gradient descent by the Adam (Kingma and Ba, 2015) optimizer. To avoid overfitting, we apply a dropout rate at 0.1 and stochastic weight averaging (Izmailov et al., 2018) to the models. Table 3 shows the hyper parameters.

Similarly with our model, as the representation of the input to BERT and BERT with multiple classifiers, we use a vector concatenating CLS embeddings obtained from the last five encoders. We implemented the models in PyTorch.

5.4 Results

Table 4 shows the performance of each model. We can observe that our proposed model outperformed all baselines. Micro and macro F_1 gains over BERT without label masking are 3.38 and 23.20 points, respectively. The significant improvement on macro F_1 score shows that the label masking is effective on various kinds of attribute-value pairs. These results show that reducing the number of irrelevant labels in training is crucial to train more accurate XMC models.

The reason why the performance of BERT with multiple classifiers trained on leaf categories is lower than ours is that the number of training examples for this model is insufficient in many leaf categories, as we mentioned. For 5,572 categories, the number of training examples is less than 64. Since parameters of BERT in this model are in common with all categories, this result implies that the classifiers are not well trained. On the other hand, the single classifier in our model is successfully trained because (general) attribute-value pairs scattered on various leaf categories are fully used to train the classifier.

Since the data sparseness problem is alleviated, BERT with multiple classifiers trained on top categories outperforms the model trained on leaf categories. Furthermore, its performance is closed to ours. We believe that the gap of the performance between the model trained on top categories and ours is from the quality of association between categories and attributes. In case of the model trained on top categories, attribute-value pairs defined for different leaf categories in the same top category are handled as relevant labels (*e.g., heel height for sneakers*). Meanwhile, our model is not affected by such attribute-value pairs. The gap implies that these erroneous relevant pairs hurt the performance.

To see the effectiveness of the label masking in detail, we categorize attribute-value pairs according to the frequency in the training data, and then check the performance for each frequency group. Table 5 shows the performance of our model in each group together with micro and macro F_1 gains over BERT. The improvement in micro and macro F_1 scores is greater for attribute-value pairs with less training examples. This means that the label masking works well for attribute-value pairs at the long-tail.

6 Conclusion

In this paper, we formalized AVE as XMC, and proposed label masking, a simple and effective method that mitigates the negative impact from the imbalanced distribution of attribute-value pairs relevant and irrelevant to products. Experimental results using a real-world dataset show that the label masking improves the performance of BERT-based XMC models; it is especially effective for attributes with less training data.

As for future work, we plan to see the effectiveness of the label masking method on other tasks in e-commerce domains such as item classification.

Acknowledgement

We thank Naoki Yoshinaga for the fruitful comments before the submission. We also thank the anonymous reviewers for their careful reading of our paper and insightful comments.

References

Lidong Bing, Tak-Lam Wong, and Wai Lam. 2012. Unsupervised extraction of popular product attributes from web sites. In *Information Retrieval Technology, 8th Asia Information Retrieval Societies Conference, AIRS 2012*, volume 7675 of *Lecture Notes in Computer Science*, pages 437–446, Berlin, Heidelberg. Springer.

Wei-Cheng Chang, Hsiang-Fu Yu, Kai Zhong, Yiming Yang, and Inderjit S. Dhillon. 2020. *Taming Pretrained Transformers for Extreme Multi-Label Text Classification*, KDD '20, page 3163–3171. Association for Computing Machinery, New York, NY, USA.

Jacob Devlin, Ming-Wei Chang, Kenton Lee, and Kristina Toutanova. 2019. BERT: Pre-training of deep bidirectional transformers for language understanding. In *Proceedings of the 2019 Conference of the North American Chapter of the Association for Computational Linguistics: Human Language Technologies*, pages 4171–4186, Minneapolis, Minnesota, USA. Association for Computational Linguistics.

Pavel Izmailov, Dmitrii Podoprikhin, Timur Garipov, Dmitry Vetrov, and Andrew Gordon Wilson. 2018. Averaging weights leads to wider optima and better generalization. In *34th Conference on Uncertainty in Artificial Intelligence 2018, UAI 2018*, 34th Conference on Uncertainty in Artificial Intelligence 2018, UAI 2018, pages 876–885. Association For Uncertainty in Artificial Intelligence (AUAI).

Ting Jiang, Deqing Wang, Leilei Sun, Huayi Yang, Zhengyang Zhao, and Fuzhen Zhuang. 2021. Lightxml: Transformer with dynamic negative sampling for high-performance extreme multi-label text classification. *Proceedings of the AAAI Conference on Artificial Intelligence*, 35(9):7987–7994.

Giannis Karamanolakis, Jun Ma, and Xin Luna Dong. 2020. TXtract: Taxonomy-aware knowledge extraction for thousands of product categories. In *Proceedings of the 58th Annual Meeting of the Association for Computational Linguistics*, pages 8489–8502, Online. Association for Computational Linguistics.

Diederik P. Kingma and Jimmy Ba. 2015. Adam: A method for stochastic optimization. In *Proceedings of the third International Conference on Learning Representations*, San Diego, California, USA.

Mikko I. Malinen and Pasi Fränti. 2014. Balanced k-means for clustering. In *Structural, Syntactic, and Statistical Pattern Recognition*, pages 32–41, Berlin, Heidelberg. Springer Berlin Heidelberg.

A. Mittal, K. Dahiya, S. Agrawal, D. Saini, S. Agarwal, P. Kar, and M. Varma. 2021a. Decaf: Deep extreme classification with label features. In *Proceedings of the ACM International Conference on Web Search and Data Mining*, WSDM '21, page 49–57, New York, NY, USA. Association for Computing Machinery.

A. Mittal, N. Sachdeva, S. Agrawal, S. Agarwal, P. Kar, and M. Varma. 2021b. Eclare: Extreme classification with label graph correlations. In *Proceedings of The ACM International World Wide Web Conference*, WWW '21, page 3721–3732, New York, NY, USA. Association for Computing Machinery.

Ajinkya More. 2016. Attribute extraction from product titles in ecommerce. In *KDD 2016 Workshop on Enterprise Intelligence*, San Francisco, California, USA.

Katharina Probst, Rayid Ghani, Marko Krema, Andrew E. Fano, and Yan Liu. 2007. Semi-supervised learning of attribute-value pairs from product descriptions. In *Proceedings of the 20th International Joint Conference on Artificial Intelligence*, IJCAI'07, pages 2838–2843, Hyderabad, India. Morgan Kaufmann Publishers Inc.

Duangmanee Putthividhya and Junling Hu. 2011. Bootstrapped named entity recognition for product attribute extraction. In *Proceedings of the 2011 Conference on Empirical Methods in Natural Language Processing*, pages 1557–1567, Edinburgh, Scotland, UK. Association for Computational Linguistics.

Martin Rezk, Laura Alonso Alemany, Lasguido Nio, and Ted Zhang. 2019. Accurate product attribute extraction on the field. In *Proceedings of the 35th IEEE International Conference on Data Engineering*, pages 1862–1873, Macau SAR, China. IEEE.

Keiji Shinzato and Satoshi Sekine. 2013. Unsupervised extraction of attributes and their values from product description. In *Proceedings of the Sixth International Joint Conference on Natural Language Processing*, pages 1339–1347, Nagoya, Japan. Asian Federation of Natural Language Processing.

Keiji Shinzato, Naoki Yoshinaga, Yandi Xia, and Wei-Te Chen. 2022. Simple and effective knowledge-driven query expansion for QA-based product attribute extraction. In *Proceedings of the 60th Annual Meeting of the Association for Computational Linguistics*. (to appear).

Qifan Wang, Li Yang, Bhargav Kanagal, Sumit Sanghai, D. Sivakumar, Bin Shu, Zac Yu, and Jon Elsas. 2020. Learning to extract attribute value from product via question answering: A multi-task approach. In *Proceedings of the 26th ACM SIGKDD International Conference on Knowledge Discovery and Data Mining*, KDD '20, pages 47–55, New York, NY, USA. Association for Computing Machinery.

Tak-Lam Wong, Wai Lam, and Tik-Shun Wong. 2008. An unsupervised framework for extracting and normalizing product attributes from multiple web sites. In *Proceedings of the 31st Annual International ACM SIGIR Conference on Research and Development in Information Retrieval*, SIGIR '08, pages 35–42, New York, NY, USA. Association for Computing Machinery.

Marek Wydmuch, Kalina Jasinska, Mikhail Kuznetsov, Róbert Busa-Fekete, and Krzysztof Dembczyński. 2018. A no-regret generalization of hierarchical softmax to extreme multi-label classification. In *Proceedings of the 32nd International Conference on Neural Information Processing Systems*, NIPS'18, page 6358–6368, Red Hook, NY, USA. Curran Associates Inc.

Huimin Xu, Wenting Wang, Xin Mao, Xinyu Jiang, and Man Lan. 2019. Scaling up open tagging from tens to thousands: Comprehension empowered attribute value extraction from product title. In *Proceedings of the 57th Annual Meeting of the Association for Computational Linguistics*, pages 5214–5223, Florence, Italy. Association for Computational Linguistics.

Ronghui You, Zihan Zhang, Ziye Wang, Suyang Dai, Hiroshi Mamitsuka, and Shanfeng Zhu. 2019. Attentionxml: Label tree-based attention-aware deep model for high-performance extreme multi-label text classification. In *Advances in Neural Information Processing Systems*, volume 32. Curran Associates, Inc.

Hanchu Zhang, Leonhard Hennig, Christoph Alt, Changjian Hu, Yao Meng, and Chao Wang. 2020. Bootstrapping named entity recognition in E-commerce with positive unlabeled learning. In *Proceedings of The 3rd Workshop on e-Commerce and NLP*, pages 1–6, Seattle, WA, USA. Association for Computational Linguistics.

Jiong Zhang, Wei-Cheng Chang, Hsiang-Fu Yu, and Inderjit Dhillon. 2021. Fast multi-resolution transformer fine-tuning for extreme multi-label text classification. In *Advances in Neural Information Processing Systems*, volume 34, pages 7267–7280. Curran Associates, Inc.

Guineng Zheng, Subhabrata Mukherjee, Xin Luna Dong, and Feifei Li. 2018. OpenTag: Open attribute value extraction from product profiles. In *Proceedings of the 24th ACM SIGKDD International Conference on Knowledge Discovery and Data Mining*, KDD '18, pages 1049–1058, New York, NY, USA. Association for Computing Machinery.

Enhanced Representation with Contrastive Loss for Long-Tail Query Classification in e-commerce

Lvxing Zhu, Hao Chen, Chao Wei, Weiru Zhang
Alibaba Group, Hangzhou, China
{lvxing.zlx, ryan.ch, weichao.wc, weiru.zwr}@alibaba-inc.com

Abstract

Query classification is a fundamental task in an e-commerce search engine, which assigns one or multiple predefined product categories in response to each search query. Taking click-through logs as training data in deep learning methods is a common and effective approach for query classification. However, the frequency distribution of queries typically has long-tail property, which means that there are few logs for most of the queries. The lack of reliable user feedback information results in worse performance of long-tail queries compared with frequent queries. To solve the above problem, we propose a novel method that leverages an auxiliary module to enhance the representations of long-tail queries by taking advantage of reliable supervised information of variant frequent queries. The long-tail queries are guided by the contrastive loss to obtain category-aligned representations in the auxiliary module, where the variant frequent queries serve as anchors in the representation space. We train our model with real-world click data from AliExpress and conduct evaluation on both offline labeled data and online AB test. The results and further analysis demonstrate the effectiveness of our proposed method.

1 Introduction

In the e-commerce search engine, query classification is a task to assign one or multiple predefined product categories to each search query. It is a fundamental component that recognizes the intent of user query and retrieves relevant products. The task of query classification can be basically viewed as a multi-label short text classification problem.

Deep learning methods are the mainstream approaches for query classification tasks nowadays. Considering the massive amount of queries and categories, it's usually too expensive to collect train data by manually labeling. Therefore, utilizing the click-through data as implicit feedback signals to build a model is the most common approach that predicts the categories of query (Shen et al., 2009; Lin et al., 2018b) . Various deep models have achieved great success in query classification (Zhang et al., 2019; Yu and Litchfield, 2020; Zhang et al., 2021). To fully utilize the mutual information between the query and categories, some models convert the multi-label classification to a multiple binary classification task and obtain superior performance (Liu et al., 2017; Nam et al., 2014).

However, the long-tail distribution of queries in e-commerce websites brings challenges to deep models. Few high-frequency queries dominate in search input while low-frequency queries have a very low probability of occurrences. These low-frequency queries are what we call long-tail queries and others are frequent queries. The users' feedback logs of long-tail queries are usually difficult to obtain and insufficient training data also result in a serious data noise problem. Moreover, the product taxonomy in e-commerce websites usually consists of thousands of categories. The large amount of categories aggravates the sparsity of long-tail query-category feedback data. Therefore, the lack and noise of training data cause the lower performance for long-tail queries compared with frequent queries in the task of query classification.

Another problem is that queries with slight lexical differences may have totally different category intents (Zhang et al., 2021). Queries in e-commerce are typically short and ambiguous (Shen et al., 2009; Lin et al., 2018b). A modification of one word in the query could entirely change the corresponding category, such as "blouse collar" and "blouse with collar", or "pearl ring" and "pearl earring". This phenomenon hinders the deep models from classifying long-tail queries because there aren't enough examples to distinguish the intents of these lexically similar queries.

In summary, query classification in real-world e-commerce scenarios differs from common text classification tasks in at least two aspects. At First,

Proceedings of The Fifth Workshop on e-Commerce and NLP (ECNLP 5), pages 141 - 150
May 26, 2022 ©2022 Association for Computational Linguistics

the supervised information is not entirely reliable especially for long-tail queries, depending on the query frequency in search logs. Secondly, most queries are short and the textual information inside queries is very limited.

Inspired by the aforementioned observations, we propose a novel method to improve the performance of long-tail query classification. The basic idea of our method is to utilize the query frequency information and transfer knowledge from frequent queries to long-tail queries, which takes advantage of the fact that the click feedbacks of frequent queries are more reliable. For each query, we select several frequent queries as the variant queries, which are lexically similar to the original query. We use an auxiliary module coupled with a contrastive loss (Chopra et al., 2005) to enhance the representation of the original query by these variant queries. The variant queries serve as anchors in vector space while the auxiliary module aligns the representation vectors between original queries and variant queries in the view of category semantics. We conduct experiments on real-world click data from AliExpress [1] and also evaluate our method on the public dataset. The results suggest that significant improvement of long-tail query classification tasks on multiple metrics. We further conduct the comparison and visualization to verify the effect of our representation enhancement.

The major contributions of this article are summarized as follows:

- We propose a novel method for long-tail query classification by transferring knowledge from multiple variant frequent queries to long-tail queries.
- Our method enhances the representations of queries with the contrastive loss which bases on the category consistence among lexical similar queries.
- We validate the effectiveness of our method in a public dataset and real-world search scenarios.

2 Related Work

2.1 Query Classification

There have been various works studying query classification in e-commerce recently. These works can be classified into three categories: statistical-based methods (Shen et al., 2009), traditional machine learning methods and deep learning methods. Lin et al. (2018b) introduce an unsupervised method to collect query classification data from click-through logs and apply several traditional methods such as SVM, XGBoost and fastText on this task. Zhang et al. (2019) design a progressively hierarchical classification framework to make use of the semantic information from a category tree and take TextCNN (Zhang and Wallace, 2015) as the base model. To incorporate information of category tree structure, Gao et al. (2020) proposes a deep hierarchical classification framework. The framework generates layer representation for each layer and shares the representation to lower layers. Yu and Litchfield (2020) propose a multi-objective method that optimizes hierarchical accuracy-depth trade-off across multi-level categories. Multi-objective optimization is adopted in post inference phase to select the deepest category whose prediction accuracy exceeds its corresponding threshold. Zhang et al. (2021) propose a framework that also focuses on long-tail query classification in e-commerce, which adds an auxiliary across-context attention module to extract external information by predicting the categories of variant queries.

2.2 Text Classification

Multi-label text classification can be viewed as the generalization of query classification, although most text classification tasks focus on long text such as web document, papers and news. CNN-based models, including traditional CNN (Liu et al., 2017) and graph-CNN (Peng et al., 2018), are the common approaches to classify text. Lin et al. (2018a) apply multi-level dilated convolution and attention-over-attention mechanism to generate higher-level semantic representations for text classification. Recurrent networks are also applied to this task, You et al. (2019) proposes a label BiLSTM-based deep learning model with multi-label attention named AttentionXML. AttentionXML uses a probabilistic label tree to handle extreme multi-label text classification (XML). X-Transformer (Chang et al., 2020) deals with XML by transformer models, which predicts labels in two steps: first, recalls the label clusters and then re-ranks the labels within the predicted clusters. LightXML (Jiang et al., 2021) and DECAF (Mittal et al., 2021) also follows the above two-stage

[1] `https://www.aliexpress.com`, a cross-border e-commerce platform of Alibaba

schema but make efforts in utilizing label metadata and dynamic negative sampling, respectively. Yang et al. (2018) and Lin et al. (2018a) apply a sequence-to-sequence model on multi-label classification to capture the correlations between label. Peng et al. (2018) use a regularized loss to model the dependency of hierarchical classes.

2.3 Contrastive Learning

The contrastive loss is first presented by Chopra et al. (2005) for the face verification task. By minimizing the contrastive loss with siamese networks, the similarity metric becomes small for pairs of faces from the same person and large for pairs from different persons. Oord et al. (2018) utilize a probabilistic contrastive loss in a universal unsupervised learning approach to extract useful representations from high-dimensional data, such as speech, images and text. Lian et al. (2018) introduce a deep model coupled with contrastive loss to learn discriminative audio representations. The principle that aligns the representation according to the categories is similar to contrast learning. Contrastive learning learns effective representations by pulling semantically close neighbors together and pushing apart non-neighbors so that "similar" points in input space are mapped to nearby points on the manifold (Hadsell et al., 2006). SimCLR(Chen et al., 2020) is a successful appliance of contrastive learning in computer vision fields and Gao et al. (2021) introduce SimCSE in NLP, which applies contrast learning to sentence embedding task of both unsupervised approach and supervised approach.

3 Methodology

We introduce our proposed method in this section. We first give an overview of our method in Section 3.1 and then demonstrate each module in detail from Section 3.2 to 3.5.

3.1 Overview

We first define the formal notation of our work. We cast query classification task as multi-label text classification in a binary manner. Given a query $q = [wq_1, wq_2, ..., wq_n]$, a sequence of words with length n, the task is to predict whether category $c \in C$ is a positive category for query q or not, where C is the set of predefined e-commerce categories. The category $c = [wc_1, wc_2, ..., wc_m]$ is also a sequence of words that is the description of the category. We denote training set as $T = \{\langle q_i, c_i, y_i \rangle \,|i = 1, 2, ..., N\}$, where $y_i \in \{0, 1\}$ is the label which indicates the pair $\langle q_i, c_i \rangle$ is a negative example or a positive example. We denote the set of all queries in training set as $Q_{ALL} = \{q| \langle q, *, * \rangle \in T\}$. We also define a frequent queries set Q_F, which is a subset of Q_{ALL} and consists of the queries with daily average page views more than $thres_q$. The other queries are regarded as long-tail queries.

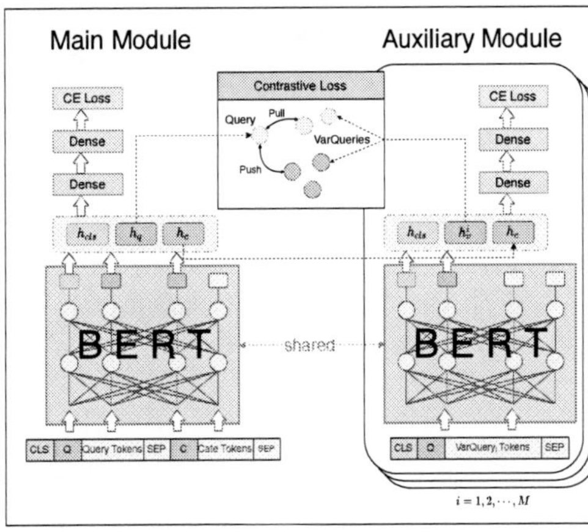

Figure 1: The overview of our proposed model.

Our proposed method consists of two components: the main module and the auxiliary module, as depicted in Figure 1. The main module is a standard text classification model which takes the tokenized sequence of query and category as input and predicts the relation between query and category in an interactive manner. The auxiliary module is to learn the representations of variant queries and transfer the representing ability to the main module with a contrastive loss function. The main and auxiliary modules are optimized simultaneously in training phase while only the main module is used in inference phase. Therefore, we do not add extra computation for prediction compared with base method. In this work, we adopt BERT (Devlin et al., 2018) as our base model because it achieves state-of-the-art performance among many NLP tasks and provides a high standard of baseline.

3.2 Main Module

The main module is basically a standard BERT to compute the relevance score between query and category via transformer architecture and we make a slight modification on input schema. Since each query and category share the same BERT model, the query input is typed by customers and the category's textual description is usually more formally written, which differs in choice of words. According to ColBERT(Khattab and Zaharia, 2020), we distinguish the input sequences by adding a special token [Q] to queries and another token [C] to category descriptions. Given a training example $\langle q, c, y\rangle$, we get the concatenated input tokens $[CLS, [Q], wq_1, ..., SEP, [C], wc_1, ..., SEP]$. After feeding the input, we obtain the output vectors from BERT of all tokens. We denote the output vectors of $[Q]$-location, $[C]$-location and CLS-location as h_q, h_c and h_{cls}, which are expected to represent the query, the category and the interactive feature between query and category respectively.

We concatenate h_q, h_c and h_{cls} as a hidden vector and feed it to fully connected networks with binary cross-entropy loss to predict the target score $\hat{y} \in [0, 1]$. The target score indicates the relevance of the query and category, as follows:

$$\hat{y} = f(W_a \cdot (h_q \oplus h_c \oplus h_{cls}) + b_a), \tag{1}$$

$$L_M = -ylog(\hat{y}) - (1-y)log(1-\hat{y}), \tag{2}$$

where W_a and b_a is the weight and bias of the fully connected network and y denotes the label of pair $\langle q, c\rangle$.

3.3 Variant Query Selection

To transfer knowledge from frequent queries to long-tail queries, we introduce variant queries that are lexically similar to the original query with several different tokens. Despite the similarity in text, those slight tokens' differences between the original query and its variant queries can lead to totally different category intents. Since variant queries and original queries may be fused in semantic space because of the lexical similarity, we use the category information from variant queries to build a better latent representation for original queries with auxiliary tasks.

We select M variant queries for each query in the training set. All the variant queries are frequent queries that are selected from the candidate set Q_F. We propose a simple but effective method with a low computational cost to select variant queries. To measure the textual similarity between query q and candidate query q_c, let T_q and T_{qc} be the set of tokens of q and q_c respectively, a weighted token similarity is calculated as follows:

$$Sim(q, q_c) = \frac{\sum_{t_i \in T_q \cap T_{qc}} w_{i,qc}}{|T_{qc}|}, \tag{3}$$

where $w_{i,qc}$ is the weight score of token t_i in query q_c. We take TF-IDF (Salton and Buckley, 1988) as the weight score:

$$w_{i,qc} = TF_{i,qc} * IDF_i, \tag{4}$$

where IDF_i is the inverse document (i.e., query) frequency of token t_i. We order all the candidate queries by their similarity score $Sim(q, q_c)$ with q and select the top M of them as the set of variant queries, denoted as V^q.

The variant queries have similar text to the original query but they are not always have same categories. These queries with different category intents become hard negative examples which are then utilized by the contrastive loss. All the work in this subsection is done in data preparing phase.

3.4 Auxiliary Module

The auxiliary module is also a BERT-based model that predicts the relevance between the given category and the variant queries. The auxiliary module shares parameters of BERT with the main module. However, to obtain the pure representation of queries, the auxiliary module only receives the tokens of variant queries as input. For each variant query $q_i^v \in V^q$, we add the special token $[Q]$ ahead to indicates a query sequence, i.e., the input sequence is $[CLS, [Q], wq_1^v, wq_2^v, ..., wq_n^v, SEP]$. We take the output of $[CLS]$-location and $[Q]$-location from BERT as the representation of variant query q_i^v , which is denoted as h_{cls}^i and h_v^i. we obtain representation of category c from the main module and concatenate h_{cls}^i and h_v^i with h_c for downstream fully connected networks. Finally, the relevance score is predicted as follows:

$$\hat{y}_i = f(W_b \cdot (h_{cls}^i \oplus h_v^i \oplus h_c) + b_b), \tag{5}$$

$$L_A = -\sum_M y_i log(\hat{y}_i) + (1-y_i)log(1-\hat{y}_i), \tag{6}$$

where $\hat{y}_i$ is the prediction value and y_i is the label that indicates whether category c is related to the variant query q_i^v. The value of y_i is from the training set where $y_i = 1$ if $\langle q_i^v, c, 1\rangle \in T$ otherwise $y_i = 0$. Through the training of the auxiliary module, we build the representations of variant queries which play an important role in the calculations of contrastive loss.

3.5 Contrastive Loss

Since we have obtained h_q and $h_i^v, i = 1,..,M$, which are the representations of original query q and its variant queries q_i^v, we apply a contrastive loss function to align their representations according to their relevance with the category c. We follow the definition of contrastive loss in (Lian et al., 2018). If the variant query q_i^v and original query q belong to the same category c, the representations of the two queries should be pulled together. Otherwise, the representations should be pushed apart. The above process is adopted by adding the contrastive loss as follows:

$$L_C = \sum_{i \in 1,...,M} y \cdot L_C^i, \quad (7)$$

$$L_C^i = \begin{cases} \|h_q - h_i^v\|_2 & y \bigwedge y_i = 1 \\ max(0, m - \|h_q - h_i^v\|_2) & y \bigwedge y_i = 0 \end{cases}, \quad (8)$$

where $\| \cdot \|$ is the L2 norm and m is the margin.

Finally, the total loss is calculated as follows, re-weighted by parameters λ_A and λ_C:

$$L = L_M + \lambda_A L_A + \lambda_C L_C. \quad (9)$$

The auxiliary module aims at transferring knowledge from frequent queries to long-tail queries. Since all the variant queries are frequent queries that have a large number of click feedback, the supervised signal derived from those feedback is more reliable and their representations are more reasonable in feature space. With the constraint of contrastive loss between the original query and lexically similar variant queries (shown in Figure 1), queries obtain better representations to recognize different category intents.

It's noteworthy that our proposed method enhances the query representations in long-tail query classification task without bringing in external information. we neither augment the training examples nor use other data except the training set.

4 Experiments

We introduce the training and evaluation data set and the setting of our experiments in section 4.1. We discuss the performance and effectiveness of our proposed method with other methods in section 4.2 and 4.3.

4.1 Data and Setting

To collect training data, we sample search queries and their clicked products' categories in recent 3 months logs from AliExpress, a cross-border e-commerce platform of Alibaba. We collect 5,000,000 $\langle query, category \rangle$ pairs and the numbers of distinct queries and categories are 3,620,000 and 6,300 respectively. All of the queries and categories are in English. Queries with daily average page view less than $thres_q = 100$ are defined as long-tail queries, which include almost 97% of queries and occupy only 56% of the whole clicked pairs. The rest 3% of queries are defined as frequent queries that contributes 44% of clicks. For each query, we choose its corresponding categories with high click-through rates as our positive training examples and replace the query or category randomly from a different pair to generate negative examples. Finally, we obtain a training data set which consists of about 33,400,000 pairs. We list several examples from the training set in Table 1 including the variant queries and their labels. The columns named "Query", "Category" and "Label" are the inputs of the main module, where the "Label" column denotes whether the pair of query and category is relevant or not. The columns named "Variant Q1/Q2/Q3" and corresponding "Label 1/2/3" are the inputs of the auxiliary module.

For evaluation, We randomly sample another 2,000 long-tail queries and collect a total of 78,226 correspondings clicked $\langle query, category \rangle$ pairs from search engine. Each pair in the evaluation set are labeled as relevant or irrelevant by human annotators.

We use the BERT-Tiny pre-trained model released by google research as our base model. We process the queries and categories by WordPiece tokenization (Wu et al., 2016). The number of variant queries M is 3. The number of frequent queries N is 100,000. Margin m in contrastive loss is 32.0 . The loss reweight parameter λ_A and λ_C are 0.1 and 0.02 respectively. We use Adam optimization method (Kingma and Ba, 2014) and set the learning rate to 1e-6 while the batchsize is 1024. All hyper-parameters are adjusted according to the performance on the held-out validation set. We train the model for a fixed number of global steps (640,000) and save models at regular intervals. Then we choose the best performance achieved by these models as the result.

Table 1: Examples of training set.

Query	Category	Label	Variant Q1	Label1	Variant Q2	Label2	Variant Q3	Label3
video game consoles 16bit	Handheld Game Players	1	game consoles	1	video game consoles	1	video	0
lure glass rattles	Fishing Lures	1	lure	1	glass	0	fishing lure	1
fine point heels	Women's Pumps	1	point	0	heels	1	fine jewelry	0
huawei p 40 lite 5g cover	Mobile Phone Cases & Covers	1	huawei	0	cover	1	huawei phone	0
612 bundles with frontal	Hair Bundles with Closures	1	bundles	1	bundles with frontal	1	613 bundles	1
0.25 eyelashes	Body Foundation	0	eyelashes	0	rover 25	0	false eyelashes	0
1 birthday boy clothes	Audio Intercom	0	birthday	0	birthday boy	0	boy birthday	0
2000s aesthetic sunglasses	Wax Fabrics	0	2000s	0	2000s aesthetic	0	sunglasses	0
pink porcelain plate	Men's Socks	0	porcelain	0	porcelain plate	0	plate porcelain	0

4.2 Performance

We use AUC (Area Under Curve), AP (Average Precision), Prec (Precision), Recall and F1 score as our evaluation metrics. The Average precision (Turpin and Scholer, 2006) is the area under the precision-recall curve and it is independent of threshold as well as AUC.

We conduct experiments on the aforementioned data set and compare our method with the baseline and existing approaches in Table 2:

- "Base" is the standard BERT model which takes the same setting as our proposed method (only preserve the main module).
- "AC(LSTM)" (Zhang et al., 2021) is the latest related work for long-tail query classification which couples with an auxiliary task to provide across-attention information. The original paper uses LSTM (Hochreiter and Schmidhuber, 1997) as the encoder and the base queries and variant queries differ in encoders.
- "AC(BERT)" is the modified version we implemented, which shares the same BERT encoder for original queries and variant queries following our proposed method setting for a fair comparison.
- "Proposed" is our proposed method.

As shown in Table 2, our proposed method outperforms the baselines by a statistically significant margin on all of the metrics. Compared with method named "Base", our method achieves +1.92% improvement on AUC, +2.48% improvement on AP and +2.27% improvement on F1 score. Our method also outperforms "AC(LSTM)" and "AC(BERT)" in all of the metrics with steady margins (range from +1.19% to +1.68%) which reflect the effectiveness. The AC methods only use one variant query to adjust the original query representation implicitly. In contrast, our proposed method

Table 2: Performance comparison between our method and baselines on evaluation set.

Method	AUC	AP	Prec	Recall	F1 Score
Base	0.7610	0.3110	0.3367	0.3463	0.3414
AC(LSTM)	0.7622	0.3132	0.3214	0.3727	0.3452
AC(BERT)	0.7681	0.3190	0.3396	0.3632	0.3510
Proposed	**0.7802**	**0.3358**	**0.3522**	**0.3767**	**0.3641**

clearly establishes the pulling or pushing relations between the original query and variant queries by contrastive constraints.

To better understand the contribution of each key component of our method, we conduct several ablation tests and each method is described as follows:

- "Proposed-Without LC" removes the contrastive loss from the proposed method.
- "Proposed-Only CLS" only uses h_{cls} as feature instead of concatenating h_q, h_c and h_{cls} in main module.
- "Proposed-Sym" means the auxiliary module uses the same input schema as the main module, which takes both variant query tokens and category tokens as input.
- "Proposed-Entire Query" takes the whole queries in the training set as variant query candidates rather than only the frequent queries.

The experimental results are listed in Table 3. The results show that our proposed method outperforms the others significantly. As contrast, the performance of "Proposed-Without LC" decreases significantly, which shows that the contrastive loss plays a key role in enhancing representations. The performance of "Proposed-Only CLS" decreases remarkably compared with our proposed method, which shows that the representations h_q and h_c can provide extra useful information for query classification. The performance of "Proposed-Sym" is dramatically lower than the results of "Proposed" method and has only slight improvement compared to the "Base" method. The result indicates that the

Table 3: Ablation test of our proposed method on evaluation set.

Method	AUC	AP	Prec	Recall	F1
Base	0.7610	0.3110	0.3367	0.3463	0.3414
Proposed-Sym	0.7650	0.3148	0.3124	**0.3791**	0.3425
Proposed-Without LC	0.7584	0.3147	0.3240	0.3780	0.3489
Proposed-Only CLS	0.7708	0.3245	0.3339	0.3699	0.3510
Proposed-Entire Query	0.7645	0.3209	0.3304	0.3589	0.3441
Proposed	**0.7802**	**0.3358**	**0.3522**	0.3767	**0.3641**

representation alignment effect of contrastive loss weakens using query tokens and category tokens simultaneously in the auxiliary module. With inputs of extra category tokens, the representation of the variant query h_i^v loses its independence and becomes sensitive to disturbance of category texts, which makes h_i^v an unstable anchor for the original query. The decreased performance of "Proposed-Entire Query" shows choosing frequent queries as variant queries can lead to better representations for long-tail queries, which implies frequent queries serve as better anchors in hidden spaces because of sufficient training data.

To investigate the effect of our method on long-tail queries, we split the evaluation set of long-tail queries into 3 sets according to their frequency levels in search logs. The set of relatively high-frequency queries is named "Long-tail Head", the set of queries with middle-frequency level is named "Long-tail Mid" and the set of rest queries is "Long-tail Tail". To compare with performance on those long-tail query sets, we also randomly sample a set of queries named "Top Freq" from frequent queries as defined in Section 4.1, which includes 28,389 pairs of 512 queries. The performance of base method and our method on the above evaluation sets are listed in Table 4. Our method outperforms the baseline by a significant margin in all the groups of long-tail queries, where the AUC improvements are +1.99%, +1.84% and +2.22% respectively. The improvement on "Long-tail Tail" set is greater than other sets, which means the greatest improvement is achieved on the queries at the far end of the tail. We notice that the improvement on "Top Freq" queries is much smaller with +0.28% on AUC, +0.37% on AP and +0.67% on F1 Score, compared with the remarkable improvement on long-tail queries. The results indicate that our method improves the effectiveness on long-tail queries more than frequent queries.

Furthermore, We evaluate our method on the public dataset released by the personalized e-commerce search challenge of the CIKM Cup 2016 [2]. This dataset contains query searching and browsing logs and product metadata including the product categories information (Wu et al., 2017). We process the data files and collect a total of 500,000 $\langle query, category \rangle$ pairs as training data for the query classification task, which have 26,137 distinct queries and 1,213 distinct categories. To collect test data, we sample 3000 long-tail queries and remove the corresponding pairs from the training set. The detailed data process is described in Appendix A. As shown in Table 5, our proposed method substantially improves multiple metrics including AUC, AP and F1 Score on this dataset, with +4.3% and +2.6% absolute improvement on AP compared with the base method and AC(LSTM) method respectively. Considering that the dataset is more sparse and its tokenization is different from the common wordpiece model (Wu et al., 2016), these performances demonstrate the effectiveness and generalizability of our method.

4.3 Discussion

To verify whether our proposed method is able to recognize the category intents of lexically similar queries, we calculate two distances: 1) the average Euclidean distance between representation vectors of original queries and their category-consistent variant queries and 2) the same metric between original queries and their category-inconsistent variant queries. We visualize the distances between the proposed method and baseline with increasing training steps in Figure 2. The curves named "PD" and "PS" are derived from our proposed method and the curves named "BD" and "BS" are from the base method. In Figure 2, the gap between the curve "BD" and "BS" are very close all the time while the curve "PD" and "PS" gradually separate from each other with a certain margin. As we mentioned ahead, the phenomenon indicates that our proposed model distinguishes different category well by pulling original query and category-consistent variant queries together and pushing them of different category further apart.

To verify whether our proposed method generates better representations for long-tail queries, we visualize the representation vectors (i.e. vector [Q] from the model) of the baseline method and our method in Figure 3. We randomly sample 100,000 long-tail queries and project their representations

[2] https://competitions.codalab.org/competitions/11161

Table 4: Performance improvement of queries grouped by frequency in search logs.

Group	base					proposed				
	AUC	AP	Prec	Recall	F1 Score	AUC	AP	Prec	Recall	F1 Score
Top Freq	0.7408	0.4615	0.4149	0.4852	0.4473	0.7436(+0.28%)	0.4652(+0.37%)	0.4177(+0.28%)	0.4973(+1.21%)	0.4540(+0.67%)
Long-tail Head	0.7558	0.3469	0.3359	0.3823	0.3576	0.7757(+1.99%)	0.3514(+0.45%)	0.3564(+2.05%)	0.3887(+0.64%)	0.3719(+1.43%)
Long-tail Mid	0.7461	0.3102	0.3214	0.3862	0.3508	0.7645(+1.84%)	0.3344(+2.42%)	0.3287(+0.73%)	0.4005(+2.43%)	0.3611(+1.03%)
Long-tail Tail	0.7742	0.2926	0.3103	0.3539	0.3307	0.7964(+2.22%)	0.3211(+2.85%)	0.3484(+3.81%)	0.3736(+1.97%)	0.3606(+2.99%)

Table 5: Performance comparison between our method and baselines on the public CIKM Cup 2016 dataset.

Method	AUC	AP	Prec	Recall	F1 Score
Base	0.9096	0.6465	0.6571	0.5716	0.6061
AC(LSTM)	0.9122	0.6637	0.6736	0.5732	0.6193
AC(BERT)	0.9129	0.6668	**0.6845**	0.5636	0.6181
Proposed	**0.9160**	**0.6897**	0.6738	**0.5969**	**0.6330**

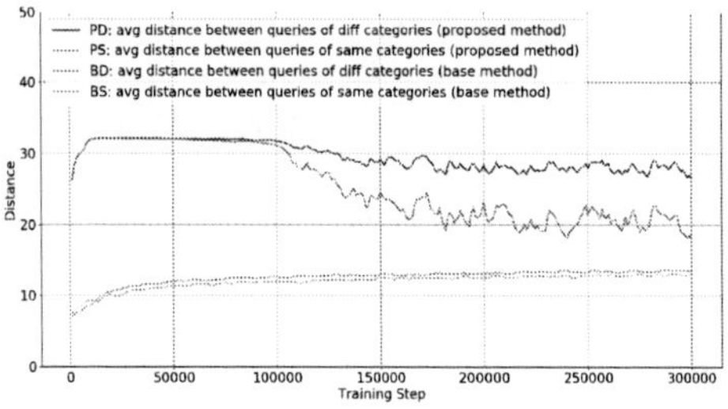

Figure 2: The Euclidean distance of category-consistent queries and category-inconsistent queries representation vector.

to 2-dimensional space by UMAP(McInnes et al., 2018) (neighbors=40, epochs=400). Each point in Figure 3 is a long-tail query colored according to its category. If a query is relevant to multiple categories, the category which has the most click logs is chosen. To simplify the figure, we only reserve queries that are relevant to the top-10 hot categories. As shown in the left box of Figure 3, a lot of the query representations are scattered around the space, and categories groups are overlapped with each other, which means the baseline method fails to preserve the category consistency of long-tail queries. In contrast, the query representations in the right figure form clusters according to their categories spontaneously. Most of these clusters are cohesive and keep away from other clusters. There are still some overlaps between query clusters, probably due to that some queries are naturally interested with multiple categories, such as T-shirt (Men) and T-shirt (Women). The visualization results indicate that our method is able to obtain reasonable representations corresponding to the category semantics of queries.

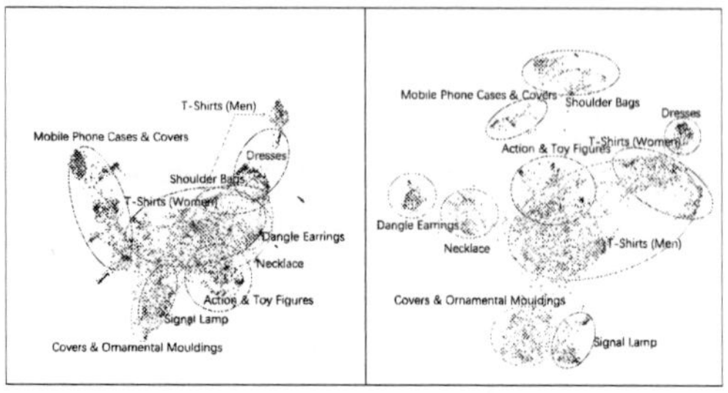

Figure 3: The visualized representation vectors of long-tail queries generated by Base model (left) and our proposed model (right).

Table 6: Online performance evaluation.

Method	CTR	RPM
Base	-	-
Proposed	+0.63%	+1.06%

4.4 Online Evaluation

We deploy online evaluation in search advertising system of AliExpress. Instead of comparing each query with the whole 6,300 categories online, we predicted categories offline beforehand and generated a query-category cached table that covers over 80% of page views. The predicted categories of queries serve as the filters of vector-based product retrieval and influence the relevance score between the queries and products in our e-commerce sponsored search system. We conducted standard A/B testing for 5 days and selected 5% of the search traffic as the test group to evaluate our proposed method. Two common metrics are calculated for evaluation: CTR (click-through rate) and RPM (revenues per mille). As shown in Table 6, the results suggest that our proposed method improves the online performance on tens of millions of user visits. The gains of CTR and RPM reflect that our method increases valid exposures of the advertisement with better quality, which finally results in the growth of users' clicks and platform revenue.

5 Conclusion

In this paper, we propose a novel method for query classification which focuses on the long-tail queries in e-commerce. Our method consists of a main module and an auxiliary module that aims at utilizing reliable information from frequent queries to help the classification of long-tail queries. The results of extensive experiments show that our proposed method outperforms the baselines by a substantial margin. Further analysis demonstrates our method can obtain better representations for long-tail queries and discriminate different category intents from lexically similar queries. In the future, We will generalize our idea to more situations in e-commerce, such as multi-language query classification and other tasks such as product retrieval or relevance classification.

References

Wei-Cheng Chang, Hsiang-Fu Yu, Kai Zhong, Yiming Yang, and Inderjit S Dhillon. 2020. Taming pre-trained transformers for extreme multi-label text classification. In *Proceedings of the 26th ACM SIGKDD International Conference on Knowledge Discovery & Data Mining*, pages 3163–3171.

Ting Chen, Simon Kornblith, Mohammad Norouzi, and Geoffrey Hinton. 2020. A simple framework for contrastive learning of visual representations. In *International conference on machine learning*, pages 1597–1607. PMLR.

Sumit Chopra, Raia Hadsell, and Yann LeCun. 2005. Learning a similarity metric discriminatively, with application to face verification. In *2005 IEEE Computer Society Conference on Computer Vision and Pattern Recognition (CVPR'05)*, volume 1, pages 539–546. IEEE.

Jacob Devlin, Ming-Wei Chang, Kenton Lee, and Kristina Toutanova. 2018. Bert: Pre-training of deep bidirectional transformers for language understanding. *arXiv preprint arXiv:1810.04805*.

Dehong Gao, Wenjing Yang, Huiling Zhou, Yi Wei, Yi Hu, and Hao Wang. 2020. Deep hierarchical classification for category prediction in e-commerce system. *ECNLP 3*, page 64.

Tianyu Gao, Xingcheng Yao, and Danqi Chen. 2021. Simcse: Simple contrastive learning of sentence embeddings. In *Proceedings of the 2021 Conference on Empirical Methods in Natural Language Processing*, pages 6894–6910.

Raia Hadsell, Sumit Chopra, and Yann LeCun. 2006. Dimensionality reduction by learning an invariant mapping. In *2006 IEEE Computer Society Conference on Computer Vision and Pattern Recognition (CVPR'06)*, volume 2, pages 1735–1742. IEEE.

Sepp Hochreiter and Jürgen Schmidhuber. 1997. Long short-term memory. *Neural computation*, 9(8):1735–1780.

Ting Jiang, Deqing Wang, Leilei Sun, Huayi Yang, Zhengyang Zhao, and Fuzhen Zhuang. 2021. Lightxml: Transformer with dynamic negative sampling for high-performance extreme multi-label text classification. In *Proceedings of the AAAI Conference on Artificial Intelligence*, volume 35, pages 7987–7994.

Omar Khattab and Matei Zaharia. 2020. Colbert: Efficient and effective passage search via contextualized late interaction over bert. In *Proceedings of the 43rd International ACM SIGIR conference on research and development in Information Retrieval*, pages 39–48.

Diederik P Kingma and Jimmy Ba. 2014. Adam: A method for stochastic optimization. *arXiv preprint arXiv:1412.6980*.

Zheng Lian, Ya Li, Jianhua Tao, and Jian Huang. 2018. Speech emotion recognition via contrastive loss under siamese networks. In *Proceedings of the Joint Workshop of the 4th Workshop on Affective Social Multimedia Computing and First Multi-Modal Affective Computing of Large-Scale Multimedia Data*, pages 21–26.

Junyang Lin, Qi Su, Pengcheng Yang, Shuming Ma, and Xu Sun. 2018a. Semantic-unit-based dilated convolution for multi-label text classification. In *Proceedings of the 2018 Conference on Empirical Methods in Natural Language Processing*, pages 4554–4564.

Yiu-Chang Lin, Ankur Datta, and Giuseppe Di Fabbrizio. 2018b. E-commerce product query classification using implicit user's feedback from clicks. In *2018 IEEE International Conference on Big Data (Big Data)*, pages 1955–1959. IEEE.

Jingzhou Liu, Wei-Cheng Chang, Yuexin Wu, and Yiming Yang. 2017. Deep learning for extreme multi-label text classification. In *Proceedings of the 40th International ACM SIGIR Conference on Research and Development in Information Retrieval*, pages 115–124.

Leland McInnes, John Healy, Nathaniel Saul, and Lukas Großberger. 2018. Umap: Uniform manifold approximation and projection. *Journal of Open Source Software*, 3(29):861.

Anshul Mittal, Kunal Dahiya, Sheshansh Agrawal, Deepak Saini, Sumeet Agarwal, Purushottam Kar, and Manik Varma. 2021. Decaf: Deep extreme classification with label features. In *Proceedings of the 14th ACM International Conference on Web Search and Data Mining*, pages 49–57.

Jinseok Nam, Jungi Kim, Eneldo Loza Mencía, Iryna Gurevych, and Johannes Fürnkranz. 2014. Large-scale multi-label text classification—revisiting neural networks. In *Joint european conference on machine learning and knowledge discovery in databases*, pages 437–452. Springer.

Aaron van den Oord, Yazhe Li, and Oriol Vinyals. 2018. Representation learning with contrastive predictive coding. *arXiv preprint arXiv:1807.03748*.

Hao Peng, Jianxin Li, Yu He, Yaopeng Liu, Mengjiao Bao, Lihong Wang, Yangqiu Song, and Qiang Yang. 2018. Large-scale hierarchical text classification with recursively regularized deep graph-cnn. In *Proceedings of the 2018 world wide web conference*, pages 1063–1072.

Gerard Salton and Christopher Buckley. 1988. Term-weighting approaches in automatic text retrieval. *Information processing & management*, 24(5):513–523.

Dou Shen, Ying Li, Xiao Li, and Dengyong Zhou. 2009. Product query classification. In *Proceedings of the 18th ACM conference on information and knowledge management*, pages 741–750.

Andrew Turpin and Falk Scholer. 2006. User performance versus precision measures for simple search tasks. In *Proceedings of the 29th annual international ACM SIGIR conference on Research and development in information retrieval*, pages 11–18.

Chen Wu, Ming Yan, and Luo Si. 2017. Ensemble methods for personalized e-commerce search challenge at cikm cup 2016. *arXiv preprint arXiv:1708.04479*.

Yonghui Wu, Mike Schuster, Zhifeng Chen, Quoc V Le, Mohammad Norouzi, Wolfgang Macherey, Maxim Krikun, Yuan Cao, Qin Gao, Klaus Macherey, et al. 2016. Google's neural machine translation system: Bridging the gap between human and machine translation. *arXiv preprint arXiv:1609.08144*.

Pengcheng Yang, Xu Sun, Wei Li, Shuming Ma, Wei Wu, and Houfeng Wang. 2018. Sgm: Sequence generation model for multi-label classification. In *Proceedings of the 27th International Conference on Computational Linguistics*, pages 3915–3926.

Ronghui You, Zihan Zhang, Ziye Wang, Suyang Dai, Hiroshi Mamitsuka, and Shanfeng Zhu. 2019. Attentionxml: Label tree-based attention-aware deep model for high-performance extreme multi-label text classification. *Advances in Neural Information Processing Systems*, 32.

Hang Yu and Lester Litchfield. 2020. Query classification with multi-objective backoff optimization. In *Proceedings of the 43rd International ACM SIGIR Conference on Research and Development in Information Retrieval*, pages 1925–1928.

Hongchun Zhang, Tianyi Wang, Xiaonan Meng, Yi Hu, and Hao Wang. 2019. Improving semantic matching via multi-task learning in e-commerce. In *eCOM@SIGIR*.

Junhao Zhang, Weidi Xu, Jianhui Ji, Xi Chen, Hongbo Deng, and Keping Yang. 2021. Modeling across-context attention for long-tail query classification in e-commerce. In *Proceedings of the 14th ACM International Conference on Web Search and Data Mining*, pages 58–66.

Ye Zhang and Byron Wallace. 2015. A sensitivity analysis of (and practitioners' guide to) convolutional neural networks for sentence classification. *arXiv preprint arXiv:1510.03820*.

A Data Process for CIKM Cup 2016 Dataset

We extract pairs of $\langle query, productID\rangle$ from the file named `train-queries.csv`, which includes user sessions from e-commerce search engine logs. Only the query-full cases are selected and each query is represented as a list of hashed tokens. The queries which appear in more than $thres_q$ sessions are regarded as frequent queries while others are long-tail queries. We then map the pairs of $\langle query, productID\rangle$ to $\langle query, categoryID\rangle$ according to the content of file `product-categories.csv` and denote the set of pairs as S. We denote the number of occurrences of query q in S as f_q and the number of $\langle q, c\rangle$ pairs in S as $f_{q,c}$ where c is the category. The pair $\langle q, c\rangle$ is regarded as a positive example when it meets the requirements of both absolute number and relative ratio, which are $f_{q,c} > thres_N$ and $f_{q,c} > \frac{f_q}{M}$. We collect all positive examples as set S^P and then generate negative examples from S^P. For each $\langle q, c\rangle$ in S^P, we replace the q and c by a random query q' and category c' respectively and repeat R times. Finally, we randomly select L long-tail queries and then take all the corresponding pairs in positive set and negative set as the test set, while the rest of pairs are training set.

Considering there is no category description in the original dataset, we group the products based on their categories and take the top-K most frequent tokens in product names as the description of the category (the hashed product name tokens are obtained from `products.csv`).

The values of above parameters are listed in Table 7. The hyper-parameters of the model are the same as Section 4.1.

Table 7: Parameters in process of CIKM Cup 2016 dataset.

Name	value	Name	value
$thres_q$	5	R	4
$thres_N$	2	L	3000
M	16	K	10

Domain-specific knowledge distillation yields smaller and better models for conversational commerce

Kristen Howell
LivePerson
khowell@liveperson.com

Jian Wang
LivePerson
jwang@liveperson.com

Akshay Hazare
LivePerson
ahazare@liveperson.com

Joseph Bradley
LivePerson
jbradley@liveperson.com

Chris Brew
LexisNexis
christopher.brew@google.com

Xi Chen
LivePerson
xchen@liveperson.com

Matthew Dunn
LivePerson
mdunn@liveperson.com

Beth Ann Hockey
LivePerson
bhockey@liveperson.com

Andrew Maurer
Amazon.com Inc
abmaurer@amazon.com

Dominic Widdows
IonQ
widdows@ionq.com

Abstract

In the context of conversational commerce, where training data may be limited and low latency is critical, we demonstrate that knowledge distillation can be used not only to reduce model size, but to simultaneously adapt a contextual language model to a specific domain. We use Multilingual BERT (mBERT; Devlin et al., 2019) as a starting point and follow the knowledge distillation approach of Sanh et al. (2019) to train a smaller multilingual BERT model that is adapted to the domain at hand. We show that for in-domain tasks, the domain-specific model shows on average 2.3% improvement in F1 score, relative to a model distilled on domain-general data. Whereas much previous work with BERT has fine-tuned the encoder weights during task training, we show that the model improvements from distillation on in-domain data persist even when the encoder weights are frozen during task training, allowing a single encoder to support classifiers for multiple tasks and languages.

1 Introduction

Encoders and language models such as BERT (Devlin et al., 2019), RoBERTa (Liu et al., 2019) and ELMo (Peters et al., 2017) are the backbone of many NLP technologies. They are typically trained on data from Wikipedia, CommonCrawl, or large homogeneous collections of text; however, language varies widely in real-world settings and the type of language used in some contexts is not well represented in the data used to train these models. In particular, the language used in e-commerce, and more specifically, conversational commerce, such as conversations pertaining to customer service in the context of online shopping or banking, exhibits both syntactic structures and vocabulary that are under-represented in the Wikipedia data used to train multilingual BERT.

At the same time, these models are too large to deploy in many industry settings, where computational resources and inference-speed are concerns. Model size is often reduced using methods such as quantization (Whittaker and Raj, 2001; Shen et al., 2020), pruning (Han et al., 2015, 2016) and knowledge distillation (Hinton et al., 2015; Sanh et al., 2019). However, even leveraging these techniques, the memory footprint of the typical encoder can easily be three orders of magnitude greater than that of the typical classifier, and it follows that encoding is much more time-intensive than classification.[1] In conversational commerce, a variety of classifiers are required to model different aspects of the conversation. In this case, it is beneficial for efficiency, to use a single encoder for all of the classifiers as illustrated in Figure 1 (left), rather than using a separate encoder for each classification task (Figure 1, right).[2] Thus text can be encoded only once and passed to any number of downstream classifiers.

Typically, domain adaptation with language models is accomplished using back-propagation during task training (see inter alia Devlin et al., 2019; Liu et al., 2019; Sanh et al., 2019). However, this approach requires a separate encoder for each classifier. Instead, we adapt the encoder to a particular domain before classifier training. We show that knowledge distillation, a common approach for reducing model size, is very adept for domain adaptation. This allows us to accomplish two goals,

[1]For example, a BERT encoder has hundreds of millions of parameters (see Table 7), while a self attention classifier like the one used in Section 8 has about 600,000.

[2]Houlsby et al. (2019), inter alios, have proposed similar architectures.

Proceedings of The Fifth Workshop on e-Commerce and NLP (ECNLP 5), pages 151 - 160
May 26, 2022 ©2022 Association for Computational Linguistics

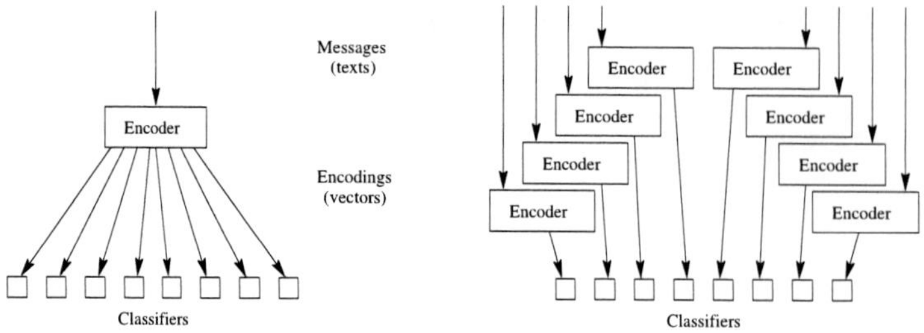

Figure 1: The difference in architecture between using one encoder for multiple tasks vs. one encoder per task

size reduction and domain adaptation, with a single training process. Evaluating on five languages and two domains, we show that distilling on unlabeled data from the domain of interest results in a smaller model that is domain-specific and outperforms the F1-score of a model distilled on domain-general data by 2.3% on average and the larger teacher model by an F1 of 1.2%. The improvement in performance persists even when relatively little training data is used. We show that the domain-adapted encoder performs better than the domain-general model both when encoder weights are fine-tuned, as in previous work, and when they are frozen, leaving them task agnostic. Furthermore, the boost in performance from distillation on in-domain data is greater than the improvement from fine-tuning the encoder during task training.

We begin with an overview of previous work in domain adaptation and knowledge distillation, highlighting the benefit of doing both at once (§2). This is followed by a description of the domains, data and tasks with which we evaluate domain adaptation through knowledge distillation (§3). We detail our approach in Section 4, investigating how much data is necessary (§5) and examining the impact of domain adaptation on sentence embeddings (§6). We evaluate on two domains and five languages in Section 8, considering both training scenarios where encoder weights are frozen for task training and where they are fine-tuned.

2 Related Work

2.1 Knowledge distillation

Many state-of-the-art NLP models have achieved high performance with increased parameters and layers, and in doing so have become too computationally expensive for some applications. Knowledge distillation addresses this problem with a "teacher-student" training approach in which a smaller "student" model learns to mimic a larger "teacher" model (Sanh et al., 2019) or an ensemble of models (Bucilă et al., 2006; Hinton et al., 2015).

In the context of reducing model size with BERT, task-specific distillation has been successful (Tang et al., 2019; Chatterjee, 2019) as has distillation of the encoder during pre-training (Sanh et al., 2019). Distillation of the pre-trained encoder is particularly beneficial as the distilled model can be applied to any number of downstream tasks. Sanh et al. (2019) released a distilled version of English BERT (DistilBERT), which is 40% smaller and 60% faster than the original model, while retaining 97% of its NLU capabilities. This was followed by DistilmBERT, distilled from mBERT using data from 104 languages, which is 24% smaller and 38% faster than its teacher. In both cases, the same data was used for knowledge distillation as for pre-training the original models. We adopt this approach, limiting our training data to the languages and domain of interest to demonstrate that less data can be used to distill a model for a specific setting.

2.2 Domain adaptation

When sufficient data is not available to train a model from scratch, a smaller amount of data can be used to adapt a domain-general model. In the context of BERT, domain adaption of the encoder through continued pre-training on in-domain data followed by task-specific fine-tuning has improved performance on domain-specific applications (Han and Eisenstein, 2019; Gururangan et al., 2020; Rietzler et al., 2020; Whang et al., 2020).

Previous work suggests that the teacher-student approach used for knowledge distillation is well suited to domain adaptation. In ASR, it has been applied to adapt models trained on clean speech to handle noisy speech, models for speech from headset mics to work for distant mics (Manohar et al., 2018), and for speaker adaptation (Yu et al., 2013). In neural machine translation, multidomain models have been distilled from single-domain specialist models (see inter alia Currey et al. 2020; Mghabbar and Ratnamogan 2020). In the context of sentiment analysis, Ruder et al. (2017) use an ensemble of models to train a domain-adapted model on unlabeled in-domain data and Ryu and Lee (2020) combine distillation with adversarial domain adaptation to mitigate over-fitting from task fine-tuning, rather than to reduce model size.

We show that knowledge distillation can simultaneously reduce the size of the model and adapt it to a domain. While, some degree of performance loss during distillation is typical, we show that focusing the training objective on in-domain data can eliminate performance loss and even improve model performance in the domain of interest. Our training objective does not require labeled data, and because we do this before task fine-tuning, the resulting model can be used for any number of in-domain tasks.

3 Use-cases and datasets

3.1 The conversational commerce use-case

Our first use case is in conversational commerce (hereafter CC), which involves messaging between customers and agents (human or automated) in a commercial customer service setting. Within CC, there are sub-domains for commercial industries, such as retail, financial services, airlines, etc.

Unlike the Wikipedia data used to train mBERT and DistilmBERT, CC is marked by questions, first and second person phrases, short responses, frequent typos and other textual and linguistic features that are more common in typed conversation. In addition to structural variation, CC data contains many product and service names that may not be common in Wikipedia data. These differences make CC a strong candidate for domain adaptation.

Our test-case is to classify customer messages as *intentful*, meaning that the message contains some actionable request, or *not intentful*. In CC, this is an important triage step that can be applied across sub-domains before sending messages to downstream classifiers. Because this classification task is applied to different sub-domains and customers say some surprising things, this task is rather challenging. Intentful messages can vary widely from requests for information, attempts to place orders or change account details, and disputes or complaints. Non-intentful messages include greetings, pleasantries, slot information that relies on a previous message for context, etc. After this triage step, intentful messages can be sent to downstream classifiers, which are specific to the industry or company, that predict specific intents such as "check order status" or "schedule appointment".

Table 1: Total amount of data used to distil each domain-adapted model in GB of uncompressed text

	Data per language (GB)					Total
model	eng	esp	jap	por	rus	(GB)
CC-Distil -mBERT	0.95	0.60	0.44	0.35	0.00	2.34
TD-Distil -mBERT	1.58	0.34	0.06	0.34	0.75	3.07

Table 2: # natural (N) and translated (T) messages per split for the CC classification task

Split	Data	eng	esp	jap	por
Train	N	4951	1364	1810	1845
	T		4306	4306	4306
Val	N	1236	255	286	323
	T		1020	1020	1020
Test	N	10078	719	908	909

3.1.1 Dataset

We use a proprietary dataset from a variety of companies that use a particular conversational commerce platform.[3,4] We distilled the encoder using 2.3GB of unlabeled text from English [ISO 639-3: eng], Spanish [esp], Japanese [jap] and Portuguese [por] as detailed in Table 1. This data came from 25 companies that span the retail, telecommunications, financial and airlines sub-domains. To verify that the encoder generalizes beyond these companies, we sampled data for the classification task from an additional 14 companies that were not used in encoder training as well as 12 that were.

Annotations classification were provided by native speakers of each language, who were trained on the task. Due to limited access to data and annotators for Japanese, Portuguese and Spanish, we supplemented natural language training data with machine-translated data from English. For evaluation, we used only naturally produced data from each language (see Table 2). The complete breakdown by class for evaluation is in Table 3.

The majority of the English, Portuguese and Spanish data is from the Americas and the remainder from Australia and Europe, while the Japanese data is primarily from Japan. Because data-use

[3]To be clarified after the anonymity period.

[4]For customer privacy, all personally identifiable information is masked before we use the data, but even after masking we cannot make the data or models publicly available.

Table 3: # messages per label in the CC evaluation set

label	eng	esp	jap	por
intentful	4050	423	475	537
not intentful	6030	298	435	373

agreements and laws vary by company and country, we could not sample evenly across regions; still, we sampled from as diverse a range of countries and company types as possible, in an effort to maximize representation of different speaker communities.[5]

3.2 The technical discussion use-case

Because our first dataset is proprietary, we repeat the experiments using data from online forums for technical discussions about programming (hereafter TD). This domain is marked by technical jargon, which includes many words that have non-technical homonyms, as we describe in Section 6. These forums also include code and urls, which can be useful for classification but are not common in the Wikipedia data used to train mBERT.

For evaluation we used a multi-label prediction task to automatically label posts with the appropriate tag or tags for the topic.[6] Because StackOverflow uses hundreds of tags, the task is limited to the ten most common, which are listed in Table 4.

3.2.1 Dataset

The data for this task comes from the anonymized dumps for the StackOverflow topics in English [eng], Japanese [jap], Portuguese [por], Russian [rus] and Spanish [esp].[7]We created classification datasets by sampling posts that contain one or more of the ten tags targeted by the task. For our validation and held-out evaluation sets for English, Spanish, Portuguese and Russian, we sampled messages such that each tag occurred in the set at least 100 times for a total of 1000 posts per set. As each post can have multiple tags, tags can occur more than 100 times. The total posts per tag for evaluation are in Table 4.[8] We then randomly selected 8000 training samples that contained at least one of the tags. Because the Japanese dump is much smaller, we created splits of half the size (500/500/4000).

Table 4: # posts per label in the TD evaluation set

label	eng	esp	jap	por	rus
c#	111	110	56	120	109
java	118	127	57	148	174
php	126	138	57	144	168
javascript	168	206	108	197	182
android	110	115	71	115	108
jquery	132	114	53	136	106
python	107	106	51	104	101
html	109	103	50	110	118
c++	104	104	51	101	116
ios	110	100	53	102	102

For encoder training, we sampled data from the remaining messages, including posts that did not contain the tags of interest. We assembled a 3GB training set (based on the results in Section 5) using all of the data for Japanese (0.055GB, 2% of the total), Portuguese (0.34GB, 11%), Spanish (0.34GB, 11%) and Russian (0.75GB. 24%), and 1.58GB (52%) for English to reach 3GB total.

4 Knowledge Distillation Method

For knowledge distillation, we use the established and open-source approach of Sanh et al. (2019),[9,10] which follows Liu et al. (2019)'s proposed best practices for BERT training. These include dynamic masking, large batches to leverage gradient accumulation and training on the masked language modeling task but not next sentence prediction.

Sanh et al.'s implementation of knowledge distillation trains the student model using the distillation loss of the soft target probabilities of the teacher. Because of this, the student model benefits from the the teacher model's full distribution during training. Due to this rich input, we expect that high performance can be achieved with less training data.

We use mBERT[11] as the teacher model and our student models have the same general architecture, hidden-size dimension and number of word embeddings. We reduce the model size by removing the token-embeddings and pooling and reducing the number of layers from 12 to 6. This reduces the total number of parameters by 43 million or 24% and increases the inference speed by 38% (Table 5).[12]

[5]We do not have access to demographic data for the users who produced the data, and cannot make any claims about how well the models generalize across speaker communities of various ages, genders, ethnicities or socio-economic groups.

[6]This task comes from https://github.com/theRajeshReddy/StackOverFlow-Classification

[7]https://archive.org/details/stackexchange

[8]The number of posts per tag for the train and validation sets can be found in the dataset's readme.

[9]Detailed instructions for training with Huggingface's Distil* module can be found at https://github.com/huggingface/transformers/blob/783d7d2629e97c5f0c5f9ef01b8c66410275c204/examples/research_projects/distillation/README.md.

[10]Here we discuss the most relevant training details, but Ibid. provides a full account of the training procedure.

[11]https://github.com/google-research/bert/blob/master/multilingual.md

[12]The change in model size and speed is equivalent to that

Table 5: Model size and and average inference speed on single-thread CPU with a batch size of 1

Model	# Params (millions)	Inf time per message (milliseconds)
mBERT	178	305
DistilmBERT	135	188
TD-DistilmBERT	135	189
CC-DistilmBERT	135	189

Whereas Sanh et al. (2019) used the same training data as the teacher model, we use only data from the domain we are adapting to. Intuitively, a model that will be deployed in a single domain does not need to learn everything the base model can do — it only needs to learn what it can do for the domain at hand. This allows us to reduce the training data and time needed for distillation.

5 Data requirements

Because knowledge distillation takes advantage of an existing model, which was already trained on a large amount of data, we expect that distillation training will be relatively economical in its use of data. Furthermore, many research objectives focus on a single domain and do not require the breadth of NLU capability of a domain-general model, but instead benefit from a depth of capability in one domain. Here we attempt to establish how much data is enough for knowledge distillation for a single domain and where we reach diminishing returns.

As a case-study, we use increasing quantities of StackOverflow English data for knowledge distillation and compare the performance of these models to both the teacher model (mBERT) and HuggingFace's multilingual distilled BERT model (DistilmBERT), which was distilled using the same approach. To measure the impact of domain adaptation from knowledge distillation alone, we freeze the encoder weights during task training and present the results in Table 6 and Figure 2.

We distilled models with English StackOverflow data, using increments of 0.3GB. We found that a minimum of 1.5GB was needed for convergence, but 2.1GB was enough to outperform DistilmBERT and perform on par with the teacher mBERT. Improvements stop after 3GB. We conclude that 2.1

in Sanh et al. 2019, however, that paper considers only the English BERT model, while we use multilingual BERT. Because the multilingual model has a significantly larger vocabulary (or number of word embeddings), which is not reduced by this distillation process, the proportionate difference in model size is for distilled mBERT models is less than for distilled BERT.

Table 6: Macro Precision, Recall and F1 on TD evaluation task for models distilled with increasing data quantities. The number in each TD model name corresponds to the GB of uncompressed text used for training.[13]

Model	Precision	Recall	F1
mBERT *	0.796	0.626	0.692
DistilmBERT *	0.796	0.602	0.679
Wiki3.0*	0.778	0.572	0.651
TD1.5	0.789	0.530	0.627
TD1.8	0.788	0.500	0.605
TD2.1	0.808	0.629	0.700
TD2.4	0.809	0.651	0.718
TD2.7	0.807	0.629	0.705
TD3.0	**0.817**	**0.664**	**0.727**
TD3.3	0.823	0.658	0.728
TD3.6	0.814	0.661	0.724
TD3.9	0.821	0.636	0.710
TD4.2	0.817	0.648	0.718
TD4.5	0.816	0.647	0.714

*=baseline model

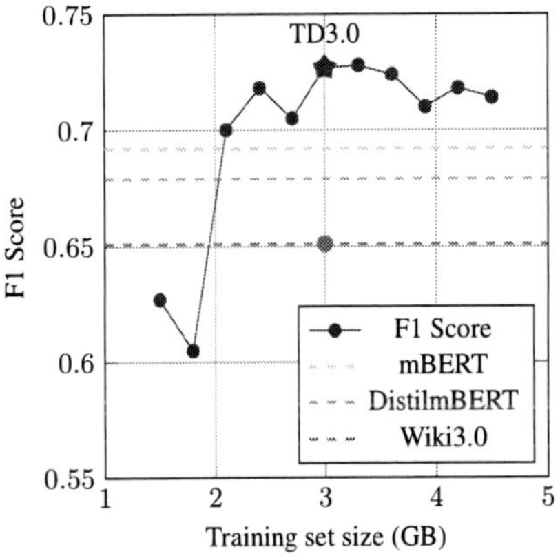

Figure 2: Training set size vs Macro F1 (see Table 6).

GB is sufficient and 3GB is optimal for adaptation to the TD domain, while more data increases training time without improving performance.

We contextualize this finding by considering the data quantity used to train mBERT and DistilmBERT. While it is hard to ascertain the exact amount of data used to train these models, we estimated by following the data sampling procedure used by the creators of those models.[14] By our best estimate, roughly 222GB of uncompressed text was used.[15] In contrast, only 2.1GB of uncompressed

[13]Here and throughout the paper, reported results are the mean of 10 random initializations.

[14]The procedure for mBERT is detailed at https://github.com/google-research/bert/blob/master/multilingual.md and DistilmBERT used data sampled in the same way (Sanh, pc).

[15]The original numbers may have been smaller as our estimate is based on the wiki data dumps on Oct. 1, 2020 and the models were trained before that time.

text was needed to outperform DistilmBERT on our in-domain task. Thus, for distillation for a single domain and language, the required amount of training data is reduced by two orders of magnitude.[16]

In this experiment, the new data matches on both domain and language. To test whether the language match is responsible for the improvement, we distilled a model on 3GB of English Wikipedia data. We sampled this data by randomly selecting 3000 1MB chunks of text from the English Wikipedia dump. This model (Wiki3.0) under-performs the one distilled on the same amount of StackOverflow data, showing that the language match alone is insufficient to explain the improved performance and suggests that the domain match is more important.

6 Vector changes under domain adaptation

To better understand the differences between an encoder trained on domain-general data versus in-domain data, we compare sentence embeddings produced by the encoder that we adapted to the technical domain (TD3.0) and the encoder distilled on the same amount of domain-general data (Wiki3.0). The TD domain has lots of homonyms like 'python' and 'float' that have both a technical word-sense and a non-technical one. We expect models trained on the TD domain to pay attention to the dominant technical word-senses, and models trained on Wikipedia to pay greater attention to the non-technical word-senses. By extension, a distance function derived from a TD model is expected to be more sensitive to technical word-senses than a distance function derived from a Wikipedia model. Thus we expect the distance function for 'python' and a non-technical synonym (i.e., 'snake') to be closer when derived from a domain-general model and the distance function between 'python' and another programming language (i.e., 'PHP') to be closer when derived from a model trained on technical data.

Because BERT embeddings are contextual, we provide a context for each word pair by creating sentences for each, such that either word may appear in the sentence. Sentences designed for technical word pairs are biased towards a technical context, and sentences for non-technical word pairs are biased towards a non-technical sense.[17] As an example, the technical sentences used to compare Java and C# are given below in list items 1 and 2 and the non-technical sentences used for java and coffee are given in list items 3 and 4.

1. I can't find any code or post on how to get traffic data in **Java** for Windows Phone 8.
2. I can't find any code or post on how to get traffic data in **C#** for Windows Phone 8.
3. Jerry can't start his day without a cup of **java**.
4. Jerry can't start his day without a cup of **coffee**.

Substituting each word from a pair into the sentence, we have a pair of sentences like items 1 and 2 and embed each with both the TD model and the domain-general model. We take the mean of the token embeddings as a representation of the sentence[18] and then take the cosine similarities between the sentence embedding produced by the TD model and the embedding from the domain-general model. These cosine similarities are given for both the technical and non-technical pairs in Table 7.

We find that cosine distance is smaller for sentences that capture the general word-sense when they are encoded by the general model. Similarly, it is smaller for sentences that capture the technical word-sense when they are encoded with the TD model. This suggests that the TD model has adapted its representations for these homonyms to their technical meanings.

7 Experiments

We compare the performance of two domain-adapted encoders that were trained using the method described in Section 4. CC-DistilmBERT was trained with data from four languages from the CC domain (§3.1.1) and TD-DistilmBERT with data from five languages from the TD domain (§3.2.1). The amount of data used to distil each model is summarized in Table 1 and determined primarily based on availability, though informed by the findings in Section 5. For each language and domain, we used as much data as was available for distillation (see §3 for details), except in the case of English TD data, in which case we had more than enough data and used only as much as was necessary to reach approximately 3GB in total.

For classifier training, we train a structured self-

[16]Training with 3 GB took $<$ 2 days using 8 A100 GPUs.

[17]The full collection of sentences is in the appendix.

[18]The embedding of the <CLS> token is often used as a sentence embedding when using BERT. However, following (Liu et al., 2019), we distill models without using the next sentence prediction task, so the embedding for <CLS> is less likely to be a good representation of the sentence.

[18]Using Euclidean distance yielded similar results.

Table 7: Each word in the first column has at least one technical and non-technical sense (e.g., 'Java') and is paired with two terms, one technical and one non-technical that can be used in the same context (e.g., 'coffee' and 'C#'). This table shows the cosine similarity between the embedding for a sentence containing the ambiguous word and the same sentences containing its technical and non-technical alternatives instead, using both the general encoder (Gen. Cosine) and domain-adapted encoder (Tech. Cosine). We show that in most cases the non-technical pairs have a greater cosine similarity when encoded with the general model and the technical pairs have a grater cosine similarity when encoded with the technical model.

Word	General Neighbor	Tech. Cosine	Gen. Cosine	Technical Neighbor	Tech. Cosine	Gen. Cosine
Java	coffee	0.01453	**0.02816**	C#	**0.01350**	0.00424
Python	snake	0.01008	**0.04663**	PHP	0.00535	**0.00687**
floats	rafts	0.00672	**0.01210**	doubles	0.00830	**0.00401**
terminal	ending	0.00527	**0.00759**	command line	**0.01341**	0.00453
classes	lectures	0.01124	**0.01512**	objects	**0.00969**	0.00447
Oracle	Prophet	0.01055	**0.01883**	DynamoDB	**0.00283**	0.00250

attention classifier head on each encoder used in evaluation. [19] We conduct two experiments: in the first, we fine-tune the encoder weights, as has been done in previous work such as Devlin et al. 2019; Sanh et al. 2019; in the second, we freeze the encoder weights to demonstrate that this approach can be used in contexts where the same underlying encoder is to be used by multiple classifiers, removing the need to encode a text every time it is classified by a different classifier.

We compare our domain-adapted, distilled models using the tasks described in Section 3 with two baselines: the teacher model used for distillation (mBERT) and Sanh et al.'s domain-general distilled model (DistilmBERT). In each case, we train and evaluate separate classifiers for each language in the dataset. We evaluate model performance two ways, first fine-tuning the encoder weights during task training and second freezing the encoder weights to test the generalizability of a single encoder to multiple classifiers.

8 Results

The results for each language and encoder are broken down for each experiment in Table 8, where encoder weights were fine-tuned or frozen during task training. On average for these two tasks, the domain-adapted model achieves an F1 score that is 1.2% greater respective to the teacher mBERT model (an absolute difference of 0.9 F1) and 2.3% better respective to the domain-general DistilmBERT model (an absolute difference of 1.7 F1).

Performance is better for all models when the encoder weights are fine-tuned during task training. Still, domain-adapted models perform better relative to the baselines in both cases. The average absolute improvement of the domain-adapted models relative to the teacher model is 1.1% and the relative improvement over the domain-general distilled model is 2.1% when the encoder weights are tuned, while these improvements are 1.3% and 2.5% when the weights are frozen. This difference between the two training scenarios may be accounted for by the encoder undergoing some degree of domain adaptation during fine-tuning. Intuitively, the domain-general models would benefit from this more than the domain-adapted models, which are already tuned to the domain. Even so, the performance of domain-adapted models relative to the domain-general models when the encoder weights are fine-tuned demonstrates that domain adaptation is still beneficial in this scenario and contributes larger improvements in model performance than fine-tuning during task training alone.

Each result in Table 8 represents an average over 10 iterations of training and evaluation. We calculate the statistical significance of the improvement between the domain adapted models and baselines using the Kolmogorov-Smirnov (KS) test, as our data is non-normal (Brownlee, 2019). We found that the improvement in F1 score due to domain adaptation for the CC-DistilmBERT model was statistically significant ($p < .05$) compared to both baselines on all languages except Japanese, despite the small size of our datasets. The TD-DistilmBERT model's improvement in F1 over the DistilmBERT baseline was also statistically significant on all languages except Japanese, although the support for each class was much smaller for the TD task.

For Japanese, in the case of the TD model, very little data was available for domain adaptation (0.06 GB; shown in Table 1). We can speculate that this

[19]Code and data for reproduction are included in supplementary materials and will be made publicly available upon publication.

Table 8: Results for freezing and fine-tuning encoder weights during classifier training. F1, Precision and Recall are for the 'intentful' class in the CC binary classification task and are macro averages for the TD multi label task. Each result is an average across 10 iterations of training and evaluation. For the CC-DistilmBERT and TD-DistilmBERT models, * indicates a statistically significant difference ($p < 0.05$) between that model and DistilmBERT and † indicates a statistically significant difference ($p < 0.05$) between that model and mBERT.

Domain	Metric	Encoder Weights	Model	eng	esp	jap	por
Conversational Commerce	*F1-Score*	Frozen	CC-DistilmBERT	**86.6***†	**82.0***†	**84.0**	**86.2***†
			DistilmBERT	84.3	79.5	**84.0**	85.2
			mBERT	85.4	78.7	83.6	85.2
		Fine-tuned	CC-DistilmBERT	**88.7***†	**82.3***†	**84.5**	**87.4***†
			DistilmBERT	85.8	79.9	83.9	85.6
			mBERT	86.7	80.7	84.1	86.3
	Precision	Frozen	CC-DistilmBERT	**89.0**	**80.2**	**81.3**†	**86.9***
			DistilmBERT	87.0	78.4	79.0	83.6
			mBERT	87.0	78.6	77.0	85.7
		Fine-tuned	CC-DistilmBERT	**90.2***†	**81.4**	**79.9**	**87.3**
			DistilmBERT	87.6	79.6	**79.9**	85.8
			mBERT	88.3	78.8	79.2	86.1
	Recall	Frozen	CC-DistilmBERT	**84.5**	**84.0**	87.0*†	85.5
			DistilmBERT	81.9	80.9	89.7	**87.0**
			mBERT	83.9	79.0	**91.6**	84.8
		Fine-tuned	CC-DistilmBERT	**87.3***†	**83.2**	89.7	**87.5**
			DistilmBERT	84.1	80.2	88.5	85.4
			mBERT	85.3	82.7	**89.8**	86.6

Domain	Metric	Encoder Weights	Model	eng	esp	jap	por	rus
Technical Discussion	*F1-Score*	Frozen	TD-DistilmBERT	**71.2***	70.1*	**67.4**	**71.2***†	**66.2***
			DistilmBERT	68.9	68.8	65.8	68.2	64.3
			mBERT	70.3	**70.9**	66.5	69.8	66.0
		Fine-tuned	TD-DistilmBERT	**72.5***	**72.9***†	66.7	**71.9***	**67.2***
			DistilmBERT	70.6	71.5	65.9	70.4	66.0
			mBERT	72.3	71.3	**67.2**	71.4	66.5
	Precision	Frozen	TD-DistilmBERT	**81.4***	**80.8**	**78.5***†	**79.8**	**78.3***
			DistilmBERT	79.7	78.5	75.7	78.6	75.5
			mBERT	80.8	79.2	76.6	78.2	77.6
		Fine-tuned	TD-DistilmBERT	**80.5***†	**81.2***†	74.7	**78.1**†	**76.5***†
			DistilmBERT	77.6	77.5	73.8	76.8	72.6
			mBERT	77.4	76.4	**74.8**	76.3	73.7
	Recall	Frozen	TD-DistilmBERT	**64.3***	63.5	**60.5**	**64.9***	**58.3**
			DistilmBERT	61.6	62.5	59.3	60.7	56.8
			mBERT	63.2	**65.4**	59.8	63.7	**58.3**
		Fine-tuned	TD-DistilmBERT	66.9†	67.6	61.5	67.3	60.7
			DistilmBERT	65.6	67.7	60.9	65.4	61.2
			mBERT	**68.7**	**68.4**	**62.6**	**67.9**	**61.7**

lack of data made adaptation via knowledge distillation less effective. In this case, adaptation via fine-tuning was relatively more effective than adaptation via knowledge distillation. For the CC model, while somewhat more Japanese data was available (0.44 GB), it is still less relative to English and Spanish, so we again attribute the less significant results for Japanese to data scarcity. We note that for this domain, even less data was available for Portuguese (0.35 GB) than Japanese, although for Portuguese the domain adapted model did show a significant improvement over mBERT. In this case, we speculate that the domain adapted model's performance on Portuguese benefited from lexical overlap with the Spanish training data.

9 Conclusion

We addressed the problem of encoder scalability in the context of conversational commerce by showing that knowledge distillation with domain-specific data reduces model size, while simultaneously improving model performance. This approach allows for the training of an encoder that can be used across a variety of languages, is smaller than a state-of-the-art model like mBERT, and performs better on domain-specific tasks. Because our approach uses only training data for the domain and languages of interest, less data is necessary for training, reducing the time, cost and environmental impact of training, while accommodating limited data availability. A key advantage of domain adaptation during encoder rather than classifier training is that it allows for the deployment of a single encoder, which can serve multiple classifiers at runtime. This reduces storage and maintenance cost, and due to the much larger size of the encoders compared with the classifiers, provides dramatically better scalability in real-world, e-commerce applications that must support multiple languages and tasks.

References

Jason Brownlee. 2019. How to use statistical significance tests to interpret machine learning results. Accessed: October 11, 2021.

Cristian Buciluǎ, Rich Caruana, and Alexandru Niculescu-Mizil. 2006. Model compression. In *Proceedings of the 12th ACM SIGKDD international conference on Knowledge discovery and data mining*, pages 535–541.

Debajyoti Chatterjee. 2019. Making neural machine reading comprehension faster. *arXiv preprint arXiv:1904.00796*.

Anna Currey, Prashant Mathur, and Georgiana Dinu. 2020. Distilling multiple domains for neural machine translation. In *Proceedings of the 2020 Conference on Empirical Methods in Natural Language Processing (EMNLP)*, pages 4500–4511.

Jacob Devlin, Ming-Wei Chang, Kenton Lee, and Kristina Toutanova. 2019. BERT: Pre-training of deep bidirectional transformers for language understanding. *Proceedings of NAACL-HLT*, pages 4171—-4186.

Suchin Gururangan, Ana Marasović, Swabha Swayamdipta, Kyle Lo, Iz Beltagy, Doug Downey, and Noah A Smith. 2020. Don't stop pretraining: adapt language models to domains and tasks. *arXiv preprint arXiv:2004.10964*.

Song Han, Xingyu Liu, Huizi Mao, Jing Pu, Ardavan Pedram, Mark A Horowitz, and William J Dally. 2016. Eie: efficient inference engine on compressed deep neural network. *ACM SIGARCH Computer Architecture News*, 44(3):243–254.

Song Han, Jeff Pool, John Tran, and William Dally. 2015. Learning both weights and connections for efficient neural network. *Advances in neural information processing systems*, 28:1135–1143.

Xiaochuang Han and Jacob Eisenstein. 2019. Unsupervised domain adaptation of contextualized embeddings for sequence labeling. In *Proceedings of the 2019 Conference on Empirical Methods in Natural Language Processing and the 9th International Joint Conference on Natural Language Processing (EMNLP-IJCNLP)*, pages 4238–4248.

Geoffrey Hinton, Oriol Vinyals, and Jeff Dean. 2015. Distilling the knowledge in a neural network. *arXiv preprint arXiv:1503.02531*.

Neil Houlsby, Andrei Giurgiu, Stanislaw Jastrzebski, Bruna Morrone, Quentin De Laroussilhe, Andrea Gesmundo, Mona Attariyan, and Sylvain Gelly. 2019. Parameter-efficient transfer learning for nlp. In *International Conference on Machine Learning*, pages 2790–2799. PMLR.

Yinhan Liu, Myle Ott, Naman Goyal, Jingfei Du, Mandar Joshi, Danqi Chen, Omer Levy, Mike Lewis, Luke Zettlemoyer, and Veselin Stoyanov. 2019. RoBERTa: A robustly optimized BERT pretraining approach. *arXiv preprint arXiv:1907.11692*.

Vimal Manohar, Pegah Ghahremani, Daniel Povey, and Sanjeev Khudanpur. 2018. A teacher-student learning approach for unsupervised domain adaptation of sequence-trained asr models. In *2018 IEEE Spoken Language Technology Workshop (SLT)*, pages 250–257. IEEE.

Idriss Mghabbar and Pirashanth Ratnamogan. 2020. Building a multi-domain neural machine translation model using knowledge distillation. *arXiv preprint arXiv:2004.07324*.

Matthew E Peters, Waleed Ammar, Chandra Bhagavatula, and Russell Power. 2017. Semi-supervised sequence tagging with bidirectional language models. *arXiv preprint arXiv:1705.00108*.

Alexander Rietzler, Sebastian Stabinger, Paul Opitz, and Stefan Engl. 2020. Adapt or get left behind: Domain adaptation through bert language model finetuning for aspect-target sentiment classification. In *Proceedings of the 12th Language Resources and Evaluation Conference*, pages 4933–4941.

Sebastian Ruder, Parsa Ghaffari, and John G Breslin. 2017. Knowledge adaptation: Teaching to adapt. *arXiv preprint arXiv:1702.02052*.

Minho Ryu and Kichun Lee. 2020. Knowledge distillation for BERT unsupervised domain adaptation. *arXiv preprint arXiv:2010.11478*.

Victor Sanh, Lysandre Debut, Julien Chaumond, and Thomas Wolf. 2019. Distilbert, a distilled version of BERT: smaller, faster, cheaper and lighter. In *NeurIPS EMC^2 Workshop*.

Sheng Shen, Zhen Dong, Jiayu Ye, Linjian Ma, Zhewei Yao, Amir Gholami, Michael W Mahoney, and Kurt Keutzer. 2020. Q-BERT: Hessian Based Ultra Low Precision Quantization of BERT. In *AAAI*, pages 8815–8821.

Raphael Tang, Yao Lu, Linqing Liu, Lili Mou, Olga Vechtomova, and Jimmy Lin. 2019. Distilling task-specific knowledge from BERT into simple neural networks. *arXiv preprint arXiv:1903.12136*.

Taesun Whang, Dongyub Lee, Chanhee Lee, Kisu Yang, Dongsuk Oh, and Heuiseok Lim. 2020. An effective domain adaptive post-training method for bert in response selection. *Interspeech 2020*, page 1585–1589.

Edward WD Whittaker and Bhiksha Raj. 2001. Quantization-based language model compression. In *Seventh European Conference on Speech Communication and Technology*.

Dong Yu, Kaisheng Yao, Hang Su, Gang Li, and Frank Seide. 2013. Kl-divergence regularized deep neural network adaptation for improved large vocabulary speech recognition. In *2013 IEEE International Conference on Acoustics, Speech and Signal Processing*, pages 7893–7897. IEEE.

A Appendix: Sentence Pairs

The sentences used to produce the embeddings compared in Table 8 are listed below.

A.1 Non-technical Sentences

1. Jerry has had a lot of late nights recently and can't start his day without a cup of {Java / coffee}.

2. I was scared to death when I saw that {Python / snake}.

3. The ship is outfitted with lots of safety features, including {floats / rafts} in case of an emergency.

4. The {terminal / ending} scene of the movie was a big surprise!

5. Emily had to drop out of school after she missed too many {classes / lectures}.

6. In times of uncertainty, people would take offerings to the temple and ask the {Oracle / Prophet} for help.

A.2 Technical Sentences

1. I can't find any code or post on how to get traffic data in {Java / C#} for Windows Phone 8.

2. I have {Python / PHP} code for shortening a URL.

3. Suppose I need to parse space delimited lists of numbers where some lists contain integers and some lists contain {floats / doubles}.

4. I am a spark newbie and I want to run a Python script from the {terminal / command line}.

5. fill up a div with this data with relevent markup - divs id's {classes / objects} surrounding this data.

6. So what I'm doing is reading a lot of data from remote Nettezza database and inserting them into another remote {Oracle / DynamoDB} database.

OpenBrand: Open Brand Value Extraction from Product Descriptions

Kassem Sabeh
Free University of
Bozen-Bolzano
ksabeh@unibz.it

Mouna Kacimi
Wonder Technology
Srl
mouna@wonderflow.ai

Johann Gamper
Free University of
Bozen-Bolzano
jgamper@unibz.it

Abstract

Extracting attribute-value information from unstructured product descriptions continue to be of a vital importance in e-commerce applications. One of the most important product attributes is the brand which highly influences customers' purchasing behaviour. Thus, it is crucial to accurately extract brand information dealing with the main challenge of discovering new brand names. Under the open world assumption, several approaches have adopted deep learning models to extract attribute-values using sequence tagging paradigm. However, they did not employ finer grained data representations such as character level embeddings which improve generalizability. In this paper, we introduce OpenBrand, a novel approach for discovering brand names. OpenBrand is a BiLSTM-CRF-Attention model with embeddings at different granularities. Such embeddings are learned using CNN and LSTM architectures to provide more accurate representations. We further propose a new dataset for brand value extraction, with a very challenging task on zero-shot extraction. We have tested our approach, through extensive experiments, and shown that it outperforms state-of-the-art models in brand name discovery.

1 Introduction

Brand name plays a very important role in influencing customers' behaviour (Chovanová et al., 2015; Shahzad et al., 2014). Typically, as customers are aware of the brand, they can deduce knowledge about other product attributes. Let us take the example of the toy shown in Figure 1. The brand of this product is "Gentle Monster". By knowing the brand, customers would have some kind of associations, like this toy would be of *"a soft and smooth wood"*, have *"bright colors"*, and contain *"small pieces which is suitable for older kids"*. So, when shopping for toys, they would pick a particular brand based on the attributes they find important. Such correlations between brands and

Figure 1: An example of a product description.

product attributes make it crucial for e-commerce applications to accurately extract brand names from product descriptions.

Retrieving brand names is addressed in the literature within the general problem of attribute-value extraction from product descriptions (Kovelamudi et al., 2011; Vandic et al., 2012; Ghani et al., 2006; Kozareva et al., 2016; Zheng et al., 2018; Xu et al., 2019). Early approaches rely on rule-based techniques which use domain-specific knowledge to identify attributes and values (Kovelamudi et al., 2011; Vandic et al., 2012; Ghani et al., 2006). Such approaches adopt a closed world assumption requiring the possible set of values to be known beforehand by mean of dictionaries or hand-crafted rules. Consequently, they are not suitable for discovering unseen values such as newly emerging brands. To tackle this problem, most recent approaches model the extraction task as sequence tagging (Kozareva et al., 2016; Zheng et al., 2018; Xu et al., 2019) and solve it using deep learning models such as BiLSTM enhanced by Conditional Random Field (CRF) and Attention layers. These new approaches achieve promising results, however, they limit the representation of their data to word embeddings which can capture context but penalizes generalizability to new brands.

In this paper, we propose to use character level embeddings in sequence tagging models for discovering brand names. In addition to word embeddings, character level embeddings were employed

Proceedings of The Fifth Workshop on e-Commerce and NLP (ECNLP 5), pages 161 - 170

in Named Entity Recognition (NER) tasks (Lample et al., 2016) to handle out-of-vocabulary words. The problem of unseen words is particularly emphasized in brands because of sub-branding, brand fragmentation, or simply emerging businesses. Unseen brand names can be completely new, like in brand fragmentation where new brands share the same parent brand maintaining minimal links between the new and the existing identities. For example, *"Audi"* and *"Porsche"* do not have any similarity although they have the same parent brand *"Volkswagen"*. By contrast, sub-branding would maintain stronger links between existing brands and the new generated ones, which can be reflected by similarities in brand names. Examples include *"Uber"* and *"UberPool"*, *"McDonalds"* and *"McCafe"*, or *"Samsung"* and *"Samsung Evo"*. Thus, the use of character level embedding is crucial for capturing variations in brand names and the occurrence of unseen brands.

We summarize the main contributions of this work as follows:

1. We propose OpenBrand, a BiLSTM-CRF-Attention model that combines word embeddings with character level word embeddings. In contrast to previous approaches, we learn character level embeddings based on CNN and LSTM architectures to obtain specific representations of our data.

2. We provide a large real world dataset[1] focusing on brand names to have a thorough analysis of the impact of character level embeddings. We experimentally show that our dataset is challenging on brand name extraction, especially those zero-shot brand values.

3. We empirically demonstrate significant improvements in F1 score over several state-of-the-art baselines on brand name extraction. Additionally, we show that OpenBrand guarantees a better generalizability over new brands and deals more effectively with compound brand names.

2 Problem Statement

In this section, we formally define the problem of open brand value extraction. Given a product title, represented as an unstructured text data, and a target attribute (eg. brand), our goal is to extract the appropriate values for the corresponding attribute from the product title. In this context, we want to discover new values that have not been encountered before. We formalize the attribute-value extraction as per the following definition:

Definition *Given a product title X. The title X is represented as a sequence of tokens* $X_t = \{x_1, ..., x_T\}$*, where T is the sequence length. Consider a target attribute A. Attribute-value extraction automatically identifies a sub-sequence of tokens from* X_t *as applicable attribute-value pair.* $A_v = \{x_i, x_{i+1}, ..., x_k\}$*, for* $1 \leq i \leq k \leq T$.

For example, consider the title for the product given in the example of Figure 1:

X = "Wooden Stacking Board Games 54 Pieces for Kids Adult and Families, Gentle Monster Wooden Blocks Toys for Toddlers, Colored Building Blocks - 6 Colors 2 Dice."

The tokenization of X yields: $X_t = \{x_1, x_2, ..., x_{25}\}$ = {"Wooden", "Stacking", "Board", .., "Dice"}, where $T = 25$. For the target attribute: A = {"Brand"}. We want to extract: Brand = $\{x_{12}, x_{13}\}$ = {"Gentle", "Monster"}.

In order to identify these sub-sequences, the sequence of tokens X_t need to be tagged to capture sequential and positional information. For this purpose, we adopt the sequence tagging model and associate a tag from a given tag-set to the sequence of input tokens X_t. We experimented with different tagging strategies and, inline with previous work in the literature (Xu et al., 2019), we found that the {B,I,O} tagging scheme produced the best results, where "B", "I", and "O" represent the beginning, inside, and outside of an attribute, respectively. (A sequence of "O" tags corresponds to the absence of an attribute). Table 1 shows an input/output example of the {B,I,O} tagging strategy.

Input	Kids	Adult	Families	Gentle	Monster	Wooden	Blocks	Toys
Output	O	O	O	B-Brand	I-Brand	O	O	O

Table 1: Example of an input/output {B,I,O} tag sequence for the brand of a product description.

3 OpenBrand Model

To address the open brand value extraction problem, we propose a BiLSTM-CRF-Attention model with character level embeddings. Figure 2 shows

[1] Data is available at https://github.com/kassemsabeh/open-brand.

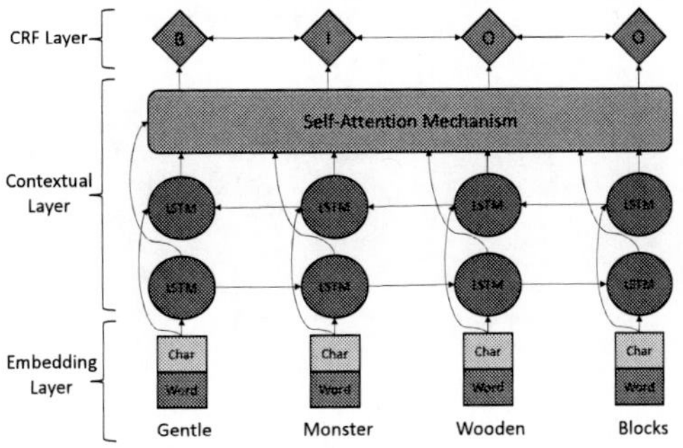

Figure 2: OpenBrand Architecture: BiLSTM-CRF-Attention with character level representations.

our OpenBrand model architecture, which is composed of three main layers: an embedding layer that encodes the input sequence, a contextual layer that captures complex relationships among the input sequence, and an output layer that produces the output labels.

3.1 Embedding Layer

In the embedding layer, we map every word in the product description into a d-dimensional embedding vector. The embeddings of the words are obtained by concatenating the word embeddings and character level embeddings. Word embeddings are obtained from the pre-trained GloVe (Pennington et al., 2014) word representations, which are trained over large unlabeled corpus. Pre-trained word embeddings, such as GloVe and Word2Vec (Mikolov et al., 2013), offer a single representation for each word, which is not useful in the case where words have different meanings depending on the context. To allow our model to learn different representations of embeddings depending on the context, we learn and generate different representations of tokens in the input sequence. For this reason, the weights of our embedding layer are considered to be learnable parameters and not fixed.

An important distinction of our approach, compared to previous work on attribute-value extraction, is that we learn character level features in our model. For character level embeddings, we use two different architectures: CNN-based and LSTM-based character level representations. Learning character level embeddings has the advantage of learning task-specific representations. Convolutional Neural Networks (CNN) are designed to discover position-invariant features and they are highly effective in extracting morphological information (ex. prefix or suffix of words) (Chiu and Nichols, 2016). On the other hand, LSTMs are capable of encoding long sequences, and are thus capable of extracting position dependent character features. These features are crucial to model the relationships between words and their characters. Given a token of our input sequence x_t, the embedding layer maps x_t in to the vector:

$$e_t = [w_t; c_t],$$

where w_t and c_t are the word and character level representations of x_t, respectively. The embedding representation of the whole input sequence X_t would be $\{e_1, e_2, ..., e_T\}$. Figure 3 illustrates the two architectures used to encode the character representations. These character representations are then concatenated with the word embeddings and fed as input to our contextual layer.

3.2 Contextual Layer

The contextual layer captures contextualized representations for every word in the input sequence. In our model, the input sequence to the contextual layer is the concatenation of the character level representations and word embeddings, both mapped by the underlying embedding layer. In this stage, we employ a BiLSTM contextual layer followed by a self-attention layer.

Long Short Term Memory Networks (Hochreiter and Schmidhuber, 1997) address the vanishing gradient problems of Recurrent Neural Networks and are thus capable of modeling long-term dependencies between tokens in a sequence. Bidirectional LSTM (BiLSTM) can capture both past and future time steps jointly by using two LSTM layers to produce both forward and backwards states, respectively. Given the input e_t (embedding of a token x_t), the hidden vector representations from the backward and forward LSTMs ($\overrightarrow{h_t}$ and $\overleftarrow{h_t}$) is:

$$h_t = \Delta([\overrightarrow{h_t}; \overleftarrow{h_t}])$$

where Δ denotes a non-linear transformation. The hidden representation of the whole input sequence X_t is $H_t = \{h_1, h_2, ..., h_T\}$.

In reality, not all hidden states generated by the BiLSTM layer are equally important for the labeling decisions. A mechanism that allows the output layer to be aware of the important features of the sequence can improve the prediction model. This is exactly what attention does. Attention mechanisms have achieved great success in Natural Language Processing (NLP) and were first introduced

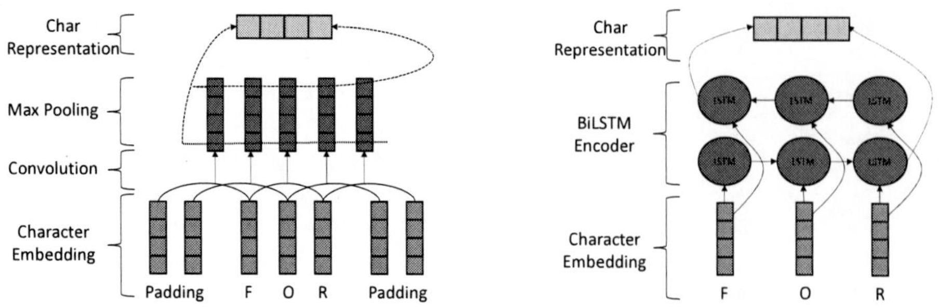

(a) CNN-based character level representation.

(b) LSTM-based character level representation.

Figure 3: Architecture of character level encoders.

in the Neural Machine Translation task (Bahdanau et al., 2015). In the contextual layer, we use a self-attention mechanism to highlight important concepts in the sequence rather than focusing on everything. The model learns to *attend* to the important parts of the input states based on the output produced so far. We first compute the similarity between all hidden states representations to obtain an attention matrix $A \in \mathbb{R}^{T \times T}$ where

$$\alpha_{t,t'} = \sigma(w_\alpha g_{t,t'} + b_\alpha)$$

is the element of matrix A representing the mutual interaction between hidden states h_t and $h_{t'}$. σ is the element-wise sigmoid function, and

$$g_{t,t'} = tanh(W_1 h_t + W_2 h_{t'} + b_g)$$

where W_1, W_2, w_α are trainable attention matrices, and b_g, b_α are trainable biases. The contextualized hidden states can be computed as

$$\widetilde{h}_t = \sum_{t'=1}^{T} \alpha_{t,t'} \cdot h_{t'}$$

The contextualized hidden state of the whole input sequence X_t is $\widetilde{H}_t = \{\widetilde{h}_1, \widetilde{h}_2, ...\widetilde{h}_T\}$.

3.3 CRF Layer

In sequence labeling tasks, it is important to consider the dependencies between output tags in a neighborhood. Conditional Random Fields (CRF) allow us to capture the correlation between labels and model their sequence jointly. For example, if we already know the tag of a token is I, then this increases the probability of the next token to be I or O, rather than being B. We feed the contextualized hidden states $\widetilde{H}_t = \{\widetilde{h}_1, \widetilde{h}_2, ...\widetilde{h}_T\}$ to our output CRF layer to get the sequence of labels with highest probabilities. The joint probability distribution of a tag y given the hidden state $\widetilde{h}_t$ and previous tag y_{t-1} is given by

$$Pr(y|x;\psi) \propto \prod_{t=1}^{T} exp\left(\sum_{k=1}^{K} \psi_k f_k(y_{t-1}, y_t, \widetilde{h}_t)\right)$$

where ψ_k is the corresponding learnable weight, f_k is the feature function, and K is the number of features. The final output label is the label with the highest conditional probability, given as

$$y^* = argmax_y Pr(y_i|x_i;\psi)$$

where $y^* \in \{B, I, O\}$ is the output tag.

In Section 5.2, we will study in detail the effect of the attention and CRF layers on the discovery of brands in comparison with the embeddings layer.

4 Experimental Setup

This section presents the experimental settings of our empirical approach for comparing state-of-the-art models on the task of brand value extraction.

4.1 Dataset

To evaluate the effectiveness of OpenBrand, we have collected a dataset that contains information about products from Amazon. Our dataset is derived from a public product collection - the Amazon Review Dataset (Ni et al., 2019) [2]. The categories of the collected dataset contained a large amount of overlapping brands, which might bias the results of the experiments. Thus, we have selected a subset to have a diverse set of brands with minimal overlapping across categories. We also processed

[2]https://nijianmo.github.io/amazon/index.html

Category	Train	Val	Test
Grocery & Gourmet Food	15679	2239	4479
Toys & Games	44314	6330	12660
Sports & Outdoors	37951	5421	10842
Electronics	33512	4787	9574
Automotive	45132	6447	12894
Total	176588	25224	50449

Table 2: Statistics of AZ-base dataset with five categories.

Category	Samples
Clothing, Shoes & Jewelry	85068
Pet Supplies	10868
Cell Phones & Accessories	78564
Total	174500

Table 3: Number of samples in AZ-new-cat dataset.

the dataset to handle noise, and removed samples with empty values. This led to a dataset comprising over 250k product titles with more than 50k unique values, which we refer to as AZ-base dataset in our experiments. The AZ-base dataset contains information about products in five main categories: *Grocery & Gourmet Food, Toys & Games, Sports & Outdoors, Electronics* and *Automotive*. We randomly sample 70% of the data for training, 10% for validation, and 20% for testing. Table 2 shows the statistical details of the AZ-base dataset.

To further examine the generalization ability of our model, we divide the AZ-base dataset into another training and test split with no overlapping brand values. In other words, none of the values in the test set are encountered during training. We refer to this data split as AZ-zero-shot, as it is designed for evaluating zero-shot extraction. The test set of AZ-zero-shot contains more than 8k new and unique brand values.

In addition, we have also chosen another subset of products from our collected data with another set of categories. The purpose of this dataset is to test the models capabilities in detecting brand values across different category domains. The dataset contains information about products in three new categories as shown in Table 3. We refer to this dataset as AZ-new-cat, as it is designed to evaluate the model on a new set of product categories.

4.2 Models Under Comparison

We implemented and compared three state-of-the-art baseline models on attribute-value extraction.

BiLSTM (Hochreiter and Schmidhuber, 1997) which uses word embeddings from pretrained GloVe (Pennington et al., 2014) for word level representation, then applies BiLSTM to produce the contextual embeddings.

BiLSTM-CRF (Huang et al., 2015) which extends the BiLSTM model by adding a CRF layer on top to model the tagging decisions jointly. This model is considered state-of-the-art sequence tagging model for NER.

OpenTag (Zheng et al., 2018) which adds a self attention mechanism between the contextual BiLSTM layer and the CRF decoding layer. OpenTag is considered the pioneer sequence tagging model for attribute-value extraction.

We compare the above baseline models with the OpenBrand models we proposed in Section 3.

OpenBrand-LSTM In this approach, character level information is obtained by applying a BiLSTM encoder on the sequence of characters in each word. This character level information is used in combination with word-level embeddings as input to the BiLSTM-CRF-Attention model.

OpenBrand-CNN This approach is similar to the above model, but CNNs are used instead of LSTMs to encode character level information in the word sequences.

We use precision P, recall R and F_1 score as evaluation metrics based on the number of true positives (TP), false positives (FP), and false negatives (FN). We use *Exact Match* criteria (Rajpurkar et al., 2016), in our evaluation, with either full or no credit. The implementation details are provided in the Appendix.

$$P = \frac{TP}{TP + FP} \quad R = \frac{TP}{TP + FN} \quad F_1 = 2 \times \frac{P \times R}{P + R}$$

5 Results and Discussion

We conducted a series of experiments on AZ-base, AZ-zero-shot, and AZ-new-cat datasets under various settings to evaluate the performance of OpenBrand.

5.1 Baseline Performance Comparison

In the first experiment, we compare the performance of OpenBrand with the three state-of-the-art baselines mentioned in Section 4.2 for identifying brand values from product descriptions. Table

Category	Models	P	R	F1
Grocery & Gourmet Food	BiLSTM	70.4	65.9	68.1
	BiLSTM-CRF	74.9	66.0	70.2
	OpenTag	76.0	65.4	70.3
	OpenBrand-LSTM	75.9	**77.5**	71.8
	OpenBrand-CNN	**77.5**	75.4	**76.4**
Toys & Games	BiLSTM	73.7	69.1	71.3
	BiLSTM-CRF	78.9	70.5	74.5
	OpenTag	79.1	70.3	74.5
	OpenBrand-LSTM	80.2	**72.4**	76.1
	OpenBrand-CNN	**81.3**	72.0	**76.4**
Sports & Outdoors	BiLSTM	80.3	75.8	78.0
	BiLSTM-CRF	84.1	75.4	79.5
	OpenTag	84.9	75.0	79.6
	OpenBrand-LSTM	85.7	76.8	81.0
	OpenBrand-CNN	**86.1**	**77.3**	**81.5**
Electronics	BiLSTM	86.2	80.4	83.2
	BiLSTM-CRF	87.8	81.5	84.5
	OpenTag	89.2	79.6	84.2
	OpenBrand-LSTM	89.1	**80.8**	84.8
	OpenBrand-CNN	**89.7**	80.5	**84.9**
Automotive	BiLSTM	88.5	84.3	86.4
	BiLSTM-CRF	90.9	85.0	87.9
	OpenTag	91.6	84.6	87.9
	OpenBrand-LSTM	91.7	85.0	88.2
	OpenBrand-CNN	**91.8**	**85.4**	**88.5**

Table 4: Performance comparison between different models on AZ-base dataset.

4 reports the comparison results of our two models (OpenBrand-LSTM and OpenBrand-CNN) and three baselines across all categories in the AZ-base dataset. From these evaluation results, we can observe that our models substantially outperform the other compared models in all categories. OpenBrand with LSTM character level and CNN character level embeddings are consistently ranked the best over all competing baselines. The overall improvement in F_1 score is up to 6.1% as compared to OpenTag. The main reason for this result is that our model learns both character and word embeddings during training, thus allowing to learn more effective contextual embeddings that are more suitable for the task of extracting brand values.

5.2 Impact of Character level Representations

To understand the effect of character level representations on brand-value extraction, we extend all baseline models with character level embeddings and test them on the AZ-base dataset. Table 5 shows the average F_1 score of baseline models on the AZ-base dataset after adding character level representations. The results show that character level embeddings significantly improve the overall

Model	Base	LSTM-char	CNN-char
BiLSTM	78.56	79.71	**79.73**
BiLSTM-CRF	80.37	81.11	**81.52**
OpenTag	80.51	81.62	**81.85**

Table 5: Effect of character embeddings on the performance of the models (F_1 score).

performances of all models. An interesting observation is that character level embeddings improve the model much more effectively than CRF or attention layers. For example, and as shown in the last two rows of Table 5, adding a CNN-representation to a BiLSTM-CRF model improves the model by 1.15%, while adding an attention layer only improves the model by 0.14%.

The experiments also show that using either CNN-char or LSTM-char both lead to an improvement with comparable overall F_1 score. However, CNNs have less training complexity as compared to LSTM models under similar experimental settings. In our experiments, the average training time of models with LSTM-char increased by 59% relative to the baseline BiLSTM-CRF-Att model, while it only increased by 22% with CNN-char, as detailed in Table 6. CNN-char also produces better performances than LSTM-char as shown in Table 5. We conclude that CNN character representations are preferable to LSTM based representations for brand-value extraction.

Model	Average Training Time per Epoch (seconds)	Difference ($\Delta\%$)
BiLSTM-CRF-Att	63	0
+LSTM-char	100	+59%
+CNN-char	77	**+22%**

Table 6: Average training time of our BiLSTM-CRF-Att models computed on a TPU.

5.3 Discovering New Brand Values

We conduct zero-shot extraction experiment to evaluate the generalization ability of our models on unseen brand values. Table 7 reports the zero-shot extraction results. It can be seen that our model achieves better performance than OpenTag on unseen data. This is because our model can leverage the sub-sequence level similarities in brand names between the train set and test set, through the character level embeddings. However, it is clear that the overall performance of all models is worse as compared to the results in Table 4, which is inline

Model	P	R	F1
OpenTag	53.80	33.82	41.53
OpenBrand-LSTM	**56.17**	35.14	43.23
OpenBrand-CNN	55.61	**35.46**	**43.44**

Table 7: Zero-shot extraction results on AZ-zero-shot dataset.

with our expectations as there are no training samples for the zero-shot brand values. This indicates that it is truly a difficult zero-shot extraction task.

To further examine the ability of OpenBrand in discovering brand values in new categories, we train the models on the AZ-base dataset, and test them on the AZ-new-cat dataset introduced in Section 4.1. Table 8 reports the results across three different categories in the AZ-new-cat dataset. It is clear that OpenBrand achieves much better performance with gains up to 2.7% in F_1 score as compared to OpenTag. This indicates that our model has good generalization and is able to transfer to other domains. Also, the results are much better than zero-shot extractions. This is because some data in the training set are semantically related to the brand values in AZ-new-cat and thus they provide hints that guide the extraction. For example, many of the brands in *Cell Phones & Accessories* category (eg. Samsung Galaxy) are sub-brands of products in *Electronics* category (eg. Samsung).

Category	Models	P	R	F1
Clothing, shoes, & Jewelry	BiLSTM	52.6	44.3	48.1
	BiLSTM-CRF	58.5	42.2	49.0
	OpenTag	60.3	43.5	50.5
	OpenBrand-LSTM	63.8	44.7	52.6
	OpenBrand-CNN	**64.5**	**45.2**	**53.2**
Pet Supplies	BiLSTM	49.1	39.4	43.7
	BiLSTM-CRF	55.0	37.3	44.5
	OpenTag	53.9	38.9	45.2
	OpenBrand-LSTM	57.3	**39.8**	**47.0**
	OpenBrand-CNN	**58.2**	38.5	46.3
Cell Phones & Accessories	BiLSTM	81.2	63.8	71.5
	BiLSTM-CRF	80.1	68.0	73.5
	OpenTag	78.3	67.4	72.4
	OpenBrand-LSTM	83.3	**70.7**	**76.5**
	OpenBrand-CNN	**85.2**	67.8	75.5

Table 8: Performance comparison between models on the AZ-new-cat dataset.

5.4 Impact of Brand Entities

We also conducted experiments to explore the relationship between the number of entities that constitute the brand and the performance of the models. Since we use *Exact Match* criteria in our evaluations, detecting brand values with more than one entity becomes very challenging in general. We divide the test set of our AZ-base dataset into four subsets according to the number of entities inside a brand (see Figure 4). While OpenTag achieves good overall F_1 performance with brand values consisting of single entities (88%), it is much worse on brand values with three or more entities (67% and 61% respectively). OpenBrand, on the other hand, still performs well even on brands with two or more entities (71% and 65% respectively).

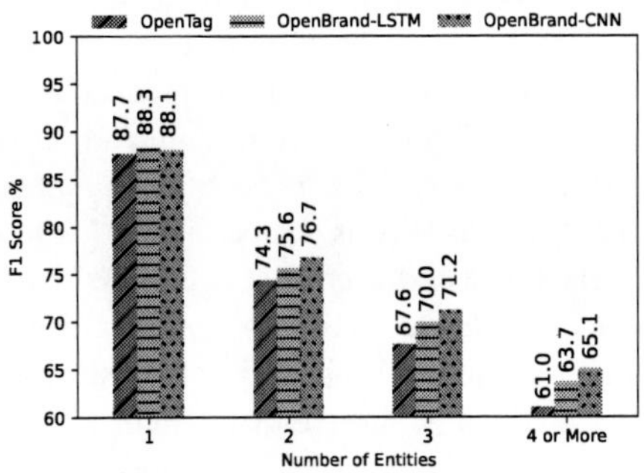

Figure 4: Impact of number of entities on the model performance.

5.5 Discussion

Our experimental results show that, for the task of extracting brand values, OpenBrand outperforms baseline approaches by a significant margin. Besides the general F1 score, the gains can be seen in both precision and recall which go up to 2.2% and 11.5%, respectively. This means that character embeddings do not only help discover more brand values but they also improve the accuracy of the extracted information. Furthermore, the gains in recall are also high for the AZ-new-cat and AZ-zero-shot datasets, reaching 3.3% and 1.46% of improvement respectively. Thus, OpenBrand performs particularly well for unseen data which confirms our initial claim that character embeddings enhance model generalizability.

Another important finding of our study is that the performance of OpenBrand depends on the product category. We can observe that, for the *Automotive* category, the gain in precision is 0.2% while it goes up to 2.2% for the *Toys & Games* category. This is mainly due to an ambiguity problem in the product descriptions of the *Automotive* category.

Some product descriptions might contain values of other brands other than the one that needs to be detected. Let us take the following product description: *"Honda Shadow 750 Aero Cobra Saddlebag Guards Supports"*. This is about a *"Saddlebag Guards Supports"* that is compatible for *"Honda"* cars. The brand of this product is *"Cobra"* but the presence of *"Honda"* in the description can be confusing for the model leading to wrong extractions.

We additionally observe that compound brand values are best handled by OpenBrand. This is due to the fact that the combination of character and word embeddings contributes to more meaningful representations. The results also show that OpenBrand-LSTM tends to perform worse, as compared to OpenBrand-CNN. This is inline with prior observations (Bradbury et al., 2017) that LSTM can be difficult to apply on long sequences of input.

6 Related Work

There has been significant research on the task of attribute-value extraction from product descriptions (Wong et al., 2009). Initial approaches (Vandic et al., 2012) formulated the problem as a classification task relying on supervised learning techniques. (Ghani et al., 2006) use a Naive Bayes classifier to extract values that correspond to a predefined set of product attributes. (Putthividhya and Hu, 2011) focus on annotating brands in product listings of apparel products on eBay. (Kovelamudi et al., 2011) propose a domain independent supervised system that can automatically discover product attributes from user reviews using Wikipedia. Similarly, (Ling and Weld, 2012) propose an automatic labeling process of entities by making use of anchor links from Wikipedia text. Other approaches exploited unsupervised learning techniques like (Shinzato and Sekine, 2013) in their task of extracting attribute-values from e-commerce product pages. Following a similar line, (Charron et al., 2016) use consumer patterns to create annotations for data-driven products. (Bing et al., 2016) focus on the discovery of hidden patterns in costumer reviews to improve attribute-value extraction. The above approaches provide promising results, however they poorly handle the discovery of new values due to their closed world assumption.

The most recent approaches (Kozareva et al., 2016; Zheng et al., 2018; Xu et al., 2019) make instead an open world assumption using sequence tagging models, similarly to NER tasks (Ma and Hovy, 2016; Huang et al., 2015). (Kozareva et al., 2016) use a BiLSTM-CRF model to tag several product attributes for brands and models with hand-crafted features. (Zheng et al., 2018) develop an end-to-end tagging model utilizing BiLSTM and CRF without using any dictionary or hand-crafted features. After that, (Xu et al., 2019) adopted only one global set of BIO tags for any attributes to scale up the semantic representation models of product titles. In this context, (Karamanolakis et al., 2020) proposed a taxonomy aware knowledge extraction model that takes advantage of the hierarchical relationships between product categories. The latest approaches extend the open world assumption also to attributes and use question answering (QA) models (Wang et al., 2020) to scale to a larger number of attributes. Sequence tagging approaches are the most relevant to our work since extracting brand names does not require scalability. However, these models did not exploit character level embeddings which are crucial for improving generalizability. In our work, we enhance such models using different granularities of embeddings.

7 Conclusion

In this paper we have addressed the problem of extracting brand values from product descriptions. Previous state-of-the-art sequence tagging methods faced the challenge of discovering new values that have not been encountered before. To tackle this issue we proposed OpenBrand, a novel attribute-value extraction model with the integration of character level representations to improve generalizability. We presented experiments on real-world datasets in different categories which show that OpenBrand outperforms state-of-the-art approaches and baselines. By exploiting character level embeddings, OpenBrand is capable of learning accurate representations to discover new brand values. Our experiments also show that CNN based representations outperform LSTM based representations in both performance and computation.

A natural extension of this work is to deal with the problem of disambiguation discussed in Section 5.5. To this end, we need to have more training data which helps understating the patterns in a better way. Moreover, we need to extend the tagging model to capture ambiguous product descriptions. This extension can be very important when brand values need to be extracted from other data sources other than concise product descriptions.

References

Dzmitry Bahdanau, Kyunghyun Cho, and Yoshua Bengio. 2015. Neural machine translation by jointly learning to align and translate. In *3rd International Conference on Learning Representations, ICLR 2015, San Diego, CA, USA, May 7-9, 2015, Conference Track Proceedings*.

Lidong Bing, Tak-Lam Wong, and Wai Lam. 2016. Unsupervised extraction of popular product attributes from e-commerce web sites by considering customer reviews. *ACM Trans. Internet Technol.*, 16(2).

James Bradbury, Stephen Merity, Caiming Xiong, and Richard Socher. 2017. Quasi-recurrent neural networks. In *5th International Conference on Learning Representations, ICLR 2017, Toulon, France, April 24-26, 2017, Conference Track Proceedings*. OpenReview.net.

Bruno Charron, Yu Hirate, David Purcell, and Martin Rezk. 2016. Extracting semantic information for e-commerce. In *The Semantic Web – ISWC 2016*, pages 273–290, Cham. Springer International Publishing.

Jason P.C. Chiu and Eric Nichols. 2016. Named entity recognition with bidirectional LSTM-CNNs. *Transactions of the Association for Computational Linguistics*, 4.

Henrieta Hrablik Chovanová, Aleksander Ivanovich Korshunov, and Dagmar Babčanová. 2015. Impact of brand on consumer behavior. *Procedia Economics and Finance*, 34:615–621. International Scientific Conference: Business Economics and Management (BEM2015).

Rayid Ghani, Katharina Probst, Yan Liu, Marko Krema, and Andrew Fano. 2006. Text mining for product attribute extraction. *SIGKDD Explor. Newsl.*, 8(1):41–48.

Sepp Hochreiter and Jürgen Schmidhuber. 1997. Long short-term memory. *Neural Comput.*, 9(8):1735–1780.

Zhiheng Huang, Wei Xu, and Kai Yu. 2015. Bidirectional lstm-crf models for sequence tagging.

Giannis Karamanolakis, Jun Ma, and Xin Luna Dong. 2020. TXtract: Taxonomy-aware knowledge extraction for thousands of product categories. In *Proceedings of the 58th Annual Meeting of the Association for Computational Linguistics*, pages 8489–8502, Online. Association for Computational Linguistics.

Diederik P. Kingma and Jimmy Ba. 2015. Adam: A method for stochastic optimization. In *3rd International Conference on Learning Representations, ICLR 2015, San Diego, CA, USA, May 7-9, 2015, Conference Track Proceedings*.

Sudheer Kovelamudi, Sethu Ramalingam, Arpit Sood, and Vasudeva Varma. 2011. Domain independent model for product attribute extraction from user reviews using Wikipedia. In *Proceedings of 5th International Joint Conference on Natural Language Processing*, pages 1408–1412, Chiang Mai, Thailand. Asian Federation of Natural Language Processing.

Zornitsa Kozareva, Qi Li, Ke Zhai, and Weiwei Guo. 2016. Recognizing salient entities in shopping queries. In *ACL*.

Guillaume Lample, Miguel Ballesteros, Sandeep Subramanian, Kazuya Kawakami, and Chris Dyer. 2016. Neural architectures for named entity recognition. In *Proceedings of the 2016 Conference of the North American Chapter of the Association for Computational Linguistics: Human Language Technologies*, pages 260–270, San Diego, California. Association for Computational Linguistics.

Xiao Ling and Daniel S. Weld. 2012. Fine-grained entity recognition. In *Proceedings of the Twenty-Sixth AAAI Conference on Artificial Intelligence*, AAAI'12, page 94–100. AAAI Press.

Xuezhe Ma and Eduard Hovy. 2016. End-to-end sequence labeling via bi-directional LSTM-CNNs-CRF. In *Proceedings of the 54th Annual Meeting of the Association for Computational Linguistics (Volume 1: Long Papers)*, pages 1064–1074, Berlin, Germany. Association for Computational Linguistics.

Tomas Mikolov, Ilya Sutskever, Kai Chen, Greg Corrado, and Jeffrey Dean. 2013. Distributed representations of words and phrases and their compositionality. In *Proceedings of the 26th International Conference on Neural Information Processing Systems - Volume 2*, NIPS'13, page 3111–3119, Red Hook, NY, USA. Curran Associates Inc.

Jianmo Ni, Jiacheng Li, and Julian McAuley. 2019. Justifying recommendations using distantly-labeled reviews and fine-grained aspects. In *Proceedings of the 2019 Conference on Empirical Methods in Natural Language Processing and the 9th International Joint Conference on Natural Language Processing (EMNLP-IJCNLP)*, pages 188–197, Hong Kong, China. Association for Computational Linguistics.

Jeffrey Pennington, Richard Socher, and Christopher Manning. 2014. GloVe: Global vectors for word representation. In *Proceedings of the 2014 Conference on Empirical Methods in Natural Language Processing (EMNLP)*, pages 1532–1543, Doha, Qatar. Association for Computational Linguistics.

Duangmanee (Pew) Putthividhya and Junling Hu. 2011. Bootstrapped named entity recognition for product attribute extraction. In *Proceedings of the Conference on Empirical Methods in Natural Language Processing*, EMNLP '11, page 1557–1567, USA. Association for Computational Linguistics.

Pranav Rajpurkar, Jian Zhang, Konstantin Lopyrev, and Percy Liang. 2016. SQuAD: 100,000+ questions for machine comprehension of text. In *Proceedings of the 2016 Conference on Empirical Methods in Natural Language Processing*, pages 2383–2392, Austin, Texas. Association for Computational Linguistics.

Umer Shahzad, Salman Ahmad, Kashif Iqbal, Muhammad Nawaz, and Saqib Usman. 2014. Influence of brand name on consumer choice & decision. *IOSR Journal of Business and Management*, 16:72–76.

Keiji Shinzato and Satoshi Sekine. 2013. Unsupervised extraction of attributes and their values from product description. In *Proceedings of the Sixth International Joint Conference on Natural Language Processing*, pages 1339–1347, Nagoya, Japan. Asian Federation of Natural Language Processing.

Nitish Srivastava, Geoffrey Hinton, Alex Krizhevsky, Ilya Sutskever, and Ruslan Salakhutdinov. 2014. Dropout: A simple way to prevent neural networks from overfitting. *J. Mach. Learn. Res.*, 15(1):1929–1958.

Damir Vandic, Jan-Willem Dam, and Flavius Frasincar. 2012. Faceted product search powered by the semantic web. *Decision Support Systems*, 53:425–437.

Qifan Wang, Li Yang, Bhargav Kanagal, Sumit Sanghai, D. Sivakumar, Bin Shu, Zac Yu, and Jon Elsas. 2020. Learning to extract attribute value from product via question answering: A multi-task approach. In *KDD '20: The 26th ACM SIGKDD Conference on Knowledge Discovery and Data Mining, Virtual Event, CA, USA, August 23-27, 2020*, pages 47–55. ACM.

Yuk Wah Wong, Dominic Widdows, Tom Lokovic, and Kamal Nigam. 2009. Scalable attribute-value extraction from semi-structured text. In *ICDM Workshop on Large-scale Data Mining: Theory and Applications*.

Huimin Xu, Wenting Wang, Xin Mao, Xinyu Jiang, and Man Lan. 2019. Scaling up open tagging from tens to thousands: Comprehension empowered attribute value extraction from product title. In *Proceedings of the 57th Annual Meeting of the Association for Computational Linguistics*, pages 5214–5223, Florence, Italy. Association for Computational Linguistics.

Guineng Zheng, Subhabrata Mukherjee, Xin Luna Dong, and Feifei Li. 2018. Opentag: Open attribute value extraction from product profiles. In *Proceedings of the 24th ACM SIGKDD International Conference on Knowledge Discovery & Data Mining*, KDD '18, page 1049–1058, New York, NY, USA. Association for Computing Machinery.

A Appendix

A.1 Implementation Details

Our models are implemented with Tensorflow[3] and Keras[4], and they are trained using TPUs on the cloud. We used the validation set of AZ-base to select the optimal hyper-parameters of our model, while the test set was used to report the final results. During training, optimization is performed with Adam optimizer (Kingma and Ba, 2015) using a $1e^{-3}$ initial learning rate. For all models, we employed pre-trained 100-dimensional word vectors from GloVe (Pennington et al., 2014). All models use a dropout layer (Srivastava et al., 2014) of size 0.3 both before and after the BiLSTM layer. The minibatch size is fixed to 128. The *BIO* tagging scheme is adopted. In the training process, we used the loss score on the validation set to assess model improvement. The models were trained for a total of 100 epochs, and early stopping was applied if there was no improvement for a period of 10 epochs. The average training time for each epoch was also recorded.

Hyper-parameter	**Value**
LSTM Units	{64, **128**, 256}
Character Embedding Size	{10, **30**, 50, 100}
Window Size	{3, 5, **10**}
Number of Filters	{10, **30**, 50}
Trainable Parameters	36420

Table 9: Hyper-parameters for OpenBrand-CNN model.

Hyper-parameter	**Value**
LSTM Units	{64, **128**, 256}
Character Embedding Size	{10, **30**, 50, 100}
Character LSTM Units	{10, **30**, 50, 100}
Trainable Parameters	526170

Table 10: Hyper-parameters for OpenBrand-LSTM model.

Tables 9 and 10 show the selected hyper-parameters in the CNN-based and LSTM-based models respectively, based on the performance on the validation set. These include the character embeddings dimension. The tables also show the total number of trainable parameters for each model. The difference in number of trainable parameters shows that CNNs have less training complexity as compared to LSTM models under similar experimental settings.

[3]https://www.tensorflow.org/.

[4]https://keras.io/.

Robust Product Classification with Instance-Dependent Noise

Huy Nguyen
Amazon.com, Inc.
Seattle, Washington, USA
nguynnq@amazon.com

Devashish Khatwani
Amazon.com, Inc.
Vancouver, British Columbia, Canada
khatwad@amazon.com

Abstract

Noisy labels in large E-commerce product data (i.e., product items are placed into incorrect categories) are a critical issue for product categorization task because they are unavoidable, non-trivial to remove and degrade prediction performance significantly. Training a product title classification model which is robust to noisy labels in the data is very important to make product classification applications more practical. In this paper, we study the impact of instance-dependent noise to performance of product title classification by comparing our data denoising algorithm and different noise-resistance training algorithms which were designed to prevent a classifier model from over-fitting to noise. We develop a simple yet effective Deep Neural Network for product title classification to use as a base classifier. Along with recent methods of stimulating instance-dependent noise, we propose a novel noise stimulation algorithm based on product title similarity. Our experiments cover multiple datasets, various noise methods and different training solutions. Results uncover the limit of classification task when noise rate is not negligible and data distribution is highly skewed.

1 Introduction

Product classification is a quintessential E-commerce machine learning problem in which product items are placed into their respective categories. With recent advancements of Deep Learning, various unimodal (i.e., text only) and multimodal (e.g., text and image) models have been developed to predict larger numbers of items and categories with better accuracy (Gao et al., 2020; Chen et al., 2021a; Brinkmann and Bizer, 2021). However, one of the fundamental assumptions behind such models is the availability of large and high-quality labeled datasets. Access to such datasets is usually costly or infeasible in some settings. Large product datasets usually suffer from annotation errors, i.e., products are assigned to incorrect categories, partially due to complex category structure, confusing categories and similar titles. The problem of noisy labels is even more severe when product category distribution is highly imbalanced with heavy-tail (Shen et al., 2012; Das et al., 2016). Therefore, a text classifier which is robust to noisy labels present in training data is critical for high-performing product classification applications.

While machine learning in the presence of label noise has been studied for decades, most of prior studies experimented in computer vision domain (Gu et al., 2021; Song et al., 2022), and only a few research was conducted in text classification (Jindal et al., 2019; Garg et al., 2021). Without an annotated dataset with manually-identified label noise, classical approaches for label noise stimulation assume class-conditional noise (CCN) where the probability of an item having label corrupted depends on the original and noisy labels. With this assumption, all products of "Men's Watches" category have the sample probability to be assigned "Women's Watches" label. This is not generally correct. For instance, product titles having phrase "men's watches" are less likely mis-labeled. Recent research addresses more general label noise, i.e., instance-dependent noise (IDN), that an item is mis-labeled with a probability depending on its original label and features.

In this paper, we present a comprehensive study on improving product title classification in the presence of IDN. We develop a simple yet effective Deep Neural Network for text classification and show that our model performs well on different product title datasets ranging from small to medium sizes, balanced to skewed distributions, and tens to over a hundred categories. To generate noisy labels for experiments, our first contribution is an IDN stimulation algorithm which flips an item's label based on its similarity to items of other categories. Noisy label data generated by our method is com-

Proceedings of The Fifth Workshop on e-Commerce and NLP (ECNLP 5), pages 171 - 180
May 26, 2022 ©2022 Association for Computational Linguistics

pared with prior IDN stimulation methods for their impact to model accuracy degradation. To make the model robust to label noise, our second contribution is a data augmentation method that reduces noise rate and thus improves model's accuracy. We compare three state-of-the-art Deep Neural Network training algorithms to train a classifier on data with label noise generated by different methods. From experimental results we discuss lessons learned for product title classification in production. To the best of our knowledge, this work is the first time that noise-resistance model training is studied in E-commerce domain, which is our third contribution.

2 Related Work

Automatic product categorization has been well studied to address its challenges including large number of items and categories, and hierarchical categories structure (Gao et al., 2020; Chen et al., 2021a; Brinkmann and Bizer, 2021). The large-scale nature of product data leads to a critical issue of noisy labels. For example, an E-commerce website reported that 15% of product listings by sellers have incorrect labels (Shen et al., 2012). Das et al. (2016) attempted to use a latent topic model to help manually inspect noisy categories and remove incorrect samples. Our current study focuses on fully automated methods for data denoising and noise-resistance training to prevent models from over-fitting to noisy samples.

Training Deep Neural Networks (DNN) with noisy labels is challenging because DNN's large learning capacity make them highly susceptible to over-fitting to noise (Arpit et al., 2017; Zhang et al., 2021a). Early work stacked DNN with layers to model noise-transition matrix assuming class-conditional noise, i.e., noisy label $\hat{y}$ only depends on true label y but not on the input x (Jindal et al., 2016; Patrini et al., 2017). Because noise transition matrix can be difficult to learn or not feasible in real-world settings, other directions targeted to selecting clean samples in each mini-batch and use them to update DNN's parameters (Jiang et al., 2018; Malach and Shalev-Shwartz, 2017). Among those, CoTeaching (Han et al., 2018) and CoTeaching^{+} (Yu et al., 2019) showed the effectiveness of cross-training two networks simultaneously in that each network sends selective samples for the other to learn. A more realistic assumption of noisy labels is instance-dependent noise (IDN) in which probability of noisy label $\hat{y}$ depends on true label y and input x (Chen et al., 2021b). Among state-of-the-art work on IDN, Self-Evolution Average Label – SEAL (Chen et al., 2021b) and Progressive Label Correction – PLC (Zhang et al., 2021b) are representatives of label refurbishment (Song et al., 2022) that uses softmax output to assign soft labels to training instances. We compare SEAL, PLC and CoTeaching^{+} on training a product title classifier with label noise.

3 Datasets

In this study, we employ 6 public datasets for product classification. While some datasets have multimodal inputs, e.g., product titles, descriptions, images, we use only product title inputs and leave other fields for a future work. This restriction may prevent us from achieving the best possible performance by incorporating other information-rich inputs (Chen et al., 2021a). However, our main motivation is to evaluate noise-resistance training approaches. For each dataset, we filter-out category labels with less than 10 samples, then apply stratified random sampling to split 10% for testing and 90% for training. We leave a study of few-shot learning for product title classification for future work. Hyper-parameters of models and training algorithms are fine-tuned within training sets when needed. In experiments with noisy labels, only training samples have label corrupted while testing sets are unchanged. This assures a realistic evaluation that model accuracies are measured against ground-truth disregarding how the model was trained. To measure skewness of data label distribution, we calculate KL-divergence from the actual category distribution to uniform distribution. Data statistics are shown in Table 1.

- Flipkart[1]: the original set contains nearly 20,000 samples but over 200 category labels are unqualified for modeling (e.g., those either have too few samples or are considered as Brand Name). Therefore we use 19,666 samples of top 28 categories.

- WDC dataset is WDC-25 Gold Standard for Product Categorization (Primpeli et al., 2019). We remove items with category label "*not-found*" and keep 23,597 samples with 24 class labels.

[1] www.kaggle.com/PromptCloudHQ/flipkart-products

Table 1: Summary of product title datasets

Dataset	#cls	#train	#test	KL
Flipkart	28	17,682	1,984	1.04
WDC	24	21,225	2,372	0.34
Retail	21	41,586	4,642	0.00
Pricerunner	10	31,773	3,538	0.03
Shopmania	147	282,095	31,437	1.49
Skroutz	12	214,346	23,824	1.10

Table 2: Models' macro F1 scores on product title data

Dataset	LSTM-CNNs	BERT-base
Flipkart	0.89	0.90
WDC	0.92	0.92
Retail	0.82	0.82
Pricerunner	0.96	0.98
Shopmania	0.83	0.87
Skroutz	0.96	0.98

- Retail dataset has 46,228 training samples with item titles, descriptions, images and category labels placed into 21 categories (Elayanithottathil and Keuper, 2021). We do not use their test data which does not have category labels.

- Pricerunner, Shopmania, Skroutz datasets[2] were collected from three online electronic stores and product comparison platforms (Akritidis et al., 2018, 2020).

As shown in Table 1, datasets Flipkart, Shopmania and Skroutz are highly imbalanced with KL-divergence greater than 1. Each of these datasets has major classes with thousands of samples and minor classes with tens of samples. WDC dataset is moderately skewed having 24 classes with number of samples ranging from 10 to 4,753. Retail and Pricerunner sets are the most balanced with KL-divergence close to zero. Retail dataset has roughly 2,200 samples per class while Pricerunner has class samples in range (2000, 6000).

4 Base Model for Product Title Categorization

We develop a product title classifier based on LSTM-CNNs architecture proposed in (Ma and Hovy, 2016). The network architecture is depicted in Figure 1. Input encoding layer is a concatenation of word-embeddings (looking-up function against GloVe pre-trained embeddings (Pennington et al., 2014)) and character embeddings (output of a Character-CNN layer). The sequence of embedding vectors is passed to a Bidirectional Recurrent Neural Network of LSTM cells (Hochreiter and Schmidhuber, 1997). Prediction is carried by a dense layer whose input is last hidden state of Bidirectional LSTM. The DNN is implemented in PyTorch (Paszke et al., 2017) and trained using Adam optimizer with Cross-entropy loss. For experiments with different datasets, we use the same set of hyper-parameters: *Glove embedding* 42B.300d, *LSTM hidden size* 100, *character embedding size* 25 with 3 convolution heads of filter sizes 2, 3, 4, *learning rate* 5e-4, *clip gradient norm* greater than 5.0. Models are trained for 10 *epoch* with *batch size* 16.

To evaluate our implementation, we compare model performance with fine-tunning the pre-trained BERT-base uncased language model (Devlin et al., 2019). Results on 6 datasets with clean label are reported in Table 2.[3] Our model performs on par with BERT-base in small datasets Flipkart, WDC, and Retail with macro F1 of less than 1 percentage point lower. For datasets Pricerunner and Skroutz, both models return great performance with BERT-base outperforming our model by 2 percentage points. Shopmania dataset observes the largest performance difference when BERT achieves F1 score 4 percentage points higher than LSTM-CNNs. Good performance of LSTM-CNNs gives us a strong base classifier which is much faster to train than BERT-base (LSTM-CNNs has approximately 6M of trainable parameters while it is 110M for BERT). We will study the impact of pre-training on noise-resistance in a future study.

5 Instance-Dependent Noise Stimulation

A common approach for automated IDN generation is to train one or a set of classifiers on clean label data, and use such classifiers to generate noisy labels for the whole dataset. Related studies can be different on how to maintain a pool of classifiers, e.g., different checkpoints of a single models or different model architectures, and label placement strategies, e.g., whether replacing clean label samples with noisy counterparts or allowing a sample

[2]www.kaggle.com/lakritidis/product-classification-and-categorization

[3]Macro F1 score is a fair evaluation metric for imbalanced data.

Figure 1: LSTM-CNNs architecture for product title classifier

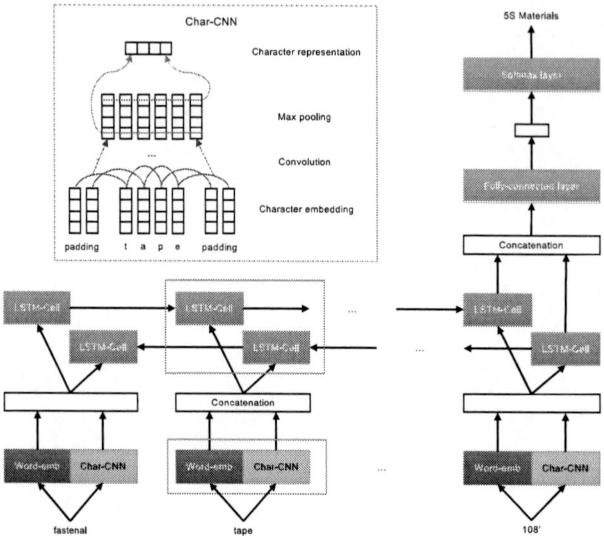

to have multiple copies with different labels. We follow (Zhang et al., 2021b; Chen et al., 2021b) to use replacement strategy which is considered a more difficult setting. We implement four different IDN algorithms, and adjust parameters to generate noisy label data with noise rates (i.e., ratio of noisy label samples over data size) in two levels: 0.2 (low) and 0.4 (medium).

Last-epoch IDN: We train a base classifier for 10 epochs to obtain the network corresponding to last epoch checkpoint. The trained network is executed on training data to obtain prediction confidence score (i.e., output of softmax layer) for every sample. Following the formula of noise type-I described in (Zhang et al., 2021b), we corrupt item category from the most confident label to the second confident label. This method uses a noise factor parameter to control noise rate, thus we run different trials to probe the noise factors that give us noise rates of interest.

Multi-epoch IDN: The base classifier is trained for 10 epochs to obtain a sequence of networks corresponding to multiple epoch checkpoints. Each sample is assigned a score as the average of prediction probabilities assigned by network sequences following the algorithm proposed in (Chen et al., 2021b). Potential noisy label should have the highest score among possible labels excluding the ground truth. In particular, data instances are sorted by scores of most likely corrupted labels, and r proportion of top instances will have labels flipped to obtain noise rate r.

Multi-model IDN: Similarly to multi-epoch IDN, we train 5 different versions of the base classifier by varying initial weights to get a network sequence, each network corresponds to last epoch checkpoint (i.e., epoch 10) of a training. Then we apply the same algorithm as in *multi-epoch IDN* to calculate noisy labels.

Similarity-based IDN: From our experience in product data analyses, we hypothesize that human annotators, and thus machine learning models, may have difficulties in categorizing similar items, e.g., "*Tara Lifestyle Chhota Bheem Printed Art Plastic Pencil Boxes*" and "*Starmark BTS Star Art Polyester Pencil Box*". Our idea is to locate highly similar items across categories and flip their category labels.

To generate noisy labels, we first calculate textual similarity between items of different categories. We implement two vector-based cosine similarity computations. First, A SentenceTransformer model (Reimers and Gurevych, 2019)[4] is used to generate embeddings of product titles. Second, a Tf-Idf model is learned from training set to generate Tf-Idf vectors of input titles. For each pair of product titles, we compare two cosine similarities calculated from sentence embedding vectors and Tf-Idf vectors. The greater score of two methods is assigned as similarity score `Sim` of two inputs. For

[4]Pretrained model *all-MiniLM-L12-v2*

each item i_c of category c, we record the maximal similarity score Maxsim between it and every item from another category c' of category set C:

$$\texttt{Maxsim}_{c'}(i_c) = max_j(\texttt{Sim}(i_c, j)) \quad j \in c'$$

The sequence of maximal similarity scores of the item is used as weight vector I_c for a multinominal distribution from which we draw a noisy label $\hat{c}$ given the item.

$$I_c = \{\texttt{Maxsim}_{c'}(i_c) \quad \forall c' \in C, c' \neq c\}.$$

$$\hat{c} \sim \texttt{Multinomial}(I_c)$$

For all items, we assign their $\texttt{Maxsim}_{\hat{c}}$ as representative scores of their corrupted labels, and we sort items by corrupted label scores from high to low. Given noise rate r, we select top r proportion of items to replace true labels by corrupted labels.

6 Experiments on Noisy Labels

6.1 Data Denoising by Corrupting Product Titles

We propose a novel data denoising method that reduces noise ratio by relabeling a sample when its prediction is certain. We say an input has certain prediction when model prediction on both original and corrupted inputs are the same. Our method relies on an idea of critical information assumption, i.e., we hypothesize that there are product titles which provide too much information that model does not need to use all words to predict their labels. For such titles, if one or more words are dropped, model should still predict the same label. There have been different studies to extract part of critical information from input to explain output of prediction models (Ribeiro et al., 2016; Lundberg and Lee, 2017; Kokalj et al., 2021). Regarding product title, leading words are consideratly more important than trailing words for recognizing product category.[5] Algorithm 1 is a simple heuristic to drop words from a product title. Statement 2 makes sure some right words are dropped even when an input is less than 15 words.

We propose Algorithm 2 to denoise training data. With clean data, model should achieves highly confident predictions on training samples. Thus, we reason that unconfident predictions on training samples (i.e., $p \leq 0.8$) are likely due to noisy labels. We note that in case of noisy training, input label is not considered ground truth generally.

[5]A common template arranges title words in order of Brand Name > Product > Key features > Size > Color > Quantity (sellerengine.com/product-title-keyword-strategies-for-new-products-on-amazon).

Algorithm 1 Drop words from a product title

1: Drop left words until dropped words have at least 5 letters in total or less then 4 words remaining
2: Drop right words until dropped words have at least 5 letters in total or less then 4 words remaining
3: Drop right words while there are more than 15 words

Steps 3 and 4 update[6] training samples while step 5 removes samples which the model is unsure. Our denoising algorithm reduces noise rate with a trade-off of smaller training data. Their impact to training data is shown in Table 3. For each dataset and input noise rate, we average noise rate and data size reductions after denoising the data corrputed by different noise stimulations.

Algorithm 2 Denoise training data

1: Run pre-trained model M on training data D: $\{L_o, P_o\} \leftarrow M(D)$ where L_o are predicted label and P_o are prediction probability
2: Run M on corrupted training data $\hat{D}$ (i.e., drops words from titles): $\{L_d, P_d\} \leftarrow M(\hat{D})$
3: Assign predicted labels to samples where predictions are confident:
InputLabel $\leftarrow L_o$ **if** $P_o \geq 0.8$
4: Assign predicted labels to samples where predictions are certain:
InputLabel $\leftarrow L_o$ **if** $L_o = L_d$
5: Remove samples where predictions are neither certain nor confident: $L_o \neq L_d$ **and** $P_o \leq 0.8$ **and** $P_d \leq 0.8$

6.2 Noise-Resistance Training Algorithms

In this study, we compare three training solutions that were developed for data with noisy labels: Self-Evolution Average Label – SEAL (Chen et al., 2021b), Progressive Label Correction – PLC (Zhang et al., 2021b) and CoTeaching$^+$ – CTp (Yu et al., 2019). The three training algorithms work independently from the underlying models.

SEAL trains a model on multiple iterations. In each iteration, SEAL optimizes model's loss against soft labels which are average predictions over epochs of the previous iteration. PLC first

[6]For efficiency, our actual implementation only update a sample when its input label is different from predicted label. This condition is ignored in pseudo code for simplicity.

Table 3: Average reduction of noise rate and data size after denoising

	Noise rate 0.2		Noise rate 0.4	
Dataset	Noise reduction	Data reduction	Noise reduction	Data reduction
Flipkart	36%	4%	29%	11%
WDC	28%	3%	21%	8%
Retail	26%	8%	30%	17%
Pricerunner	48%	3%	43%	11%
Shopmania	50%	7%	43%	12%
Skroutz	44%	6%	33%	7%

Table 4: Models' macro F1 scores on product title data with noisy labels. Highest scores are bold. API shows average performance improvement compared to base classifier.

	Noise rate 0.2					Noise rate 0.4				
					Last-epoch IDN					
Dataset	**Base**	**DeN**	**SEAL**	**PLC**	**CTp**	**Base**	**DeN**	**SEAL**	**PLC**	**CTp**
Flipkart	0.74	**0.82**	0.81	0.78	0.81	0.55	0.67	**0.69**	0.62	0.66
WDC	0.86	0.86	**0.88**	0.87	**0.88**	0.68	0.71	0.71	0.73	**0.77**
Retail	0.72	0.76	**0.78**	**0.78**	**0.78**	0.59	0.66	0.70	0.66	**0.71**
Pricerunner	0.89	**0.94**	**0.94**	0.93	**0.94**	0.71	0.87	0.90	0.79	**0.91**
Shopmania	0.74	0.71	0.73	**0.76**	0.68	0.59	0.62	0.62	**0.63**	0.56
Skroutz	0.90	0.94	0.94	0.93	**0.95**	0.77	0.86	0.86	0.78	**0.92**
API	-	3.7%	4.8%	4.2%	3.8%	-	12.9%	15.3%	8.5%	16%
					Multi-epoch IDN					
Flipkart	0.73	0.73	0.74	**0.75**	**0.75**	0.61	0.59	**0.64**	0.62	0.63
WDC	0.81	0.82	**0.83**	**0.83**	0.82	0.65	0.66	0.66	0.65	**0.68**
Retail	0.79	**0.80**	0.79	0.79	**0.80**	0.73	0.73	**0.76**	0.74	**0.76**
Pricerunner	0.91	0.91	**0.92**	**0.92**	**0.92**	0.80	0.82	0.84	0.82	**0.85**
Shopmania	0.76	0.75	0.76	**0.77**	0.67	0.63	**0.65**	**0.65**	0.62	0.57
Skroutz	**0.95**	**0.95**	**0.95**	**0.95**	**0.95**	0.88	**0.90**	**0.90**	0.88	**0.90**
API	-	0.2%	0.8%	1.3%	-0.9%	-	1%	3.5%	0.6%	1.8%
					Multi-model IDN					
Flipkart	0.72	0.74	**0.75**	0.74	**0.75**	0.57	0.61	**0.64**	0.61	0.63
WDC	0.82	**0.83**	**0.83**	0.82	**0.83**	0.65	0.65	**0.67**	0.66	**0.67**
Retail	0.78	0.79	**0.80**	0.79	0.79	0.70	0.73	**0.76**	0.73	0.74
Pricerunner	0.90	0.91	**0.92**	0.91	**0.92**	0.80	0.81	**0.84**	0.81	**0.84**
Shopmania	0.76	0.75	**0.78**	0.77	0.68	**0.66**	0.65	**0.66**	0.64	0.57
Skroutz	**0.95**	**0.95**	**0.95**	**0.95**	**0.95**	0.90	**0.92**	0.91	0.91	**0.92**
API	-	0.8%	2.1%	1%	-0.2%	-	2.2%	5%	2%	2.1%
					Similarity-based IDN					
Flipkart	0.73	0.76	0.76	0.77	**0.78**	0.55	0.58	0.61	0.65	**0.67**
WDC	0.73	0.74	0.75	0.75	**0.76**	0.58	0.58	0.59	0.59	**0.60**
Retail	0.69	0.75	**0.77**	0.76	**0.77**	0.57	0.66	**0.72**	0.70	**0.72**
Pricerunner	0.86	0.91	**0.93**	0.92	**0.93**	0.72	0.83	0.85	0.82	**0.86**
Shopmania	0.70	0.70	0.71	**0.73**	0.65	0.57	0.59	0.57	**0.59**	0.50
Skroutz	0.84	**0.89**	0.85	0.84	0.88	0.68	**0.76**	0.72	0.69	**0.76**
API	-	4.3%	4.8%	4.9%	4.7%	-	8.6%	10.4%	10.2%	11.7%

Table 5: Models' macro F1 scores averaged over different noise stimulations. Highest scores are bold.

	Noise rate 0.2					Noise rate 0.4				
Dataset	**Base**	**DeN**	**SEAL**	**PLC**	**CTp**	**Base**	**DeN**	**SEAL**	**PLC**	**CTp**
Flipkart	0.73	0.762	0.765	0.76	**0.772**	0.57	0.6125	0.645	0.625	**0.647**
WDC	0.805	0.812	0.822	0.817	**0.822**	0.64	0.65	0.6575	0.657	**0.68**
Retail	0.745	0.775	**0.785**	0.78	**0.785**	0.6475	0.695	**0.735**	0.707	0.732
Pricerunner	0.89	0.917	**0.927**	0.92	**0.927**	0.757	0.832	0.857	0.81	**0.865**
Shopmania	0.74	0.727	0.745	**0.757**	0.67	0.612	**0.627**	0.625	0.62	0.55
Skroutz	0.91	**0.932**	0.9225	0.917	**0.932**	0.807	0.86	0.8475	0.815	**0.875**

trains noisy label data normally for a number of epochs, i.e., warm-up phase, with expectation that model can learn from clean labels before over-fits to noisy labels. Then PLC corrects input labels after each epoch for cases that it yields a confidence score above a threshold. CoTeaching$^+$ is an upgrade of CoTeaching paradigm that cross-trains two models using only small-loss samples in each mini-batch. CoTeaching$^+$ further prevents the two models from convergence by passing only samples whose predictions disagree among small-loss data to loss optimization step.

6.3 Experiment Results

Experimental results of individual models are shown in Table 4. We first train the base classifier directly on noisy label data and record Macro F1 score on column *Base*. We then denoise[7] training data before training the base classifier, and enter performance into column *DeN*. Next columns report F1 scores of models trained by noise-resistance algorithms on noisy label data (i.e., not desnoised).

As expected, label noises degrade model performance significantly. Noise rate 0.2 reduces performance of base model from 5% (Skroutz) - 18% (Flipkart), while the performance reduction is 17% (Skroutz) to 46% (Flipkart) given noise rate 0.4. Pricerunner and Skroutz have lowest performance degradation which is reasonable because these two datasets are the easiest (see Table 2).

Evaluating impact of different IDN methods, similarity-based IDN degrades performance of base classifier the most in comparison with other IDN methods. Comparing performance of noise-resistance training methods with base classifier, we report average performance improvement (API) over different datasets in percentage point. Noise-resistance training methods have the most difficulty in improving multi-epoch and multi-model IDNs. In particular, performance improvements are at most 2% and 5% when multi-epoch and multi-model IDN rates are 0.2 and 0.4 respectively. Such noise-resistance training methods achieve much higher performance improvements when noisy labels are generated by other two IDN methods. Particularly, average performance improves are at least 4% and 8% when last-epoch and similarity-based IDN rates are 0.2 and 0.4 respectively.

Denoising data before training show improvements but performance improvements are lower for multi-epoch and multi-model IDN's than for last-epoch and similarity-based IDN's. Although our data denoising implementation is basic, it helps improve performance more than PLC in many settings, e.g., higher API in last-epoch, multi-epoch and multi-model IDN's. This encourage us to explore more advanced classifiers for better noise reduction results.

Table 5 summarizes the results by grouping by dataset name then averaging over different noise stimulation methods. It is shown that CoTeaching$^+$ performs better than other methods in many datasets, e.g., 5 datasets with noise rate 0.2 and 4 datasets out of 6 with noise rate 0.4. DeN performs worse than three noise-resistance training methods despite a fact that noise rate was reduced significantly as shown in Table 3. We hypothesize that regular training cannot recover from noisy instances that denoising algorithm is unable to correct/remove.

Comparing different datasets, we observe that Shopmania is the most difficult. Among denoising and noise-resistance training algorithms, the best approach could only improve performance by 4% and 7% when noise rate is 0.2 and 0.4 respectively. CoTeaching$^+$ even performed worse than base classifier on this dataset. As shown in Table 1, Shopmania is the largest dataset, has the most num-

[7]We run pre-trained model reported in column Base on training data to collect prediction outputs as described in Algorithm 2.

Table 6: Models' macro F1 scores on product title data with noise rate 0.6. Scores are averaged over IDN methods.

Dataset	Base	CTp	API (%)
Flipkart	0.41	0.45	10%
WDC	0.42	0.46	9%
Retail	0.52	0.60	15%
Pricerunner	0.51	0.54	6%
Shopmania	0.42	0.42	0%
Skroutz	0.58	0.64	10%

ber of classes and the most imbalanced distribution. Regarding imbalanced data, noisy labels in a minor class might be harder to address due to its small number of instances.

Finally, prediction performance at high noise rate 0.6 is briefly shown in Table 6. We only compare base classifier to CoTeaching$^+$ which is the best performing approach in this setting. While noise-resistance training algorithms do improve performance, overall performance is low. In our opinion, such a performance score is too low for an product title classification application. Thus we do not find any of the three training algorithms or our denoising algorithm can work reasonably well with high noise rate in product data.

6.4 Future Work

Data denoising algorithm opens new opportunities for us to further improve product title classification with noisy labels. We plan to improve data denoising by several techniques: (1) run denoising algorithm using a base model trained with small number of epochs to prevent over-fitting to noise, (2) use more advanced base classifier, and transformer-based model is a good candidate. Stacking data denoising and noise-resistance training is another extension, and we can approach this in two ways: (1) data denoising provides less-noisy data for noise-resistance training, (2) noise-resistance training provides better base model to denoise data.

7 Conclusion

In this paper, we evaluate a denoising algorithm and three training approaches for product title classification with category labels corrupted by instance-dependent noise. We introduce a new IDN stimulation algorithm and compare with three IDN algorithms from prior studies to explore model performance on a wider range of noise type. Therefore our study can evaluate model robustness to IDN more reliably. Overall we find that CoTeaching$^+$ achieves highest average improvement and be our recommendation when applying to new product data without prior knowledge of noise cause or true distribution. SEAL can be a good method when we have clean validation data to evaluate. However, all methods studied in this paper have difficulties to address noise in large scale data with highly imbalanced class distribution, especially when noise rate is high. For such extreme setting, application of data denoising and noise-resistance training algorithms could not yield to reasonable performance for applying to production. For a future work, we plan to combine multiple techniques including transformer-based classifier as a more advanced model and stacking data denoising with noise-resistance training.

References

Leonidas Akritidis, Athanasios Fevgas, and Panayiotis Bozanis. 2018. Effective Products Categorization with Importance Scores and Morphological Analysis of the Titles. In *2018 IEEE 30th International Conference on Tools with Artificial Intelligence (ICTAI)*, pages 213–220.

Leonidas Akritidis, Athanasios Fevgas, Panayiotis Bozanis, and Christos Makris. 2020. A self-verifying clustering approach to unsupervised matching of product titles. *Artificial Intelligence Review*, pages 1–44.

Devansh Arpit, Stanis\law Jastrzundefinedbski, Nicolas Ballas, David Krueger, Emmanuel Bengio, Maxinder S. Kanwal, Tegan Maharaj, Asja Fischer, Aaron Courville, Yoshua Bengio, and Simon Lacoste-Julien. 2017. A Closer Look at Memorization in Deep Networks. In *Proceedings of the 34th International Conference on Machine Learning - Volume 70*, ICML'17, pages 233–242. JMLR.org. Event-place: Sydney, NSW, Australia.

Alexander Brinkmann and Christian Bizer. 2021. Improving hierarchical product classification using domain-specific language modelling. In *Proceedings of Workshop on Knowledge Management in e-Commerce*.

Lei Chen, Houwei Chou, Yandi Xia, and Hirokazu Miyake. 2021a. Multimodal Item Categorization Fully Based on Transformer. In *Proceedings of The 4th Workshop on e-Commerce and NLP*, pages 111–115, Online. Association for Computational Linguistics.

Pengfei Chen, Junjie Ye, Guangyong Chen, Jingwei Zhao, and Pheng-Ann Heng. 2021b. Beyond Class-Conditional Assumption: A Primary Attempt to Combat Instance-Dependent Label Noise. In *Proceedings of the AAAI Conference on Artificial Intelligence.*

Pradipto Das, Yandi Xia, Aaron Levine, Giuseppe Di Fabbrizio, and Ankur Datta. 2016. Large-scale taxonomy categorization for noisy product listings. In *2016 IEEE International Conference on Big Data (Big Data)*, pages 3885–3894.

Jacob Devlin, Ming-Wei Chang, Kenton Lee, and Kristina Toutanova. 2019. BERT: Pre-training of Deep Bidirectional Transformers for Language Understanding. In *Proceedings of the 2019 Conference of the North American Chapter of the Association for Computational Linguistics: Human Language Technologies, Volume 1 (Long and Short Papers)*, pages 4171–4186, Minneapolis, Minnesota. Association for Computational Linguistics.

Febin Sebastian Elayanithottathil and Janis Keuper. 2021. A Retail Product Categorisation Dataset. _eprint: 2103.13864.

Dehong Gao, Wenjing Yang, Huiling Zhou, Yi Wei, Y. Hu, and H. Wang. 2020. Deep Hierarchical Classification for Category Prediction in E-commerce System. *ArXiv*, abs/2005.06692.

Siddhant Garg, Goutham Ramakrishnan, and Varun Thumbe. 2021. Towards Robustness to Label Noise in Text Classification via Noise Modeling. *Proceedings of the 30th ACM International Conference on Information & Knowledge Management.*

Keren Gu, Xander Masotto, Vandana Bachani, Balaji Lakshminarayanan, Jack Nikodem, and Dong Yin. 2021. A Realistic Simulation Framework for Learning with Label Noise. *ArXiv*, abs/2107.11413.

Bo Han, Quanming Yao, Xingrui Yu, Gang Niu, Miao Xu, Weihua Hu, Ivor Tsang, and Masashi Sugiyama. 2018. Co-teaching: Robust training of deep neural networks with extremely noisy labels. *Advances in neural information processing systems*, 31.

Sepp Hochreiter and Jürgen Schmidhuber. 1997. Long Short-Term Memory. *Neural Comput.*, 9(8):1735–1780. Place: Cambridge, MA, USA Publisher: MIT Press.

Lu Jiang, Zhengyuan Zhou, Thomas Leung, Li-Jia Li, and Li Fei-Fei. 2018. MentorNet: Learning Data-Driven Curriculum for Very Deep Neural Networks on Corrupted Labels. In *ICML*.

Ishan Jindal, Matthew Nokleby, and Xuewen Chen. 2016. Learning deep networks from noisy labels with dropout regularization. In *Data Mining (ICDM), 2016 IEEE 16th International Conference on*, pages 967–972. IEEE.

Ishan Jindal, Daniel Pressel, Brian Lester, and Matthew Nokleby. 2019. An Effective Label Noise Model for DNN Text Classification. In *Proceedings of the 2019 Conference of the North American Chapter of the Association for Computational Linguistics: Human Language Technologies, Volume 1 (Long and Short Papers)*, pages 3246–3256, Minneapolis, Minnesota. Association for Computational Linguistics.

Enja Kokalj, Blaž Škrlj, Nada Lavrač, Senja Pollak, and Marko Robnik-Šikonja. 2021. BERT meets Shapley: Extending SHAP Explanations to Transformer-based Classifiers. In *Proceedings of the EACL Hackashop on News Media Content Analysis and Automated Report Generation*, pages 16–21, Online. Association for Computational Linguistics.

Scott M. Lundberg and Su-In Lee. 2017. A Unified Approach to Interpreting Model Predictions. In *Proceedings of the 31st International Conference on Neural Information Processing Systems*, NIPS'17, pages 4768–4777, Red Hook, NY, USA. Curran Associates Inc. Event-place: Long Beach, California, USA.

Xuezhe Ma and Eduard Hovy. 2016. End-to-end Sequence Labeling via Bi-directional LSTM-CNNs-CRF. In *Proceedings of the 54th Annual Meeting of the Association for Computational Linguistics (Volume 1: Long Papers)*, pages 1064–1074, Berlin, Germany. Association for Computational Linguistics.

Eran Malach and Shai Shalev-Shwartz. 2017. Decoupling "when to update" from "how to update". In *NIPS*.

Adam Paszke, Sam Gross, Soumith Chintala, Gregory Chanan, Edward Yang, Zachary DeVito, Zeming Lin, Alban Desmaison, Luca Antiga, and Adam Lerer. 2017. Automatic differentiation in PyTorch. In *NIPS-W*.

Giorgio Patrini, Alessandro Rozza, Aditya Krishna Menon, Richard Nock, and Lizhen Qu. 2017. Making deep neural networks robust to label noise: A loss correction approach. In *Proceedings of the IEEE conference on computer vision and pattern recognition*, pages 1944–1952.

Jeffrey Pennington, Richard Socher, and Christopher D. Manning. 2014. GloVe: Global Vectors for Word Representation. In *Empirical Methods in Natural Language Processing (EMNLP)*, pages 1532–1543.

Anna Primpeli, Ralph Peeters, and Christian Bizer. 2019. The WDC Training Dataset and Gold Standard for Large-Scale Product Matching. In *Companion Proceedings of The 2019 World Wide Web Conference*, WWW '19, pages 381–386, New York, NY, USA. Association for Computing Machinery. Event-place: San Francisco, USA.

Nils Reimers and Iryna Gurevych. 2019. Sentence-BERT: Sentence Embeddings using Siamese BERT-Networks. In *Proceedings of the 2019 Conference on Empirical Methods in Natural Language Processing*. Association for Computational Linguistics.

Marco Tulio Ribeiro, Sameer Singh, and Carlos Guestrin. 2016. "Why Should I Trust You?": Explaining the Predictions of Any Classifier. In *Proceedings of the 22nd ACM SIGKDD International*

Conference on Knowledge Discovery and Data Mining, San Francisco, CA, USA, August 13-17, 2016, pages 1135–1144.

Dan Shen, Jean-David Ruvini, and Badrul Sarwar. 2012. Large-Scale Item Categorization for e-Commerce. In *Proceedings of the 21st ACM International Conference on Information and Knowledge Management*, CIKM '12, pages 595–604, New York, NY, USA. Association for Computing Machinery. Event-place: Maui, Hawaii, USA.

Hwanjun Song, Minseok Kim, Dongmin Park, Yooju Shin, and Jae-Gil Lee. 2022. Learning from Noisy Labels with Deep Neural Networks: A Survey. *IEEE Transactions on Neural Networks and Learning Systems*.

Xingrui Yu, Bo Han, Jiangchao Yao, Gang Niu, Ivor Tsang, and Masashi Sugiyama. 2019. How does disagreement help generalization against label corruption? In *International Conference on Machine Learning*, pages 7164–7173. PMLR.

Chiyuan Zhang, Samy Bengio, Moritz Hardt, Benjamin Recht, and Oriol Vinyals. 2021a. Understanding Deep Learning (Still) Requires Rethinking Generalization. *Commun. ACM*, 64(3):107–115. Place: New York, NY, USA Publisher: Association for Computing Machinery.

Yikai Zhang, Songzhu Zheng, Pengxiang Wu, Mayank Goswami, and Chao Chen. 2021b. Learning with Feature-Dependent Label Noise: A Progressive Approach. In *ICLR*.

Structured Extraction of Terms and Conditions from German and English Online Shops

Tobias Schamel
Technical University of Munich
tobias.schamel@tum.de

Daniel Braun
University of Twente
d.braun@utwente.nl

Florian Matthes
Technical University of Munich
matthes@tum.de

Abstract

The automated analysis of Terms and Conditions has gained attention in recent years, mainly due to its relevance to consumer protection. Well-structured data sets are the base for every analysis. While content extraction, in general, is a well-researched field and many open source libraries are available, our evaluation shows, that existing solutions cannot extract Terms and Conditions in sufficient quality, mainly because of their special structure. In this paper, we present an approach to extract the content and hierarchy of Terms and Conditions from German and English online shops. Our evaluation shows, that the approach outperforms the current state of the art. A python implementation of the approach is made available under an open license.

1 Introduction

Terms and Conditions (T&Cs) of online shops are rarely read and even more rarely understood (Bakos et al., 2014), although we all still accept them. In recent years, the automated analysis of T&Cs has become an interesting field of research (Braun and Matthes, 2021; Lippi et al., 2019). A structured extraction of T&Cs from online shops is a necessary prerequisite for such further processing in an NLP pipeline.

Content extraction is a well-researched task and numerous open source libraries are available. Existing approaches are predominantly designed for or based on news articles and blog posts. In this paper, we will show that the existing approaches are not well-suited to deal with T&Cs, partially because of the strict hierarchical structures that can be found in such legal documents, which are not common in other types of content such as news articles.

In this paper, we present a domain-specific content extraction approach for T&Cs, that combines both, *Content Extraction* and *Hierarchy Extraction*, and an open source Python library that implements this approach. needs to combine both. Our evaluation shows that the library outperforms general-purpose content extraction approaches on T&Cs from German and English online shops. The library is available on GitHub: `https://github.com/sebischair/LowestCommonAncestorExtractor`.

2 Related Work

The existing work on content extraction has been mainly focused on news articles or generic content extraction, often based on the dataset of the cleaneval competition (Baroni et al., 2008). To the best of our knowledge, no work exists that specifically targets or is evaluated on T&Cs.

Gibson et al. (2007) described the process of content extraction as a sequence labeling problem on a document broken down into a sequence of blocks. Each block needs to be classified as either *Content* or *NotContent*. Kohlschütter et al. (2010) work with a more detailed four-class separation. Another approach is a Boundary Detection Method where a heuristic needs to determine a *Start*- and *End*-Block framing the whole content, i.e. everything between *Start*- and *End*-Block is considered *Content* whereas everything else is discarded as *NotContent*. According to Jiménez et al. (2018), the classification needs to take both HTML structure and the actual content into account. "Purely text-based or purely HTML-based approaches do not have perfect results."

Several approaches for classifying blocks as *Content* or *NotContent* can be found in the literature.

Kohlschütter et al. (2010) propose a classification inspecting the text on a functional level using a set of so-called shallow text features. Shallow text features are statistical calculations on block-level looking at domain and language independent features like link density, the average sentence length, the uppercase ratio, etc. Jiménez et al. (2018) introduce an improvement to this algorithm by also

Proceedings of The Fifth Workshop on e-Commerce and NLP (ECNLP 5), pages 181 - 190

taking the HTML tree structure into account.

Pomikálek (2011) introduced a similar approach using a low amount of features to determine the likelihood of a block being *Content* or *NotContent*. Uncertainties are dealt with within the next step, which involves an analysis of the relative position of a block in the HTML tree including the classification of its neighbors. This step is based on the assumption that *Content* blocks are to be found near other *Content* blocks (and vice versa).

Pasternack and Roth (2009) tried to solve the task by finding a maximum subsequence in tokenized HTML documents, where each token is assigned a score determined by token-level classifiers. Different classifiers like simply assigning predefined scores to words and tags and more advanced classifiers which combined Naive Bayes classification with features of the surrounding tokens were investigated.

There is a number of synonyms to the process of "content extraction" (Gibson et al., 2007; Barbaresi, 2019) like *boilerplate detection/removal* (Kohlschütter et al., 2010), *template matching* (Sano et al., 2021) and *cleaning* (Lejeune and Zhu, 2018; Kilgarriff, 2007).

In addition to extracting the content, a (relatively small) number of approaches also try to extract the hierarchy of the content. According to Manabe and Tajima (2015), the nested hierarchy of an HTML document can contribute some information to hierarchy extraction but does not necessarily coincide with the actual hierarchical structure of an HTML document. The HTML tags originally meant to structure a document and indicate headings are often misused for SEO or not used at all.

Manabe and Tajima (2015) introduced a segmenting method extracting the hierarchical structure of HTML documents based on the differences in the visual styles in hierarchical headings. They defined a set of rules based on the way humans read hierarchically structured content. According to them, headings a characterized by more prominent visual styles (the same on one level of hierarchy) preceding the blocks they describe.

Sano et al. (2021) used a similar approach with only nine parameters. The parameters include the number of child nodes, text length of nodes and the styling of succeeding content.

1. headings have few child nodes
2. headings have a short text length
3. the width of headings is greater than their height
4. the size of a heading is smaller than the size of the following content block underneath it

3 Requirements

In order to derive requirements for the extraction of T&Cs, we compared existing extractors and our expected results. In addition, we manually inspected T&C pages to detect patterns and domain-specific characteristics. The test data was sampled from the data set by Braun and Matthes (2020) which is available under the CC BY-SA 3.0 license on GitHub[1]. We investigated the extraction results of the T&Cs pages of 30 German and 20 English online shops. 15% of the English sample had to be adjusted, as the URL from the data-set did not point to the actual T&Cs page.

3.1 Content Extraction

Through visual inspection of the T&Cs page and the DOM tree, we identified some prevalent patterns: While news articles are often interrupted by references to similar articles and advertisements, all cases examined in the sample of T&Cs pages displayed the relevant legal document without any interruptions on a rather simply structured page. For T&Cs of German online shops, the content is not always grouped within a single large paragraph but often divided into multiple paragraphs, e.g., *1. Allgemeine Geschäftsbedingungen* (German for general terms and conditions) and *2. Kundeninformation* (customer information), where both contain relevant information. Generally speaking, German T&Cs tend to be more structured than their counterpart in English online shops. In most of the cases, the relevant content shared a common style (font size and style) and could be found in the same depth of the DOM tree. This same style was used in the footer of the page in rare cases. Exceptions to these observations are headlines and differently styled withdrawal forms, which are contained in a number of T&C pages. These withdrawal forms are often comprised of underscores, blank spaces, and text. A small number of T&C pages had content that needed to be unfolded making and purely visual approach insufficient, as parts of the relevant content are not seen without further interaction with specific elements of the website.

[1] `https://github.com/sebischair/TC-Detection-Corpus/`

3.1.1 Existing Solutions

We compared the content extraction performance of three existing libraries on the data set. The extraction results were quantified by classifying the extraction quality for the following properties (quality sorted from *correct* to *most severe* error):

- content start: *correct, too early, too late*
- content end: *correct, too late, too early*
- main content: *correct, missing content* (links & addresses), *none-content* (whole paragraphs or sentences), *missing & none-content*

If the content start is detected earlier than it actually is, noise is added to the content, however, if the content start is detected later than it actually is, content is cut off and information lost. The latter is the more severe error. For the end of the content, the reverse is true.

The following three content extraction libraries were tested:

Boilerpipe We compared three different extractors implemented in *Boilerpipe*[2]:

ArticleExtractor The end of the main content was often identified too early, i.e., content towards the end of the pages was cut off. This was often caused by addresses and other contact information. Less frequently, *ArticleExtractor* also had problems identifying the start of the main content.

CanolaExtractor The *CanolaExtractor* was trained on the KrdWrd Canola corpus[3], which is created from random webpages across various domains (Stemle, 2009). It recurrently extracted cookie information or the footer of the web pages. The main content was usually detected but the extracted text was interrupted many times. This occurred for some short paragraphs, headings, addresses and withdrawal forms.

LargestContentExtractor The *LargestContentExtractor* extracts a continuous piece of content in all cases. This connected part is not a single HTML node but a consecutive series of HTML nodes. By nature, the extraction performance for the center of the extracted content is excellent. However, the performance on the identification of the start and end of the main content is the worst observed in comparison with the other extractors.

JusText The performance of *JusText*[4] Pomikálek (2011) was similar to the results of the Boilerpipe CanolaExtractor. The main content was usually detected but the extracted text was interrupted, as *JusText* classified many headlines, addresses, and paragraphs containing links as boilerplate.

Trafilatura *Trafilatura*[5] performed best among the investigated solutions. However, *Trafilatura* ignored some of the paragraph headlines. In addition, there were problems with content that was not visible to a user without unfolding them in the browser manually.

6 of 20 sampled web pages from the English sample were not extractable due to malformed HTML. As small mistakes in the HTML structure are not uncommon and are usually fixed by browsers rendering them, this should not be the case. The proposed solution should be robust when encountering that type of problem. The detailed results can be found in Tables 2 and 3.

3.1.2 Derived Requirements

Based on the identified patterns in the data and the problems of the existing approaches, we derived the following reuqirements for a domain-specific content extraction approach for T&C:

1. extract (largest) continuous part of HTML document
2. extract the content sharing a common style and depth in HTML tree
3. extract the withdrawal form/information with different style and different depth
4. extract address information
5. always extract both of the sections *1. Allgemeine Geschäftsbedingungen* (general terms and conditions) and *2. Kundeninformation* (customer information) in German T&Cs
6. extract *hidden* content which needs to be unfolded in the browser (e.g. by clicking an expand button)
7. robust against malformed HTML

[2] https://code.google.com/p/boilerpipe

[3] https://krdwrd.org/

[4] https://code.google.com/archive/p/justext/

[5] https://github.com/adbar/trafilatura

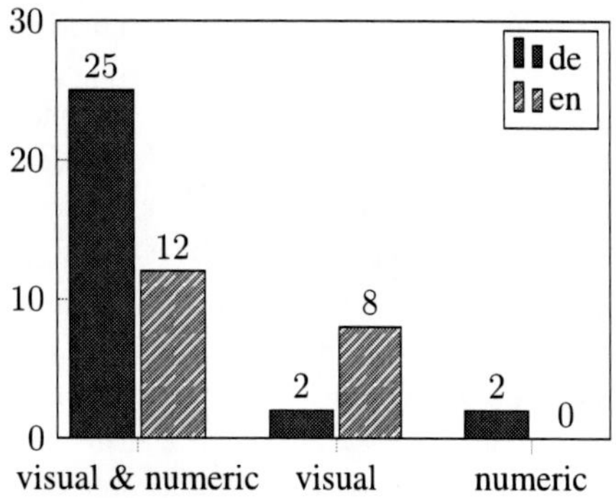

Figure 1: Occurrences of different hierarchy styles in the German and English sample

3.2 Hierarchy Extraction

Data on the visual and HTML-based representations of the hierarchical structure of web pages containing T&Cs were gathered in a manual review. The results found in the English sample and the German sample differed slightly. The following hierarchy representation classes were defined:

Visual page is structured using visual separators and different text styles

Numeric page is structured using a numeric scheme (Arabic, Latin/Roman, alphabetic, etc.)

Visual & Numeric a combination of both *Visual* and *Numeric* elements are used to structure the page

The analysis showed, that German shops were much more likely to use a combination of *Visual & Numeric* features to structure the content (see Figure 1).

Based on our observations, we formulated the following requirements:

1. extract subclauses grouped in their own paragraph forming HTML tag (block elements)
2. detect numeration patterns (alphabetic, Arabic, Latin/Roman, section sign, etc.)
3. extract styling (CSS) of titles to determine associated content
4. ignore enumerations for the table of contents

4 Approach and Implementation

This section covers the approach we developed based on the identified requirements and the design and implementation of the *StructuredLegalExtraction* library that implements the approach in Python.

4.1 Architecture

The extraction library consists of two main components described in Section 4.3 and Section 4.4 which serve to extract the content and the hierarchy of a given T&C page. In addition, there is an auxiliary component that serves to download the web page and one that transforms the HTML content into a DOM tree which is by far more useful for further processing. Another auxiliary component is used to generate the target structure relying on another auxiliary component to segment sentences.

At first, the content is downloaded using the *Downloader* component. The downloaded content is processed by the *DOMParser* to achieve the desired DOM tree holding no more information than those actually needed during later processing steps. The *ContentExtractor* component is responsible for detecting and extracting the main content of the downloaded page based on the parsed DOM tree. The *HierarchyExtractor* component uses the main content node of the DOM tree to build its hierarchy tree based on visual information (CSS attached to DOM nodes) and numerical patterns in the text. In the last step, the hierarchy tree needs to be transformed to the target format by the *TargetFormat* component, which uses the *SentenceSegmenter* component to tokenize and segment the content.

4.2 Additional Technologies

Some generic tasks can be solved by using existing solutions. The requirements and selected libraries are presented in this section.

4.2.1 Web Page Download

In an effort to determine the main content of a web page, the entire content must first be downloaded. The following requirements have been identified:

- download full HTML file representing the web page
- extract CSS style information on the content
- full XML Path Language (XPath) support to navigate the dom tree

Selenium[6] is a well-known library usually used for website testing. By this, it allows full interaction with the website using X-Path by controlling a browser. This also allows us to use the

[6]https://github.com/SeleniumHQ/selenium/

browser's HTML error correction when downloading the HTML. However, the `find_by_xpath (path)` method does not support text elements. Text can be extracted by accessing an element's `.text` attribute. Unfortunately, text segments (complete text - direct and indirect children - under the current node) cannot be mapped to the individual nodes so that one could track down which text has which style. This will require another library.

An outstanding feature of selenium is its capability of extracting CSS style information. The high number of visual represented hierarchies (see Figure 1) makes this a crucial feature.

4.2.2 HTML Parser

As Selenium does not support text nodes in its X-Path functionality, there is a need for a dedicated parser with the following requirements:

- full XPath support to navigate the DOM tree
- XPath generation from DOM tree nodes

lxml[7] an XML-parser offering dedicated HTML-parsing functionality. Due to its full XPath support, it also allows extracting all child nodes including the text nodes of a DOM-node using the XPath `child::node()`. The library also allows generating XPath for elements relative to a given parent element which makes it possible to link it to other libraries capable of XPath for style extraction (see Section 4.2.1).

4.2.3 Sentence Segmentation and Tokenising

The content of the document needs to be segmented into sentences which themselves need to be tokenized for the target format. This requires reliable segmenting and tokenizing with respect to text elements like references to laws or address information common in the domain of T&Cs.

According to Braun (2021), *SoMaJo*[8] performed best in the domain of T&Cs .

LangID[9] is used, as *SoMaJo* requires knowledge on the language of the text to segment and tokenize. LangID's multinomial naive Bayes model is trained to determine a text's language among 97 languages including German and English (Lui et al., 2021).

4.3 Content Extraction

As described in Section 3, the main content of a T&Cs page usually shares a common style. The main content makes up for the largest visible content block most of the time. Therefore, the extraction approach can be built upon this knowledge.

In a first step, we determine the MCS (Most Common Style) by traversing the DOM tree nodes while collecting a mapping of styles to number of characters. Different approaches to determine and approximate the style of a given node were investigated.

Naïve Style The first naïve approach is combining the HTML tag and all the attributes (incl. CSS classes and ids). However, this is just an approximation, as CSS style information is passed to child nodes of the parents holding them. This approach is rather efficient but less accurate.

Naïve Style and Short Text Exclusion As navigation bars and headlines consist of nodes holding only one to two words, it can be dangerous to include them when determining the MCS, as nested navigation elements hold large amounts of characters. Excluding short text nodes (<4 words) can solve that issue

Rendered Style Using *Selenium* allows the retrieval of the rendered style information.

It turned out, that the *Naïve Style and Short Text Exclusion*'s approximation is almost as accurate as the *Rendered Style* approach. Using the *Naïve Style and Short Text Exclusion* approximation, we can limit the time-intensive rendered style extraction through *Selenium* to the actual main content for hierarchy extraction (see Section 4.4). The number of nodes for which the rendered style needs to be extracted can be reduced by approximately 69% in the German sample and by approximately 71% in the English sample.

After the MCS is identified, the tree is traversed to identify a node covering at least 85% (this threshold is variable) of the characters of the MCS. Once this node is identified, all descendants are classified as *Content*. This decision is justified by the findings in Section 3: T&Cs are usually continuous texts often structured into a container (e.g. a `<div>`) by content management systems.

The selection of the right (domain-specific) threshold is crucial for the success of this extraction algorithm. A threshold too low can result in only a part of the main content being extracted; a threshold too high can make it impossible to find a node covering the given amount of MCS characters

[7] https://github.com/lxml/lxml/

[8] https://github.com/tsproisl/SoMaJo/

[9] https://github.com/saffsd/langid.py

and thereby triggering a fallback solution described later. After investigating the MCS (*Naïve Style and Short Text Exclusion*) coverage of the nodes holding the main content and the next largest child in the German and English samples from Section 3, the lower bound of the interval of possible threshold values is found to be limited to approximately 83.65% by the English sample (lowest MCS coverage of the next largest MCS coverage in a main content's child node). The upper bound of this interval is defined by the lowest coverage of the main content node above 83.65%, which can also be found in the English sample with a value of approximately 91.01%. Therefore, the threshold is set to 85%.

In some rare cases, the algorithm will not find a node covering at least 85% of the MCS, as the webpage does not use a dedicated container to hold the main content. Instead, individual containers for each of the paragraphs are placed as direct descendants of the `<body>` node. By identifying the longest subsequence containing the MCS, one can most likely extract the main content while excluding boilerplate content like the navigation bar and footer. This fallback solution provides much worse results than the actual content extraction algorithm.

We call the extraction algorithm *LowestCommonAncestorExtractor*

4.4 Hierarchy Extraction

The hierarchy extraction is based on the idea presented by Manabe and Tajima (2015). The visual style of the text is used to identify headings and their associated text blocks. In some cases, T&Cs are also structured using enumerations or a combination of visual style and enumerations (see Figure 1). Thus, this information needs to be considered, too. For the actual hierarchy extraction information from both, the enumerations and the visual styles, need to be taken into account in a rule-based approach in order to produce accurate results. Information from the DOM tree does not provide reliable information on the hierarchy. Given the data from Figure 1, the hierarchy extraction algorithm will focus on visual features and use numeric patterns for verification and adjustments.

In a first step, the DOM (sub-)tree identified as the main content is converted to a list of content blocks where each block has its own style. A block is a sequence of characters ending with a forced newline. This forced newline could be a `<br>` tag, the start or end of a paragraph (`<p>`), or any other element with `block` as the standard level for the `display` property. The style of a block corresponds to the style that the majority of the characters in it are part of (excluding the anchor tag `<a>`).

The style attached to a block is determined by extracting the rendered style retrieved through *Selenium*. The style is defined by font-decorations, font-weight, font-size, font-family and font-color.

For each of the blocks, possible enumeration patterns are identified and attached to the blocks by using the following regular expression:

```
\s[\(§]?(([IVXLivxl]{1,7})|
([0-9]{1,2})|[a-zA-Z])
([\.\-,:](([IVXLivxl]{1,7})|
([0-9]{1,2})|[a-zA-Z]))*[\-:\.)]?
\s
```

Arabic enumeration Arabic numbers are the most common enumeration used in the domain of T&C structuring. They can easily be extracted from a string and transformed into an integer representation.

Roman enumeration Since in a few cases Roman numerals were also used for numbering, these must be converted into Arabic numerals. In all investigated cases Roman numerals were not bigger than 20. By limiting the allowed Roman enumeration characters to *I*, *V*, *X* and *L*, the risk of mixing up alphabetic and roman enumeration can be reduced, as *I* would only be used in alphabetic enumerations larger than 8.

Alphabetic enumeration As alphabetic enumeration is only applicable for single characters, there is no need for extensive conversion. Letters are mapped to their position in the alphabet.

Lists `<li>` elements are automatically separated into blocks, however, enumerations rendered by the browsers when using `<ol>` tags are not part of the textual content of the blocks. Thus, the information about list enumerations is attached to the block as regular enumeration information.

The following assumptions by Manabe and Tajima (2015) are used as a basis for the visual hierarchy extraction:

1. headings appear at the beginning of the corresponding blocks

2. headings are given prominent visual styles
3. headings of the same level share the same visual style

A section's start is identified by determining its headline, i.e. a line with a different style than the MCS identified during content extraction. A headline is only allowed a maximum of 10 words. The section ends whenever the next line styled like the current section's headline occurs. The content in between these two lines forms the provisionally content of the upper headline. Each of the identified sections is then grouped into subsections using the same algorithm (see Appendix, Algorithm 1) until no more prominent style is visible in between two headlines. Assuming, that no section is interrupted by another section and later continued, content in between two headlines, respectively the last headline and the end of the main content, is assumed to be the content of the upper headline.

Enumerations extracted during the conversion to the block list are used to correct and validate the existing hierarchy which was extracted visual features. In the first step, the blocks assigned to each of the visually separated sections are examined for possible numerical hierarchies. List enumerations are treated in a special way, as we allow them to interrupt a section that is continued after the list element blocks. Given that the section can be divided into further subsections based on the enumeration patterns found in the blocks, these subsections are processed in the same way. After the initial enumeration-based segmentation within the nodes' content blocks, all headlines on the same level of the tree are checked for enumeration patterns. If there are different enumeration patterns on one level, the tree is modified in order to have consistent enumeration.

An enumeration pattern is only considered if there are at least two consecutive numberings of that pattern whose numerical values reflect a valid step. Invalid steps or enumeration patterns occurring only once are most likely to be detected due to an error in the enumeration detection and thus ignored.

4.5 Target Format

The tree-like results from content and hierarchy extraction are converted to JSON after being segmented and tokenized.

	too late	too early	correct
start	3	0	46
end	0	2	47

Table 1: Extraction performance for the LowestCommonAncestorExtractor on the test set. 49 out of 50 web pages in the test set could be processed.

5 Evaluation

The performance of the developed algorithms is evaluated in this section. Besides the sample used to derive the requirements, there is also another sample to evaluate the library to prelude overfitting.

5.1 Content Extraction

The content extraction algorithms were tested with a focus on the correct identification of the start and end of the content, as the center is always identified correctly given the functionality of the previously introduced *LowestCommonAncestorExtractor* with *NaïveStyle*, *ShortTextExclusion*, and a threshold of 85%. The results of the evaluation are shown in Table 1.

During the evaluation, the following three reasons were identified as the main drivers of extraction errors: (1) **threshold too high**: Whenever the threshold is too high for the page, the fallback algorithm is triggered; (2) **no container for main content**: Whenever the T&C page lacks a container wrapping the whole main content, the fallback algorithm is triggered; (3) use of different tags: The NaïveStyle approach cannot handle the usage of different tags rendering to the same actual style used for the main content. If one of the tags is held in its own container, as often is the case in lists, only this container is extracted.

However, the *LowestCommonAncestorExtractor* performed significantly better than the previously examined extractors, as shown in Tables 2 and 3.

5.2 Hierarchy Extraction

The hierarchy extraction algorithm was, similar to the content extraction, evaluated with the sample used to derive requirements and a test sample created for the purpose of evaluation. Errors arising from a failed content extraction are ignored in this section, as they provide no information on the quality of the algorithm applied during hierarchy extraction.

The algorithm showed good results (see Ap-

	too late	too early	correct	processing error
LowestCommonAncestorExtractor	**1**	3	**45**	**1**
Boilerpipe ArticleExtractor	16	4	24	6
Boilerpipe LargestContentExtractor	29	2	13	6
Boilerpipe CanolaExtractor	7	15	22	6
JusText	6	11	25	6
Trafilatura	5	**2**	37	6

Table 2: Performance of detecting the start of T&Cs (for "correct", higher numbers are better, for all others, lower numbers are better).

	too late	too early	correct	processing error
LowestCommonAncestorExtractor	**3**	2	**44**	**1**
Boilerpipe ArticleExtractor	23	13	8	6
Boilerpipe LargestContentExtractor	32	**1**	11	6
Boilerpipe CanolaExtractor	**3**	27	14	6
JusText	8	15	19	6
Trafilatura	5	4	35	6

Table 3: Performance of detecting the end of T&Cs (for "correct", higher numbers are better, for all others, lower numbers are better).

pendix A.2). In most cases, small extraction errors can be found in the hierarchy. However, their impact on the overall result can be described as minor. A precise analysis of the sources of errors showed the following reasons for erroneous hierarchy extraction:

1. Use of bold text: Some pages used bold text elements to highlight whole sections or just some blocks. This can screw up the whole result as the bold blocks might be identified as headlines.
2. Wrong enumeration: A surprisingly large amount of T&C pages contain errors in their enumerations. As the algorithm requires a strict sequence of numerations, this can lead to problems in the hierarchy extraction.
3. Violation of the assumption "Sections are not interrupted": The algorithms assume that there is no more content of a section after one of its subsections.
4. Use of tables: Whenever tables occurred on a page (often in the context of shipping costs), the algorithm separated each cell into its own block resulting in a large number of blocks with different styles. A high frequency of numbers occurring in the table worsened the results as the vast amount of detected enumeration patterns triggered further adjustments to the table.
5. Failed style extraction: In order to link the custom DOM tree structure to the Selenium tree, each DOM node is attached with its full XPath. As some pages render elements after a short time span, they may not be included in the parsed DOM tree. At the time the algorithm starts style extraction, new elements can render and tackle the validity of the XPath attached to the DOM node making the extracting of visual features impossible.

6 Conclusion

We introduced a new content extraction algorithm that performs better than existing solutions in its specific domain of T&C web pages. Since the algorithm is based on some domain-specific assumptions, it is unclear how successful it would operate on a generic web corpus. Further research in the field could answer this question. Initial small tests looked promising under the assumption that the content of the page is not interrupted. The style extraction, which is currently based on *Selenium* can be considered the performance bottleneck, as retrieving certain CSS properties takes a rather long time. One should look for a more efficient solution to extract the rendered style. In addition, several content extraction threads can operate in parallel. The general functionality of the rule-based approach to hierarchy extraction could be demonstrated. The general idea of Manabe and Tajima (2015) was extended by an enumeration detection due to the frequent usage of enumerations to structure T&C pages. It is much more difficult to achieve similar success rates in hierarchy extraction as with content extraction, due to the many irregularities in visual representation. This is probably due to the fact that the operators of different online shops often want to highlight very different elements from the contract text visually. In cases where such outliers do not occur in the visual representation, hierarchy extraction yields good results.

Acknowledgements

The project was supported by funds of the Federal Ministry for the Environment, Nature Conservation, Nuclear Safety and Consumer Protection (BMUV) based on a decision of the Parliament of the Federal Republic of Germany via the Federal Office for Agriculture and Food (BLE) under the innovation support programme.

References

Yannis Bakos, Florencia Marotta-Wurgler, and David Trossen. 2014. Does anyone read the fine print? consumer attention to standard-form contracts. *The Journal of Legal Studies*, 43:1–35.

Adrien Barbaresi. 2019. Generic web content extraction with open-source software. In *Proceedings of the 15th Conference on Natural Language Processing, KONVENS 2019, Erlangen, Germany, October 9-11, 2019*.

Marco Baroni, Francis Chantree, Adam Kilgarriff, and Serge Sharoff. 2008. Cleaneval: A competition for cleaning web pages.

Daniel Braun. 2021. *Automatic Semantic Analysis, Legal Assessment, and Summarization of Standard Form Contracts*. Ph.D. thesis, Technical University of Munich.

Daniel Braun and Florian Matthes. 2020. Automatic detection of terms and conditions in german and english online shops. In *16th International Conference on Web Information Systems and Technologies, WEBIST 2020*. SciTePress.

Daniel Braun and Florian Matthes. 2021. NLP for consumer protection: Battling illegal clauses in German terms and conditions in online shopping. In *Proceedings of the 1st Workshop on NLP for Positive Impact*, pages 93–99, Online. Association for Computational Linguistics.

John Gibson, Ben Wellner, and Susan Lubar. 2007. Adaptive web-page content identification. pages 105–112.

Francisco Viveros Jiménez, Miguel A. Sánchez-Pérez, Helena Gómez-Adorno, J. Posadas-Durán, G. Sidorov, and Alexander Gelbukh. 2018. Improving the boilerpipe algorithm for boilerplate removal in news articles using html tree structure. *Computación y Sistemas*, 22.

Adam Kilgarriff. 2007. Last words: Googleology is bad science. *Computational Linguistics*, 33(1):147–151.

Christian Kohlschütter, Peter Fankhauser, and Wolfgang Nejdl. 2010. Boilerplate detection using shallow text features. pages 441–450.

Gaël Lejeune and Lichao Zhu. 2018. A new proposal for evaluating web page cleaning tools. *Computación y Sistemas*, 22.

Marco Lippi, Przemysław Pałka, Giuseppe Contissa, Francesca Lagioia, Hans-Wolfgang Micklitz, Giovanni Sartor, and Paolo Torroni. 2019. Claudette: an automated detector of potentially unfair clauses in online terms of service. *Artificial Intelligence and Law*, 27(2):117–139.

Marco Lui, Timothy Baldwin, and Nicta Vrl. 2021. Cross-domain feature selection for language identification.

Tomohiro Manabe and Keishi Tajima. 2015. Extracting logical hierarchical structure of html documents based on headings. *Proceedings of the VLDB Endowment*, 8:1606–1617.

Jeff Pasternack and Dan Roth. 2009. Extracting article text from the web with maximum subsequence segmentation. pages 971–980.

Jan Pomikálek. 2011. *Removing boilerplate and duplicate content from web corpora*. Ph.D. thesis, Masaryk University, Faculty of informatics, Brno, Czech Republic.

Hiroyuki Sano, Shun Shiramatsu, Tadachika Ozono, and Toramatsu Shintani. 2021. A web page segmentation method based on page layouts and title blocks.

Egon Stemle. 2009. The krdwrd annotation framework – gathering training data for sweeping web pages: the canola corpus.

A Appendix

A.1 Hierarchy Extraction Algorithm

Algorithm 1: Extract hierarchy based on headlines (recursive).

```
Input: List of blocks (blockList)
Result: Children of a Node
/* Determine headline style of
   current level and gather all
   headlines on this current level.
   */
headlineStyle ← getNextHeadlineStyle(blockList);
headlineList ← [];
for block in blockList do
    if block.style = headlineStyle then
        headlineList.append(block);
    end
end
/* Create children list for current
   node by adding the blocks
   associated to the current node
   and by extracting the lower
   level nodes.                    */
children ← [];
children.append(blockList[0 : headlineList[0].index];
for headline in headlineList do
    cChildren ←
      extractHierarchy(blockList[(headline.index +
      1) : headline.next.index];
    children.append(Node(headline, cChildren));
end
return children;
```

Error Score	German	English
0	12	5
(0; 0.05]	12	4
(0.05; 0.1]	1	1
(0.1; 0.15]	2	2
(0.15; 0.2]	1	0
(0.2; 0.3]	1	0
(0.3; 0.5]	1	1
(0.5; 1]	0	0
Failed	0	6

Table 4: Distribution of error scores for the hierarchy extraction of the German and English requirements sample.

A.2 Hierarchy Extraction

The deviations of the hierarchy extraction algorithm from the expected results are determined by assigning the following scores to the extracted nodes:

- 0: each section with correct parent, correct content, and correct title
- 0.4: wrong parent
- 0.5: wrong content
- 0.1: wrong title

As different T&C pages contain different amounts of sections, the score is divided by the total amount of sections identified by the algorithm. An error score of 0 accounts for a perfect extraction.

The meaning of the brackets used in Tables 4 and 5 is the following:

$$x \in [a; b) \mid x \geq a \wedge x < b$$

Error Score	German	English
0	8	9
(0; 0.05]	11	3
(0.05; 0.1]	1	2
(0.1; 0.15]	1	1
(0.15; 0.2]	1	2
(0.2; 0.3]	1	2
(0.3; 0.5]	5	1
(0.5; 1]	0	0
Failed	2	0

Table 5: Distribution of error scores for the hierarchy extraction of the German and English test sample.

"Does it come in black?"
CLIP-like models are zero-shot recommenders

Patrick John Chia[*]
Coveo, Montreal
pchia@coveo.com

Jacopo Tagliabue
Coveo Labs, New York
jtagliabue@coveo.com

Federico Bianchi
Bocconi University, Milan

Ciro Greco
Coveo Labs, New York

Diogo Goncalves
Farfetch, Porto

Abstract

Product discovery is a crucial component for online shopping. However, item-to-item recommendations today do not allow users to explore changes along selected dimensions: given a query item, can a model suggest something similar *but* in a different color? We consider item recommendations of the *comparative* nature (e.g. "something darker") and show how CLIP-based models can support this use case in a zero-shot manner. Leveraging a large model built for fashion, we introduce `GradREC` and its industry potential, and offer a first rounded assessment of its strength and weaknesses.

1 Introduction

Recommender systems (RSs) are one of the most ubiquitous applications of machine learning (ML) in e-commerce (Tsagkias et al., 2020), recently featuring novel benchmarks and extensive use of deep neural networks in item-to-item, user-to-item, and comparison RSs (de Souza Pereira Moreira et al., 2019; Chia et al., 2021; Tagliabue et al., 2021). While details differ between neural architectures, they all share the principle that products are represented as points in a latent space, learned from user behavior, item meta-data or a combination of both (Bianchi et al., 2021c; Yi et al., 2019). Fig. 1 represents item-to-item recommendations *as movements in the product space*: starting from a query item – the *white dress* –, RSs help shoppers to move either around their current location, or "jump" to a different one. Adding to the blooming literature on substitute, complementary, popularity and exploration-based RSs (Chen et al., 2020; Hao et al., 2020; Ramachandran, 2020; Barraza-Urbina, 2017), *this* work presents `GradREC`, a new type of recommendation that introduces explicit directionality into the mix, by allowing exploration in selected directions *through natural language*: "something darker" will move the user from the *white dress* to the *grey dress*. In particular, we summarize our contributions as follows: **First**, we introduce `GradREC` as a new type of recommendation experience *and* a technical contribution – to the best of our knowledge, `GradREC` is the first *zero-shot* approach for language-based comparative recommendations, showing that CLIP-like (Radford et al., 2021) models may enable recommendations to be generated on the fly *without the need of explicitly defined labels for training* or behavioral data. **Second**, we devise both qualitative and quantitative evaluations to offer a first rounded assessment of the strengths and weaknesses of our proposal, and supplement our analysis with extensive visual examples. **Third**, as part of our submission, we release to the community our fine-tuned weights, publish an interactive web-app for exploration, and open source our code to help reproducing our findings and building on them [1].

While we present our results as a *preliminary* investigation into the untapped capabilities of CLIP for retail, we *do* believe our methods to be interesting to a broad set of practitioners: those exploring recommendations for conversational and interactive commerce, and those leveraging deep learning for horizontally scalable SaaS products[2]. Finally, while motivated by very practical concerns, this work contains new insights on the topology of the information encoded by over-parameterized neural networks, which could help our understanding of the kind of regularities that these models learn about our world.

[*] GradRECS started as a (failed) experiment by JT; PC actually made it work, and he is the lead researcher on the project. FB, CG and DC all contributed to the paper, providing support for modelling, industry context and domain knowledge. PC and JT are the corresponding authors.

[1] Artifacts are available at `https://github.com/patrickjohncyh/gradient-recs`.

[2] As a context for this global market, Algolia and Bloomreach both raised more than USD200M in the last two years (Techcrunch, 2021; Bloomreach, 2022), and Coveo raised more than CAD200M with its IPO (Marotta, 2021).

Proceedings of The Fifth Workshop on e-Commerce and NLP (ECNLP 5), pages 191 - 198
May 26, 2022 ©2022 Association for Computational Linguistics

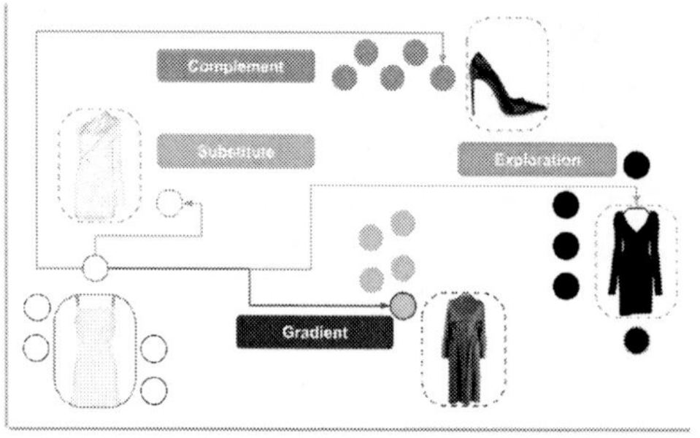

Figure 1: Recommendation as movements in the latent space, starting from a query item (*red*): substitute, complementary and exploration-based strategies are depicted in orange, blue and violet; GradREC is in gray.

2 An Industry Perspective

The intersection of product recommendation and natural language is a blooming research area: advances in neural NLP have been recently used for content-based recommendations (Iqbal et al., 2018), cold-start scenarios (Tagliabue et al., 2020), language grounding (Bianchi et al., 2021b,a), and explainable RSs (Chen et al., 2021). A relatively new use case is provided by the growth in the market of interactive technologies, as intelligent virtual assistants (IVAs) are expected to handle recommendations that increasingly encompass the expressiveness of natural language (Jannach et al., 2021). While interaction is an opportunity, the limited real estate available to display recommendations is a constraint for IVAs (Lin et al., 2021): since scrolling is limited, strategies for moving from one product to another (as in Fig. 1) are crucial for IVAs market penetration. In *this* work, we consider recommendations which are of the *comparative* form: given an item of focus – in a chat, a product page, etc. –, the shopper makes use of natural language queries to retrieve a second item (e.g. "shorter", "darker", etc.), related to the first but different along the specified attribute. While state-of-the-art IVAs can already provide very simple recommendations through language (Amazon, 2022), we are the first to suggest the existence of an entire new dimension and depth to mimic the interactions typical of a real-life shopping experience.

When thinking about applying this method in a multi-tenant SaaS context, it is worth noting how small are the assumptions GradREC actually makes about the underlying inventory: while in the case of FashionCLIP and its dataset it is true that products often contain information about an attribute's intensity (e.g. "knee-length shorts"), the *relationship* between them is not explicitly encoded, yet it is inferred by GradREC. Moreover, when applying these models across new catalogs, there is no guarantee descriptions would be as rich, or even using the same lexicon to describe the same attribute ("bermudas" vs "knee-length"). These considerations further highlight the strength of using a latent space derived from a general and flexible multi-modal model, and the non-trivial nature of extracting comparative recommendations.

3 Related Work

Our work sits at the intersection of various recent technical advances in *latent space manipulation* and *iterative IR*. Many recent works explore latent space manipulation of Generative Adversarial Networks (GANs) for purposes of fine-grained image editing (Shen et al., 2020; Patashnik et al., 2021); Jahanian et al. (2020) also studied latent space traversal in GANs to measure GAN generalization. We extend this line of research by providing a clear e-commerce use case, a focus shift from generative modeling to recommendation, and new insights on CLIP-based representations.

The idea of iterative search refinement using comparative information and attribute ranking is not new (Kovashka et al., 2012; Yu and Grauman, 2015). However, previous work sit in the standard *fully supervised* "learning-to-rank" tradition. Conversely, our approach operates in a zero-shot fashion by using *both* CLIP retrieval and CLIP representations to generate suggestions on-the-fly. Finally, our work builds on top of the recent wave of contrastive-based methods for representational learning: while latent product representations have been extensively studied from multiple angles (Bianchi et al., 2020; Xu et al., 2020), CLIP-like models are still very new in this domain: *GradREC* leverages the space learned by FashionCLIP, a fashion-fine tuning of the original CLIP (Chia et al., 2022).

4 Gradient Recs

4.1 Overview

GradREC, builds upon the multi-modal space induced by FashionCLIP. GradREC aims to traverse the latent space such that the intensity of an attribute of interest varies monotonically for products along that path, allowing us to make fine-grained recommendations that require comparative knowledge. There are independently grounded reasons to expect this method to work. *First*, we have solid evidence that embedding spaces are able to encode recognizable "concepts" (e.g. lexical knowledge in *word2vec* (Mikolov et al., 2013), facial expressions in GANs (Ding et al., 2018)). *Second*, we perform an extensive evaluation of the `FashionCLIP` product space, focusing on attributes such as *color* and *occasion*: our qualitative assessment (Section 4.2) verified that embeddings are indeed often clustered, further suggesting that movements in the "concept space" can be represented as paths in the latent space.

4.2 FashionCLIP exploration

As discussed in Section 4.1, there are pre-existing theoretical reasons to think that embedding spaces encode in their geometry interesting regularities. In order to validate this hypothesis, we run visual investigations on `FashionCLIP` space as seen in Figure 2, which shows TSNE projections of product image embeddings for four attributes: Pants Length, Shirt Color, Heel Height and Occasion. For each attribute, we retrieve products possessing negative, neutral and positive attribute intensities. Figure 2 demonstrates that the projected products from the corresponding attribute intensities do indeed form meaningful clusters, suggesting that it is possible to trace a path from one cluster to another in the latent space.

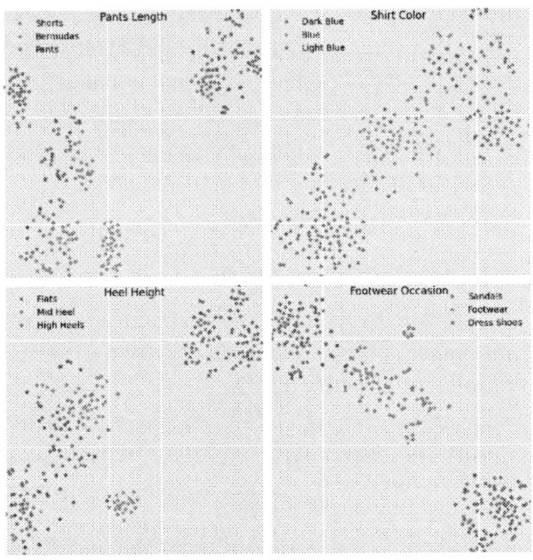

Figure 2: Sample TSNE projections of product image vectors: products are colored based on attribute strength.

4.3 Method

In what follows, we focus on the core task of gradient recommendations[3]. Assuming a target inventory of fashion products, a starting item and a pair of natural language queries whose difference captures the comparative dimension of interest (e.g. the difference between "dark red shirt" and "red shirt" captures the dimension of "darker"[4]), `GradREC` should return a new item in the "same style" as the starting item, varying along the specified dimension; in particular, `GradREC` can leverage CLIP representations but has no access to labels or co-purchasing data. Providing now a formal description, we decompose our approach into two components: a *traversal function*, $\mathbf{\Phi}$ and a *traversal direction vector*, $\mathbf{v}_c$.

Traversal Function: given a product t, represented in the CLIP space by either its L2 normalized textual vector $\mathbf{t}_t$ or image vector $\mathbf{i}_t$, and some attribute c we want to explore, our goal is to compute a function $\mathbf{\Phi}$, such that given a starting point $\mathbf{v}_t$ and some vector $\mathbf{v}_c$, returns a new point $\mathbf{v}_{t+1}$ in the latent space that is increasing or decreasing in strength of attribute c. Given the new position $\mathbf{v}_{t+1}$, we use cosine-based k-nearest neighbors $(KNN(\cdot,\cdot))$ to retrieve suggested products: if we iterate this process, we would travel along the dimension of attribute c, discovering products as we move along. We define $\mathbf{\Phi}$ as vector addition, with a scale factor λ to control step size; additionally, we use the mean of the current point's nearest neighbours $(K\bar{N}N(\mathbf{v}_t, k))$ as a regularizing term. The two terms are balanced by taking a convex combination of the direction vector and the regularizing term. In our notation, $\hat{\mathbf{v}}$ refers to $\mathbf{v}$ normalized to unit length. Note that all vectors are of dimension 512. Our definition is summarized in Eq.1:

$$\begin{aligned}\mathbf{v}_{t+1} &= \mathbf{\Phi}(\mathbf{v}_t, \mathbf{v}_c) \\ &= \mathbf{v}_t + (1-\rho)\cdot\lambda\hat{\mathbf{v}}_c \\ &\quad + \rho \cdot K\bar{N}N(\mathbf{v}_t, k)\end{aligned} \tag{1}$$

Traversal Vector: the construction of $\mathbf{v}_c$ relies on two main ingredients. First, given a pair of

[3]We realize that a more ecological setting – such as IVA – would require additional steps to handle stateful interactions: those steps are however general open problems in IVA, whose solution is independent of the interaction we model here.

[4]Different ecological settings may provide these queries more or less explicitly; `GradREC` may be used naturally in the context of multi-turn systems such as IVAs, or, for example, as support to standard manually defined facets for IR use cases, such as product search.

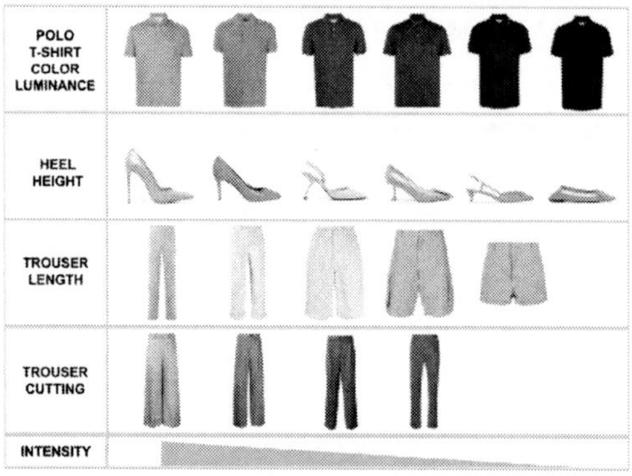

Figure 3: A sample of the qualitative results obtained by applying GradREC for four different attributes: the *intensity / strength* of the attribute decreases from left to right.

queries which semantically captures the attribute c ("darker"), we use the zero-shot retrieval capabilities of FashionCLIP to construct two small datasets: one comprising the image embeddings closest to the FashionCLIP encoding of the neutral class ("a blue shirt"), and one from an exemplar class for c ("a dark blue shirt"). We define the retrieved image vectors for the neutral and exemplar prompts as $\mathbf{I}_n = \{\mathbf{i}_n^1 ... \mathbf{i}_n^M\}$ and $\mathbf{I}_e = \{\mathbf{i}_e^1 ... \mathbf{i}_e^N\}$ respectively. Second, we adopt the channel importance measure from Wu et al. (2021) to determine channels[5] which encode the differences between the neutral class and exemplar class. The method measures the channel-wise Signal-to-Noise Ratio (SNR) between the mean neutral class vector (i.e. $\bar{\mathbf{I}}_n$) and the exemplar class vectors (i.e. $\{\mathbf{i}_e^1 ... \mathbf{i}_e^N\}$). The intuition is that channels with high SNR correspond to channels which encode the differences between images from the neutral and exemplar class, and hence the attribute c. Our implementation departs from theirs by retaining the sign of the differences for each channel. Finally, to obtain $\mathbf{v}_c$, we normalize the vector formed by the channel-wise SNR values[6].

5 Experiments

To investigate GradREC strengths and weakness, we offer a preliminary assessment of its capabilities over important fashion dimensions, such as product discovery.

5.1 Dataset and Pre-trained Space

Our pre-trained space is FashionCLIP, an adaptation of CLIP obtained by fine-tuning the original embeddings over fashion products provided by *Farfetch*, a world leading platform for online luxury fashion shopping. The dataset comprises of over 800k fashion products across dozens of item types and more than 3k brands. In addition to a standard product image over white background, the dataset contains natural language descriptions of the stylistic properties (e.g., "cotton-blend", "high waist", "belt loops") and categorical information (e.g. "layered track shorts") of products[7]. FashionCLIP shares the same architecture as Radford et al. (2021), i.e. a multi-modal model comprising an image and a text encoder. We refer to Chia et al. (2022) for details on training and retrieval / classification capabilities: since FashionCLIP has independent value in the industry, GradREC does not require any *specific* pre-training.

5.2 Qualitative Analysis

We consider four different attributes of interest: *shirt color luminance*, *heel height*, *trouser length* and *trouser cutting*. For each attribute, we traverse the latent space between both extremes of the attribute of interest and present the results in Fig. 3 for visual validation. We observe that the products retrieved form a monotonic change in the attribute's strength that aligns well with human intuition: i.e. t-shirts in the first row do indeed follow a gradient going from lighter to darker shades of blue. It is interesting to note that the latent space of FashionCLIP appears to encode and organize these geometric and physical regularities despite not having been trained to do so explicitly, pointing to further questions about what and how these self-supervised models learn.

5.3 Quantitative Analysis

We quantitatively assess GradREC by measuring its efficiency in product discovery along an attribute of interest, to verify that the path it discovers is semantically meaningful. We generate three datasets ($N = 100$) using FashionCLIP retrieval capabilities to represent products from the negative, neu-

[5]Each channel corresponds to one of the 512 dimensions of an embedding.

[6]We refer the reader to Wu et al. (2021) for the original discussion.

[7]FashionCLIP weights and training code will be released with the original publication. At the moment of writing this paper, the original training dataset is scheduled to be released as well: please check https://github.com/Farfetch for updates.

tral and positive intensities of an attribute[8]. For example, to generate datasets for shirt color *luminance* we would issue the following queries – "dark blue polo shirt", "blue polo shirt", "light blue polo shirt" – to FashionCLIP and retrieve N products for each query. In Figure 4 we visualize a sample of the products retrieved for each of the above queries.

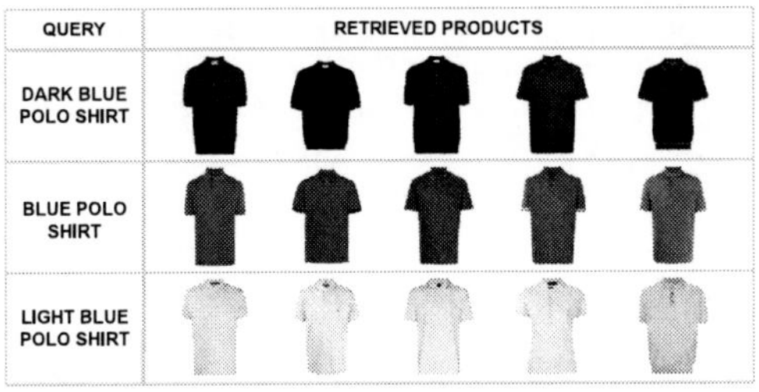

Figure 4: Products retrieved for queries on a spectrum of intensity.

We apply GradREC, starting a traversal from a negative product in the direction of neutral intensity products, simulating product discovery by logging the top $k = 10$ unseen products found at each step. We then compute the intersection cardinality of the three datasets along the simulated trajectory with a sliding window of 50 products: a model which traverses a meaningful path should produce three peaks, one for each level of intensity. As a baseline, we use visual similarity in the CLIP image-space (KNN over image embeddings) and simulate the product discovery trajectory as traversing the list of nearest neighbors of the same seed product in the order of increasing distance.

In Figure 5 we see the result of applying our analysis to the discovery path for *luminance* of blue polo shirts. We observe that GradREC explores well this path as seen by its three distinct modes of intersected products, where each peak for *light blue*, *blue* and *dark blue* respectively, corresponds to the correct *order* of decreasing luminance. Conversely, we see that visual similarity fails to produce a similar product discovery pattern as GradREC, which spans a wider range of the luminance spectrum. In fact, visual similarity struggles to discover products from *blue* and *light blue*, highlighting the merits of the directionality induced by GradREC (Appendix A.2).

[8]The exact definitions of negative and positive are relative; We are more concerned here with capturing the opposing extremes of an attribute's spectrum i.e. *dark* and *light*.

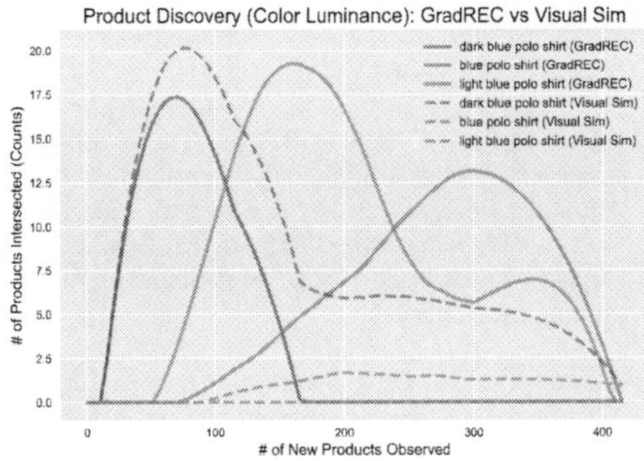

Figure 5: Quantitative analysis comparing GradREC to Visual Similiarty on product discovery for the attribute *color luminance* of blue shirts.

5.4 Limitations & Future Work

While GradREC performances are encouraging – especially when considering that no attribute has been explicitly taught –, limitations highlight several areas of improvement. First, the performance of the model is sensitive to the quality of the retrieval phase. For example, to construct $\mathbf{v}_c$ for *trouser length*, using queries "shorts" and "pants" yielded better performance than "shorts" and "bermudas". Second, our definition of $\mathbf{\Phi}$ is not optimal: as we traverse the image space, the cosine distance between our position and all the products increases, suggesting that we are not traversing the latent manifold in the most efficient way. Third, while we observe that GradREC moves in a semantically meaningful direction, it does not, nor is it currently designed to, provide guarantees on the monotonicity of the products it returns along the path. Finally, GradREC does not account for uncertainty and thus does not possess a confidence measure for its recommendations: while we may be confident in its ability with geometric and physical concepts, and less so for more abstract notions (e.g. "for colder weather"), it is hard to know *a priori* what GradREC does not know.

6 Conclusion

We introduced GradREC, a zero-shot approach for comparative recommendations, that showed promising results in our initial investigations. While further evaluation – especially, involving relevance judgments by humans – is needed to fully assess GradREC capabilities, we *do* believe that our work provides preliminary but novel insights into innovative application of large models in important industry use-cases.

References

Amazon. 2022. Style by Alexa.

Andrea Barraza-Urbina. 2017. The exploration-exploitation trade-off in interactive recommender systems. In *Proceedings of the Eleventh ACM Conference on Recommender Systems*, RecSys '17, page 431–435, New York, NY, USA. Association for Computing Machinery.

Federico Bianchi, Ciro Greco, and Jacopo Tagliabue. 2021a. Language in a (search) box: Grounding language learning in real-world human-machine interaction. In *Proceedings of the 2021 Conference of the North American Chapter of the Association for Computational Linguistics: Human Language Technologies*, pages 4409–4415, Online. Association for Computational Linguistics.

Federico Bianchi, J. Tagliabue, Bingqing Yu, Luca Bigon, and Ciro Greco. 2020. Fantastic embeddings and how to align them: Zero-shot inference in a multi-shop scenario. *ArXiv*, abs/2007.14906.

Federico Bianchi, Jacopo Tagliabue, and Bingqing Yu. 2021b. Query2Prod2Vec: Grounded word embeddings for eCommerce. In *Proceedings of the 2021 Conference of the North American Chapter of the Association for Computational Linguistics: Human Language Technologies: Industry Papers*, pages 154–162, Online. Association for Computational Linguistics.

Federico Bianchi, Bingqing Yu, and Jacopo Tagliabue. 2021c. BERT goes shopping: Comparing distributional models for product representations. In *Proceedings of The 4th Workshop on e-Commerce and NLP*, pages 1–12, Online. Association for Computational Linguistics.

Bloomreach. 2022. With $175 million in funding, bloomreach is authoring the next chapter of e-commerce.

Hanxiong Chen, Xu Chen, Shaoyun Shi, and Yongfeng Zhang. 2021. Generate natural language explanations for recommendation. *CoRR*, abs/2101.03392.

Tong Chen, Hongzhi Yin, Guanhua Ye, Zi Huang, Yang Wang, and Meng Wang. 2020. *Try This Instead: Personalized and Interpretable Substitute Recommendation*, page 891–900. Association for Computing Machinery, New York, NY, USA.

Patrick John Chia, Giuseppe Attanasio, Federico Bianchi, Silvia Terragni, Ana Rita Magalhães, Diogo Goncalves, Ciro Greco, and Jacopo Tagliabue. 2022. Fashionclip: Connecting language and images for product representations.

Patrick John Chia, Bingqin Yu, and Jacopo Tagliabue. 2021. Are you sure?: Preliminary insights from scaling product comparisons to multiple shops. In *SIGIR eCom 2021*.

Gabriel de Souza Pereira Moreira, D. Jannach, and Adilson Marques da Cunha. 2019. On the importance of news content representation in hybrid neural session-based recommender systems. In *INRA@RecSys*.

Hui Ding, Kumar Sricharan, and Rama Chellappa. 2018. Exprgan: Facial expression editing with controllable expression intensity. *AAAI*.

Junheng Hao, Tong Zhao, Jin Li, Xin Luna Dong, Christos Faloutsos, Yizhou Sun, and Wei Wang. 2020. P-companion: A principled framework for diversified complementary product recommendation. In *Proceedings of the 29th ACM International Conference on Information & Knowledge Management*, CIKM '20, page 2517–2524, New York, NY, USA. Association for Computing Machinery.

Murium Iqbal, Adair Kovac, and Kamelia Aryafar. 2018. A multimodal recommender system for large-scale assortment generation in e-commerce. In *The SIGIR 2018 Workshop On eCommerce co-located with the 41st International ACM SIGIR Conference on Research and Development in Information Retrieval (SIGIR 2018), Ann Arbor, Michigan, USA, July 12, 2018*, volume 2319 of *CEUR Workshop Proceedings*. CEUR-WS.org.

Ali Jahanian, Lucy Chai, and Phillip Isola. 2020. On the "steerability" of generative adversarial networks. In *International Conference on Learning Representations*.

Dietmar Jannach, Ahtsham Manzoor, Wanling Cai, and Li Chen. 2021. A survey on conversational recommender systems. *ACM Comput. Surv.*, 54(5).

Adriana Kovashka, Devi Parikh, and Kristen Grauman. 2012. Whittlesearch: Image Search with Relative Attribute Feedback. In *Proceedings of the IEEE Conference on Computer Vision and Pattern Recognition (CVPR)*.

Ying Lin, Han Wang, Jiangning Chen, Tong Wang, Yue Liu, Heng Ji, Yang Liu, and Premkumar Natarajan. 2021. Personalized entity resolution with dynamic heterogeneous KnowledgeGraph representations. In *Proceedings of The 4th Workshop on e-Commerce and NLP*, pages 38–48, Online. Association for Computational Linguistics.

Stefanie Marotta. 2021. Canada's latest tech public debut swings amid soft ipos.

Tomas Mikolov, Wen-tau Yih, and Geoffrey Zweig. 2013. Linguistic regularities in continuous space word representations. In *Proceedings of the 2013 Conference of the North American Chapter of the Association for Computational Linguistics: Human Language Technologies*, pages 746–751, Atlanta, Georgia. Association for Computational Linguistics.

Or Patashnik, Zongze Wu, Eli Shechtman, Daniel Cohen-Or, and Dani Lischinski. 2021. Styleclip: Text-driven manipulation of stylegan imagery. In *Proceedings of the IEEE/CVF International Conference on Computer Vision (ICCV)*, pages 2085–2094.

Alec Radford, Jong Wook Kim, Chris Hallacy, Aditya Ramesh, Gabriel Goh, Sandhini Agarwal, Girish Sastry, Amanda Askell, Pamela Mishkin, Jack Clark, Gretchen Krueger, and Ilya Sutskever. 2021. Learning transferable visual models from natural language supervision. In *ICML*.

Lakshmi Ramachandran. 2020. *Behavior-Based Popularity Ranking on Amazon Video*, page 564–565. Association for Computing Machinery, New York, NY, USA.

Yujun Shen, Jinjin Gu, Xiaoou Tang, and Bolei Zhou. 2020. Interpreting the latent space of gans for semantic face editing. In *CVPR*.

Jacopo Tagliabue, Ciro Greco, Jean-Francis Roy, Federico Bianchi, Giovanni Cassani, Bingqing Yu, and Patrick John Chia. 2021. Sigir 2021 e-commerce workshop data challenge. In *SIGIR eCom 2021*.

Jacopo Tagliabue, Bingqing Yu, and Federico Bianchi. 2020. *The Embeddings That Came in From the Cold: Improving Vectors for New and Rare Products with Content-Based Inference*, page 577–578. Association for Computing Machinery, New York, NY, USA.

Techcrunch. 2021. Search api startup algolia raises $150 million at $2.25 billion valuation.

Manos Tsagkias, Tracy Holloway King, Surya Kallumadi, Vanessa Murdock, and Maarten de Rijke. 2020. Challenges and research opportunities in ecommerce search and recommendations. In *SIGIR Forum*, volume 54.

Zongze Wu, Dani Lischinski, and Eli Shechtman. 2021. Stylespace analysis: Disentangled controls for stylegan image generation. In *IEEE Conference on Computer Vision and Pattern Recognition, CVPR 2021, virtual, June 19-25, 2021*, pages 12863–12872. Computer Vision Foundation / IEEE.

Da Xu, Chuanwei Ruan, Evren Korpeoglu, Sushant Kumar, and Kannan Achan. 2020. *Product Knowledge Graph Embedding for E-Commerce*, page 672–680. Association for Computing Machinery, New York, NY, USA.

Xinyang Yi, Ji Yang, Lichan Hong, Derek Zhiyuan Cheng, Lukasz Heldt, Aditee Ajit Kumthekar, Zhe Zhao, Li Wei, and Ed Chi, editors. 2019. *Sampling-Bias-Corrected Neural Modeling for Large Corpus Item Recommendations*.

A. Yu and K. Grauman. 2015. Just noticeable differences in visual attributes. In *2015 IEEE International Conference on Computer Vision (ICCV)*, pages 2416–2424, Los Alamitos, CA, USA. IEEE Computer Society.

A Appendix

A.1 A worked-out traversal example

Fig. 6 showcases an example of successful traversal when using the methods in Section 4.3 applied to skirt length. In particular, we can see the query item, an intermediate one and a final one, along the path of products that was traced (the path of products are denoted by $\times$ markers, and the order of observation/direction of traversal is denoted by the darker to lighter hue). Note that a simple visual similarity search would have moved us from the first query item to a nearby region.

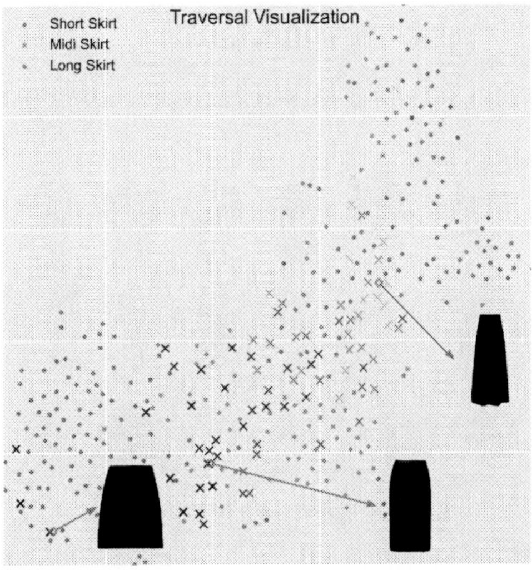

Figure 6: TSNE Projection of 3 ranges of skirt lengths and the traversed product path by GradREC along the attribute *skirt length* as shown by $\times$ markers (dark to light denotes direction of traversal). Corresponding product images along the traversed path are visualized.

A.2 Additional Experiments

We ran our product discovery analysis for the attribute *heel height* and report the result in Fig. 7.

A similar pattern as Fig. 5 emerges with GradREC having three peaks and Visual Similarity struggling to discover "high heel". Unlike Fig. 5, however, we observe a lower cardinality of intersection for GradREC and "women's high heels", since GradREC preserves the style of the seed product (red colored shoes, in this example) while the products retrieved by "women's high heels" are of varying color.

We also provide additional qualitative examples in Fig. 8. We observe GradREC working across colors, in different product sortals (e.g., Dress), and having the ability to preserve visual style (e.g., Denim).

In Fig. 9, we instead give an example of the limitations of GradREC. Indeed, we see a failure mode where GradREC, while increasing the strength of

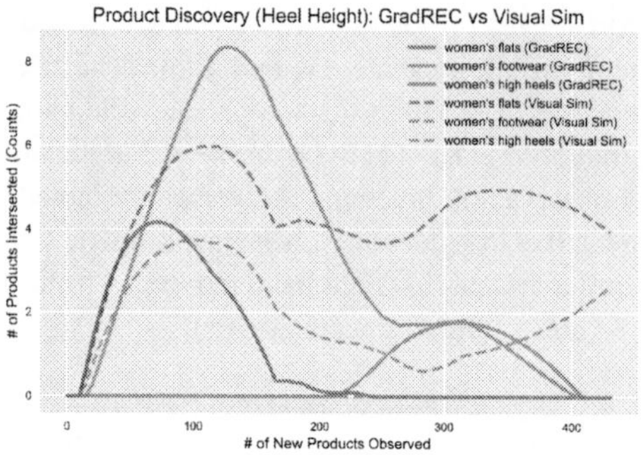

Figure 7: Product discovery analysis for *heel height*.

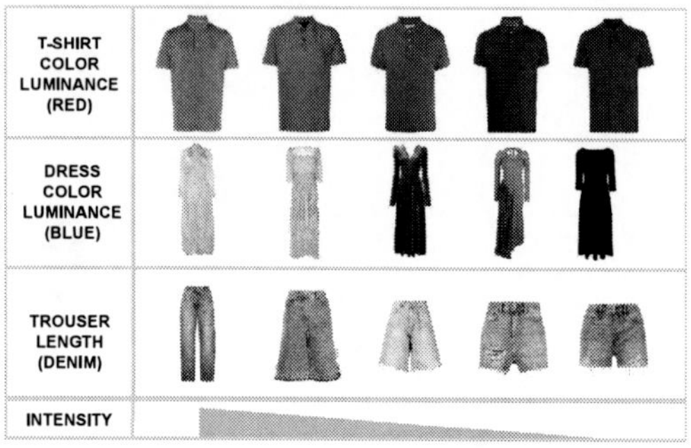

Figure 8: Extra qualitative examples.

formality correctly, is however unable to preserve the visual style of the footwear correctly. As we have highlighted in Section 5.4, `GradREC` performance is sensitive to the initial dataset retrieval performance: in this instance, the query "formal shoes" retrieves predominantly black, leather dress-shoes, thereby steering the traversal in that direction.

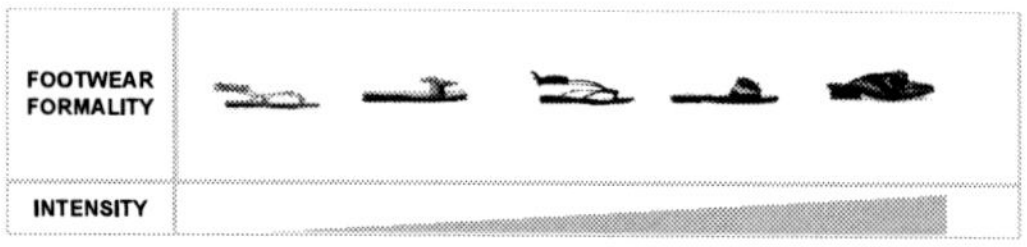

Figure 9: Failure mode of `GradREC` for *formality* attribute. While *formality* is appropriately increased, the product changes visual appearance from pink to black.

Clause Topic Classification in German and English Standard Form Contracts

Daniel Braun
University of Twente
Department of High-tech Business
and Entrepreneurship
d.braun@utwente.nl

Florian Matthes
Technical University of Munich
Department of Informatics
matthes@tum.de

Abstract

So-called standard form contracts, i.e. contracts that are drafted unilaterally by one party, like terms and conditions of online shops or terms of services of social networks, are cornerstones of our modern economy. Their processing is, therefore, of significant practical value. Often, the sheer size of these contracts allows the drafting party to hide unfavourable terms from the other party. In this paper, we compare different approaches for automatically classifying the topics of clauses in standard form contracts, based on a data-set of more than 6,000 clauses from more than 170 contracts, which we collected from German and English online shops and annotated based on a taxonomy of clause topics, that we developed together with legal experts. We will show that, in our comparison of seven approaches, from simple keyword matching to transformer language models, BERT performed best with an F1-score of up to 0.91, however much simpler and computationally cheaper models like logistic regression also achieved similarly good results of up to 0.87.

1 Introduction

So-called standard form contracts, i.e. contracts that are drafted unilaterally by one party of the contract, usually a company, like terms and conditions of online shops or terms of services of social networks, are cornerstones of our modern economy. While the concept of a contract that is completely decided upon by one party might seem unfair and inherently flawed, its existence is a necessity in our modern economy. It would simply not be possible for companies like Amazon, Facebook or Google, to negotiate individual contract terms with each of their customers.

It is largely acknowledged, that most consumers do not read such contracts before buying something online or registering for a service. The actual share of consumers that regularly read such contracts ranges from as little as 3.5% (Plaut and Bartlett III, 2012) to 9% (Braun, 2021) in the literature. In acknowledgement of this fact, lawmakers around the world have tightly restricted the provisions that can be made by standard form contracts in a bid to protect consumers. This makes them an interesting subject for different Natural Language Processing (NLP) tasks, because they have a high economical and therefore practical relevance, but are still somewhat restricted with regard to their content. In this work, we use contracts that have been drafted under the jurisdiction of the European Union (EU). Many of the regulations applying to standard form contracts in this jurisdiction originate from the Council Directive 93/13/EEC of 5 April 1993 on unfair terms in consumer contracts.

While standard form contracts are relevant in almost all kinds of business-to-consumer transactions, like banking, insurances, and data processing, we here focus on Terms and Conditions (T&C) from online shops for three reasons: They have high economical relevance, they are publicly available in large quantities on the internet in a machine-readable format, and they are among the contracts which are least likely to be read, compared to a contract for life insurance, for example.

Being able to automatically classify the topics of clauses in T&C could help consumers to find relevant regulations faster and make more informed decisions, but it could also support legal professionals, like lawyers specialising in consumer protection law, in their work.

2 Related Work

Contract review is one of the main commercial applications of NLP in the legal domain (Dale, 2019). Unlike standard form contracts, "normal" contracts, i.e. contracts that have been negotiated by all contracting parties, allow for more variation and are less regulated, especially in business-to-business contexts. Therefore, building a taxonomy of clause

Proceedings of The Fifth Workshop on e-Commerce and NLP (ECNLP 5), pages 199 - 209

topics and performing topic classification (i.e. a supervised approach), would be less suitable for such contracts.

For reasons of data availability, most research projects use publicly available contracts, which happen to be standard form contracts, like T&C from online shops, Terms of Services (ToS) from online platforms, and, since the introduction of the General Data Protection Regulation (GDPR) in the EU, one particular focus has been on privacy policies. Although, legally, it is not settled whether they have a contractual status or not (Raysman and Brown, 2010), from an NLP perspective, they can be treated as a special variety of standard form contracts.

Most of the existing research on the analysis of standard form contracts is focusing on automatically finding void clauses. The CLAUDETTE project (Lippi et al., 2019), for example, focuses on finding so-called "unfair clauses", which are void under EU legislation, in ToS from large online platforms like Facebook or Netflix. Later, they also applied their approach to privacy policies (Liepina et al., 2019). Similarly, Braun and Matthes (2021) focus on finding void clauses in T&C from online shops by using a fine-tuned BERT model, in earlier work, they summarised specific aspects of T&C using an abstractive summarisation approach (Braun et al., 2017). In comparison to these works, which try to make a fully automated decision on the validity of clauses, the classification of clause topics could be used to support humans in the decision-making process, by helping them to find relevant clauses faster.

In the area of privacy policies, approaches are more diverse. Ravichander et al. (2019), for example, presented a Q&A system that can answer user questions about privacy policies. Binary assessments in classes like valid or void are less desirable in the domain of privacy policies where, especially before the introduction of the GDPR, much of what was legally allowed was still undesired by users.

3 Taxonomy

For a topic classification approach, i.e., a supervised approach, rather than an unsupervised topic modelling approach, a taxonomy of clause topics is needed. At first, this might seem like a limitation of the approach, because, in theory, a contract can regulate arbitrary aspects. In practice, however, standard form contracts underly strong limitations, because, under EU jurisdiction, clauses that are "unexpected" are automatically void under the Unfair Contract Terms Directive (93/13/EEC). Therefore, if a taxonomy is extensive enough, the information that a clause is not covered by one of the topics in the taxonomy is already important information in itself, because it means that the clause is very likely void.

To build such an extensive taxonomy for T&C from online shops, we used contract templates from legal literature (Sommer and von Stumm, 2017; Fingerhut, 2009) and industry associations (IHK Munich and Upper Bavaria, 2020; Schirmbacher, 2018), as well as a commercial T&C generator[1] and analysed which topics are present in these templates, because they are used by many online shops.

For each of these sources, two legal experts with experience in consumer protection law went through the templates and annotated each clause with one or more fitting topic and zero or more fitting subtopic label(s). In the end, the topic labels from the different annotators were aligned by the authors. By the combination of the above-described sources, we derived a taxonomy of 22 classes (topics) and 36 sub-classes (subtopics). The differentiation between topics and subtopics was mainly based on the structure of the sources, i.e. the organisation in sections and subsections in the templates. A topic, for example, could be "delivery" and subtopics could be the delivery time or the delivery costs.

To get an estimate of how extensive our taxonomy is, we used it to manually annotate more than 6.000 clauses from real T&C (see section 4). Of these more than 6,000 clauses, the taxonomy was able to cover 90.08%. The remaining clauses (336) fell into only two classes: 285 clauses contained information regarding vouchers and gift cards, and 51 clauses contained information about codes of conduct. We added both classes to the taxonomy. The final taxonomy, therefore, consists of 23 labels for topics and 37 labels for subtopics. All labels in the taxonomy are shown in Table 2.

4 Corpus

Since no corpus of topic-annotated clauses from T&C existed, we had to build our own corpus. For this, we parsed the list of merchants from two German price comparison websites ("Idealo"[2] and

[1] https://www.trustedshops.com

[2] www.idealo.de

"Geizhals"[3]) that also offer a localised version of their respective websites in English, targeted to the British market[4]. On these websites, shop operators manually report the URLs to their T&C, which we extracted with a web-crawler. We randomly selected 142 German T&C and 30 English T&C from these pages. Each clause from these contracts was subsequently copied into an Excel file, in which each row contains one clause. In addition to the text of the clause itself, each row contains a unique id, an id for the contract the clause belongs to, (if existing) the title of the superordinate paragraph and (if existing) the title of the clause.

4.1 Size

The corpus we built consists of 5,020 German clauses and 1,040 English clauses. In both languages, a contract, therefore, consists of roughly 35 clauses on average. All German clauses together consist of 351,903 words, which is an average of 2,478 words per contract (see Table 1). The English corpus contains 55,392 words which equals to an average of 1,846 words per contract. This means German clauses are, on average, significantly longer than English ones. 5,013 clauses (or 99.9% of all clauses) in the German corpus have a paragraph or clause title (or both), which we can use for the topic classification. In the English corpus, that is the case for 989 clauses or 95.1%.

4.2 Annotation

Each clause of both corpora was labelled with its topics and subtopics according to the taxonomy described in Section 3. First, each clause was labelled by a student using only the classes from the first level (topics) of the taxonomy. Then, where applicable, classes from the second level of the taxonomy (subtopics) were added. In a second step, this process was repeated by the authors, i.e., each clause was again first labelled with classes from the first level and then, where applicable, with classes from the second level. A clause can be labelled with more than one topic and subtopic. A clause can also be assigned to a topic without necessarily having to be assigned to a subtopic of it (but not the other way round). An example of such a clause from the corpus is "The warranty is subject to the relevant statutory provisions.", which is assigned the topic warranty, but not to one of its subtopics.

[3]www.geizhals.de

[4]www.idealo.co.uk, www.skinflint.co.uk

Cases where the two annotators disagreed, were presented to (and finally decided by) consumer protection lawyers with many years of experience in advising consumers. The inter-annotator agreement was relatively high at 87%, i.e., only 13% of all clauses had to be decided by the lawyers. In this way, four people together spend more than 100 hours and generated more than 24,000 labels, which were consolidated into two corpora, one for each language, with 11,777 labels in total. The distribution of topics and subtopics is shown in Table 2.

The annotation also revealed local differences, e.g., almost none of the English contracts contained a model withdrawal form, the only two that did contain such a form were from companies based in Germany, while many German contracts contained one. On the other hand, clauses about loyalty schemes were almost non-existing in German contracts and far more popular in the English corpus. It is worth reminding that our English data set was collected specifically from a UK perspective, i.e., the shops are either based in the UK or specifically targeted at the UK market. English contracts from other markets, like the USA or Australia, would most likely look very different. Since the T&C we annotated are protected by copyright law, we are, unfortunately, not able to publish the corpus.

5 Approaches

We compared seven different approaches to the classification of clause topics in standard form contracts from German and English online shops: Rule-based keyword matching, Logistic Regression, Random Forest, Multilayer Perceptron (MLP), Long short-term memory (LSTM), and Bidirectional Encoder Representations from Transformers (BERT). In the following sections, we will shortly introduce how we used the different approaches. For each of the approaches, we trained two classifiers, one which only classifies topics and one which only classifies the subtopics. Experiments we conducted with joint classification models, i.e., models that classify topics and subtopics at the same time turned out to decrease the classification quality for both, topics and subtopics.

We split both corpora into a training (80%) and a test (20%) set, using scikit-multilearn (Szymański and Kajdanowicz, 2017) to make sure the representation of labels is balanced between the training and the test set and reflects the original distribution.

	contracts	clauses	words	∅ clauses/contract	∅ words/contract
German	142	5,020	351,903	35	2,478
English	30	1,040	1,846	34	1,846

Table 1: Statistics on the German and English corpus

For the stochastic approaches, we performed a grid search with a k-fold cross-validation on the training data to find the optimal parameters for each approach.

Our initial hypothesis, based on similar research, was, that with increasing complexity of the models, the performance would also increase, i.e. we expected BERT to perform best, followed by LSTM, MLP, and the "classic" ML approaches.

5.1 Rule-based

As a baseline, we first developed a rule-based classification approach. We used a simple keyword-matching approach. For each topic and subtopic in the taxonomy, we asked the consumer protection lawyers to provide a list of keywords that are distinctive for the topic/subtopic. The list can contain independent keywords (OR), keywords that should appear together (AND), and keywords that should not appear (together) (NOT).

We pre-processed the clauses using SoMaJo (Proisl and Uhrig, 2016) to split the clauses into sentences and the sentences into tokens. Afterwards, we lemmatised all tokens using the Stanford Lemmatizer (Manning et al., 2014) for English and the Mate tools Lemmatizer (Björkelund et al., 2010) for German before applying the rules. In German, we noticed that lemmatisation (but also stemming) face big challenges, especially in the legal domain, when it comes to compound nouns, i.e., nouns that are combined to create new nouns, like "Vertragspartner" (contractual partner) is a combination of "Vertrag" (contract) and "Partner" (partner). Compound nouns can be inflected internally ("Vertrag**s**partner"), and splitting them into their constituents is not trivial. A "Druckerzeugnis" (printed matter) could, for example, lexically speaking either be a "Druck-Erzeugnis" (print - matter) or a "Drucker-Zeugnis" (printer - certificate). While there are existing approaches on how to automatically split compound words into their respective parts (e.g., by Baroni et al. (2002), Koehn and Knight (2003), Daiber et al. (2015), Sugisaki and Tuggener (2018), and Weller-Di Marco (2017)), the problem is far from being trivial and is not yet addressed in our implementation.

5.2 Logistic Regression

Second, we trained a logistic regression classifier, which we implemented using Scikit-learn (Pedregosa et al., 2011). As input, we used a Tf–idf vector representation of the concatenation of clause text and titles. Before transforming the clauses into these vectors, we removed stopwords using "Stopwords ISO"[5]. Since logistic regression does not inherently support multi-label classification, we used a "one-vs-the-rest" approach. Instead of training one classifier, we train one classifier for each class, which performs a binary classification against all remaining classes and combined all results to decide which labels are predicted for a given input.

We grid search with a 10-fold cross-validation on the training data to find the best parameter for the regularisation strength for the classification of topics. We performed multiple iterations on both languages to narrow down the search space. In German, we achieved the best results with $C = 1,000$ and in English with $C = 45,000$. The values are rather high for both languages but especially for the smaller English data-set. Since C is the inverse of the regulator $(1/\lambda)$, a high value for C means a low value for λ and hence poses the risk of overfitting. We performed the same procedure for the classification of subtopics and found that $C = 100$ performed best in both languages, which is significantly lower and therefore less prone to overfitting.

5.3 Random Forest

Logistic regression is computationally efficient and generalises well, and is, therefore, a good baseline. However, its inability for "real" multi-label classification is a drawback in our use case. Decision trees do inherently support multi-label classification and also are inherently explainable. However, they are not as efficient as logistic regression and are more prone to overfitting. Instead of training just one decision tree, we use a random forest approach, where multiple independent randomised

[5] `https://github.com/stopwords-iso/stopwords-iso`

Label	DE	EN	Total
age	38	5	43
applicability	253	33	286
applicableLaw	137	23	160
arbitration	155	13	168
changes	13	12	25
codeOfConduct	55	1	56
conclusionOfContract (cOc)	800	146	946
cOc:binding	328	39	367
cOc:changeOfOrder	58	6	64
cOc:definition	103	4	107
cOc:restrictions	42	7	49
cOc:steps	256	58	314
cOc:withdrawal	95	20	115
delivery	839	164	1003
delivery:brokenPackaging	134	10	144
delivery:costs	247	57	304
delivery:customs	43	6	49
delivery:destination	96	16	112
delivery:methods	160	17	177
delivery:partial	32	5	37
delivery:time	143	41	184
description	86	30	116
disposal	51	16	67
intellectualProperty	45	24	69
language	124	11	135
liability	439	140	579
party	157	21	178
payment	898	112	1010
payment:fee	50	3	53
payment:late	48	1	49
payment:loyalty	7	22	29
payment:methods	435	53	488
payment:restraint	46	1	47
payment:vouchers	301	14	315
personalData	213	49	262
personalData:cookies	6	3	9
personalData:duration	8	1	9
personalData:information	48	12	60
personalData:reason	50	11	61
personalData:update	7	4	11
personalData:usage	57	16	73
placeOfJurisdiction	117	19	136
prices	158	56	214
prices:currency	17	13	30
prices:vat	119	24	143
retentionOfTitle	222	13	235
severability	42	12	54
textStorage	152	11	163
warranty	540	25	565
warranty:options	69	5	74
warranty:period	155	10	165
withdrawal	484	202	686
withdrawal:compensation	94	27	121
withdrawal:effects	97	12	109
withdrawal:exclusion	100	27	127
withdrawal:form	131	37	168
withdrawal:model	41	2	43
withdrawal:period	126	40	166
withdrawal:shippingCosts	118	43	161
withdrawal:shippingMethod	74	13	87
Total lvl 1	6018	1138	7156
Total lvl 2	3941	680	4621

Table 2: Distribution of topic and subtopic labels among the German (DE) and English (EN) corpus

decision trees are trained, and a majority vote is used for classification. As input, we again used Tf-idf vectors.

We again performed a grid search with stratified 10-fold cross-validation on the training data to find the best performing values for the parameters: number of estimators (i.e., the numbers of trees), the maximum depth of the trees, the minimum number of samples per internal node that is needed for a split, and the minimum number of samples per leaf. As usual, we performed several iterations to narrow down the search space before, in the final iteration, we found the following values to perform best. In German: number of estimators = 2,000, maximum depth = ∞, samples per node = 2, samples per leaf = 1 and in English: number of estimators = 1,000, maximum depth = 100, samples per node = 2, samples per leaf = 1.

5.4 Neural Networks

For the different approaches using neural networks, we also evaluated different input encodings, namely different kinds of word embeddings. To train domain-specific embeddings, we used a larger corpus than the one described in Section 4, because the data does not have to be annotated. We collected the corpus in the same way as the other corpus from the price comparison websites, however, it is more than 30-times bigger, consisting of 5,412 contracts, 4,869 in German and 543 in English.

We used the following embeddings:

- German
  - Word2Vec embeddings with 300 dimensions based on the German Wikipedia[6]
  - GloVe embeddings with 300 dimensions based on the German Wikipedia[7]
  - Word2Vec embeddings with 300 dimensions we trained from scratch on the above described corpus of T&C
- English
  - Word2Vec embeddings with 300 dimensions based on the Google News Corpus (Mikolov et al., 2013)
  - GloVe embeddings with 300 dimensions based on Wikipedia and Gigawords 5 (Pennington et al., 2014)

[6] https://gitlab.com/deepset-ai/open-source/word2vec-embeddings-de

[7] https://gitlab.com/deepset-ai/open-source/glove-embeddings-de

– Word2Vec embeddings with 300 dimensions we trained from scratch on the above described corpus of T&C

Training neural networks is computationally much more expensive than, e.g., logistic regression and at the same time depends on more parameters. To manage the increasing complexity, we changed our approach for the parameter optimisation by reducing the 10-fold cross-validation to a 5-fold cross-validation. Additionally, we fixed parameters that always performed best or almost best, independent from other parameters, as early as possible in order to reduce the search space and converge faster to a local optimum.

5.4.1 MLP

The hyper-parameters we optimised of the MLP were the number of layers, the number of neurons per layer, the dropout, the batch size and the number of epochs. The results of the hyper-parameter studies can be found in Appendix A.

5.4.2 LSTM

For the LSTM network we optimised the sequence length, the number of LSTM layers and the number of neurons in them, the number of dense layers and the number of neurons in them, the dropout, the batch size, and the number of epochs. The best performing parameters we found for the topic and subtopic classification can be found in Appendix A.

5.5 BERT

Finally, we evaluate an approach using a transformer model for the clause topic classification, more specifically, the BERT language model (Devlin et al., 2019). We used the HuggingFace transformers library (Wolf et al., 2019) to fine-tune the pre-trained language models and implement the classification.

For English, we used the "bert-base-uncased" pre-trained model, provided by the original authors Devlin et al. (2019). The model, which is trained on lower case English texts, has 12 hidden layers with a size of 768, 12 attention heads per attention layer, and 110 million parameters. For German, we used the "bert-base-german-cased" model from Chan et al. (2020). It is trained on cased German texts and, like the original model, has 12 hidden layers with a size of 768, 12 attention heads per attention layer, and 110 million parameters.

The original BERT language model was trained on the English Wikipedia and the BookCorpus by Zhu et al. (2015), which consists of 11,038 fiction books that are available for free on the internet. The German language model we are using was pretrained on a more diverse set of sources, among which are the German Wikipedia and a web corpus gathered by Suárez et al. (2019), which account for more than 90% of the data the model was trained on. However, the model was also trained on the Open Legal Data set from Ostendorff et al. (2020), which consists of more than 100,000 German court decisions. We also briefly evaluated a multilingual approach with the Multilingual Universal Sentence Encoder transformer model, which was used by Braun and Matthes (2020) for the multilingual automated detection of T&C, however, first tests on German and English were not promising, so we did not follow through on the approach.

We used our training data to fine-tune both language models, the English and the German, for the topic classification task. In order to find the best hyper-parameters, we split 20% off the training data as validation set. We started our search with the values suggested in the original BERT paper: batch size 16 or 32, learning rate 5e-5, 3e-5 or 2e-5, and 2, 3 or 4 epochs (Devlin et al., 2019). However, the authors also note that the optimal hyper-parameters are task-specific and that small data sets (which they define as less than 100,000 labels) are more sensitive to the choice of parameters than larger ones. For our data sets and task, we found a smaller batch size with a slightly higher number of epochs to work better than the suggested parameters in both languages. We found a batch size of eight and a learning rate of 5e-5 to perform best for the topic and subtopic classification in both languages. In German, eight epochs performed best for the topic classification and six for the subtopic classification. In English, six epochs for the topic classification and 21 epochs for the subtopic classification performed best. All other parameters were kept equal to the original pre-trained model.

6 Evaluation

Our baseline approach of using keywords achieved an F1-score of 0.78 in German for topic classification and 0.64 for subtopic classification. The performance in English was worse with an F1-score of 0.72 for topics and 0.46 for subtopics. We noticed that, in German, the list of keywords

Approach	A	P	R	F1
BERT	0.84	0.93	0.89	0.91
Log. Regression	0.77	0.95	0.80	0.87
Random Forest	0.73	0.97	0.72	0.83
MLP	0.75	0.89	0.74	0.81
LSTM	0.73	0.90	0.72	0.80
Rule-based	0.64	0.77	0.80	0.78

(a) German

Approach	A	P	R	F1
BERT	0.79	0.89	0.82	0.85
Log. Regression	0.71	0.88	0.73	0.80
LSTM	0.72	0.80	0.74	0.77
MLP	0.72	0.79	0.73	0.76
Rule-based	0.57	0.76	0.69	0.72
Random Forest	0.57	0.88	0.58	0.70

(b) English

Table 3: Best clause topic classification results for each approach, ordered by F1-score (A = accuracy, P = precision, R = recall, F1 = F1-score)

Approach	A	P	R	F1
BERT	0.79	0.89	0.83	0.86
Log. Regression	0.75	0.91	0.78	0.84
Random Forest	0.68	0.91	0.67	0.77
MLP	0.73	0.86	0.66	0.75
LSTM	0.69	0.85	0.63	0.72
Rule-based	0.47	0.74	0.56	0.64

(a) German

Approach	A	P	R	F1
BERT	0.68	0.79	0.68	0.73
MLP	0.67	0.76	0.66	0.71
LSTM	0.67	0.78	0.65	0.70
Log. Regression	0.54	0.80	0.59	0.68
Random Forest	0.44	0.85	0.43	0.57
Rule-based	0.28	0.39	0.49	0.43

(b) English

Table 4: Best clause subtopic classification results for each approach, ordered by F1-score (A = accuracy, P = precision, R = recall, F1 = F1-score)

mostly consisted of domain-specific compound nouns, like "Widerrufsrecht" (right of withdrawal) or "Gefahrenübergang" (transfer of risk), which are very distinctive for their respective topics and make the classification relatively easy.

This is also a possible explanation for why the logistic regression classifier, with Tf-idf vectors as input, performed so well on the German corpus. With an F1-score of 0.87 for topics and 0.84 for subtopics, it was only surpassed by the BERT model. All other approaches performed comparable to each other in German, with F1-scores between 0.8 and 0.83 for topic classification and 0.72 to 0.77 for the subtopic classification (see Table 3 and 4).

In English, the picture was less clear, with logistic regression still performing best for topic classification (F1-score 0.80) but being surpassed by the neural network approaches for subtopic classification. However, the clear overall winner, with the best performance on both languages and classification levels was BERT, which scored up to 0.91.

For the approaches we evaluated with different inputs, i.e. the MLP and LSTM, the values in Table 3 and 4 represent the best results achieved. There was no clear pattern visible of which word embedding model performs best. All of them achieved comparable results and no one performed best or worse in all settings.

7 Transferability

Due to their practical relevance and availability, we focused on T&C from online shops in this paper. However, there is no reason why the same technology could not be applied to other types of standard form contracts, e.g. from banks and insurances. At the same time, the taxonomy we developed and the models we trained have a component that is specific to online shopping, broken packaging, for example, is a topic, that is not relevant for banking.

To get an idea of how domain-specific the taxonomy and the models are, we annotated the T&C of three of the largest German banks (Commerzbank, Deutsche Bank, and Sparkassen) in the same way described in Section 4.2: first, a student, then authors annotated the all clauses of the contracts independently with their topics and subtopics, then conflicting labels were resolved by the team of experts. We used the taxonomy described in Section 3 for the classification, however, we added a class "n.a." to mark clauses that cover a topic that is not represented by any of the classes in the taxonomy.

The three contracts consist of 214 clauses, about 71 clauses per contract, and 13,681 words, an aver-

Topic	#clauses
applicability	3
applicableLaw	3
arbitration	2
changes	5
liability	9
n.a.	143
payment	14
placeOfJurisdiction	6
prices	1
withdrawal	27

Table 5: Topics of clauses in the general business conditions of banks

Topic	P	R	F1
applicability	0.60	1.00	0.75
applicableLaw	1.00	1.00	1.00
arbitration	1.00	1.00	1.00
changes	1.00	0.83	0.91
liability	0.41	1.00	0.58
payment	0.16	1.00	0.28
placeOfJurisdiction	0.00	0.00	0.00
prices	0.00	0.00	0.00
withdrawal	0.54	1.00	0.70
TOTAL	0.28	0.97	0.43

Table 6: BERT clause topic classification results on the banking corpus

age of 2,478 words per contract. The contracts from the online shops, in comparison, consisted of an average of 35 clauses per contract. The 214 clauses consist of 13,681 words, which equals 4,560 words per contract. The fact that the banking contracts contain much more clauses per contract already suggests, that our taxonomy will, most likely, not be able to cover all of them.

The annotation process confirmed this assumption. Of the 214 clauses, only 71 (or 33%) are concerned with a topic that is covered by our taxonomy (see Table 5). The other clauses are concerned with a wide range of banking specific topics, from deposit protection funds to banking confidentiality. This means that, even if we would correctly classify all the other clauses, we could never achieve a recall above 0.33. We can already conclude, that the taxonomy we developed can not simply be applied to other types of standard form contracts without adaption.

Since the taxonomy is still able to cover one-third of the banking contracts, we wanted to test how well the classifiers we trained would perform on this data set. Therefore, we took the best performing topic classifier, i.e., the BERT model, and applied it to the new corpus. The evaluation of the results is shown in Table 6. We can see that for some of the topics, e.g., applicability, applicableLaw, arbitration, and changes, the performance is very good, even tough our model has never seen this type of contract before.

8 Conclusion

In this paper, we compared different approaches to classify the topics of clauses in standard form contracts from online shops, based on a taxonomy of clause topics and subtopics we developed and a bilingual corpus of more than 6,000 clauses we gathered and annotated. Our evaluation showed, that our initial hypothesis, that the model performance would increase with complexity, did not hold.

While BERT did indeed perform best for both languages, the much simpler logistic regression approach showed the second-best performance. Considering the computational time and power that is needed to not only train the more complex model but also during inference of the labels, the simple logistic regression approach might for some practical application be the better choice.

We were surprised to find that multilingual approaches, using the German and English data together, did not seem to bring any improvements for this task, even though earlier work in the legal domain, e.g. by Niklaus et al. (2021) and Braun and Matthes (2020), have shown that multilingual models can improve performance. This aspect needs further investigation.

While the taxonomy we developed and the models we trained are domain-specific for eCommerce, first tests suggest that the approaches can be transferred to other types of standard form contracts and that event the models can partially be transferred to other domains, at least for more "technical" clauses concerning the contract itself. This could apply to all types of consumer standard form contract within a highly regulated domain, like insurances, housing, and employment, and is something we would like to investigate further in the future.

Acknowledgements

The project was supported by funds of the Federal Ministry for the Environment, Nature Conservation, Nuclear Safety and Consumer Protection (BMUV) based on a decision of the Parliament of the Federal Republic of Germany via the Federal Office for Agriculture and Food (BLE) under the innovation support programme.

References

Marco Baroni, Johannes Matiasek, and Harald Trost. 2002. Predicting the components of german nominal compounds. In *ECAI 2002: 15th European Conference on Artificial Intelligence*, pages 470–474.

Anders Björkelund, Bernd Bohnet, Love Hafdell, and Pierre Nugues. 2010. A high-performance syntactic and semantic dependency parser. In *Coling 2010: Demonstrations*, pages 33–36, Beijing, China. Coling 2010 Organizing Committee.

Daniel Braun. 2021. *Automated Semantic Analysis, Legal Assessment, and Summarization of Standard Form Contracts*. Dissertation, Technische Universität München, München.

Daniel Braun and Florian Matthes. 2020. Automatic detection of terms and conditions in german and english online shops. In *Proceedings of the 16th International Conference on Web Information Systems and Technologies - WEBIST,*, pages 233–237. INSTICC, SciTePress.

Daniel Braun and Florian Matthes. 2021. NLP for consumer protection: Battling illegal clauses in German terms and conditions in online shopping. In *Proceedings of the 1st Workshop on NLP for Positive Impact*, pages 93–99, Online. Association for Computational Linguistics.

Daniel Braun, Elena Scepankova, Patrick Holl, and Florian Matthes. 2017. SaToS: Assessing and summarising terms of services from German webshops. In *Proceedings of the 10th International Conference on Natural Language Generation*, pages 223–227, Santiago de Compostela, Spain. Association for Computational Linguistics.

Branden Chan, Stefan Schweter, and Timo Möller. 2020. German's next language model. *arXiv preprint arXiv:2010.10906*.

Joachim Daiber, Lautaro Quiroz, Roger Wechsler, and Stella Frank. 2015. Splitting compounds by semantic analogy. In *Proceedings of the 1st Deep Machine Translation Workshop*, pages 20–28, Praha, Czechia. ÚFAL MFF UK.

Robert Dale. 2019. Law and word order: Nlp in legal tech. *Natural Language Engineering*, 25(1):211–217.

Jacob Devlin, Ming-Wei Chang, Kenton Lee, and Kristina Toutanova. 2019. BERT: Pre-training of deep bidirectional transformers for language understanding. In *Proceedings of the 2019 Conference of the North American Chapter of the Association for Computational Linguistics: Human Language Technologies, Volume 1 (Long and Short Papers)*, pages 4171–4186, Minneapolis, Minnesota. Association for Computational Linguistics.

Michael Fingerhut. 2009. *7. Teil: Allgemeine Geschäftsbedingungen*, 12th edition edition. Carl Heymanns Verlag.

IHK Munich and Upper Bavaria. 2020. Allgemeine Geschäftsbedingungen für einen Webshop. `https://www.ihk-muenchen.de/ihk/documents/Recht-Steuern/Vertragsrecht/AGB-Webshop_2020.docx`. Last accessed 2020-07-09.

Philipp Koehn and Kevin Knight. 2003. Empirical methods for compound splitting. In *Proceedings of the Tenth Conference on European Chapter of the Association for Computational Linguistics - Volume 1*, EACL '03, pages 187–193, Stroudsburg, PA, USA. Association for Computational Linguistics.

Ruta Liepina, Giuseppe Contissa, Kasper Drazewski, Francesca Lagioia, Marco Lippi, Hans-Wolfgang Micklitz, Przemysław Pałka, Giovanni Sartor, and Paolo Torroni. 2019. Gdpr privacy policies in claudette: Challenges of omission, context and multilingualism. In *Proceedings of the Third Workshop on Automated Semantic Analysis of Information in Legal Texts co-located with the 17th International Conference on Artificial Intelligence and Law (ICAIL 2019)*.

Marco Lippi, Przemysław Pałka, Giuseppe Contissa, Francesca Lagioia, Hans-Wolfgang Micklitz, Giovanni Sartor, and Paolo Torroni. 2019. Claudette: an automated detector of potentially unfair clauses in online terms of service. *Artificial Intelligence and Law*, 27(2):117–139.

Christopher Manning, Mihai Surdeanu, John Bauer, Jenny Finkel, Steven Bethard, and David McClosky. 2014. The Stanford CoreNLP natural language processing toolkit. In *Proceedings of 52nd Annual Meeting of the Association for Computational Linguistics: System Demonstrations*, pages 55–60, Baltimore, Maryland. Association for Computational Linguistics.

Tomas Mikolov, Kai Chen, Greg Corrado, and Jeffrey Dean. 2013. Efficient estimation of word representations in vector space. In *1st International Conference on Learning Representations, ICLR 2013, Scottsdale, Arizona, USA, May 2-4, 2013, Workshop Track Proceedings*.

Joel Niklaus, Ilias Chalkidis, and Matthias Stürmer. 2021. Swiss-judgment-prediction: A multilingual legal judgment prediction benchmark. In *Proceedings of the Natural Legal Language Processing Workshop 2021*, pages 19–35, Punta Cana, Dominican Republic. Association for Computational Linguistics.

Malte Ostendorff, Till Blume, and Saskia Ostendorff. 2020. Towards an open platform for legal information. *arXiv preprint arXiv:2005.13342*.

Fabian Pedregosa, Gaël Varoquaux, Alexandre Gramfort, Vincent Michel, Bertrand Thirion, Olivier Grisel, Mathieu Blondel, Peter Prettenhofer, Ron Weiss, Vincent Dubourg, et al. 2011. Scikit-learn: Machine learning in python. *the Journal of machine Learning research*, 12:2825–2830.

Jeffrey Pennington, Richard Socher, and Christopher D. Manning. 2014. Glove: Global vectors for word representation. In *Empirical Methods in Natural Language Processing (EMNLP)*, pages 1532–1543.

Victoria C Plaut and Robert P Bartlett III. 2012. Blind consent? a social psychological investigation of non-readership of click-through agreements. *Law and human behavior*, 36(4):293.

Thomas Proisl and Peter Uhrig. 2016. SoMaJo: State-of-the-art tokenization for German web and social media texts. In *Proceedings of the 10th Web as Corpus Workshop*, pages 57–62, Berlin. Association for Computational Linguistics.

Abhilasha Ravichander, Alan W Black, Shomir Wilson, Thomas Norton, and Norman Sadeh. 2019. Question answering for privacy policies: Combining computational and legal perspectives. In *Proceedings of the 2019 Conference on Empirical Methods in Natural Language Processing and the 9th International Joint Conference on Natural Language Processing (EMNLP-IJCNLP)*, pages 4947–4958, Hong Kong, China. Association for Computational Linguistics.

Richard Raysman and Peter Brown. 2010. Contractual nature of online policies remains unsettled. *New York Law Journal*, 10.

Martin Schirmbacher. 2018. Allgemeine geschäftsbedingungen (online-shop). `https://www.bevh.org/fileadmin/content/01_leistungen/rechtshilfen/muster-agb/muster-agb-internetshop-2018.pdf`. Last accessed 2020-07-10.

Barbara Sommer and Ferdinans von Stumm. 2017. Fernabsatz von waren und dienstleistungen. In Wolfgang Weitnauer and Tilman Mueller-Stöfen, editors, *Beck-šches Formularbuch IT-Recht*, 4 edition, chapter J, pages 715–761. C. H. Beck Verlag, Munich.

Pedro Javier Ortiz Suárez, Benoît Sagot, and Laurent Romary. 2019. Asynchronous pipeline for processing huge corpora on medium to low resource infrastructures. In *7th Workshop on the Challenges in the Management of Large Corpora (CMLC-7)*. Leibniz-Institut für Deutsche Sprache.

Kyoko Sugisaki and Don Tuggener. 2018. German compound splitting using the compound productivity of morphemes. In *14th Conference on Natural Language Processing-KONVENS 2018*, pages 141–147. Austrian Academy of Sciences Press.

P. Szymański and T. Kajdanowicz. 2017. A scikit-based Python environment for performing multi-label classification. *ArXiv e-prints*.

Marion Weller-Di Marco. 2017. Simple compound splitting for German. In *Proceedings of the 13th Workshop on Multiword Expressions (MWE 2017)*, pages 161–166, Valencia, Spain. Association for Computational Linguistics.

Thomas Wolf, Lysandre Debut, Victor Sanh, Julien Chaumond, Clement Delangue, Anthony Moi, Pierric Cistac, Tim Rault, Rémi Louf, Morgan Funtowicz, Joe Davison, Sam Shleifer, Patrick von Platen, Clara Ma, Yacine Jernite, Julien Plu, Canwen Xu, Teven Le Scao, Sylvain Gugger, Mariama Drame, Quentin Lhoest, and Alexander M. Rush. 2019. Huggingface's transformers: State-of-the-art natural language processing. *ArXiv*, abs/1910.03771.

Yukun Zhu, Ryan Kiros, Rich Zemel, Ruslan Salakhutdinov, Raquel Urtasun, Antonio Torralba, and Sanja Fidler. 2015. Aligning books and movies: Towards story-like visual explanations by watching movies and reading books. In *Proceedings of the IEEE international conference on computer vision*, pages 19–27.

A Appendix: Model Parameters

See Table 7 to 10, activation function for all was `tanh` and optimiser `adam`.

Language	Input	Layers	Neurons	Dropout	Batch	Epochs
German	T&C	2	200, 200	0.4	100	500
	Word2Vec	3	200, 150, 200	0.4	100	300
	GloVe	1	110	0.3	200	200
English	T&C	2	200, 150	0.2	20	300
	Word2Vec	3	200, 150, 200	0.3	100	500
	GloVe	3	100, 200, 100	0.2	50	400

Table 7: Hyper-parameters used for the topic classification with the Multilayer Perceptron on different inputs

Language	Input	Layers	Neurons	Dropout	Batch	Epochs
German	T&C	1	150	0.3	500	400
	Word2Vec	3	100, 200, 100	0.4	300	500
	GloVe	1	80	0.3	300	500
English	T&C	1	150	0.3	500	400
	Word2Vec	3	100, 200, 100	0.4	150	300
	GloVe	3	200, 150, 200	0.3	150	400

Table 8: Hyper-parameters used for the subtopic classification with the Multilayer Perceptron on different Inputs

Lang.	Input	Sequ. Length	LSTM Layers	Neurons	Dense Layers	Neurons	Dropout	Batch	Epochs
DE	T&C	35	1	300	2	200, 50	0.3	300	30
	W2V	50	1	300	1	50	0.3	40	30
	GloVe	50	1	300	1	50	0.3	40	13
EN	T&C	100	1	300	2	200, 50	0.3	150	100
	W2V	40	1	45	0		0.6	10	50
	GloVe	65	1	200	1	65	0.7	15	100

Table 9: Hyper-parameters used for the topic classification with the LSTM on different inputs

Lang.	Input	Sequ. Length	LSTM Layers	Neurons	Dense Layers	Neurons	Dropout	Batch	Epochs
DE	T&C	35	1	250	1	50	0.4	15	20
	W2V	45	1	200	1	50	0.4	15	20
	GloVe	45	1	105	1	50	0.3	15	10
EN	T&C	45	1	200	1	50	0.3	20	15
	W2V	50	1	250	1	50	0.4	25	25
	GloVe	40	1	150	1	50	0.3	15	10

Table 10: Hyper-parameters used for the subtopic classification with the LSTM on different inputs

Investigating the Generative Approach for Question Answering in E-Commerce

Kalyani Roy[1], **Vineeth Kumar Balapanuru**[1], **Tapas Nayak**[2*] and **Pawan Goyal**[1]
[1]Indian Institute of Technology Kharagpur, India
[2]TCS Research, India
kroy@iitkgp.ac.in, Vineethkumar6001@gmail.com
tnk02.05@gmail.com, pawang@cse.iitkgp.ac.in

Abstract

Many e-commerce websites provide Product-related Question Answering (PQA) platform where potential customers can ask questions related to a product, and other consumers can post an answer to that question based on their experience. Recently, there has been a growing interest in providing automated responses to product questions. In this paper, we investigate the suitability of the generative approach for PQA. We use state-of-the-art generative models proposed by Deng et al. (2020) and Lu et al. (2020) for this purpose. On closer examination, we find several drawbacks in this approach: (1) input reviews are not always utilized significantly for answer generation, (2) the performance of the models is abysmal while answering the numerical questions, (3) many of the generated answers contain phrases like "I do not know" which are taken from the reference answer in training data, and these answers do not convey any information to the customer. Although these approaches achieve a high ROUGE score, it does not reflect upon these shortcomings of the generated answers. We hope that our analysis will lead to more rigorous PQA approaches, and future research will focus on addressing these shortcomings in PQA.

1 Introduction

With the increase in e-commerce shopping, customer-generated product queries are also growing. Manually answering the questions in real-time is infeasible, and also some questions go unanswered for an extended period. It is necessary to answer the user queries in the e-commerce business automatically. The user reviews are a vast source of information with diverse opinions, and they can be used to answer user queries. Earlier works on product question answering (PQA) focus on retrieval-based approaches and binary answer prediction tasks. McAuley and Yang (2016); Fan et al. (2019); Yu and Lam (2018) aim to predict the answer as "yes/no" based on the relevant reviews, customer ratings, aspects in the reviews, etc. Retrieval-based approaches try to find the most relevant review snippet as the answer (Chen et al., 2019a) and use a ranked list of review snippets as the response for a given question (Yu et al., 2018). With the success of machine translation (Sutskever et al., 2014) and summarization (See et al., 2017), the PQA approaches are shifting towards natural answer generation from relevant product reviews (Gao et al., 2019; Chen et al., 2019b; Deng et al., 2020; Lu et al., 2020; Gao et al., 2021). In this work, we analyse the answer generated from state-of-the-art generative models OAAG(Deng et al., 2020) and CHIME(Lu et al., 2020) in detail beyond their traditional scores on popular metrics such as ROUGE (Lin, 2004). We find that despite achieving a good score on these metrics, generated answers have several drawbacks that can lead to user dissatisfaction.

2 A State-of-the-art Generative PQA Model

2.1 PQA Dataset

The Amazon Question Answering dataset (McAuley and Yang, 2016) contains around 1.4 million questions from different categories with multiple customer-written answers and opinion labels, such as positive, negative, and neutral. The Amazon Product Review dataset (Ni et al., 2019; He and McAuley, 2016) includes users' reviews along with a rating of the product given by the same user. The Product ID is used to align the question with its reviews.

2.2 PQA Models

We use Opinion-aware Answer Generation (OAAG) model (Deng et al., 2020) and Cross-passage Hierarchical Memory Network (CHIME)

* This work was carried out while author was a postdoctoral researcher at IIT Kharagpur.

Proceedings of The Fifth Workshop on e-Commerce and NLP (ECNLP 5), pages 210 - 216
May 26, 2022 ©2022 Association for Computational Linguistics

model (Lu et al., 2020) for our analysis. Following the generative approach, these two models achieve state-of-the-art performance on the Amazon Question Answering dataset. There are thousands of products in each category in the Amazon Product Review dataset, and each product has thousands of reviews. All the reviews may not be relevant for a particular query, and therefore, to answer a product-related question, models need to filter out the irrelevant reviews first. OAAG and CHIME use the BM25 algorithm to retrieve and rank all the review snippets of a product, and the top k relevant snippets (we use top 10 reviews snippets) for that question are taken as the premise of the answer.

2.2.1 OAAG Model

Upon retrieving the relevant reviews, OAAG uses an encoder-decoder model for answer generation. OAAG encodes the question and each review corresponding to that question using a Bi-LSTM (Hochreiter and Schmidhuber, 1997) network. They apply a co-attention mechanism over these encodings to get the question and review representations. They utilize the ratings of the retrieved reviews to mine the general opinion about the question using the attention mechanism. Finally, they employ a multi-view pointer-generator network that copies words from the question as well as from the reviews and fuses the opinion by re-weighting the attention scores of the words in reviews to generate an opinionated answer. They report ROUGE-based scores to compare the model performance against the previous approaches (Chen et al., 2019b; Gao et al., 2019).

2.2.2 CHIME Model

CHIME uses a transformer-based encoder-decoder model to generate the response. It extends pretrained XLNet (Yang et al., 2019) with an auxiliary memory module that consists of two components: the *context memory*, and the *answer memory*. Given a question with K review passages, it creates K training instances, each consisting of the question, a review passage, and the reference answer. Each training instance is fed into an XLNet encoder to get the hidden representations that are used to update the two memories. The *context memory* mechanism sequentially reads the review passages and gathers the cross-passage evidences to identify the most prominent opinion in reviews. The *answer memory* works as a buffer to gradually refine the generated answers after reading each (*question, review passage*) pair. After reading the last review, the *answer memory* is fed to the decoder to get a final response.

3 Research Questions

We empirically analyse the OAAG model with dynamic fusion and CHIME model to answer the following research questions:

RQ1 : Are the retrieved review snippets significantly utilized for generating the answers?

RQ2 : Is the model performing similarly for a heterogeneous group of questions?

RQ3 : Is the generative model biased towards more frequently occurring phrases?

RQ4 : Can ROUGE capture the correctness of generated answers?

4 Experiments

We use two product categories, namely, *Home&Kitchen* and *Sports&Outdoors* for our analysis from the dataset mentioned in Section 2.1 after combining the question-answer and review dataset with the Product IDs. We will denote the two categories as *Home* and *Sports*, respectively. We use the same data split from OAAG[1] to retrain the models. Since there is no validation dataset, we take the 10% of the train data as validation data. Table A.1 in the Appendix shows the details of training, validation, and test split. We keep all the hyper-parameters the same as the OAAG and CHIME. We train all the OAAG models for 20 epochs and CHIME models for 3 epochs, and the model that performs the best on the validation set is used to evaluate the test set. We evaluate the model with ROUGE metric and report the F1 scores for ROUGE-1 (R1) and ROUGE-L (RL), which measure the word overlap and the longest common sequence between the reference answer and the generated answer, respectively. We obtain the ROUGE scores using `rouge-score` [2] package.

5 Analysis & Discussion

5.1 Answer to RQ1 (Utilization of retrieved review for generating the answers)

Both the models use the BM25 algorithm to retrieve relevant reviews using the questions in the test dataset. We refer to this test setting as *BM25Q*.

[1]https://github.com/dengyang17/OAAG

[2]https://pypi.org/project/rouge-score/

For answering RQ1, at inference time, we replace these reviews with four sets of review snippets: (i) *TrainA*: We use BM25 to find the closest question to the test question in the train data, and we take the answer of it as the generated answer. (ii) *RandomOD*: We randomly choose the review snippets from any other product of that category except the product for which the question is asked. (iii) *RandomID*: We randomly select review snippets from the review sentences of that particular product. (iv) *BM25QA*: We retrieve the review snippets using the BM25 algorithm that uses the question and reference answer in the test dataset.

OAAG uses the opinion along with the reviews. We also select the opinion of the corresponding review sentence while replacing the reviews. Both the models utilize the top 10 reviews for training and evaluation.

		Sports		*Home*	
		R1	RL	R1	RL
	TrainA	13.01	10.13	14.36	11.35
OAAG	BM25Q	15.01	**11.99**	14.44	11.91
	RandomOD	14.25	11.38	14.04	11.53
	RandomID	14.71	11.69	14.42	11.85
	BM25QA	**15.09**	11.97	**14.53**	**11.93**
CHIME	BM25Q	**18.53**	**13.19**	**18.99**	**13.84**
	RandomOD	18.10	12.87	17.83	13.11
	RandomID	17.95	12.81	17.98	13.17
	BM25QA	17.99	12.84	17.85	13.11

Table 1: Performance of the OAAG and CHIME models with various sets of review snippets.

Table 1 shows the result of this experiment. The TrainA does not utilize either of the models to generate the answer. It shows the answer from the most similar train question, and its performance is competitive with other methods, especially in *Home*. In both the categories, the performance of both the models is almost similar in RandomOD and RandomID. RandomID shows marginally better performance than RandomOD for OAAG. For CHIME, BM25Q performs the best in both categories. For OAAG, BM25QA performs the best in *Home* while in *Sports*, BM25QA performs the best in R1, and BM25Q performs the best in RL, but the difference is minute. The results are quite surprising: the performance of the models is very similar when the answers are generated with random reviews vs. when the answers are generated with the reviews obtained from BM25. Hence, it is not clear if the model is effectively utilizing the retrieved review snippets.

5.2 Answer to RQ2 (Models' performance on heterogeneous questions)

Different types of questions are asked on the Amazon product page like numerical, "yes/no", descriptive. The generative model may not be suitable for answering all kinds of questions. So, we categorize the questions as template-based and descriptive.

		Sports		*Home*	
		R1	RL	R1	RL
OAAG	Template	13.15	10.99	12.38	10.33
	Descriptive	**15.67**	**12.34**	**15.11**	**12.21**
CHIME	Template	16.72	12.79	17.68	13.67
	Descriptive	**19.17**	**13.33**	**19.37**	**13.89**

Table 2: Performance of OAAG and CHIME models on template-based, descriptive categories of questions.

For template-based questions, the answer can be yes or no without any explanation. We filter the questions where the answer starts with 'yes', 'yeah', 'no', 'nope' and mark these as template-based questions. Both categories contain ~75% descriptive questions. Table 2 summarizes the result of the template-based and generative questions. Both models' performance in descriptive questions is better than the template-based questions.

Furthermore, we categorized the questions into numerical and non-numerical questions. We consider a question to be numerical if there are numbers in the question or in the reference answer. The test datasets of both the categories have ~19% numerical questions. The OAAG model performs better in answering non-numerical questions, while CHIME performs better in answering numerical questions. Although the ROUGE scores are close in numerical and non-numerical questions for both the models, on analyzing the numerical answers, we find that the words in generated and reference answers might match, but the numbers generally do not match. [3] We present some examples of numerical questions with their answers in Table A.4 of Appendix.

5.3 Answer to RQ3 (Bias in model)

We observe that some phrases are frequently occurring in the reference answers as well as in the generated answers. We find that in the training data of both categories, ~2.4% of the reference answers

[3]We manually check 400 numerical question answers for OAAG, and only 2 answers turn out to be correct. We check 100 random numerical question answers for CHIME, but none are correct.

start with the phrase "I don't think so", but 12.29% of responses in *Sports* and 35.64% responses in *Home* begin with this phrase. This ∼2.4% repetition of the same phrase in the training data makes the generative model biased towards this phrase.

		Sports		*Home*	
		R1	RL	R1	RL
OAAG	BM25Q	**15.01**	**11.99**	14.44	11.91
	BM25Q-IDK	14.87	11.71	**16.16**	**12.73**
CHIME	BM25Q	**18.53**	**13.19**	18.99	13.84
	BM25Q-IDK	18.50	13.21	**19.44**	**14.12**

Table 3: Performance of OAAG and CHIME models when trained with and without phrases that are not meaningful (IDK phrases).

Many of the reference answers in the training data contain "I don't know", "I have no idea", "I can't say". These kinds of answers do not give any meaningful information to the user. Together, we denote these phrases as IDK. On analysis of the dataset, we find that in *Sports*, there are 3.04%, 2.9%, and 6.9% IDK phrases in train dataset answers, test dataset answers, and generated answers, respectively. In *Home*, the answers in the train and test dataset contain 3.64% and 3.60% IDK phrases, respectively, but 16.31% of the answers are generated as IDK phrases. So, in the generated answers, the appearance of IDK phrases has increased by three to five folds which clearly shows that the model is biased towards these frequent phrases.

To see the effect of these phrases on the models, we remove the questions from the training dataset which have IDK in their reference answer [4] and retrain the models. We denote this model as BM25Q-IDK. Table 3 shows the result of BM25Q, the model trained on the original training data, and BM25Q-IDK. *Home* had 16.31% and *Sports* had only 6.9% IDK phrases, and consequently, when the IDK phrases are removed, it has more impact on *Home* which drops the bias towards these phrases and improves the ROUGE score, whereas, in *Sports*, BM25Q and BM25Q-IDK have close ROUGE scores due to lesser IDK phrases in the generated answer.

5.4 Answer to RQ4 (Correctness of generated response)

For answering RQ4, we look into the generated response with high R1 scores and check their correctness with respect to the reference answer. In OAAG model, 15.36% predictions in *Home* and 13.34% predictions in *Sports* have R1 score above 20. We manually analyse the reference and generated answers of randomly chosen 100 question-answers with a high ROUGE score (> 20), and we find that 54% are answered incorrectly. In CHIME model, 46.87% predictions in *Home* and 46.15% predictions in *Sports* have R1 score above 20 and 56% of 100 randomly chosen question-answer pairs (whose ROUGE score > 20) turn out to be incorrect.

Question	is this box made of polypropylene? can photos and mementos be safely stored in it ?
Ref. Ans.	i can't comment on the material it is made of, but the top does not stay on tight. it is not a decent storage container for anything requiring a top or to be airtight.
OAAG.	it says "made in china" on the bottom of the box . it says "made in china" on the bottom of the box . hope that helps . (26.22)
CHIME.	yes, it is polypropylene and can be stored in the box if you want to store them in a safe environment that is not toxic to you and/or your pets or food they will be exposed (27.77)
Question	What is the width at the base?
Ref. Ans.	Width across the bottom/base is approximately 3 inches.
OAAG.	The width of the top of the base is about 1.5 inches . the base of the pitcher is 9 inches. the top of the pitcher is about 1.5 inche.' (25.00)
CHIME.	itś about 12 " wide at the base and about 10.5 inches deep (26.08)

Table 4: Examples of generated answers with high R1 score, but having incorrect answer. The R1 score is mentioned within the parenthesis.

Table 4 shows two examples where the generated responses result in high R1 scores, but the answers are incorrect. Both models predict irrelevant answers in the first question, and the predicted dimension is incorrect in the second question. It shows that it is not possible to infer from ROUGE scores if the generated answer is accurate to the reference answer, i.e., the word count overlap is not an indicator of an accurate answer. We show some more cases with high R1 scores in Tables A.2 and A.3 in the Appendix.

6 Conclusion

In this paper, we extensively analyze the generative approach of question-answering in e-commerce using a state-of-the-art OAAG model (Deng et al., 2020) and CHIME model (Lu et al., 2020). We find many shortcomings which need to be addressed for a reliable PQA system. We try to address four re-

[4] Phrases such as "I don't think so" can be considered as valid reference answers. Therefore, we do not remove it from the training data.

search questions related to the generative approach for PQA, such as how the models utilize the reviews, how it performs on diverse question types, whether it is biased toward frequent phrases in training data, and the correctness of the generated response. We hope that our analysis will lead to more rigorous PQA research.

References

Long Chen, Ziyu Guan, Wei Zhao, Wanqing Zhao, Xiaopeng Wang, Zhou Zhao, and Huan Sun. 2019a. Answer identification from product reviews for user questions by multi-task attentive networks. In *Proceedings of the AAAI Conference on Artificial Intelligence*.

Shiqian Chen, Chenliang Li, Feng Ji, Wei Zhou, and Haiqing Chen. 2019b. Review-driven answer generation for product-related questions in e-commerce. In *Proceedings of the Twelfth ACM International Conference on Web Search and Data Mining*.

Yang Deng, Wenxuan Zhang, and Wai Lam. 2020. Opinion-aware answer generation for review-driven question answering in e-commerce. In *Proceedings of the 29th ACM International Conference on Information & Knowledge Management*.

Miao Fan, Chao Feng, Mingming Sun, Ping Li, and Haifeng Wang. 2019. Reading customer reviews to answer product-related questions. In *Proceedings of the 2019 SIAM International Conference on Data Mining*.

Shen Gao, Xiuying Chen, Z. Ren, Dongyan Zhao, and Rui Yan. 2021. Meaningful answer generation of e-commerce question-answering. *ACM Transactions on Information Systems*.

Shen Gao, Zhaochun Ren, Yihong Zhao, Dongyan Zhao, Dawei Yin, and Rui Yan. 2019. Product-aware answer generation in e-commerce question-answering. In *Proceedings of the 12th ACM International Conference on Web Search and Data Mining*.

Ruining He and Julian J. McAuley. 2016. Ups and downs: Modeling the visual evolution of fashion trends with one-class collaborative filtering. In *Proceedings of the 25th International Conference on World Wide Web*.

Sepp Hochreiter and Jürgen Schmidhuber. 1997. Long short-term memory. *Neural computation*.

Chin-Yew Lin. 2004. ROUGE: A package for automatic evaluation of summaries. In *Text Summarization Branches Out*. Association for Computational Linguistics.

Junru Lu, Gabriele Pergola, Lin Gui, Binyang Li, and Yulan He. 2020. CHIME: Cross-passage hierarchical memory network for generative review question answering. In *Proceedings of the 28th International Conference on Computational Linguistics*.

Julian McAuley and Alex Yang. 2016. Addressing complex and subjective product-related queries with customer reviews. In *Proceedings of the 25th International Conference on World Wide Web*.

Jianmo Ni, Jiacheng Li, and Julian McAuley. 2019. Justifying recommendations using distantly-labeled reviews and fine-grained aspects. In *Proceedings of the 2019 Conference on Empirical Methods in Natural Language Processing and the 9th International Joint Conference on Natural Language Processing (EMNLP-IJCNLP)*.

Abigail See, Peter J. Liu, and Christopher D. Manning. 2017. Get to the point: Summarization with pointer-generator networks. In *Proceedings of the 55th Annual Meeting of the Association for Computational Linguistics (Volume 1: Long Papers)*. Association for Computational Linguistics.

Ilya Sutskever, Oriol Vinyals, and Quoc V. Le. 2014. Sequence to sequence learning with neural networks. In *Proceedings of the 27th International Conference on Neural Information Processing Systems - Volume 2*, NIPS'14.

Zhilin Yang, Zihang Dai, Yiming Yang, Jaime Carbonell, Russ R Salakhutdinov, and Quoc V Le. 2019. Xlnet: Generalized autoregressive pretraining for language understanding. *Advances in neural information processing systems*, 32.

Qian Yu and Wai Lam. 2018. Review-aware answer prediction for product-related questions incorporating aspects. In *Proceedings of the Eleventh ACM International Conference on Web Search and Data Mining*.

Qian Yu, Wai Lam, and Zihao Wang. 2018. Responding E-commerce product questions via exploiting QA collections and reviews. In *Proceedings of the 27th International Conference on Computational Linguistics*.

A Appendix

A.1 Dataset Statistics

We downloaded the dataset from the Github repository of OAAG (https://github.com/dengyang17/OAAG). We use the same data split, but as there were no validation dataset, we use 10% train data as validation data. The deails of training, validation, and test split is shown in Table A.1.

	Sports	*Home*
Train	$40,517$	$73,118$
Validation	$4,502$	$8,125$
Test	$5,001$	$9,026$

Table A.1: Dataset statistics.

Question:	does the sight come with batteries ? if not what batteries do i need to buy ?
Ref. Ans.:	the sight did come with a battery , but if needed it would be a cr2032 .
Gen. Ans.:	no , it does not come with a batteries . you need to buy a separate batteries . it 's a great scope for the money but it 's not worth it . (31.82)
Question:	is it lined ?
Ref. Ans.:	it does n't have a liner in it , but still makes for a very nice light winter coat ...
Gen. Ans.:	no , it is not lined . it is a very nice jacket and i do n't think it 's too big for it . it 's a great deal . (22.22)
Question:	does the bottle sweat ? and , does the straw have a cover ?
Ref. Ans.:	does it sweat ? a little . not hardcore . just a little condensation on the bottom . and the straw does n't have a cover ...
Gen. Ans.:	no , it does not have a sweat straw . it is a very good straw and i have n't had any issues with it . i have n't had any issues with it . (24.62)
Question:	is it wood ?
Ref. Ans.:	it is gorgeous , and yes it is wood
Gen. Ans.:	no it is not wood . it 's a very nice piece of furniture . i would n't buy it again . it 's a very nice piece of furniture . (22.22)
Question:	how many watt ?
Ref. Ans.:	i do n't know but i am disappointed in mine . i wanted it to keep my coffee hot but it only keeps it warm .
Gen. Ans.:	i do n't know , but i do n't know if it does n't work for me . i 've had mine for over a year and it works great . (39.29)

Table A.2: Examples of answers generated by the OAAG model with high R1 scores. The R1 scores are within the parenthesis.

A.2 Generated Answers with High R1 Score

Table A.2 and Table A.3 shows some examples where the generated answers have a high (> 20) R1 score. In Table A.2, in the first and the second example, the generated answers are exactly the opposite of the reference answers. In the third example, the question was about sweating of the bottle and straw cover, but the answer does not address any of these. In the fourth example, the answer is ambivalent. The last example contains a frequently occurring phrase "I don't know" with a very high R1 score.

Question:	will it melt or bubble in the microwave ?
Ref. Ans.:	it never has with me and i have a high power microwave. really love to freeze in them. no ice buildup in them .
Gen. Ans.:	i have not tried it in the microwave but it does melt and bubble a little when you press on. (32.55)
Question:	does this actually comes with storage box as shown which is not in description ?
Ref. Ans.:	mine did not come with a storage box. and, it was not a very good knife. it grinds rather than cuts.
Gen. Ans.:	yes, it comes with a storage box as shown in picture.it is very easy to use and easy to take apart and put back together (38.29)
Question:	does it have an attachment to clean windows?
Ref. Ans.:	there is a wider flat piece that you could use on windows... it works nicely .
Gen. Ans.:	no, it does not have an attachment to clean windows but you can use a hose to do so if you need to clean them with water or something similar like that in your kitchen .(20.40)
Question:	could i have a red one ?
Ref. Ans.:	they do come in red, white and cream colors. whoever you buy it from, email them right after you place your order so you have a better chance of getting red .
Gen. Ans.:	i don't know if you can get a red one but it is a great product and is easy to use with any size pasta or sauce you want to make in your kitchen . (27.27)
Question:	is the under side a refrigerator as well or just storage ?
Ref. Ans.:	its a storage not a refrigerator you can only store cups or water bottles .
Gen. Ans.:	it's a refrigerator, but you can put it in the freezer or in your car to cool off water and then use it for storage .(35.00)

Table A.3: Examples of answers generated by the CHIME model with high R1 scores. The R1 scores are within the parenthesis.

Similarly, in the case of Table A.3, the second and the fifth examples have high R1 scores, but the generated answers are exactly opposite of the reference answers. In the first question, the model wrongly predicts that it would melt and bubble up a little in the microwave, and in the third question, it predicts an entirely different answer. The response to the fourth question is "I don't know," which is a frequently occurring phrase.

Question:	why do the dimensions say 2″ when the description says 3″ ? is the thickness of the mattress 3 inches or 2 ?
Ref. Ans.:	3″ .. seems amazon just copy and pasted from the other products in the line-up .
OAAG:	the thickness of the mattress is 3″ and the 3″ 3″ is the same as the picture of the mattress . it is a very nice pillow .
CHIME:	it's 3 " and 2.5 inches thick.i love this bed and it is perfect for my son who sleeps on his bed with no problem
Question:	what is the width and length of the rubbermaid 5576 slide and stack ?
Ref. Ans.:	the outside measurements are : 14 in . wide by 20 in . long . the inside of the basket is 123/4 in . wide by 163/4 to 181/2 in . long ...
OAAG:	it 's about 14″ long by 12″ wide by 12″ deep by 4″ high . hope that helps . i am very happy with this purchase .
CHIME:	the dimensions of the slide and stack are 11.5 inches wide by 8.5 inches deep by 7.75 inch tall.
Question:	how big of a pot can you put on it , 12″ ?
Ref. Ans.:	the cooking top measures 10.5″ × 10.5″ . the burner is an 8″ diameter circle . a 12″ pot would extend over the control panel if it were centered .
OAAG:	i have n't measured it , but i do n't think it would be too big to fit in a pot . i use it for that purpose and it works great .
CHIME:	it's 12 inches long and 12 inches wide and about 2 inches deep at the bottom of the pans.
Question:	what is the exact weight of it and how strong is the pocket clip ?
Ref. Ans.:	it 's about 3 oz . and it 's just as strong as any other clip i 've seen
OAAG:	it 's about 7.5″ long . it 's a great knife . it 's a great deal . it 's a great knife and i love it . it 's a great deal .
CHIME:	i'm not sure about the exact weight but it is very light and is very easy to use with ease .
Question:	does this fit a 2 year old ?
Ref. Ans.:	it fit my two year old who has a pretty normal size head . the multiple thicknesses of pads that are included really make it a great long term helmet !
OAAG:	yes it will , it 's a very tight fit . i do n't think it would be too big for a 2″ 2″ . it 's a great helmet .
CHIME:	i bought this for my son and he loves it so much he bought another one for his 2 year-bean .

Table A.4: Examples of numerical questions with their reference answer and the answer generated by OAAG and CHIME models.

A.3 Examples of Numerical Questions

We present some examples of numerical questions with their answers in Table A.4. In the first example, the generated answer is right, but none of the answers are correct for the rest of the questions.

Utilizing Cross-Modal Contrastive Learning to Improve Item Categorization BERT Model

Lei Chen*, Hou Wei Chou*
Rakuten Institute of Technology
Boston, MA, USA
{lei.a.chen,houwei.chou}@rakuten.com

Abstract

Item categorization (IC) is a core natural language processing (NLP) task in e-commerce. As a special text classification task, fine-tuning pre-trained models, e.g., BERT, has become a main stream solution. To improve IC performance further, other product metadata, e.g., product images, have been used. Although multimodal IC (MIC) systems show higher performance, expanding from processing text to more resource-demanding images brings large engineering impacts and hinders the deployment of such dual-input MIC systems. In this paper, we proposed a new way of using product images to improve text-only IC model: leveraging cross-modal signals between products' titles and associated images to adapt BERT models in a self-supervised learning (SSL) way. Our experiments on the three genres in the public Amazon product dataset show that the proposed method generates improved prediction accuracy and macro-F1 values than simply using the original BERT. Moreover, the proposed method is able to keep using existing text-only IC inference implementation and shows a resource advantage than the deployment of a dual-input MIC system.

1 Introduction

Item categorization (IC) is a core natural language processing (NLP) technology in e-commerce. Since millions types of products are provided in e-commerce markets, it is important to map these products to their locations in a product category tree efficiently and accurately so that buyers can easily find their interested products. Therefore, IC models with a high accuracy are needed for the success of e-commerce business. In spite that IC shares the same setup as a text classification task, it possesses its unique aspects, including (a) handling a large number of prediction labels, (b) a severe long-tailed distribution of labels, and (c) noisy raw inputs due to the fact that these inputs are generally provided by merchants in a heterogeneous way. These unique aspects make IC be a challenging task in practice.

Fine-tuning pre-trained models, e.g., BERT (Devlin et al., 2019), has become a main stream approach on building high-performance NLP applications. When using this paradigm to build IC models, is there any way to achieve an even higher performance? This is the first research question we tackled in this paper. One approach to improving IC models that generally use products' text titles alone is utilizing products' images. Previously, multimodal IC models using both text and image inputs have been actively investigated and applied in practice. However, such dual-input multimodal IC models bring more burden to the operation. Comparing to handling text data, the resource needed for storing/transferring/processing image data is much higher. For industry-scaled IC systems, adding image processing in its inference stage is costly. Is there any other way to get benefits by utilizing products' associated images but not paying such a high cost? This is the second research question we focused in this paper.

To tackle these two questions, inspired by (Zhang et al., 2020; Fang et al., 2020), we propose a solution of running a cross-modal contrastive learning, a special self-supervised learning (SSL), between products' images and text titles, to adapt pre-trained models to fit the IC task domain better. Then, the adapted pre-trained models will be used to build IC models using the fine-tuning paradigm. Moreover, by using the cross-modal SSL training, images can be used to improve text-based pre-trained models in the model training stage and a series of costly changes/operations in the inference stage can be avoided.

* Equal contributor

Proceedings of The Fifth Workshop on e-Commerce and NLP (ECNLP 5), pages 217 - 223
May 26, 2022

2 Related works

Fine-tuning pre-trained models has been becoming a main stream method for building high quality IC systems. For example, in a recent data challenge for building multimodal IC systems, which was organized in the SIGIR'20 e-commerce workshop[1], fine-tuning BERT models (Devlin et al., 2019) has been used by most of the participants (Bi et al., 2020; Chordia and Vijay Kumar, 2020; Chou et al., 2020).

In order to improve IC performance, one direction has been exploring utilizing more metadata associated with products. (Zahavy et al., 2016) is a seminal work where multi-label classification using both titles and images was conducted on products listed on the Walmart.com website. They used a convolutional neural network (CNN) to extract representations from both titles and images, and designed several policies to fuse the outputs of the two models. This led to improved performance over individual models separately. In the SIGIR'20 multimodal IC data challenge, different text-image fusion methods have been explored. Roughly in order of increasing complexity, the methods included simple decision-level late fusion (Bi et al., 2020), highway network (Chou et al., 2020), and co-attention (Chordia and Vijay Kumar, 2020). By reviewing the experiment results from several teams, we can observe that (a) dual-input IC models show higher performance than any uni-modal IC model, (b) performance gains brought by using images are limited but not neglectable. When considering IC performance's profound impacts on e-commerce business values, including products' visual information is necessary.

Contrastive learning (CL) has been found to be an effective self-supervised learning (SSL) approach for training high-quality representations. For example, in computer vision, SimCLR (Chen et al., 2020) uses the consistence between an anchor image and its transformed version and the in-consistence between the anchor and other instances in a batch (negative instances) to guide learning visual representations. Without using labels, it achieves visual representations with a quality on par or even higher than the ones trained based on traditional supervised learning. Inspired by the success of SimCLR in computer vision, CL-based text representation learning has been a hot research topic in NLP. Both SimCSE (Gao et al., 2021) and (Liu et al., 2021) used dropout operations existing in Transformer architecture (Vaswani et al., 2017) to be an effective text augmentation way and obtained effective text representations.

The SSL idea has been tried in the NLP domain for further improving BERT models. For example, (Fang et al., 2020) proposed using SSL to improve the pre-trained BERT model prior to running down-stream NLP tasks, e.g., various tasks in the GLUE benchmark test. When generating augmented instances for providing positive pairs, a back-translation method is used. The CL setup was based on MoCo architecture by using a momentum mechanism (He et al., 2020). (Su et al., 2021) also used the SSL to improve pre-trained BERT model for more accurate relation extraction (RE) task. When doing text augmentation, it considered the RE task's unique property and proposed a task-specific augmentation method. In these two works, SSL training was found to be useful for improving follow-up fine-tuning tasks' performance.

Regarding the SSL methods being used, an interesting trend is considering cross-modal signals. (Zhang et al., 2020) proposed Contrastive VIsual Representation Learning from Text (ConVIRT) model to use text descriptions associated with medical images to help training more accurate medical image representations. Note that in the medical image domain, the annotated image data size is much limited, in a contrast, medical text notes are more adequate. (Radford et al., 2021) is a seminal work from OpenAI. By using a massive set of image-text pairs, about 350 million, CLIP used a simple cross-modal contrastive learning to pretrain a quite powerful vision-language joint model. The trained model shows many impressive applications, like superior performance on many zero-shot image classification tasks.

3 Model

Figure 1 depicts our proposed model in a concise way. From a pre-trained BERT model, denoted as BERT_{origin}, a self-supervised learning (SSL) is applied to further adapt the BERT_{origin} fitting to the fine-tuning task better. When selecting the data set used in the SSL step, note that due to the self-supervised nature, we don't need human-annotated labels. Then, the adapted BERT is used to initialize the BERT model (serving as a textual feature encoder) in the fine-tuning stage. The final IC model,

[1] `https://sigir-ecom.github.io/ecom2020/data-task.html`

consisting of BERT and a linear classifier on top of it, is learned jointly by using a cross-entropy loss on the fine-tuning data set.

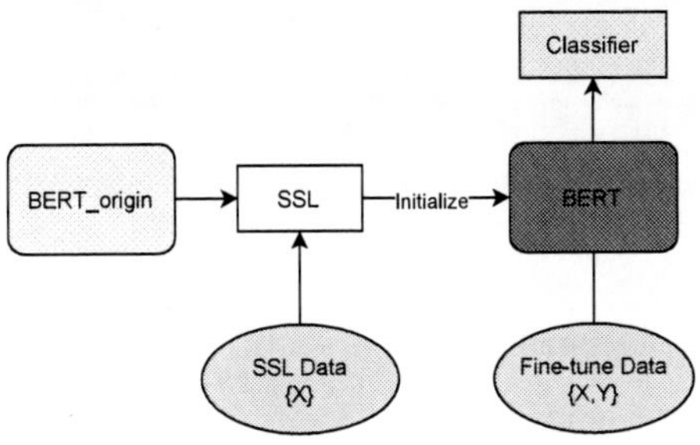

Figure 1: Self-Supervised Learning (SSL) is applied to improve pre-trained BERT, BERT_{origin}, for fitting the fine-tuning task better. Then, a conventional fine-tuning is conducted to jointly update both BERT (for representation learning) and classifier training.

3.1 SSL SimCSE

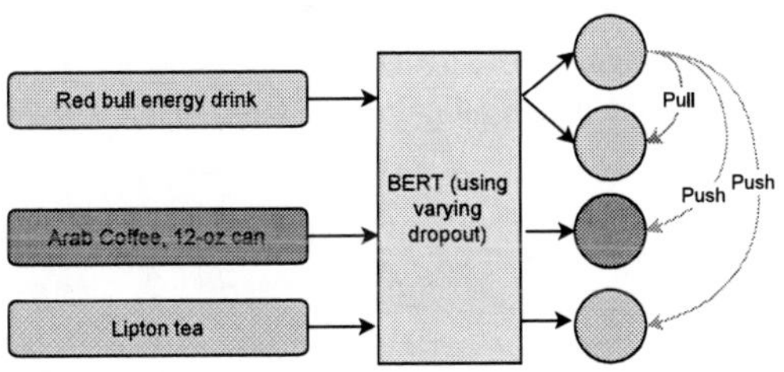

Figure 2: An illustration showing how SimCSE works. Note that we only show contrastive pairs, i.e., both positive and negative, to the top product "red bull energy drink".

For a text title $\mathbf{x}_t$, we obtain a text representation $\mathbf{t}$ with a BERT encoder $f_t(, d)$ where d is a dropout mask, and a projection function g_t, which uses a simple multiple layer perception (MLP) structure.

$$\mathbf{t} = g_t(f_t(\mathbf{x}_t, d)) \tag{1}$$

To obtain a positive pair, SimCSE just runs the same text title throughout the Transformer encoder pipeline with a different dropout mask d^+.

$$\mathbf{t}^+ = g_t(f_t(\mathbf{x}_t, d^+)) \tag{2}$$

For ith text title, the training objective of SimCSE is like:

$$\mathcal{L}_i^t = -log \frac{exp(sim(\mathbf{t}_i, \mathbf{t}_i^+)/\tau)}{\sum_{j=1}^{N, j \neq i} exp(sim(\mathbf{t}_i, \mathbf{t}_j)/\tau)} \tag{3}$$

for a mini-batch of N text titles, where $sim()$ represents a similarity computation and τ is a temperature parameter. The total loss computed by SimCSE is an average among all text titles

$$\mathcal{L}_{simCSE} = \sum_{i=1}^{N} \mathcal{L}_i^t / N \tag{4}$$

in the mini-batch.

As shown in Figure 2, the top title serves as an anchor and is sent to a BERT model twice to obtain two similar but varying text representations because of using varying dropout masks. The augmented version serves as a positive pair to the anchor while other two titles in the batch serve as negative pairs. Through using an infoNCE loss (Oord et al., 2018), BERT encoder is changed to pull positive pairs closer while pushing negative pairs away. Clearly, without any supervision, BERT encoder can be further adapted to provide a representation better fitting to the SSL data set.

3.2 SSL ConVIRT

In the SSL SimCSE method, both positive and negative pairs are from the text domain. Inspired by the cross-modal contrastive learning in (Zhang et al., 2020), we use product images that co-exist with text titles to provide self-supervision signals.

Regarding the visual encoder used to process product images to visual representation vectors, we choose a newly emerging encoder based on Transformer like BERT model. In recent years, Transformer based visual models have become popular (Han et al., 2020). Among the many visual Transformer models, we selected the ViT model (Dosovitskiy et al., 2020), which is a pure Transformer that is applied directly on an image's $P \times P$ patch sequence. In the implementation, it follows the original Transformer's design as much as possible. ViT utilizes the standard Transformer's encoder part as an image classification feature extractor and adds a MLP head to determine the image labels. The ViT model is pre-trained using a supervised learning task on a massive image data set. The size of the supervised training data set impacts ViT performance significantly. When using Google's in-house JFT 300M image set, ViT can reach a performance superior to other competitive ResNet (He et al., 2016) models. After converting a product image to $P \times P$ patches, ViT converts these patches to visual tokens. After adding a special [CLS] visual token to represent the entire image, the $M = P \times P + 1$ long sequence is fed into a ViT model to output an encoding as $\mathbf{v} = (v_0, v_1, v_2, ...v_M)$, where $M = P \times P$.

For a product i with a text title x_t and an image x_v, we obtain its visual representation by running through a visual processing pipeline including a ViT image encoder f_v and a projection layer g_v, which is also an MLP.

$$\mathbf{v} = g_v(f_v(x_v)) \quad (5)$$

Based on text and image representations, we compute a contrastive loss from text to image direction (denoted as $t \rightarrow v$).

$$\mathcal{L}_i^{t \rightarrow v} = -log \frac{exp(sim(\mathbf{t}_i, \mathbf{v}_i)/\tau)}{\sum_{j=1}^{N, j \neq i} exp(sim(\mathbf{t}_i, \mathbf{v}_j)/\tau)} \quad (6)$$

Similarly, a contrastive loss from the other direction, image to text (denoted as $v \rightarrow t$), can be computed as

$$\mathcal{L}_i^{v \rightarrow t} = -log \frac{exp(sim(\mathbf{v}_i, \mathbf{t}_i)/\tau)}{\sum_{j=1}^{N, j \neq i} exp(sim(\mathbf{v}_i, \mathbf{t}_j)/\tau)} \quad (7)$$

$$\mathcal{L}_{ConVIRT} = \sum_{i=1}^{N} (\alpha \mathcal{L}_i^{t \rightarrow v} + (1-\alpha) \mathcal{L}_i^{v \rightarrow t})/N \quad (8)$$

where α is a hyper-paramter to control two contrastive losses in the range [0,1].

As shown in Figure 3, for the anchor with a text title as "red bull drink", we use its corresponding product image to be a positive pair. Images from other in-batch products serve as negative pairs. By using the ConVIRT objective, we can adapt both BERT and ViT encoders to better fit the SSL data set. Note that in a contrast to (Zhang et al., 2020), our goal is on using the adapted BERT on text domain in the follow-up fine-tuning task.

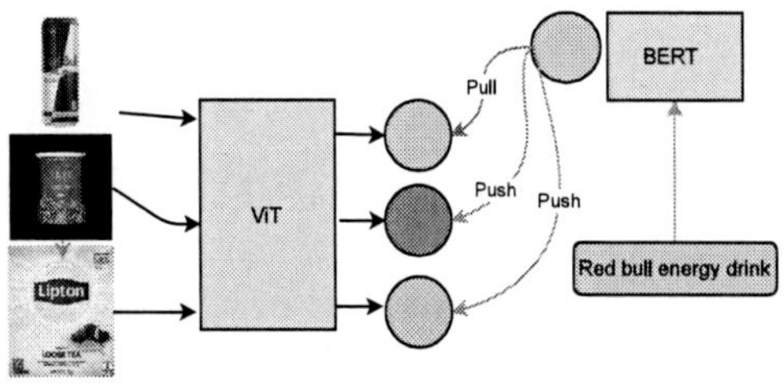

Figure 3: An illustration of ConVIRT. Note that we only showed text→image direction.

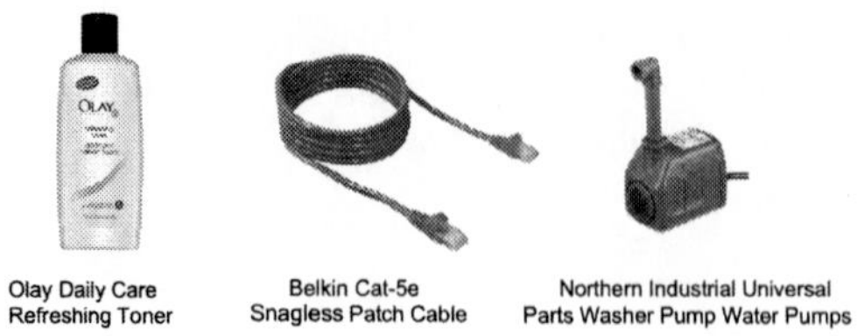

Figure 4: Example titles and images from Amazon Review Dataset

4 Experiment

4.1 Setup

Data set: The experimental data consisted of products from Amazon Review Dataset (McAuley et al., 2015; He and McAuley, 2016), focusing on three major product categories, i.e., Automotive, Beauty, and Electronics. Each product contains a text title and a product image that is downloaded from Amazon website from a set of associated images. Figure 4 provides some concrete examples. Our task, a multi-class classification problem, is to predict product categories from their titles. More details of the experimental data are shown in Table 1.

Root genre	# Class	# Data	Len. (ave.)
Automotive	953	200,907	9.91
Beauty	229	199,757	10.26
Electronics	500	107,947	14.88

Table 1: Statistics of the data obtained from Amazon Review Dataset, including the number of labels, the number of instances, and average lengths of text titles

Models: We built IC models by following the paradigm of fine-tuning pre-trained models. Three different pre-trained models were compared.

- origin: using the origin English BERT base model[2].
- SSL SimCSE: the origin BERT model is adapted by using the SimCSE SSL method described in Section 3.1.
- SSL ConVIRT: the origin BERT model is adapted by using the ConVIRT SSL method described in Section 3.2. Note that we used ViT-L-16[3] 16 means that we used 16×16 patches when feeding images.

[2]https://huggingface.co/bert-base-uncased

[3]https://github.com/asyml/vision-transformer-pytorch

Implementation details: For each root genre, from entire data set, we allocate 50% instances for SSL training while keep the remaining 50% instances for fine-tuning, i.e., 30% for Train, 10% for Dev and 10% for Testing. To test model performance on different sizes of fine-tuning data, we then incremental increased fine-tuning set from 5%, 10%, 25%, 50%, 75%, and 100% on the Train set (containing 30% of the entire data size). The fine-tuned IC classifiers were tested on the entire Testing set. Our primary evaluation metric is accuracy. In addition, to make sure all labels can be properly detected, we also evaluate macro-F1 metric. Our models are implemented in PyTorch using 4 GPUs for training and evaluation. At SSL stage, for each dataset, we use the AdamW optimizer (Loshchilov and Hutter, 2017) with an initial learning rate of $1e^{-5}$ and weight decay of $1e^{-8}$. Different from (Zhang et al., 2020), We use Vit as vision encoder and give more weights (higher α) on text-to-image contrastive loss. We set τ=0.1, α=0.75 and train 50 epochs for ConVIRT. The Transformer encoders are followed by a mean-pooling layer and a projection layer with an output dimension $d = 768$. At the fine-tuning stage, we use Adam optimizer with an initial learning rate of $5e^{-5}$, and a weight decay of $1e^{-8}$ for 30 epochs. A fixed batch size of 32 is used on both stages.

Genre	FT%	origin	SimCSE	ConVIRT
Beauty	5	0.526	0.525	**0.599**
	10	0.577	0.577	**0.623**
	25	0.618	0.616	**0.633**
	50	0.642	0.643	**0.663**
	75	0.659	0.659	**0.670**
	100	0.661	0.669	**0.676**
Auto.	5	0.473	0.499	**0.563**
	10	0.563	0.574	**0.617**
	25	0.648	0.646	**0.668**
	50	0.685	0.690	**0.697**
	75	0.702	0.709	**0.712**
	100	0.718	0.720	**0.721**
Elec.	5	0.319	0.344	**0.483**
	10	0.428	0.441	**0.533**
	25	0.539	0.533	**0.581**
	50	0.575	0.583	**0.601**
	75	0.599	0.604	**0.619**
	100	0.615	0.618	**0.626**

Table 2: Accuracy by fine-tuning BERT models from (a) origin, (b) intra-modal self-supervised by using SimCSE, and (c) cross-modal self-supervised by using ConVIRT on three genres. The underline shows that BERT after SSL cannot show further performance gains. The bold fonts suggest that BERT after SSL can bring further performance gains.

4.2 Result

Table 2 reports on accuracy metrics on the three genres. We compared the three fine-tuning methods, including (a) routine fine-tuning using BERT_{origin}, (b) fine-tuning on the BERT self-supervised by using the SimCSE method on texts only, and (c) fine-tuning on the BERT self-supervised by using the ConVIRT method on both texts and product images. We incrementally increased fine-tuning portions from 5% to 100% of the Train set. Comparing with method (a), both methods using SSL methods show performance gains in most of cases. Between the two SSL methods, we found that using cross-modal contrastive learning is more effective, especially when fine-tuning portion is low. Success of a SSL method depends on effectiveness of augmentation operation. Compared to the dropout used in SimCSE, the cross-modal CL losses in ConVIRT may be more genuine and powerful. This is also suggested by recent success of using cross-modal contrastive signals, such as (Radford et al., 2021).

Figure 5 plots macro-F1 values on the two label groups. Based on instance sizes belonging to class labels, we divide all of the labels into two categories, *head* (labels contain 80% of instances) and *tail* (labels only contain 20% of instances). We observed ConVIRT SSL training helps on improve $F-1$ on both head and tail labels. However, SimCSE SSL training does not show noticeable F-1 increases comparing to the baseline of using origin BERT. On tail labels, the gains brought by SSL are quite consistent no matter how large portion of data was used in fine-tuning. This shows that SSL benefit to mitigate long-tailed issue in the item classification task.

5 Discussion

With the success of pre-trained models like BERT (Devlin et al., 2019) on many NLP tasks, fine-tuning BERT models has become an leading approach. To further improve fine-tuned IC model performance, inspired by related works (Fang et al., 2020), self-supervised learning (SSL) is used to adapt original BERT models to better match with the IC task. Regarding the SSL method, we com-

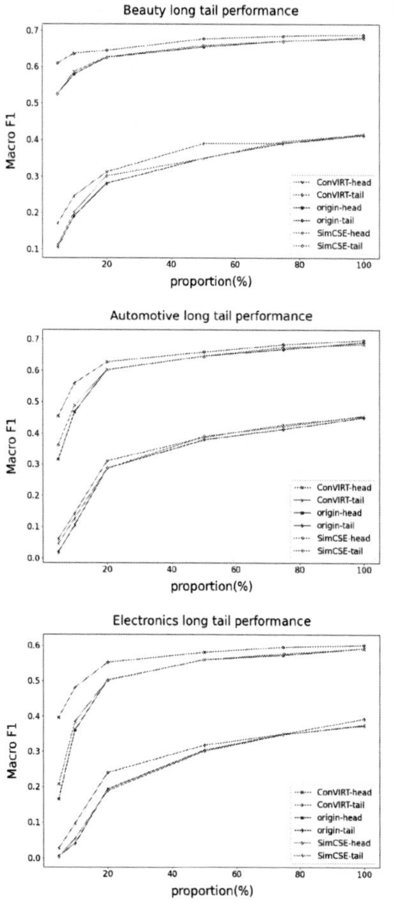

Figure 5: On head class labels (#instance $\geq$ 80%) and tail class labels (#instance $\leq$ 20%), we measured macro-F1 on the three methods, i.e., (a) fine-tuning on BERT$_{origin}$, (b) intra-modal self-supervised using SimCSE, and (c) cross-modal self-supervised using ConVIRT.

pared two approaches. The first approach is unsupervised SimCSE (Gao et al., 2021) that only uses text titles. The SimCSE provided a simple but effective way to generate semantically similar pairs (positive) by feeding the same product title into a BERT model with varying dropout masks. Using other titles in the mini-batch to be negative pairs, the BERT model can be adjusted by minimizing the infoNCE loss (Oord et al., 2018). To improve SSL further, we proposed using the cross-modal contrastive learning to utilize product images to bring additional modeling power to improve our text representations. Following (Zhang et al., 2020), for a product title, we use its associated product image to be a positive pair while other products' images to be negative pairs. The same cross-modal computation was also applied on a product image to provide contrastive signal from the other direction.

Our experiments on the three genres in the Amazon Review Dataset show that both SSL enriched BERT models have higher fine-tuning performance. Between the two SSL methods, the SSL using ConVIRT method is more effective. Moreover, this new way of utilizing images means that we only need process images during the model training stage and can only deploy text-only BERT (enriched by ConVIRT SSL training) in our inference stage. This will dramatically reduce engineering and computation costs compared to the method of deploying a dual-input MIC systems.

One limitation of our research is that we only explored the SimCSE method when using unlabeled text data. It is possible that other semi-supervised learning methods like UDA (Xie et al., 2019) may help on improving the final fine-tuning performance. We will leave the exploration on more semi-supervised learning methods in future. In addition, there are several directions to extend the current work in the future, including (1) improving contrastive learning based SSL, for example using nearest neighbor to get better positive pairs similar to (Li et al., 2021), and (2) improving our algorithms to better address training set bias such as high label noise and very imbalanced data set in real IC data.

References

Ye Bi, Shuo Wang, and Zhongrui Fan. 2020. A Multimodal Late Fusion Model for E-Commerce Product Classification. *arXiv preprint arXiv:2008.06179*.

Ting Chen, Simon Kornblith, Mohammad Norouzi, and Geoffrey Hinton. 2020. A simple framework for contrastive learning of visual representations. In *International conference on machine learning*, pages 1597–1607. PMLR.

V. Chordia and B.G. Vijay Kumar. 2020. Large Scale Multimodal Classification Using an Ensemble of Transformer Models and Co-Attention. In *Proc. SIGIR'20 e-Com workshop.*

H. Chou, Y.H. Lee, L. Chen, Y. Xia, and W.T. Chen. 2020. CBB-FE, CamemBERT and BiT Feature Extraction for Multimodal Product Classification and Retrieval. In *Proc. SIGIR'20 e-Com workshop*.

Jacob Devlin, Ming-Wei Chang, Kenton Lee, and Kristina Toutanova. 2019. BERT: Pre-training of Deep Bidirectional Transformers for Language

Understanding. *arXiv:1810.04805 [cs]*. ArXiv: 1810.04805.

Alexey Dosovitskiy, Lucas Beyer, Alexander Kolesnikov, Dirk Weissenborn, Xiaohua Zhai, Thomas Unterthiner, Mostafa Dehghani, Matthias Minderer, Georg Heigold, and Sylvain Gelly. 2020. An image is worth 16x16 words: Transformers for image recognition at scale. *arXiv preprint arXiv:2010.11929*.

Hongchao Fang, Sicheng Wang, Meng Zhou, Jiayuan Ding, and Pengtao Xie. 2020. CERT: Contrastive self-supervised learning for language understanding. *arXiv preprint arXiv:2005.12766*.

Tianyu Gao, Xingcheng Yao, and Danqi Chen. 2021. SimCSE: Simple contrastive learning of sentence embeddings. In *Proceedings of the 2021 Conference on Empirical Methods in Natural Language Processing*, pages 6894–6910, Online and Punta Cana, Dominican Republic. Association for Computational Linguistics.

Kai Han, Yunhe Wang, Hanting Chen, Xinghao Chen, Jianyuan Guo, Zhenhua Liu, Yehui Tang, An Xiao, Chunjing Xu, and Yixing Xu. 2020. A Survey on Visual Transformer. *arXiv preprint arXiv:2012.12556*.

Kaiming He, Haoqi Fan, Yuxin Wu, Saining Xie, and Ross Girshick. 2020. Momentum contrast for unsupervised visual representation learning. In *Proceedings of the IEEE/CVF Conference on Computer Vision and Pattern Recognition*, pages 9729–9738.

Kaiming He, Xiangyu Zhang, Shaoqing Ren, and Jian Sun. 2016. Deep residual learning for image recognition. In *Proceedings of the IEEE conference on computer vision and pattern recognition*, pages 770–778.

Ruining He and Julian McAuley. 2016. Ups and downs: Modeling the visual evolution of fashion trends with one-class collaborative filtering. In *proceedings of the 25th international conference on world wide web*, pages 507–517.

Yangguang Li, Feng Liang, Lichen Zhao, Yufeng Cui, Wanli Ouyang, Jing Shao, Fengwei Yu, and Junjie Yan. 2021. Supervision exists everywhere: A data efficient contrastive language-image pre-training paradigm. *arXiv preprint arXiv:2110.05208*.

Fangyu Liu, Ivan Vulić, Anna Korhonen, and Nigel Collier. 2021. Fast, effective, and self-supervised: Transforming masked language models into universal lexical and sentence encoders. In *Proceedings of the 2021 Conference on Empirical Methods in Natural Language Processing*, pages 1442–1459, Online and Punta Cana, Dominican Republic. Association for Computational Linguistics.

Ilya Loshchilov and Frank Hutter. 2017. Decoupled weight decay regularization. *arXiv preprint arXiv:1711.05101*.

Julian McAuley, Christopher Targett, Qinfeng Shi, and Anton Van Den Hengel. 2015. Image-based recommendations on styles and substitutes. In *Proceedings of the 38th international ACM SIGIR conference on research and development in information retrieval*, pages 43–52.

Aaron van den Oord, Yazhe Li, and Oriol Vinyals. 2018. Representation learning with contrastive predictive coding. *arXiv preprint arXiv:1807.03748*.

Alec Radford, Jong Wook Kim, Chris Hallacy, Aditya Ramesh, Gabriel Goh, Sandhini Agarwal, Girish Sastry, Amanda Askell, Pamela Mishkin, Jack Clark, et al. 2021. Learning transferable visual models from natural language supervision. *arXiv preprint arXiv:2103.00020*.

Peng Su, Yifan Peng, and K Vijay-Shanker. 2021. Improving bert model using contrastive learning for biomedical relation extraction. In *Proceedings of the 20th Workshop on Biomedical Language Processing*, pages 1–10.

Ashish Vaswani, Noam Shazeer, Niki Parmar, Jakob Uszkoreit, Llion Jones, Aidan N. Gomez, \Lukasz Kaiser, and Illia Polosukhin. 2017. Attention is all you need. *Advances in neural information processing systems*, 30:5998–6008.

Qizhe Xie, Zihang Dai, Eduard Hovy, Minh-Thang Luong, and Quoc V. Le. 2019. Unsupervised data augmentation for consistency training. *arXiv preprint arXiv:1904.12848*.

Tom Zahavy, Alessandro Magnani, Abhinandan Krishnan, and Shie Mannor. 2016. Is a picture worth a thousand words? A Deep Multi-Modal Fusion Architecture for Product Classification in e-commerce. *arXiv preprint arXiv:1611.09534*.

Yuhao Zhang, Hang Jiang, Yasuhide Miura, Christopher D Manning, and Curtis P Langlotz. 2020. Contrastive learning of medical visual representations from paired images and text. *arXiv preprint arXiv:2010.00747*.

Towards Generalizable Semantic Product Search by Text Similarity Pre-training on Search Click Logs

Zheng Liu, Wei Zhang, Yan Chen, Weiyi Sun, Michael Du, Benjamin Schroeder
Wayfair LLC
4 Copley Place, Boston, MA USA 02116
{zliu2,wzhang5,ychen4,wsun1,tdu1,beschroeder}@wayfair.com

Abstract

Recently, semantic search has been successfully applied to e-commerce product search and the learned semantic space(s) for query and product encoding are expected to generalize to unseen queries or products. Yet, whether generalization can conveniently emerge has not been thoroughly studied in the domain thus far. In this paper, we examine several general-domain and domain-specific pre-trained Roberta variants and discover that general-domain fine-tuning does not help generalization, which aligns with the discovery of prior art. Proper domain-specific fine-tuning with clickstream data can lead to better model generalization, based on a bucketed analysis of a publicly available manual annotated query-product pair data.

1 Introduction

Semantic Search has been widely studied recently as a promising competitor to token-based inverted index search that had dominated information retrieval (IR) and question answering (QA) for decades. However, in e-commerce product search, the quality of the learned embedding space is not well understood, especially on the quality of generalization to unseen queries, unseen products, or even unseen query-product pairs. The generalization is particularly interesting and important because in Wayfair 80% of queries are new in the monthly basis, and new products are added everyday. In this paper, we will investigate the generalization issue by seeking answers to the two following questions:

1. How well does the learned space generalize to unseen queries/products/query-product combinations?
2. Are we able to improve generalization by pre-training, and how?

Arguably, some pre-trained models, especially the ones pre-trained with domain-specific clickstream data, may outperform the others on generalization. To validate the hypothesis, we train two-tower semantic search models using three different categories of base models for comparison: not pre-trained (Roberta-base (Liu et al., 2019), Roberta-large), general-domain pre-trained with text similarity (SimCSE (Gao et al., 2021)) and domain-specific pre-trained with text similarity (SimCSE that are continuously pre-trained with clickstream data).

To observe how the models perform, we take a publicly available product search dataset (Chen et al., 2022) and partition the data into buckets according to whether the query/product/query-product pairs have been visited during training. By comparing the performance of the above models, we observe that query representations may have been insufficiently learned during two-tower semantic search fine-tuning as opposed to product representations, and the model variant which is pre-trained on query-query text similarity has a visible impact on models' generalization power.

This paper is organized as follows: 1) we first introduce related work, then 2) explain the proposed pre-training approach, and finally 3) discuss results and analysis.

2 Related Work

Semantic search in product search Recently, semantic search has been explored in e-commerce product search (Nigam et al., 2019; Huang et al., 2020; Zhang et al., 2020; Li et al., 2021), in which queries and products are embedded as vectors through representation learning and search is then conducted in the vector space. These implementations generally follow a two-tower approach: one group of stacked neural network layers, usually referred to as "tower", processes the query, and another tower processes the product. This approach is favored in production due to its ability of decoupling query and product embedding process, so

Proceedings of The Fifth Workshop on e-Commerce and NLP (ECNLP 5), pages 224 - 233
May 26, 2022

that products can be embedded offline and search can be accelerated in real-time services. In search systems, the semantic search is usually used as candidate generators focusing on core-relevance, and often followed by dedicated ranking layers that capture other e-commerce attributes such as price, popularity, quality, etc. The two tower model of this work is described in Section 3.5.

Generalization for two-tower neural models Deep Passage retrieval has become a popular approach recently for IR. In Question Answering, Lewis et al. (2021) observed that when using the two-tower approach for relevant passage retrieval stage, deep learning models tend to memorize training instances and perform substantially worse on unseen questions or unseen answers. They argued the generalization on questions is the major issue, which is similar to our observation in product search. Mao et al. (2021) tried to address the issue by explicitly retrieving question-related texts as query expansions and showed improvements on model generalization to unseen question/answers, yet we take the route of query similarity learning by using automatically mined query pairs from product co-click behaviors.

Pre-training for Neural Retrieval Chang et al. (2020) pre-trained neural retrieval-based QA models with carefully designed synthetic tasks, followed by Guu et al. (2020) with a knowledge-augmented training task and Sachan et al. (2021) with combining ICT and masked salient spans training. Oğuz et al. (2021) instead enhanced training with domain-matching Reddit post comment pairs to pre-train a dense retrieval model and also observed positive influences to open domain QA. Differently, our approach explores the clickstream graph structure instead of mining additional data.

Text Representations Learning Our approach closely relates to the graph node embeddings within texts (Mikolov et al., 2013) or the linked graphs (Hamilton et al., 2017) rather than node embeddings that involve node relation types (Bordes et al., 2013) or graphical neural networks that aggregate neighbouring nodes in a parametric fashion (Li et al., 2016; Kipf and Welling, 2016). Recently, noisy contrastive learning has enjoyed significant success (Gao et al., 2021) for regularizing text encoders, and shows that such encoders can effectively serve as a starting point for downstream task fine-tuning. In retrieval tasks, Gao and Callan (2021) pre-trained text encoders with synthetic passage similarity tasks using noisy contrastive loss, assuming that in Wikipedia two adjacent passages in the same article are similar in semantics rather than those from two different articles. In contrast, in product search, we assume two queries leading to the same product browse, or two products purchased under the same query, are similar.

3 Approach

This section describes how models are pre-trained, fine-tuned, and evaluated on clickstream data. Section 3.1 sets up preliminaries and math notations for the product search problem; Section 3.2, 3.3 and 3.4 describe three different pre-training approaches; Section 3.5 discusses how the model is fine-tuned and evaluated in the product search problem.

3.1 Preliminaries

A click graph is denoted as $\mathcal{G} = \{V, E\}$ where V is the set of nodes either being a query q or a product p which is the concatenation of title, brand name, and class name [1]. An edge E connecting q and p suggests a customer showed interest to product p when searching with query q.

The core of semantic search is to learn query and product representations. Intuitively, a good representation that generalizes may put similar concepts (p or q) closer in the semantic space, while dissimilar ones further apart.

There are three node type combinations (p, p), (q, q), and (p, q), the last of which is the goal of semantic search. Arguably, learning solely on (p, q) may cause generalization issue when (p, p) and (q, q) relations can not be implicitly learned from (p, q) objective. To verify if this hypothesis holds in our semantic search problem, we design three pre-training tasks to warm up Transformers: the (q, q) pre-training task, the (p, p) pre-training task, and the (q, q) and (p, p) pre-training task. Afte pre-training, we fine-tune the model on the (p, q) learning objective. In the remaining of this section, we describe the three pre-training and the fine-tuning approaches.

3.2 Query Similarity Learning

qq Model If two queries q_1 and q_2 link to the same product p in graph $\mathcal{G}$, we regard (q_1, q_2) as

[1] A product can have multiple class names with hierarchical structure (e.g. class "sofa" belongs to class "living room furniture"). Here we used the high level product class name (e.g. "living room furniture").

first query	second query	relation	score
girls study desk	outdoor shed	Entirely different intents	0
bathroom window curtains short	curtains bedroom	Similar (not entail/co-intent)	1
52 inch ceiling fan with light	Ceiling fans with lights	Entailment	2
Fishing storage	Fishing tackle storage	Same intent	3

Table 1: Query similarity manual annotation samples. Note that first and second query is order-sensitive. However, as similarity strength, we disregard directionality.

one co-clicked query pair. After collecting the pairs, we use them to fine-tune a SimCSE-large (Gao et al., 2021) model to obtain a model we call **qq** model.

Pair Sampling We follow the 3 steps below to mine pairs: 1) sample q_1 by $P(q)$, the query distribution obtained from data; 2) for q_1, we collect top-K popular products $p_1, ...p_K$ by frequency, and uniformly sample one product p from them [2], and 3) at last, for p, we collect all its related queries and sample one query as q_2 uniformly. We repeat this process N times to obtain N pairs where N is set to 1 million.

Training We train the model with a noisy contrastive learning objective as in (Gao et al., 2021) with default settings. We train the model with 3 epochs. We fine-tune on top of the unsupervised SimCSE-large model and observe the additive effect of open-domain and domain-specific learning.

Similarity Evaluation To evaluate the query representation, we invite 3 domain experts to annotate the degree of query pairs into 4 relation types: not related (0), similar but not entail (1), entailment (2) and identical (3), where the number represents the semantic strengths, the higher the more related they are. A total of 1056 random query pairs are extracted from click sessions and the relation types are evenly distributed. The inter-annotator agreement was 90% after 2 rounds of annotation and curation. A sample of the annotation data is shown in Table 1.

We calculate vector cosine between two queries as similarity score, and compare it to the groundtruth by Spearman Rank Correlation with significant tests. The result is shown in Table 2. As we can see, the model fine-tuned with co-click data achieves the best performance. Surprisingly, "Ours-unsup" learning noisy contrastive loss by masking a single query twice and learning their similarities (similar to SimCSE-unsup with open-domain texts), does not lead to a better performance on query pairs, suggesting that the key of query similarity learning is to capture rich domain-specific text similarity knowledge rather than text robustness and regularity in semantic space. This message encourages us to further extend it to product similarity learning (this time, without manual evaluation).

Model	SP (P-value)
Roberta-large	0.287 (1.8e-21)
SimCSE-large-unsup	0.467 (2.9 e-58)
SimCSE-large-sup	0.426 (7.9e-48)
Ours-unsup	0.458 (2.2e-48)
Ours-sup (co-click)	0.546 (5.8e-82)

Table 2: Comparison of different Models's Spearman Rank Correlation on representation evaluation data. SimCSE–large-unsup is the representation learned *unsupervisedly* with noisy contrastive loss; SimCSE-large-sup is subsequently learned from *supervised* text entailment data. In our settings, the definition of unsup and sup changed a bit: Ours-unsup is the model learned with unsupervised objective (masked language modeling) with noisy contrastive loss, where Ours-sup is learned from query co-click data described in section 3.2.

3.3 Product Similarity Learning

pp Model The product representation learning is performed similarly to the query representation learning. We start from SimCSE-large-unsup model, and fine-tune (p, p) pairs that are obtained from the process similar to the sampling approach in section 3.2 with the role of query and product swapped. The created 1 million pairs are used to fine-tune the SimCSE model and obtain a model dubbed **pp** model. Different from **qq** model, we did not obtain manual annotation data for **pp**, thus we let the model train 2 epochs until convergence.

[2] "Uniformly" as a reasonably simple yet arguably effective approach to mitigate exposure bias without complex user behavior modeling

3.4 A Combined Model

qq+pp Model In this approach, we sequentially pre-trained the model with both (q, q) data and (p, p) data, to examine the additive effect where a model is fine-tuned with both query similarities and product similarities. We take the **qq** model and continue to pretrain it with the above (p, p) data until convergence, and obtain a model called **qq+pp**. Indeed, we may risk catastrophic forgetting since arguably the (p, p) pairs may overwrite the captured (q, q) information. Although we have observed such forgetting to happen, its effect is mild at best.

3.5 Fine-tuning for Semantic Search

pq Learning After pre-training, the semantic search model was fine-tuned on product search tasks: given a search query, the task is to retrieve a list of relevant products from the product catalog. Specifically, both queries and products were represented as vectors in the same latent space, and products were retrieved according to cosine similarities w.r.t. the queries.

As shown in figure 1, we adopted a two tower approach to fine-tune the semantic search model: a user tower embeds search queries into vectors, while a product tower embeds product information (e.g. product name, product brand name, product class name) into vectors. The two towers share the same tokenizer and transformer model. We took the last hidden layer's CLS token representation and L2-normalized it as the final output embedding vector. Then, the relevance score was calculated as the cosine similarity between search query embedding and product embedding vectors.

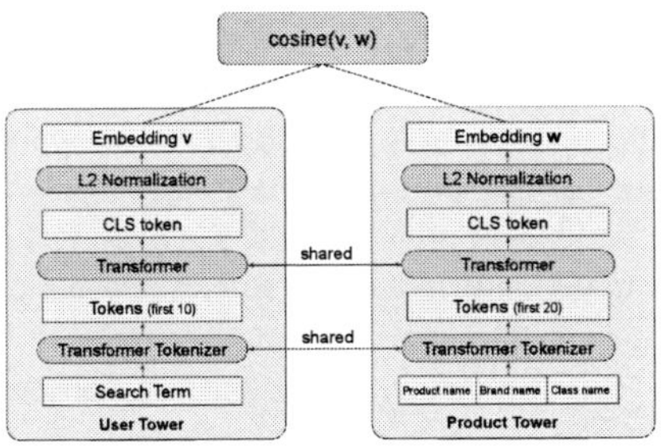

Figure 1: Structure of semantic search models on product search tasks

To train the model, we adopted the contrastive framework and utilized the cross-entropy objective with in-batch negatives (Chen et al., 2020). In each mini-batch, we sampled n semantically relevant (query, product) pairs $D = \{(q_i, p_i)\}_{i=1}^{n}$, and calculated the training objective for the i'th pair (q_i, p_i) as:

$$l_i = -\frac{cos(f(q_i), g(p_i))}{\tau} + log \sum_{j=1}^{n} e^{\frac{cos(f(q_i), g(p_j))}{\tau}} \quad (1)$$

f, g represent the user and product tower respectively. τ is a temperature hyperparameter. All layers of Transformer models are fine-tuned in the product search task.

Data In the experiment, (q, p) pairs are collected from click graph $\mathcal{G}$. As show in table 3, each search query and its resulted add-to-cart products (if any) are constructed as semantically relevant (query, product) pairs. The training dataset contains 31M pairs from 2019 and 2020 records of a e-commerce search engine, and the dev dataset contains 100k pairs randomly sampled from 2021. We evaluated model's performance on the *WANDS* dataset (Chen et al., 2022), which is a human annotated dataset for evaluating product search relevance. It contains (query, product) pairs with relevance labels annotated by humans in three different levels: relevant, partially relevant, and irrelevant. Table 4 shows details about the training, dev and test dataset.

Training and Evaluation 6 different Roberta variations are fine-tuned in this experiment. They are Roberta base, Roberta large (Liu et al., 2019), unsupervised SimCSE based on Roberta large (Gao et al., 2021), and three in-house pretrained models based on the SimCSE model using query-query, product-product, and query-query plus product-product similarity data respectively.

All of the models have the same training setup. For each model, we ran 4 epochs on the training dataset with mini-batch size of 256. Model checkpoints were saved every 6000 mini-batches, for the purpose of model selection. Adam optimizer with learning rate of $1e^{-5}$ was used to train the model. The temperature hyperparameter was set as 0.07.

In model selection, for each model we select the best performing checkpoint on the dev dataset to be the final trained model. The evaluation metric is the top-k retrieval accuracy, defined as the ratio of *(query, product)* pairs for which the top-k retrieved products of the *query* contains the corresponding *product*. The retrieval space for dev dataset is the unique products in dev dataset.

query	product
rose gold wing chair	alyka adonis wingback chair, red barrel studior, accent chairs
led lights strip lights	doynton strip light, the holiday aisle, under cabinet lighting
sun shelter	messina aluminum patio gazebo, sojag, canopies & gazebos

Table 3: Example of semantically relevant (query, product) pairs

	train	dev	test
total pairs	32M	100K	234K
unique queries	9.5M	76K	483
unique products	2.1M	88K	43K
unique pairs	21M	99K	234K

Table 4: Dataset summary. Train and dev datasets are collected from historical browsing contexts; the test dataset (WANDS) is a human annotated dataset for evaluating product search relevance (Chen et al., 2022).

To evaluate the final trained model, we calculated nDCG@k scores on the WANDS dataset. The ground truth relevance score is derived from human annotation labels: relevant is 1, partial relevant is 0.5, and irrelevant is 0.

For both the retrieval accuracy and nDCG scores, we set $k = 50$, which roughly equals to the number of products shown on the first page of search results.

4 Results

We evaluated the models' performance on the WANDS dataset. As noted in Table 4, this dataset contains 234k annotated (query, product) pairs. We further expand this dataset exhaustively to $20.6M$ pairs so that it contain every possible combination of unique query and unique product from the WANDS dataset. If a (query, product) pair is not annotated, we assume its relevance score is 0. Then, we assign these (query, product) pairs into different buckets, according to whether the query, the product, or the (query, product) pair exists in the training data or not. Details about bucket assignments are shown in Table 5. Finally, for each bucket, we calculate the averaged per-query nDCG@50 score.

RQ1: How well does the learned semantic space generalize? Table 5 shows each model's $nDCG@50$ scores on different buckets of the WANDS dataset. The "seen" bucket has much higher nDCG scores than the "unseen" bucket, indicating a large opportunity area of generalization for all models. By looking further into the amortized unseen sub-buckets, it shows that queries and products follow very different generalization behaviors. For example, the queries seen in the training data (q+, bucket 4, 5) usually performs better than the unseen queries (q-, bucket 6, 7). Yet counter-intuitively, the products seen in training under-perform the unseen ones (bucket 4 vs 5, 6 vs 7), which is against the common understanding where seen products may perform better than unseen ones. Arguably, this difference between query and products can be naively explained as products being relatively well learned compared to queries. We will revisit this point in analysis by graphical evidence.

RQ2: Are we able to improve generalization by pretraining? In Table 4, two domain-pretrained models (the qq model, and the qq+pp model) achieved top-two overall scores, showing the effectiveness of domain-specific pretraining approach. This, again, suggests the importance of query representation learning. Also, the SimCSE-large model performs worse than the Roberta-large model, suggesting that not all general-domain pretrainings are beneficial for domain-specific tasks, which may be due to the fact that the task of semantic search relies on asymmetric query-product relation encoding more than symmetric point-wise similarity. In contrast to SimCSE-large, the domain-specific query-query pretraining may have served the purpose of injecting domain knowledge mined from graph structure into text encoders, rather than a means for representation regularization, and such consistent improvement may have opportunity to be further improved given its moderate improvements over other models. Last, the Roberta-large model outperforms the Roberta-base model as expected due to a larger model capacity, yet the capacity for memorization is a draw between the two, based on the numbers in bucket 2.

5 Analysis

To understand why queries and products follow different generalization pattern in terms of nDCG scores observed in RQ1, we further analyzed the

Bucket index	1	2	3	4	5	6	7
				Unseen sub-buckets			
Bucket name	Overall	Seen	Unseen	q+, p+	q+, p-	q-, p+	q-, p-
Bucket ratio	100%	0.03%	99.9%	29.87%	31.60%	18.72%	19.79%
Roberta base	0.7812	0.9335	0.7722	**0.7539**	0.7894	0.6962	0.7249
Roberta large	0.7830	0.9337	0.7730	0.7511	0.7893	0.6942*	0.7177
SimCSE large	0.7775*	0.9315	0.7679*	0.7491	0.7875	0.6884*	0.7179*
Query-query (qq) pretrain	**0.7866**	**0.9351**	**0.7760**	0.7477*	**0.7918**	**0.7057**	**0.7276**
Product-product (pp) pretrain	0.7802*	**0.9351**	0.7700*	0.7460*	0.7875	0.7003	0.7201
qq+pp pretrain	0.7845	0.9319	0.7747	0.7489	0.7886	0.7006	0.7270

Table 5: nDCG@50 of fine-tuned models on product search tasks, evaluated by the WANDS dataset. The model names indicate the base model before fine-tuning. The "overal" bucket contains all (query, product) pairs in the testing dataset, the "seen" bucket contains (query, product) pairs from the testing dataset that also exist in the training dataset, and the "unseen" bucket contains (query, product) pairs from testing dataset that does not exist in the training dataset. The "unseen" bucket is further split into four different sub-buckets, according to whether the specific query or product exists in the training dataset or not. "q" represents query, "p" represents product; "+" represents existing in the training dataset, "-" represents not existing in the training dataset. Bucket ratio represents the size of current bucket with respect to the entire test dataset. In nDCG scores, "*" indicates that number is statistically smaller than that column's largest (bold-faced) number, tested by one-side t-test with 0.05 p-value. nDCG results at other k's are presented in the Appendix A.

query-product cosine score distribution for different buckets. To make distribution comparison fair across buckets, in each bucket we only keep a subset of (query, product) pairs that are annotated as "partial relevance". The model we used to generate the cosine score distributions is the SimCSE-large model that is first **qq**-pretrained and then **pq** fine-tuned on click graph data, the best model according to Table 5.

First, the models perform better on seen query-product combinations than unseen combinations (the query and the product has been individually seen in training, but not the combination). The bucket 2 from Figure 2 shows a well learned cosine score distribution for seen query-product pairs, and the scores concentrate around a high similarity range around 0.65. In contrast, for bucket 4, although queries and products are individually seen by the models during training, the combination is novel to them, and it increases the models' uncertainty, which is demonstrated by a significant similarity score spread-out accompanied by a shift to a lower median around 0.3. In general, the figure shows the difficulty of generalization of deep learning-based semantic search models on even the simpler task of dealing with unseen combinations. This suggests the generalization may be beyond the discussion of learning representations for an individual query or product, and rather about the geometry of the semantic space to properly maintain the distance between seen and unseen texts after semantic search as asymmetric embedding learning that "disturbs" a well-defined text representation space to encode text rankings.

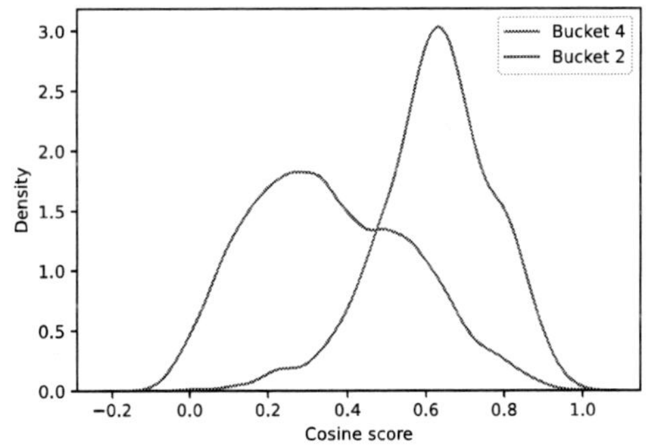

Figure 2: Query-product cosine score distribution for different buckets. The model is firstly pretrained by query-query similarity data, then fine-tuned in the product search task. Bucket 2 represent (query, product) pairs already seen by the model in training. In bucket 4, both query and product are seen, but the combination is not seen by the model in training. Bucket 2's mean cosine score (0.6253) is significantly higher than bucket 4 (0.3562).

Second, as shown in Figure 3, the visibility of queries and products in training data poses opposite impacts to a model's behavior.

1) For seen products, comparing the curves of

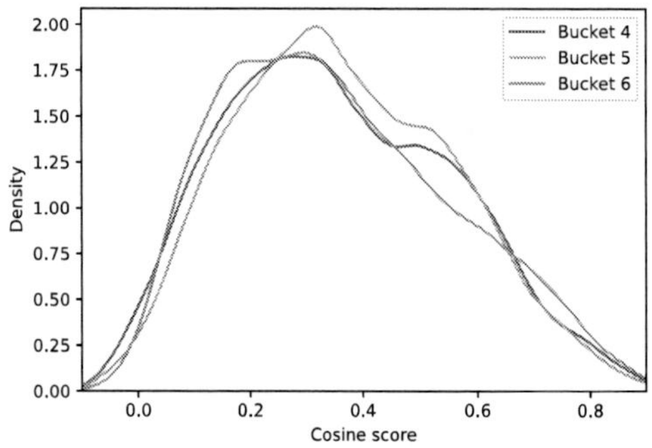

Figure 3: Query-product cosine score distribution for bucket 4, 5 and 6. Their mean cosine scores are 0.3562, 0.3655, and 0.3556 respectively. In bucket 4, both query and product are seen, but the combination is not seen by the model in training. In bucket 5, only the query is seen by the model in training. In bucket 6, only the product is seen by the model in training.

bucket 5 and 4, 1) counter-intuitively, we observe that 4 have a lower peak of around 0.25 as opposed to that of bucket 5 of around 0.3, which suggests that seen products have been "attracted" to seen queries in the training data, thus leading to a biased product representation. Yet, unseen products do not get to go through such an attraction process, and the representation may have maintained a neutral and generalize-able status in semantic space, leading to an overall higher and concentrated peak of 5 as opposed to a flat and lower peak of 4. This phenomenon might have suggested that a large semantic space may be over-parameterized that separately adjusting an individual product's representation without affecting its geometrically closer neighbours may have become easy. Thus, an un-generalizable learning in generalizable models might have happened.

2) For seen queries, however, by comparing the cures of bucket 6 and 4 (the same as 7 and 5), we found that queries that have been seen in the training data lead to better semantic similarity with products in general than unseen queries, demonstrated by the distribution mass of the blue curve towards a higher similarity range than the green curve. The green line's peak being extended towards the lower cosine score range demonstrates that the representation of seen queries may have improved instead of overfit. In other words, this may also suggest that query representation may have not been fully learned. From Table 5 we can also observe a similar hint that query-query pre-trained model is the most effective at improving semantic search performance from product ranking's perspective. In stark contrast to seen products being overfit, seen queries gets to be learned and improved during semantic search's **pq** learning process.

By comparing the above two cases, we have seen that queries may have learned slower than products in semantic search. The reason may be due to the fact that queries are usually much richer and more diverse (we have tens of times more unique queries than unique products), requiring a text encoder to observe way more cases for a query to learn representation well; whereas products are relatively fewer, well-formed and limited in diversity in product search. However, for a company that has billions of products in inventory, this observation may not hold true. Yet, the observation indeed resonates with that of question answering and web search, which suggests learning generalizable semantic search through improving query representation learning may still be a promising direction to follow.

6 Conclusions and Future Work

This paper examines the encoder generalization problem in the setting of semantic product search. We observe that query representation learning still is the bottle neck compared to the product representation learning under the semantic search training objective, the problem of which is surfaced by the superior performance of the domain-specific query pair pre-trained encoder model. We also surprisingly found that large, general-domain and unsupervisedly regularized Roberta variants such as SimCSE do not guarantee superior performance compared to Roberta-base or large, which may have suggested that semantic search is an *asymmetric* relationship learning task rather than symmetric, similarity learning task, since the semantic space has to encode much more complex relations (e.g. node priorities in a list) beyond point-wise similarity.

Although being a proof of concept, the proposed pre-training approach could start the conversation about how to properly pre-train encoders for semantic product search, and the results suggest that the knowledge hidden in the click graph can be better explored by defining proper training tasks, either transforming the task into a sequential task learning setting or a multi-task setting. In the future, a transfer learning setting that leverage richer domain knowledge and semantic structures from relevant sources such as class and class taxonomy of queries may be promising. Also, data augmentation to enhance query representation learning, or novel learning curriculum/objective/regularization that can help balance query and product learning in the semantic search objective may also be valuable for exploration.

Acknowledgements

The authors would like to acknowledge previous and current members of the Wayfair Search and Recs team for full support on this research: Shujian Liu, Archi Mitra, John Castillo, Pooja Ranawade, John Murray, Avanti Patil, Zhilin Chen, Jeremy Myrland, and Matt Herman. We would also love to thank the suggestions and comments from reviewers to improve this paper.

References

Antoine Bordes, Nicolas Usunier, Alberto Garcia-Duran, Jason Weston, and Oksana Yakhnenko. 2013. Translating embeddings for modeling multi-relational data. *Advances in neural information processing systems*, 26.

Wei-Cheng Chang, Felix X. Yu, Yin-Wen Chang, Yiming Yang, and Sanjiv Kumar. 2020. Pre-training tasks for embedding-based large-scale retrieval. *CoRR*, abs/2002.03932.

Ting Chen, Simon Kornblith, Mohammad Norouzi, and Geoffrey Hinton. 2020. A simple framework for contrastive learning of visual representations. In *International conference on machine learning*, pages 1597–1607. PMLR.

Yan Chen, Shujian Liu, Zheng Liu, Weiyi Sun, Linas Baltrunas, and Benjamin Schroeder. 2022. Wands: Dataset for product search relevance assessment. In *Proceedings of the 44th European Conference on Information Retrieval.*

Luyu Gao and Jamie Callan. 2021. Unsupervised corpus aware language model pre-training for dense passage retrieval. *CoRR*, abs/2108.05540.

Tianyu Gao, Xingcheng Yao, and Danqi Chen. 2021. SimCSE: Simple contrastive learning of sentence embeddings. In *Proceedings of the 2021 Conference on Empirical Methods in Natural Language Processing*, pages 6894–6910, Online and Punta Cana, Dominican Republic. Association for Computational Linguistics.

Kelvin Guu, Kenton Lee, Zora Tung, Panupong Pasupat, and Ming-Wei Chang. 2020. REALM: retrieval-augmented language model pre-training. *CoRR*, abs/2002.08909.

Will Hamilton, Zhitao Ying, and Jure Leskovec. 2017. Inductive representation learning on large graphs. *Advances in neural information processing systems*, 30.

Jui-Ting Huang, Ashish Sharma, Shuying Sun, Li Xia, David Zhang, Philip Pronin, Janani Padmanabhan, Giuseppe Ottaviano, and Linjun Yang. 2020. Embedding-based retrieval in facebook search. In *Proceedings of the 26th ACM SIGKDD International Conference on Knowledge Discovery & Data Mining*, pages 2553–2561.

Thomas N Kipf and Max Welling. 2016. Semi-supervised classification with graph convolutional networks. *arXiv preprint arXiv:1609.02907*.

Patrick Lewis, Pontus Stenetorp, and Sebastian Riedel. 2021. Question and answer test-train overlap in open-domain question answering datasets. In *Proceedings of the 16th Conference of the European Chapter of the Association for Computational Linguistics: Main Volume*, pages 1000–1008.

Sen Li, Fuyu Lv, Taiwei Jin, Guli Lin, Keping Yang, Xiaoyi Zeng, Xiao-Ming Wu, and Qianli Ma. 2021. Embedding-based product retrieval in taobao search. In *Proceedings of the 27th ACM SIGKDD Conference on Knowledge Discovery & Data Mining*, pages 3181–3189.

Yujia Li, Richard Zemel, Marc Brockschmidt, and Daniel Tarlow. 2016. Gated graph sequence neural networks. In *Proceedings of ICLR'16*.

Yinhan Liu, Myle Ott, Naman Goyal, Jingfei Du, Mandar Joshi, Danqi Chen, Omer Levy, Mike Lewis, Luke Zettlemoyer, and Veselin Stoyanov. 2019. Roberta: A robustly optimized bert pretraining approach. *arXiv preprint arXiv:1907.11692*.

Yuning Mao, Pengcheng He, Xiaodong Liu, Yelong Shen, Jianfeng Gao, Jiawei Han, and Weizhu Chen. 2021. Generation-augmented retrieval for open-domain question answering. In *Proceedings of the 59th Annual Meeting of the Association for Computational Linguistics and the 11th International Joint Conference on Natural Language Processing (Volume 1: Long Papers)*, pages 4089–4100, Online. Association for Computational Linguistics.

Tomas Mikolov, Ilya Sutskever, Kai Chen, Greg S Corrado, and Jeff Dean. 2013. Distributed representations of words and phrases and their compositionality. *Advances in neural information processing systems*, 26.

Priyanka Nigam, Yiwei Song, Vijai Mohan, Vihan Lakshman, Weitian Ding, Ankit Shingavi, Choon Hui Teo, Hao Gu, and Bing Yin. 2019. Semantic product search. In *Proceedings of the 25th ACM SIGKDD International Conference on Knowledge Discovery & Data Mining*, pages 2876–2885.

Barlas Oğuz, Kushal Lakhotia, Anchit Gupta, Patrick Lewis, Vladimir Karpukhin, Aleksandra Piktus, Xilun Chen, Sebastian Riedel, Wen-tau Yih, Sonal Gupta, et al. 2021. Domain-matched pre-training tasks for dense retrieval. *arXiv preprint arXiv:2107.13602*.

Devendra Sachan, Mostofa Patwary, Mohammad Shoeybi, Neel Kant, Wei Ping, William L. Hamilton, and Bryan Catanzaro. 2021. End-to-end training of neural retrievers for open-domain question answering. In *Proceedings of the 59th Annual Meeting of the Association for Computational Linguistics and the 11th International Joint Conference on Natural Language Processing (Volume 1: Long Papers)*, pages 6648–6662, Online. Association for Computational Linguistics.

Han Zhang, Songlin Wang, Kang Zhang, Zhiling Tang, Yunjiang Jiang, Yun Xiao, Weipeng Yan, and Wen-Yun Yang. 2020. Towards personalized and semantic retrieval: An end-to-end solution for e-commerce search via embedding learning. In *Proceedings of the 43rd International ACM SIGIR Conference on Research and Development in Information Retrieval*, pages 2407–2416.

A Appendix: Additional nDCG scores of product search performance

Extending the results of Table 5, this section showed three more k values to the nDCG performance of fine-tuned models on product search tasks. Table 6 shows nDCG@1, Table 7 shows nDCG@20, and Table 8 shows nDCG@100.

The results from nDCG@20 and nDCG@100 are consistent with nDCG@50, such that the qq model achieves the best performance on both seen and unseen (query, product) pair segments. However, in nDCG@1 the Roberta-large model performs the best. This reveals that information gained from domain-specific pre-training makes it more difficult for the model to optimize the highest relevance score range; however, it helps the model to produce a generally better ranked list. Since semantic search models are usually used as candidate generators and followed by dedicated ranking models, the nDCG@1 performance is not as important as nDCG@50 or nDCG@100, and thus we still think domain-specific pre-training is a suitable approach to improve encoders' performance.

Bucket name	Overall	Seen	Unseen	Unseen sub-buckets q+, p+	q+, p-	q-, p+	q-, p-
Roberta base	0.7845	0.8858	0.7793	**0.7988**	0.8061	0.7204	0.7446
Roberta large	**0.7969**	**0.9032**	**0.7892**	0.7811	0.807	0.7231	0.746
SimCSE large	0.7876	0.8829	0.7793	0.7862	0.8019	0.7124	0.7554
Query-query (qq) pretrain	0.7919	**0.9032**	0.7816	0.7736	**0.8123**	**0.746**	**0.7742**
Product-product (pp) pretrain	0.7949	0.9017	0.7886	0.787	0.812	0.7272	0.7433
qq+pp pretrain	0.7764	0.8916	0.7712	0.771	**0.8123**	0.7164	0.7392

Table 6: nDCG@1 of fine-tuned models on product search tasks. Please refer to Table 5 for notation definitions.

Bucket name	Overall	Seen	Unseen	Unseen sub-buckets q+, p+	q+, p-	q-, p+	q-, p-
Roberta base	0.7884	0.921	0.7807	**0.7686**	**0.8053**	0.7012	0.7269
Roberta large	0.7888	0.9203	0.7809	0.7641	0.8023	0.7051	0.7216
SimCSE large	0.7818	0.9183	0.7739	0.7631	0.7978	0.6941	0.7223
Query-query (qq) pretrain	**0.7914**	**0.9229**	**0.7829**	0.7607	0.8009	**0.7165**	**0.7316**
Product-product (pp) pretrain	0.7863	0.9221	0.7771	0.7598	0.7988	0.7072	0.7288
qq+pp pretrain	0.7877	0.9188	0.78	0.7628	0.8007	0.7151	0.7298

Table 7: nDCG@20 of fine-tuned models on product search tasks. Please refer to Table 5 for notation definitions.

Bucket name	Overall	Seen	Unseen	Unseen sub-buckets q+, p+	q+, p-	q-, p+	q-, p-
Roberta base	0.7681	0.9386	0.7593	**0.7603**	0.7887	0.7138	0.7321
Roberta large	0.7678	0.9392	0.7583	0.7539	0.7842	0.7102	0.7284
SimCSE large	0.7643	0.9372	0.7545	0.7525	0.7834	0.7059	0.7279
Query-query (qq) pretrain	**0.7721**	**0.9407**	**0.7624**	0.7523	**0.7913**	**0.7229**	**0.7334**
Product-product (pp) pretrain	0.7664	0.9406	0.7571	0.7529	0.7846	0.7157	0.7308
qq+pp pretrain	0.7703	0.9377	0.7609	0.7539	0.789	0.7199	0.7315

Table 8: nDCG@100 of fine-tuned models on product search tasks. Please refer to Table 5 for notation definitions.

Can Pretrained Language Models Generate Persuasive, Faithful, and Informative Ad Text for Product Descriptions?

Fajri Koto[1] **Jey Han Lau**[1] **Timothy Baldwin**[1,2]
[1]The University of Melbourne
[2]MBZUAI
ffajri@student.unimelb.edu.au, jeyhan.lau@gmail.com, tb@ldwin.net

Abstract

For any e-commerce service, persuasive, faithful, and informative product descriptions can attract shoppers and improve sales. While not all sellers are capable of providing such interesting descriptions, a language generation system can be a source of such descriptions at scale, and potentially assist sellers to improve their product descriptions. Most previous work has addressed this task based on statistical approaches (Wang et al., 2017), limited attributes such as titles (Chen et al., 2019; Chan et al., 2020), and focused on only one product type (Wang et al., 2017; Munigala et al., 2018; Hong et al., 2021). In this paper, we jointly train image features and 10 text attributes across 23 diverse product types, with two different target text types with different writing styles: bullet points and paragraph descriptions. Our findings suggest that multimodal training with modern pretrained language models can generate fluent and persuasive advertisements, but are less faithful and informative, especially out of domain.

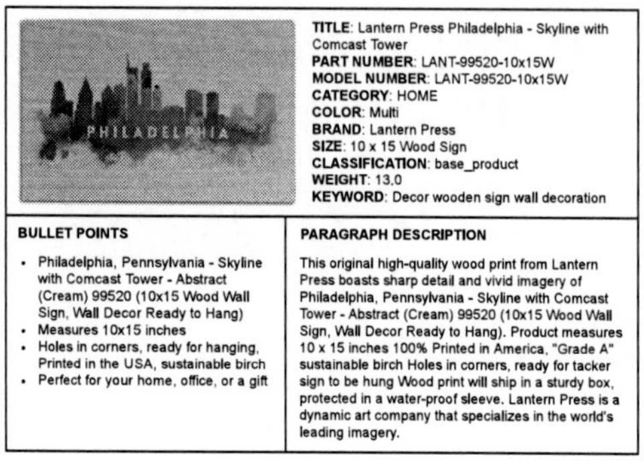

Figure 1: **Top**: Input consisting of an image and textual attributes of a product. **Bottom**: Two target texts: bullet points and a paragraph description

1 Introduction

Generative pretrained language models such as GPT-2 (Radford et al., 2019), T5 (Raffel et al., 2020), and BART (Lewis et al., 2020a) have led to impressive gains in language generation applications beyond machine translation, such as story geneneration (Fan et al., 2018; Goldfarb-Tarrant et al., 2020), summarization (Zhang et al., 2020; Qi et al., 2020), and dialogue systems (Ham et al., 2020). Although such transformer-based language models (Vaswani et al., 2017) are capable of generating fluent texts through a sequence-to-sequence framework, they still suffer from unfaithfulness and factuality issues (Maynez et al., 2020; Wang et al., 2020; Moradi et al., 2021).

In this paper, we comprehensively discuss the utility of modern pretrained language models over an ad text generation task for product descriptions, with a focus on faithfulness, persuasiveness, and informativeness. While previous work has been limited to short ad generation tasks conditioned on titles (Chen et al., 2019; Chan et al., 2020), and used traditional neural models (Munigala et al., 2018; Zhang et al., 2019a) or statistical approaches (Wang et al., 2017), we focus on a data-to-text generation approach to product description generation for an English e-commerce service. Specifically, we explore various textual attributes and images as the input, and generate two types of product descriptions: (1) bullet points, and (2) paragraph descriptions (see Figure 1). Bullet points provide a list of key information regarding a product, while paragraph descriptions are made up of sentences structured into a coherent narrative.

We argue there are two underlying motivations for the ad text generation task, especially for product descriptions. Application-wise, the utility is to improve the seller experience for e-commerce services when registering a new product. The generated descriptions can reduce the need for manual data entry, and potentially improve sales due to better descriptions (in terms of attractiveness, structure, and persuasiveness). Research-wise, ad

Proceedings of The Fifth Workshop on e-Commerce and NLP (ECNLP 5), pages 234 - 243
May 26, 2022

text generation is an under-studied task, and arguably a good proxy for persuasive text generation (Wei et al., 2016; Rehbein, 2019; Luu et al., 2019; El Baff et al., 2020).

While previous work has discussed ad text generation of e-commerce service for a few product types such as fashion (Munigala et al., 2018), computers (Wang et al., 2017), and house decor (Hong et al., 2021), in this work, we use twenty diverse product types and an additional three product types for out-of-domain prediction. With this setting, we aim to study model generalization and robustness over in-domain and out-of-domain test sets.

To summarize our contributions: (1) we study the application of modern pretrained language models based on data-to-text generation for product description in an e-commerce service; (2) we explore multimodal training by incorporating image features for ad generation and perform automatic and manual evaluation; (3) we study model robustness for out-of-domain prediction; and (4) we conduct analysis of attributes that significantly contribute to ad text generation.

2 Related Work

Data-to-text generation is the task of translating a semi-structured table to natural text, and has been applied in different real-world scenarios, such as weather forecasting reports (Liang et al., 2009), sport (Puduppully et al., 2019), health-care descriptions (Hasan and Farri, 2019), and biographies (Wang et al., 2020). While the goal of most previous tasks is to generate descriptive text, there are few studies (Wang et al., 2017) on data-to-text generation for the advertisement domain, and the work that has been done has tended to focus exclusively on the product type of *computer* and be based on pre-neural statistical approaches and template-based techniques.

Previous work has mostly used titles of e-commerce products to generate short ads in Chinese (Chen et al., 2019; Chan et al., 2020) and English (Munigala et al., 2018; Kanungo et al., 2021). Similarly, Zhang et al. (2019a) generate a product description for Chinese e-commerce, conditioned on the title and a small number of attributes (with an average length of six words).[1] In this work, we comprehensively study product description generation in English based on ten diverse attributes (*à la* a data-to-text scheme, with the average number of

[1] These attributes are not clearly described in the paper.

Attributes	Coverage (%)	#words max	μ	σ	|Vocab|
TITLE	100	95	15.7	6.22	193,649
PRODUCT TYPE	100	1	1	0	20
CLASSIFICATION	100	1	1	0	3
BRAND	99.49	17	1.58	0.88	46, 552
KEYWORD	92.17	958	32.32	55.72	292,372
COLOR	80.19	32	1.44	1.01	18,839
SIZE	69.96	16	1.82	1.44	15,187
MODEL NUMBER	33.75	9	1.15	0.52	67,215
PART NUMBER	47.64	12	1.08	0.41	91,084
WEIGHT	20.76	1	1	0	1,786
BULLET POINTS	100	766	86.8	67.9	225,784
PARAGRAPH DESC.	100	516	90.9	72.9	472,711

Table 1: Statistics of attributes. For BULLET POINTS, the average number of bullets in the overall dataset is 5.

Component A	Component B	% of novel *n*-grams 1	2	3	4
10 attr.	BP	86.7	96.3	98.1	98.7
10 attr.	PD	85.1	93.7	95.2	95.9
BP	PD	66.2	86.9	90.9	92.7

Table 2: Abstractiveness of BULLET POINTS (BP) and PARAGRAPH DESCRIPTIONS (DP) based on novel *n*-gram overlap. "10 attr." means the concatenation of all attributes, and values in the table are calculated relative to component B.

concatenated attributes being 64 words in Table 1) that incorporates joint training over images of the product.

3 Data Construction

We use 200,000 e-commerce products spanning 20 different product types as described in Figure 2. For copyright reasons we are not able to release this data to the public. This dataset is randomly split into 180K/10K/10K training, development and test instances, respectively. We also create an Xtreme test set (4,266 samples) in which we filter out test samples that have overlapping descriptions with the training data. Lastly, we additionally use three different product types as an out-of-domain test set, comprising 1,000 products of each of the three produce types: SAREE, COMPUTER, and CELLULAR_PHONE. In total, there are three different test sets: (1) main; (2) Xtreme; and (3) out-of-domain.

In Table 1, we show the overall statistics of ten product atttributes and two target texts: BULLET POINTS and PARAGRAPH

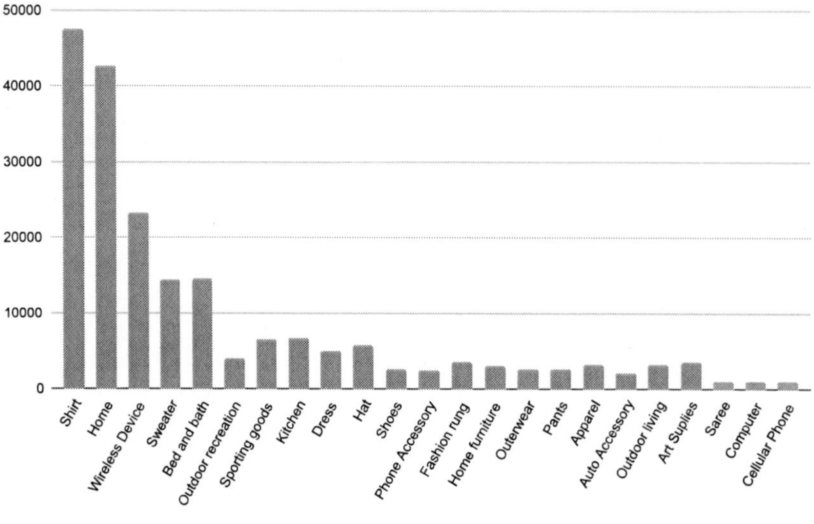

Figure 2: Distribution of 20 product types in the main dataset and 3 additional product types from the out-of-domain test set. The main and additional data is in English, and gathered from different regions (countries).

DESCRIPTIONS. The selection of product attributes is based on a minimum coverage of 20% in the dataset. Overall, the five attributes with the highest coverage are TITLE, PRODUCT TYPE, CLASSIFICATION, BRAND, and KEYWORD.[2] The average length of BULLET POINTS and PARAGRAPH DESCRIPTIONS is 87 and 91, respectively, significantly longer than most previous work except Wang et al. (2017) who focused on the product type of *computer* and tested only pre-neural statistical approaches (see Table 3).

To understand the abstractiveness of our dataset, in Table 2 we show the percentage of novel n-grams in BULLET POINTS and PARAGRAPH DESCRIPTIONS. Overall, we observe that the two target texts are highly abstractive, with more than 85% of novel n-grams, computed relative to the concatenated attributes. We also found that there is a high proportion of novel n-grams between the two target texts.[3] We suspect, though, that the low lexical overlap between the two text types in this task might not be attributed to paraphrasing or lexical choice, but rather to content selection.

Work	Lang.	Product Types	#words of source (μ)	#words of target (μ)
Zhang et al. (2019a)	ZH	N/A	18	25
Chan et al. (2020)	ZH	N/A	18	22
Hong et al. (2021)	ZH	1	N/A	76
Wang et al. (2017)	EN	1	N/A	117
Munigala et al. (2018)	EN	1	6	18
Kanungo et al. (2021)	EN	1	19	6
This work	EN	23	64	87 & 91

Table 3: Dataset comparison between our work and previous work

4 Model

Problem Formulation. As discussed in Section 3, a product in our dataset consists of up to ten attributes $\{a_1, a_2, a_3, ..., a_{10}\}$, one image I, and two target texts $\{t_1, t_2\}$. The goal of this work is to learn a function that estimates the probabilities $P(t_1|a_1, a_2, a_3, ..., a_{10}, I)$ and $P(t_2|a_1, a_2, a_3, ..., a_{10}, I)$.

Architecture. This work relies on pretrained language models such as BERT (Devlin et al., 2019), T5 (Raffel et al., 2020), and BART (Lewis et al., 2020a). To perform data-to-text generation, we formulate a structured input based on special tokens that are randomly initialized before the fine-tuning. The textual input is the concatenation of each attribute preceded by each corresponding special token (see Figure 3).

To accommodate multimodal training, we fol-

[2] CLASSIFICATION means other categories such as base product or different variation.

[3] We also note that no previous work reported on the abstractiveness of their data.

low Xing et al. (2021) in extracting n **R**egions **o**f **I**nterest (RoIs) (i.e. bounding boxes) of the image using `detectron2`, a pretrained masked R-CNN (He et al., 2017).[4] Formally, an Image I is chunked by `detectron2` into $\{\mathrm{RoI}_1, \mathrm{RoI}_2, ..., \mathrm{RoI}_n\}$. We obtained a fixed-size latent representation of each RoI based on intermediate features of `detectron2` (ResNet-101 (He et al., 2016)). To align the embedding size with pretrained language models we use a linear layer. Similar to the textual input, we also introduce a special token `[IMAGE]` that is concatenated at the beginning of the input.

For the target texts, we introduce special tokens `[BULLET POINTS]` and `[DESCRIPTION]` as the start token. Specifically, for bullet points, we concatenate all points with token <q> as the separator. Finally, for the encoder-decoder, we use BERT-base with raw decoder following (Liu and Lapata, 2019), BART-base, and T5-base, and train the model with standard cross-entropy loss.

5 Experiments

5.1 Set-Up

We experiment in three settings: (1) training with the text input only; (2) training with the image features only; and (3) multimodal training incorporating both text and image features, as depicted in Figure 3. For the text features, we encode the text using the three pretrained LMs of BERT, BART, and T5, while for the other two we only experimented with BART because of its higher performance in the first experiment. For image feature extraction, we experimented with $\{10, 20, 30, 40, 50\}$ RoIs, and tuned based on the development set. We report results of 50 and 20 RoIs for the second and third experiment, respectively.

For `TITLE`, `KEYWORD`, and other attributes, we set the maximum token length to 30, 100, and 10 based on the statistics in Table 1. This results in a maximum token length of 220 for the source text (including the special tokens). For the two target texts, we set the maximum token length to 250, and train them separately. Our preliminary experiments show that performing multi-task training (i.e. using both target texts at the same time) performs worse than single-task training.

We use the huggingface PyTorch framework (Wolf et al., 2020) for our experiments with three pretrained language models: BERT-base[5] (Devlin et al., 2019), T5-base[6] (Raffel et al., 2020), and BART-base[7] (Lewis et al., 2020a). All experiments are run on 4×V100 16GB GPUs.

For the BERT model, we follow Liu and Lapata (2019) in adding a randomly-initialized transformer decoder (layers = 6, hidden size = 768, feed-forward = 2,048, and heads = 8) on top of BERT, and train it for 200K steps. We use the Adam optimizer and learning rate lr $= 2e^{-3} \times \min(\mathrm{step}^{-0.5}, \mathrm{step} \times 20,000^{-1.5})$ and $0.1 \times \min(\mathrm{step}^{-0.5}, \mathrm{step} \times 10,000^{-1.5})$ for BERT and the transformer decoder, respectively. We use a warmup of 20,000, a dropout of 0.2, a batch size total of 200 (10 × 4 GPUs × gradient accumulation of 5), and save checkpoints every 10,000 steps. We compute ROUGE scores (R1) to pick the best checkpoint based on the development set.

For T5 and BART, we train them for 30 epochs (around 20K steps) with an initial learning rate of $1e^{-4}$ (Adam optimizer). We use a total batch size of 300 (15 × 4 GPUs × gradient accumulation of 5), a warmup of 10% of total steps, and save checkpoints for every 1,000 steps. We also compute ROUGE scores (R1) to pick the best checkpoint based on the development set.

5.2 Evaluation

As discussed in Section 3, we use three different test sets: main, Xtreme, and out-of-domain. For automatic evaluation, we use ROUGE-1/2/L (Lin, 2004), BLEU-4 (Papineni et al., 2002), METEOR (Banerjee and Lavie, 2005), and BERTScore (Zhang et al., 2019b). For BERTScore we compute the F1 score using `roberta-large` (layer 17) as recommended by Zhang et al. (2019b).

For manual evaluation, we first obtain 50 random samples for each of the three test sets, ensuring there is no overlap between the main and Xtreme test sets. We hire four expert workers with Master degree qualifications to annotate four descriptions for each product: (1) gold; (2) BART; (3) BART+image; and (4) image only. The total number of annotations is 2 workers × 4 models × 150 samples × 2 descriptions = 2,400 annotations. One worker was asked to work on either bullet points or paragraph descriptions, and was paid $50.

There are five aspects that are manually evaluated by our workers: (1) Fluency: the description is fluent and grammatically correct; (2) At-

[4]https://github.com/facebookresearch/detectron2

[5]`bart-base-uncased`

[6]`t5-base`

[7]`facebook/bart-base`

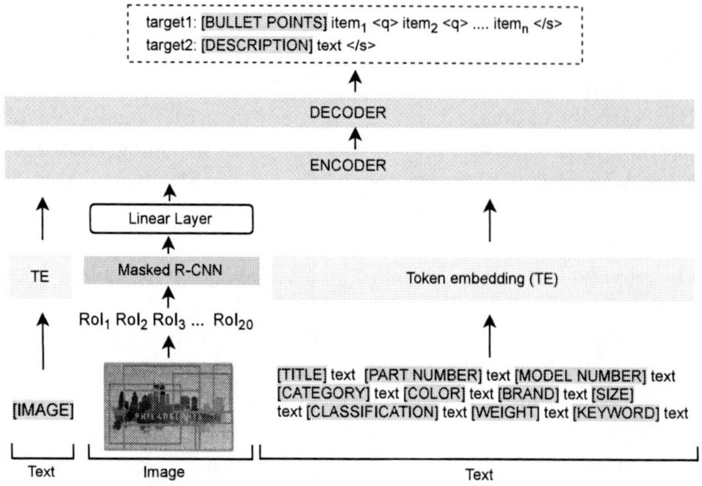

Figure 3: Model architecture used in this work.

Model	Main Test						Xtreme Test						Out-of-domain Test						Avg.
	R-1	R-2	R-L	B-4	M	BS	R-1	R-2	R-L	B-4	M	BS	R-1	R-2	R-L	B-4	M	BS	
BULLET POINTS																			
BERT	51.8	40.7	50.6	32.6	25.0	88.7	35.1	20.7	33.5	15.6	14.1	85.5	11.9	2.4	11.1	1.5	3.3	80.5	33.6
T5	45.4	34.7	44.1	30.6	28.9	87.4	28.2	30	31.1	13.4	13.3	83.4	12.6	4.2	10.8	2.3	4.4	79.2	32.4
BART	58.9	48.5	57.7	43.5	38.5	90.7	39.8	24.8	38.1	20.8	19.6	86.5	**17.5**	**6.1**	**16.5**	**3.0**	**5.0**	**81.5**	38.7
Image only	43.4	30.9	32.3	27.5	25.3	87.3	27.6	13.5	26.1	11.4	11.6	83.8	9.9	0.7	9.0	0.8	2.9	79.4	29.1
BART+Image	**59.3**	**48.9**	**58.1**	**43.7**	**38.6**	**90.8**	**40.1**	**24.9**	**38.4**	**21.0**	**19.7**	**86.6**	**17.5**	5.9	16.4	2.8	4.9	81.4	**38.8**
PARAGRAPH DESCRIPTIONS																			
BERT	41.0	30.1	35.5	24.2	19.4	86.4	27.5	15	21.4	10.9	10.5	83.3	10.9	1.5	7.2	0.9	2.5	79.6	28.2
T5	40.7	31.9	36.7	28.6	29.3	85.8	23.8	14.2	19.8	11.5	12.6	81.2	10.8	4.4	9.1	2.2	4.6	77.8	29.2
BART	54.8	45.1	50.1	40.2	37.7	90.1	**36.1**	**22.6**	**29.5**	**18.3**	**18.2**	**85.9**	16.5	**5.6**	12.0	**2.8**	5.5	81.1	36.2
Image only	41.1	29.4	35.4	26.6	25.6	86.9	24.7	10.9	18.2	9.1	10.1	83.1	12.2	0.8	7.4	0.8	3.3	79.9	28.1
BART+Image	**54.9**	**45.3**	**50.3**	**40.4**	**37.9**	**90.2**	35.8	22.4	29.3	**18.3**	18.0	85.8	**17.2**	**5.6**	**12.3**	2.7	**5.6**	**81.5**	**36.3**

Table 4: Main experimental results of automatic metrics. R-1, R-2, R-L, B-4, M, and BS are ROUGE-1, ROUGE-2, and ROUGE-3, BLEU-4, METEOR, and BERTScore, respectively.

tractiveness: the description is interesting and eye-catching; (3) Persuasive words: the description uses persuasive words or phrases; (4) Faithfulness: information in the description is captured by the image and the attributes; and (5) Informativeness: the description is informative and complete relative to the available attributes. Except for the third aspect which is binary (yes/no), we use a slider scale with values between 0–100 for all aspects.

In manual evaluation, workers were presented the product image and list of text attributes with four different descriptions. The four descriptions are shuffled, so the model information of each description is not apparent to the worker. Workers were asked to carefully read each description, and then asked to put the evaluation scores in the available field.

5.3 Results

Table 4 shows the experimental results based on the automatic metrics. Overall, we observe similar trends for both `BULLET POINTS` and `PARAGRAPH DESCRIPTIONS`, namely that BART is substantially better than T5 and BERT across the three test sets. Using only image features for generating both ad text types yields a comparable score to T5, but tends to be lower for almost all test sets and metrics. The multimodal training (i.e. "BART+image") slightly improves BART performance for the main test set, but achieves mixed results for the Xtreme and out-of-domain test sets with both `BULLET POINTS` and `PARAGRAPH DESCRIPTIONS`. We also observe that Xtreme and the out-of-domain test sets are harder, with high performance gaps, relative to the main test set.

Model	Main Test					Xtreme Test					Out-of-domain Test					Avg.
	Flu.	Att.	Per.	Fa.	Inf.	Flu.	Att.	Per.	Fa.	Inf.	Flu.	Att.	Per.	Fa.	Inf.	
BULLET POINTS																
Gold	0.62	0.59	0.77	0.54	0.52	0.58	0.56	0.74	0.57	0.55	0.62	0.58	0.51	0.59	0.60	0.59
Image only	0.63	0.61	**0.82**	0.43	0.43	0.65	0.61	**0.87**	0.43	0.44	**0.64**	**0.56**	**0.74**	0.13	0.27	0.53
BART	0.63	0.59	0.78	0.56	0.53	0.61	0.58	0.64	0.58	**0.56**	0.48	0.42	0.27	0.53	0.52	0.55
BART+image	**0.66**	**0.63**	0.79	**0.58**	**0.56**	**0.64**	**0.62**	0.72	**0.57**	0.54	0.44	0.42	0.30	**0.55**	**0.54**	**0.57**
PARAGRAPH DESCRIPTIONS																
Gold	0.82	0.52	0.29	0.60	0.48	0.74	0.46	0.31	0.53	0.47	0.84	0.49	0.18	0.52	0.48	0.44
Image only	0.77	0.43	0.29	0.42	0.38	**0.81**	0.43	**0.34**	0.43	0.41	**0.74**	0.25	**0.20**	0.17	0.16	0.33
BART	**0.82**	**0.53**	0.31	**0.62**	0.50	0.74	0.50	0.21	**0.60**	**0.53**	0.69	0.39	0.16	0.53	**0.42**	0.44
BART+image	0.81	**0.53**	**0.33**	0.60	**0.51**	0.76	**0.52**	0.23	0.59	**0.53**	0.71	**0.41**	0.15	**0.56**	0.41	**0.45**

Table 5: The primary experimental results for manual evaluation. Flu., Att., Per., Fa., and Inf. denote Fluency, Attractiveness, Persuasiveness, Faithfulness, and Informativeness, respectively. The presented scores are the average of two annotations. Entries in bold refer to the best overall score (excluding Gold texts).

Aspects	BULLET POINTS	DESCRIPTION
Fluency	0.51	0.50
Attractiveness	0.50	0.42
Persuasiveness	0.39	0.32
Faithfulness	0.51	0.41
Informativeness	0.34	0.45

Table 6: Pearson correlation scores between two annotators in manual evaluation. For persuasiveness we present the Kappa score.

For example, in BULLET POINTS, ROUGE-1 of BART drops substantially by -19.1 and -41.4 in the Xtreme and out-of-domain test sets, resp., implying that the model does not generalize well to different test sets.

In Table 6 we show the inter-annotator agreement of manual evaluation in the form of Pearson correlation for fluency, attractiveness, faithfulness, and informativeness; and the Kappa score for persuasiveness. Overall, we found that annotators have moderate correlation and agreement. In Table 5, scores of the Gold text can be interpreted as the upper bound of the manual evaluation. Note that for faithfulness and informativeness, these aspects are only evaluated based on the ten selected attributes.

For the main and Xtreme test sets in Table 5, most models generate fluent, attractive, persuasive, faithful, and informative texts for BULLET POINTS and PARAGRAPH DESCRIPTIONS, *relative to the performance of the gold texts*. When using only image features (the "image only" model), the model's faithfulness and informativeness decrease markedly, indicating the importance of textual attributes for this task. BART and BART+image models yield comparable results with the gold texts, with slightly better faithfulness and informativeness.[8]

For the out-of-domain test set, we observe that the human evaluation performance over the three models (Image only, BART, and BART+image) is generally lower than the gold text. Interestingly, we find that the "image only" model generates fluent and persuasive texts, but with substantially low faithfulness and informativeness. It is also worth mentioning that the BART model's performance is not as good as for the main test set, which indicates the out-of-domain challenge in applying models in real world scenarios.

In addition, we calculated the average performance of the manual evaluation, and found that the BART+image model performs best for both target texts. These results are in line with the averaged automatic evaluation scores in Table 4.

Based on the manual evaluation results in Table 5, the relatively low faithfulness scores for the gold texts (around 0.5–0.6) suggests that they contain new information that is not found in the input attributes. Although this means the gold texts are not faithful, they are likely to be still *factually correct*, as they are written by the product sellers (Maynez et al., 2020). Taking the faithfulness scores of the gold texts as the upper bound, we could conclude that the BART models are performing as well as they could (seeing that they are trained on not very faithful target texts in the first place). Ultimately, our results in this task high-

[8]These results are to be expected in the manual evaluation, since both aspects are only examined based on the ten selected attributes.

BULLET POINTS

TITLE: Yosoo Digital Clock Portable Electronic Bell with Backlight LCD Screen Display Alarm Clock Car Desk Table Decoration Clock(Pink)
PART NUMBER: Yosoo6wkf82orh7
CATEGORY: HOME
BRAND: Yosoo
CLASSIFICATION: base_product
WEIGHT: 43.0
KEYWORD: LCD Digital Clock, Digital Alarm Clock, Portable Digital Clock,Table Desk Digital Clock, Digital Clock

Gold:

- Large LCD screen for an easy and accurate reading of time Display the current time, week clearly, with alarm function and snooze function
- Press the light button at the back of the clock, the backlight will bright 3 seconds or so, convenient for you to read time at night
- Built with a clip and stand, you can put it on your desk or table
- Light weight and compact size, multi-colors are available. A good choice to improve concept of punctuality

BART:

- Delivery Time 10-15 Days
- Return Range 30 Days
- If you have any questions, please feel free to contact us and we will get back to you within 24 hours.
- The clock is made of high-quality materials, durable and easy to clean.

BART + image:

- This digital clock is made of high quality materials, durable and easy to clean.
- The clock is equipped with backlight LCD screen display, which is very convenient to read.
- It can be used in bedroom, living room, kitchen, office, etc. It is also a good gift for your family and friends.
- If you have any questions, please feel free to contact us and we will reply you within 24 hours.

PARAGRAPH DESCRIPTION

TITLE: LJSWG Men's Oklahoma Flag Oklahoma National T-shirt Asphalt L
CATEGORY: SHIRT
COLOR: Asphalt
BRAND: LJSWG
SIZE: Large
CLASSIFICATION: base_product
KEYWORD: Personalised Cheap Men Tee Casual Cotton, Girls Games Plus Size Clothing Captain America: Civil War AKON, Oklahoma City

Gold:

Men's Oklahoma Flag Oklahoma National Custom Text, ID, Name Or Message On High Quality Hanes Cotton T-Shirts. 100% Preshrunk Cotton Takes The Worry Away From Shrunk-age. Seamless Rib At Neck And Collar. Double-needle Stitching For Dorabiltiy. This Classic Crew Neckline T-shirtis Is Great For Every Occasion And Situation.The Design Is Printed With Advanced Printing Technology. It Is Printed With A Water-soluble And Eco-friendly Ink.Trendy, Brightly Colored Graphics. A Unique Gift Idea For A Friend Or Family Member.

BART:

100% Soft Cotton Fabric With A Soft Touch And Quality Printing Techniques.It Will Never Fade, Peel Or Crack And Can Be Machine Washed & Ironed.This Customized T Shirt Will Be The Best And Sincere Gift For Your Family,friends And Team.

BART + image:

Oklahoma Flag Oklahoma National T-shirt. Art Heat Press Print On Front. Wash Inside Out In Cold Water, Hand Dry Recommended. Most Of Our Designs Are Available In Men's Sizes.Please Check Our Store For All Other Varieties.

Figure 4: Example of generated BULLET POINTS and PARAGRAPH DESCRIPTIONS.

lighted the fact that our current human faithfulness evaluation does not always capture factuality, prompting further questions on how we can assess this dimension, which we leave for future work.

Figure 4 depicts some example outputs of the BART models for BULLET POINTS and PARAGRAPH DESCRIPTIONS. The first example shows that the prediction of the BART+image model contains better content than the BART text-only model, with a description of the LCD screen and usage examples. Similarly in the second example, the BART+image model generates more specific content for the t-shirt product by mentioning *Flag Oklahoma National*.

6 Analysis

Which attributes contribute to ad generation? To answer this question, we performed an ablation study using the BART models. We decode both BULLET POINTS and PARAGRAPH DESCRIPTIONS using different numbers of attributes as context, and report the average automatic performance in Table 7.

We observe there are three prominent attributes for this task — TITLE, BRAND, and KEYWORD — for both BULLET POINTS and PARAGRAPH DESCRIPTIONS. Interestingly, using only TITLE can produce 32.98 and 29.93 average performance, and adding KEYWORD to the input boosts performance by 11.05 and 10.57, for BULLET POINTS and PARAGRAPH DESCRIPTIONS, respectively.

7 Discussion and Conclusion

In this work, we described the first attempt at multimodal training for ad generation by incorporating image representations and text embeddings as input. We found that multimodal training yields the best performance in terms of overall scores in the both automatic and manual evaluation. We observe that modern pretrained language models can generate fluent advertisements, but are less faithful and

Attributes (#Attr)	BULLET POINTS		PARAGRAPH DESCRIPTIONS	
	Avg.	Δ	Avg.	Δ
TITLE (1)	32.98	**32.98**	29.93	**29.93**
prev. + PRODUCT TYPE (2)	34.53	1.55	31.38	1.45
prev. + CLASSIFICATION (3)	34.53	0.00	31.38	0.00
prev. + BRAND (4)	39.75	**5.22**	39.33	**7.95**
prev. + KEYWORD (5)	50.80	**11.05**	49.90	**10.57**
prev. + COLOR (6)	51.63	0.83	50.15	0.25
prev. + SIZE (7)	53.15	1.52	51.03	0.88
prev. + PART NUMBER (8)	55.12	1.97	52.32	1.28
prev. + MODEL NUMBER (9)	56.30	1.18	52.77	0.45
prev. + WEIGHT (10)	56.30	0.00	52.77	0.00

Table 7: Ablation study on the main test set using BART by incrementally adding different attributes. Avg means the average score of ROUGE-1, ROUGE-2, ROUGE-L, BLEU-4, METEOR, and BERTScore. Δ means the difference score between the given and previous row. The bold entries are the top-3 highest Δ scores.

informative, especially in out-of-domain settings.

Can pretrained language models generate persuasive, faithful, and informative ad text for product descriptions? The answer to this question is *yes to a certain extent*, particularly for in-domain scenarios. And although the BART models have similar human faithfulness performance to the gold texts, we believe that it does not necessarily imply that they are factually correct and further validation is necessary. One way forward may be to allow human judges to have access to some external knowledge (e.g. search engines or product catalogues), which will help them assess the factuality of the generated texts.

Furthermore, since the product descriptions in our e-commerce dataset might introduce new information, retrieval augmented generation (Lewis et al., 2020b; Kim et al., 2020; Shuster et al., 2021) is one potential direction for future work. This is because information on some products is likely to be available on the Internet, and incorporating it into the generation model could potentially improve the resulting ad text.

References

Satanjeev Banerjee and Alon Lavie. 2005. METEOR: An automatic metric for MT evaluation with improved correlation with human judgments. In *Proceedings of the ACL Workshop on Intrinsic and Extrinsic Evaluation Measures for Machine Translation and/or Summarization*, pages 65–72, Ann Arbor, Michigan. Association for Computational Linguistics.

Zhangming Chan, Yuchi Zhang, Xiuying Chen, Shen Gao, Zhiqiang Zhang, Dongyan Zhao, and Rui Yan. 2020. Selection and generation: Learning towards multi-product advertisement post generation. In *Proceedings of the 2020 Conference on Empirical Methods in Natural Language Processing (EMNLP)*, pages 3818–3829, Online. Association for Computational Linguistics.

Qibin Chen, Junyang Lin, Yichang Zhang, Hongxia Yang, Jingren Zhou, and Jie Tang. 2019. Towards knowledge-based personalized product description generation in e-commerce. In *Proceedings of the 25th ACM SIGKDD International Conference on Knowledge Discovery & Data Mining*, pages 3040–3050.

Jacob Devlin, Ming-Wei Chang, Kenton Lee, and Kristina Toutanova. 2019. BERT: Pre-training of deep bidirectional transformers for language understanding. In *Proceedings of the 2019 Conference of the North American Chapter of the Association for Computational Linguistics: Human Language Technologies, Volume 1 (Long and Short Papers)*, pages 4171–4186, Minneapolis, Minnesota. Association for Computational Linguistics.

Roxanne El Baff, Henning Wachsmuth, Khalid Al Khatib, and Benno Stein. 2020. Analyzing the Persuasive Effect of Style in News Editorial Argumentation. In *Proceedings of the 58th Annual Meeting of the Association for Computational Linguistics*, pages 3154–3160, Online. Association for Computational Linguistics.

Angela Fan, Mike Lewis, and Yann Dauphin. 2018. Hierarchical neural story generation. In *Proceedings of the 56th Annual Meeting of the Association for Computational Linguistics (Volume 1: Long Papers)*, pages 889–898, Melbourne, Australia. Association for Computational Linguistics.

Seraphina Goldfarb-Tarrant, Tuhin Chakrabarty, Ralph Weischedel, and Nanyun Peng. 2020. Content planning for neural story generation with aristotelian rescoring. In *Proceedings of the 2020 Conference on Empirical Methods in Natural Language Processing (EMNLP)*, pages 4319–4338, Online. Association for Computational Linguistics.

Donghoon Ham, Jeong-Gwan Lee, Youngsoo Jang, and Kee-Eung Kim. 2020. End-to-end neural pipeline for goal-oriented dialogue systems using GPT-2. In *Proceedings of the 58th Annual Meeting of the Association for Computational Linguistics*, pages 583–592, Online. Association for Computational Linguistics.

Sadid A Hasan and Oladimeji Farri. 2019. Clinical natural language processing with deep learning. In *Data Science for Healthcare*, pages 147–171. Springer.

Kaiming He, Georgia Gkioxari, Piotr Dollár, and Ross Girshick. 2017. Mask R-CNN. In *Proceedings of the IEEE International Conference on Computer Vision*, pages 2961–2969.

Kaiming He, Xiangyu Zhang, Shaoqing Ren, and Jian Sun. 2016. Deep residual learning for image recognition. In *Proceedings of the IEEE Conference on Computer Vision and Pattern Recognition*, pages 770–778.

Yunsen Hong, Hui Li, Yanghua Xiao, Ryan McBride, and Chen Lin. 2021. SILVER: Generating persuasive Chinese product pitch. In *PAKDD (2)*, pages 652–663. Springer.

Yashal Shakti Kanungo, Sumit Negi, and Aruna Rajan. 2021. Ad headline generation using self-critical masked language model. In *Proceedings of the 2021 Conference of the North American Chapter of the Association for Computational Linguistics: Human Language Technologies: Industry Papers*, pages 263–271, Online. Association for Computational Linguistics.

Jihyeok Kim, Seungtaek Choi, Reinald Kim Amplayo, and Seung-won Hwang. 2020. Retrieval-augmented controllable review generation. In *Proceedings of the 28th International Conference on Computational Linguistics*, pages 2284–2295, Barcelona, Spain (Online). International Committee on Computational Linguistics.

Mike Lewis, Yinhan Liu, Naman Goyal, Marjan Ghazvininejad, Abdelrahman Mohamed, Omer Levy, Veselin Stoyanov, and Luke Zettlemoyer. 2020a. BART: Denoising sequence-to-sequence pre-training for natural language generation, translation, and comprehension. In *Proceedings of the 58th Annual Meeting of the Association for Computational Linguistics*, pages 7871–7880, Online. Association for Computational Linguistics.

Patrick Lewis, Ethan Perez, Aleksandra Piktus, Fabio Petroni, Vladimir Karpukhin, Naman Goyal, Heinrich Küttler, Mike Lewis, Wen-tau Yih, Tim Rocktäschel, et al. 2020b. Retrieval-augmented generation for knowledge-intensive NLP tasks. *Advances in Neural Information Processing Systems*, 33:9459–9474.

Percy Liang, Michael Jordan, and Dan Klein. 2009. Learning semantic correspondences with less supervision. In *Proceedings of the Joint Conference of the 47th Annual Meeting of the ACL and the 4th International Joint Conference on Natural Language Processing of the AFNLP*, pages 91–99, Suntec, Singapore. Association for Computational Linguistics.

Chin-Yew Lin. 2004. ROUGE: A package for automatic evaluation of summaries. In *Text Summarization Branches Out*, pages 74–81, Barcelona, Spain. Association for Computational Linguistics.

Yang Liu and Mirella Lapata. 2019. Text summarization with pretrained encoders. In *Proceedings of the 2019 Conference on Empirical Methods in Natural Language Processing and the 9th International Joint Conference on Natural Language Processing (EMNLP-IJCNLP)*, pages 3730–3740, Hong Kong, China. Association for Computational Linguistics.

Kelvin Luu, Chenhao Tan, and Noah A. Smith. 2019. Measuring online debaters' persuasive skill from text over time. *Transactions of the Association for Computational Linguistics*, 7:537–550.

Joshua Maynez, Shashi Narayan, Bernd Bohnet, and Ryan McDonald. 2020. On faithfulness and factuality in abstractive summarization. In *Proceedings of the 58th Annual Meeting of the Association for Computational Linguistics*, pages 1906–1919, Online. Association for Computational Linguistics.

Pooya Moradi, Nishant Kambhatla, and Anoop Sarkar. 2021. Measuring and improving faithfulness of attention in neural machine translation. In *Proceedings of the 16th Conference of the European Chapter of the Association for Computational Linguistics: Main Volume*, pages 2791–2802, Online. Association for Computational Linguistics.

Vitobha Munigala, Abhijit Mishra, Srikanth G Tamilselvam, Shreya Khare, Riddhiman Dasgupta, and Anush Sankaran. 2018. Persuaide! an adaptive persuasive text generation system for fashion domain. In *Companion Proceedings of the The Web Conference 2018*, pages 335–342.

Kishore Papineni, Salim Roukos, Todd Ward, and Wei-Jing Zhu. 2002. Bleu: a method for automatic evaluation of machine translation. In *Proceedings of the 40th Annual Meeting of the Association for Computational Linguistics*, pages 311–318, Philadelphia, Pennsylvania, USA. Association for Computational Linguistics.

Ratish Puduppully, Li Dong, and Mirella Lapata. 2019. Data-to-text generation with entity modeling. In *Proceedings of the 57th Annual Meeting of the Association for Computational Linguistics*, pages 2023–2035, Florence, Italy. Association for Computational Linguistics.

Weizhen Qi, Yu Yan, Yeyun Gong, Dayiheng Liu, Nan Duan, Jiusheng Chen, Ruofei Zhang, and Ming

Zhou. 2020. ProphetNet: Predicting future n-gram for sequence-to-SequencePre-training. In *Findings of the Association for Computational Linguistics: EMNLP 2020*, pages 2401–2410, Online. Association for Computational Linguistics.

Alec Radford, Jeffrey Wu, Rewon Child, David Luan, Dario Amodei, Ilya Sutskever, et al. 2019. Language models are unsupervised multitask learners. *OpenAI blog*, 1(8):9.

Colin Raffel, Noam Shazeer, Adam Roberts, Katherine Lee, Sharan Narang, Michael Matena, Yanqi Zhou, Wei Li, and Peter J Liu. 2020. Exploring the limits of transfer learning with a unified text-to-text transformer. *Journal of Machine Learning Research*, 21:1–67.

Ines Rehbein. 2019. On the role of discourse relations in persuasive texts. In *Proceedings of the 13th Linguistic Annotation Workshop*, pages 144–154, Florence, Italy. Association for Computational Linguistics.

Kurt Shuster, Spencer Poff, Moya Chen, Douwe Kiela, and Jason Weston. 2021. Retrieval augmentation reduces hallucination in conversation. In *Findings of the Association for Computational Linguistics: EMNLP 2021*, pages 3784–3803, Punta Cana, Dominican Republic. Association for Computational Linguistics.

Ashish Vaswani, Noam Shazeer, Niki Parmar, Jakob Uszkoreit, Llion Jones, Aidan N Gomez, Łukasz Kaiser, and Illia Polosukhin. 2017. Attention is all you need. In *Advances in Neural Information Processing Systems*, pages 5998–6008.

Jinpeng Wang, Yutai Hou, Jing Liu, Yunbo Cao, and Chin-Yew Lin. 2017. A statistical framework for product description generation. In *Proceedings of the Eighth International Joint Conference on Natural Language Processing (Volume 2: Short Papers)*, pages 187–192, Taipei, Taiwan. Asian Federation of Natural Language Processing.

Zhenyi Wang, Xiaoyang Wang, Bang An, Dong Yu, and Changyou Chen. 2020. Towards faithful neural table-to-text generation with content-matching constraints. In *Proceedings of the 58th Annual Meeting of the Association for Computational Linguistics*, pages 1072–1086, Online. Association for Computational Linguistics.

Zhongyu Wei, Yang Liu, and Yi Li. 2016. Is this post persuasive? ranking argumentative comments in online forum. In *Proceedings of the 54th Annual Meeting of the Association for Computational Linguistics (Volume 2: Short Papers)*, pages 195–200, Berlin, Germany. Association for Computational Linguistics.

Thomas Wolf, Lysandre Debut, Victor Sanh, Julien Chaumond, Clement Delangue, Anthony Moi, Pierric Cistac, Tim Rault, Remi Louf, Morgan Funtowicz, Joe Davison, Sam Shleifer, Patrick von Platen, Clara Ma, Yacine Jernite, Julien Plu, Canwen Xu, Teven Le Scao, Sylvain Gugger, Mariama Drame, Quentin Lhoest, and Alexander Rush. 2020. Transformers: State-of-the-art natural language processing. In *Proceedings of the 2020 Conference on Empirical Methods in Natural Language Processing: System Demonstrations*, pages 38–45, Online. Association for Computational Linguistics.

Yiran Xing, Zai Shi, Zhao Meng, Gerhard Lakemeyer, Yunpu Ma, and Roger Wattenhofer. 2021. KM-BART: Knowledge enhanced multimodal BART for visual commonsense generation. In *Proceedings of the 59th Annual Meeting of the Association for Computational Linguistics and the 11th International Joint Conference on Natural Language Processing (Volume 1: Long Papers)*, pages 525–535, Online. Association for Computational Linguistics.

Jingqing Zhang, Yao Zhao, Mohammad Saleh, and Peter Liu. 2020. PEGASUS: Pre-training with extracted gap-sentences for abstractive summarization. In *ICML 2020: 37th International Conference on Machine Learning*, volume 1, pages 11328–11339.

Tao Zhang, Jin Zhang, Chengfu Huo, and Weijun Ren. 2019a. Automatic generation of pattern-controlled product description in e-commerce. In *The World Wide Web Conference*, pages 2355–2365.

Tianyi Zhang, Varsha Kishore, Felix Wu, Kilian Q Weinberger, and Yoav Artzi. 2019b. BERTScore: Evaluating text generation with BERT. In *International Conference on Learning Representations*.

A Simple Baseline for Domain Adaptation in End to End ASR Systems Using Synthetic Data

Raviraj Joshi
Flipkart, Bengaluru
raviraj.j@flipkart.com

Anupam Singh
Flipkart, Bengaluru
anupam.s@flipkart.com

Abstract

Automatic Speech Recognition(ASR) has been dominated by deep learning-based end-to-end speech recognition models. These approaches require large amounts of labeled data in the form of audio-text pairs. Moreover, these models are more susceptible to domain shift as compared to traditional models. It is common practice to train generic ASR models and then adapt them to target domains using comparatively smaller data sets. We consider a more extreme case of domain adaptation where text-only corpus is available. In this work, we propose a simple baseline technique for domain adaptation in end-to-end speech recognition models. We convert the text-only corpus to audio data using single speaker Text to Speech (TTS) engine. The parallel data in the target domain is then used to fine-tune the final dense layer of generic ASR models. We show that single speaker synthetic TTS data coupled with final dense layer only fine-tuning provides reasonable improvements in word error rates. We use text data from address and e-commerce search domains to show the effectiveness of our low-cost baseline approach on CTC and attention-based models.

1 Introduction

End-to-end speech recognition models simplify the speech recognition process by folding multiple components into a single model. These models directly convert the speech utterance into the spoken text (He et al., 2019). The major end-to-end architectures include CTC-based, attention-based, and transducer-based approaches (Graves et al., 2013; Graves, 2012; Chan et al., 2015). These all neural approaches are competitive in terms of performance however they require a large amount of supervised data to achieve generalization. A model trained on a single application domain doesn't work well on other target domains. Examples of such applications domains include e-commerce, voice search, medical, etc. Since it is not feasible to prepare supervised data for all the application domains, it is common to train models on large out of domain corpus followed by a small amount of in-domain finetuning (Bell et al., 2020). However, this approach still requires the availability of small labeled data. In the most basic form, the unlabelled text data from the target domain can be used to build domain-specific language models (LMs). The domain LMs are combined with the end-to-end ASR model using shallow fusion (Kannan et al., 2018; Shan et al., 2019; Meng et al., 2021). This approach has limited benefits since the main ASR model is not tuned to the target domain. Another popular technique is to prepare synthetic data using a Text to Speech (TTS) system and the target domain text data (Sim et al., 2019). This requires a sophisticated multi-speaker TTS system followed by the addition of representative noise to make the data usable. The idea is to make synthetic data as close as the real-world data. However, this approach is prone to overfitting as the synthetic data does not exactly resemble real-world noisy conditions. Different fine-tuning approaches have been explored using synthetic data to alleviate the overfitting problem.

In this work, we are concerned with domain adaptation techniques when a text-only corpus from the target domain is available (Gao et al., 2021). We present a simple baseline approach using single speaker synthetic TTS data followed by final dense layer only fine-tuning. The synthetic data is created using a single speaker TTS system which is commonly available and also easier to build in-house. The data is not subjected to any noise and is directly used to fine-tune the neural network. Although such single speaker data is easy to build it is not usable for the training of end-to-end networks. We, therefore, propose dense-only fine-tuning for effective fine-tuning. The approach solely relies on final dense layer fine-tuning

Proceedings of The Fifth Workshop on e-Commerce and NLP (ECNLP 5), pages 244 - 249
May 26, 2022

to avoid over-fitting on single speaker and acoustic conditions. We refer to the dense layer projecting the intermediate embedding onto vocabulary space as the final dense layer. Since the acoustic encoder of the neural network is frozen, the network only learns about the linguistic characteristic of the target domain. Similar approaches have been explored in literature where only the decoder part of the neural network is fine-tuned. However, this approach is not applicable to CTC-based neural networks (Graves et al., 2006) which do not follow an encoder-decoder architecture. We present our approach in the context of CTC and Listen-Attend-Spell (LAS) based neural network architectures. For LAS-based network, we also compare dense only and decoder only fine-tuning. We consider the text from address (for delivery of e-commerce products) domain and voice search (of e-commerce products) domain (Joshi and Kannan, 2021) for fine-tuning the model trained on a generic multi-domain dataset. Although encoder only fine-tuning has been widely studied in the literature (Mimura et al., 2018), this is the first work to exploit dense-only fine-tuning which is more relevant to the CTC-based systems. Moreover, we demonstrate a way to build an ASR system for the Address domain which is not explored in the literature.

2 Related Work

Our work is at the intersection of data augmentation using the TTS system and domain adaptation. In this section, we review the recent work in these two areas. The synthetic data generated using the TTS system was used to improve the recognition of out of vocabulary (OOV) words in (Zheng et al., 2021). Both synthetic data containing OOV words and original data were used together to train the best RNN-T model. Encoder freezing and elastic weight consolidation were further shown to provide extra benefits. Similarly, (Peyser et al., 2019) used a TTS system to generate numeric training data and improve the ASR performance on the out of vocabulary numeric sequences. The importance of data augmentation over semi-supervised learning was shown in (Laptev et al., 2020). In this work, the TTS system was trained on the same supervised ASR data set and used to generate synthesized samples on a wider set. The work also highlights the importance of multi-speaker TTS systems and noise addition to build usable systems. Other data augmentation techniques like spec augment (Park et al., 2019) were shown to be complementary with TTS based augmentation in (Rossenbach et al., 2020). Effective training strategies for using synthetic data were proposed in (Fazel et al., 2021). In order to avoid catastrophic forgetting, multi-stage training was used. The encoder layers were frozen in the initial stage followed by full fine-tuning in later stages. An elastic penalty was also added to the loss function so to avoid large deviation in learned parameters.

Similar approaches have been proposed for domain adaptation as well with a bais towards fine-tuning based transfer learning approaches. An LSTM-based domain classifier was trained to select an appropriate domain adapted language model in (Liu et al., 2021). The corresponding domain-specific language model was used for second pass re-scoring. The transfer learning approaches for domain adaptation and cross-language adaptation were evaluated in (Huang et al., 2020). They compare the fine-tuning of the pre-trained QuartzNet model with the corresponding model trained from scratch. They concluded that large pre-trained models performed better than small pre-trained models and the models trained from scratch. Another form of transfer learning involves partial fine-tuning of the model instead of the entire model. The decoder only fine-tuning for domain adaptation in Listen-Attend-Spell (LAS) based model was evaluated in (Ueno et al., 2018). The model is first trained on the source domain followed by decoder only fine-tuning on the target domain. The partial fine-tuning is shown to work better than the full fine-tuning and from the models trained from scratch. An adaptation technique specific to RNN-T networks using text-only data was proposed in (Pylkkönen et al., 2021). The prediction network of RNN-T is viewed as a neural language model and is adapted using text-only corpus while keeping the encoder and joint network fixed. Another approach for adapting RNN-T network using text-only data was proposed in (Li et al., 2020). The fine-tuning of prediction and the joint network was performed using synthetic TTS domain-specific data. Partial fine-tuning was shown to work better than full fine-tuning approaches. These works mainly used RNNT-based systems and employ a multi-context multi-speaker TTS system. In this work, we use a single speaker TTS system with a focus on CTC and attention-based models. Moreover, we focus on dense only fine-tuning instead of decoder fine-tuning studied in these works.

3 Methodology

The flow of our process is depicted in Figure 1. We follow a simple pre-training and fine-tuning approach. The model is first trained on general out-of-domain data. The target domain text data is converted into audio using a single speaker TTS engine. The synthetic samples are then used to fine-tune the final dense layers of ASR models. We consider two model types i.e CTC based models and Attention-based models. The model architecture and TTS system description are provided in the following sub-sections.

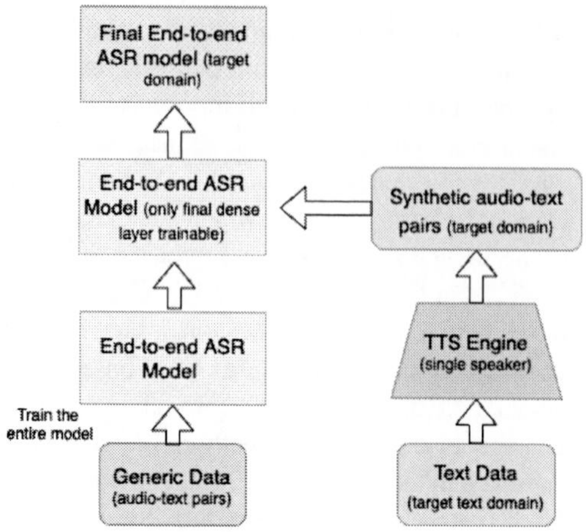

Figure 1: Domain Adaptation Process

3.1 Model Architecture

We consider CTC and attention-based ASR models which follow the same pre-processing steps (Joshi and Kannan, 2021). The audio is segmented into 20ms chunks with an overlap of 10ms. Log-mel features are computed and provided as input to the model. Standard spec-augment is used for time and frequency masking of the spectrograms (Park et al., 2019). An 80-dimensional log mel feature is computed per time step. Three consecutive features are stacked to give a final feature of size 240. The output vocabulary size consists of sub-word units of size 5000. The sentence piece library is used to train the subword model using the generic out-of-domain data (Kudo, 2018).

The CTC-based model consists of a series of stacked LSTM layers followed by a final dense layer projecting the hidden vectors onto the vocabulary space. The LSTM consists of 700 units at all levels. A total of 12 LSTM layers are present with a final dense layer of size 700 x 5001. The final vocabulary element is reserved for the blank token. The CTC loss function is used to train the model.

The attention-based model follows a transformer LAS architecture. It consists of 10 encoder layers and 2 decoder layers. All the layers are standard transformer blocks. The internal model dimension is 512 units and the feed-forward dimension is 2048 units. Each block has 4 attention heads with 1024 units each. The final dense layer on the decoder side has a size of 512 x 5000. The same generic vocabulary is used for all the experiments. This sequence to sequence model is trained using the cross-entropy loss function.

A single speaker TTS system is used to generate the synthetic data. The system is based on Tacotron2 architecture (Shen et al., 2018) and a Clarinet (Ping et al., 2018) based vocoder. The Tacotron2 sub-system converts a sequence of phonemes to a mel-spectrogram. The generated mel-spectrogram is converted into a time-domain using a Clarinet-style vocoder. In-house single speaker studio recordings are used to train this model. Both Hindi and English queries were recorded using the voice of the same artist and the text was represented in Devnagari script. The TTS system could therefore be used to convert both English and Hindi text to audio.

3.2 Dataset Details

The train data consists of a multi-domain generic audio corpus and two domain-specific synthetic data sets. The generic data consists of crowd-sourced read speech corpus. It consists of around 4 million samples amounting to 6500 hours of data. The domain-specific data were synthetically created using a single speaker TTS engine. The two domains under consideration are the voice search domain and address domain. The search domain corresponds to the Flipkart e-commerce product search domain. The address domain corresponds to the pan India delivery address. Both the domains contain around 3 million samples which are approximately 4000 hours of data for VS domain and 5000 for the address domain. The address domain queries are longer as compared to voice search queries. All the datasets consist of queries in both English and Hindi. All the text is represented in the Devanagari script. The test data was real-world domain-specific data recorded on the Flipkart application. The test data is multi-speaker

Model	Test WER	Test WER + LM Rescoring	N-Best WER
LAS-Gen	25.31	22.18	13.71
LAS-Dense	16.25	15.55	7.6
LAS-Decoder	13.65	**13.36**	5.82
CTC-Gen	31.84	25.58	13.83
CTC-Dense	20.32	17.66	8.24

Table 1: Word Error Rate(WER) for different model variations using Voice Search Domain. The N-Best WER indicates the best WER in the top N=10 beams.

Model	Test WER	Test WER + LM Rescoring	N-Best WER
LAS-Gen	39.42	31.62	25.35
LAS-Dense	22.57	16.38	11.01
LAS-Decoder	18.96	**12.54**	8.17
CTC-Gen	31.08	22.81	19.74
CTC-Dense	22.43	15.42	12.15

Table 2: Word Error Rate(WER) for different model variations using Address Domain. The N-Best WER indicates the best WER in the top N=10 beams.

data recorded in a noisy environment and it is very different than the single speaker TTS data recorded in noise-free studio settings. The test audio data was manually transcribed by the operations team. The voice search test data consisted of 25000 examples and address test data had 7000 examples. Except for linguistic overlap, the synthetic train and real test datasets represent completely different environments, and hence improvements reported in this work are not dependent on the quality of the TTS system as long as it is a single speaker.

4 Results

In this work, we evaluate dense only fine-tuning baseline for CTC and attention-based models. The domain adaptation approach is presented on two datasets from voice search and address domain. The word error rates(WER) is used to compare the different approaches. The WER is word-level Levenshtein distance between ground truth text and output text. The results for voice search domain and address domain are shown in Table 1 and Table 2 respectively. The models are first trained on the generic multi-domain dataset and represented as CTC-Gen and LAS-Gen. These pre-trained models are then fine-tuned single speaker synthetic dataset. We show that dense only fine-tuning provides considerable improvement in accuracy while at the same time avoiding over-fitting on single speaker data. The dense-finetuned models are referred to as CTC-Dense and LAS-Dense. We also evaluate decoder-only fine-tuning for LAS models termed as LAS-Decoder. We report WER with and without external language model rescoring. A kenLM based language model is trained using text transcripts for both the domains individually. The N-Best WER is computed by picking the best beam from the top N=10 beam elements.

The results show that LAS-Dense provides around 30% relative improvement in WER over LAS-Gen for VS domain and around 50% relative improvement for the address domain. The LAS-Decoder further improves the results by 14% for VS domain and 23% for the address domain. Similarly, CTC-Dense provides an improvement of 30% and 32% for VS and address domain respectively over CTC-Gen. Note that the WER of LAS-Gen evaluated on address domain is considerably high as compared to VS domain. Moreover, this simple fine-tuning and LM-rescoring provides high improvements in WER. This shows that the text distribution of address data is very different from the initial multi-domain data. Also, the variety of named entities is very high in address data as compared to VS data. Overall we show that dense only fine-tuning can provide us a reasonable baseline for domain adaptation. For encoder-decoder architectures, decoder fine-tuning serves as a better option. This is expected as the encoder part can also be seen as the acoustic network is frozen and the decoder network which can be seen as a contextual language model is fine-tuned. For CTC-based networks, we observe that extending fine-tuning to even a single lower LSTM layer results in over-fitting and degradation in performance. Therefore for CTC networks dense only fine-tuning is the optimal approach to avoid over-fitting.

5 Conclusion

In conclusion, we demonstrate a simple baseline approach for domain adaptation using a text-only corpus from the target domain. We show that the final dense layer only fine-tuning using single speaker TTS data provides considerable improvements over the generic model. The results are shown on two different domains of voice search and address domain. For both CTC and attention-based models we show that dense-only fine-tuning is a reasonable approach for domain adaptation. Although the technique is more relevant to CTC-based models it can also be used with encoder-decoder type models. For encoder-decoder models, the decoder only fine-tuning performs better.

References

Peter Bell, Joachim Fainberg, Ondrej Klejch, Jinyu Li, Steve Renals, and Pawel Swietojanski. 2020. Adaptation algorithms for neural network-based speech recognition: An overview. *IEEE Open Journal of Signal Processing*, 2:33–66.

William Chan, Navdeep Jaitly, Quoc V Le, and Oriol Vinyals. 2015. Listen, attend and spell. *arXiv preprint arXiv:1508.01211*.

Amin Fazel, Wei Yang, Yulan Liu, Roberto Barra-Chicote, Yixiong Meng, Roland Maas, and Jasha Droppo. 2021. Synthasr: Unlocking synthetic data for speech recognition. *arXiv preprint arXiv:2106.07803*.

Changfeng Gao, Gaofeng Cheng, Runyan Yang, Han Zhu, Pengyuan Zhang, and Yonghong Yan. 2021. Pre-training transformer decoder for end-to-end asr model with unpaired text data. In *ICASSP 2021-2021 IEEE International Conference on Acoustics, Speech and Signal Processing (ICASSP)*, pages 6543–6547. IEEE.

Alex Graves. 2012. Sequence transduction with recurrent neural networks. *arXiv preprint arXiv:1211.3711*.

Alex Graves, Santiago Fernández, Faustino Gomez, and Jürgen Schmidhuber. 2006. Connectionist temporal classification: labelling unsegmented sequence data with recurrent neural networks. In *Proceedings of the 23rd international conference on Machine learning*, pages 369–376.

Alex Graves, Abdel-rahman Mohamed, and Geoffrey Hinton. 2013. Speech recognition with deep recurrent neural networks. In *2013 IEEE international conference on acoustics, speech and signal processing*, pages 6645–6649. Ieee.

Yanzhang He, Tara N Sainath, Rohit Prabhavalkar, Ian McGraw, Raziel Alvarez, Ding Zhao, David Rybach, Anjuli Kannan, Yonghui Wu, Ruoming Pang, et al. 2019. Streaming end-to-end speech recognition for mobile devices. In *ICASSP 2019-2019 IEEE International Conference on Acoustics, Speech and Signal Processing (ICASSP)*, pages 6381–6385. IEEE.

Jocelyn Huang, Oleksii Kuchaiev, Patrick O'Neill, Vitaly Lavrukhin, Jason Li, Adriana Flores, Georg Kucsko, and Boris Ginsburg. 2020. Cross-language transfer learning, continuous learning, and domain adaptation for end-to-end automatic speech recognition. *arXiv preprint arXiv:2005.04290*.

Raviraj Joshi and Venkateshan Kannan. 2021. Attention based end to end speech recognition for voice search in hindi and english. In *Forum for Information Retrieval Evaluation*, pages 107–113.

Anjuli Kannan, Yonghui Wu, Patrick Nguyen, Tara N Sainath, Zhijeng Chen, and Rohit Prabhavalkar. 2018. An analysis of incorporating an external language model into a sequence-to-sequence model. In *2018 IEEE International Conference on Acoustics, Speech and Signal Processing (ICASSP)*, pages 1–5828. IEEE.

Taku Kudo. 2018. Subword regularization: Improving neural network translation models with multiple subword candidates. In *Proceedings of the 56th Annual Meeting of the Association for Computational Linguistics (Volume 1: Long Papers)*, pages 66–75.

Aleksandr Laptev, Roman Korostik, Aleksey Svischev, Andrei Andrusenko, Ivan Medennikov, and Sergey Rybin. 2020. You do not need more data: Improving end-to-end speech recognition by text-to-speech data augmentation. In *2020 13th International Congress on Image and Signal Processing, BioMedical Engineering and Informatics (CISP-BMEI)*, pages 439–444. IEEE.

Jinyu Li, Rui Zhao, Zhong Meng, Yanqing Liu, Wenning Wei, Sarangarajan Parthasarathy, Vadim Mazalov, Zhenghao Wang, Lei He, Sheng Zhao, et al. 2020. Developing rnn-t models surpassing high-performance hybrid models with customization capability. *arXiv preprint arXiv:2007.15188*.

Linda Liu, Yile Gu, Aditya Gourav, Ankur Gandhe, Shashank Kalmane, Denis Filimonov, Ariya Rastrow, and Ivan Bulyko. 2021. Domain-aware neural language models for speech recognition. In *ICASSP*

2021-2021 IEEE International Conference on Acoustics, Speech and Signal Processing (ICASSP), pages 7373–7377. IEEE.

Zhong Meng, Sarangarajan Parthasarathy, Eric Sun, Yashesh Gaur, Naoyuki Kanda, Liang Lu, Xie Chen, Rui Zhao, Jinyu Li, and Yifan Gong. 2021. Internal language model estimation for domain-adaptive end-to-end speech recognition. In *2021 IEEE Spoken Language Technology Workshop (SLT)*, pages 243–250. IEEE.

Masato Mimura, Sei Ueno, Hirofumi Inaguma, Shinsuke Sakai, and Tatsuya Kawahara. 2018. Leveraging sequence-to-sequence speech synthesis for enhancing acoustic-to-word speech recognition. In *2018 IEEE Spoken Language Technology Workshop (SLT)*, pages 477–484. IEEE.

Daniel S Park, William Chan, Yu Zhang, Chung-Cheng Chiu, Barret Zoph, Ekin D Cubuk, and Quoc V Le. 2019. Specaugment: A simple data augmentation method for automatic speech recognition. *arXiv preprint arXiv:1904.08779*.

Cal Peyser, Hao Zhang, Tara N Sainath, and Zelin Wu. 2019. Improving performance of end-to-end asr on numeric sequences. *arXiv preprint arXiv:1907.01372*.

Wei Ping, Kainan Peng, and Jitong Chen. 2018. Clarinet: Parallel wave generation in end-to-end text-to-speech. *arXiv preprint arXiv:1807.07281*.

Janne Pylkkönen, Antti Ukkonen, Juho Kilpikoski, Samu Tamminen, and Hannes Heikinheimo. 2021. Fast text-only domain adaptation of rnn-transducer prediction network. *arXiv preprint arXiv:2104.11127*.

Nick Rossenbach, Albert Zeyer, Ralf Schlüter, and Hermann Ney. 2020. Generating synthetic audio data for attention-based speech recognition systems. In *ICASSP 2020-2020 IEEE International Conference on Acoustics, Speech and Signal Processing (ICASSP)*, pages 7069–7073. IEEE.

Changhao Shan, Chao Weng, Guangsen Wang, Dan Su, Min Luo, Dong Yu, and Lei Xie. 2019. Component fusion: Learning replaceable language model component for end-to-end speech recognition system. In *ICASSP 2019-2019 IEEE International Conference on Acoustics, Speech and Signal Processing (ICASSP)*, pages 5361–5635. IEEE.

Jonathan Shen, Ruoming Pang, Ron J Weiss, Mike Schuster, Navdeep Jaitly, Zongheng Yang, Zhifeng Chen, Yu Zhang, Yuxuan Wang, Rj Skerrv-Ryan, et al. 2018. Natural tts synthesis by conditioning wavenet on mel spectrogram predictions. In *2018 IEEE International Conference on Acoustics, Speech and Signal Processing (ICASSP)*, pages 4779–4783. IEEE.

Khe Chai Sim, Françoise Beaufays, Arnaud Benard, Dhruv Guliani, Andreas Kabel, Nikhil Khare, Tamar Lucassen, Petr Zadrazil, Harry Zhang, Leif Johnson, et al. 2019. Personalization of end-to-end speech recognition on mobile devices for named entities. In *2019 IEEE Automatic Speech Recognition and Understanding Workshop (ASRU)*, pages 23–30. IEEE.

Sei Ueno, Takafumi Moriya, Masato Mimura, Shinsuke Sakai, Yusuke Shinohara, Yoshikazu Yamaguchi, Yushi Aono, and Tatsuya Kawahara. 2018. Encoder transfer for attention-based acoustic-to-word speech recognition. In *INTERSPEECH*, pages 2424–2428.

Xianrui Zheng, Yulan Liu, Deniz Gunceler, and Daniel Willett. 2021. Using synthetic audio to improve the recognition of out-of-vocabulary words in end-to-end asr systems. In *ICASSP 2021-2021 IEEE International Conference on Acoustics, Speech and Signal Processing (ICASSP)*, pages 5674–5678. IEEE.

Lot or Not: Identifying Multi-Quantity Offerings in E-Commerce

Gal Lavee
eBay Research
glavee@ebay.com

Ido Guy
Ben-Gurion University of the Negev
idoguy@acm.org

Abstract

The term *lot* in e-commerce is defined to mean an offering that contains a collection of multiple identical items for sale. In a large online marketplace, lot offerings play an important role, allowing buyers and sellers to set price levels to optimally balance supply and demand needs. In spite of their central role, e-commerce platforms often struggle to identify lot offerings, since explicit lot status identification is frequently not provided by sellers. The ability to identify lot offerings plays a key role in many fundamental e-commerce tasks, from matching offerings to catalog products, through ranking e-commerce search results, to providing effective pricing guidance. In this work, we seek to determine the lot status (and lot size) of each offering, in order to facilitate an improved buyer experience, while reducing the friction for sellers posting new offerings. We demonstrate experimentally the ability to accurately classify offerings as lots and predict their lot size using only the offer title, by adapting state-of-the-art natural language techniques to the lot identification problem.

1 Introduction

The term *lot* has its origins in the world of live auctions, where it describes the atomic unit for sale. Each such lot usually has an associated multiplicity (or *lot size*). In global e-commerce marketplaces, the variety of products for sale is several orders of magnitude larger than that of live auctions. In this latter setting, the atomic unit for sale is referred to as an *offering* or *listing* , and does not usually have an associated multiplicity (i.e., only one object is for sale). Thus, in the e-commerce setting, the term *lot* (or lot offering) is redefined to describe those offerings that contain a collection of multiple identical items. That is, not every offering is a lot. We further define the term *lot size* as the multiplicity of identical items in the collection for sale.

We adopt the definition for a lot offering given by eBay in its guidelines[1] to sellers:

> *A "lot" is a group of similar or identical items that are sold together to one buyer*

Amazon uses a similar definition for the related term *multi-packs*.[2]

Lots, or multi-packs, are distinguished from *bundle* offerings, which contain multiple *distinct* (rather than *identical*) items (Tzaban et al., 2020).

The ability to list lot offerings provides great flexibility to sellers. One reason for this is that many products come from the manufacturer as lots (e.g., a box of pencils). Another reason is that lot offerings provide the seller an additional degree of freedom (the lot size), in addition to price, to maximize marketplace value by adapting to the demand of the market for their particular product.

Online marketplaces strive to distinguish between lot and non-lot offerings for several reasons. The first reason is to enable discovery of lot offerings as first class citizens in the electronic marketplace. That is, a local retail entrepreneur may be looking for lots of products independent of what the actual product happens to be, seeking to gain profit by buying lots and reselling the component items individually.

Another important scenario is allowing price-per-unit comparison in aggregate. E-Commerce buyers, seeking the best value, may be willing to consider purchasing a larger quantity of a product in return for a per-unit discount. Consider the offerings for protective masks depicted in Figure 1. Without detecting and considering the lot size of these comparable offerings, it is difficult for a customer to recognize that some offers cost much more on a per unit basis.

[1] https://www.ebay.com/pages/cn/help/sell/contextual/lots.html

[2] https://tinyurl.com/y6kej274

Proceedings of The Fifth Workshop on e-Commerce and NLP (ECNLP 5), pages 250 - 262
May 26, 2022

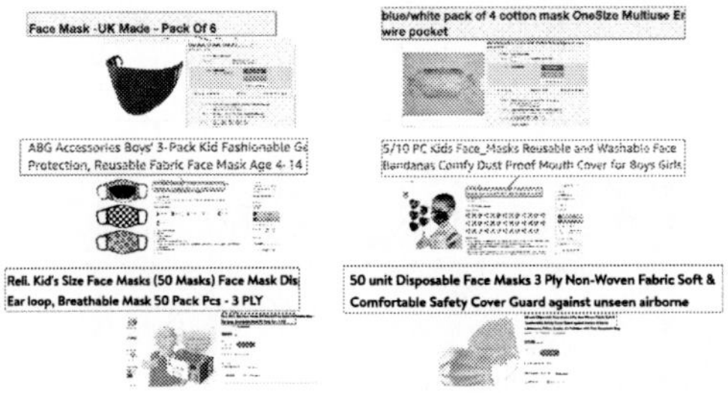

Figure 1: A comparison of lot offerings for protective masks across 3 e-commerce sites: `ebay.com`, `amazon.com`, and `walmart.com` The price per unit varies across these offerings from $0.40 to $5.00.

This work is motivated to automatically detect lot offerings, but a critical reader may ask, why not ask the sellers to explicitly designate their lot offerings (and provide an explicit lot size)? In fact, such an option does exist on many e-commerce platforms. eBay[3] , for example, has a standalone interface for sellers to input lot entries. Unfortunately, the adoption of this feature among the seller population is quite low. While sellers often have an incentive to clearly designate their offering as a lot, in practice interfaces to specify structured lot metadata are difficult to navigate. These interfaces are often unfamiliar to sellers and not standardized across marketplaces. This issue becomes more acute when sellers upload their offerings in (often large) batches, using a non-visual interface, to multiple marketplaces.

Rather than mark the offering as a lot explicitly, a common practice of many e-commerce sellers is to declare the lot status (and lot size) in the offering title using natural language. Since the title field exists across all e-commerce platforms and is prominently displayed to potential buyers, sellers can apply this technique to convey important offering information (such as lot status and size), without needing to understand the nuance of any particular marketplace interface, as well as its own terminology and attribute definitions. Table 1 illustrates example titles of lot offerings, which were not explicitly designated as lot offerings by the sellers. The examples in the table demonstrate the diversity of offerings that contain lots and the unique and colorful language of jargon and abbreviations to specify the lot status (and lot size) of the offering.

In this work, we seek to determine the lot status (and lot size) of each offering, in order to facilitate the scenarios enumerated above for buyers, while reducing the friction for sellers. Although e-commerce offerings contain multiple sources of information (e.g. images, descriptions, etc.) our methods focus exclusively on the offering title. The first reason for this is the presence of powerful natural language cues for lot status and size. This is anecdotally demonstrated in Table 1. Another reason is broad applicability: while many offerings are incomplete to some degree, with lacking or altogether-missing attributes (Ghani et al., 2006), descriptions (Novgorodov et al., 2019) and images (Goswami et al., 2012), the vast majority of offerings contain a valid title. We show experimentally that methods based on recent advances in natural language processing, but adapted to the problem of lot identification, are able to achieve high-performance on our tasks of interest.

Our main contributions can be summarized as follows:

- We introduce the first comprehensive study of lot identification in e-commerce.
- We release a dataset with nearly 20,000 offering titles across multiple categories, each labeled with lot status and lot size.
- We propose an adaptation of the naive regression approach to lot-size prediction, based on binary sequence models, which achieves high accuracy on this task.
- We empirically evaluate the performance of our proposed approach across several e-commerce domains and compare performance of several state-of-the-art methods.

2 Related Work

In this work, we apply a variety of natural language processing methods to offering titles to address the lot identification task. Accordingly, we review related work in two areas: research related to lots or multipacks in electronic commerce, and text representation and classification approaches relevant to our task.

2.1 Lots in E-Commerce

Despite their central role in online marketplaces, the current literature on lots or multipacks is very sparse. In a study from 1996, Lindskog and Lundgren (Lindskog and Lundgren, 1996) examined the use of multipacks in 41 physical stores in the UK

[3]https://pages.ebay.com/sell/lots/

Table 1: Examples of lot offering titles. The lot size (highlighted for emphasis) is often included somewhere in the title in sometimes colorful shorthand.

Lot Size	Title	Category
3	Lot of **3** Vtg. 1974 ENESCO IMPORT Rustic Metal Sculptures Wagon Telephone MailBox	Collectibles
5	**5** PACKETS EPIL-STOP PERFECT FINISH NEUTRALIZING AFTER WASH FREE SHIPPING USA NEW	Health & Beauty
20,000	Antique German Doubled Baked Ceramic Bricks **20000** pcs	Antiques
1000	(**1000**) CD Disc Jewel Case Bin Divider Cards - 5-5/8"x6" - White HEAVY DUTY 30mil	Music
2	Genuine OEM **2** Pack Canon PG-220 Black PGI-220BK Ink Tank NEW	Computers/Tablets & Networking
22	ALL BRAND NEW...LOT OF **22** KIDS GIFT ITEMS	Toys & Hobbies
50	Varian 1210-2046 Analytichem Bond Elut box of **50** SEALED BOX	Business & Industrial
28	LOT **28x** 459512-002 375863-010 HP 146GB 3G SAS 10K SFF 2.5" HDD HARD DRIVE NR	Computers/Tablets & Networking
2	Pier 1 Curtain Panels (set of **2**) gold, burgundy, green with geo design 84" long	Home & Garden

and Sweden. They discussed the different benefits, mostly related to production costs, packaging, storage, distribution, and increased sales due to the discounted prices. In their work on matching offerings to catalog products, Shah et al. (Shah et al., 2018) note that lots make data ambiguous, since, for example, "*a number in a product description could refer to a lot quantity or variation of product edition*". They state that such product offerings exhibit another level of complexity and require special treatment or a separate model to identify, but do not further explore this task. Zentes et al. (Zentes et al., 2017) mention multipacks as one of the main strategies for price reductions, but do not further characterize it compared to other promotion approaches, such as coupons or price packs.

A key research challenge in the e-commerce domain is the extraction of structured key-value attributes, such as brand, model, size, or color, from the titles of products or offerings.Techniques to approach this general problem vary from using attribute-specific gazetteers to applying sequence labeling for named entity recognition, as well as applying ideas from search and question answering (Ghani et al., 2006; More, 2016; Putthividhya and Hu, 2011; Xu et al., 2019; Wang et al., 2020). The lot identification task could be modeled as the extraction of a binary attribute. One of the main studies in the area mentions "package quantity" as an example attribute (More, 2016), but does not further explore its extraction.

Related areas of study in the commerce literature are "bundling" (Adams and Yellen, 1976; Hanson and Martin, 1990; Yadav, 1994; Tzaban et al., 2020), tying together multiple distinct products, and "price packs" (Kwok and Uncles, 2005; Tellis, 1998), which are monetary promotions that offer savings by combining multiple items.

2.2 Text Representation and Classification

The literature on representation and classification of text data spans many disciplines and several decades. For a recent general survey on text classification the reader is referred to (Kowsari et al., 2019). Specific applications of these methods include document retrieval (Schütze et al., 2008), document categorization (Sebastiani, 2002) , question answering (Rajpurkar et al., 2018), and sentiment analysis (et al., 2002). The research area of *text representation* is devoted to methods for encoding a passage of text data in a machine-interpretable way. Most methods involve tokenization (Manning et al., 2014), breaking up a document into a collection of substrings, often corresponding to the words or word combinations in the document.

Word embedding has been an area of study that produces models, such as word2vec (Le and Mikolov, 2014; Mikolov et al., 2013), which include a distributed representation of words as part of their learned output. Other popular embedding models include dependency-based embedding (Levy and Goldberg, 2014) and GloVe (Pennington et al., 2014).

Language Modeling considers the problem of predicting unseen texts from context. Early language models were based on word and n-gram frequency (Jelinek and Mercer, 1980; Katz, 1987). Neural language modeling (Bengio et al., 2000) uses fully connected neural nets to predict the next word in a sentence. Other works propose models that use word-embedding resemblance in a similar setup (Le and Mikolov, 2014; Mikolov et al., 2013). Language models applying recurrent neural architectures are proposed in (Graves, 2013) (RNN) and (Merity et al., 2018a) (LSTM). These approaches also learn word embeddings as a component of their network architecture. A more recent architecture for language modeling that has gained much popularity is the transformer (Vaswani et al., 2017), which uses neural attention mechanism instead of recurrence to encode the relevant context. BERT (Bidirectional Encoder Representations from Transformers) (Devlin et al., 2019) is a variant of a transformer, which allows bi-directional training by masking random words in the training set, rather than trying to predict the next word in a sequence.

The upper layer output of language models, such as transformers and recurrent networks, can be used as a sentence embedding. This leads to the idea of *fine-tuning* (Howard and Ruder, 2018). The idea is to train large models in domains where a large volume of text data exists (e.g. Wikipedia). The parameters in the lower layers of the resulting models are then frozen and the upper layers are trained in a specialized domain where only a small amount of data is available (e.g., travel tips). The resulting model yields a useful representation of text in the specialized domain, without having to collect vast amounts of data.

3 Datasets

Recall from our discussion in the introduction, many lot offerings are not explicitly designated as lots by the seller, and thus this explicit signal cannot be relied upon. As such, we employed human agents to manually label offerings sampled at random.

We collected a number of examples of lot and non-lot offering titles from across several categories on eBay, one of the world's largest online marketplaces. The label was acquired by allowing a human evaluator to look at the entire offering page, which includes the title, but also additional structured information on the offering attributes and possibly an image and description. The evaluator then provided the lot-size label for each offering under consideration.

3.1 Lot Dataset

Table 2 describes the datasets used in our experiments. Each dataset is named for the category of e-commerce from which the offering title examples are taken. The *Heterogeneous* dataset is the largest dataset and contains examples from a number of different e-commerce categories. For the categories we considered, the lot class was severely underrepresented in the labeled data. Thus, we create a balanced evaluation set, containing roughly equal numbers of lot and non-lot offerings.

Table 2: Datasets

Category	Training Size
Health & Beauty	4,370 (40.7% Lots)
Business & Industrial	1,754 (38.8% Lots)
Heterogeneous	18,742 (14.5% Lots)

Figure 2: Distribution of lot size across categories. The distribution displays a classic power-law behavior across all categories (note the log scale in the axes.)

3.2 Lot Characteristics

We present additional empirical analysis of lot offerings in e-commerce with the hope of providing additional insight into their properties. To this end, we used the offerings explicitly designated as lots by the seller. While this is a noisier signal, it allows us to analyze many millions of offerings.

Figure 2 displays the the lot-size distribution of these same offerings, across several categories. The figure shows that the majority of lot offerings have a small lot size. In fact, the distribution displays a classic power-law behavior (note the log scale in the axes.)

To provide a sense of how titles of lot offerings differ from title of non-lot offerings, we set out to explore the most characterizing terms of lot titles versus non-lot titles. To this end, we used Kullback-Leibler (KL) divergence, which is a non-symmetric distance measure between two given distributions (Berger and Lafferty, 1999). Specifically, we calculated the unigrams and bigrams that contribute the most to the KL divergence between the language model of the lot titles versus the language model of the non-lot titles in our dataset. Table 3 presents the results. It can be seen that the top unigrams and bigrams represent diverse language, with very substantial differences between their occurrence in lot versus non-lot titles. As we will later show, due to this diverse language, a rule-

Table 3: Most distinctive unigrams and bigrams according to KL divergence over a sample of 4 million lot versus 4 Million non-lot titles. xxnum is a special token added by the tokenizer ahead of any numeric quantity. In addition, the portion of lot titles containing the unigram/bigram and the non-lot titles containing the unigram/bigram are presented.

Unigram	%lot	%non-lot	Bigram	%lot	%non-lot
lot	35.30%	2.73%	of xxnum	25.39%	2.18%
of	31.62%	7.32%	lot of	21.23%	1.27%
xxnum	90.04%	66.30%	lot xxnum	4.21%	0.38%
pcs	8.51%	1.21%	" lot	3.09%	0.16%
x	15.00%	5.48%	pack of	2.64%	0.16%
pack	5.80%	0.98%	- pcs	1.38%	0.01%
)	14.86%	8.93%	(pack	1.97%	0.05%
&	11.25%	6.14%	(xxnum	7.67%	3.20%
(	14.79%	9.37%	- xxnum	15.54%	10.48%
set	7.19%	3.44%	set of	3.13%	0.71%

based approach using regular expressions is not effective enough, and more advanced supervised approaches are required.

4 Methods

In this section, we formalize our research problem, and propose an approach for identifying lot offerings and lot size. In order to conserve space and focus the discussion, we defer the details of our novel tokenization (Section A.1) , training procedure (Section A.2), and model architectures (Section A.3) to the appendix.

4.1 Problem Definition

We formalize two variants of the lot classification task. Both accept only the offering title as input and are distinguished by their output.

1. *Binary Classification* – the decision function determines whether the title represents a lot offering or not. That is, are multiple identical items for sale in this offering?

2. *Lot Size Prediction* - in this, more challenging, formulation, the decision function outputs the *lot size*, the number of identical products for sale in the offering described by the title. This is a generalization of the first formulation, as non-lot offerings will have a lot-size of one.

4.2 Identifying Lot Offerings

The problem definition above suggests using natural language processing techniques that given offering titles would output either the classification or the lot size prediction. However, in this work we propose several innovations specifically tailored to the problem of identifying lot offerings.

Table 4: Binary Accuracy across datasets. * indicates statistical significance at 0.05 level.

	Health&Beauty	Business&Industrial	Heterogeneous
RegExp_FC	0.600	0.696	0.544
NGram_FC	0.843	0.845	0.815
FastText_FC	0.845	0.861	0.785
LSTM_Basic_SZ	0.889	0.881	0.872
ENC_LSTM_BIN	0.889	**0.928**	0.917
ENC_LSTM_SZ	0.915	0.897	0.898
TRANS_ENC_SZ	**0.944***	**0.933**	**0.945***

4.2.1 Lot size prediction as sequence labeling

While the lot size prediction problem is ostensibly a regression problem in that its output is a quantity, lot sizes are positive (more accurately ≥ 2), integer-valued, and distributed across a wide range of possible values (see Figure 2). Further, our defined business objective is exact lot-size accuracy. That is, an error in predicted lot-size of magnitude 1 should have equal cost to an error of magnitude 100 (which is very different from common regression objectives like squared error). We also note that, the lot-size information is very often present in the offer title exactly, and can (often) be made to be contained in a single token with sufficiently clever tokenization (see above).

For these reasons, rather than formalize the lot-size prediction problem as a naïve regression, with continuous output, we propose formalizing the approach as a sequence labeling problem. That is, the model output is a sequence of binary predictions. Each decision in the output sequence corresponds to a token in the input sequence, and encodes the probability that the corresponding token describes the lot size of the offering. Note that this objective is different from the eventual goal we measure in our experiments of predicting the lot size. We describe how to convert a per-token binary prediction to a lot-size prediction in Section A.3.2.

5 Experiments and Results

In our empirical evaluation, we examine the performance of the various model architectures described in Section A.3 on the lot classification problem variants defined in Section 4.1: Binary Classification and Lot Size Prediction.

To this end, we consider the following metrics:

1. Binary Accuracy (**BAcc**) - The number of times a title was classified Lot/ Not Lot correctly as a fraction of the evaluation set.

Table 5: Lot Size Accuracy across datasets. * indicates statistical significance at 0.05 level.

	Health & Beauty	Business & Industrial	Heterogeneous
LSTM_Basic_SZ	0.870	0.820	0.845
ENC_LSTM_SZ	0.905	0.840	0.874
TRANS_ENC_SZ	**0.932***	**0.892***	**0.922***

2. Lot Size Accuracy (**LAcc**) - The number of times the lot size was predicted (exactly) correctly as a fraction of the evaluation set.

When considering Binary Accuracy, we evaluate the Binary Classification Model architectures as well as the Binary Sequence Model architectures, which, as previously described, can be post-processed in a straightforward manner to yield a binary classification decision. We further evaluate the accuracy of the binary sequence model architectures in the Lot Size Prediction Problem. Recall that we approach this problem as a token classification problem. The token with the highest score is parsed for a numeric quantity, and this quantity is considered the predicted lot size. In this formulation, small errors in the lot size prediction are weighted equally to large errors. We computed statistical significance using a two-proportion z-test (Sprinthall and Fisk, 1990), with a significance level of 0.05.

Table 4 examines binary accuracy of the various models across the datasets, while Table 5 examines the lot size accuracy of the relevant models.

Examining Tables 4 and 5, we observe that the TRANS_ENC_SZ model achieves the best performance across all datasets. This may be because for this family of tasks, the transformer encoder architecture, which only considers word ordering indirectly, is more appropriate than the recurrent encoder architecture (ENC_LSTM_SZ), which explicitly models the word ordering. In other words, local word structure is more important than global word structure for this class of problem.

Furthermore, the results indicate that the pre-trained class of models (TRANS_ENC_SZ, ENC_LSTM_BIN, ENC_LSTM_SZ) leverage their indirect access to much larger general-purpose datasets to achieve better performance than models that were trained "from scratch" with random weight initialization. We can also observe that modeling the binary task directly does not improve binary performance and in fact, 3 of the top 4 performers on the Lot Classification task are sequence models, whose output is post-processed to reach a binary decision. This indicates that the value of the additional information (the lot size) and structure used during training the sequence model outweighs the cost of additional complexity incurred by expanding the decision space.

Another, somewhat surprising, result is that lot size prediction accuracy for all sequence models is quite close in magnitude to the binary classification accuracy (e.g., 0.932 compared to 0.944 for the *Health and Beauty* dataset and TRANS_ENC_SZ model). Thus, the models are able to predict the precise lot size correctly almost exactly as well as they are able to classify the offer as *Lot or Not*.

Generalizing from the results a bit, we observe that a large improvement is gained by modeling all n-grams (NGram_FC) and/or sub-words (FastText_FC) over a simple collection of heuristic features (RegExp_FC). A smaller additional gain is made by using a recurrent architecture to explicitly model the temporal dynamics of the offer title (LSTM_Basic_SZ). Finally, an additional gain is achieved by introducing pre-trained high-capacity encoder architectures (ENC_LSTM_SZ, TRANS_ENC_SZ).

5.1 Complexity vs Accuracy

An additional analysis we carried out considers the complexity–accuracy tradeoff that exists in the models we considered. The reader of Section A.3 will no doubt observe that some of the architectures are significantly more complex than others. The more complex models generally achieve better quantitative performance in our empirical evaluation. However, how much of this complexity is needed is an important practical question, as often very complicated models are difficult to deploy and maintain in a production environment. In such cases, if a simpler model only slightly underperforms the more complicated model, in many cases it is preferred. To quantify this question of "bang for the buck" we plot the **BAcc** metric of experiments with different architectures against the "complexity" of the method as measured by the number of learnable parameters in the architecture.[4] Figure 3 shows a plot of this tradeoff across several

[4]This method is not without faults, e.g., fastText uses a hashmap of 1M vectors to represent all possible sub-words, so technically has 300 (embedding size) times 1M learnable parameters, even though much fewer are updated in practice during training.

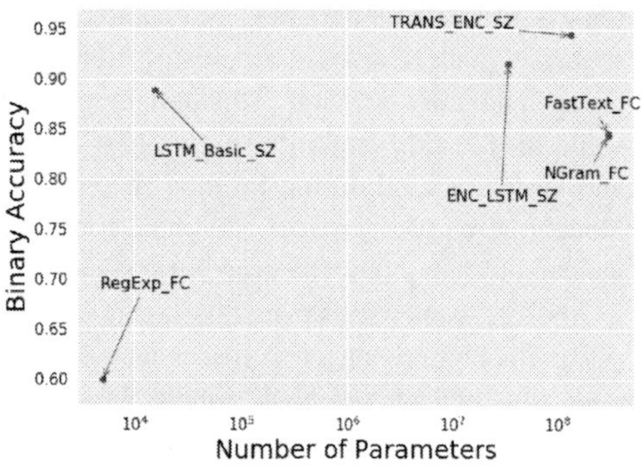

Figure 3: Comparing model complexity and binary accuracy on the *Health and Beauty* dataset.

different training runs of different architectures on the *Health & Beauty* dataset (similar relative performance is observed on other datasets.)

The plot accentuates the benefit of the relatively simple LSTM architecture, `LSTM_Basic_SZ`. This architecture, while among those with the least learnable parameters, achieves performance (on both the binary and size prediction tasks) within 10% of the leading approach, while performing better than several other approaches with more parameters. Further, this architecture is much more flexible to augmentation as it does not rely on any pre-training. Thus, for a practical production scenario, which emphasizes "bang for buck", `LSTM_Basic_SZ` may be preferable to the other more complex alternatives.

5.2 Error Analysis

To gain additional insights into the performance, we present examples where the model disagrees with the ground truth labels in Figure 4. We focus on three types of such disagreements. "*false positive*" disagreements occur when an offering title is labeled as a lot incorrectly by the model. Examining the top rows of the figure, we observe that these types of mistakes often occur on titles that include phrases and language often associated with lot offerings. In many cases, using only the title information, a human evaluator may tend to agree with the model. Thus, we conjecture that these kinds of mistakes are largely due to the gap between the information available to the model and information available to the human labelers (which includes multiple modalities such as offering image, description, and more).

"*False negative*" mistakes occur when the model incorrectly labels an offering title as "not a lot".

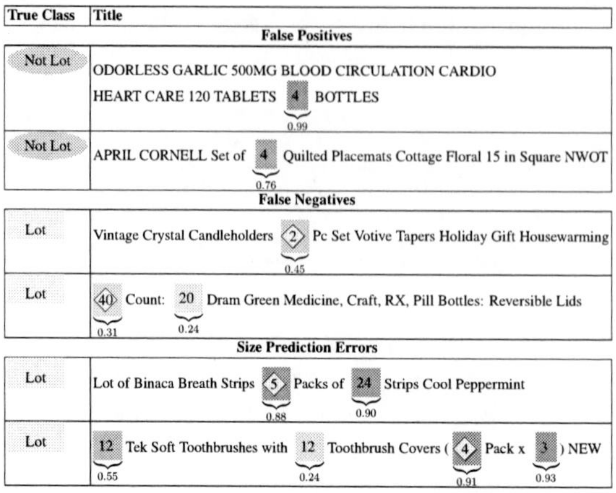

Figure 4: Error Analysis. ◇ indicates the lot-size token for each *Lot* title. ▒ indicates the most likely lot-size tokens according to the model. The model score associated with each token is indicated below the token (when non-negligible).

As Figure 4 demonstrates, the model often detects the "lot-size token" with non-negligible probability. However, this probability does not rise above the threshold needed to classify the offer as a lot. We used a threshold of 0.5 for this purpose, but this hyper-parameter can be tuned lower in order to correctly classify the examples in the figure. This type of tuning represents an opportunity to trade off false positive errors for false negative errors, as appropriate for the particular business scenario.

The third type of mistake we consider is "*size prediction error*". This type of error occurs when the model correctly identified an offering as a lot, but gets the lot size wrong. Examining the figure we can observe that this type of error occurs when the offer title is very complex, and specifically contains many numbers. It may be possible to detect this situation by considering the relative scores of different tokens.

We present the different types of errors for analysis, however, one should note that the different types do not occur with the same frequency. In our evaluation, false negative errors were more common then the other error types. Specifically, in the *Heterogeneous* test set, the top performing model had 36 false positive, 71 false negatives, and 7 size prediction errors (out of 2,082 test examples).

5.3 Impact of Tokenization

Tables 4 and 5 show that `TRANS_ENC_SZ` outperforms all baseline architectures over all datasets. In additional experiments (not described), we ob-

Table 6: Lot size prediction accuracy over the heterogeneous dataset across different architecture depths and tokenization methods. Boldfaced results are statistically tied best models at significance level of 0.05.

Number of layers	Simple Tokenization	BPE tokenization
6	**0.937**	0.901
12	**0.930**	0.918
24	**0.928**	0.909

served that this architecture also outperforms the original BERT model (Devlin et al., 2019) pre-trained on orders of magnitude more documents. One reason for this performance gap is the difference in tokenization. `TRANS_ENC_SZ` uses the custom tokenization described in Section A.1, while the original BERT tokenization is based on a trainable WordPiece tokenizer (Al., 2016), which uses sub-word level tokens. However, a confounding factor could be that the corpus used to train our model, a collection of 10 Million English language e-commerce titles (about 150M words), is more appropriate for our task than BERT's corpus of general natural language ($\sim$ 3B words).

To isolate the impact of the choice of tokenizer, we pre-trained language models with different tokenization variants: 1) the "Simple" tokenization is a plain rule-based tokenization that splits on punctuation and white spaces (see Section A.1); 2) the "BPE" tokenization is a "BERT-style" byte-pair-encoding scheme that tokenizes text into sub-word tokens based on the frequency statistics of bytes in a corpus. We also hypothesized that the depth (number of layers) of the language model is related to the performance of a tokenization approach. To evaluate this hypothesis we varied the number of layers along with the tokenizer.

Table 6 shows the result of this comparison for lot size prediction accuracy on the *Heterogeneous* dataset. Simple tokenization outperforms BPE tokenization by statistically significant margins. Notably, the depth of the transformer language model does not play a role, with all network depths achieving similar performance.

We conjecture that the reason for this performance increase is that sub-word tokenization is inappropriate for the lot classification task (at least for English text), as the important tokens are usually discovered by simple rules, and complex tokenization schemes, such as BPE, without this foreknowledge of the application, can potentially break an important "lot-size token" into multiple tokens, making a successful lot-size prediction impossible.

The table also shows that a "shallow" 6-layer transformer with Simple tokenization can perform just as well as much deeper models for this task. This combination is also more efficient computationally, due to the fewer tokens and layers.

6 Conclusions and Future Work

In this work, we consider the task of identifying *lots*, e-commerce offerings that contain multiple identical items. This application has the potential to improve the online e-commerce experience for millions of users. In our experiments, we apply a number of state-of-the-art natural language processing approaches to analyze the offering titles. We show that binary sequence models, which are aimed at identifying the lot-size token within the title, are especially effective for achieving high accuracy on both Lot Classification and Prediction tasks across multiple e-commerce domains.

Our models reach high performance based on title only, which is an advantage since almost all offers contain a valid title (as opposed to image, description, or key-value attributes). That said, the ability to detect lot offerings can potentially be further improved by using additional signals available for each offering beyond its title. The offer's price may also help achieve a further performance gain.

The methods developed herein rely on the availability of data to perform effectively. A large amount of unlabeled domain title data is necessary to build the language model, and a smaller amount of labeled data is required to fine-tune the model to the lot identification task. In other areas, where such data is available, specifically e-commerce data in languages other than English, we conjecture that this approach can generalize well.

Finally, the methods developed for analyzing titles in the pursuit of lot identification are useful in other problems that arise in the curation of a large and heterogeneous e-commerce catalog, including matching offerings to products and enabling product search.

References

William James Adams and Janet L Yellen. 1976. Commodity bundling and the burden of monopoly. *The quarterly journal of economics*, pages 475–498.

Yonghui Wu Et Al. 2016. Google's neural machine translation system: Bridging the gap between human and machine translation.

Yoshua Bengio. 2012. Practical recommendations for gradient-based training of deep architectures. In *Neural networks: Tricks of the trade*, pages 437–478. Springer.

Yoshua Bengio, Réjean Ducharme, Pascal Vincent, and Christian Janvin. 2000. A neural probabilistic language model. *J. Mach. Learn. Res.*, 3:1137–1155.

Adam Berger and John Lafferty. 1999. Information retrieval as statistical translation. In *Proc. of SIGIR*, pages 222–229.

Piotr Bojanowski, Edouard Grave, Armand Joulin, and Tomas Mikolov. 2017. Enriching word vectors with subword information. *Transactions of the Association for Computational Linguistics*, 5:135–146.

Jacob Devlin, Ming-Wei Chang, Kenton Lee, and Kristina Toutanova. 2019. Bert: Pre-training of deep bidirectional transformers for language understanding. In *NAACL-HLT (1)*.

Bo Pang et al. 2002. Thumbs up? sentiment classification using machine learning techniques. In *Proceedings of EMNLP*, pages 79–86.

Thomas Wolf et al. 2019. Huggingface's transformers: State-of-the-art natural language processing. *ArXiv*, abs/1910.03771.

Rayid Ghani, Katharina Probst, Yan Liu, Marko Krema, and Andrew Fano. 2006. Text mining for product attribute extraction. *ACM SIGKDD Explorations Newsletter*, 8(1):41–48.

Anjan Goswami, Sung H Chung, Naren Chittar, and Atiq Islam. 2012. Assessing product image quality for online shopping. In *Image Quality and System Performance IX*.

Alex Graves. 2013. Generating sequences with recurrent neural networks. *ArXiv*, abs/1308.0850.

Ward Hanson and R Kipp Martin. 1990. Optimal bundle pricing. *Management Science*, 36(2):155–174.

Sepp Hochreiter and Jürgen Schmidhuber. 1997. Long short-term memory. *Neural Comput.*, 9(8).

Jeremy Howard and Sebastian Ruder. 2018. Universal language model fine-tuning for text classification. In *Proceedings of the ACL*, Melbourne, Australia.

Fred Jelinek and Robert L. Mercer. 1980. Interpolated estimation of Markov source parameters from sparse data. In Edzard S. Gelsema and Laveen N. Kanal, editors, *Proceedings, Workshop on Pattern Recognition in Practice*, pages 381–397. North Holland, Amsterdam.

M. Jimenez, C. Maxime, Y. Le Traon, and M. Papadakis. 2018. On the impact of tokenizer and parameters on n-gram based code analysis. In *2018 IEEE International Conference on Software Maintenance and Evolution (ICSME)*.

Slava M. Katz. 1987. Estimation of probabilities from sparse data for the language model component of a speech recognizer. *IEEE Trans. Acoustics, Speech, and Signal Processing*, 35:400–401.

Diederik P. Kingma and Jimmy Ba. 2015. Adam: A method for stochastic optimization. In *Proc. of ICLR*.

Kowsari, Jafari Meimandi, Heidarysafa, Mendu, Barnes, and Brown. 2019. Text classification algorithms: A survey. *Information*, 10(4):150.

Simon Kwok and Mark Uncles. 2005. Sales promotion effectiveness: the impact of consumer differences at an ethnic-group level. *Journal of Product & Brand Management*, 14(3).

Quoc Le and Tomas Mikolov. 2014. Distributed representations of sentences and documents. In *International conference on machine learning*, pages 1188–1196.

Omer Levy and Yoav Goldberg. 2014. Dependency-based word embeddings. *Proceedings of the 52nd Annual Meeting of the Association for Computational Linguistics (Volume 2: Short Papers)*.

Johan Lindskog and Jessica Lundgren. 1996. Multi-pack - a growing packaging concept. an analysis of the market, the distributions/handling & cost.

Yinhan Liu, Myle Ott, Naman Goyal, Jingfei Du, Mandar Joshi, Danqi Chen, Omer Levy, Mike Lewis, Luke Zettlemoyer, and Veselin Stoyanov. 2019. Roberta: A robustly optimized bert pretraining approach.

Ilya Loshchilov and Frank Hutter. 2017. Sgdr: Stochastic gradient descent with warm restarts. In *Proc. of ICLR*.

Christopher Manning, Mihai Surdeanu, John Bauer, Jenny Finkel, Steven Bethard, and David McClosky. 2014. The stanford corenlp natural language processing toolkit. In *Proc. of ACL*, pages 55–60.

Stephen Merity, Nitish Shirish Keskar, and Richard Socher. 2018a. Regularizing and optimizing lstm language models. In *International Conference on Learning Representations*.

Stephen Merity, Nitish Shirish Keskar, and Richard Socher. 2018b. Regularizing and optimizing lstm language models. In *International Conference on Learning Representations*.

Stephen Merity, Caiming Xiong, James Bradbury, and Richard Socher. 2016. Pointer sentinel mixture models. *arXiv preprint arXiv:1609.07843*.

Tomas Mikolov, Kai Chen, Greg Corrado, and Jeffrey Dean. 2013. Efficient estimation of word representations in vector space.

Ajinkya More. 2016. Attribute extraction from product titles in ecommerce. *arXiv preprint*, abs/1608.04670.

Slava Novgorodov, Ido Guy, Guy Elad, and Kira Radinsky. 2019. Generating product descriptions from user reviews. In *Proc. of WWW*, pages 1354–1364.

Jeffrey Pennington, Richard Socher, and Christopher Manning. 2014. Glove: Global vectors for word representation. *Proceedings of the 2014 Conference on Empirical Methods in Natural Language Processing (EMNLP)*.

Duangmanee Pew Putthividhya and Junling Hu. 2011. Bootstrapped named entity recognition for product attribute extraction. In *Proc. of EMNLP*.

Pranav Rajpurkar, Robin Jia, and Percy Liang. 2018. Know what you don't know: Unanswerable questions for squad. *Proceedings of the 56th Annual Meeting of the Association for Computational Linguistics (Volume 2: Short Papers)*.

Hinrich Schütze, Christopher D Manning, and Prabhakar Raghavan. 2008. Introduction to information retrieval. In *Proceedings of the international communication of association for computing machinery conference*, volume 4.

Fabrizio Sebastiani. 2002. Machine learning in automated text categorization. *ACM computing surveys (CSUR)*, 34(1):1–47.

Kashif Shah, Selcuk Kopru, and Jean David Ruvini. 2018. Neural network based extreme classification and similarity models for product matching. In *Proc. of NAACL:HLT*.

Leslie N. Smith. 2017. Cyclical learning rates for training neural networks. *2017 IEEE Winter Conference on Applications of Computer Vision (WACV)*.

Richard C Sprinthall and Stephen T Fisk. 1990. *Basic statistical analysis*. Prentice Hall Englewood Cliffs, NJ.

Gerard J Tellis. 1998. *Advertising and sales promotion strategy*. Prentice Hall.

Hen Tzaban, Ido Guy, Asnat Greenstein-Messica, Arnon Dagan, Lior Rokach, and Bracha Shapira. 2020. Product bundle identification using semi-supervised learning. In *Proc. of SIGIR*, page 791–800.

Ashish Vaswani, Noam Shazeer, Niki Parmar, Jakob Uszkoreit, Llion Jones, Aidan N. Gomez, Lukasz Kaiser, and Illia Polosukhin. 2017. Attention is all you need.

Qifan Wang, Li Yang, Bhargav Kanagal, Sumit Sanghai, D. Sivakumar, Bin Shu, Zac Yu, and Jon Elsas. 2020. *Learning to Extract Attribute Value from Product via Question Answering: A Multi-Task Approach*, page 47–55. Association for Computing Machinery, New York, NY, USA.

Huimin Xu, Wenting Wang, Xin Mao, Xinyu Jiang, and Man Lan. 2019. Scaling up open tagging from tens to thousands: Comprehension empowered attribute value extraction from product title. In *Proc. of ACL*, pages 5214–5223, Florence, Italy. Association for Computational Linguistics.

Manjit S Yadav. 1994. How buyers evaluate product bundles: A model of anchoring and adjustment. *Journal of Consumer Research*, 21(2):342–353.

Joachim Zentes, Dirk Morschett, and Hanna Schramm-Klein. 2017. Pricing. In *Strategic Retail Management*, pages 279–306. Springer.

A Appendix

A.1 Tokenization

An important preprocessing step in many natural language processing approaches is tokenization, transforming the raw text input into an ordered sequence of discrete tokens (often mapped to a finite-size dictionary). The choice of tokenization method can have significant impact on results in the downstream task (Jimenez et al., 2018). Specifically, applying tokenization that is catered to the downstream task may improve the overall performance. We therefore devise a unique tokenization scheme tailored to our scenario, processing offering titles in a general e-commerce marketplace. These titles (see Table 1) contain their own set of rules and idiosyncrasies, and can be quite different than English natural language text. As such, using general-purpose English language tokenization may be less desirable.

To understand our tokenization approach consider the following example title corresponding to a lot offering:

```
BOBBIN WINDER TIRE (2pk) Brother PC8895 ...
```

Clearly the numerical tokens are important to separate, but as the example illustrates, many numbers appear in lot offering titles that have nothing to do with the lot size, usually model numbers or various specification quantities. Further, the lot quantity often appears in important context, such as adjacent to specific punctuation (e.g., within parentheses) or close to one or more context tokens (e.g. `Lot of` or `pcs`). These may or may not be separated by a whitespace token.

To deal with these phenomena, we developed several unique approaches to tokenization. First, we separate all punctuation into its own token. Then, we separate tokens with a numeric **prefix** into two separate tokens. Finally, we add a special token to indicate a numeric quantity. Note that this special token is added only when another token contains just digit characters. Thus, the token `pc8895`, for example, would not trigger a special token. This token does not replace the original numeric quantity, but rather is added next to it. This strategy is designed to allow generalizing from patterns often seen in offering titles.

With the application of such principles, the title above may be tokenized as follows:

```
bobbin | winder | tire | ( |
xxnum | 2 | pk | ) | brother | pc8895
```

where `xxnum` is the special token adding numerical context. Note that, in the example, the token `pc8895` is not split, as it does not begin with a digit character.

A.2 Techniques for Training Lot Models

Before describing specific neural architectures, we discuss key techniques that we applied in training our models that helped achieve the performance reported in the experiments section. While not all techniques are applicable to all model architectures, they play a key role in allowing our models to be trained to high performance.

A.2.1 Dynamic Learning Rates

We use a stochastic gradient descent variant (specifically, Adam (Kingma and Ba, 2015)) to optimize the parameters of the model architectures considered in this paper. Following (Bengio, 2012) , we employ several techniques to determine good values for the learning-rate parameter. The first of these is using *differential learning rates*, i.e. each parameter layer has a different learning rate. Another innovation that yields improved results is working with cyclical learning rates (Smith, 2017) combined with "cycle restarts" (Loshchilov and Hutter, 2017). That is, at the beginning of each epoch the learning rate is relatively large and begins to decay with each update. Another technique we employ is an interactive approach to finding the base learning rate called *The Learning Rate Finder* (Smith, 2017), a technique in which several batches of training are run with increasing learning rate, until the training error begins to increase. The process described above for training our models is interactive, and based on the performance of the network on such metrics as training and validation error.

Table 7: Techniques used by our different models.

Model	Dynamic Learning Rate	Pre-Training	Fine Tuning	Tokenization
RegExp_FC	✓	✗	✗	✗
NGram_FC	✓	✗	✗	✓
FastText_FC	✓	✗	✗	✓
ENC_LSTM_BIN	✓	✓	✓	✓
LSTM_Basic_SZ	✓	✗	✗	✓
ENC_LSTM_SZ	✓	✓	✓	✓
TRANS_ENC_SZ	✓	✓	✗	✓

A.2.2 Pre-Training and Fine Tuning

A well-accepted practice for improving the performance of neural models for natural language is the use of pre-trained language models (Howard and Ruder, 2018). These models are often quite large in terms of the number of parameters they contain, as well as the amount of training data they were trained on. Given a supervised text classification task, especially one where the amount of labeled training data is limited, we can use the language model to generate a useful representation of the text. This is often achieved by "chopping off" the top layer of the language model and using the continuous values of the activations in the second-to-last layer as the representation of the text. Using this representation, which is assumed to encode universal properties of word tokens, allows the primary task to utilize significantly less data.

The technique known as *Fine Tuning* introduces another step in this process. Essentially, the pre-trained language model is used as a language model on an additional corpus of text data, usually more relevant to the task of interest than the original corpus the model was pre-trained on (which is general in nature). Once this step is complete, the fine-tuned language model is used as before for the primary supervised task. Fine-tuning is especially useful when a large corpus of task-specific unlabeled data is available alongside the (often small) task-specific labeled data.

A.3 Model Architectures

We evaluated a number of different model architectures for the two problems described in Section 4.1. Each of the architectures, applied some subset of the techniques described above. Table 7 specifies the precise correspondence between models and techniques applied.

The approaches can be divided into two logical groups (1) binary classification models, and (2) binary sequence models. These groups are named according to their output type. The former group outputs a single quantity corresponding to the probability that a title corresponds to a lot offering. The latter group outputs multiple quantities, each corresponding to a token in the input sentence. An important note is that binary classification models can only be used for the binary Lot Classification task and cannot address the Lot Size Prediction task. On the other hand, binary sequence models can be used for both the Lot Size Prediction task and the binary Lot Classification task.

A.3.1 Binary Classification Models

1. `RegExp_FC` – this model corresponds to a naïve baseline for the Lot Classification task. We represented the text as a set of binary features. Each such feature corresponded to whether we were able to match with a regular expression designed to fit important patterns pertaining to lots in the offering titles. For example, one such regular expression was the following : `pack of \d+` (where \d+ represents one or more digit characters). We made use of 15 such regular expressions. We fed this representation into a fully-connected neural network with a single hidden layer (size 300).

2. `NGram_FC` – here we represented the text as a bag of n-grams (using n=2 or n=3). Each n-gram corresponds to a binary feature (does the n-gram appear in the title). Although the space of possible n-grams is very large, in practice only a small sub-set appears. However, in order to enable unseen n-grams and keep the model size consistent, we used a hashmap of size 1M to map between each n-gram and its corresponding feature. That is, potentially multiple n-grams will map to the same binary feature, although such collisions rarely occur in practice. For each title, only a few n-grams of the many possible will be active. Thus, a sparse vector of size 1M represents each title. This representation was fed into a fully-connected neural network with one hidden layer (of size 300). We applied the lot-specific tokenization and dynamic learning rate techniques when learning the parameters of this architecture.

3. `FastText_FC` – in this model, we represented each word token as a vector of size 300, which is computed as a sum of its sub-word embeddings, which are learned separately. A sub-word is essentially a sub-string that can be constructed by only considering a subset of the characters composing the token. Sub-word information can be useful for generalizing tokens with similar roots that appear in different forms (e.g. the tokens `lot` and `lots`). Since there are many possible sub-words, as above in the n-grams model, we used a hashtable of size 2M to keep the model size fixed and allow generalization to sub-words that are unseen during the training phase. Each title is represented as a simple average of its word tokens. This representation was then processed by a fully connected linear layer. The architecture is equivalent to the fastText approach described in (Bojanowski et al., 2017) , although we used our own tokenization and training procedure.

4. `ENC_LSTM_BIN` – in this approach, we employed an LSTM-based encoder (specifically we employed the bi-directional multi-layered architecture described in (Merity et al., 2018b)), which yields a representation of the text using the sequence information explicitly. This approach uses pre-training a language model on a large corpus of text (specifically, the *WikiText 103* (Merity et al., 2016) dataset of English text) and then fine-tuning the learned representation on available e-commerce offering title data (not necessarily those offerings with known lot labels). We then attached a linear layer to the final layer of this architecture (which is a concatenation of the representation at each token), and trained the model on the available supervised data, to obtain the final binary classification model. We applied our own tokenization of the text before pre-training. During training, we made use of dynamic learning rate techniques described in Section A.2.1.

A.3.2 Binary Sequence Models

As discussed in Section 4.2.1, we address the lot size prediction problem with models that output a sequence of binary decisions (one for each token in the input). To obtain the final prediction from such output, we apply the heuristic of choosing the maximum output value (assuming it passes some threshold) in the sequence and parsing the corresponding input token for a quantity. If no such token exists then the title does not represent a lot offering (and the predicted lot size is 1).

1. `LSTM_Basic_SZ` – in this approach, we used a basic LSTM model (Hochreiter and Schmid-

huber, 1997), which takes into account the token ordering. The LSTM learns its own embedding for each word token. The final state vector is processed by a linear layer that outputs a binary decision per token. This method makes use of our custom tokenization (Section A.1) and dynamic learning rate (Section A.2.1).

2. `ENC_LSTM_SZ` – in this approach, we used the same encoder architecture as described for `ENC_LSTM_BIN` above. That is, we applied custom tokenization, pre-trained the encoder component of the model on a large corpus of general English text, and then fine-tuned using in-domain text data. However, instead of a binary classification head, this architecture attaches a binary sequence head on top of the encoder, which provides a binary decision for each of the tokens in the sequence.

3. `TRANS_ENC_SZ` – in this approach, we used the well-known BERT (Devlin et al., 2019) transformer architecture, and specifically its RoBERTa variant(Liu et al., 2019). The innovation of BERT over classical transformers is the combination of multiple self-supervision tasks, Masked Language Model and Next Sentence Prediction when training the encoder. The version we made use of is consistent with the common "base" architecture of BERT (et al., 2019), which is composed of a 12-layer encoder with 768 hidden nodes and 12 attention heads per layer, for a total of approx 132 million parameters. The model uses our custom tokenization scheme, which we believe is more appropriate for our research problem. Our model is pre-trained on 10 million English language e-commerce offering titles. As the pre-training is done on in-domain data, no additional fine-tuning step was performed.

Author Index

Association for Computational Linguistics
209 N. Eighth Street
Stroudsburg, Pennsylvania 18360

ISBN 978-1-7138-6736-4

CURRAN ASSOCIATES INC.
proceedings.com